Burned Bridge

Burned Bridge

How East and West Germans
Made the Iron Curtain

EDITH SHEFFER

Foreword by Peter Schneider

OXFORD
UNIVERSITY PRESS

OXFORD
UNIVERSITY PRESS

Oxford University Press, Inc., publishes works that further
Oxford University's objective of excellence
in research, scholarship, and education.

Oxford   New York
Auckland   Cape Town   Dar es Salaam   Hong Kong   Karachi
Kuala Lumpur   Madrid   Melbourne   Mexico City   Nairobi
New Delhi   Shanghai   Taipei   Toronto

With offices in
Argentina   Austria   Brazil   Chile   Czech Republic   France   Greece
Guatemala   Hungary   Italy   Japan   Poland   Portugal   Singapore
South Korea   Switzerland   Thailand   Turkey   Ukraine   Vietnam

Copyright © 2011 by Edith Sheffer

Published by Oxford University Press, Inc.
198 Madison Avenue, New York, NY 10016

www.oup.com

Oxford is a registered trademark of Oxford University Press

Library of Congress Cataloging-in-Publication Data
Sheffer, Edith.
Burned Bridge : how East and West Germans made the Iron
Curtain / Edith Sheffer; foreword by Peter Schneider.
p.   cm.
Includes bibliographical references and index.
ISBN 978-0-19-973704-8
1. Germany (East)—Relations—Germany (West).
2. Germany (West)—Relations—Germany (East).
3. Neustadt bei Coburg (Bavaria, Germany)—History—20th century.
4. Sonneberg (Thuringia, Germany)—History—20th century.
5. Boundaries—Social aspects—Germany—History—20th century.
6. Germany—History—1945–1990. I. Title.
DD258.85.G35S44   2011
943.087—dc22   2011005112

1 3 5 7 9 8 6 4 2

Printed in the United States of America
on acid-free paper

Before I built a wall I'd ask to know
What I was walling in or walling out
  —Robert Frost, "Mending Wall"

CONTENTS

ACKNOWLEDGMENTS

It is a true pleasure to thank the generous individuals and institutions that made this book possible.

I am grateful to phenomenal mentors. Margaret Lavinia Anderson and John Connelly guided this entire study with compassion and commitment, shaped my thinking and vision as a scholar, and gave unreserved help. Robert Moeller has read drafts of the work many times over, offering warm suggestions, enthusiasm, and encouragement on a daily basis. I also treasure the unconditional support of my late advisor, Gerald Feldman, who believed in this project even when it was not clear it would be feasible. Gerry never saw the dissertation completed, but his openheartedness has sustained my endeavor throughout.

Several organizations extended wonderful opportunities for writing and research. The dissertation was funded by a German Chancellor Scholarship from the Alexander von Humboldt Foundation, as well as by fellowships from the University of California's Institute on Global Conflict and Cooperation, Institute of European Studies, Institute of International Studies, and the Berkeley History Department. The early stages of my graduate work, and of this study, were assisted by an Andrew W. Mellon Fellowship in Humanistic Studies, a Mellon Foundation Prospectus Fellowship, and a Humanities Research Grant from the University of California. A Stanford University Andrew W. Mellon Fellowship in the Humanities supported the preparation of this manuscript.

The findings of this book must be credited to the dedicated archivists who went out of their way to assist this research. I thank Heike Büttner and Waltraud Roß at Sonneberg's City Archive, Annett Spörer at the Records of the State Security Service (Stasi) in Suhl, Horst Gehringer at Coburg's State Archive, Norbert Moczarski at the Thuringian State Archive in Meiningen, Amy Schmidt at the United States National Archives and Records Administration, Gerhard Fürmetz at the Bavarian Central State Archive in Munich, and Kerstin Risse at the Federal Archive in Berlin. I especially thank Hannelore Glaser at Sonneberg's

County Archive and Christina Simmen at Neustadt bei Coburg's City Archive for their friendship and sleuthing—and for sharing their desks with me month after month.

I encountered tremendous generosity in Sonneberg and Neustadt bei Coburg. So many people offered help, shared their stories, and welcomed me into their homes. Neustadt mayor Frank Rebhan and Sonneberg mayor Sibylle Abel graciously granted access to their cities' communal files. Frank Altrichter, Elisabeth and Christian Freyer, Ulrich Gwosdzik, Adolf Hoßfeld, Isolde Kalter, Stefan Löffler, Heidi Losansky, Wolfgang Schneider, Rainer Schubert, Thomas Schwämmlein, Johannes Seifert, Dieter Seyfarth, Hans-Jürgen Schmidt, the Schmitt family, Hans-Dieter Thein, and Beate Züllich provided astute insights and pivotal assistance.

This project owes much to the spirited engagement of scholars throughout its evolution. For inspirational conversations at the inception of this topic, I thank Alf Luedtke, Peter Sahlins, Yuri Slezkine, and Kim Voss. For early advice and opportunities to present the work, I thank Frank Biess, Roger Chickering, Andreas Daum, Elizabeth Heineman, Ulrich Herbert, Konrad Jarausch, Cristoph Kleßmann, Jan Palmowski, Patrice Poutrous, and Richard Wetzell. This study benefited from lively discussions at the German Historical Institute's Transatlantic Doctoral Seminar and colloquia at the University of Freiburg, the University of Göttingen, and the Center for Research on Contemporary History (ZZF) in Potsdam. It gained immeasurably from the suggestions of faculty and students in the history departments of UC Berkeley and Stanford University, in formal workshops as well as in casual hallway conversations. Participating in these intellectual communities has been a rare gift. I am also grateful to my undergraduate instructors at Harvard University—David Blackbourn, Peter Burgard, James Gussen, James Engell, Andrew Port, Edmund Spevack, and Maria Tatar—and to Earl Bell and Gregor Heggen from the University of Chicago Laboratory Schools, for leading me to history. Great educators really can change someone's life.

A number of friends and colleagues contributed materially to this book. My great thanks go to Keith Baker, James T. Campbell, Astrid Eckert, Katharina Matro, Norman Naimark, Laura Stokes, Annette Timm, and Tara Zahra for reading and commenting extensively on the entire manuscript. For generous feedback, advice, and assistance, I thank Eliza Ablovatski, Lanier Anderson, Emily Banwell, the late Daphne Berdahl, Monica Black, Daniela Blei, Mark Bremer, Scott Bruce, Chad Bryant, Philippe Buc, Hubertus Büschel, Winson Chu and Karolina May-Chu, Alex Cook, Adrian Daub, Simone Derix, Paula Findlen, Eagle Glassheim, David Gramling, David Holloway, Molly Wilkinson Johnson, Patrick Major, Brian McCook, Jack Rakove, Richard Roberts, Priya Satia, Sagi Schaeffer, Gerhard Schätzlein, Paul Steege, Maren Ulrich, Jun Ushida,

James Ward, Kathryn Ward, Amir Weiner, Caroline Winterer, and Lisa Zwicker. I am also indebted to Susan Ferber, Ken Ledford, and Susan Rabiner for their conviction in publishing this material, and to Seth Lerer and James Sheehan for welcoming me into the Stanford community.

In this book about the importance of everyday actions, I extend special acknowledgment to the colleagues who offered daily help and camaraderie during its completion. For continuous exchange, guidance, and friendship, I thank J. P. Daughton, Alan Mikhail, and Bradley Naranch. For unlimited emotional support, I thank Allyson Hobbs, Anne Lester, and Elizabeth McGuire more than I can say.

I would also like to express my gratitude to my cousin Tracey Ledel, who sparked the idea for this project with her wedding present of a world atlas. Upon unwrapping the volume and glancing at the former border between East and West Germany, I noticed the adjacent cities of Sonneberg and Neustadt bei Coburg and wondered: what happened there?

My parents, Robert and Carol Replogle, have assisted all my endeavors wholeheartedly. They inspired, fostered, and partook in my long education. I believe my mother, the consummate English professor, has edited every draft of everything I have ever written, from elementary school to this book. I can only hope to repay their generosity by offering my own children the same.

I am grateful to little Eric and Alice. They enjoy life so immensely and are so eager for all it has to hold. I am grateful to Scott, my husband, beyond words. Day in and day out, his steadfast enthusiasm, understanding, and sacrifice have meant the world. For this, and for his love, I dedicate this book to him.

FOREWORD

PETER SCHNEIDER

One of the impressive aspects of Edith Sheffer's major work is her method. Instead of writing a general historical overview of Germany's division and reunification—of which there are dozens—she takes one exemplary case and delves deeply into it. Rather than focusing a wide lens on German division as a whole, she provides a close-up of two small neighboring towns in the central German provinces. With great care and narrative skill, she follows the local history of her two "protagonists"—the neighboring towns of Sonneberg and Neustadt bei Coburg—which became the border towns between two hostile world powers. Using an extraordinary wealth of archival material and an eye for detail, the American author successfully paints a portrait of rural Germany in the great tradition of Studs Terkel.

The questions that Edith Sheffer investigates are interesting not only from a historical perspective but also from human, even literary, points of view. How do the inhabitants of two neighboring towns, who previously shared "one heart and one soul," behave when a strange twist of history suddenly turns them into outposts of competing world orders? How do their relationships develop when they are unwillingly subjected to a powerful social experiment? When Neustadt, the city to the west of "Burned Bridge," lives according to the rules of the capitalist West, while Sonneberg, the city on the other side, must follow the principles of "really existing socialism"? Sheffer looks at the questions raised by this parallel research in terms of a large-scale experiment that was conducted, in a sense, by history itself and that is still not finished twenty years after reunification: which is stronger, nature or nurture? Which influence has proven more enduring after sixty years of political division and twenty-eight years of separation by the Wall—shared traditions and history, or the effects of two different, even contrary, political systems and ways of life? One might, as some researchers and observers have done, see communism as a kind of freezer, putting traditional values and emotions on ice. According to this theory, the old passions and feelings pick up where they left off, unchanged, once the freezer is set to defrost. But is this theory accurate? Is there not also a secret life within the ice—bacteria, perhaps, that break down and transform the "essentials" of a society during its years in deep freeze? It is a testament to Edith Sheffer's thoroughness and curiosity that she does not fall prey to a single, all-encompassing interpretation. Her work also benefits from the fact that she does not restrict her view of Neustadt and Sonneberg to their years of separation by the fortifications. Is it possible that the two communities aligned themselves with the borders drawn by the Allies long before the Wall was built, distancing themselves from one another? Was the border built up by both sides from within, even before it was constructed in concrete? And how long will it take to break down this much older inner wall after the fall of the physical Wall?

Edith Sheffer develops a biography of this border, investigating its many different influences on the lives of those who lived in its shadow—and on their ways of thinking. With an ethnographer's eye, she traces the astounding adaptations that people underwent in order to gradually accept, and even guard, the violent border that was forced upon them. She gives stunning examples of people's "participation" in their own oppression. For example, many East German refugees who sought a path to the West through Sonneberg were turned in not by GDR border guards but by the residents of Sonneberg themselves. Then there are the examples of being reunited—such as the happy discovery after the fall of the Wall that the long-separated neighbors were still speaking the same dialect, although each had incorporated new words that the others had never heard. There are also sobering realizations: after a short period of embracing one another, the people of Neustadt and Sonneberg became better acquainted and found that they considered each other more foreign than during the time when they were separated. The "Wessis," the Neustadt residents, said that they felt closer to the Turkish inhabitants of Neustadt than to their brothers and sisters on the other side, whom they saw as "German Russians"—while Sonneberg citizens could not get used to the foreigners who had moved into their neighborhoods. It was so hard for the two sides to agree on shared initiatives and investments that two shopping malls, very similar in style, were built on either side of Burned Bridge. Finally, there is the puzzling example of celebrations on both sides for the twentieth anniversary of Germany's reunification in 2009. The residents of the two towns actually held separate events for the holiday, each with its own small audience—reenacting the old familiar division in close proximity to one another.

Edith Sheffer has written a nuanced, exciting German "family history" based on the twin cities of Neustadt and Sonneberg. Of course the story has not yet ended. Even the small towns of Neustadt and Sonneberg may be examples of the kind of "trend reversal" that is already in full swing in Germany's capital, Berlin.

Behind the scenes of mutual shyness and disenchantment with the German reunification, a process I call "the Easternization of the German West" is under way. The victor's illusion always held that reunifying the two German states would change only the former East Germany, not the old Federal Republic of Germany, from the ground up. Ignorance and sheer pride led the "Wessis" to mistakenly believe that their brothers and sisters in the East would adopt the West German world view and historical perspective along with the Deutschmark and the West German Constitution. From the start, it was clear that much more would remain of the GDR than just the famous right-turn traffic sign. In *The Culture of Defeat*, historian Wolfgang Schivelbusch argued that those who were historically "defeated" were able to impose a good deal of their own culture and values upon the "victors" as a result of their greater flexibility, as well as their creative need to invent myths about their "defeat." In Berlin, the supposed losers have a palpable and growing influence on the city's fortunes, and this phenomenon may, in time, transform even Neustadt and Sonneberg.

Burned Bridge on Germany's Iron Curtain

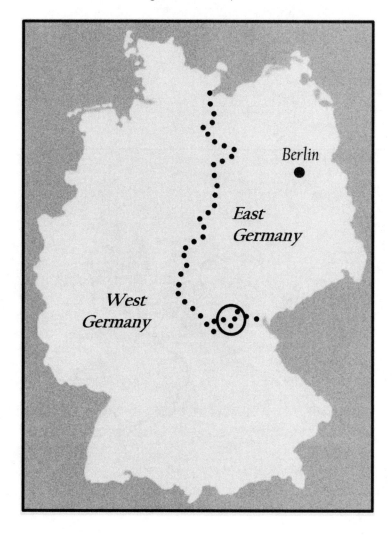

Sonneberg and Neustadt bei Coburg

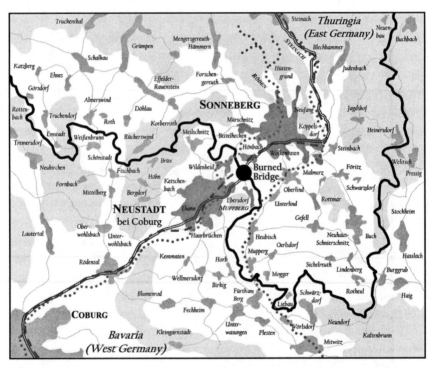

View from Sonneberg to Neustadt.

Burned Bridge following World War II. Johannes Seifert.

Burned Bridge

Introduction

Burned Bridge—*Gebrannte Brücke*—spanned a tranquil marsh in the heart of Europe. This short stretch of road, built in the Middle Ages out of logs burned to resist rot, connected two adjacent German towns, Sonneberg and Neustadt bei Coburg, for nearly a millennium. The sister cities were remarkably similar and entwined. Townspeople intermarried, spoke the same dialect, cooked the same traditional dishes, labored in the same toy industry, and saw themselves as one community. They often said they shared "one heart and one soul."[1] With their town halls less than five kilometers apart, residents crossed Burned Bridge to work, trade, and see loved ones, passing tall chestnut trees and modest slate-covered houses.

Improbable as it may seem, Burned Bridge became a fault line in the Cold War, a hotspot on the most notorious border in the world. After victorious Soviet and American armies occupied either side of the crossing at the end of World War II, differences intensified at the boundary between them. Townspeople watched, and participated, as division grew. Burned Bridge, originally built to last, became a site of disconnection. Families and friendships came apart. Smuggling, spying, fleeing, kidnapping, and killing raged. Minefields and electric fences scarred the land. Then, in 1989, the Iron Curtain unexpectedly fell, and relations shifted again. Now rival malls face off across the site. A McDonald's oversees the former barrier, at the center of another new Germany and another new Europe.

This is a story about the incremental nature of astonishing change. It traces the rise and fall of the Iron Curtain between Sonneberg in East Germany and Neustadt in West Germany, a population center of around fifty thousand that was the largest divided community outside Berlin. Uncovering the interactions of townspeople behind and across the border, it explores how two new nations formed out of one cohesive region, how people took part in their own partition, and how, in so doing, they normalized the monstrosity in their midst.

What follows is a biography of a border and of a divided society. Burned Bridge represented Germany's Cold War transformations over half a century from Nazism to democracy as well as to communism and its collapse. It marked a crossroads of social disorder and political change, where makeshift policies had unforeseen and

3

far-reaching consequences. And it marked the juxtaposition of irreconcilable realities—of freedom and captivity, rich and poor, peace and bloodshed, past and present—and the muddled attempts to wall off these diverging worlds.

What made these walls? Germany's "wall in the head," a mental divide
between East and West, has famously outlasted the physical barrier.[2] Though
fractured identity is commonly viewed as a consequence of severance, Burned
Bridge suggests it was likewise a cause. The wall in the head formed early and
propelled the wall on the ground. Geopolitics created the conditions for Germany's Iron Curtain. But nervous Germans, riven by war, National Socialism,
and foreign occupation, came to accept and enforce it against other Germans.
Their new mentalities helped give the boundary form.

The goal of this book is to explore the mutual intensification of physical and
mental divides. The Iron Curtain was not as iron, the Cold War was not as cold,
divided Germany was not as divided, and totalitarianism was not as total as our
metaphors imply. Life was and is far less coherent than that, even along the Iron
Curtain, that enduring emblem of monolithic division. Although Germans
thought their partition was made solely of iron, this story reveals it was also
human. Behavior and belief buttressed the barrier; they were central to how it
was built and to how it fell down.

The history of Burned Bridge challenges the conventional image of the Iron
Curtain in Germany. The physical border between East and West was not simply
imposed by Cold War superpowers but was also an improvised outgrowth of
anxious postwar society. While devised in Moscow and Washington, Berlin and
Bonn, the border gained shape and meaning from the wary residents who lived
along it, prisoners who became witting and unwitting wardens. The daily choices
of ordinary people helped construct and sustain a barrier more lasting and lethal
than anyone foresaw. This layered look exposes a division deeper than military
and political confrontation. In the wake of the Third Reich, Germany's Iron Curtain shared a social core with other twentieth-century tragedies.

The Cold War was much more than a static standoff between superpowers.[3] But
the Iron Curtain—the Cold War's central symbol—still stands strong. In popular imagination, an impenetrable barrier divided the European continent.
Imposed by communism, it prevented Soviet bloc residents, especially East Germans, from escaping to freedom in the West.[4] Widespread celebrations of its fall
in 1989 only reinforced the image of how unyielding it had been.

However, the very term "Iron Curtain" is misleading. In 1946, a year after the
end of World War II, Winston Churchill declared that "from Stettin in the Baltic
to Trieste in the Adriatic, an iron curtain has descended across the Continent,"
signifying a military and political schism between western Europe and Soviet-
occupied eastern Europe.[5] Churchill's Iron Curtain was not an actual barrier, nor

did it sever Germany, whose future was still uncertain. Contemporaries soon extended the metaphor as the demarcation line between the Soviet and western zones of occupation proved contentious, and it acquired particular salience in the split nation.

The 1,393-kilometer border between Germany's two halves—the distance, roughly, from Chicago to New Orleans—became a juncture of postwar military, economic, political, and social tension. Neither East nor West had a blueprint for its management, let alone a coherent concept. Policies developed ad hoc, in response to each other's moves and countermoves. The invisible zonal boundary was to have been temporary, yet it hardened bit by bit amid postwar tumult. Its uses changed over time. Initially a measure to enforce military occupation, the border became a means of economic protection and then an instrument of political legitimacy for the two emergent German states. To stabilize the chaotic frontier, East Germany built barbed wire fences and deported "undesirable" residents in 1952, measures long practiced on Soviet borders, and became increasingly concerned about flight.[6] So although images of a rigid Iron Curtain circulated widely, its porous fences evolved erratically, and spanned just 70 percent of the frontier by the end of the fifties.

Meanwhile, Berlin, located inside East Germany, was politically divided between the two German states but remained physically open. Throughout the 1950s East Germans fled west through the city in droves, up to 2,500 a day by mid-1961. In order to stop the hemorrhaging, on August 13, 1961, the East German regime built the Berlin Wall overnight.[7] The abrupt partition of the city—dividing families, friends, and neighborhoods—drew an international outcry. Sensational escapes made headlines, and at least 136 people died along the fortifications over the decades.[8] For the West, the Berlin Wall came to underpin the moral consensus of the Cold War, from John F. Kennedy's "Ich bin ein Berliner" declaration in 1963 to Ronald Reagan's exhortation in 1987, "Mr. Gorbachev, tear down this wall!"[9] The legacy of the Berlin Wall has even transcended the Cold War, its primitive brutality now invoked as a universal symbol of oppression.

But the Berlin Wall was only one part of Germany's Iron Curtain. It was the most visible portion, to be sure, yet the shock of its sudden construction has obscured understanding of the rest. The genealogy of the Berlin Wall lay in the longer 1,393-kilometer fence that had been developing haphazardly between the two Germanys for sixteen years. After 1961, the inter-German border, too, solidified. Hundreds died or sustained serious injuries trying to escape across its mines and electric fencing. By the mid-1970s, fewer than one hundred people a year reportedly succeeded, less than 10 percent of all flight attempts.[10] The barrier appeared an impervious military installation.

Viewed up close, however, the Iron Curtain was dynamic. Frontier residents adapted to geopolitical changes and became part of the border apparatus, weaving it into the fabric of local communities. Their adjustments altered everyday life, including their sense of themselves and of those on the other side. In time, their accumulated acclimations—from petitioning to patrolling—inadvertently built and sustained a barrier that most did not want. As Karl Marx said, people make their own history, but not in circumstances of their choosing.[11]

A diversity of actors and actions constituted Germany's Iron Curtain, generating a range of events almost too fantastic to be believed. There were curious confrontations: between Neustadt and Sonneberg, American soldiers in 1949 forcibly held back a crowd of twenty thousand easterners trying to cross, while their communist leaders urged them westward; in 1953, East German border guards joined West German neo-Nazis (who had just won 47 percent of Neustadt's vote) at a torchlight rally to burn the barrier at Burned Bridge. There was serendipity: in 1963, a lost two-year-old toddled west across a minefield, merely losing a shoe. There was tragedy: in 1968, a mine gravely injured the legs of a sixteen-year-old boy, who lay bleeding for four hours while a crowd watched. There was cunning: in 1982, one young man stole across the Iron Curtain twenty-three times in six months, staying days at a time inside Sonneberg's strict Prohibited Zone, helped by his father, who worked for the Stasi, East Germany's secret police. These are but a fraction of the border's peculiar passages. Each contributed to the evolution of Germany's border, and each revealed the human underpinnings of a supposedly iron barrier.

This book contests traditional views of Germany's Iron Curtain as unilaterally imposed by the East, illustrating how open-ended the form of the early border actually was, and the West's role in its solidification. It suggests that division penetrated more than was realized, as Germans rapidly felt oppositional identities of East and West. And it shows how the brutal barrier emerged not just from coercion but also from the mundane attitudes and actions of ordinary people. Thus a community came to accept, and uphold, the strange line that suddenly split it. The wall was more than a symbol of political failure; it was a symbol of social breakdown.

This reinterpretation of the Iron Curtain can enrich understanding of the Cold War, postwar Germany, and borders around the world. Informing all three is a particular way of looking at the intersection of public events and private choices. Without denying the centrality of high politics, Burned Bridge shifts the perspective. It spotlights the geopolitics accumulated in small, local actions. Put another way, it argues for the geopolitical significance of accumulated small, local actions.[12]

This study continues to widen the paradigm of the Cold War in Europe, proposing that the story of the Cold War is also a story about postwar society. Certainly Stalin, Churchill, Roosevelt, and Truman drew the lines on the map and ordered the boots on the ground. But the continent's division unfolded within war-torn populations, desperate for stability, that implemented, cemented, and appropriated the ad hoc provisions of conferences at Teheran, Yalta, and Potsdam. Their anxieties gave life and longevity to international structures and ideologies—and communities were profoundly transformed in the process. This recasts the Cold War as an outcome of postwar vulnerabilities and contributes to new histories that emphasize the tenuousness of the postwar world.[13]

Burned Bridge offers a critical vantage point on the Cold War and Germany's division. Its history does not accent the hotspots of European conflict: the Berlin blockade and airlift, revolt in Hungary, the Berlin Crisis, the Prague Spring, the Helsinki accords, and Poland's Solidarity movement. Those events are already well told. Rather, this parallel story evokes how the Cold War was lived and how people on its front line experienced their own pressures and motivations, apart from major events.[14] The Cold War looks different at Burned Bridge. Here are discoveries of local improvisation, such as the makeshift measures of the early postwar period, the 1952 border escalations as a turning point before the construction of the Berlin Wall in 1961, and East German officials' evolving tactics of population retention.

Burned Bridge also advances a history of an entangled postwar Germany, an entity that most people believed had ceased to exist. Recent work has complicated the image of two German states normalizing after the Third Reich, of West Germany as a model of western markets and democracy, and of East Germany as a model socialist state.[15] It is clear that Cold War division shaped society, infusing politics, culture, memory, identity, and personal relationships.[16] But Germany's severance is still seen as a geopolitical tragedy that did not *reflect* society. While this book eschews notions of German particularity, it does propose that the Iron Curtain arose from a specific historical context.[17] The barrier emerged from the National Socialist past: a product of world war, military occupation, and social coarsening. And it remained tied to the National Socialist past: representing an "antifascist defensive wall" in the East and a totalitarian "concentration camp wall" in the West.[18] The postwar period appears less peaceable from the Iron Curtain. As the two Germanys evolved, the boundary between them grew more brutal.

The volatile borderland became a transformational space. It marked a fault line between capitalism and communism, a contact zone through Europe's heart that was not at war but also not at peace. Here was a third Germany that bound and buttressed its disparate halves. The fragility and fissures of this strip of land, where one society came apart, shaped the new states' consolidation, as well as the relation of each to the other.[19] Burned Bridge depicts the interactivity of East and West, exposing a belt of violence at the center of Cold War Germany.

Although the Iron Curtain appears a central fact of postwar development, its evolution outside Berlin has remained curiously marginal to histories of Germany. Political studies have traced the border's diplomatic origins;[20] popular studies have outlined its apparatus;[21] military studies have examined its security dimensions;[22] remembrance studies have explored its identities and public com-memorations;[23] and local studies, story collections, and traveler narratives have chronicled its events.[24] Since the fall of the wall, several exciting works began to sketch the boundary's complicated development.[25] But it is only now, more than two decades after the fall of the Iron Curtain, that research on it has started in earnest, with a number of projects newly completed and others under way.[26] Each, in different ways, stresses the border's complexity: in border enforcement, dy-namic policy development rural resistance, public controversies over killings, and West German responses to the border.[27] Research on the Iron Curtain outside Germany likewise describes a multidimensional evolution between Czechoslova-kia and Germany, Hungary and Austria, Yugoslavia and Italy, and Turkey and the Soviet Union.[28] As the field takes shape, this book, the first social history of Ger-many's Iron Curtain that spans the Cold War, proposes some central questions.

Burned Bridge also contributes to understandings of East Germany and com-munism—helping to broaden the focus from "vertical" power relations between state and society to "horizontal" pressures within society.[29] Since 1989, heated debate has revolved around citizens' autonomy vis-à-vis the state. Emphasis on government repression in a "thoroughly ruled society" was challenged by schol-arship on "the limits of dictatorship" that explored how people maneuvered inside and around the regime.[30] Recent work continues to integrate state and society—to the point of describing a "welfare dictatorship" or "participatory dictatorship."[31] The productive concept of *Eigen-Sinn*, or "stubborn self-reliance," suggested individual meanings behind public actions.[32] It is within this compli-cation of "above" and "below" that Burned Bridge highlights a sideways dimen-sion: the effect of citizens on one another. Borderland communities reveal the role of neighbors in both conformity and defiance, from self-policing and de-nunciation to subcultures of border crossers. People felt the pull and tug of other people as well as of the state. So while Burned Bridge illustrates both regime re-pression and individuals' agency, it likewise calls attention to the shifting social milieu in which the Iron Curtain arose.

To the study of boundaries, Burned Bridge demonstrates how borders shape identities and, more unexpectedly, how identities shape borders.[33] In the absence of linguistic, cultural, or religious distinctions, boundaries may foster differences by generating frictions between, rather than by isolating, separated communities. Policies and affiliations are not simply crafted centrally and disseminated outward but take form in significant ways along the periphery.[34] Even arbitrary borders have transformative power. Partitions of cohesive communities—Catalans between France and Spain, Jivaro between Peru and Ecuador, and Hausa between Niger and Nigeria—have generated divergent identities.[35] Continued contact can create a heightened interaction zone around frontiers, a zone distinct from, and perhaps a threat to, state interiors, such as that between the United States and Mexico.[36] The Iron Curtain has been seen as an exception, its rigidity precluding a transboundary "border culture."[37] But in many ways, the Iron Curtain was a boundary like any other. In the case of Burned Bridge, fraught interactions and mentalities within the border zone actually propelled partition. Though unpopular, the barrier became a product of the people who lived it, whose daily hopes, fears, and motives gave form to, and continued to be formed by, the line that divided them.

Underlying each of these arguments is an idea of improvisation: aggregate actions that are not necessarily designed nor coerced but which arise unexpectedly from cumulative personal decisions, particularly in times of crisis. The border gained emergent authority. It served different purposes at different times, a solution to an array of problems in which both East and West developed a stake. In outlining the complex creation of the Iron Curtain, the history of Burned Bridge describes how individual disconnections, however comprehensible, can amass into something colossal. That is why the circumstances of society, as well as its political structures, matter so much.

This book follows the Iron Curtain's unpredictable cascade of consequences in Germany, tracing how an invisible territorial demarcation expanded into an enduring perceptual boundary. Burned Bridge was an accident of geography, but it was very much of a piece with the rest of the inter-German border. There were areas with heavier traffic (Helmstedt), greater security concerns (the Fulda Gap), and better-known cultural and social ties (the Eichsfeld). There was even one partitioned village of under one hundred inhabitants (Mödlereuth) that claimed much greater public attention. While Neustadt and Sonneberg were more urban and densely populated than elsewhere on this variegated border, perhaps intensifying mobility and tensions, state records on both sides suggest that the region broadly reflected interactions that occurred, in varying forms, along Germany's Iron Curtain.

Part One of this book covers the period 1945–52 and argues that the unfenced "green border" was itself a catalyst of division, compounded by the crises it created. Burned Bridge had linked Neustadt and Sonneberg for centuries, but the towns rapidly diverged under foreign military governments at the end of World War II. The Soviet army occupied Sonneberg and the American army occupied Neustadt. Their differences became self-reinforcing on the demarcation line, where violence—shootings, abductions, rapes, and killings—led to demands for greater border control on both sides. It was, in fact, the American military that built the first barriers in the region. Economic inequality grew between East and West, especially in the wake of currency reform and the Berlin blockade in 1948–49.[38] Western animus grew toward poorer easterners, who crossed daily as smugglers, begging children, refugees, and undocumented workers. Borderland

hostilities led to early East-West stereotypes and the local policing and prosecution of border crossers. It was the weakness of central authority on the border
that allowed residents to take initiative. As the East and West German states
developed after 1949, the boundary became a conduit of political skirmishing,
propaganda, and mass crossings. Three divides were overlaid into one, exacerbating each other: military insecurity, economic inequality, and political threat.
Locals' growing acceptance of border measures, a product of a post-dictatorial
society facing tumult, readied the way for more extreme measures.[39]

Part Two covers 1952–61 and shifts the focus to the East, with perhaps the
most overlooked turning point in Germany's Cold War history—East Germany's closure of the inter-German border and forced deportation of more than
eight thousand "unreliable" frontier residents inland in 1952, almost a decade
before the construction of the Berlin Wall. The disorganized East German regime
relied on border populations to build fences, to keep the peace, and to deport
their neighbors, co-opting locals into creating their own captivity. Although
there was widespread resistance during Action Vermin (*Aktion Ungeziefer*) and
the communities that rebelled saw fewer inhabitants expelled, the events of 1952
shocked residents into quiescence. Borderland discipline remained intact even
during East Germany's nationwide uprisings of 1953, a factor shoring up the
shaky regime. Throughout the 1950s, a "living wall" continued to grow between
East and West. The border was still physically porous, but everyday actions
helped solidify it. Quotidian concerns blurred the distinction between victims
and perpetrators, intensifying social controls. Because East Germans could still
flee over the weak fortifications and through Berlin, local officials endeavored to
retain people individually, customizing incentives and punishments. The border
became a defining principle of citizenship, as new taxonomies of transgression
defined legal rights and status. Growing complexity resulted in multiple modes
of communist rule, encompassing dictatorial repression as well as individual autonomy. This customization worked, to an extent, evidenced by the success of
the December 1957 Pass Law in reducing defections by almost 40 percent. Due
to the everyday accommodations of the fifties—anticipatory compliance in the
East and increasing complacency in the West—the barrier escalations that came
in 1961 divided a society that already saw itself as divided.

Part Three covers the years from 1961 to 1989 and begins with East Germany's second major round of border construction and deportations in 1961, culminating in the erection of the Berlin Wall. These escalations saw nowhere near the
level of resistance of 1952, as the die was already cast. Over the decades, the border progressively hardened from a weak barbed wire fence into a mined, multilayered, militarized zone, sustained by the progressive coercion and acceptance of
local populations. Within a generation, dictatorial border strictures came to seem
almost normal, integrated into daily life. East Germany succeeded in creating a

self-policing society in the Prohibited Zone, a virtual panopticon, where one in ten residents was tasked to keep watch on neighbors. Even at the height of the border's fortifications, less than a fifth of arrests were reportedly made by the guards at the border itself. Most escapees were caught by transport and local police further inland, and up to a quarter were turned in by frontier civilians: Voluntary Border Helpers and ordinary residents. A few locals who knew the terrain still hopped over the Iron Curtain in dozens of impulsive, often inebriated crossings that neither side registered in flight tallies nor publicized in the press. So this strong border was oddly porous for some of the very same people who made it possible. Meanwhile, the boundary entrenched estrangements between East and West where, paradoxically, increasing contact through western border tourism and cross-border travel resulted in a greater sense of difference. By the time the Iron Curtain fell in 1989, differences ran deep indeed. The disappointment of desired connections resulted in the creation of a new "wall in the head" with reunification.

As this book explores all the little ways the Iron Curtain became a fact, it weaves together a range of sources and perspectives: East and West, local and national, personal and political. It draws stories from documents in fourteen archives, private papers and memoirs, newspapers and journals, regional studies, a survey mailed to five hundred people, and more than fifty interviews of residents ranging from border officials to border victims.[40] Each source base has limitations, and they frequently conflict, even about the same event. But the gaps themselves speak volumes, suggesting the confusion, fears, and assumptions that propelled much of the border's development. The contingencies of small-town research underscored these gaps, such as the four boxes of border trials in a forgotten corner, or a required interview with the mayor before being given access to files. Relevant record collections were often lost, destroyed, or uncataloged. The uneven source base partly explains the shift in emphasis in this book toward East Germany in later chapters. Eastern records grew far more voluminous and were publicly available, as opposed to the legal restrictions of a thirty-year waiting period to access western documents.[41] Also, because the inter-German border has been so under-researched, the priority of this project became to unearth and frame a range of new material rather than to focus on specific laws, procedures, or agencies. In time, the archival picture may well be more complete.

Yet oral sources will soon be lost, and with them, a vital perspective. People's focus on normalcy and victimization in the borderland contrasts with the crises and complicities described in the archival record. Sonnebergers and Neustadters were eager to share their version of events, concerned that government files misrepresented how their lives were actually lived. Wariness of official reports was most pronounced in the former East, where Sonneberg's city and county archivists proposed and arranged initial interviews. Most subsequent interviews were with people who, after this project was publicized in regional newspapers, radio, and television, contacted these outlets. Chance acquaintances at the post office or the bratwurst kiosk also initiated discussions, volunteering insights and home-cooked meals. People shared letters, photographs, memorabilia, and personal Stasi files. Conversations were accompanied by nostalgia, laughter, and tears. Children and grandchildren listened in, curious about a past that was not exactly taboo, but about which they had never heard.

Because of the sensitive nature of this past, this book uses pseudonyms for all interviewees and private citizens referenced in the text.[42] The goal of this protection, and the varied use of source quotations, is to convey the diversity of life in the borderland. Perspectives in East and West, among officials as well as citizens, differed starkly. They still do. Certainly, enthusiasm for a history of the boundary by an "outside" American researcher—described as "exactly the neutral person, sought for so long, for this kind of difficult scholarly work"—was striking, indicating not only the lasting significance of division but also the frustrations in coming to terms with this past.[43] This project is now a file of its own in the two cities' archives. It is necessarily subjective and generalized. Yet I hope that the residents who read it may feel that it reflects some of what they lived.

Burned Bridge offers an unusual story about a world turned upside down, part of a narrative of the twentieth century that emphasizes rapid transitions, the rise of radical regimes, and the building of societies anew. It begins in 1945, a moment when Europe was shattered, reeling from the most destructive war in history and dominated by two ideological adversaries on the brink of yet another. From this perceived "zero hour," it sketches the emergence of the border as an answer to problems that then assumed momentum of its own. The account tracks civilians and soldiers as they structured their daily lives around border escalations, as they sneaked across meadows, arbitrated disagreements, and guarded frontier farms, their choices unfolding tentatively within a network of others' tentative choices. Small actions, each individually understandable, added up to something hard to comprehend. Soon the grotesque barrier allowed for the creation of two new realities adjacent to each other. People a stone's throw apart experienced different sights, sounds, and smells, lived different identities, beliefs, and ways of being.

On the one hand, Burned Bridge represents remote communities on the margins of two societies that no longer exist. On the other, it represents the complex core of a postwar Germany that was defined by the interaction of its two halves as well as by their segregation. Its perspective on the postwar period, with East and West together, helps shift perspective on the Cold War, calling attention to the role of ordinary people and local events. More broadly, it speaks to the importance of social fabric. It demonstrates the fragility of a community in crisis: the institutionalization of violence among neighbors, popular participation in a system that was deeply unpopular, and the creation of difference where there was no difference.

The following is a tale of how people in one insular valley, between their farms, villages, and workshops, realized the Iron Curtain. It does not argue that a little more small-town pluck could have undone a geopolitical division, nor does it offer a tidy pattern of who did what, since daily actions were often inconsistent, even for the same individuals. Rather, the story of Burned Bridge illustrates how daily actions constituted the border, making it a reality. It points to the predominance of situational factors within uncertainty, the extent to which mentalities are malleable and mentalities matter. And it points to the ephemeral insecurity from which events can unexpectedly arise. As the bottom dropped out again and again in Europe's wars and reconstructions, Burned Bridge suggests the everyday workings behind the momentous doings, and undoings, of modern times.

PART ONE

DEMARCATION LINE, 1945–1952

‖ 1 ‖

Foundations: Burned Bridge

Burned Bridge was always a crossroads. It lay midway along the medieval trade route between Nuremberg and Leipzig, and it linked distinct landscapes, spanning the last lowlands of Upper Franconia before the steep hills of the Thuringian Forest. It conveyed armies, governments, and practices that local residents then assimilated and influenced. What stands out most in the long history of Burned Bridge is the plasticity of change. New developments wedged differences between Sonneberg and Neustadt, presaging in milder forms the cities' eventual divergence.

A Millennium of Connection and Competition

There are conflicting legends about Burned Bridge, and almost everyone has a story of its origins. But it is agreed that, at least since its first recorded history in 1162, Burned Bridge was a border crossing.[1] A "new city on the heath," *Nuowensthat vf der Heyde*, developed around its customs office after 1248. It became a natural rest stop for travelers, as merchants paid well for supplies, repairs, accommodations, and safe passage into the mountains. While Neustadt profited from its border location, Sonneberg, further from the toll station, remained under its older sister's jurisdiction and developed in its shadow. Sonneberg's city charter of 1349 was even modeled on Neustadt's. The towns developed symbiotically as a borderland, linked by the road, the moor, and the meandering river Röden.[2]

Burned Bridge was well trafficked in early modern times. Peddlers, buyers, vagabonds, scholars, and dignitaries all traveled on the trade road, which carried Martin Luther in 1530 and Holy Roman Emperor Charles V in 1547.[3] During the Thirty Years' War, pillaging troops arrived on the thoroughfare, wreaking devastation from which the cities were slow to recover. In the war's wake, townspeople increasingly supplemented poor harvests, the curse of the region's sandy soil, by crafting wooden objects for sale to Nuremberg traders. They carved utensils, tools, toys, and figurines during the long winter months at the base of the Thuringian Forest, launching the toy and doll industries for which the area became famed.[4]

In 1735, Neustadt and Sonneberg's fortunes diverged when a dynastic inheritance dispute divided them into the Duchies of Saxe-Coburg-Saalfeld and Saxe-Meiningen, respectively. The new border, like most new borders, altered the balance of political and economic power in the region—the area erupting into violence as Neustadters repelled Saxe-Meiningen's attempts to claim it with pitchforks, axes, and stones in its *Dreschflegelkrieg,* or "Thresher War."[5] The towns remained enmeshed in daily life, however, and borderland administrators continued to delineate territory with natural markers such as trees and creeks.[6] But the partition did grant Sonneberg administrative independence from Neustadt, ending its four hundred years of subordination and leading to alternative paths of development.

Over the course of the eighteenth century, separation spurred competition. Neustadt craftsmen and traders feared cheaper wares produced in Sonneberg and retrenched into protectionist guilds. They limited new products and practices, and they excluded non-Neustadt artisans. Whereas Sonneberg's less-developed toy industry profited from its openness, Neustadt's grew more isolated. When Sonnebergers switched to making papier-mâché doll and animal heads by 1800, reducing labor and costs, Neustadters rejected the technique for decades. Their eventual adaptation to market conditions was too little, too late.[7]

In the nineteenth century, the cities had contrasting approaches to city development: Neustadt's leaders sought to preserve provincial ways, and Sonneberg's aggressively refashioned them. After ruinous fires in 1839 and 1840, Neustadt rebuilt the winding streets of its medieval center, while Sonneberg relocated its downtown to flatter land on a modern grid plan.[8] The towns also had opposite responses to the arrival of the railroad in 1858. Sonneberg had formed a Railroad Association a decade earlier to lobby for access, and then built a grand new city square around its depot. Neustadt was ambivalent, building a small station on the town's periphery.[9]

Sonneberg's boldness transformed it into a world-class center of toy and doll making. As nineteenth-century changes in middle-class domesticity and child-rearing practices spurred demand for toys, catapulting the industry to imperial Germany's thirteenth-largest export, Sonneberg grew quickly. The number of toy-manufacturing firms increased tenfold between 1880 and 1907 to around 3,400, and toy exports more than quadrupled between 1870 and 1913 to 45 million marks.[10] Unusually close ties to the United States fueled this expansion. A hundred Sonnebergers a year had immigrated to America from 1845 to 1871, fleeing poverty as cottage industry workers; this toy-making diaspora then helped bring a U.S. consulate and seven American export firms back to Sonneberg, including a massive Woolworth's distribution center.[11]

By the turn of the twentieth century, the cities' positions had reversed. Sonneberg merchants were buying up more than 80 percent of Neustadt's toys and dolls, and Neustadters felt demoted to "slaves" in their sister city's "workshop."[12] Toy experts derided Neustadt crafts as "significantly cheaper and also naturally worse," while Sonneberg proclaimed itself the "World Toy Capital."[13] Ranked first in German toy production on the eve of World War I, the region claimed one-fifth of total global toy sales, perhaps the most widely known historical fact among locals today.[14] And with its ascent, Sonneberg's population grew faster, quintupling between 1800 and 1900 to 13,225, more than double Neustadt's 6,250.[15] Outwardly, the cities looked quite different.

But ordinary townspeople were not themselves that different. The vast majority of inhabitants led similar everyday lives. Since Sonneberg's wealth was concentrated in a clique of wealthy export families, most Sonnebergers, like Neustadters, were poor small-scale crafts workers.[16] One visitor was not fooled by Sonneberg's pretensions, seeing a "prosaic provincial city peculiarly interrupted by giant American buildings."[17] For the most part, large families worked long hours for low wages, casting doll bodies or stuffing animal patterns in cramped home workshops for sale to the major trading houses. These vestiges of the putting-out system endured long after the Industrial Revolution transformed other industries in Germany. Well into the early twentieth century, around four in five toy manufacturers in Sonneberg and Neustadt were home workshops employing fewer than four workers.[18] More than half the cities' residents worked in the toy industry, with at least 40 percent of all children under fourteen in child labor, and wages among the lowest in Germany through the 1930s.[19]

The lives of Sonnebergers and Neustadters were also interconnected. Locals commonly claim that two-thirds of residents had close relatives living in the other city. There was a daily back-and-forth of shopping, trading, and visiting, as townspeople shared pubs, clubs, associations, schools, and festivals, and telephoned each other just as often as they telephoned among themselves.[20] Over 95 percent Protestant, Neustadt and Sonneberg communities shared churches and parishes. Rivalries surfaced over resources such as toy museums and industrial schools; to some extent, locals identified with their cities' external images, with stereotypes of provincial, easygoing Neustadters versus industrious, reserved Sonnebergers resonating even today.[21] Yet a basic sense of affinity underlay these differences. Travel books promoted a unified "Sonneberg-Neustadt Doll and Toyland" as a "paradise for children's dreams . . . where dolls and bears peek out of the windows."[22] Combined itineraries showcased "two industrious cities that complement each other in all things, and form one economic unit."[23] This close-knit region, from its variation of Thuringian Sunday dumplings, or *Klöße*, to its distinctive Main-Franconian dialect, had its own unique culture.[24]

The border at Burned Bridge remained inconsequential in everyday life. Sonneberg and Neustadt were in different duchies, yet parallel development of local laws and governance intertwined basic infrastructure such as gas, electricity, water, and postal delivery. Absent any natural barrier such as a hilltop or river, few people even knew where the boundary lay. Eighteenth-century border stones were irregular and inaccurate, their authenticating porcelain and glass tiles long pilfered from underneath them.[25] At lighthearted "border inspections," community leaders and musicians led schoolchildren along the boundary and boxed their ears so they would remember the route, an old tradition followed by food, drink, and dancing.[26] In contrast to these quaint practices, however, the 1920 state border at Burned Bridge would have far-reaching consequences.

The State Border and Nazism

After Germany's defeat in World War I, the Treaty of Versailles and the end of monarchy redrew the nation's external and internal boundaries. Dynastic territories reorganized into larger federal states. Sonneberg's Duchy of Saxe-Meiningen decided in 1920 to join Thuringia, while Neustadt's Duchy of Saxe-Coburg held Germany's first democratic referendum and voted overwhelmingly for Bavaria. Ninety-one percent of Neustadters and 88 percent of the duchy overall favored the southern state over Thuringia.[27]

The landslide results were somewhat surprising, given Coburg's centuries of dynastic ties to the north. Regional histories, especially during the Cold War, suggested that Coburg was culturally closer to conservative Bavaria; socialist, unstable Thuringia was "too red."[28] Yet short-term economic interests appear to have loomed largest. Bavaria had promised the Coburg region administrative autonomy, industrial subsidies, and agricultural surpluses. Plus, bad harvests had aggravated food distribution problems with Thuringia, and the "belly question" was paramount.[29] Because, as one contemporary jingle put it, "the hunger suffering of Thuringia—is not to be found in Bavaria," Neustadters and Sonnebergers had been day-tripping over Coburg's southern border in order to "hamster," or forage for food, in Bavaria.[30]

After Coburg joined Bavaria on July 1, 1920, this border barter shifted northward, between Sonneberg and Neustadt. Hungry Sonnebergers now "hamstered" in their sister city, while Neustadt farmers profited, leading to tensions and stronger police controls. Consciousness of a new divide grew. Within a year, there was even talk of renaming Neustadt "Grenz," or "Border-Neustadt."[31] The 1920 state border cannot reasonably be compared to the Iron Curtain, but it foreshadowed local scuffles over scarcity after 1945—as well as how swiftly political realignments could create economic imbalances, which in turn shaped oppositional interests and identities.

Germany's instability during the early Weimar Republic exacerbated the importance of the new state boundary. The young democracy was on the brink of collapse, racked by revolution, putsches, hyperinflation, and widespread unrest. Even Burned Bridge came into the crosshairs of conflict between Bavaria and Thuringia. In October 1923, Bavaria's far-right administration sent paramilitary groups to Neustadt to secure the border against the socialist and communist coalition government in Thuringia, which sent eighteen leftist units to Sonneberg. Local National Socialists and communists joined the fray, and Neustadt's Emergency Police sported swastikas and organized "cleansing operations" that targeted leftists. The showdown led to violence and exchanges of fire over Burned Bridge.[32] So despite the reality of crisscrossing allegiances among townspeople, images of the fascist threat in Bavarian Neustadt and the Bolshevist menace in Thuringian Sonneberg endured throughout the twenties, and would resurface with force during the Cold War.

While Burned Bridge—like many border areas—became a lightning rod for national tensions, politics inside Neustadt and Sonneberg remained similar. Traditionally, both cities were "red," Germany's Social Democratic Party receiving over 50 percent support since the turn of the century.[33] After the collapse of toy exports in the wake of World War I, tough times spurred extremist movements, particularly on the right. The region embraced National Socialism unusually early, propelled by industrial underdevelopment, monarchical tradition, Bavaria's leniency toward groups on the far right, and the weakness of local Catholicism and its moderating Center Party. Within a few years, both Neustadt and Sonneberg converted from "red" to "brown."[34]

Nazism grew rapidly in the area. The cities' party organizations formed in tandem, opening branch offices in 1923–24 and attracting strong support. Neustadt was, in fact, a National Socialist "fortress," with the highest rate of "golden badge" carriers in Germany—sixty-eight of its residents were among the party's first one hundred thousand members.[35] Sonneberg's Nazi movement, while more constrained by Thuringia's restrictions, received logistical help from its Bavarian neighbor and was among the earliest to organize outside Bavaria. The cities shared funds, rallies, and a newspaper for the "Franconian-Thuringian Border Region."[36] Local propaganda, songs, poems, and stories blended Franconian and Thuringian themes.[37] Adolf Hitler himself evoked cross-border ties at a rally for fifteen hundred people in Neustadt in 1927, envisioning "a state that no longer recognizes the border posts set for us . . . *That is our fatherland!*"[38]

National Socialism gained momentum during Germany's depression of 1929–32. As toy exports and tax revenues halved, Neustadt and Sonneberg's unemployment rates ranked among the highest in Bavaria and Thuringia.[39] Escalating poverty and criminality radicalized political culture, and successions of raucous Nazi, socialist, and communist meetings, marches, and rallies mobilized the populace.[40] Voting trends in Neustadt and Sonneberg were parallel. Within a few years, support for socialist and moderate parties declined from over half to one-third of the electorate, communists drew almost a fifth of voters, and National Socialist tallies skyrocketed by 40 percent. By July 1932, around half of Neustadters and Sonnebergers voted Nazi, with the party receiving up to 60 percent of the vote in surrounding rural communities—well over the national average of 37 percent.[41]

The Nazi seizure of power in 1933 reduced the significance of the state boundary between Sonnebergers and Neustadters, to the point that the government halted demarcation efforts the following year. But the Third Reich created brutal political and racial demarcations within a new *Volksgemeinschaft*, or national community.[42] Nazi enthusiasts and opportunists in the cities denounced and rounded up dozens of Social Democrats and Communists, who were sent to concentration camps at Bad Sulza and Dachau.[43] Resistance in the region was negligible, especially when it came to the regime's escalating anti-Semitism and persecution of Jews. The few Jews who lived in the towns, around forty in Sonneberg and two in Neustadt, were assimilated and well regarded; Hugo Karl Limann was even mayor of Sonneberg for sixteen years, from 1893 to 1909.[44] Yet many townspeople participated in, or turned a blind eye to, the incremental exclusion of their neighbors from city life. A few did not, leading local newspapers to publish the names of people who continued to patronize Jewish businesses. In one well-known instance of opposition, Karl Kiesewetter refused to hang an anti-Semitic sign in his Neustadt cinema in 1933 (e.g., "Jews and Dogs Not Allowed"), for which he was paraded through the streets with a poster around his neck: "I Insulted the Regime."[45] On the Night of Broken Glass, the nationwide Kristallnacht pogrom of November 9, 1938, Sonneberg Nazis vandalized Jewish stores and, the next day, marched a group of Jews in a "triumphal procession" into the main square for public humiliation and beatings. The event was attended by school groups and scores of citizens.[46] The persecution of Jews soon became more radical. Sonneberg officials oversaw the seizure, or "Aryanization," of the city's fifteen Jewish businesses, as well as the arrest and deportation of the remaining Jews to concentration camps.[47]

During World War II, thousands of imprisoned foreign workers, prisoners of war, and Jewish concentration camp inmates worked as laborers in Neustadt and Sonneberg. The cities had lobbied the National Socialist government in the mid-1930s to relieve unemployment, and had gained two large state-of-the-art factories.[48] This employment boon soon led to labor shortages, though, especially with the onset of war. The government moved toy workers into war production and—notwithstanding patriotic Hitler Youth, SS, and SA dolls that cried "Heil Hitler"—banned toy manufacture after 1943.[49] The cities requested ever more workers. The Reich government obliged, transporting people mainly from eastern Europe. By 1944 in Sonneberg, more than forty-two hundred forced laborers and prisoners of war from at least nineteen different countries worked in thirty local businesses and on numerous private farms.[50] As elsewhere in Germany, slave labor was a part of ordinary life.

In September 1944, the cities opened Buchenwald satellite camps, two of thousands of small concentration camps scattered throughout Germany. Conditions were dreadful for the 450 Jewish women laboring at Neustadt's Siemens factory and the more than 450 Jewish men forced to work at Sonneberg's Reinhardt gear factory. In Sonneberg, around twenty prisoners died each month.[51] Townspeople would see the inmates at work and on the streets, marched to and from the factory in grimy striped uniforms and wooden clogs. Locals also remember the camps' hurried evacuations in early April 1945 on "death marches." Columns of prisoners were hounded by SS dogs. Those too weak to walk perished or were shot. Trudging an average of thirty-five kilometers a day, less than half of Sonneberg's inmates survived the six weeks until their liberation on May 7, 1945, fifty kilometers outside Prague.[52]

For all these upheavals, most Neustadters and Sonnebergers remained relatively unscathed by World War II. The Allies did not bomb the area until February 1945, and civilian deaths and damage were far lower than average in Germany. Local casualties from Allied bombings were in the dozens, and less than 7 percent of the towns' buildings were hit, compared to over 50 percent in larger cities and industrial regions.[53] Here, perhaps more than anywhere else, Germans' macabre popular joke was particularly apt: "Enjoy the war—the peace will be terrible!"[54]

1945: "Zero Hour"

The end of World War II brought more instability to Burned Bridge than had the war itself. Invasion and occupation by American and Soviet armies transformed everyday life, a rupture that Germans described as "zero hour."[55] Soon, foreign administration set Sonneberg and Neustadt on paths toward the construction of two new and very different societies.

The initial arrival of U.S. forces on April 11–12, 1945, was peaceful, since most of Germany was already in Allied hands. When the advancing 101st Infantry Regiment called Sonneberg's town hall from nearby Bettelhecken, two low-level officials surrendered the city by telephone.[56] There was little opposition. The Volkssturm, Germany's national militia, had built a barricade at Burned

Bridge, sacrificing the beloved chestnut trees along the road, but American tanks maneuvered around it through the flat fields. Neustadters and Sonnebergers accepted defeat, lining the streets with improvised white flags, sheets, and towels. Some local women paired off with American soldiers that same night, to the dismay of resentful members of the Hitler Youth, who noted their names.[57]

The peace, however, became progressively tumultuous. People were aghast as "looting, rape, thefts, etc. plagued" the cities.[58] Townspeople raided warehouses and the Luftwaffe depot for military boots, gloves, and coats. Though at the time, public discourse blamed the "terror" and "heinous deeds ... of vandalistic devastation" on liberated foreign workers ("Poles") and Germans expelled from their homes in eastern Europe who were pouring in from the countryside.[59] Thousands of newcomers—housed provisionally in schools, factories, and barracks—received higher rations, strained scarce resources, and swelled the towns' populations by 30 to 50 percent.[60] Locals begrudged the imposition as infrastructure collapsed. Railroad, telephone, and postal services were disrupted, news was distributed by a primitive caller and signal system, and disease and infant mortality escalated.[61] Administrative purges aggravated the "anarchy," as the cities hastily appointed new officials who were ill-prepared to handle the crisis.[62] In the words of Curt Ortelli, literally recruited off the street by U.S. officials to be Sonneberg's new mayor because he spoke English: "Nothing seemed certain, it was chaos."[63]

American forces tried to assert control over the confusion. Their sudden arrests, house-to-house searches, property confiscations, housing requisitions, street patrols, warning sirens, public registrations, and military shows of force took townspeople aback. Their curfews, six-kilometer county travel boundary, and restrictions on driving and bike riding limited everyday movement.[64] A bonfire of confiscated bicycles fueled locals' ire. American occupiers also put their mark on the towns. They plastered posters announcing new orders and regulations and renamed streets, buildings, playgrounds, mountains, and, of course, Sonneberg's Hitler Square.[65]

Many found the U.S. Army's initial ban on fraternization "extraordinarily embarrassing."[66] They resented troops' aloofness and abuses, and bristled at the rule of "Negroes and mixed-breeds."[67] Soldiers reveled in their power. In the words of one former private, "Cigarettes were gold, you could buy up the whole country-side for a pack ... you could get services out of them, you know. We had a German captain and he'd come clean our boots."[68] Some accounts, propagated by East German histories of Sonneberg, accuse Americans of snapping up weapons, cameras, liquor, and other booty, as well as intentionally allowing looting to continue and orchestrating the large-scale transport of Sonneberg's toy inventories to the West.[69]

After three months of American occupation, Sonneberg, along with other areas of Thuringia and Saxony, was turned over to Soviet military administration.

Germany's zonal boundaries had been set in the London Protocol of September 1944, and Stalin, Roosevelt, and Churchill agreed to them at Yalta in February 1945. So on July 1, 1945, Soviet forces entered Sonneberg, and the U.S. Army withdrew into Neustadt. Locals perceived American and Soviet forces oppositely, contrasting images of bighearted Americans distributing gum and chocolate from tanks with images of brutish Soviet soldiers in tattered horse-drawn wagons.[70] Townspeople chuckled at how "chic" the Americans seemed, and were "astonished" by their modern equipment, smart uniforms, and access to types of food not seen for years. They mocked the Soviets for "primitiveness"—for naive delight in watches or for washing potatoes in the toilet.[71]

At first, the cities' separation into different occupation zones felt temporary. One of the first stories townspeople tell about the Iron Curtain, although there is no apparent archival record of the event, is that Soviet forces tried to enter Neustadt because their map showed that the Coburg region belonged to their zone. Allegedly, American forces stopped them at Burned Bridge, and the two armies confronted each other. Once a passerby helped explain that the Soviet map was outdated, printed before Coburg joined Bavaria in 1920, the crisis passed, with Neustadt amicably claimed for the American zone.[72] Apocryphal or not, this popular story evokes the prevailing sense of haphazardness about the towns' fates, and uncertainty over the meaning of those fates.

The arrival of the Soviet army brought a second round of abrupt changes to Sonneberg. Locals were surprised. One wrote in her memoir, "Suddenly, it's the Russians are coming to Thuringia, we didn't want to believe it . . . the communists smeared the streets with banners like 'we greet our liberators!'"[73] Within days, the Soviet command replaced city personnel with local communists. Sonnebergers understood that "new ideologies demanded new men," but many disliked "uneducated people" ascending to power.[74] After twelve years of virulent anti-Soviet propaganda, it was unnerving to see Stalin portraits and communist slogans covering the city's roads and buildings, which the military government renamed after socialist heroes. Incessant broadcasting from twenty-two newly erected loudspeakers, with news, music, and lectures beginning at seven in the morning, annoyed residents.[75] Sonnebergers also faced sweeping demands. Soviet forces confiscated household items—books, lightbulbs, and soccer balls— and issued sudden work orders to clean streets, chop wood, or provide services such as hair styling to Soviet officers.[76]

For war reparations, the military authority transported to the Soviet Union around 30 percent of the Soviet zone's industrial capability, removing machinery from numerous Sonneberg factories in 1945–46. The swift dismantling of Sonneberg's prized gear factory became legend, as Soviet troops rounded up a hundred men off the street to ship off the plant overnight.[77] Yet Sonneberg was less affected by economic restructuring than other regions of the Soviet zone. Since the county had few large businesses and fewer large farms, nationalization of industry and land redistribution in the area, while unpopular, were relatively mild.[78]

Everyday violence in Sonneberg was not mild, however. Certainly stereotypes of American friendliness and Soviet brutality were overdrawn. Soldiers on both sides had diverse relationships with Germans, and American troops could be belligerent, "beating up German civilians (mostly while intoxicated)."[79] But on the whole, violence in the Soviet zone was far greater. Sonneberg, occupied three months after invasion, was spared the brunt of Red Army aggression. Still, its residents suffered daily assaults, arbitrary arrests, and thefts that produced "great fear and insecurity."[80] Hundreds, perhaps thousands, of townspeople fled to the American zone in the summer and autumn of 1945. Soviet violence remained especially acute in the borderland. Because of high troop levels on the demarcation line, in the words of one Bavarian report, "the masses are absolutely fair game."[81]

Political purges were fearsome. In the Soviet zone, authorities targeted not just Nazi leaders but thousands of others deemed hostile to socialism. Many fled west. Yet Soviet internment camps still held 1.3 percent of the population (where a third perished from disease and starvation), compared to 0.5 percent of the populace interned in the western zones.[82] Arbitrary roundups in Sonneberg generated widespread "fear and panic," especially the deportation of seventy-seven innocent teenagers in the winter of 1945–46.[83] Boys convicted as "Werewolves," or Nazi resistance fighters, were sentenced to ten to twenty-five years of internment. Arrests were notoriously groundless, arising from the machinations of local Communist Party organizations. Oberlind's vice mayor reportedly received 2,000 reichsmarks (RM) for each of the fifteen youths he denounced, so while next-door Unterlind had only four arrests, Oberlind's totaled twenty-seven.[84]

The youths' interrogations at the old city hall became the "people's nightmare."[85] Screams from beatings could be heard on the street, where parents, siblings, and school friends gathered, hoping to glimpse their loved ones.[86] As police raided communities and dance halls looking for boys, people developed warning signals so that young men could hide, or sent their sons over the border to disappear in Neustadt.[87] Even the West was not always safe. Bernd Meusel was kidnapped and returned to Sonneberg by four Neustadt policemen and a communist Neustadt city councilor (who received 1,000 RM each) and was later executed.[88] This climate of mistrust had a lasting impact on Sonneberg and on the boys. Jakob Ziegler, who at age sixteen was denounced by a neighbor and sent to Buchenwald's Soviet "Special Camp" in 1946, was released in 1950 weighing 110 pounds, deaf in one ear, and with his lungs damaged from tuberculosis. More than fifty years later, he said he still could not sleep at night; "I just can't get it out of my head."[89] Yet he was among the lucky. More than half of Sonneberg's innocent teenagers died: twenty-nine in camps, one during transport to the Soviet Union, and nine from execution.[90]

Soviet sexual violence was also terrifying. Rape in the Soviet zone was endemic during the early months of occupation and, though the incidence had been reduced by the time soldiers arrived in Sonneberg in July 1945, interviewees describe victimized neighbors, sisters, and mothers.[91] Sonnebergers also explain matter-of-factly that billeted Soviet officers had expectations of sex. Women unlucky enough to live nearby regarded it not as rape but more as par for the course. The mayor of Mengersgereuth-Hämmern claimed the Soviet command removed him from office because he "did not provide young women."[92]

In both the Soviet and American occupations, soldiers' physical and economic dominance fused through sex, giving rise to a complicated continuum from coercion to semiprostitution to profitable dating. The devastated postwar economy, as well as the skewed ratio of young German men to women (verging on two to three), worked in the soldiers' favor, as did their access to goods and privileges.[93] Troops took full advantage, a culture of coupling arising especially in the American zone. In the words of one former U.S. soldier in Neustadt, "You could get the women to do anything for a cigarette."[94] Most encounters were short-lived, yet German families could also go to great lengths to "find an American to take care of them." One former soldier boasted of his good fortune in finding a girlfriend whose father worked at the nearby Hummel factory; the father arranged three visits for the soldier, with three complimentary figurines.[95] Another said his seventeen-year-old girlfriend's mother always served them breakfast in bed.[96]

Sex between soldiers and German women—both coerced and consensual— was contentious. Discretion was hard to come by in close-knit communities, where housing shortages meant an average of two to three people per room, and "lying in" a potato field could lead to a police report.[97] Compromised women became symbols of Germany's submission and humiliation, with images of Soviet "rape" versus American "fraternization" expanding into metaphors of occupied rule more broadly.[98] Angry verses addressed to "chocolate-wenches," disseminated near Neustadt, raged:

> We do not want to be raped,
> So we go out with Amis [Americans] to be buffered . . .
> Six years the men have fought
> Six years long for you have suffered
> Have you since really so forgot
> And now think about devouring chocolate![99]

Newspapers in both zones cast sex with soldiers as voluntary, apart from physical or economic pressure. Articles railed against the "sinking morals" of "women who aren't women," and reported prosecutions for abortions, drunkenness, and loitering outside clubs.[100] The tenants of one apartment block banned American soldiers and lobbied Coburg's Moral Police to raid their premises repeatedly.[101]

Venereal disease became a kind of scarlet letter, a mark of personal and national disgrace. Prevention efforts, public throughout Germany, were especially invasive in the borderland.[102] High frontier traffic and troop concentrations meant higher rates of sexually transmitted diseases—and each side pointed to the other as the source of contagion. Sonneberg's county council claimed that half of local cases originated in the West.[103] In both zones, posters, exhibitions, lectures, and articles stigmatized contaminated women. Sonneberg's newspaper urged readers to report people they suspected of infection, not as a "denunciation" but as a "necessity."[104] The U.S. Army began the "screening of fräuleins" for venereal disease (and Nazi influence) for admittance at American clubs, while troops posted photographs of infected local women.[105]

Police on each side raided bars, cafés, and dance halls, retaining suspects and sometimes expelling women of "loose moral character" to "special house[s] of correction."[106] American and Soviet zone authorities ordered hundreds of locals, overwhelmingly women, to submit to testing or face arrest.[107] Those on Coburg-area "VD suspect lists" were apprehended in "Moral Controls," and if they were infected, they were confined and treated for six days.[108] If a U.S. soldier became "sweet on" a girl, he could ask a "buddy in the medics" to have her picked up, tested, and treated.[109] American troops also rounded up "unescorted" women on the street at random. Once, soldiers seized sixty-five theatergoers, transporting them for testing at Coburg's hospital. Because this raid affected "ladies from good circles," including the mayor's daughter, granddaughter, and daughter-in-law (and yielded only one case of syphilis), there was temporary outrage.[110] But for the most part, women on both sides of the border bore the blame, and shame, of a sexualized occupation.

This was not the first time that fears of outsider influence, social anxiety, and a recriminatory political culture intersected to create new categories of transgressors at Burned Bridge. Nor would it be the last. Social fabric unraveled swiftly in this post-dictatorial, insecure postwar world. Denunciations of all kinds "flourished."[111] Neustadt's police were so inundated with anonymous accusations that the Neue Presse asked people to stop sending them.[112] Fear and mistrust bred more fear and mistrust. It was within this shattered society that the American and Soviet military governments began to impose widely disparate systems.

American Versus Soviet Rule

Life in Neustadt and Sonneberg changed dramatically after 1945 and began to diverge. Socialist authority soon dominated the Soviet zone, where the Soviet Union loomed as a polarizing model that attracted active enthusiasts yet, after the Third Reich's demonization of communism, provoked alarm and animosity among many Germans. In the American zone, more fluid goals of democratization and decentralization made for a bigger tent, drawing reformers and reactionaries alike. Measures were milder in all of Germany's western zones—American, British, and French—as were ambitions for political, social, and economic restructuring.[113]

Yet for all their obvious contrasts in ideology and approach, the Soviet and American military governments shared similar logistical constraints. Regional offices were stretched thin, overcome by disorganization and inexperience, and muddled through conflicting policies, supply shortages, and rotating personnel. Coburg County had eight American administrators in 1946, reduced to three in 1947, for 100,000 people, plus the "extra work caused by the border."[114] Soviet officials were even more disorganized in Sonneberg, where Mayor Geyer asked neighboring cities for guidance in helping to structure the Soviet command.[115] In both zones, ad hoc, decentralized policy implementation relied heavily on German expertise and manpower, allowing for a lot of local leeway.

The limitations of military rule limited political restructuring in both zones. The Allies planned to purge Nazis from influential positions in society; the Americans focused on individual guilt, aiming to reform rather than replace the administration, while the Soviets blamed the crimes of fascism on capitalism and wanted to revolutionize the system. The borderland magnified their dissimilarities, as newspapers in Neustadt and Sonneberg criticized each other's denazification trials.[116] However, denazification in both zones had similar outcomes, turning out to be less extensive than either occupier intended. The Soviet military administration sought a sweeping purge of bourgeois professions, but flawed tribunals, expedient shortcuts, and community tensions impeded full removal of the "reactionary forces" that supposedly endangered "democratic construction."[117] Denazification records in Sonneberg are sparse, and much of the city's Nazi hierarchy had already fled west; still, it appears that Sonneberg's commission handled half as many cases as Neustadt's (470 to 1,031), despite the city's much larger population, and demoted or removed 234 people from their jobs. Many were rehired after a few months.[118]

The West was gentler to ex-Nazis. Initially, American efforts at denazification involved 28 percent of the zone's adult population, though pragmatism and halfhearted prosecution disproportionately hurt the "small fry" while "big fish" got away.[119] In the "very Nazified community" of Neustadt, it was difficult to find enough "clean" Neustadters willing to serve on denazification tribunals, let alone to give testimony as public witnesses.[120] Besides, strict enforcement would have crippled reconstruction, since 70 percent of small business owners in the area were subject to dismissal.[121] So although more than ten thousand Neustadters qualified for denazification procedures, only 121 received meaningful convictions.[122] Willi Dietzel, a Nazi Party member since 1925 (number 10,653), who operated two factories with Jewish slave labor in Czechoslovakia, was declared a "fellow traveler," or *Mitläufer*, and fined 1,000 RM.[123] Local Nazis reentered public life easily. Neustadters voted four former party members into the city council in 1948, and former Nazi mayor Friedrich Schubart (1934–45), who had overseen dozens of summary arrests and the deportation of nine men to Dachau, won 47 percent of the vote for mayor in 1952.[124]

As local realities constrained occupier ambitions, the two military governments had opposite responses to their own insufficiencies. Soviet authorities sought control over a subservient bureaucracy, intolerant of even minor improvisation. When Councilor Heß of Sonneberg suggested billeting border police in regular homes to protect the local economy, instead of at Farmer Schmidt's barn and coal business, Lieutenant Petrov reportedly warned: "It is irrelevant what German offices deem reasonable or unreasonable.... Any hesitation is sabotage."[125] Soviet officials were even less interested in the opinions of ordinary citizens, whom they berated for raising concerns, rather than going through German channels.

By contrast, American authorities encouraged Germans to take the initiative, promoting engagement in order to dismantle "machine government."[126] In fact, the U.S. Coburg Office refrained from intervening in the day-to-day activities of local agencies, even when they took actions contrary to its precepts.[127] This laissez-faire approach could be confusing, especially since many Germans presumed that Americans would seek the same degree of control as had Nazi officials. Civilian requests, down to petitions for apartments, jobs, mattresses, and drill machines, fused democratic buzzwords with the alarmist tone characteristic of the Third Reich. One disabled refugee insisted the U.S. Coburg Office owed him a free bicycle so "that I can get my rights, too."[128] Rather than dismissing such demands, director Sanford Sussell wrote didactic replies. Urging citizens to solve their own problems through local meetings, media, and petition drives, he insisted that because American officials "seek to interfere as little as possible in German affairs," governance "becomes the responsibility of people such as yourself."[129]

While the Soviet and American military governments diverged in their goals and means for achieving socialism and liberal democracy, each hoped its ideology would permeate German society to become "a way of life, not [just] a form of government."[130] To convert hearts and minds, both sides promoted grassroots activism from above, a difficult undertaking. The Soviet zone mobilized citizens into mass organizations, following communist and National Socialist strategies for civic homogeneity. American authorities sought heterogeneity, with community associations advancing not the power of the state but the independence of individuals. These mirror images of political engagement took shape in numerous areas of local life. In Sonneberg, for example, children were to join the Free German Youth (FDJ), which, like the Soviet Komsomol, organized uniform socialist instruction. In Neustadt, however, children were to learn "democratic thinking" from informal soap-box derbies, 4-H Clubs, Boy Scouts, baseball, and other American pastimes.[131] Town meetings also diverged. In Sonneberg, they became stylized rituals intended not for open discussion, as propaganda claimed, but to instill seamless "solidarity" and "trust" in government. Sonnebergers learned to watch what they said, since "a reasonable person could have nothing to add" to officials' "convincing arguments."[132] Conversely, American authorities wanted critique and debate at town meetings. They even pressured Neustadt's city council to open its sessions to the public. But Mayor Woltz insisted citizens were "not disciplined enough," and American officials continued to complain about Germans' political passivity.[133]

Actually, pervasive apoliticism disappointed both occupiers. American and Soviet administrators had presumed that, given the right conditions, their respective ideologies would flourish. Yet when the new rulers lifted the supposed yoke of the Third Reich, most Germans did not rise up in spontaneous movements in either's desired direction. The occupiers' efforts failed to ignite political passions. Far from it: Sonneberg's first postwar municipal election was noteworthy not for revolutionary fervor but for free bratwursts and ice cream.[134] Locals tended to privilege their own "household-horizon."[135] Frieda Löffler threw hot water on members of the Young German Order singing outside her window not because she objected to their beliefs but to stop the noise.[136] After twelve years of National Socialism and six years of war, people were wary of ambitious ideologies. Less concerned with lofty rhetoric than food, housing, and reconstruction, Neustadters and Sonnebergers tended to judge the occupation governments by their practical achievements.

Support for socialism, in particular, decreased.[137] Communists in Sonneberg had difficulty wooing frontier residents who saw a more peaceable U.S. zone right next door. In fact, Sonneberg had the lowest party membership rate in all of Thuringia in late 1945, with recruitment lagging behind even Coburg County, which was in American hands.[138] Reprimanded by the district leadership, Sonneberg cadres were told to emphasize not ideology but how the American zone was (just as) bad, with economic misery, military confiscation of the best houses, and ongoing violence. They claimed that "Negro rapes of women are daily occurrences."[139] The increased borderland effort of Sonneberg's Communist Party (KPD) saw some success, as did the forced merger with the popular Social Democrats into the Socialist Unity Party (SED).[140] In 1946, in the last comparatively open elections, more than 60 percent of Sonnebergers voted for the SED, above Thuringian and Soviet zone averages of around 50 percent.[141] Sonnebergers soon learned that communist rule meant "conflicts are not allowed" and, adjusting to an "excessive increase of bureaucratization," became circumspect in their daily utterances and activities.[142] Soviet-style authoritarianism disappointed many idealists who believed in a communism of Christian communalism. In the words of one, "The real, old comrades in Sonneberg, we didn't want it to turn out like this."[143]

In Neustadt, socialist support dwindled rapidly. Leftists had polled well at first, the KPD receiving more than 10 percent and Social Democrats at least 50 percent of the vote in 1946, double the Bavarian average. But the far right was strong, too. More than a quarter of Neustadters voted for Free Democrats, the party of most former Nazis, while 16 percent of county residents cast invalid votes for the Nazi Party itself.[144] Neustadt's frontier location pushed the city further rightward. As Neustadters witnessed firsthand the alarming developments in the Soviet zone, local communists were disdained as strange marginal elements, or "lazy dogs."[145] Neustadt's KPD leadership admitted that proximity to the border put it "in a difficult position."[146] Increasingly moderate Social Democrats distanced themselves from increasingly strident Communists and, like elsewhere in the American zone, authorities' mistrust and limitations on leftist activities grew.[147]

For all that American and Soviet authorities wanted grassroots political engagement, neither side wanted activism that challenged its core ideology. Especially along the demarcation line, both military governments became intolerant of opposition. Notwithstanding an ongoing rhetoric of openness, political systems in the zones hardened, and ultimately governed from the top down. Moreover, as tensions mounted between the American and Soviet administrations ahead of the Cold War, the sides formed in reaction to the other. The military governments began to regard Germans in their zones more as allies than as enemies, and adjusted reconstruction priorities accordingly. Both occupiers portrayed the other as an anti-model, propelling a dynamic of reciprocal influence that was particularly pronounced in the borderland and which exaggerated differences over time. So although administrative constraints and political exigencies meant U.S. and Soviet policies fell short of their goals, their improvisations still transformed each zone.

* * *

Burned Bridge, originally a landmark of connection, became a symbol of severance with foreign occupation in 1945. Neustadters and Sonnebergers had hoped the boundary between the American and Soviet zones would resemble previous borders between them: an administrative demarcation that little affected everyday life. But efforts to construct opposite societies dwarfed historical partitions and set the foundations of the Iron Curtain. As the cities diverged, a barrier emerged.

‖ 2 ‖

Insecurity: Border Mayhem

At first, the demarcation line between Soviet and American zones at Burned Bridge was an invisible "green border," or *grüne Grenze*. It had scant infrastructure from 1945 to 1948, leading to chaos and conflict as the occupying powers imposed vastly different governments on either side. Residents and officials in both East and West came to regard the zonal boundary as a wild frontier. Violence and instability prompted security escalations as well as everyday adjustments. Paradoxically, Germany's early border generated the insecurity that propelled its own expansion, lending it ever greater legitimacy.

Problems of Partition

Stalin, Roosevelt, and Churchill had decided on the principle of Allied occupation zones at the Teheran Conferences in late 1943 but differed as to the exact location of the zonal boundaries. When a joint European advisory commission began meeting in January 1944 to draw the lines, it rather hastily accepted the proposals of Britain's Lord William Strang, which followed historical provincial borders and left Berlin, in the Soviet zone, under four-power control. The plan met with "little discussion and early agreement," and came into being with the London Protocol of September 1944 and the approval of the Big Three at Yalta in February 1945.[1] Germany's eventual shape remained uncertain, however. External borders seemed tenuous, most notably Stalin's moving of the Polish boundary westward to the Oder and western Neisse rivers. And Germany's internal zonal boundaries seemed even "more temporary."[2]

Following the end of hostilities, the Allies began imposing travel restrictions between their military zones. Begun as short-term population control, the measures lent force to zonal boundaries. In the spring of 1945, the American military government enacted Law No. 161 to limit the movement of refugees, displaced persons, German soldiers, Nazi officials, and intelligence personnel into its territory, blocking some roads and footpaths with barriers. When traffic proved unmanageable—1.6 million people leaving the Soviet zone for the western zones between October 1945 and June 1946—the western Allies established a Travel Security Board in December 1945 to systematize regulations. The Soviet Union eventually persuaded the Allied Control Council to shut all zonal boundaries to unauthorized travelers on June 30, 1946.[3] The guarded borders between the U.S., British, and French zones remained relatively unproblematic. Their traffic was manageable, liaison relationships were solid, and everyday conditions were comparable. The western Allies reduced enforcement of these borders. The demarcation lines between the Soviet and western military governments, though, soon proved intractable.

At Burned Bridge, the American-Soviet zonal boundary aggravated postwar anxieties. With the U.S. and Soviet armies massed on either side, it seemed a potential flash point that might lead to World War III. Borderland newspapers urged "stupid people" not to believe rumors of war; "rumor mongering" was a crime punishable by five years' imprisonment in the Soviet zone and ten in the American zone.[4] But it was hard not to be nervous. The very course of the demarcation line was unclear. Sometimes American and Soviet forces made ad hoc agreements over contested parcels of land. Or obscured stone markers, unreliable in wetter areas, occasioned Soviet land grabs. In one seizure, the Soviet army claimed 740 acres of Neustadt forest, which was returned only because of the "courageous" negotiations of Meilschnitz's mayor.[5] Amid the ongoing uncertainty, a number of eastern border towns requested to transfer to Bavaria, promising western authorities "extremely industrious" inhabitants.[6] In October 1945, Soviet troops actually withdrew from Liebau and Heldburg, which protruded almost completely into the American zone. The towns remained in territorial limbo for months, yet appeals for western "protection" ultimately came to naught.[7]

The cities of Sonneberg and Neustadt did not change hands again after July 1945, though separate administration itself wreaked logistical havoc. The demarcation line even put the cities in different time zones initially, an hour's difference, spottily observed, that created headaches.[8] Moreover, Soviet-American disagreements delayed the resumption of basic services: post, rail, and electricity, even milk and school blackboard deliveries.[9] Gas negotiations were particularly heated. The Franconian-Thuringian Gas Works, located in Neustadt but jointly owned by the cities, operated at only 10 percent capacity for months due to heavy bomb damage; the sides could not reach a stable arrangement.[10] The most pressing problem of partition was food. Scarce throughout Germany at the war's end, daily rations in Coburg County hovered at just over a thousand calories.[11] Food was scarcer at Burned Bridge. Neustadters, living at the last railway stop in Bavaria, accused other cities of siphoning off more than their share. Sonneberg was cut off entirely from its main supply, since the county, largely wooded, had imported two-thirds of its food from Bavaria.[12]

In fact, the zonal boundary disrupted Sonneberg more than Neustadt, transforming it into "an island, shut off from the rest of the world."[13] The city had always oriented itself toward the south, its main transportation networks passing through Neustadt to the larger Franconian cities of Coburg, Bamberg, and Würzburg. The Thuringian Forest hemmed it in to the north, west, and east, and the Volkssturm had destroyed bridges along its already inadequate rail and road links. The demarcation line in 1945 not only severed Sonneberg from Neustadt but cut it off from much of Germany, throwing local life into upheaval.

Disconnection made for a massive refugee problem. As hundreds of thousands of people sought to leave the Soviet zone and resettle in the West, the Allies placed severe limits on legal crossing. Although places like Halle, in the Soviet zone, still mistakenly sold train tickets in September 1945 to Coburg, Bamberg, and Munich in the American zone, travelers without interzonal passes were stopped at demarcation line.[14] With nowhere else to go, travelers found themselves stranded in border towns. Sonneberg's overflowing Red Cross station began turning people away. They slept in barns and sheds, in "unbearable" hygienic conditions, and faced locals' ire for theft and food shortages.[15] Far fewer people headed into the Soviet zone than out of it, but Neustadt had its share of marooned travelers as well, especially discharged soldiers unable to return home. Local farmers mostly welcomed these able-bodied young men for their labor.[16]

To stabilize the postwar population, both the American and Soviet military governments sought a stronger boundary. Each began to conceive of its borderland as a separate security area. The U.S. European Command ultimately scrapped proposals for a "Prohibited Frontier Zone" in November 1945 as logistically problematic.[17] But the Soviet military did establish a "Forbidden Zone" in July 1945. Encompassing twenty-two of Sonneberg's fifty-nine municipalities, the restricted area, while haphazardly enforced, was modeled on the Soviet system of restrictive curfews, ordinances, and permits for work or residence on the frontier.[18] Soviet troops were "to use firearms" if people entered the Forbidden Zone without authorization.[19] Trusting only long-standing residents to live there, the Soviet army ordered those who had arrived after 1941 to be "evacuated," giving them twenty-four hours to pack their belongings.[20]

The American army built the first roadblocks and border posts at Burned Bridge. The newly formed U.S. Constabulary conducted a comprehensive survey of the zonal boundary in mid-1946 to clarify territorial disputes, since American and Soviet patrols, even watchtowers, could be on the wrong side of the border by up to several hundred meters. Then U.S. forces reinforced the line with physical barriers, severing 104 roads and innumerable footpaths that crisscrossed the frontier in the region. Although military government authorities worried that systematizing the border would have "serious international political implications" and would be "looked upon as an unfriendly act," the Constabulary was more concerned with curbing illegal traffic.[21] In response, Soviet officials increased troop strength, built their own barriers and markers (higher than the Americans' 1.8 meters), and in some locations added fences and barbed wire.[22]

So while Winston Churchill declared in 1946 that the Soviet menace had created a metaphorical Iron Curtain between East and West, American and Soviet armies together constructed a physical border at Burned Bridge. Significantly, both sides enlisted civilians, drafting frontier residents to clear trees, build barriers, and erect roadblocks.[23] Alongside geopolitical maneuvering, local actions actually constituted the border, fixing rough-hewn wooden posts into the postwar landscape. This expansion of the zonal boundary, however, failed to mitigate the problems it was meant to solve.

Border Guard Violence

Since border marking did little to curb illegal crossings, and even less to stabilize the boundary, the task of border control fell to Allied and German border guards. Far from taming the wild frontier, though, these unruly overseers clashed with frontier residents and with each other. Their lapses intensified occupiers' and civilians' desire for security on both sides, so the protectors of East and West themselves became part of the tumultuous cycle of division.

American authorities complained of U.S. troops' "arrogance and immaturity" on the border.[24] Stefan Taubert, who with his German shepherd tagged along with frontier patrols as a boy, recalled Americans' many on-duty antics.[25] Off-duty there were yet more. "I was an eighteen-year-old kid at the time," one former private remembered, "we had the Russian Army a few yards from us, and could not have cared less. Lots of refugees, black market, wine, women and song."[26] Americans would chat with eastern sentries while raking the border's twenty-foot plow strip. Guards drank (heavily) together after hours inside the U.S. zone—"you could get by with a lot of things."[27] While forces from opposite sides got along, sharing pantomimed conversations and bonfires during cold nights at Burned Bridge, inebriated exchanges could turn hostile.[28] When three U.S. troops tried to cajole Soviet guards to let them "meet their girls" in Sonneberg, their attempted bribe (cigarettes and liquor) and the quip "By fall we'll drink vodka in Moscow" led to a scuffle.[29] Such American insouciance made for diplomatic complications, as joy-riding and intoxicated soldiers strayed into the Soviet zone and got detained for several days, cited for border violations and brawls with eastern forces.[30]

The Bavarian Border Police, created on November 15, 1945, to assist American patrols, translation, and intelligence, did not do much to calm the situation. The German guards were almost four times more numerous in Neustadt than elsewhere on the Bavarian border (one per 0.8 kilometer versus one per 2.7 kilometers), but they failed in "completely sealing the border" because they had little authority.[31] The U.S. military government forbade Bavarian sentries from using weapons within a kilometer of the demarcation line "regardless of circumstances," even when fired upon.[32] Because the border remained so volatile, the German guards were stripped of firearms completely in early 1947, though they remained armed on the French and British zonal borders.[33] This triggered more problems than it solved. Bavarian sentries were powerless to intercept marauding Soviet troops, and became targets of eastern forces' harassment and intelligence abductions. Civilian crossers, too, subjected them to insults and assaults. Cars stopped at the Burned Bridge checkpoint peeled off before they could be searched.[34] Bavarian police lacked respect from their own communities. It was "common knowledge," according to one report, that the guards "may be bought with a few scarce items."[35] And since Bavarian sentries were often native to the areas they patrolled (contrary to the Soviet zone's preference for guards from outside the region, who were believed less susceptible to corruption or flight), overfamiliarity turned some towns into "hot beds of smuggling."[36] Meanwhile, meager salaries and poor provision of uniforms, shoes, and vehicles meant that Bavarian policemen cast "a very poor appearance" and were "openly laughed at in border towns."[37]

By contrast, eastern guards' excess of power proved destabilizing. The Soviet military administration established the German Border Police on December 1, 1946, as a branch of the People's Police, and stationed roughly one guard per kilometer of zonal border.[38] Like Bavarian guards, they were badly clothed and equipped, though they had a reputation for trying to monopolize the choicest food, furniture, and housing in frontier towns, running roughshod over local government.[39] Locals, bristling at their "arrogant behavior" and "unreasonable demands," were punished for not handing over their homes or cooking meals for the "plague" of young policemen.[40] Eastern sentries, too, were known for black marketeering and "dark business."[41] On one hand, they could be a "lubricant" for border smugglers, safeguarding secret paths.[42] On the other hand, they were allowed to keep 10 percent of goods they seized from illegal crossers as incentive pay, and Sonnebergers doubted much of the rest made it into government warehouses.[43]

Of greater concern, though, was eastern guards' brutality. Locals complained that they were "much worse than the Russians," an assertion not corroborated by the archival record, but one that likely reflected surprise at fellow Germans' severity.[44] Indeed, the People's Police had oral instructions "to open fire on border violators who fail to heed the call to stop, regardless of who it is."[45] This was the 1947 root of the so-called *Schießbefehl,* or "license to kill"—an assemblage of evolving orders that "permitted" fatal shots and claimed hundreds of victims over the decades. However, eastern guards often did not want to be on the border any more than locals wanted them there. The flight of sentries to the West was an embarrassing problem for East Germany throughout its history.[46]

The most disruptive force on the border was the Soviet army. Troop violence, endemic throughout the Soviet zone, was especially pronounced along the frontier due to high force concentrations. Plus, the Soviet military administration asserted its authority to pursue illegal crossers up to one kilometer inside American territory. This dubious claim, with its unsettling effects, provoked intense interzonal dispute that culminated in a protest by U.S. military governor General Clay to Soviet military governor Marshal Sokolovsky in early 1948.[47]

Soviet incursions ranged from petty to perilous. Soviet soldiers would venture into the American zone for fun. They frequented Neustadt's Mountain Mill Tavern, located on the Bavarian side of the demarcation line, and popped up at local pubs and festivals.[48] More often, poorly provisioned Soviet troops crossed to pilfer food from western fields, or demanded meals and liquor from Bavarian families. Some stole livestock, watches, jewelry, bicycles, and cars.[49] Soviet soldiers allegedly broke one grain mill dam, owned by a man from Wildenheid, eight times in two weeks, and then required bacon, eggs, butter, and bread from him each time he came near the border to repair it.[50]

Intelligence gathering brought more invasive forays into the American zone. Soviet troops abducted Neustadters into the East for up to several days, interrogating them about politics, public opinion, and western force deployments. They kidnapped people at gunpoint from frontier streets, taverns, and fields.[51] One soldier entrapped a man by asking him to inspect a hare near the border, then pulled him across the line.[52] In another case, Soviet soldiers shot a Bavarian guard during tree stump removal, dragged him across the border, and exploited his long hospitalization in Sonneberg for interrogations.[53] Armed U.S. soldiers were less vulnerable to outright seizure than defenseless members of the Bavarian Border Police. But a few were arrested when Soviet troops moved demarcation posts to catch them patrolling the wrong side of the border.[54] Not all abductions were for military intelligence, though. Soviet forces also ransomed American and Bavarian sentries for cigarettes or a bottle of whiskey.[55]

Some Soviet abductions were political arrests. Eastern forces pursued wanted individuals several kilometers into American territory, forcing them from private homes and businesses. Several cases involved covert operatives from the U.S. Counter Intelligence Corps, but less is known about these disappearances because victims often did not return.[56] And because there were Soviet zone collaborators in Neustadt, locals were reluctant to discuss the incidents with authorities. Fragmentary evidence suggests that the scope of such abductions was considerable, with more than one hundred people estimated to have been kidnapped from Bavaria in 1945–46 alone.[57]

Soviet shootings were widespread along the frontier. Near Burned Bridge, there were shooting incidents every week, with sixty-five reported from June 1946 through June 1947.[58] Exchanges of fire with western forces were typically shows of force, not deadly conflicts. Yet German civilians were not so fortunate. Soviet soldiers killed numerous crossers, as well as people who they believed intended to cross. When Ulrich Imhof, handicapped and on crutches, asked a Soviet soldier from 150 meters inside Bavaria if he could reunite with his wife in the Soviet zone, he was shot and killed after advancing five paces.[59] Locals more familiar with individual guards and frontier ways tended to stay safer than travelers, yet still fell prey to unpredictable violence. Elsa Krueger, hard of hearing, did not heed one Soviet soldier's shouted warning, and was shot and killed walking along the church path in Weissenbrunn, three hundred meters inside the American zone.[60] Although there are no systematic records for these early years, and incidents were likely underreported, western forces documented at least one or two killings a month in the region from 1945 to 1947.[61]

Rape by Soviet soldiers was likewise pervasive on the border. A problem throughout the Soviet zone, rape was especially frequent in the borderland because of high troop levels—and, concealed by the demarcation line, soldiers could kill victims and witnesses with relative impunity. Locals had warned seventeen-year-old Ida Niemeyer not to cross the frontier alone at night, but she was eager to find her parents in the French zone; Soviet soldiers raped her in the middle of a frontier forest and shot her in the head. Her body was found three weeks later.[62] While Sonnebergers cautioned women "not to cross the border without a man," male protectors were just as vulnerable.[63] Soviet troops killed a crosser who happened upon the rape of two women and tried to intervene.[64] Once, six crossers were found together murdered; all three of the women had been "criminally assaulted."[65]

Soviet soldiers sometimes raped western residents inside the American zone. Troops were even less accountable for their actions across the border due to poor relations between the U.S. and Soviet military governments. One group of Soviet soldiers raped a twelve-year-old girl harvesting potatoes near the border in Wildenheid. They hung up her work pants as a trophy at their guard post, and she was hospitalized with critical abdominal bleeding.[66] It is difficult to estimate the incidence of cross-border rape because police files are more oblique about it than about other forms of Soviet violence, except in cases of death or extreme injury. And, as elsewhere in Germany, some were reticent to report sexual assault. Neustadt's *Neue Presse* outright doubted one woman who said she was raped by two Soviet soldiers while walking to work but who could not provide further details because during the assault her face was covered by a thick blue rag.[67]

From what attacks were reported, it is clear Soviet violence on the frontier was frequent and fearsome. In one month in 1946, western forces recorded nineteen Soviet border violations near Burned Bridge: five shootings, one death, one attempted rape, five abductions, two thefts, and several instances of harassment and assault.[68] These forays unsettled daily life in Neustadt. Locals avoided working or walking close to the border lest they encounter impulsive sentries in frontier fields and forests.

It did not seem that much could be done to stop capricious Soviet violence. Eastern authorities denied it was even an issue. They blamed the Soviet zone's ongoing shootings, rapes, and deaths on elusive "Polish bandits" and "perpetrators from the West." People's Police records document implausibly few "warning shots" fired by Sonneberg forces (two to five per month), with fewer than five injuries for the entire state of Thuringia.[69] Plus the Soviet military authority seemed unwilling and, to some extent, unable to rein in its border forces. Such obduracy strained U.S.-Soviet relations, as Soviet commanders "always promised corrective action but [showed] no actual results."[70] Western officials were seldom able to even get the names of offending troops, let alone hold them accountable. Of the thirty-seven reported Soviet border killings in the Neustadt area between August 1945 and September 1947, Coburg's district attorney could pursue only five cases, with limited success.[71]

Western residents lobbied the Bavarian and American occupation governments for stronger border protections. This local pressure had an impact. The mayor of Wildenheid, complaining of Soviet raids for food and alcohol, gained a new U.S. "outpost" for the town.[72] Near Rodach, western leaders demanded an entire "station" of U.S. reinforcements because villagers had become "quite agitated and uncertain" as a result of ongoing Soviet incursions. For two days in March 1946, more than twenty Soviet troops even tried to occupy the western hamlet of Grattstadt. They fired upon Bavarian Border Police, "drove inhabitants into their homes," and threatened to burn down the village.[73] Frontier violence was so disruptive that both zones authorized yearly security increases not only to curb crossers but also to avoid being outnumbered by the other side.

Successive force expansions further destabilized the early frontier. Since American soldiers were ill-prepared, Bavarian Border Police ill-equipped, Thuringian People's Police ill-managed, and Soviet troops ill-contained, poor protectors wound up exacerbating the area's insecurity. As protracted one-upmanship spurred locals' calls for escalations, the border's insufficiencies, ironically, enhanced its legitimacy. Popular desire for law and order stemmed from the utter lack of it.

Beyond Control

Though frontier residents desired a regulated border between East and West, coordination remained elusive in the early postwar years. The absence of administration added to frontier disorder, especially in an intertwined and densely populated region such as Neustadt and Sonneberg. So while the armed forces of East and West had too much engagement, their overseeing officials had too little. The result was much the same: rendering the border beyond control.

Much of the difficulty stemmed from confusion in border policy. Daily governance along the frontier necessitated trade-offs between security and economic pragmatism, two vital yet often conflicting priorities. Border problems tended to compound in unexpected ways. When, for example, Soviet authorities banned motor vehicles from the Forbidden Zone in Mogger, impeding harvests, the prospect of rotting produce during a food shortage incensed inhabitants. Residents lobbied the West for assistance.[74]

But American and Soviet zone authorities had difficulty even meeting to discuss frontier matters. The Soviet commander of Sonneberg could not attend talks in Coburg because his interzonal pass stretched just six kilometers.[75] Moreover, eastern officials were fearful of overstepping their limited authority. At one failed meeting near Neustadt in 1946, "characteristic of most attempts for coordination," the ranking Soviet officer refused to provide either his own name or his unit's name.[76] Sonneberg's German administrators were on a tighter leash, prohibited from engaging in basic correspondence about border logistics with western offices and businesses.[77] Soon, "most liaison" between Neustadt and Sonneberg was conducted not in person but by exchanging notes at border posts, so "even simple problems require[d] days and weeks."[78]

The lack of frontier regulation was a major problem in the region, which had long depended on the everyday back-and-forth of families, workers, and farmers. For the first year after capitulation, the occupation governments placed "petty frontier traffic," or *kleiner Grenzverkehr*, in the hands of local authorities and whatever ad hoc systems they managed to devise. Some border towns cobbled together interim travel booklets or passes. In Fürth am Berg, the mayor resorted to trading shoes and boots to Soviet officers for crossing allowances.[79] Confusion hampered economic recovery, since manufacture and agriculture had been so entwined. In tiny western Meilschnitz, population 250, twenty-five families had worked fields in Sonneberg, while fourteen village farms had Sonneberg tenants—though there was no central provision for daily traffic until mid-1946.[80] The rules were relaxed for a few days at harvest time, but hardly enough to make up for diminished yields.[81] The lack of legal crossing provisions was hardest on divided families. Eastern forces forbade

Crossing the border to tend fields. Landesbibliothek Coburg.

A western border guard comes between mother and son at the barrier between
Wildenheid and Hönbach. Grenzerfahrungen Kompakt, Salier Verlag, Rainer Krebs
collection.

Giesela Greiner from returning her two-year-old granddaughter, who had been visiting in Sonneberg, to her mother over the border in Wildenheid.[82]

The advent of Control Council Directives in June 1946 did little to facilitate legal crossing. The occupiers had sought to rectify "the piteous state of USSR-US agreements" and to rationalize interzonal passage, but the understanding broke down within months.[83] Crossing permits remained difficult to come by, requiring political clearance and evidence of economic necessity, a labyrinthine process whose ever-evolving parameters were subject to much Allied dispute. Burned Bridge, one of a handful of official checkpoints along the demarcation line, remained lightly trafficked. In the immediate postwar years, just eight to ten local commuters and five to fifteen interzonal travelers passed through it each day. By the early 1950s, commuter traffic at the checkpoint increased to between fifty and one hundred a day, and interzonal traffic to between fifty and two hundred.[84] Of Neustadt's seventeen thousand residents, only 250–350 a year legally registered as visitors in Sonneberg, and Sonnebergers were able to visit Neustadt much less frequently.[85] Local workers, civil servants, farmers, friends, and families soon lost everyday contact with the other city.[86]

Even if Neustadters and Sonnebergers did manage to procure commuter or travel permits, occupier conflicts interrupted their passage. Amid growing Allied tensions, border procedures became proxy diplomacy, a means for each side to grandstand, rebuke, and game economic advantage. For example, although Soviet zone authorities allowed Neustadters to work in Sonneberg companies, they were less keen on Neustadters working in Sonneberg fields, as their harvests would then go to the American zone. So when Sonneberg's Soviet commander required Neustadt farmers to have photograph IDs, local American officials launched "retaliatory measures" to ban Sonneberg farmers from tending their fields in the U.S. zone entirely—which they believed would hurt the Soviet zone more.[87] Western reports increasingly brimmed with frustration at Soviet officials' checkpoint closures, rejections, and harassment of crossers. Ever sharper disagreements characterized the "nonexistent" border cooperation, embroiling the upper echelons of the American and Soviet military governments well in advance of the Berlin blockade in 1948.[88]

In the absence of legal regulations, frontier residents resorted to crossing illegally. The "green border" was still porous, and most people were never intercepted. An estimated three hundred to nine hundred people crossed illicitly near Burned Bridge each day, fifty to one hundred of whom were apprehended by guards on either side.[89] This was a considerable, though not unusual, amount of unregulated traffic, representing less than 10 percent of illegal crossing along the entire demarcation line between the Soviet and western zones.[90] People crossed for a variety of reasons, ranging from working to berry picking to visiting family to dancing to "Negro music" in the West.[91] More than 90 percent, though, appear to have been Soviet zone refugees and small-time smugglers.[92] Illegal traffic was highly seasonal, with fewer people crossing in the colder months, except for December, a peak period of family visits and toy and Christmas ornament smuggling.

Initially, both zones' prevention and prosecution efforts were haphazard. When western guards apprehended illegal crossers, they noted their names and released the vast majority.[93] Just 1 to 3 percent of all intercepted traffic—repeat offenders and large-scale black marketeers—faced formal charges. Sentencing varied. Early on, local courts showed "extreme leniency" and "light sentences" of one to two weeks' imprisonment and fines of 50 to 200 RM (the same as in the Soviet zone), while Coburg's U.S. military government court issued sentences of up to six months in jail and tried 100–150 border cases each month (over half of its caseload), leading to overcrowding of borderland prisons.[94] Soviet zone enforcement was more severe but no less chaotic. Sonnebergers remember "entire processions of border-goers with backpacks, suitcases, and packages marched through the streets by Russian soldiers toward the military prison."[95] Punishments could be unofficial bribes or requests. One Soviet officer propositioned a detained woman to escort him to a local festival; when she refused, he ordered her to clean the soldiers' quarters for two days.[96] More often, a bottle of liquor or a couple of western cigarettes sufficed to avoid Soviet arrest.[97]

Although the border was unfenced and posed "no serious obstacle," most Neustadters and Sonnebergers still chose not to cross it.[98] Out of fear or on principle, many obeyed the new restrictions. Westerners, in particular, seldom went into the Soviet zone. Since the archival record is largely silent on the compliant, it is hard to estimate their proportion. But the vast majority of locals said they had little connection to their sister city after 1945. In a mailed survey, 62 percent of Neustadters and 35 percent of Sonnebergers who lived in the region in 1945–52 (105 respondents) said they had "never" crossed the border—either legally or illegally—during those seven years. And youths had been among the most frequent crossers. Fewer claimed to have crossed one to four times (31 percent of Neustadters and 39 percent of Sonnebergers), and the smallest proportion crossed five or more times (7 and 26 percent, respectively). There are no records of how often people went back and forth before 1945, yet it was by all accounts much more frequent. Indeed, 75 percent of this same subset of survey respondents stated that after reunification they crossed the former boundary at least once a month.[99] The "green border," while mostly invisible, divided Burned Bridge from the outset.

Everyday Accommodations

The porous boundary suffused and recast communal life. Neustadters had long spent their paychecks in Sonneberg, enjoying its better-appointed shops and entertainment, while Sonnebergers had frequently gone on weekend excursions in Neustadt, enjoying its better-situated hiking, hunting, swimming, and beer gardens. As the border interrupted long-standing linkages, townspeople adjusted their routines. Locals switched to new churches, schools, and banks, down to finding a new "hairdresser, cobbler, tailor."[100]

The demarcation line also reshaped the landscape, giving rise to unique border spaces and cultures. The land became less trafficked, since gathering wood or hunting was dangerous and even forbidden, and bilberry bushes, for example, grew unchecked—a windfall for Sonneberg's enterprising "berry people," who could sell a kilo for 2 West marks: "the opportunity!"[101] Previously mundane occurrences gained new meaning, such as when the Neue Presse reported a western pig's "dumb mistake" of wandering into the Soviet zone.[102] Locals also restructured and reconceived familiar places. The newspaper printed zigzag directions to Neustadt's Mountain Mill Tavern, detailing where the border "jumps over the road at a right angle," then "goes back diagonally across the path to the west side of the sawmill and then bends again to the south."[103] Yet because Soviet soldiers continued to attack, arrest, and shoot at patrons, the owner built new stairs at the back of the popular watering hole.[104]

The border also changed the tempo of life in Neustadt and Sonneberg. The hubbub of boundary sirens, customs houses, and guard stations penetrated household rhythms. Günter Oppinger remembers trying to sleep with spotlights beamed through his bedroom window near Burned Bridge.[105] Even small acts, such as chatting over the demarcation line, became incorporated into daily practices, a new mode of sociability. Local youths would hang out, gossip, and flirt over the road barrier near Hönbach's cemetery, while divided friends and families met up on the border on weekends.[106] These meetings could be hazardous, too, provoking Soviet abductions or shootings. By 1949, frontier chats required a special permit at Burned Bridge, though this proved impossible to enforce.[107]

On the frontier, the extraordinary became everyday. Residents became acclimated to the assaults, abductions, rapes, and killings—to stumbling upon corpses in shallow graves, under leaves, or in the spring snow melt months after their demise. According to townspeople, "everyone knew of certain dangers" and "got used to the road barrier, the travel permits, and the shots at night."[108] Kurt Geis described finding a severed hand one day while playing in this "Wild West" near his grandparents' house at Burned Bridge.[109] In hindsight, locals tended to downplay the early border, the demarcation line of their childhoods appearing a quaint construct from an age of innocence. Many said with a shrug that it simply "was not so painful."[110] They remember their families' fears but overflow with stories of adventures and treats from Allied soldiers. As one explained, it was "not normal, but it was daily life."[111]

Border brutality was not a subject of much public discussion. Neustadt's Neue Presse might publish a single line noting that someone had been shot or a corpse had been found, positioning it adjacent to long columns on new recipes or fashion advice. Sonneberg's *Thüringer Volk* suppressed such stories completely, though it did warn, vaguely, that illegal crossers risked being shot, and that "criminal elements" menaced the borderland. But for the most part, frontier "incidents, disappearances, arrests, and pursuits" were "not discussed out loud," only "whispered behind one's hand."[112] This reserve contrasted sharply with the outrage and political protest expressed over less frequent killings in subsequent years.

In fact, there was little open questioning of the border's legitimacy in the immediate postwar period. The *Neue Presse* and even *Thüringer Volk* occasionally urged greater "understanding" for border policies, but local opinion pieces, political speeches, and city government records in both East and West shied from overt commentary.[113] The lack of public critique reflected real and perceived pressures of censorship, particularly in the Soviet zone. The silence could also suggest a certain level of acceptance. People may have seen division as retribution for war and the Third Reich, a non-negotiable reality. Most Neustadters and Sonnebergers were surprised by the question of whether they had seen the early border as illegitimate. They feared the Soviet army and felt they had little choice but to acquiesce to the new reality. One former Bavarian Border Police officer was confused when asked if he had ever had second thoughts about his job. Crossing was illegal, and while he "pitied" the crossers, he had "no problems—we were hungry too."[114] The validity of the border would be challenged only later, once it was firmly established.

During the period from 1945 to 1948, when the demarcation line was still in flux, locals portrayed it as almost incontrovertible. Since neither East nor West was yet publicly blaming the other for the border, it appeared as an immutable power unto itself, its "ways" more "mysterious" than God's.[115] Speeches and writings decried its existence in the abstract but did not confront it as a concrete, solvable problem. Sonneberg's *Thüringer Volk* rarely addressed the boundary at all, tending to represent it as a regrettable, "unnatural," and "senseless" inevitability.[116] The freer *Neue Presse* discussed it more often, though casting it as an inhumane monstrosity, an image that endured throughout the decades: "Borderland! Borderland fate! I cannot continue."[117] Fatalistic pieces grieved over (newly) long-lost land: "'Once upon a time!!' . . . Memory! I look and dream."[118] After just a few years of partition, articles presented the boundary as an already inescapable reality. One Neustadter mourned, "We have lost a piece of our home. The farmer who plows his fields below plows in another country."[119] Neustadt and Sonneberg were not in separate countries yet. But the border seemed entrenched.

As the physical border emerged, it expanded in people's imaginations—and concentrated postwar anxieties. After all, Germany's most pressing problems all converged on the demarcation line: violence, refugees, economic collapse, political instability, and Allied conflict. Frontier residents whispered of barrier escalations, territory transfers, troop movements, and World War III.[120] Dramatist Tankred Dorst depicted Burned Bridge as a maelstrom of epic proportions in his play *Die Villa*. While the characters huddled together in a metaphorical Noah's Ark, the piece opened with the lead pacing back and forth "like in a cage. Exactly the same. And perfectly senseless."[121] Germany's unfenced border of 1945–48 was not a static "cage," and locals were not mere bystanders to the changes around them, yet individuals understandably felt helpless. The boundary crystallized all that had gone wrong since capitulation and, more ominously, represented a future too chaotic to comprehend.

Public discussion began marginalizing the frontier, and its crossers, as a shadowy underworld. Shrouded in mystery and danger, it became a nefarious space. Sonneberg's *Thüringer Volk* warned of border profiteers, provocateurs, and various forms of pestilence from the West, such as polio, foot-and-mouth disease, and potato beetles. Newspapers on each side warned of the "road plague" of "venereal diseased" women who lurked along the boundary, decrying trespassers who "sank the morals of our people" through their "brazenness and impertinence."[122] Western guards apprehended Sonneberg women seeking "male acquaintances" in Neustadt, and in one case destroyed, rather than merely confiscated, smuggled glass figures in erotic poses.[123] The borderland became an imagined haunt of criminals and contagion, a breeding ground for literal and symbolic "epidemics of all kinds."[124]

Soon, official discourse blamed crossers for the dangers of the frontier, newspapers warning that "'dark' border-goers make the region unsafe."[125] Not only were crossers the most visible effects of the boundary, but they also deflected potential criticism away from government failures in providing security. So while western officials lamented how serial killers roamed the borderland—three in the Neustadt region allegedly boasted twenty murders among them—there was little discussion of the conditions that made this possible.[126] In the Soviet zone, authorities simply blamed frontier woes on western fascists. Former Nazis "sit here along the zonal boundary" as "smugglers and rumormongers in order to sabotage the construction of socialism."[127] Residents associated border crossers with the dangerous frontier landscape, a shady place that drew shadier characters. In a self-fulfilling prophecy, the border became emblematic of Germany's disorder, a consequence of defeat.

Neustadters and Sonnebergers often said that the immediate postwar years were so tumultuous, they had to believe the border was a temporary problem. Consumed by daily needs and anxieties, they could not think the crisis could persist or worsen. At one level, locals indeed may have seen (or wanted to see) the boundary as temporary. But at the same time, townspeople adapted to the specter in their midst, the frontier incorporated into their mental maps of the postwar world.[128] After all, the ratio of American zone residents believing Germany would reunite in the near term dropped from 70 percent in the winter of 1945–46 to under 20 percent just two years later.[129] Already in 1947, the *Neue Presse* launched a column on Sonneberg entitled "A Look over There."

A growing sense of separateness manifested itself in subtle yet ubiquitous ways. Contentious issues such as food shortages fed cross-border contrasts. Food remained scarce in the region, leading to harvest requisitions on both sides and the creation of food watch groups in Sonneberg that endured for years.[130] Sonneberg officials begged citizens not to believe "false rumors" of plenty in the West, claiming Neustadt was "substantially worse than here."[131] Meanwhile, Neustadt leaders worried about the "political danger" of its food strikes, as well as its residents' not-so-lighthearted reputation as *Hundefresser*, or "dog eaters." The newspaper published that the veterinarian still counted plenty of canines in the city.[132] Political parties campaigned on images of divergence. Local officials stressed the interests of "our" economy or "our people"; borderland policies justified "specific rights" based on proximity to the opposite zone."[133] Though it was mild in comparison to what the Cold War idiom would soon become, Neustadters and Sonnebergers operated within an early vocabulary of difference.

Germany's physical partition emerged from postwar tumult. At Burned Bridge, anxious occupiers, local governments, and ordinary people improvised increasingly divisive measures to fix the boundaries of East and West. The frontier's failures drove its expansion, requiring ever more intervention and appearing ever more a fait accompli. Residents, in turn, reoriented their lives around the demarcation line. Not only did the border create the borderland, but the borderland created the border. Soon, attempts to quell the chaos transformed the tenuous demarcation line into an entrenched barrier.

3

Inequality: Economic Divides

How did the inter-German border, in just a few years, become one of the most notorious boundaries in the world? The early border was not fenced, but in the wake of National Socialism's "Thousand-Year Reich," Germans on both sides broadly accepted it and enforced it against other Germans. Between 1948 and 1952, the hastily drawn demarcation line between Allied zones of occupation expanded into a social, legal, economic, and political boundary in which both East and West developed a stake. These nascent divisions helped make possible East Germany's later closure of the border.

As the Cold War divide hardened, the boundary proved useful to divergent constituencies, gaining importance after 1948 as citizens and governments solidified East-West differences. The Cold War divide hardened. The influx of American Marshall Plan aid into western Europe after April 1948, a spur to currency reform in Germany's western occupation zones in June 1948, marked the foundation of two economic systems. The measures helped stabilize and cohere western Germany, signaling a stark separation from Stalin's postwar priorities of extracting reparations and creating socialist command economies in eastern Europe. When the Soviet Union pulled out of the Allied Control Council in March 1948 over the rift, it closed off western Berlin's land and rail routes in the Berlin blockade, resulting in the western Allies' effort to fly in food and supplies in the Berlin airlift of 1948–49.

The division of Germany, already an economic and military fact, became a political reality with the creation of two German states. The western zones became the Federal Republic of Germany (FRG) on May 23, 1949. Its ostensibly provisional Basic Law provided for a representative parliamentary democracy that, after free elections in August 1949, resulted in the chancellorship of Konrad Adenauer. Soon thereafter, on October 7, 1949, the German Democratic Republic (GDR) was declared in the Soviet zone. To keep the option of reunification open, its initial constitution was superficially compatible with West Germany's Basic Law. Yet under direction of SED leader Walter Ulbricht, East Germany became increasingly socialist and undemocratic. East and West formed competing supranational organizations: the western Organisation for European Economic Co-operation (OEEC) in 1948 and North Atlantic Treaty Organization (NATO) in 1949 (without West Germany), versus the Soviet-led Council for Mutual Economic Assistance (Comecon) in 1949 and eventual Warsaw Pact in 1955. The two German states remained very much a part of their respective Cold War blocs, only semisovereign until 1955.

While geopolitics created the conditions for Germany's division, it did not determine the shape of the actual border between East and West. That remained uncertain, as governments and citizens fumbled toward solutions to the problems that partition created. Local responses are vital to understanding how the boundary actually developed.

Economic inequality, a common borderland phenomenon, had striking consequences along the inter-German boundary in the late 1940s. Material contrasts were particularly visible between the sister cities of Neustadt and Sonneberg, compared to other, more rural borderland regions.[1] Each day, hundreds of black marketeers, undocumented workers, refugees, and begging children crossed illegally near Burned Bridge, overwhelming eastern and western forces. As governments on both sides criminalized this *Grenzgängerei*, or "border-going," frontier residents began to enforce and denounce each other for the new crime. Initiatives against social vagrancy were, of course, nothing new in Germany, predating the rise of National Socialism. But rather quickly, Neustadters and Sonnebergers accepted border transgression as a category of offense and extended its stigma to their neighbors. In so doing, frontier communities inadvertently reinforced East-West divergences, as well as the very notions of East and West.

Black-Market Border

Germany's unfenced "green border"—taking shape with posts, guards, policies, and rhetoric—was clearest when violated. To many, there were gradations of border transgression, with habitual crossers the worst offenders. Locals who crossed for special family or social events were considered the most innocuous, since they posed little threat to the stability of either zone. Some who crossed out of desperation also found compassion, such as those looking for loved ones, and easterners making emergency "hamster," or foraging, trips to support their families.[2] Neustadt's *Neue Presse* depicted sympathetic "women with small children, enduring fear still in their eyes," who braved the "dark" "border forest," where "bitter happenings occur almost daily and hourly." Kindly westerners offered them "their first drink of water" or the chance to "wash themselves in the kitchen."[3] Passage was a major event for infrequent crossers. Their stories convey breathless exhilaration, featuring individual courage in the face of a formidable frontier, from persisting through fog to outsmarting stern sentries, as well as a communal, us-against-them sense of banding with helpful strangers.[4] Also, border officials tolerated intermittent border-goers, conceding, "It is difficult to treat such people as criminals . . . without building an actual wall along the entire border."[5] Often Allied and German guards "just let them go."[6]

Regular crossers, however, were more suspect. The border was a crime zone, and anyone who willingly and repeatedly crossed it could be engaged in some sort of unsavory activity, most likely smuggling. The black market, enormous everywhere in postwar Germany, was especially active on the frontier, feeding off the uncertainty and underregulation of cross-border barter, arbitrage, and dumping. Coburg County conservatively estimated that at least 20 to 30 percent of agricultural production and 5 to 15 percent of industrial production in the region flowed through illicit channels, with estimates for Neustadt and Sonneberg ranging as high as 80 percent.[7] The black market enveloped everyday life. American cigarettes became a standard currency in East and West, one worth almost a quarter of the average weekly wage. At American bars, young women dumped ashtrays into small sacks at closing time. On the streets, boys fought over butts soldiers tossed away—"If you'd drop a cigarette you'd about get knocked down."[8] Although Neustadters and Sonnebergers, like Germans elsewhere, tended to associate black marketeering with outsiders and criminals, most still participated in one form or another.

Border smuggling involved every stratum of the community. Around 90 percent of crossers were easterners, using oversized straw backpacks to carry toys, glass, and other wares that they typically exchanged for food. But a range of westerners facilitated or orchestrated the exchanges. Certain Neustadt businesses, hotels, and taverns, required by law to report nonlocal patrons, were known for their side deals. Lorenz Zwick supposedly "got rich" from his inn, providing shelter for smugglers, space for contraband storage, and a ready sales channel.[9] Private families, too, got in on the action. Crossers paid Günter Oppinger's parents in goods to stay overnight; the border police knew but never did anything about it.[10] Right at Burned Bridge, the grandparents of Kurt Geis used their well-situated house for operations. Their seven grown children—four in Neustadt and three in Sonneberg—deputized the grandchildren to procure items such as cameras or panty hose, and exchanged wares in the cellar under the nose of checkpoint sentries.[11] People came to feel entitled to their activities. When the mayor of Meilschnitz tried to crack down on milk smuggling with the Soviet zone in 1946, ten men showed up on his doorstep to intimidate him, one armed with a club.[12]

Within the tumult, townspeople launched creative side businesses. Locals familiar with frontier paths and patrols became "border guides," leading groups

An illegal border crosser smuggling Christmas ornaments faces a western border guard near Ebersdorf. Stadtarchiv Neustadt bei Coburg.

of crossers for around 20 RM apiece; farmers with commuter passes smuggled wares in their hay or manure carts; city officials on both sides took bribes and falsified travel documents.[13] In Neustadt, border bellhops proliferated, a "legal and apparently very lucrative children's enterprise" of carrying crossers' baggage on handcarts and other "improvised vehicles" between the train station and the demarcation line. However, some complained that the youths created a "traffic obstruction" on the train platform, and that their "effortless income" of 20 to 50 RM for the fifteen-minute walk was "impertinent," even unethical.[14]

Borderland black marketeering became even more rampant in June 1948, following currency reform in the western zones. A new deutsche mark (DM) would replace the worthless reichsmark to create a solid foundation for a separate West German economy, a critical turning point in the development of the border as well as in Germany's division and in the Cold War. For citizens in both East and West, many of whom had lost their life savings in the hyperinflation of 1923, "nervousness had no bounds."[15] Amid the "currency hysteria," the Soviet zone feared a rash of black marketeering from easterners who wanted western banknotes as well as from westerners who might spend unused reichsmarks in the East.[16] The Soviet army closed the border as soon as it learned of western intentions on June 15, before currency reform was publicly announced on June 18 or the new notes distributed on June 21. Eastern forces barricaded Burned Bridge with logs, harassed authorized travelers, and restricted commuter traffic to people on foot or bicycles.[17] Sonneberg's *Thüringer Volk* warned that border sentries had been posted "deep into the hinterland," so any crossing would be "extremely dangerous."[18] Still, both sides reported a spike in illegal traffic.[19]

Overnight, currency reform expanded not only the physical divide between East and West but an economic divide as well. People sensed Neustadt was gaining surer footing, compared to increased crime and uncertainty in Sonneberg.[20] Plus, currency reform exacerbated the asymmetries of border smuggling. As western merchants began to sell food and wares that had only been available on the black market, and the deutsche mark rendered eastern wares even less expensive to western buyers, eastern border-goers flocked west in ever greater numbers. In fact, currency reform rendered the new "D-Mark a magnet on the zonal border."[21] Despite tightened border controls, the volume of illegal traffic escalated with the growing economic disparity between East and West. Illegal crossing was so endemic that authorities had difficulty even estimating its volume. Together, eastern and western forces apprehended more than two hundred people a day in the region around Burned Bridge, with total traffic believed to be two to five times that. In the twelve months following currency reform, eastern forces arrested almost half a million crossers. Illegal crossing all along the demarcation line proved much more common than on external German boundaries, representing 99 percent of all East Germany's border violations.[22] Although the East German government continued to claim that most were poverty-stricken westerners heading east, police records on both sides estimated that 90 to 95 percent were easterners, the vast majority of whom were involved in black marketeering.[23] Entrenching an elaborate illicit economy, some Sonnebergers crossed up to twice a week in "carrying convoys." "The addiction to western money was enormous," one recalled.[24]

Smuggling Stigma

Frequent crossing might have had the potential to bring people on both sides closer together, but the frictions of border-going magnified the growing rift between East and West. As people took advantage of economic divergences,

they came to be associated with those divergences. Crossers reinforced notions of an impoverished East versus a "promised land" in the West.[25] Early
images of East and West formed not just from ideology but also from material
disparity.

Many frontier residents came to resent crossers and their impact on the local
economy. Sonnebergers protested that border-goers bought out inventories
(stockings, material, carpets, etc.) at the city's modest state stores for smuggling,
so "honest customers" had scant access to goods.[26] The eastern People's Police
conducted undercover spot checks, targeting western food, cigarettes, and
alcohol sold at Sonneberg restaurants, pubs, and hotels. And the communist
SED adapted state goods to the border black market, seeking to increase the
supply of items bought in the West (food specialties such as herring) while limiting goods smuggled from the East (e.g., typewriters and motorcycles).[27] As
border-goers' earnings climbed higher than average wages, townspeople on
both sides disliked that the crossers could buy up food and wares at will.[28] In
Neustadt, merchants profited from border-goers' "indiscriminate" buying (they
didn't "know the value of a mark"), but most residents were not "laughing"
about the astronomical sums easterners paid for the most basic items, because
it drove up prices for everybody.[29]

Neustadt and Sonneberg officials invoked a language of moral economy
when combating border dealings.[30] Neustadt's Mayor Paul Weppler worried
that black marketeering had "greatly impaired the morals" of residents who
had "grown accustomed to shirking proper work to live from illegal earnings."[31]
Sonneberg officials organized neighborhood People's Control Committees to
encourage denunciations "in the interest of the public."[32] Newspapers in both
cities portrayed "sordid business" at the heart of the boundary's physical, economic, and ethical dangers, publishing quantities of seized contraband and
the sentences of caught crossers.[33] Neustadt's *Neue Presse* decried "calories
wandering over the border" and sensationalized the milieu of border-going,
with investigative reports on the tactics of frontier camouflage, hitchhiking,
police impersonation, and voice and light signals.[34] To "astonish" the hungry
masses, Sonneberg's *Thüringer Volk* itemized food uncovered at "hamster
nests" and "plague spots" in mouth-watering detail; its long-nosed, cigar-
smoking (capitalist) caricature of "Mr. Profiteer" leered, "The border area suits
my needs wonderfully."[35] Public images, fears, and resentments approached
moral panic.[36]

Local animus toward border transgressors was perhaps starkest in the case
of the most innocuous crossers: children.[37] Because youths were generally
exempt from frontier arrest, eastern children frequently "hamstered," smuggled, and begged across the boundary, especially after currency reform in
1948. Youth crossing reached "catastrophic proportions" for the Soviet zone,

most of all in Sonneberg, where every day an estimated three hundred local kids crossed into Neustadt.[38] As young as six or seven years old, they skipped school; as a result, "seldom even half the pupils were present."[39] Some teachers even excused absences in exchange for goods. Many Sonnebergers recalled their youthful exploits fondly. Götz Emrich, later responsible for border construction in the 1980s, savored his first West mark as a ten-year-old and the delectable milk drop he bought.[40] Hannelore Reuther, who smuggled glass doll eyes in her preteen brassiere, remembered that Neustadters gave her money out of "pity," but she admitted, like most other former child crossers, that she and her sisters went door-to-door mostly for "adventure," pocket money, and ice cream.[41] Most tellingly, the children "dressed up as 'east-zonal,'" with ill-fitting shoes and ripped clothing, "in order to arouse sympathy."[42] Suggesting the strength of early East-West stereotypes, westerners already expected easterners to appear needy, and easterners were already well aware of it.

Neustadters soon lost patience with eastern youths' exploits. The press detailed the crimes of these "small thieves" and "juvenile pickpockets," the contraband at their train station "stock exchange," and their "social and moral uprooting."[43] Neustadt's Mayor Weppler, never one to mince words, proclaimed that "through their thefts of great audacity, brazen behavior, and begging, the crossing children have become a plague."[44]

As Neustadters became "no longer as generous and accommodating," Sonneberg children began venturing further into the American zone, to Coburg, Bamberg, Würzburg, and even Munich.[45] But westerners in these larger cities likewise complained that "wayward" youths evidenced "a critical level of moral degradation," and took action against their "begging and loafing."[46] City governments sent lists of children's names to Sonneberg's criminal police. Bamberg went so far as to commit the youths until their parents could travel to Bavaria and cover the cost of their institutionalization, a tall order.[47] Its Catholic diocese even inquired "whether it might be possible" for the Soviet zone to better patrol the frontier.[48]

Sonneberg's leaders scrambled to end the humiliating "vagabonding."[49] They blamed "asocial elements" and censured parents of the "work-shy" children, threatening them with fines of 150–300 RM, special talks at schools and city hall, legal action by the district attorney in Rudolstadt, and "harsh proceedings" from Soviet authorities and secret police.[50] The *Thüringer Volk* campaigned against children's "spiritual and moral ruin," as did Party neighborhood groups in "public parents' evenings."[51]

However, these "relatively mild measures" did little to stop the crossing children.[52] Sonneberg legislators took the issue to Thuringia's state parliament, warning that since the West had handled "this shameful problem quite publicly," border-going youth "through their behavior and poor clothing" endangered the "political reputation of the East Zone."[53] After talks with Bavarian officials, Sonneberg agreed to build a "transit home" on the border for compulsory committals of the "willful youths."[54] This was a controversial and embarrassing move for the fledgling socialist government, unable to feed, reform, or contain the young border-goers. Many objected to its harshness, threatening to leave the Party. Eventually Sonneberg's city councilors negotiated construction of the youth home further east toward Kronach, away from the more visible checkpoint at Burned Bridge.[55] Yet the home created as many difficulties as it solved, and Sonneberg's young "wanderers" and "adventurers" remained a problem for border control for decades.[56]

Stigmatizing crossers—even children—contributed to early notions of East and West. As easterners crossed because they saw divergences between the Soviet and western zones, and as westerners took advantage or disdained them, the asymmetries both revealed and reinforced a sense of difference. Just as Soviet zone officials warned that bedraggled crossers gave "a false impression of our living conditions," *Thüringer Volk* admonished its readership neither to beg in Neustadt telling "fairy tales" of hardship nor to let western journalists photograph them.[57] In other words, border-going gave rise to divisive images, practices, and institutions that progressively strengthened one another. New East-West patterns of perception penetrated, and expanded, in daily life.

Crossing Crackdown

The criminalization of border-goers escalated frontier security in both East and West. Sonneberg and Neustadt police regularly raided public streets and train stations—as well as hotels, restaurants, pubs, dance halls, and cinemas—in order to uncover crossers without proper identification or travel permits. These *Razzias*, or "control actions," reportedly yielded high returns. They could even close down locales for weeks, such as Neustadt's Rear Swan Tavern, "because all kinds of dark riffraff and border-goers met there."[58]

There was some popular support for authoritarian police practices in the borderland. Though public opinion is difficult to gauge, particularly for Sonneberg, four thousand residents of Neustadt joined one "powerful" protest, the largest the city had ever seen, to demand the closure of all "profiteering and illicit trading locales." The demonstrators reportedly declared, with National Socialist overtones, that "asocial elements of all kinds belonged in a work camp."[59] Criminalizing vocabulary seeped into everyday conversation on both sides. Frontier residents began defining each another by their boundary transgressions, as

"border-goers," "border-violators," and "border-profiteers." Growing intoler-
ance had tangible consequences. The Bavarian Border Police said that one "surveillance increase" of patrols up to ten kilometers inside the American zone was
"actually requested by the populace."[60]

Western border guarding was not nearly as harsh as what took place in the
East, either in the number of arrests or in the treatment of detainees.[61] While the
archival record of this early period in Sonneberg is sparse, newspaper articles
about major border trials suggest their severity. Indeed, eastern administrators
trumpeted "tough" punishments for "profiteers and saboteurs"; in one such "big
warning" in Sonneberg, glass smuggler Franz Greiner was sentenced to seven
years in prison.[62]

Although western enforcement did not approach the levels of East Germany's
emerging police state, western animus toward the eastern "plague" of border-
goers led to a border policy that was tougher than is popularly remembered.[63] To
combat the surge in smuggling after currency reform, Neustadt's city council, for
instance, issued a "cry for help" to Bavarian and American offices in November
1948, warning that border black marketeering endangered the food supply and
"robbed" the city of vital tax revenue.[64] Mayor Weppler "emphatically request[ed]"
the "immediate strengthening of the Border Police," as well as augmented judicial enforcement in a system of "effective summary courts."[65] The Bavarian government promptly responded and, at talks in Coburg on December 6, 1948,
devised new legal procedures for border trials, including the key decision to
prosecute the "attempted export of wares."[66]

Neustadt's summary trials were not the venue for serious border crimes, such
as smuggling counterfeit money or insulin, but rather for local black marketeering in stuffed animals, doll hair, toy voice boxes, festival masks, and so forth.[67]
They were also not the venue for serious legal deliberations. To publicize the
new measures, the newsreel *Welt im Film* documented how fifteen eastern glass
smugglers from Lauscha—"all of them apathetic, tired, with emaciated, haggard
faces"—were each found guilty and sentenced in less than ten minutes.[68] The
vast majority of Neustadt's border trials were similarly abridged. In fact, court
proceedings were so insubstantial that Coburg's state archives had slated the
records for disposal.

But these files reveal a great deal about the East-West dynamic on the
early border.[69] The brunt of Neustadt's new summary procedures fell on
local easterners. Of its 650 defendants between January 1949 and October
1950, 91 percent were from Thuringia, with 84 percent from Sonneberg
County and 51 percent from quite near the border, from frontier villages or
the city of Sonneberg. Only 7 percent were Bavarians, with 5 percent from
Neustadt, mostly transplanted Sonnebergers trading with former networks
in the East.

In the trials, black marketeering dwarfed all other concerns. Ninety-five percent of the defendants reportedly had crossed for economic reasons. They carried an average of 100 DM of wares or food per person, and at least four in ten transported Sonneberg-produced toys, dolls, and Christmas ornaments. Just 9 percent of defendants also cited social and familial reasons for crossing, 1 percent said they were leaving the East permanently, and there were hardly any political cases. Virtually all of those apprehended traveled on foot and in darkness; 70 percent crossed in the more heavily populated areas near Burned Bridge (between Ebersdorf and Wildenheid). Bavarian guards typically registered first-time offenders, bringing charges on the second or third offense for "repeated delinquent behavior."

Western forces caught just half (51 percent) of defendants near the frontier, apprehending the rest well inside the West.[70] Patrolling Bavarian Border Police would stop suspicious-looking passersby for ID checks on the street or conduct raids at the Neustadt train station, especially the 3:50 a.m. train. Almost a third of crossers apprehended in Neustadt were arrested inside private apartments, workshops, or taverns. The police patrolled residences, barns, pubs, and workshops "known" to harbor border-goers.[71] Observant patrons and neighbors issued what they considered "'justified' denunciations" of easterners.[72] Officers could work several nights or even months to apprehend offenders.[73] Margarete Carl from Lauscha received a deferred sentence for crossing in November 1949 because she was eight months pregnant. But when she failed to return to Neustadt after the birth of her child, the court issued a warrant for her arrest in East Germany in 1951, and she spent two months in Sonneberg's prison, barred from seeing her baby.[74]

Prosecutions had serious ramifications. Neustadt and Sonneberg police cooperated in the name of frontier security, routinely sharing investigations and defendants' criminal files. Moreover, a conviction in Neustadt's border court had consequences in East Germany, registered in citizens' records, and ranking in offense alongside theft. Within the West, those deemed guilty faced partial or total confiscation of their wares (depending on whether their smuggling was for personal "need" or commercial "profiteering"), and also had to pay the costs of the trial (2.50 DM). The court fee was not problematic for westerners, but easterners, in a catch-22, sometimes resorted to further smuggling to raise the money. Defendants also typically received several weeks' probation provided they lived "a lawful and orderly life in the future," or a choice between a 10–20 DM fine or two nights in jail. Still, western police complained to U.S. offices that summary court penalties were too lenient.[75]

Meanwhile, western enforcement went easy on western businessmen who profited from Sonnebergers' personal risks. Smuggling was lucrative for Neustadt firms, especially exporters. A dozen Christmas ornaments that cost 1.20

DM to manufacture in the West, for instance, could be purchased from eastern border-goers for 0.30 to 0.80 DM, and then retail for around 5 DM.[76] Arrangements varied, from ad hoc dealings with backpack crossers to full-fledged smuggling rings with trucks driving into the woods in the middle of the night. Smuggling and enforcement intertwined with complicated social networks that spanned the border. Certain firms were well known for buying illegal wares, yet police were often unable—or unwilling—to prove that the smuggling occurred with the bosses' knowledge.[77]

Even when it was clear that westerners had directed the smuggling, Neustadt's court was sympathetic to businessmen's flimsy justifications. After border police intercepted five illicit toy deliveries to Joachim Hammer in two months, he claimed he smuggled not out of "filthy greed" but from "humanitarian sympathy with our often suffering and hungry brothers from the East Zone." The court not only acquitted Hammer but also returned his sixty-six dozen confiscated toy sailboats.[78] Arguing economic expedience also worked. Venerated doll manufacturer Jürgen Meyer had used an eighty-year-old Sonneberg woman to smuggle glass doll eyes in her farmer's cart, but the Neustadt court allowed it for the "fulfillment of an extremely urgent, short-term export contract."[79] Businessmen got away with pleading economic hardship, too. When Hubert Noetzel complained the difficulties of interzonal commerce forced him to smuggle (2,500 dozen Christmas ornaments in three months), Neustadt's court determined that he had acted out of economic need, and acquitted him. Yet it convicted Noetzel's eleven helpers, mainly easterners who had acted out of greater economic need.[80]

Border enforcement in Neustadt was, in fact, a win-win proposition for westerners. Neustadt businessmen profited from smuggling and, if caught, faced minimal repercussions. Even if their wares were not released, the Bavarian Border Police sold them off at steep discounts—up to 50 percent off black market prices—so Neustadters could buy back confiscated toys, dolls, and ornaments more cheaply than they could directly from eastern border-goers. Westerners reportedly "pushed and shoved into the border police office" for access to the booty.[81] In turn, Neustadt's border police brought in an extra 1,150 DM a week from selling the contraband.[82] This improvisation was just one of many ways in which Neustadters manipulated the border to their advantage.

Antismuggling measures in Neustadt were of a piece with western actions elsewhere along the demarcation line. West German offices, facing pressure for increased security from a number of frontier towns, as well as an estimated yearly tax revenue loss of 800 million DM from smuggling, determined in 1949 that "strengthening the border is urgent everywhere."[83] West Germany's Ministry of the Interior launched a public relations campaign against the "moral brutalization and degeneration" of "so-called backpack smuggling," in which the rhetoric of "sinister dealings" with an "enemy [who] is clever, changeable, and unscrupulous" did not differ greatly from East Germany's.[84] The customs police acquired extensive executive powers on the border in 1949.[85] Amid successive force increases, along with the creation of the Federal Border Guard (Bundesgrenzschutz, or BGS) in mid-1951, western guards gained authority within ten kilometers of the boundary to stop citizens for ID controls, initiate baggage and strip searches, and conduct house inspections without a judicial warrant. In some locations, western forces put up barbed wire fences and other border "barriers." [86]

These escalations passed without much comment in Neustadt. The "watchful eyes of the bureaucracy" were an irritant, but the restrictions did not unduly disrupt westerners' everyday lives. Some even tried to deploy the new laws for personal ends. One Neustadter, irked by drunken carousers on city streets, suggested in the newspaper that border police exercise their new powers for "nighttime peace," ensuring "order and peace" and restful sleep.[87] What began as provisional regulations metastasized in unforeseen directions—and authoritarian border measures became part of a new normalcy.

Border Profits

Growing inequality between East and West exacerbated not only smuggling over the border but also the migration of undocumented easterners to the West. Both sides decried this mass movement. As the emergent East and West German states constructed economies in opposition to each other, they sought to detangle their industries and populations.

Yet detangling was difficult at Burned Bridge, a poor and close-knit region. Sonneberg County was in dire straits, its artisans cut off from export markets in western Europe and the United States, and marginalized as unessential in socialism's "workers' and peasants' state." Many Sonnebergers who found themselves out of work simply left for Neustadt. Moreover, the border interrupted the enmeshed geography of manufacture. Traditionally, it took several villages to make a doll: the body might be made in Neustadt and painted in Wildenheid, sent to Sonneberg-Bettelhecken to an eye inserter, then back to Neustadt to a doll hairdresser, then over to Sonneberg-Oberlind to a doll clothes maker and cobbler.[88] This interconnection left locals vulnerable to frontier vicissitudes, not to mention rapidly diverging currencies, laws, and business climates. It also facilitated postwar mobility. Since crafts did not require expensive machinery but did need portable skilled labor, Sonneberg artisans and exporters took advantage of their ready-made networks in the West and left in disproportionate numbers.[89]

The East German Ministry for Trade and Supply deemed Sonneberg's high migration and unemployment rates a pressing "political problem."[90] Because only one-third of Sonnebergers worked in nationalized enterprises in 1950—two-thirds in 2,600 small and artisan businesses, with around 1,300 in home workshops—officials decided it was these "production modes of early capitalism" that made "petty bourgeois" Sonnebergers susceptible to western influences.[91] The state moved to "strengthen industrialization" in Sonneberg and other border counties.[92] However, as elsewhere in East Germany, the introduction of state-owned enterprises, new industries and factories, higher production plans, and trade cooperatives was a "difficult and complicated process." It provoked "open resistance" among the region's ten thousand crafts workers, resulting in "severe punishments."[93] Sonneberg also had to change its public image. Whereas the newsreel of its six hundredth jubilee, in 1949, focused on quaint toy-making traditions, by 1952 central authorities prohibited the city from branding itself a "toy capital," and wanted it to diversify into other, more practical industries, such as clothing and radio manufacture.[94] Yet the regime's heavy-handed construction of socialism did little to keep frontier residents at home. If anything, it further alienated them.

By 1951, at least 1,400 Sonnebergers worked illegally across the border.[95] Typically, men labored at rock-bottom wages in Neustadt for long stretches, returning home to their wives and children once a month to claim ration cards. That so many easterners "risked life and limb" to work in the West is testament to the economic gap between the cities and to how difficult life in Sonneberg had become.[96] While locals had become desensitized to the disparities, outsiders were often struck by the gulf between former neighbors. One American visitor from the Department of Defense argued it was "unfair" that Neustadt refused to extend lodging, financial assistance, and legal security to Sonnebergers.[97]

But for the most part, Neustadters did not want eastern undocumented workers. The initial postwar years had been hard on the city, with unemployment high (12 percent in 1950) and the departure of businesses unwilling to contend with the border's uncertainty and distribution costs.[98] While currency reform improved the city's long-term prospects, the short-term demise of small, "inferior" workshops, with toy industry layoffs of up to 60 percent, raised locals' defenses.[99] Neustadters resented competition and wage pressures from Sonnebergers. The city council passed laws against their admittance, worried that "undesirable elements" would settle in the West, bring over their families, and drain municipal coffers.[100]

In Neustadt itself, community leaders complained of the "economic disadvantages of this 'hole in the border,'" and lamented it was not "hermetically sealed."[101] Local businessmen, irate that Munich and Bonn were not doing enough to protect "our economy" and "our currency" in this "state of emergency," urged the city council to take enforcement into its own hands. So on the heels of its 1948 border court reorganization, Neustadt launched in 1949 a series of initiatives to limit the "dangers" of "dirty competition" from the East.[102] At the same time, it cherry-picked people and products from Sonneberg to best position the town, each time invoking the border as pretext. In one shrewd agenda for a "Conference on Zonal Border Problems," Mayor Weppler summed up the city's border strategy in his own words:

- Transfer of important and desired enterprises from the East Zone
- Keeping away unwanted and unreliable companies from the East Zone
- Moving allowances and accommodation for important skilled workers from the East Zone
- Departure of incorrectly placed and regionally burdensome workers into more prosperous regions
- Prevention of illegal mass imports of goods from the East Zone
- Legalization of important special imports for export needs.[103]

Neustadt's aggressive protectionism was multifaceted. City leaders selected from a variety of policies, blaming the border for each, to dictate the cross-border movement of workers, refugees, businesses, and trade with unimpeachable justifications. At the same time the city council denied entrance to many easterners in the name of border defense, it recruited individuals skilled in "critical" industries, wheedling from the border police work authorizations or at least "unofficial tolerance." Skilled workers' residence in the West was contingent on remaining at their initial job. If fired or fickle, they were to be sent back to East Germany.[104]

Neustadt was similarly selective in admitting eastern businesses. More than fifty Sonneberg firms had opened branch offices in the city after 1948, drawn by close access to free trade privileges in the West.[105] Neustadters worried that Sonneberg franchises, whose manufacturing costs were half that of westerners', could now sell directly to American and west European buyers, and thus reap double the profits. The *Neue Presse* complained this "unfair competition is a danger and undermines community spirit."[106] Neustadt city councilors and businessmen created a special committee in 1950 to "control" eastern companies' relocations, determining which were "redundant" (i.e., competing toy and doll makers and wholesalers) and could not open branch offices.[107] Moreover, Neustadt audited thirty-two Sonneberg branches for tax evasion, wage violations, and illegal workers. Officials suspected yet more as "sham enterprises," fronts for smugglers or, worse, communists. Neustadt businessmen also enlisted government to head off sources of eastern competition, from denying Sonneberg firms display opportunities at the Nuremberg toy fair to restricting eastern exports.[108] In the end, the city denied relocation for dozens of Sonneberg companies.

Neustadt's machinations in the glass industry reveal the potential profitability of border maneuvering. Lauscha, in the forested north of Sonneberg County, was renowned before 1945 as the inventor and primary source of glass Christmas ornaments, marbles, and eyes for dolls and stuffed animals. Because the tight-knit community revolved around autonomous home workshops (specializing in birds with short necks, birds with long necks, and so on) residents grew angry at the Soviet zone's centralization of their "uncontrollable" industry in late 1948.[109] Neustadt capitalized on Lauscha's disruption to create its own glassmaking industry where none had existed before.

Western firms had been smuggling Lauscha's glass wares over the border, but smuggling Lauschaers ultimately proved more efficient. Neustadt firms built workshops to employ glassmakers as intermittent, illegal workers. Eastern officials agonized about the loss of skilled labor, worried that remaining residents were becoming "intractable," and took punitive measures against the crossing craftsmen, whom they labeled "egoists," "vermin," and "industrial thieves."[110] Still, Neustadt successfully wooed dozens of Lauschaers "in the interest of the city." Although local leaders worked to keep out eastern workers in general, they wrangled for glassblowers' authorizations or "tacit allowances" from border police.[111]

Yet all was not solved by easing the flow of glassblowers. Since most glass eyes continued to be crafted in Lauscha, trade restrictions after 1951 meant that Neustadt's dolls had to remain sightless. The doll eye shortage received state and media attention. The city worked to win import exceptions from Munich and Bonn, and asked local customs offices to turn a blind eye to illicit sourcing.[112] Eye smuggling increased, leading in the East to ever sharper controls and punishments for glassmakers and to growing tensions with the West.[113]

Ultimately, Neustadt resolved to "become the center in place of Sonneberg" and lobbied for state and federal funds to simply "transfer" the glass industry across the border. The city was "not only a cultural, but above all an economic display window of the West."[114] In the early 1950s Neustadt constructed a state-of-the-art facility, training school, and housing settlement for eastern glassblowers.[115] Ironically, the Lauscha craftsmen are today seen as escaped refugees, not the trophies of a clever city strategy.

Thus Neustadt tailored the border to its needs, catapulting to prosperity beyond West Germany's broader "economic miracle." In manipulating the cross-border movement of workers, businesses, and industries, the western town emerged in the 1950s as the hub of toy, doll, and glass exports that Sonneberg had been before. Contemporaries felt this marked shift in fortunes. Decades later, a number of interviewees and a majority of survey respondents maintained that while Sonneberg "had it better" before 1945, the border quickly proved to be "good" for Neustadt.[116] Over the years, the blending of economic self-interest and Cold War rhetoric proved a powerful combination.

Certainly, Neustadt saw a "remarkable revitalization" with the influx of Sonneberg workers and businesses after currency reform.[117] From 1948 to 1951, the city ran a positive budget balance and total municipal revenue rose from 1.15 to 2.9 million DM, an average of 36 percent a year.[118] This prosperity did not stop local officials from lobbying for subsidies or bombarding Munich and Bonn with proclamations of economic doom. Yet continual complaints about material conditions failed to convince central authorities to prioritize "Christmas ornaments over steel."[119] Neustadt did not originally qualify for federal Borderland Assistance because it was too well off.

City leaders "deplored Neustadt's neglect" as a remote "Bavarian Siberia," and decided to revamp their rhetoric, adopting a new marketing strategy of plucky political struggle.[120] In an April 1950 lecture, "How Neustadt Promotes Itself," Mayor Weppler urged city councilors, businessmen, and the local Working Group for Advertising and Sales to emphasize the town's "fighting optimism" against the Iron Curtain.[121] Locals duly put on a brave face for journalists and, rather than grousing about economic hardship, began to moralize about the communist menace and the harrowing plight of refugees. Soon a parade of important officials traipsed through the region, from Bavarian minister-president Hans Ehard to U.S. commissioner George Shuster, and posed for pensive photographs at Burned Bridge, gazing upon the East through military binoculars. Within a month of launching the new campaign, Bavarian culture minister Alois Hundhammer was sufficiently impressed with Neustadt's martyrdom to promise assistance "in the dead corner of a vast concentration camp wall."[122]

Bavarian and federal officials began to regard the border not just as an economic demarcation but also as an ideological and cultural bulwark. Material matters became ever more politicized. State authorities heeded calls for self-defense in an "ethnic struggle and economic battle" (*Volkstumskampf*) along the West's new "border with Asia"—rhetoric similar to future chancellor Konrad Adenauer's 1946 observation that "Asia stands on the Elbe," and long associated with fears of Mongol hordes from the Soviet Union. West Germany expanded frontier assistance from its initial economic mandate.[123] In fact, borderland funds grew out of a Nazi-era program in eastern regions to protect against Slavic influence. Since eastern threats were "diverse," borderland subsidies became likewise diverse, from building schools to supporting industries. Evidently, communism had already transformed East Germany into a foreign nation, necessitating protection against the "endangerment of Germandom."[124]

Neustadt, in Sonneberg's shadow for over a century, maximized the demarcation line to its advantage. Through subventions and selectively opening and closing the border to easterners, westerners remade the region's economy within just a few years. Residents repositioned around the new boundary so effectively that partition even came to appear in their self-interest.

Neighbors

Increasing inequality between East and West also manifested itself in population movements. Millions of easterners headed west for greater economic and political freedom, as well as for personal safety. Sonneberg and Neustadt, the largest population center on the demarcation line, bore the brunt of the frontier's transient traffic. Animus toward refugees was common in postwar Germany—but its intensity and East-West cast appear to have been particularly acute at Burned Bridge.[125]

Immediately after the war, Neustadt absorbed between twenty-five hundred and three thousand Germans from eastern Europe who had fled or been expelled from their homes with Germany's defeat. Accounting for 17 percent of Neustadt's population, the newcomers spoke different dialects and were Catholic rather than Protestant. They strained resources, especially housing. Crowded homes, averaging two to three people per room, often doubled as toy workshops. Conflicts became so nasty that the city's Housing Commission had to obtain rooms "using compulsory measures." When a dentist prevented one couple from moving into his empty exam areas, two U.S. soldiers broke in with machine guns.[126] American authorities launched a special investigation of Neustadt officials' misconduct, sending local leaders "and their wives" on tours through the city's refugee camps to impress upon them the refugees' "suffering and misery."[127] Still, up through the early 1950s, five hundred to seven hundred expellees remained in Neustadt's three unsanitary refugee centers, one of which had been the Buchenwald satellite camp. Because residents had difficulty finding legal employment, the camps gained a reputation "city-wide" as "centers of profiteering and black-marketing."[128] Mayor Weppler warned it was "absolutely necessary to immediately reduce the number of inmates" for "upholding order and security at this border town." He lobbied to dissolve the Clubhouse Camp, closest to the frontier, because it was "a hiding place for black-marketers, illegal border trespassers, and similar obscure individuals." Besides, city space was needed for "cultural purposes."[129]

Of greater long-term concern, however, was an influx of refugees Neustadt faced from next door in eastern Germany. As more than 1.5 million easterners headed west between 1945 and 1951, disproportionately more left from Sonneberg than from elsewhere in the Soviet zone.[130] They were familiar with the frontier terrain and able to reconstruct their lives right across the border. Local farmers owned western land, toy makers had western networks, and many lived with western friends and family. There were many reasons *not* to go, of course. People were "rooted" to lives and loved ones in Sonneberg, or remained optimistic about socialism. Others believed "the Americans would come back," or that they would always be able to leave; "the border wasn't taken so seriously," one recalled.[131] Many worried about starting over from scratch in the West. Tankred Dorst's semiautobiographical character in *Die Villa* conveys the complex emotions: "There is our factory that my grandfather started. . . . we won't let it simply be taken and sneak away in the night like criminals! Over the border! What would I do over there!"[132] Because Sonnebergers usually made quiet arrangements for moving west, or moving back east, it is not known how many resettled in Neustadt between 1945 and 1952. Locals guessed it ran into the thousands.

In the early years, the Soviet military administration did not do much to stop the exodus. Its emigration policies were unclear and contradictory.[133] In Sonneberg, city councilors disliked the disorder of illegal traffic but were amenable to legal departures. In fact, some believed legal resettlement in the West "should be supported for procuring housing space."[134] This goal was so self-evident that one official justified taking emigration bribes because it was "only to provide living quarters" in the overcrowded city.[135] Hundreds of Sonnebergers left the Soviet zone legally in the late 1940s and, despite corruption and bureaucracy, managed to ship their household effects along with them.[136] Moreover, Sonneberg officials did not want them to come back. They begrudged the costs of providing "returnees" with ration cards and finding them new homes, protesting to Thuringia's State Ministry that "such vagabonding requires more intervention."[137] Soviet zone administrators were even less receptive toward westerners wanting to move east. They restricted entrance and residence permits, a cavalier attitude toward population gain and loss that, within a few years, would be completely reversed.[138]

Western officials, from Neustadt to the highest circles of the Bavarian and U.S. military governments, likewise did not want to swell their populations with border transgressors.[139] Authorities could be sympathetic to easterners who feared political persecution, labor conscription, or deportation to the Soviet Union. But they suspected most crossers of opportunism, pursuing "self-interest and personal gain." One American report estimated that just 2 percent held "legitimate fear of Soviet action against them."[140] According to one observer, western guards, "intensely suspicious of all border crossers, scrutinized every 'story' with the precision of a microscope."[141]

Beleaguered authorities came to disdain easterners as "illegals" and "asocials" who "commit[ted] thefts, sexual crimes, and other offenses" and became a "dangerous . . . burden on the state."[142] Western administrators would issue newcomers conditional residence permits, with failure to work in the jobs assigned by the Labor Office to result in deportation back to the Soviet zone.[143] Some even "presumed" that East Germany tried to "get rid of" or "dump into the lap of West Germany" people "not 100 percent fit to work."[144] Bavaria's state secretary for refugee affairs, Wolfgang Jaenicke, went so far as to call their emigration a Soviet conspiracy. He speculated that "mass flight to Bavaria is fostered with the intention to create chaotic conditions in our housing sector and economy and thus prepare political events"—and urged a "uniform blockage of the western zones from the Russian Zone."[145]

Western officials forcibly sent back "illegal refugees" on buses and trains. But because the Soviet zone did not want these people either, and regularly refused entry, the American military government worried there would be "an increase in illegal border crossers if it becomes known that we cannot return them."[146] In the Neustadt region, authorities detained easterners for weeks and months at the overcrowded Moschendorf camp near Hof. There was some public comment on their treatment. One American witness worried that illegal crossers returned from this "barbed wire cage" to the Soviet zone could face "imprisonment, deportation, or death."[147] One writer for the *Neue Presse* objected that they were not "criminals," describing cramped train shipments of hundreds back east each week that carried "women with bare purple legs, ragged children, and hollow-cheeked men."[148] But for the most part, the arrest, internment, and deportation of eastern neighbors passed without much discussion or dissent.

The West also tightened frontier security to stem the influx of easterners. While agencies clashed over specific policies and enforcement was ad hoc, there was nevertheless broad agreement among American and Bavarian officials that the best strategy for population containment was prevention and, ultimately, "stronger controls on the border."[149] In fact, Bavaria's parliament initiated force increases and border escalations in 1947 expressly to halt eastern refugee traffic, believing "a close blockage of the state and/or zonal borders is absolutely necessary."[150]

After 1949, the West no longer returned "illegal refugees" by force, but held them at camps and strongly encouraged them to leave on state transports.[151] Federal officials accepted fewer than 40 percent of refugee applicants.[152] That figure overstated refugees' rate of admission in the West, since officials on the border could decide who was eligible to be considered for asylum. When one easterner crossing to Neustadt declared himself a political refugee, a Bavarian sentry reportedly "drove him like a cow back over the border." He muttered, "We have enough of your sort here."[153]

Westerners also put up barriers to easterners already in the West. The national media played up their cost (2 DM per person per day, 6 million DM per month), in addition to sensational scams and crimes.[154] Easterners found "difficult starting conditions," with "rigidity, distrust, and lack of understanding" marked in western border regions.[155] This was especially true for Neustadt. The city reluctantly housed more than 550 officially registered easterners in addition to the remaining expellees, and lobbied for state help in refugee matters well into the 1950s.[156] Certainly, individuals, church groups, and other voluntary associations in Neustadt launched charitable initiatives. Interviews and private papers, rather than government archives, suggest extensive informal support.[157] Yet city leaders remained tightfisted with economic assistance and residence permits. Even American intervention could not persuade Neustadt's refugee commissioner to admit one easterner who had two relatives already living in Neustadt.[158]

Sonnebergers said westerners were "unwelcoming" and "greatly displeased" by their presence. Though of higher status than "third-class" expellees, many felt like "second-class citizens."[159] Sonnebergers tended to turn to each other and developed their own social, housing, and support networks. Inge Mulzer remembered how the Sonneberg refugee community helped her find a job at a bowling alley, and her Neustadt sister-in-law's resentment of her quick success. Even after sixty years in Neustadt, she said, she "always remained a Sonneberger." Westerners still regarded her as from "another country."[160]

Within just a few years, East and West Germany *seemed* like different countries. After 1949 they were, in fact, different states, in which different forms of civil society were taking shape. Alongside border tensions, Neustadters and Sonnebergers experienced different ideologies and forms of socialization in education, community organizations, and trade union movements. As diverging systems and economies collided, the unstable frontier revealed the widening fissure between East and West, mirroring and magnifying early Cold War tensions. Though this was not intended, border residents nevertheless felt a divide, and through a multitude of quotidian actions helped to entrench it. In 1949, the mayor of neighboring Coburg publicly stated that "enormous problems would result from the fall of the 'Iron Curtain.' The completely prostrate East Zone would endanger the West Zone."[161]

The border at Burned Bridge aggravated growing inequality between the two Germanys, producing oppositional interests and identities. Stereotyped images of East and West formed early along the frontier—based mainly on material differences rather than ideological ones, and personified by the smugglers, undocumented workers, and migrants who transgressed the boundary. Neustadters and Sonnebergers had not wanted a demarcation line to sever their cities, but when it did, they accommodated and instrumentalized its precepts. While local and state governments on both sides criminalized crossing and escalated enforcement, measures in the West are particularly noteworthy, and contradict popular images of the border as an entirely eastern construct. The emergence of a two-sided economic boundary in the late 1940s, then, propelled the expansion of a two-sided political divide.

4

Kickoff: Political Skirmishing

East and West's maneuvering over the unfenced "green border" became ever more elaborate from 1949 to 1952. Whereas in the immediate postwar years each side had focused on stabilizing the frontier, states and citizens grew sophisticated in their tactics, adapting to and exploiting the wide field of play. Oppositional moves on the frontier entrenched Cold War conflicts. As the porous boundary proved mutually threatening, both sides switched to defense, restricting contact and hardening the border between them.

Political skirmishing on the border accompanied the political formation of the two German states, the Federal Republic in the West and the German Democratic Republic in the East. The broad contours of the new countries were set in 1949: parliamentary democracy versus Marxist-Leninist "democratic centralism." But exactly what form they would take was unclear. There were conflicting voices within each state, as well as among the western Allies and Soviet Union. The leaders who emerged in both East and West Germany rendered unification less likely. Christian Democrat Konrad Adenauer prioritized integrating the Federal Republic into the West, as well as market-driven economic growth and conservative "chancellor democracy." Hard-line communist leader Walter Ulbricht steered East Germany toward the model of the Soviet Union. He consolidated power over a Stalinist system marked by political repression and the creation, in 1950, of the Ministry for State Security (MfS, or Stasi) and a centralized five-year economic plan. The western Allies and the Soviet Union became increasingly invested in, and concerned about, the outcome of the "German question." The extent to which the governments of Stalin or Truman may have been open to German unification or planned to re-create their Germanys in their own images is debatable. In the nascent Cold War, uncertainty over the German question exacerbated ideological, economic, military, and political conflict.

Cold War tensions were pronounced on the boundary between the emerging East and West German states. As international, national, and local conflicts converged, each side enlarged its frontier policing and supervisory agencies.

West Germany created the Federal Customs Service (Bundeszollverwaltung) in September 1949 and the Federal Border Guard (Bundesgrenzschutz, or BGS) in May 1951 to reinforce the Land Border Police and U.S. Army. East Germany's Border Police (Deutsche Grenzpolizei), backed by the Soviet army, became centralized after 1948 and quadrupled in size within two years, eventually numbering eighteen thousand guards. For all of these escalations, however, the two states struggled to contain the fractious border.

In 1949, geopolitical conflict along the early Iron Curtain converged in an unusual cross-border soccer game that reveals much about larger stakes for both East and West. The match kicked off a succession of extraordinary yet half-forgotten mass crossings, the largest breaches in the border's history before 1989, that escalated each side's propaganda and security efforts. Most striking is the interactivity, and potential, of these borderland contests, especially in contrast to how rapidly each side was then able to contain them.

1949: One Soccer Game and Four Mass Crossings

On July 31, 1949, Sonneberg and Neustadt hosted a joint soccer match near Burned Bridge. The game was to span the U.S. and Soviet zones, with the border as the midfield line, so that easterners and westerners could watch the game from their own sides without interzonal permits. Of course, the athletes would need passes to legally run back and forth on the field.[1]

In the July 1949 soccer game, the border was to be the midfield line. Max Weyh.

The game was an unusual and exciting East-West event. Twenty-five thousand spectators came, more than the population of either Sonneberg or Neustadt. Some climbed atop nearby trees for a better vantage point. Thirty-five flags emblazoned the field, an array of new postwar political patterns and colors. There were lavish offerings of local beer, bratwursts, cigarettes, and ice cream, especially on the Bavarian side.[2] The players entered to spirited applause, the Sonneberg team carrying a placard proclaiming, "We want German unity!" while Neustadt's declared, "And we do too." Play was fierce. Though Neustadt was favored in the cities' long-standing rivalry, Sonneberg won an unexpected 2–0 victory.[3]

After the game, Sonneberg's Soviet commander, dressed in civilian clothes, announced the border would be open for the day. Thousands of easterners over-whelmed western forces and rushed across the demarcation line, "pouring into the 'golden West.'"[4] Some reunited with loved ones, but the majority headed to Neustadt stores with wares and devalued East marks for barter. Merchants obtained permission to open that Sunday, "and it paid."[5] Most shops sold out, even of their window displays. Gerd Jahn, who headed Sonneberg border secu-rity in later decades, savored his first ice cream for 50 pfennigs.[6] People then returned home that night, and the demarcation line closed again.

Locals have remembered the 1949 soccer game and border opening as a spontaneous protest against a closing Iron Curtain, commemorated in commu-nity histories, articles, and exhibitions. But a different story unfolded behind the scenes. First, the soccer match did not actually span the border; it took place entirely inside the Soviet zone. Spectators did not know where the border lay in the open field.[7] Second, the official score was suspect, as Sonneberg reportedly made another goal that was not counted.[8] And third, interest was lopsided between East and West. Westerners accounted for less than a fifth of spectators at the game. Only four hundred to five hundred Neustadters ventured into the Soviet zone after the border opened, compared to the tens of thousands of east-erners headed west.[9] Many westerners were not thrilled with eastern crowds overrunning their city, either. One native Sonneberger, who had fled to Neustadt in 1946, said that although she had enjoyed seeing her family again, she, like many, was "happy when the Sonnebergers went back home again."[10]

Moreover, the event was far from a joint local initiative. The Soviet zone's communist SED had orchestrated it centrally.[11] In fact, the newly elected Third People's Congress "embarrassed" Sonneberg's city council by declaring it just days in advance, forcing the city to reschedule a festival already set for that day, to the councilors' "astonishment" and "strong irritation."[12] Sonneberg leaders had worried the border opening would spiral out of control. Organizing the event "behind the backs" of western authorities would lead to "incidents" and "failure," and the ferment of mass crossing would overshadow "good propa-ganda."[13] But the People's Congress had explained that the soccer match "must be organized quickly" in order to "surprise" Bavarian border forces two weeks before West Germany's first federal parliamentary elections.[14] Indeed, the Soviet zone staged propaganda events all along the border on July 31, 1949, part of its campaign for "German unity" in the wake of West Germany's formation on May 23.[15] These borderland meetings, musical events, bonfires, and torchlight parades drew as many as several thousand people. They generated nowhere near the level of participation as at Burned Bridge, though, where Soviet zone newspapers, posters, special trains, and buses brought outsiders, and fueled rumors of an impending border opening.[16]

Western officials had worried about the Soviet zone's plans for the soccer game. They expected a cross-border onrush, since "numerous" easterners had been illegally attending Neustadt events all summer.[17] They also distrusted the event's communist sponsorship. The city council had agreed to lend Neustadt's flag for the soccer match, but Mayor Weppler refused to provide further support and did not himself attend.[18] The Bavarian Border Police warned that the Soviet zone intended "to unsettle the border population."[19]

The event did unsettle. The July 31 soccer match kicked off a spate of interzonal games between smaller teams the next week, leading to a steady stream of illegal crossings between the cities. American authorities cancelled an August 7 rematch between Sonneberg and Neustadt to prevent "border trespassing in masses." Loudspeakers in both East and West announced the day before that Neustadt was to play tiny Mengersgereuth-Hämmern instead.[20] However, Sonneberg players substituted in protest, a switch that the U.S. Coburg Office and Mayor Weppler learned of only after the game.[21] Amid the resultant finger-pointing, the Soviet zone mocked the "much vaunted 'freedom of the West.'"[22] The final score, a 3–3 tie, reflected the East-West deadlock.

The Soviet zone raised the stakes on September 1 with "Peace Day" celebrations, holding border rallies and openings at several points along the demarcation line. Once again, Sonneberg and Neustadt were unusually eventful. While Sonneberg's borderland factories and houses donned "festive garb" of "flags, banners, slogans," loudspeaker trucks directed citizens to meet at the border near Burned Bridge.[23] The restless crowd hardly paid attention to the speeches on the "misery of the masses" in the West. Easterners wanted to get to the West.[24] People pressed against road barriers beginning at 7:00 a.m., growing to an "impatient and threatening" crowd of between fifteen thousand and twenty thousand that stretched along the border for two-and-a-half kilometers.[25]

American soldiers and Bavarian Border Police held back the line of easterners for hours, repelling attempted breaks and apprehending 2,365 people who rushed across.[26] Ever more "aggressive," the crowd hurled "curses and insults" at western forces. Soldiers of the U.S. Constabulary fired warning shots and brought in reinforcements of three armed vehicles with machine guns.[27] By afternoon, the crowd gained critical mass and overran western defenses. According to Neustadt's *Neue Presse*, "nothing could counter the onslaught."[28] Within hours, twenty thousand to thirty thousand easterners crossed near Burned Bridge, an "invasion" that dwarfed border openings elsewhere that day. The *New York Times* chided western security for being "unable to halt the mobs of Germans forcing their way through barriers and police road blocks."[29]

Westerners once again confronted Sonnebergers' shopping binge. Many Neustadters disdained the "20,000 Thuringian pilgrims to the West," with their humble offerings of eastern toys, ornaments, and furniture for barter. In their eagerness, easterners ate bratwursts that were not always fully cooked.[30] The delights of the West even enticed political demonstrators away from the dwindling communist parade, as they, too, joined the "unstoppable throng of gazers and shoppers."[31]

Eastern officials became alarmed at what they had unleashed. The Soviet zone had instigated the border opening, which originally was to last three days, and maximized propaganda photographs of armed Americans confronting crowds of peaceful Germans.[32] But eastern authorities immediately reinstated frontier controls. The next day, on September 2, Thuringian police joined western guards in

American forces preventing eastern crowds from crossing the border; publicized by the Soviet Zone's *Neue Berliner Illustrierte*, September 3, 1949. University of Pennsylvania Libraries.

Easterners lined up along the "green border," beginning to break through to the West.
Stadtarchiv Neustadt bei Coburg.

holding back a crowd of easterners, estimated at between fifteen hundred and
two thousand, gathered at Burned Bridge.[33]

Still, the Soviet zone planned a third mass crossing one month later, on October 1–2, 1949, for World Peace Day. Though it was downplayed in Sonneberg's
press, in contrast to the July 31 and September 1 crossings, word of the impending opening spread informally. Anticipation grew. People from all over Thuringia
traveled to Sonneberg on packed trains and buses, overwhelming hotels and restaurants. They loaded up wares for trade in overstuffed carts, boxes, and backpacks. In Neustadt, locals improvised kiosks along the road from Burned Bridge
to sell shoes, food, and household goods to easterners at exorbitant prices. City
officials planned to impress visitors with floats and feasting to "demonstrate a
difference in the kind of festivals 'here' and 'there.'"[34]

The night of October 1, a crowd of easterners began to gather at Burned Bridge.
It continued to grow the next morning in the course of a boisterous political demonstration. U.S. Constabulary and Bavarian Border Police reinforcements held the
line for several hours at the "main point of attack," enduring taunts.[35] Then, when
one American soldier tried to wave back the encroaching crowd, people misinterpreted the gesture as a signal to go ahead. They ran through. The Soviet zone
opened several points along the inter-German border, but once more Sonneberg
and Neustadt's unique proximity proved a lightning rod for the largest "storm."[36]

Eastern crowds transformed Neustadt into a "wonderland" for a third time.[37]
Onlookers gaped, as the city "was not Neustadt any more, isolated in 'Bavarian

Siberia,'" but teemed with Thuringians making the most out of their few hours in the West.[38] Easterners rushed to buy meat, butter, and fur coats before stocks sold out, some even hopping trains south to Coburg, where prices were less inflated. Westerners grumbled that Neustadt "resembled an anthill," with all the "surging, flooding, and pushing."[39] And eating: visitors reportedly consumed "20,000 bratwursts and 10,000 liters of beer."[40] To avoid easterners sleeping off their hangovers in western streets, the *Neue Presse* speculated, the Soviet zone announced the border would close at three o'clock that afternoon. Yet revelers stayed in the West until well past dark, not heeding the call to return.[41] So as the Soviet zone prepared to declare itself the German Democratic Republic the next week, its border population—and the border itself—proved beyond the new state's control.

The mass crossings took on a life of their own. A month later, a fourth breach occurred against the East German government's prohibition. Eastern authorities had renounced the mass crossings in the press, yet rumors of an opening for the anniversary of the socialist revolution on November 9 led Sonnebergers to gather at Burned Bridge the night before. The next morning, reinforced sentries from both East and West held back frustrated citizens. In the dense fog, "the air crackled" with tension.[42] The crowd yelled at guards to open the border. Eastern police stood with Kalashnikov assault rifles ready, and Sonneberg party chairwoman Olga Brückner yelled at the crowd from a jeep to leave the border area. There were "many tanks, tanks over here and over there . . . utter chaos!"[43] Together, eastern and western guards managed to hold back the initial throng of six thousand to eight thousand until eleven o'clock, when around a thousand broke through and ran into Neustadt. Forces regained control, but in early afternoon

Eastern crowds in Neustadt streets after a mass crossing. Stadtarchiv Neustadt bei Coburg.

they could no longer contain the growing crowd. The sentries stood aside, and more than twenty thousand easterners "stormed across the frontier," an "onslaught" on a "wide front."[44] Despite other attempts elsewhere, Burned Bridge was the only successful mass breach along the inter-German border that day.

The ensuing spectacle in Neustadt was now "a familiar image."[45] The *Neue Presse* likened it to a gold rush in a "Wild West novel," with "lethal crowding" at stores and kiosks.[46] Western reports, bemused by the material gap between East and West, focused on easterners' enchantment with western products. One widow reportedly tried to trade her husband's lovingly preserved stamp collection for a few West marks in order "to for once have the food that's so rare and so good over here." Sonneberg's SED tried to organize a demonstration in Neustadt but found few participants because members were queued for bratwursts at the stand nearby.[47] The *New York Times* compared the crowd of "shabby people" to a "swarm of locusts" who "frantically" sold all they had for western goods or hard currency.[48] However, the western press largely ignored government actions. For example, West German Customs Directorate president Vögele, furious at the free-for-all, ordered the Bavarian Border Police to close Neustadt's shops and to confiscate all bags and boxes from illegal crossers, an unlawful command that his subordinates refused.[49]

Over time, townspeople simplified the story of Burned Bridge's four border openings in 1949. The Cold War's iron narrative of eastern brutality versus local and western resistance overshadowed each side's crisscrossing motivations. The breaches are remembered, and celebrated, as straightforward demonstrations of neighborly solidarity, showcasing the "spirit of German fraternity" and "warm togetherness."[50] In a mailed survey, 81 percent of 112 respondents born before 1945 said the mass crossings were "initiated by both communities," as opposed to just 9 percent who stated, correctly, that they were "organized by the SED."[51] In a television feature, one former crosser was more than skeptical about the party's involvement. "In sixty years, I've never heard that," he said.[52]

Moreover, the 1949 openings resonated much less than other events that better fit the standard narrative of the Iron Curtain. Whereas later generations can recount the details of border shootings and escapes, only 13 percent of 141 survey respondents born after 1945 had heard of the mass crossings. By contrast, 61 percent knew of East Germany's forced evacuations of six hundred Sonnebergers in 1952 and 1961.[53] This selective amnesia is curious, because the border openings were major events at the time. Eastern crowds gained autonomous, subversive momentum—with the world press watching—and posed one of the most significant challenges to the Iron Curtain until 1989.

1949: Opening Responses

The mass crossings fizzled as quickly as they had begun. The fledgling governments of both East and West Germany reacted sharply to the fourth border breach of November 9—which, unlike the others, involved no government planning. The East German regime, barely two weeks old, threatened its population the next day with "sharp measures," and blamed the breach on western "enemy agents" who wanted to derail the GDR.[54] The new hard line was confusing. The first three openings, after all, had been organized by the East in order to disrupt the West. Now "things were turned upside-down."[55] The regime redressed this "lack of clarity" by rebuking citizens, in direct contradiction to its propaganda just a month earlier, that it was "false and absurd to regard . . . the mass push to the border provoked on November 9 as building a bridge between East and West."[56] The party penalized comrades who had crossed, and worried about growing unrest, vandalism, and insubordination in the wake of the openings. The People's Police erected a second road barrier at Burned Bridge.[57]

The fallout from the November 9 breach reached beyond Sonneberg, and the measures of local party leadership to restrict cross-border contacts affected border regulation throughout East Germany. On November 11, two days after the opening, Sonneberg county began reviewing all commuter passes and limiting authorization for the two thousand farmers, workers, and businessmen who had dealings across the border. Even Mayor Geyer had to turn in his daily permit.[58] Thuringian interior minister Willy Gebhardt sought to widen this local crackdown, warning East Germany's Interior Ministry, People's Police, and Soviet Control Commission that "the Sonneberg incident necessitated screening in other border counties" as well.[59] Under new "political inspection," any frontier pass holder suspected of being an "enemy to democratic development" would lose his or her permit. Gebhardt also argued that the "Sonneberg occurrences" called for a "political campaign for better discipline among the population on the demarcation line," a forerunner of reinforcement measures in 1952.[60] Gebhardt's proposals met with approval in Berlin, where Interior Ministry state secretary Johannes Warnke signed off on the new frontier regulations for all of East Germany.[61] Ironically, Sonneberg's border openings, which began as state-sponsored propaganda, led to greater controls along the brand-new state's frontier.

The breach at Burned Bridge also hardened border security in the West. To Bavarian interior minister Willi Ankermüller, it was "untenable" that crossers "simply ran over" the border police, who required reinforcements and operational improvements.[62] The mass crossings were further evidence of the West's vulnerability at its periphery. The West German state instituted a number of border escalations in the aftermath, alongside its broader efforts against eastern smuggling and migration.

Meanwhile, in Neustadt itself, politicians and merchants begged U.S. and Bavarian offices to protect the town from the "invasions" and "excesses" of easterners. They insisted on the "urgently needed strengthening of customs and border security."[63] Aghast at their neighbors' "unimaginable appetite for shopping," Neustadt merchants demanded state recompense for depleted inventories and warned of the "danger of sabotage."[64] Neustadt artisans fretted that the influx of cheap eastern Christmas ornaments, toys, and dolls during the "mass breaks had caused a true inflation of wares." By the November 9 opening, customs police broke up the lines of easterners selling to western wholesalers.[65] Neustadt procurers did raging business nonetheless. The truth was that while eastern "flooding" threatened Neustadt's small-scale toy and doll makers, larger exporters made fatter profit margins.[66] Yet Mayor Weppler did not mention this in his impassioned appeals for state help.

For all of Neustadt's clamoring for border security and financial assistance, it is not clear the city suffered during the mass crossings. In many ways it benefited. While shopkeepers complained of being "robbed of necessary foods" such as butter, sugar, and flour by unfavorable exchanges, actual currency conversions ranged well above the official rate, with 1 DM trading for 6–10 East marks.[67] Because of these high prices, merchants petitioned to stay open during the crossings. When the city decided to get in on the action, charging each vendor 5 DM per hour they did business, many happily paid up. City leaders even tried to create a monopoly for Neustadt merchants, keeping out the "wild" kiosks of non-Neustadt entrepreneurs by blocking the city's southern entrance.[68] Neustadt did such a "very good business" that Bavarian Border Police head Karl Riedl concluded the openings had the opposite outcome of the East's intention to "cause difficulties."[69]

The 1949 mass crossings were one of many examples of Neustadt manipulating the border to its advantage. Throughout this period, city leaders exploited the double-sided opportunity of the boundary. They profited from the desperation of Sonneberg neighbors even as they pleaded desperation to Munich and Bonn. Meanwhile, local officials pressed for ever greater subsidies and frontier security, based less on the reality of past experience than playing upon future fears.

The new governments of West and East Germany worked to prevent future border breaches. Both sides denied rumors of a fifth border opening at Burned Bridge on December 21 for Stalin's seventieth birthday, and sent extra guards—around five hundred to Sonneberg and one hundred to Neustadt. The western "police cordon" was to arrest, detain, and return crossers, but "avoid resorting to violent methods and incidents of any kind." The Eastern People's Police were at the highest level of alert, with increased latitude for firing warning shots.[70] In contrast to November 9, reinforcements easily deterred the smaller gathering of December 21. Only forty Sonnebergers attempted to cross, and they were promptly arrested. Western forces declared the prevented opening a "remarkable success."[71]

Border discipline returned to normal. Fundamentally, the openings had not altered frontier life. There was no mass violence, no permanent exodus to the West, and little change in everyday compliance. The increased warnings, the guard escalations, and the advent of winter cooled the crossings. Despite ongoing whisperings and smaller incidents, the 1949 breaches at Burned Bridge remained the largest in the border's history.[72]

In retrospect, the mass crossings appear notably one-sided and short-lived. Perhaps more surprising than four mass crossings in four months is how swiftly they were then contained. After all, the "green border" was still unfenced. But at Burned Bridge, Germany was already divided—and the 1949 crossings exposed and deepened the extent of the divergence. Stereotypes of a poor East and a rich West were so fixed that while tens of thousands of easterners rushed to sample wares in Neustadt, only a few hundred westerners ventured to Sonneberg. Moreover, partition had become enough of an established reality for the mass crossings to generate incredible excitement and anxiety. In contrast to the Berlin blockade, where border closure was extraordinary, at Burned Bridge it was ephemeral openings that were extraordinary. They were astonishing and disruptive precisely because border discipline had become an internalized fact of postwar life.

What, then, did the crossings mean to the crossers? Notwithstanding western portrayals of mass shopping sprees, their enormous size and idealized memory suggest that more was at work. Even decades later, Sonnebergers retold their adventures with a gleam of triumph, recollecting less the materialism of the event than their participation in something singular. They likened the magical "festival atmosphere" of 1949 to the euphoria of the fall of the Berlin Wall.[73] Though not a direct protest, the border breaches felt empowering, a carnivalesque release from reality.

A Sonneberg Christmas skit from 1949 conveyed this sense of the world reversed.[74] In it, a man rushed into the mayor's office requesting a cross-border entry permit for his baby; his pregnant wife had eaten "too many bratwursts" in Neustadt during a border opening and suddenly given birth. Their newborn was stranded in the West. As the mayor inquired bureaucratically whether the infant was registered with the requisite institutions, a second man barged in. His wife had likewise eaten "too many bratwursts and drunk too much strong beer" in Neustadt, and she, too, had given birth in the West. While the mayor regretted he could not admit either newborn, his secretary announced that her sister, visiting from Neustadt, had just given birth to twins. The sketch ends with the babies happily adopted into new families.

Obviously the Sonneberg skit mocked the absurdity of border regulations and divided families. Yet its message was not entirely subversive. The mass crossings appeared as momentary extravagances, with western overconsumption inducing inopportune labor and birth. Ultimately, the characters played by the rules and accepted that the border could shape their lives, trumping family relationships. It was not the border but the border openings that upset regular life and caused the babies to be born on the wrong side. A new normalcy was in place.

That is the significance of the 1949 crossings: border closure, not border opening, seemed normal. And Sonnebergers and Neustadters did not recognize the stakes of the boundary that already divided them. Perhaps more than at any other point before 1989, Germans were in a position to challenge the Iron Curtain. On four occasions, tens of thousands faced off against weak border forces loath to risk bloodshed, and prevailed. The new East German state felt threatened by the forces it launched, as socialist demonstrations became capitalist celebrations and as autonomous crowds gained strength and international attention.

The 1949 mass crossings exposed not the strength of border security but its vulnerability to local unrest. That such breaches were possible, time after time, makes their cessation all the more revealing. Frontier discipline soon recovered. The border remained unfenced for several more years, dependent on local compliance. Had Germans, or the West, known what the next forty years would bring, the mass crossings might well have turned out differently.

Propaganda Border

By 1949, the border was part of everyday life. As the new states of East and West Germany established themselves, the geopolitical match between communism and capitalism was everywhere, on the ground and in the air. The 1949 mass crossings were but one part of a larger propaganda contest, as East and West increasingly grandstanded about, through, and on the frontier.

Each state's ever more dramatic tactics transformed the borderland into an early theater of the Cold War. To impress westerners, Sonneberg officials placed a "brightly illuminated peace dove" on the tower of city hall for the 1951 campaign against West German remilitarization. They also spray-painted doves and slogans such as "Ami go home," against American forces, on vehicles passing through the city.[75] To impress easterners, Neustadt youth groups synchronized a "freedom fire" atop the Muppberg hill, with western bonfires along the Iron Curtain.[76] Both sides launched flashy "balloon actions" against the other, floating over the border thousands of anticommunist or anticapitalist propaganda leaflets with each mass release.[77] Both sides held border demonstrations, ranging from parties' election campaigns to May 1 celebrations, and featured torchlight parades, speeches, and singing, or sometimes "humorously constructed road barrier scenes."[78] After the 1949 breaches, Sonneberg authorities shied away from events directly on the frontier. Lest one 1950 Neustadt event attract eastern onlookers, they turned off street lamps, closed Burned Bridge, and ushered people indoors.[79] But eastern officials found more surreptitious ways to convey propaganda across the frontier.

Indeed, the borderland became a battleground for transmitting political images and ideas. Since East and West had banned each other's publications in May 1948, each fought to spread its ideologies illicitly. The East was especially vigorous, even treacherous. At least two easterners who distributed western newspapers in Sonneberg went missing, one after having already fled west.[80] By late 1950, East

Germany was mailing more than a million missives directly to westerners each month. Sonneberg border communities, schools, workers, and political parties wrote form letters to assigned counterparts in the West.[81] Because of high postage costs, though, most propaganda in the region was smuggled over the border—inside farmers' carts or hollow doll bodies. Transporting propaganda was so common that Bavarian authorities struggled to keep a blacklist of those caught, who were to be denied interzonal passes in the future. Plus activists passed out leaflets to travelers at the train station or on the street. In all, an estimated one thousand pounds of eastern propaganda went to and through Coburg County each month.[82] U.S. officials, worried about the border region's vulnerability to "indoctrination" and fearful that eastern newspapers were "more common than American zone" publications, established an America House center in Coburg to "counterbalance" socialist "influence."[83]

The contest between communism and capitalism permeated frontier life. Locals grew accustomed to exaggerated rhetoric in newspapers and official utterances, in which both sides played up the threat of the other. Neustadt leaders warned that East Germany plotted to create "instability" in the West "in order to recruit followers," foment "radical ideas," and prepare invasion, holding Neustadters in a "psychosis of fear."[84] While western rhetoric built upon preexisting anxieties about communism, eastern propaganda had to challenge prevailing stereotypes of peace and prosperity in the West. Contradicting Sonnebergers' firsthand experiences in Neustadt was an uphill battle, to say the least. Sonneberg's newspaper tried to reveal hidden "truths" of western lawlessness, violence, and poverty. One column that ran almost daily, "The Latest from Neustadt," denounced high unemployment and the prevalence of "USA Gangsters" in the "Wild West."[85] Amid both sides' warnings about the dangers of exposure to the other, governmental relations between Neustadt and Sonneberg became minimized and ritualized. From anniversary celebrations to gas and water distribution discussions, each city tracked the cash value of gifts exchanged or the import of things said.[86] Mayor Langer of Coburg, cynical about these stilted summits, sniped to Sonneberg's city council in 1951 that they were of little use: "East and West have developed differently since 1945" and, after six years, "can hardly understand each other anymore."[87]

Burned Bridge itself became a focus of borderland propaganda. Upon reopening after the Berlin blockade, frontier crossings, in the words of Thuringian minister-president Werner Eggerath, attained "serious political meaning."[88] Border posts, road barriers, and guardhouses were repainted, repaired, and rejuvenated.[89] The efforts made an impression. Western visitors could not help noticing the "very colorful" slogans and portraits of Stalin, Marx, and Lenin at the checkpoint.[90] The interminable controls became ever more invasive. Travelers complained of full-body searches, vehicle checks, and arbitrary fines. Officials confiscated easterners'

West marks and westerners' East marks, and required currency exchanges at unfavorable rates. Eastern authorities established a political gauntlet at Burned Bridge, stripping travelers of western publications, pressuring them to sign political statements, and stationing National Front "enlighteners" to discuss the virtues of socialism.[91] Westerners soon lost interest in braving the "lonesome and desolate" checkpoint. Passengers dwindled on the grim, "modern," "steel-gray" bus between Neustadt and Sonneberg, as fewer "desired to look behind the 'Iron Curtain.'"[92] Upon returning home, westerners professed to "breathe freely again," happy to be "finally back in America."[93]

The movement of people was particularly contentious in the frontier propaganda battle. While East Germany tried to shut the border to ordinary citizens, it barraged the boundary with leftist political activists. The government paid the way for thousands of westerners to attend eastern demonstrations and meetings, spending around 1.5 million DM in 1951 alone.[94] All-expenses-paid getaways to Berlin or sporting events lured not only western communists and Free German Youth enthusiasts but also curious teenagers and union workers. Local officials, too, organized cross-border events, such as the feting of Neustadt railroad employees at the Day of the Railroader celebration in Sonneberg.[95] Because American authorities denied passes for such "political" travel, East Germany helped westerners cross illegally. They were to "avoid" going near Burned Bridge because it was too "visible," but a number came through Neustadt and Sonneberg nonetheless. Eastern travel packages would bus West Germans from larger Bavarian cities to Neustadt, divide them into small groups of three to five, and take them across the unfenced border on foot with the help of party guides and eastern border guards.[96]

Political crossings could attract as much attention as the events to which the crossers were headed. Certainly East Germany encouraged illegal crossings by westerners as a kind of demonstration or performance, provoking West Germany to react with what could be publicized as western belligerence. In May 1950, the *Washington Post* reported that ten thousand "cold and begrimed" West German "red youths" trying to return home from a rally in Berlin faced off near Lübeck against western border police. Further south at Helmstedt, "scattered violence" erupted between crossing western teenagers and several thousand local anticommunists.[97]

Border tensions spiked in the summer of 1951, during East Germany's World Youth Sports Festival in Berlin. West Germany braced for a "stampede" of crossings by teenagers, placing sentries on the highest level of alert and inaugurating the BGS to "hermetically shut off the East Zone."[98] Sonnebergers prepared to aid twenty-five hundred to three thousand "West German friends" in crossing the frontier. Party comrades erected signs pointing to special transit camps where adolescents could enjoy three cigarettes, "a refreshing drink," ping-pong, chess, and other board games. Although Sonneberg was one of the "best collection points in the Republic," relatively few youths wound up braving the heavily reinforced area around Burned Bridge.[99] Tens of thousands "stormed" the border elsewhere. One thousand, armed with clubs and brass knuckles, tried to cross all at once in the nearby forests of Maroldsweisach, leading to violent clashes and even shootings, one of many confrontations the East German press played up as "terror under the western occupying powers."[100]

Yet East Germany's attempts to incite western border brutality never got very far, especially since eastern brutality was far more severe and targeted ordinary citizens. Besides, publicizing violence went both ways. When East German guards shot Erich Sperschneider from the Mengersgereuth-Hämmern crossing near Meilschnitz in 1951 and left him to bleed to death in an open field, six hundred locals from both sides came to his funeral—the pastor deeming his murder a "crime against humanity."[101] To most border residents, blocking the crossings of ragtag leftists paled in comparison.

As East Germany inundated the border with activists and event attendees, political crossers became a priority for Neustadt border authorities. Smuggling continued but was no longer the dominant concern as the western economy stabilized and East German enforcement grew harsher. The change was reflected in changing the targets of Neustadt border prosecutions: from local eastern smugglers to nonlocal western activists. Previously, from January 1949 to October 1950, more than 90 percent of court defendants had been easterners who crossed for economic reasons. After November 1950, 81 percent of defendants were political, mostly western leftists transporting propaganda or going to events in East Germany. The proportion of easterners and economic crossers dropped to 7 percent.[102]

Border enforcement also became more acrimonious. Western authorities were far less forgiving toward unapologetic political crossers than toward eastern crossers deemed to be in need, and tended to handle the former more severely. Small-time smugglers had seldom resisted or protested their arrests, but the files of political activists were replete with "sharp and spiteful" insults, threats, depositions, and appeals.[103] Neustadt's Border Police had difficulty simply keeping in custody seventy-two western "left radicals" returning from the First German Peace Congress in 1950.[104] Sometimes sentries could not even make arrests. When one Bavarian guard boarded a bus to apprehend twenty westerners headed to a Free German Youth meeting in Berlin, the driver started the engine and the guard had to jump off.[105]

Bavarian officials tried to preemptively arrest people for intending to cross the border. Two visiting young women drinking coffee at the Mountain Mill Tavern were sentenced to one week's probation for this thought crime.[106] Bavarian interior minister Wilhelm Hoegner even urged Bonn to create a federal law that, building upon a 1942 Nazi-era decree, would "consider an unauthorized stay in [border] districts an attempt of illegal crossing" and thereby render the intent to cross a punishable offense.[107]

Western border enforcement did not go that far and approached nowhere near the severity of eastern enforcement. Still, political defendants unfamiliar with the borderland were surprised by the strictness of western forces, especially since they received nothing but encouragement to cross from eastern police. In their court appeals, these western political crossers argued not their innocence but the injustice of the boundary. Some echoed East Germany's borderland propaganda message of peace and German unity, and many leveled their own critiques. One defendant argued that western forces violated the original intent of the demarcation line, which was to curb population disorder in the aftermath of war. A second warned that "honest" officials "would later regret" implementing border laws, just as they had the criminal laws of the Third Reich.[108] Another pointed to the absurdity of "Germans who punish Germans because they are visiting Germans in Germany, just because the colonial masters want them to."[109]

Yet few frontier residents voiced such objections, especially as fears of communism grew in Neustadt. The city's Communist Party (KPD), derided as inept and innocuous in the immediate postwar years, seemed progressively more threatening amid reports that agents were "slipping across" the border and that "Moscow had a long arm."[110] The East German regime was, in fact, expanding its western political and intelligence operations, or *Westarbeit*, in the region.[111] People worried about communist "infiltrees" along the frontier. Plus eastern authorities retaliated against wayward westerners. One Neustadter quit the Free German Youth after serving three weeks in jail for smuggling eastern songbooks and pamphlets. Then, during a legal trip to visit family in Oberlind, East German police arrested him as a "saboteur" and "dangerous criminal" collaborating with American intelligence.[112]

Communism remained unpopular in Neustadt, where townspeople increasingly saw communists as fringe activists. West Germany restricted KPD activities after 1950, legally outlawing the party in 1956; its electoral support in Neustadt shrank to 3 percent, with low attendance at meetings.[113] Accusations of socialist leanings could be a damning political charge. Neustadt residents "insulted, molested, and even threatened" one troop of Boy Scouts after mistaking them for Free German Youth because of their blue shirts.[114] Political sympathies, instead, tended to the far right. In April 1952's mayoral election, Friedrich Schubart, Neustadt's unrepentant Nazi local group leader and a former mayor (1926, 1934–45), nearly ousted the SPD incumbent, Weppler, who himself was hardly soft on communism. The former Nazi leader won 47 percent of the vote.[115]

As both West and East grandstanded about the evils of the other side, hypocrisy prevailed. Neustadt's *Neue Presse* belabored stories of people wrongly detained by eastern police, yet gave at best perfunctory coverage, if any, to western abuses. Sonneberg authorities condemned the West's use of "terror" against leftist western crossers, yet threatened their own citizens with dire punishment for attempting passage.[116] Townspeople adjusted to the escalations, often reflexively, sometimes cynically. The border was the law and, as Neustadt's newspaper claimed, an "unalterable reality"—"officials are just following orders."[117] What was to have been a temporary demarcation line had become an established boundary between two new states.

Stronger Security

East German policing on the frontier grew increasingly severe. Even as the regime facilitated leftist political crossings in the name of open borders and international harmony, it cracked down on all other forms of crossing in the name of protecting socialism. Here was the defense to frontier offense. Eastern officials repressed cross-border contacts that threatened the state's image and development, regulating ever more interactions. The border had become an instrument of Cold War politics, and life became harsher for the residents who lived along it.

Amid growing tensions with the West, the Soviet zone expanded its border forces in March 1948.[118] As the number of guards more than tripled, Sonnebergers bristled at the arrival of more than a thousand sentries from Saxony. They resented the new arrivals' broad authority, unintelligible dialect, and additional requisitions of homes and property.[119] Locals detested the stricter controls, watchdogs, orders to shoot violators, and increasing surveillance. For county police, now the "most urgent task" was to keep tabs on "exactly who has dealings in the other zone."[120] At Burned Bridge, a new guardhouse, barracks, and "triumphal arch" rendered these changes visible to all.[121]

Sonnebergers became alarmed at the clampdown, and rumors swirled of evacuations and war preparations. The regime tried to calm fears through newspaper articles and town meetings. Supposedly the border escalations were to keep western "bands" and "bandits"—"dark people with darker pasts"—from smuggling, "robbing, looting, and even murder" in the Soviet zone.[122] Controls were also to prevent the "mass crossing of hungry people" from the West heading to a more prosperous East, an inversion of the actual dynamic of crossing.[123] These claims convinced few, however, and kept anxieties high.

Eastern border security intensified with currency reform and the Berlin blockade. As the Soviets sealed off access to the capital on June 24, 1948, leading to the Berlin airlift, security tightened at the inter-German border, too. In Neustadt and Sonneberg, the blockade closed Burned Bridge to interzonal travel and severed cargo and passenger rail, leading to major dislocations. Sonneberg's leaders appealed to Thuringian authorities to resume coal and gas deliveries from Neustadt, but in vain.[124]

Border controls remained tough after the Berlin blockade ended on May 12, 1949. Burned Bridge reopened as one of five checkpoints between the American and Soviet zones, and just 150 to 400 people crossed there with a travel pass each day, mostly westerners.[125] A handful were Neustadters (two thousand a year), though demand was at least double that. While Neustadt's city council blamed the U.S. military government for authorizing only business and emergency trips, many found the city's opportunistic price increase on passes to 4 DM prohibitively expensive, creating "public unpleasantness."[126] For Sonnebergers, permits were much more difficult to obtain. In the entire county, its population of sixty thousand three times the size of Neustadt's municipality, fewer than five hundred people a year received travel passes.[127]

Eastern authorities also restricted and politicized citizens' everyday *Westkontakte*, or ties to the West. Around 850 Sonneberg commuters legally crossed the border each day. As the East German government progressively restricted them, workers and farmers chafed at unpredictable checkpoint administration, closures, harassments, intelligence interrogations, and even abductions.[128] The regime also meddled with cross-border working conditions. It issued wage restrictions, mandated unfavorable currency exchanges, and authorized strip searches.[129] Of greatest concern in the region were the difficulties of the 80 to 250 western miners who worked in East Germany's Lehesten slate quarry, and the 100 to 200 eastern porcelain workers who were employed in West Germany's Tettau region. But the American high commissioner and West German officials had a rather tepid response to East Germany's clampdown on the commuters. They themselves were not enthusiastic about high volumes of daily traffic on the frontier.[130]

The East German government increasingly regulated citizens' exposure to westerners. It monitored communications with loved ones across the border. Mail between Sonneberg and Neustadt spent a week in transit along a circuitous five-hundred-kilometer route.[131] The regime pulled out the handful of Sonneberg children attending western schools because of the danger of "false beliefs."[132] It shut down Neustadt's Steinachtelbahn, a western railroad line that ran inside Sonneberg territory for four kilometers. It closed local routes and footpaths that even briefly meandered over the boundary. Because fifty meters of road between adjacent Mogger and Mupperg lay in Bavaria, visiting villagers had to detour two and a half kilometers through Oerlsdorf.[133] Most people felt they had little choice but to accept these limitations, especially since East Germany regarded those contaminated by western contact with the "utmost caution" and started to discriminate against them.[134]

Still, some openly rebelled against repressive frontier measures. Local officials would say, outright, that the border system held community government "in its clutches." Eastern guards were so "greatly hated by the civilian population" that they themselves became targets of violence.[135] Unknown perpetrators near neighboring Heldburg shot seven border policemen in three weeks, killing at least two, which led to severe force escalations.[136]

Increasingly, easterners lived on the border at the pleasure of the regime. East Germany's SED leader, Walter Ulbricht, stressed the need for political reliability in "cities near the zonal boundary."[137] In fact, the government began purging borderland residents in several Sonneberg frontier towns (Oerlsdorf, Heubisch, Mupperg, Mogger, Liebau, Heinersdorf, and Effelder), with waves of arrests, house searches, and property seizures.[138] Border residents were also to police themselves, reporting crossers to local control committees and keeping their "eyes and ears open" for suspicious activities. The People's Police lauded them for helpful "cooperation."[139]

Most unnerving, eastern officials co-opted locals into abducting neighbors who had escaped to the West. Seizures took myriad forms. For example, after Thuringian guards shot two border violators near Burned Bridge, killing one, they tasked the mayor of Unterlind to send "men from the community" into western territory to drag back the wounded man and the body of the other.[140] One Sonneberger visited a former coworker who had fled west and lured him near the border while on a walk; then People's Police hiding in the bushes abducted him over the boundary.[141] In another case, Dr. Oliver Albrecht, who had fled to Neustadt, asked Horst Nagel, a border guard whose family he had treated, to retrieve belongings from his home and to meet him at the demarcation line. Nagel betrayed him, allegedly for just 150 East marks. As Albrecht reached out to shake hands after the trade, Nagel's partner pulled him over the border into East Germany. His twelve-year-old daughter, Ursula, stood there, thunderstruck.[142] While eastern abductors surely feared the consequences of noncompliance, actual repercussions may not have been dire. One People's Police officer was released after a day of incarceration for refusing to kidnap a man who had escaped to the West from a Soviet prison.[143] It would seem the regime enlisted abductors mainly by asking them, and pervasive anxiety did the rest.

This was the paradox of East Germany's early border security: it was widely detested but depended upon widespread observance in order to work. In the late 1940s, it was not clear that eastern forces could contain the frontier. But in the early 1950s, the regime had come to believe it could, and should, assert control.

1951: Failed Mass Crossings

By 1951, border skirmishing at Burned Bridge had become elaborate indeed. Officials and citizens vied to outposition one another, and launched a dizzying succession of mass, abortive, and contested crossings. These breaches were on a much smaller scale than previous ones, but the sheer breadth of the maneuvering revealed how quickly people had learned to play the game.

East Germany initiated a spate of cross-border events in the spring of 1951 as propaganda ahead of a June referendum on West German remilitarization. It was the most East-West interaction in Neustadt and Sonneberg since 1949, with lively gymnastics and handball matches and May 1 demonstrations along the border.[144]

In Rottenbach, in the northern hills of Sonneberg County, East German police unexpectedly opened the boundary in the midst of a May 13 Whitsunday festival. Five hundred easterners went "storming" across, only to be stopped by Bavarian Border Police.[145] Western guards restricted the easterners to a beer garden thirty meters inside West Germany. Wary of "trouble" from "heavily drunken" revelers, western forces added a "confining barrier" behind the pub. When some "unlawfully crossing" easterners were reluctant to leave the West, saying they would "rather" be "locked up than to go back," law-minded western sentries "prevailed upon [them] to return."[146]

Word of the Rottenbach crossing spread like wildfire, heightening hopes of future border openings in Sonneberg. An East German choral festival near Burned Bridge on May 20 drew unusual excitement. When American officials refused to allow singers from Wildenheid to participate, a special edition of Sonneberg's *Das Volk* proclaimed that the westerners would cross nonetheless. Eastern police prepared to prevent East Germans from crossing, however, and put up road barriers, fenced in the festival site, and stationed 450 policemen around the singers. But more Sonnebergers turned out than expected, and they wanted to cross. A crowd of several thousand "whistled and jeered" at the People's Police as "filthy pigs," and shouted, "Three cheers for America!" The easterners knocked down the fences, rushing over the border.[147] A crossing on this scale had not occurred since 1949.

Westerners were not thrilled about the border breach. As in 1949, many disdained the easterners' shopping "spree," which "beleaguered taverns and pork sausage stands."[148] The *Washington Post* headlined, "4000 Germans Crash Police Lines for Beer"—beer that then proved "too potent" for visitors "accustomed to the watered beer of East Germany."[149] For Sonnebergers such as Jakob Ziegler, though, buying a shirt and dancing at the Hunter's Rest Tavern was less about consumption than about the feeling of defiance.[150] That is precisely what worried

Thuringian police, who decided not to arrest returning crossers for fear that doing so would "antagonize the entire county of Sonneberg against us and create unrest."[151] After "consultation" with the newly created Ministry for State Security the next day, Thuringia banned assemblies within five hundred meters of the border. Apprehensive Sonneberg police extended the prohibition to four kilometers, even closing the soccer field near Burned Bridge.[152]

Still, Sonneberg's May 1951 crossings fueled rumors of additional openings. Twice in the next month, hundreds of Sonnebergers massed on the border to cross for Wildenheid's choral festival (June 17) and a Neustadt-Sonneberg soccer game (June 21). On both occasions, Soviet and East German forces, in camouflage and on horseback, rebuffed the crowds, firing at and injuring several people.[153] Some Sonnebergers managed to cross—though western forces returned around twenty-five of them.[154] While Neustadters watched the scuffles from the border, the episodes were hardly mentioned in the western press, and they remain marginal in local border memory. East German officials took swift action against the June crossers and, even as they encouraged thousands of westerners to cross that summer for the World Youth Sport Festival, continued to shut the border to their own citizens.[155]

Then, in another twist on 1949, a politicized Neustadt-Sonneberg soccer game contributed to the closure of the checkpoint at Burned Bridge. The match was scheduled for September 1951 in Sonneberg, but Bavaria's district of Upper Franconia denied Neustadt athletes travel passes, supposedly due to fears of

East Germans and American soldiers at Burned Bridge, 1951. Archiv Klaus Bauer.

polio across the border. Eastern authorities did not inform Sonnebergers of the cancellation until the day of the game. So five thousand to six thousand expectant soccer fans assembled at the city stadium in the rain. Sonneberg's leadership capitalized on their indignation to call the western polio accusations "nonsense" (the nearest case was 160 kilometers away) and the "meanest kind of politics."[156] The western travel ban exacerbated concurrent East-West trade tensions, and East Germany closed regional checkpoints at Burned Bridge and Probstzella on October 1.[157] Though Upper Franconia lifted the polio prohibition three months later, the damage had been done. Burned Bridge would not reopen until the fall of the Berlin Wall.

Border games between East and West continued, and remained hotly contested. One Sonneberg-Neustadt soccer match had to stop early because two westerners "scandalously" assaulted the eastern referee for a call (Sonneberg had been winning 2–1) and spectators grew belligerent.[158] The high stakes of frontier skirmishing were becoming increasingly clear to all.

In one final overtime maneuver, soccer enthusiasts in Sonneberg broke borderland rules and organized an East-West match between adjacent Neuhaus-Schierschnitz and Burggrub for May 1, 1952. This was a compound offense: a major event would take place too close to the border, on *the* socialist holiday, and without the party's permission. Sonneberg's SED leadership learned of the game only the day before. Aghast at this "enormous political mistake," officials cancelled it.[159] That night, western Burggrub players illegally crossed to commiserate at an eastern pub. Together with Neuhaus-Schierschnitzers (including local party members), they yelled insults at eastern border guards, leading to "brawling" and general "tumult."[160] The morning after this "mess," Neuhaus-Schierschnitz's May 1 demonstration was rather dismal. Soccer players refused to join in. Though others showed up to claim their ten East marks for participating in the holiday events, most soon left for the local tavern. "Worst," though, was that some malcontents tore down banners and portraits of Stalin and President Wilhelm Pieck.[161] Border permeability become untenable. A month later, when East Germany closed the boundary and deported "unreliable" frontier residents further inland, twenty-five Neuhaus-Schierschnitzers, several of whom had been involved in the May 1 opposition, were slated for "evacuation." All but one managed to flee west.[162]

By June 1952, border games had run their course. Citizens and governments had engaged in increasingly aggressive play, developed divergent tactics, and established positions that were mutually threatening. Faced with constant conflict, the East German regime abruptly built a fence through the porous "green border." In one stroke, the border transformed from the heated midfield line between two evolving states into the fortified periphery of two new nations.

The instability of Germany's unfenced "green border" between 1945 and 1952 propelled security escalations in both East and West. Partial partition

PART TWO

"LIVING WALL," 1952–1961

|| 5 ||

Shock: Border Closure and Deportation

A decade before the Berlin Wall, the East German regime attempted hermetic closure of the unfenced inter-German border. In the spring of 1952, it abruptly sealed the 1,393-kilometer frontier with West Germany, building barbed wire fences and severing transit links. It declared the borderland a militarized Prohibited Zone, forming an intensified police state within the police state. The government also launched deportations code-named Aktion Ungeziefer, or Action Vermin, that expelled to inland counties more than eighty-three hundred border residents it deemed unreliable. The measures of 1952 led to uprisings, violence, suicides, and mass flight all along East Germany's supposedly iron border. Yet they remained little known to the outside world, especially in comparison to the construction of the Berlin Wall in 1961.

East Germany's 1952 border fortification was a critical turning point in German division, if not *the* turning point. The measures stabilized the western boundary, the young state's greatest zone of liability, and shocked frontier communities into quiescence for decades. During the escalations, the situation had been extremely fluid on both sides of the border. Uncertainty predominated. Because of this uncertainty, the manner in which measures unfolded, as much as their immediate effects, set a template for the rest of Germany's partition, allowing for a cascade of previously unimagined possibilities.

Early border closure was so transformational for the same reason it has been so overlooked: local participation. Because state power in the borderland was clumsy and disorganized, East Germany used frontier residents to construct fences, keep the peace, and denounce neighbors, relying on their compliance. There was some room for resistance. Eastern communities that rebelled could derail border measures, and individuals who dared were able to rescue their neighbors. Western protest and assistance, while much less common, also had an impact. But opportunities for opposition were difficult to perceive amid the upheaval. Fear blurred the relationship between victims and perpetrators, creating a potent form of social discipline that buttressed the Iron Curtain for years to come.

In short, 1952 was no neat, tidy story of a monolithic barrier descending upon a detached populace, the narrative associated with the Berlin Wall in 1961. To the contrary, it reveals a populace enmeshed in a confusing chain of events, with actors and consequences unclear. Even though border residents detested the new measures, could disrupt their implementation, and could defy authorities, partition still worked. The events of May and June 1952, as chaotic as they were, revealed the division of Germany to be feasible.

The Front Line of Building Communism

In early 1952, Germany's future still seemed undecided. East and West advanced competing visions of communism and capitalism, yet both rhetorically supported reunification. Many Germans hoped the formation of East and West Germany in 1949 was provisional. The intentions of the western Allies, the Soviet Union, and two German states were unclear to contemporaries, and remain so. Scholars have debated for decades who bears ultimate responsibility for Germany's division. Most blame Soviet belligerence, seeing little possibility for a different outcome, while some suggest that western inflexibility thwarted potential negotiations, such as with the Stalin Note of March 1952, Stalin's unexpected (and likely insincere) overture for a unified neutral Germany.[1]

It is clear, though, that by 1952 the political groundwork was set for Germany's physical partition. That spring, the deterioration of international relations propelled East Germany's establishment as a sustainable state. First Secretary Walter Ulbricht had pushed for a crash course toward socialism that would follow the path of massive restructuring taken in communist eastern Europe. Accepted by Stalin and the Second Conference of the SED, it called for the nationalization of industry, collectivization of agriculture, limitations on private enterprise, and increased political control and policing.[2]

The new campaign to "build socialism" also meant defending against capitalism, an ideological intensification that turned the inter-German boundary into East Germany's longest front in its now "permanent conflict" with the West. Strengthening the border would strengthen communism and, by extension, the East German state. Everyday smuggling and illegal crossing took on a different cast in official rhetoric. Representations of the frontier shifted from a petty crime zone to an ominous source of western threats. In this view, the border was a conduit of capitalism that had to be contained.

Stalin himself declared that controlling the western boundary was essential to socialism's success, telling East German leaders on April 7, 1952, "You too need to organize an independent state. The demarcation line between East and West Germany should be considered a border—and not just any border, but a dangerous one. We need to strengthen the defense of this border."[3] His infamous pronouncement triggered a series of high-level planning meetings over the following month. On May 26, just minutes after western leaders signed over greater sovereignty to West Germany in the General Treaty, East Germany's Politburo used this as a pretext to enact the new border decree.[4] Its preamble proclaimed the western agreement a "Treaty of War" that necessitated border escalations against an expected influx of "enemy agents."[5] Few believed the East German claim, since the regime frequently invoked enemy infiltration as a cover for domestic worries.

Yet perhaps East Germany's rhetoric about western infiltration should be taken seriously. Arguably, the creation of a militarized border zone initially had less to do with keeping easterners *in* than with keeping capitalist influences *out*. In 1952, flight was not as great a concern as the frontier instability that arose from constant contact with the West.[6] The regime's sudden severance of western ties, aggressive ideological campaigning, classification of borderland populations, and removal of "unreliable" residents appear not as straightforward attempts to retain population but rather as efforts to secure the frontier in order to build a self-sufficient socialist state.[7]

The East German government envisioned the borderland as a zone of total security and ideological purity. A "special regime" would govern a hierarchy of three exclusion areas, which together encompassed almost four hundred thousand citizens. The outermost layer was to be a five-kilometer *Sperrgebiet*, or Prohibited Zone, that required a special permit for entry and subjected residents to intensified political, security, and surveillance measures. The second layer, a five-hundred-meter *Schutzstreifen*, or Protection Strip, would have even more restrictive admission requirements, as well as early curfews, closure of public locales, and (initially) prohibitions on either visiting West Germany or receiving western visitors. Life in the third layer, a ten-meter *Kontrollstreifen*, or Control Strip, was to be extinguished entirely. In what the West called the "Death Strip," trees and other plants, roads, and houses would be destroyed, and violators would be shot. A barbed wire fence and enlarged border police force would guard the border itself. Berlin was to stay open, but East Germany cut other travel routes, leaving only five roads and six rail lines intact between all of East and West Germany. At the same time, the regime secretly planned to expel 10,300 undesirable border residents, more than 2.5 percent of the Prohibited Zone population, to counties further inland.

The border escalations of 1952 suggest an attempt at social reengineering. They appear to have had more in common with previous National Socialist efforts to purge enemies of the state and to forge a purified new national community than with East Germany's later, more defensive efforts in population retention that toned down ideological rhetoric and emphasized blanket controls.

After all, regime tactics in 1952 presupposed that a reliable majority of the border population would cooperate to contain a small, border-transgressing minority. This contrasted with subsequent border measures, in which the police and military acted to contain the entire population.

Perhaps because of the 1952 measures' historical echoes of the Third Reich, some frontier residents initially may have understood them to be aimed at a discrete group. Potentially seeing themselves within a relatively safe "us" as opposed to a targeted "them," people may not have wanted the border escalations, though they may have felt the measures did not threaten their personal well-being. After twelve years under National Socialism and seven years under Soviet hegemony, Sonnebergers had experience with the sudden segmentation of internal enemies. An expectation of limitation could help explain why social discipline prevailed in many places before and during the crackdown. It could also explain the growing panic during the action as it became clear that East Germany's new border regime would affect everyone.

"The Evacuations *Will Be* Carried Out!"

Sonneberg residents sensed that border changes were imminent well before East Germany's decree of May 26, 1952. Rumors of escalations began to swirl in mid-May, especially after a "stream of leading SED" luminaries arrived and checked into the Central Hotel.[8] Suspicions grew as the Border Police increasingly disrupted cross-border travel and commuter traffic. State functionaries also launched a series of frontier "inspections," documenting all East-West linkages in business, agriculture, public utilities, and political parties.[9]

In late May, the regime launched a new public relations campaign on the frontier. Sonneberg's newspaper announced plans for extravagant socialist construction projects, including a gargantuan housing development, stadium, swimming pool, and sports hall, and touted the city's future economic superiority over "crisis"-ridden Neustadt in the West.[10] Propaganda began demanding defense against western influences, claiming to represent a groundswell of popular support. Yet a rally in Sonneberg's market square for "border fortification" was "only very poorly attended," and a series of screaming headlines, such as "We Demand Protection from Saboteurs and Agents," failed to drum up much enthusiasm.[11] The doublespeak exacerbated anxieties and fooled no one.

East German officials worried about unrest upon the actual announcement of the May 26 border decree. They had a multipronged strategy to keep the population under control, involving National Front neighborhood meetings and Communist Party "agitators" canvassing frontier schools and communities.[12] But communications did not go as planned. The first day, since passes into the new Prohibited Zone were limited, out-of-town activists could not even enter the border towns they were supposed to be enlightening. They were arrested by "Soviet friends" at security checkpoints.[13] When party members did attend meetings, their resolve could appear slack. At least, Sonneberg leaders complained their comrades from state and central offices arrived late to town assemblies and remained on the sidelines, letting local officials take the blame for border measures: "Not one spokesperson from Berlin talked."[14]

There was widespread unease along the frontier. County officials tried to create more "enlightenment groups" to pacify the border population, though their many meetings on "keeping the peace" attracted few attendees and did little to alleviate anxiety.[15] Party reports describe ubiquitous "negative discussion" in Sonneberg communities. "Panic buying" of flour, sugar, and oil caused stores to limit sales of staples.[16] On May 28, Sonnebergers grew further "alarmed" by police registrations that summoned everyone in the Prohibited Zone to report for specially stamped permits. Several town mayors simply did not announce the measure, while apprehensive communities, seeking safety in numbers, went to the registrations together to head off potential detention.[17] In the end, the police registered 31,485 residents in Sonneberg's five-kilometer zone, including 8,226 in the five-hundred-meter Protection Strip. Oddly, several hundred people received permits with a stamp from the People's Police in Jena, 155 kilometers away. Most did not think much of it, but they would find out what that portended in a week's time.[18]

For all of these disturbing measures, border residents appear not to have realized the magnitude of what was happening. Things stayed quiet even after word got out that some frontier residents, even entire villages, would be "vacated."[19] Some knew firsthand what the regime was planning. Sonneberg's Border Police drew up long lists of "suspicious people," local officials tipped off friends who had been placed on the lists, and Soviet officers went door-to-door in frontier communities, asking for details about each family.[20] Rumors of deportations crisscrossed the border, Neustadt's newspaper publishing on June 1 that certain Sonneberg residents would be "evacuated inland."[21] Still, most could not imagine that average law-abiding citizens would be affected. One resident recalled, "Everyone still thought nothing could happen to them."[22]

Even after the party officially announced the imminent removal of all "unreliable elements" from the borderland, people remained anxiously detached. Sonneberg party chairman Hildebrandt chided his fellow comrades on June 2 for "smiling unbelievingly" at the news: "You laugh and don't believe it, but some of you will also be among them. . . . You can count on it, the evacuations *will be* carried out!"[23] But the advance warnings were hard to believe, and many were blindsided by what happened just a few days later.

Action Vermin

East Germany's borderland deportations came as a shock. At four o'clock in the morning on June 5, scores of paramilitary units began entering Sonneberg frontier communities. With five to eight policemen and local civilian helpers each, they pounded on the doors of the 357 households on their lists, often waking the neighborhood. Officials informed the occupants to pack at once, that they were being relocated to new homes in Jena, three counties away.[24] Police took their identification cards and left behind only a slip of paper decreeing they had twenty-four hours left at home.

Targeted individuals were stunned. At one stroke, they lost their rights, homes, jobs, and communities.[25] Officials made few exceptions. The frail, the elderly, and even one woman who had just given birth were to be evacuated immediately.[26] The critically ill were to be transferred to hospitals outside the Prohibited Zone.[27] When one deportee had a nervous breakdown and lost consciousness, the police simply carried him back into his house and returned for him in a few hours.[28]

Some victims took their own lives, although it is unknown exactly how many. Stories abound, but Sonneberg County reported four suicides officially. In one case, the mayor's brother in Effelder hid as police units came for him, but his wife, from whom he was estranged, did not know she would be spared and hung herself from a crossbeam.[29] News traveled quickly about the Schueler family, who faced deportation for running a hotel that hosted border crossers. Caught trying to escape west, they killed themselves that night with their young son, Ludwig, sitting together around the kitchen table.[30]

Fear spread throughout the borderland. Some listed individuals refused to leave. They threatened to burn down their houses and dared the police to take them by force or to shoot them on their doorsteps. Almost everyone in Sonneberg had a relative, neighbor, colleague, or classmate who was being deported. Rumors ricocheted that people were being sent to Poland and Siberia, that war with the West was imminent, and that local youths would be arrested in the middle of the night. It seemed that second, third, and fourth waves of expulsions would follow.[31]

The action appeared massive. Columns of young men, helpers from neighboring communities, piled the personal effects of targeted families onto the 350 transport vehicles and four cargo trains reserved in Sonneberg for the operation. County officials inventoried the property the victims had to leave behind, itemizing furniture, appliances, equipment, and livestock to be placed under trusteeship of the state.[32]

The operation also felt terrifyingly random. Sonneberg's newspaper had declared that "all *enemies of the people* (RIAS radio listeners), prostitutes, and

An East German unit loading up one border resident's belongings in the name of "peace and freedom." Stadtarchiv Neustadt bei Coburg.

criminal elements should be expelled and relocated."[33] Yet many upstanding citizens were targeted, even as known troublemakers were spared. Sonnebergers shuddered to see friends impugned as former Nazis or border crossers when they were no such thing. Maybe neighbors had denounced them out of "envy or revenge."[34] No one knew whom to trust.

Neighbors' collaboration was one of the most terrifying aspects of Action Vermin. Not only were local party and Stasi officials supervising the transports, but people also realized that Sonneberg administrators must have helped draft the deportation lists: "Berlin did not know anyone's name."[35] Arguably, it was local participation that made Action Vermin possible. In Sonneberg County, two thousand civilian "helpers" and "agitators" reinforced police and Soviet troops, ensuring that "the loading went smoothly.[36] When it was "not feasible" to load deportees with "the few forces on hand" in Neuhaus-Schierschnitz, one official "brought a truck with around fifty helpers," who got the job done in five hours.[37]

Action Vermin seemed formidable in part because pervasive participation made it seem that way. Yet the East German regime had resorted to local help out of weakness. The party and armed forces were not equipped to go it alone, as they would later do in the 1961 deportations. In enlisting the population, the very thing that meant the regime was weak, ironically, made the regime appear strong. The appearance of strength helped make it so. However, the archival record exposes the underlying fragility of regime efforts. Thus while Action Vermin felt overpowering to those who lived it, in hindsight its many shortcomings become visible—as does the extent to which border communities themselves gave shape to the operation.

Action Confusion

The East German government designed, initiated, and enforced Action Vermin. But even in the most notorious action in the history of the inter-German border, there were elements of local improvisation. Citizens played a greater role in events than they realized. Government disorder created power vacuums that left room for both widespread participation and widespread resistance. State confusion made space for local action, producing new sets of conditions. In other words, how border residents reacted at each step helped determine the next.

First, local officials changed the targets of Action Vermin, altering its core strategy. Berlin's initial blueprint recalled the excising language and tactics of the Third Reich. Overnight deportations would "eradicate" all "asocial elements" for the population's own protection.[38] Most of the groups slated for removal resembled National Socialist categories. Though there were no explicit references to race or Jewishness, and East Germany also targeted citizens with large landholdings and close ties to capitalism, the deportation orders specified foreigners, stateless persons, political opponents, convicts, suspected agents, black marketeers, and, particularly in Sonneberg, Jehovah's Witnesses.[39]

Actual expulsion lists in Sonneberg differed, though. County leaders were more interested in upholding law and order on the frontier than in creating political purity. Local lists were full of social vagrants (the "unteachable," the "work-shy," and "notorious boozers") and frontier transgressors (border crossers, guides, and lodgers).[40] In fact, 70 percent of deportees targeted in Sonneberg, and in Thuringia overall, did not meet any of the regime's six official criteria for expulsion. They were named for "other reasons," perhaps for "hostile attitudes" or for being the spouse or relative of someone who had fled west.[41]

Local officials also influenced the length of the lists. As commissions from each border county reviewed draft rosters from People's Police offices, they tended to trim numbers. Most counties in Thuringia cut police deportation lists by 20 to 40 percent, sparing about 1,550 people. Sonneberg was one of just two Thuringian counties that did not reduce original targets and in fact initially increased them, from 985 to 1,116.[42] After bungling the evacuations, however, Sonneberg officials retroactively reduced their quota to 850.[43]

Time pressure and bureaucratic muddle led to more list deviations. Rosters were based on obsolete or inaccurate demographic information, with name and address mix-ups leading to mistaken deportations. Several listed individuals were long dead, had fled to the West, or lived apart from divorced spouses.[44] Plus, much was left to local discretion, such as whether deportees' eighteen-year-old children were allowed to stay. Such life-changing decisions were made in the rush of the moment. Presiding officials often did not know why certain people had been picked; some of those officials had "no idea what was going on" or were themselves targets.[45] There were plenty of shenanigans. Leaders in Mengersgereuth-Hämmern, for instance, created a second deportation list after the police had already ordered the expulsion of fifteen villagers. In the uncertainty, one newly listed twenty-year-old grabbed his mother and a truck and raced over the border.[46] Things were so confused that, after the operation, counties had to rewrite their records, clarifying exactly who had been taken.[47]

Botched execution meant that Action Vermin hardly lived up to regime plans. Available statistics are contradictory and likely minimize regime failings, yet it appears that as many as one in five selected East Germans three in five selected Sonnebergers managed to escape deportation. In all, the regime planned to expel more than 10,300 border residents inland, around 2.6 percent of its Prohibited Zone population (3.2 percent in Sonneberg). However, a reported 8,369 border residents were evacuated, while an additional 5,585 (1.4 percent of East Germany's five-kilometer zone) immediately fled west.[48] Eighty-five percent of this flight was from Thuringia, whose southern borderland had greater ties to western communities and no natural barrier, such as the Elbe River in the north.[49] Implementation in Sonneberg was especially difficult. The county was more densely populated than other border counties, with 8 percent of East Germany's Prohibited Zone population, and was unusually intertwined with the West. Sonneberg units managed to expel only 375 residents, as over 60 percent escaped deportation. Moreover, a reported 885 Sonnebergers fled across the border. The actual number of escapes to the West was likely higher.[50]

Conservatively, some 4 percent of the border population in Sonneberg and the rest of East Germany lost their homes overnight, facing unknown fates as refugees in the West or as deportees inside East Germany.[51] A numerical summary, however, cannot begin to convey the extent of the unrest unleashed. Action Vermin may have targeted a fraction of the population, but its turbulent execution involved entire communities and left everyone feeling vulnerable.

Uneven Unrest

From the regime's point of view, the most "critical mistake" was announcing the deportations a day in advance.[52] This gave people time to flee and resist, causing "utter commotion" on the streets.[53] Because Sonneberg County was such an unruly "combustion point," it saw one of the highest rates of disrupted expulsions in East Germany.[54]

Although Action Vermin may have felt inexorable, border residents actually did a lot to "create difficulties" for the operation and to alter its course.[55] Individual acts had cumulative effects. Civilian helpers, border police, and transport workers rejected orders, walked off the job, or fled west. Local leaders refused to collaborate or intervened to alter the lists, though some then found themselves penciled in on the deportation rosters.[56] Neighbors, too, negotiated on behalf of victims or assisted their escape. Residents cut phone lines to disrupt the operation, organized strikes "at a number of businesses," and even physically attacked the police. Villagers in Mupperg rang church bells to alert the community and to draw western help. A couple of communities became so raucous that the police had to call in dozens of "assault troops."[57]

Western border residents also played a role. When word reached Knauer's Pub in Neustadt that eastern People's Police were about to seize Willy Schmidt's property, "ready friends" in the West "rushed in at lightning speed." They shuttled most of his livestock, equipment, and personal effects over the border within an hour. Locals celebrated their "bravery and vigor."[58] Yet the relative ease with which a handful of inebriated Neustadters thwarted East German police units raises the question of what more derring-do might have accomplished.

Local memory and popular accounts tend to mythologize heroic resistance in the face of unalterable border repression.[59] But borderland opposition was not futile. It threw Action Vermin off balance and spared thousands from deportation. In fact, the outcome of Action Vermin in each community depended largely on the extent to which locals caused trouble. Overall, Sonneberg County deported fewer than 40 percent of those on its lists, yet there was huge variance among the region's twenty-nine targeted municipalities. Places that remained relatively calm, such as Schalkau, Effelder, and Heubisch, saw deportation rates of 65 to 85 percent. By contrast, in several trouble spots the ratio of removed victims was less than 10 percent.[60] These cases of community opposition suggest wide parameters of what was possible.

In Heinersdorf, for instance, protest on both sides of the border disrupted Action Vermin, as well as basic governance. The town council unanimously refused to support the deportations. Its defiance spurred the "entire population to foment civil disturbances" and a wave of families fled west.[61] Sonneberg People's Police called in troop reinforcements to stop the crossings. As they held around eighty Heinersdorfers at the border, the standoff drew attention in adjacent western Welitsch. One thousand westerners, backed by 150 Bavarian Border Police and seventy American military vehicles, gathered on the boundary and shouted "provocations" to East German guards. Such border protest in the West was rare, and this was the only case of its kind documented in the region. But it worked.

Western support "emboldened" Heinersdorfers to attempt crossing en masse, and half of them, around forty, got through.[62] Panicked, Sonneberg's party leadership called a public meeting to retain the eight hundred or so Heinersdorfers who remained in the town. Yet when rumors spread that the party was drawing up a second deportation list, more than one hundred additional people fled over the border that night. Thus, of the thirty-one Heinersdorf families targeted for deportation, the police managed to take only one person. The rest fled west, along with twenty-four other families who had not been listed.[63] June 5 in Heinersdorf became known as "Black Thursday." The town lost two hundred people within twenty-four hours, nearly one in five residents.[64] Here East Germany's 1952 frontier measures looked untenable indeed.

Upheaval was even greater in Liebau. The Lilliputian village lay on a narrow finger of land that protruded into West Germany and had long been problematic. East German officials now planned to locate the ten-meter Control Strip behind Liebau and effectively sever its sixty-six residents from East Germany. When Soviet and East German border guards withdrew from the area on June 3 and 4, villagers had no idea what was happening and began "sleeping in their clothes." One county employee told Mayor Bayer that Liebau was being transferred to West Germany, but the next day, a police commander informed him that U.S.-Soviet negotiations in Neustadt had broken down."[65]

County chairwoman Olga Brückner—who oversaw Action Vermin in Sonneberg—illicitly warned Mayor Bayer on June 5 of Liebau's imminent evacuation, a security breach still decried by some former functionaries.[66] That night, Liebauers decided to flee west at once, together. Three elderly residents stayed behind, while the hamlet's sixty-three other inhabitants crossed the border and found refuge with friends and family in neighboring Neustadt communities.

The vanished village confounded eastern border authorities and was deeply embarrassing. Liebau was now as empty as the "Sahara," a strangely serene no-man's-land deserted by eastern forces.[67] Neustadt's newspaper ran stories about escaped Liebauers sauntering back east to gather the rest of their possessions, peaceably loading up furniture, appliances, and livestock (115 cattle, 66 pigs, and 3 horses) to take west.[68] In the cross-border fallout from this fiasco, East German officials halted plans for Liebau's demolition. Instead, they poured resources into repopulating the ghost town.

The East German regime did have successes thwarting border unrest, brutal successes.[69] Streufdorf, adjacent to Sonneberg County, saw the arrival of Soviet tanks. Ironically, the town's rebellion stemmed from regime propaganda. The party had heavily promoted a film, *The Condemned Village*, in the Thuringian borderland because it hoped westerners would cross illegally to watch it and then foment unrest back home. However, it had the opposite effect. In the film, the U.S. Army planned to demolish a West German town in order to build a military training ground but was prevented from doing so by villagers who banded together, barricaded the streets, and rang church bells to call neighboring towns for help.[70] Although Streufdorf officials hastily replaced the film on June 2 with *The Merry Wives of Windsor*, it had planted a seed. So a few days later, when police units entered the town to deport thirteen families, one man reportedly shouted, "Let's do what happened in the film."[71]

Life imitated art. More than half the town took to the streets in "utter rebellion."[72] As Streufdorf's three church bells clanged, residents removed deportees' furniture from trucks, ripped up roads, and blocked access routes with lumber and farm machinery. Armed with axes, scythes, pitchforks, and stones, Streufdorfers managed to hold off deportations until 120 Soviet troops, 500 People's Police, and 100 to 300 Party "agitators" arrived, leading to violent clashes. Brute force and water cannons ultimately squelched the uprising. Dozens of Streufdorfers fled over the border that day, and others followed in the ensuing days and weeks. Several additional families found themselves expelled. At least twelve "ringleaders" were arrested and sentenced in show trials.[73]

Clearly, border opposition carried enormous risks, and organized unrest such as that in Heinersdorf, Liebau, and Streufdorf was exceptional along the frontier. Resistance remained dispersed over a broad, remote, and rural region. Residents, having only patchy information, tended to see opposition as isolated incidents. Although some communities did have success disrupting Action Vermin, the arrival of Soviet tanks in several towns suggests the likelihood that greater mutiny merely would have been met with more tanks. At the same time, the unrest of 1952 reveals the fragility of East Germany's early border measures. It also suggests a point at which fortification may not have been militarily or politically workable for either the East or the West.

Most frontier communities, however, reacted with scared submission. Neighbors watched nervously as friends and family were put on wagons and cargo trains, exiled to an uncertain future. One young deportee was hurt to see the predominant passivity, remembering how "relatives and neighbors stood around us, their eyes blank with fear. . . . No one waved as our truck pulled away. Everyone retreated into their houses and closed the doors safely behind them. . . . The places we drove through were like ghost towns. We didn't see anyone in the streets, in their yards, or at their windows."[74] For those left behind, it was "traumatizing to see the women and children sitting and standing in the wagons, sobbing." When their cries created "too great a sensation," the police tried to close the doors, concealing the deportees.[75] Yet these glimpses of expulsion left a lasting impression, such as the orderly loading of neighbors on the seventy to eighty freight cars at Sonneberg's train station.[76] Border residents are still haunted by their terror. Some are also haunted by their complicity, a former operation helper admitting, "Never in my life had I been so ashamed of myself."[77] Yet most felt powerless to do anything, viewing acts of resistance in terms of the regime's invincibility, not as any sort of possibility.

The Specter of Deportation

While social discipline prevailed during Action Vermin, the East German government worried about further erosion in its aftermath. It had kept the deportations secret from most of East Germany's inland population. But in the borderland, to prevent additional unrest and flight, it launched a broad public relations campaign justifying the action. Damage control efforts portrayed the expulsions as necessary and finite, removing just the community's bad apples. *Das Volk* listed the names and addresses of "smugglers" and "reactionaries" deported from Sonneberg. It denounced as "Anglo-American warmongering" rumors that "beloved" and "respectable names" were on the lists.[78] At "overflowing" town meetings, the party told thousands of anxious Sonnebergers that only "foreigners, stateless persons, criminals, and prostitutes" were taken.[79] But in the face of "considerable indignation," authorities conceded that "some reputable citizens who had strong connections to West Germany"(which would be "inconsequential in normal times, but highly dangerous in the present situation") had been removed "for their own protection."[80] To stabilize the situation and to build trust in the regime, the government wound up softening some new border policies. It also decided to "suspend evacuations to assure Prohibited Zone residents of their legal basis to live there."[81]

Eastern officials tried to win back *Rückkehrer*, or "returnees," who had fled west during Action Vermin. Sonneberg authorities organized assemblies, demonstrations, enlightenment committees, and house-to-house visits that encouraged residents to convince loved ones to come home. They promised amnesty to defectors who returned to East Germany right away, saying that those not on the original deportation lists would face neither judicial nor economic consequences for their flight. Many took the regime up on this offer. *Das Volk* triumphantly published the names of Sonnebergers who returned vowing their loyalty to East Germany and condemning western "lies" about border brutality.[82] In Heinersdorf, where recruiting efforts were especially intense, at least sixteen people came back in the first five days. There was a great deal of back-and-forth, however, as people changed their minds and still others decided to flee. Ultimately, more than 90 percent of eligible Sonnebergers declined the amnesty offer, as only thirty-nine returned to East Germany within the first two weeks. That several of them were arrested upon their homecoming likely dissuaded additional returnees.[83]

The regime's false promises exacerbated frontier anxieties. Everyone feared additional deportations. Worries were so widespread that on June 17, 1952, all of East Germany's daily newspapers published a carefully worded statement censuring "scurrilous" rumors of looming "mass evacuations" and reassuring readers that, for the moment, "no evacuations along the demarcation line are foreseen."[84] But Sonnebergers continued to whisper of imminent police actions. Some no longer slept in their homes, but spent their nights in "all conceivable hiding places." Others escaped west. Dozens of families from nearby Billmuthhausen, Poppendorf, and Streufdorf crossed overnight on June 20 in convoys with their furniture and livestock.[85] The reverberations of Action Vermin unsettled the borderland almost as much as the deportations themselves.

The bleak fate of banished neighbors reverberated as well. Sonneberg relatives and officials soon heard that deportees suffered rough transport on trucks and freight trains to Jena County. Household possessions such as lamps, dishware, and furniture were "badly destroyed" in the journey.[86] Arriving late on the night of June 6, evacuees faced grimy and crowded living quarters, sometimes in barracks.[87] Given just 10 marks per day for ten days, they were told to find work quickly. Yet by June 20, only a third of the 198 deportees from Sonneberg who were eligible for work (and a third of 1,420 Thuringians) had found employment, many in the Zeiss optical factory.[88] Everyday life proved difficult in the new communities. Deportees tended to remain outsiders, stigmatized by their diminished circumstances, Franconian southern accents, and suspiciously compulsory move from the borderland. One survey reported that in the seven East German counties that accepted deportees, 70 percent of respondents saw the expulsions as "justified."[89]

Exiled Sonnebergers inundated local, district, and central offices with hundreds of heartbreaking appeals to return home. They pleaded mitigating circumstances, false accusations, infirmities, or the need to care for a family farm or sick loved one in Sonneberg. Most petitioners did not challenge the regime's basic premise of banishing "criminals" but objected that they, as "decent people," also had been deported.[90] Others admitted to waywardness as Jehovah's Witnesses or border crossers and vowed to reform and join the party—"to prove my positive attitude toward today's state."[91]

Appeals could involve personal compromises. Believing her spouse to be the cause of her deportation, one woman promised to divorce her husband.[92] Another petitioned to return to Sonneberg after her husband fell ill; languishing in Jena's university clinic, he seemed unlikely to be able to work again, and the situation was "no longer bearable."[93] Some pointed the finger at others. Peter Grohmann not only insisted he had been a model citizen but suggested that his neighbor Bernhard Grohmann, "known as a criminal element," likely had "abused [Peter's] good name in the course of his criminal acts" and should have been deported instead.[94]

The randomness of the deportations was the "bitterest pill of all."[95] Petitioners demanded to know the reason for their expulsions, presuming a certain lawfulness or orderliness to the action, or some legal path to prove their innocence. After all, as one woman argued, "even murderers are told the reasoning behind their punishment."[96] Banishment seemed a moral judgment, a condemnation for which people had to pay for the rest of their lives. East German officials were aware deportations had been arbitrary, but regime policy was to deny that any mistakes had been made. They sent petitioners form letters with tautological justifications: "You fall into the category of persons to be evacuated. Therefore your evacuation ensued justly."[97] They gave most rejections verbally, in "individual discussions," warning deportees to "settle down" and accept their new lives or face consequences as "work-shy antidemocratic elements."[98] Some functionaries recoiled from these practices, uncomfortable with giving "notifications orally, let alone such weighty decisions without any valid formal juridical reason."[99] But qualms did not result in much administrative softening. A year later, official guidelines were to deny outright "all applications for return," with "new petitions no longer to be processed or answered."[100]

The regime's "chilly, vacant" responses left deportees "hanging and twisting in constant torment," appealing for years in the hopes that someone might "explain straight out, 'why and wherefore!'"[101] Yet, as previously noted, presiding officials themselves often did not know why some deportees had been targeted, let alone the exact scope of the transports. Since regional "data" on Action Vermin were "in no way consistent," central authorities ordered counties to rewrite their records, which "must be in exact accord to address complaints, queries, and reports."[102]

The appeals process was itself confused, and decisions made by different branches and levels of government frequently contradicted one another. Two imprisoned Sonnebergers were allowed to return home to the Prohibited Zone after their acquittal—but their deported wives and children, who had never fallen afoul of the law, were not allowed to return.[103] One blind Sonneberger was allowed back after lengthy deliberations, but another disabled man, who had been sterilized and imprisoned during the Third Reich as an antifascist, could not return. No longer "quite right in the head," he mysteriously disappeared the following winter.[104] Regime rulings remained inscrutable. Petitioners would give up trying, and their frustrated loved ones in Sonneberg would uproot themselves and join them in Jena. Only a handful of deportees received permission to return to Sonneberg in the early 1950s—in cases of obvious mix-ups, the death of an offending spouse, or significant changes in family circumstances. More gained readmittance with a thaw in border policy in the mid-fifties. Yet by 1956, only 10 percent of deported Sonnebergers had returned.[105]

The plight of expelled neighbors continued to haunt frontier residents. Deportees would be desperate to maintain ties, writing letters and postcards to loved ones and illegally sneaking back to Sonneberg for visits and special occasions. However, for wary friends and relatives still living inside the Prohibited Zone, "contact with evacuees was undesirable," lest they themselves arouse suspicion. Many just "drifted apart."[106] Exiles lost not only their homes but also their personal relationships. Ordinary Sonnebergers could feel complicit in their banishment. One woman uneasily remembered how, as a child, her parents forbade her to write to her deported best friend, so she did not. Although she was relieved to run into her friend years later in another city, where they briefly hugged and reminisced, she was always troubled by the memory.[107]

Most Sonnebergers did not see their former neighbors again. Even those who stayed in touch had difficulty comprehending what deportees' lives had become. Although the victims of Action Vermin were out of sight, they were not out of mind. Like specters never visible, they became cautionary tales that helped inculcate borderland compliance over the decades.

Flight West

The trauma of Action Vermin was exacerbated by the fate of the other population it displaced: border residents who fled west. At least 885 Sonnebergers escaped across the boundary on June 5 and 6, 1952. Half had been slated for deportation, while the others—large landholders, successful businessmen, and the politically outspoken—left because they thought it only a matter of time before they were targeted. While the overnight exodus west of 3 percent of Sonneberg's Prohibited Zone population added to frontier upheaval, mass flight likely deflated direct opposition. Going to the West was a safety valve for dissident Sonnebergers, and in 1952 it was certainly a safer option than sparring with the People's Police in the East.

Flight, too, carried considerable risks and repercussions. Terrifying stories spread like wildfire, and western newspapers breathlessly enumerated escapes from Sonneberg.[108] One young man from Oberlind drove his car through the road barrier, dodging dozens of People's Police and bullets that struck the driver's-side door.[109] Eighteen-year-old Gudrun Gebhardt was not as lucky. When border guards shot at her family, who were crossing near Hönbach, she fainted three meters inside Bavaria, and eastern guards carried her back into Sonneberg. Her parents and siblings watched, aghast, from further inside western territory.[110]

Watching Action Vermin from the West was chilling. Neustadters saw the violence and personally knew Sonnebergers who fled. The local press printed detailed reports on shootings, abductions, spying, and East German incursions into Bavaria.[111] Even as articles sympathized with eastern neighbors as "no-man's-land Germans" living in perpetual "uncertainty," reports often conveyed a sense of distance and difference.[112] When one Sonneberg family altruistically carried their neighbors' two-year-old over the border, for example, the *Neustadter Tageblatt* marveled: "There are also good people over there!"[113]

Following harrowing escapes, refugees arrived in Neustadt "exhausted and covered in sweat." Some had managed to bring with them "carts, rucksacks, and bags," while others came barefoot and half dressed.[114] Once in Neustadt, they often did not know where to go. Escapees stood "dazed" outside the Bavarian Border Police station, "describing their experiences and flight routes through tears."[115]

The sudden influx of refugees was of immediate concern to Neustadt's leadership. After years of accommodating eastern defectors, officials become protective of city resources. By mid-morning on June 6, when eighty Sonnebergers had arrived, Mayor Weppler preemptively telephoned Bavarian state authorities to say Neustadt could not take any more. He warned, "The border zone must absolutely be kept free of all new assemblages of refugees. I can in no way accept the establishment of a new camp here."[116]

Makeshift admissions procedures compounded tensions. In the days following Action Vermin, more than twelve hundred easterners registered with Coburg County's border police. Around six hundred filed for local support, at least two hundred more found private sanctuary with friends and relatives, and the remaining hundreds passed through the county to the refugee camp in Giessen.[117] Escapees were supposed to go directly to Giessen, 175 miles away, for official acceptance into West Germany and assignment to other cities. But many felt "too proud" or too weary for the trek. After losing everything in Sonneberg, Hannelore Reuther explained that her father said, "I cannot, I just cannot go through a camp."[118] Refugees who did not go to Giessen faced repercussions for "'illegal' residence" and the loss of potential refugee benefits.[119] Yet abiding by the rules meant hardship, too. One family escaped Action Vermin in Unterlind only to wind up spending more than a year in a refugee camp before being allowed to settle back in Neustadt.[120] There were ways around the system. Men would go alone to Giessen while their families stayed anchored in Neustadt, and Coburg County did eventually accommodate many of the three hundred or so Sonnebergers who simply refused to leave Neustadt.[121] However, the route to settled status and residence in West Germany for Action Vermin escapees was often convoluted and traumatic.

Dislocated Sonnebergers also faced local resentments. Refugee assistance, distribution, and regional quotas had long been hot-button issues in Neustadt—and in one stroke, Action Vermin essentially doubled the number of easterners. In 1952, the municipality already counted between six hundred and nine hundred easterners, 5 to 8 percent of the population (in addition to 2,350 expellees from eastern Europe).[122] Notwithstanding a number of civic and charitable initiatives, as well as warm support within families and communities, public

Sonneberg refugees with their possessions at Burned Bridge, shortly after the Action Vermin deportations. Landesbibliothek Coburg.

discourse about East German refugees appears to have toughened.[123] Neustadt newspaper articles and government records document ongoing skirmishes over refugees' benefits, housing, and farmland. Residents openly fretted the borderland was "overflowing" with easterners, and editorialized, "This can't work anymore!"[124]

The borderland was, indeed, chaotic with crossers in the year following Action Vermin, as Sonnebergers continued to flee the new Prohibited Zone. More than two thousand defected in 1952–53, almost ninety Sonnebergers a week.[125] Increased flight and brutality in East Germany prompted a shift in West Germany's federal refugee policy. Reconceiving defectors as victims of terror rather than as economic migrants, western offices began accepting almost all asylum applicants—from under 40 percent in 1949–51 to 79 percent in 1952 and 96 percent in 1953. Border officials were to stop charging eastern crossers for unauthorized crossing and petty smuggling.[126]

In practice, western border guards still discriminated. There were "constant complaints" over the summer of 1952 that Bavarian police arrested and punished eastern refugees for "illegal border crossing" despite the policy change.[127] Adolescent crossers, especially, were a gray area for western officials, who "could not in good conscience apply the protections of political refugees," and returned many "sobbing" back to East Germany.[128] Decisions were seldom clear-cut. One eleven-year-old boy arrived in Wildenheid with his father's address on a note hanging around his neck, his mother having sent him walking from Sonneberg to find his dad in the West.[129] Through the mid-1950s, Neustadt and Sonneberg leaders worked to coordinate the return of local minors to East Germany.[130]

West German authorities also denied refugee status to troublesome adults who were "unwanted for police reasons" and returned them to East Germany.[131] Bavarian border officials used to simply send such crossers back over the border on their own. After June 1952, western authorities began to worry that "deporting undesirable people in the previous way" put them at risk of being shot by eastern forces. So they offered unwanted easterners a choice: either be handed over to East German forces for certain punishment or take their chances crossing the border on their own. To head off potential legal difficulties, crossers who opted for the latter were to sign a form accepting their "personal responsibility and danger for returning over the green border."[132]

Tensions over East German refugees grew. Neustadt continued to absorb an unusually high number of newcomers in the year following Action Vermin, with roughly 30 to 40 percent of Sonneberg defectors settling nearby in the western borderland.[133] On one hand, it did not seem fair that easterners who arrived with their property and livestock intact, as had many Action Vermin refugees, were able to insert themselves into communal life a rung or two above expellees and native Neustadters who had been working for years to get ahead. On the other hand, poorer easterners who worked illegally drove down wages, for which westerners sought counteracting legislation from the federal government.[134]

By 1953, Neustadt was accepting only 40 percent of asylum applications, even though nationally the rate had risen to 96 percent.[135] Mayor Weppler complained publicly that since the refugees exacerbated Neustadt's "catastrophic housing emergency and uncertain labor market," the city's "generosity" was bearing "rotten fruit."[136] The local press "unmasked" easterners who reportedly tried to claim benefits under false pretenses. Wrangling over refugee housing and federal subsidies continued for years.[137]

Relocated Sonnebergers tried to combat local prejudices. They formed the district's Union of Soviet Zone Refugees to redress westerners' "misjudgments" and "unfavorable views" and to emphasize their victimization under "Bolshevism." But such efforts did not get very far due, in part, to rocky relations with Mayor Weppler.[138] East German refugees became increasingly conciliatory, "seldom going public" and voicing few demands. They assured Neustadters in meetings that their "presence in the Federal Republic was only temporary"—they would go back east once the border crisis had passed. As former Sonnebergers minimized their differences, their "passivity" contrasted with the attitudes of other organized groups, such as German expellees from eastern Europe or war veterans. At the end of the decade, Neustadt did not even have an organization for "Soviet zone refugees."[139]

Easterners' assimilation also stemmed in part from West Germany's "economic miracle" and ever-expanding labor needs in the 1950s. Whereas in the late 1940s, Neustadters had complained about competition from incoming Sonneberg craftsmen, westerners increasingly worried about the "catastrophic shortage of skilled workers" in the toy industry. Because teddy bear contracts were not being fulfilled on time, experienced Sonneberg artisans became a welcome source of labor.[140] Their position improved. Still, most relocated Sonnebergers said they continued to feel like second-class citizens in Neustadt, never really at home.[141] Mass flight in the wake of East Germany's 1952 border fortifications had contributed to the growing divide—and the growing sense of divide—between East and West.

Border escalation in 1952 was pivotal in Germany's Cold War. Since it unfolded in rural regions with scattered protest, it has not received much attention. But it was decisive to the course of German division, marking a moment at which a fortified partition became conceivable as well as a reality. In both East and West, the border brutality of 1952 became propaganda, legend, and identity, so integrated into daily practice that Sonnebergers and Neustadters did not realize the extent to which it structured their lives.

Action Vermin caused a shift in borderland relations. At first, the deportations seemed to be targeting discrete enemies of the state, echoing National Socialist and communist roundups of certain racial, political, and social groups. Like other midcentury attempts across Europe to purge and purify populations, the definition of internal enemies was slippery. It nonetheless presumed a safe majority versus a persecuted minority.[142] The East German government's intention of limitation, as well as the populace's expectation of it, may account for why social discipline held in 1952 to the extent that it did.

Failures in implementation made Action Vermin more indiscriminate and thus more terrifying than the regime had planned. In its wake, border residents felt anyone could be expelled, at any time, for any reason. Uncertainty became insidious. County chairwoman Olga Brückner lamented that Sonnebergers began regarding one another with "conspicuous restraint," as "everyone suspected everyone else of being an informant." In their "panic," some preemptively denounced neighbors for future deportations.[143] Remembering his terror, one elderly Sonneberger explained that although most people were "always inwardly opposed" to the border measures, they "had to adjust." Today it is impossible to grasp how it was, he said.[144] The capriciousness of state action, though the product of weakness, bred a transformative "illness" in the borderland: *paranoia socialistica*.[145] What was to be a finite measure of social engineering in 1952, the creation of a reliable security zone, became through unintentional arbitrariness an experience of mass imprisonment, in which everyone was a potential victim as well as a potential collaborator. This dispersing of power and punishment bred atomization—and continued to unravel the social fabric.[146]

Despite the very real fear that border residents felt, state authority in East Germany remained vulnerable. Eastern authorities had difficulty countering Sonneberg's few instances of organized opposition. They failed to transport more than 60 percent of people on the deportation lists, and could not prevent the overnight escape of 3 percent of the borderland population west. The boundary escalations had not been about stemming flight, yet the exodus that resulted wound up making flight a paramount border concern.

Border closure in 1952 exposed the tenuousness of government control within the formation of East Germany. Although frontier turmoil gave residents greater agency, it led them to perceive that they had less. Action Vermin, particularly, suggests the paradoxical fragility and terror of self-policing systems, cementing along the Iron Curtain the *"power* of the powerless" that came to typify communist rule in the Soviet bloc.[147] Both easterners and westerners ascribed to East Germany's new border regime more control than it had. This presumed invincibility discouraged citizens and officials on each side from taking greater risks. It also eclipsed the more complicated explanation of events: that amid endemic fear and confusion, border residents inadvertently contributed to their own captivity.

6

Shift: Everyday Boundaries

On a January night in 1953, neo-Nazis burned Burned Bridge. More than six hundred people in Neustadt joined a rally for the German Block, one of the most fanatic far-right parties in West Germany. After a torchlight "march to the border," the boisterous crowd pledged "loyalty to the Reich," sang National Socialist songs, and decried Germany's "border of disgrace."[1] Party head Rudolf Jungnickel first took an axe to the road barrier, then doused it with gasoline and lit it on fire. To cheers, he and another leader crossed the boundary and set the eastern barrier on fire, too. An East German officer then joined the arsonists and called out to the demonstrators: "You Neustadters are brave chaps—friendship!" The crowd returned the expression of goodwill with shouts of "Germany!"[2]

Mainstream western leaders and newspapers denounced the far-right protest as illegal and even treacherous. Because the German Block had a sizable following in Neustadt, more than one-third of the electorate, it was suspicious that city and border police had failed to contain, monitor, or even report the demonstration. The pyrotechnics also suggested collusion with communists. Otto Peltzer, a known "peace fighter" sympathetic to East Germany, had "used" his "popularity" as an Olympian and fifteen-time national track champion to broker the burnings with East German guards. This was an odd favor to neo-Nazis from someone who had been imprisoned for four years in the Mauthausen concentration camp because of his homosexuality.[3] According to the western press, the German Block had overstepped West German bounds of decency, not so much in its unabashed pro-Nazi agenda but in its "friendly relations" with East Germany and its disregard for border law. After fiery public reaction, Neustadt's municipal court charged the arsonists with "illegal border crossing" and "destruction of property," legitimizing the legality of the Iron Curtain it condemned.[4]

Germany's unstable border of the 1950s made for strange bedfellows. A leftist concentration camp victim helped a neo-Nazi party. East German guards burned their own barrier. A West German democracy, which espoused open borders and freedom of speech, put men on trial for asserting both. In fact, protesting the border discredited the extreme right and left alike. It was fine to bemoan the cruelty of the Iron Curtain, but acting against it was reckless, the unsavory province of fringe elements, and remained a punishable offense in West Germany for the barrier's entire history.

While this peculiar episode was itself minor, it reveals the cautious reflexes that underpinned an uncertain age. In East and West, responsible politics and citizenship came to mean accepting the status quo of division. What law-abiding border residents did not realize, though, was the precariousness of the early boundary—and how sensible accommodations helped entrench what became an insensible barrier.

Cold War Divide

In the 1950s, Cold War realities split apart East and West German states. Their superpower patrons, the Soviet Union and United States, chose to cultivate reliable allies rather than to run the geopolitical risk of uniting a neutral Germany, the solution that emerged for a smaller Austria in 1955. Leaders still paid lip service to the idea of unification, yet the prospect became increasingly unthinkable. German politicians themselves envisioned a divided future. First Secretary Walter Ulbricht was as committed to building communism in East Germany as Chancellor Konrad Adenauer was to orienting the Federal Republic toward the West. Each state progressively integrated into opposite supranational blocs. West Germany joined the European Coal and Steel Community in 1951 and, with the Treaty of Rome in 1957, became a founding member of the European Economic Community, the forerunner of the European Union. In 1955 it gained complete sovereignty, formed the Federal Army (Bundeswehr), and joined NATO. East Germany, a member of the Council for Mutual Economic Assistance (Comecon) since 1950, gained full sovereignty in 1954 and, in 1956, formed the National People's Army (Nationale Volksarmee, or NVA) and joined the Warsaw Pact. The two Germanys' separate trajectories seemed set, especially after differences at the Geneva Conference of 1955 and Adenauer's announcement of the Hallstein Doctrine, which declared the end of West Germany's diplomatic relations with any country, except the Soviet Union, that recognized East Germany. There was resistance within each state to these bloc alignments. The Korean War exacerbated a pacifist *"ohne mich,"* or "without me," stance toward rearmament and remilitarization in West Germany.[5] In East Germany, deep opposition to the Ulbricht regime resulted in nationwide unrest in 1953 and extreme rifts within state leadership in 1956. In both cases, the crushing of uprisings by Soviet tanks— in East Germany on June 17, 1953, and in Hungary in 1956—reinforced Ulbricht's rule. The two Germanys' division, and opposite trajectories, appeared inevitable.

While Germany's political partition was expected, physical partition was not. Neither East nor West had a blueprint for their common boundary in the fifties, or a coherent strategy. Policies developed bit by bit, in response to each side's actions. As the two states consolidated, orderly borders became essential to orderly government. Precisely because border populations were so entangled, asserting statehood meant establishing state control over an array of everyday interactions. Resulting clashes led to greater tensions and infrastructure. The border continued to propel its own elaboration. The source of its escalation shifted from the early postwar period. What began as a solution to social disorder increasingly became an instrument of political legitimacy. Yet the effect was much the same. Frontier populations saw few alternatives and adjusted, entrenching a barrier most did not want.

The border's emergence is all the more striking because physically it seemed so tenuous. East Germany had officially closed the boundary with West Germany in 1952, but there was still no Iron Curtain, at least not in the sense that western headlines claimed. People could cross fairly easily. The barbed wire fences were crude and, by the end of the decade, spanned just over 70 percent of the frontier.[6] Beset by logistical problems and widespread disobedience, it was remarkable that the border system worked at all. Only in August 1961, with the construction of the Berlin Wall, did the East decisively fortify its frontier.

Although the actual barrier between East and West remained weak in the fifties, the boundary grew in significance. It became a military and symbolic

East German guards plow an unfenced section of the border Control Strip in 1959. Johannes Seifert.

front line in the conflict between communism and capitalism, dividing two states, two blocs, and two ways of life. It also became a political football. East Germany declared it an international state boundary, or *Staatsgrenze*, while West Germany continued to insist it was an internal "zonal border," or *Zonengrenze*, to deny the legitimacy of the "East Zone."[7] The boundary seemed less and less an imposition of external powers, especially as German forces on both sides assumed responsibility for its security in 1955. The border also defined interactions between the Germanys. Since the two states did not share diplomatic relations in the first half of the Cold War—West Germany did not recognize the East German government until 1970—the frontier became a conduit of communications large and small. Here was a 1,393-kilometer contact zone through the heart of Germany, an interface that neither side at first knew how to control, but with which each had to contend.

East and West both improvised. The two states reinforced their border lines with borderlands, engineering frontier communities to guard and showcase rival ideologies. While East Germany's harsh Prohibited Zone was the mirror opposite of West Germany's coddled Zonal Peripheral Area, the underlying concept was similar: transforming the borderland into a social, economic, and political bulwark. In the words of Jakob Kaiser, West Germany's minister for all-German Questions, "The border population is to be made into a living wall."[8]

A "living wall" emerged on both sides. In myriad ways, the barrier became a fact in everyday life, suggesting how human boundaries formed in conjunction with the barrier on the ground. The makeshift fences of 1952 were not that different from the fences of early 1961, but attitudes about the Iron Curtain changed considerably over the decade. The sense of partition deepened as easterners and westerners came to imagine themselves inhabiting different worlds. In 1961, the Berlin Wall would divide two societies that were already divided.

Border Confusion, 1952

The year 1952 was a time of profound anxiety throughout the Eastern bloc, the height of Stalinism's political, economic, and social repressions. On communism's newly fortified border with capitalism, East Germany's frontier population was reeling from the June 1952 security escalations and Action Vermin deportations. Rules shifted quickly, and no one could predict what lay ahead. Even the location of the border was contested. Soviet and East German forces broke several ad hoc agreements made at the war's end and crossed to occupy a number of western towns and territories overnight. As Soviet and American officials untangled competing claims, both sides vied to mark their territory, striating the frontier with color-coded posts, roadblocks, warning signs, and painted boulders and trees—white rings in the East and orange stripes in the West. Still, the line remained unclear in some places, and the mistaken destruction of the odd woodland or potato field could erupt into an international dispute.[9]

Border violence increased. Soviet and East German forces had expanded dramatically in May 1952, followed by hasty American and West German increases in June, leading to incidents throughout the summer and fall. The People's Police crossed into the West and kidnapped Sonnebergers who had fled. They also shot at or detained dozens of Neustadters who stepped over the border accidentally, gathering wood or herding cows.[10] In a "scuffle" with three inebriated westerners one night, eastern guards fired seven shots and killed a man; his widow received an urn with his ashes days later.[11] Reporting at least forty-one frontier incidents in eight weeks, Neustadt issued to Bonn a "call for help" for this "unbearable little war on the border." Local leaders clamored for additional western forces.[12] The confrontational atmosphere complicated interpersonal relations, as rumors swirled about neighbors "provoking" each other across the boundary, or about mines stored under Mupperg's village church.[13]

Barrier construction added to the unease. The East German regime tasked local governments to clear the ten-meter Control Strip and to build barbed wire fences, a massive undertaking. Ordinary citizens were diverted from their regular jobs to "voluntary" stints on the frontier. They chopped down trees and uprooted smaller plants, tore out roads, and demolished houses, in effect building their own prison.[14] Many did not comply. Especially during the first week of fortification, some civilians and guards fled west during their shifts. Others refused orders, with few reported repercussions. Workers took two-hour lunch breaks and threatened to walk off the job over poor provisions (skimpy liverwurst sandwiches). One day, hundreds crossed into western Kleintettau "in order to sample Bavarian beer one more time," and spent the afternoon drinking in local pubs.[15] There was less outright defiance after Action Vermin, but work on Sonneberg's ninety-three kilometers of border remained conspicuously sluggish throughout the summer of 1952. Locals would steal logs from the Control Strip or congregate there to chat, westerners offering eastern brigades beer and cigarettes. This could be risky, though. East German border guards abducted and detained one western entrepreneur for two days for selling capitalist candy on socialism's new line of defense.[16]

Things were also tense behind the frontier, as East Germany imposed strict laws on the borderland. It limited entry into the five-kilometer Prohibited Zone to residents and visitors with special permits, barricading roads and putting up yellow signs threatening that violators would be shot without warning.[17] The five-hundred-meter Protection Strip was particularly restrictive. The government imposed curfews—as early as eight o'clock in the evening in some towns—and closed all bars, restaurants, hotels, cinemas, soccer fields, and other public spaces.

Procedures for admission into the area were lengthy and difficult. Notwithstanding "serious failings" in enforcement, nonresidents, including border guards, had to apply weeks in advance to so much as visit someone for coffee.[18] The regime also cut telephone lines to the Protection Strip. Residents appealed, but still had to conduct even government and business calls from police stations.[19]

The division of Sonneberg into different security zones was a logistical nightmare. Ostensibly, the state was "doing a favor" for the county by letting most residential areas of Sonneberg city remain outside the Prohibited Zone.[20] But the city's industrial area, with forty-eight businesses, fell inside it. Ten thousand Sonnebergers suddenly needed passes to get to work. At the same time, local trains ended service inside the zone, enraging commuters. Farmers went through even greater contortions to access their fields around all the blocked routes. In Heinersdorf, locals needed rope hoists to lift their wagons up the steep detour paths.

Border residents contested the new measures. Prohibitions on livestock grazing and agricultural machinery inside the Protection Strip led to "sharp and combative" altercations with the People's Police.[21] Angry communities could wrangle some concessions. Most notably, officials in nearby Eisfeld convinced Berlin to let it out of the Prohibited Zone altogether, warning that the traffic, work delays, and petty arrests of unauthorized entrants were straining resources and endangering the state's five-year plan for economic development.[22] East Germany's fumbled implementation of the new border regime definitely left room to maneuver.

The flight or deportation of more than twelve hundred Sonneberg residents in 1952 brought additional confusion. Empty homes were vulnerable to theft, and looting was endemic. Even People's Police officers stole and sold items from houses under their watch. Westerners, too, crossed to pilfer the odd chandelier or drainpipe.[23] Sonneberg County was inundated by petitions for compensation from dislodged owners, from easterners who had lost everything, and from westerners who could no longer access their land in East Germany. The county also had to administer all the untended workshops, mills, fields, cattle, pigs, and chickens.[24] Twelve percent of Prohibited Zone farmland in Sonneberg (9 percent in East Germany overall) was now vacant, in the middle of the growing season.[25] Locals made arrangements with relatives on the other side of the border to tend their fields, or exchanged land in formal agreements.[26] Sonneberg authorities also searched for local "caretakers," without much success. Custodianship was a thankless task: why take on extra work when the embittered owners were just across the border in Neustadt and potentially could return? Officials wooed settlers from elsewhere in East Germany by promising them larger farms. But newcomers did not always adjust well to the Prohibited Zone. Ludwig Nagel from Elxleben took over one deportee's land and, within months, found himself deported without warning. All in all, this was a most "muddled situation."[27]

Sonneberg's frontier around Liebau was particularly turbulent. Since all but three of the village's residents fled west overnight during Action Vermin, the embarrassed regime decided not to raze Liebau, as planned, but to resettle it as a "display window" of the East."[28] Officials tried to convince the Liebauers who had left to return home, an invitation no one accepted.[29] Few others were willing to move there. After all, the hamlet was surrounded by border on three sides, the sole access road severed because it meandered into western land. The county prioritized building a new road as Sonneberg's "first socialist construction project." It also sought to grace Liebau with a "model life," including new buildings visible to the West, "first-rate Soviet agricultural machines," and the county's first collective farm.[30] When people in other villages began to resent this "special attention," Liebau settlers complained their neighbors had a "bad attitude." Liebauers alleged "arrogant and snippy" remarks, even "sabotage" of bread deliveries and electricity that amounted to a "huge class war."[31]

In the chaotic borderland, the East German government worked to shore up ideological commitment. Surveillance intensified, with community policemen (ABVs) and Voluntary Border Helpers increasingly enmeshed in local affairs.[32] The government began tracking daily grumblings about everything from food prices to international relations, and purged around sixty Sonnebergers from high-profile positions. By the end of 1952, it seemed, "political commissars" directed the minutiae of life along the frontier.[33] The regime also forbade church services in the Protection Strip, stationed political "enlighteners" in border towns and schools, and launched cultural events to "raise the consciousness of the frontier population."[34] A traveling border cinema was a success, but onerous permit requirements made live theater unfeasible. Despite plans for dances and libraries, most village "cultural rooms" held only "empty, cold tables and naked walls."[35] Efforts to win over frontier residents with better food, as well as extra rations of meat, fat, and sugar, likewise proved fruitless. Border security interfered with grocery deliveries, so provisions were often worse than what was available inland.[36]

One initiative that resonated, though, was the 15 percent salary bonus for borderland residents: "Yes, that was something!"[37] Actually, it was so popular that it proved politically untenable to amend, despite its high cost. When one private company announced after six months that it could no longer afford to pay the bonuses, all but one of its fifty-seven employees voted to strike. Berlin stepped in and placed the firm under trusteeship.[38] Sonnebergers also jockeyed for eligibility. The policy was unclear, and dispensations—for border zone residents who worked outside, or nonresidents who worked inside the zone, as well as different payments for different categories of workers and employers—resulted in intense "frustrations."[39] In fact, many people were willing to forgo freedoms to join the Prohibited Zone outright. Its residents had "all the perks," with 15 percent more pay as well as greater freedom of movement. They did not need permits to visit loved ones, to go to work, or to see their hairdressers and dentists inside the zone, as nonresidents did.[40] These advantages created frictions between neighbors who had unequal privileges but lived the same distance from the border, as in adjacent Oberlind and Unterlind. A number of citizens, including the entire community of Sonneberg-West, sought incorporation into the Prohibited Zone.[41]

Such confusion was hardly what the party had envisioned. Frontier communities were supposed to be a "paradigm that radiates over the nearby border" and confirms "our way is the right one!"[42] But in the borderland especially, administrations were shaky and citizens were unhappy. Residents were leaving in droves. Just 2 percent of East Germany's population, they represented 13 percent of all flight west in July 1952.[43] The young police state was exceedingly vulnerable at its perimeter.

June 1953: Frontier (In)action

The vulnerability of the East German government was soon put to the test. The regime's aggressive campaign for the "construction of socialism" had taken its toll by 1953. The forced socialization of industry and agriculture, mass arrests, show trials, repression of religion, deteriorated standard of living, and daily shortages of food and consumer goods led to widespread discontent. That spring, the number of East Germans heading west reached crisis proportions, more than doubling to over one thousand per day.[44]

Potential for unrest was perhaps greatest in the borderland, where things were particularly bleak. Certainly hostility seethed just beneath the surface in Sonneberg County. "Class enemies" posted fifty oppositional leaflets in Steinach, drew swastikas on public buildings, prank-called party comrades, and chalked houses with the phrase "Down with Stalin," leading to "gloating and smirking among the residents."[45] Dissent was ubiquitous. In one brawl involving seven teenagers and law enforcement, the crowd "baited the ruffians against the People's Police." "No one" supported the officers.[46] People were angry and barely suppressed it.

Everyone hated the new border measures. Everyone, from farm workers to party leaders, railed against security interference in community affairs. Political parties formally appealed frontier ordinances and the deportation of their members in Action Vermin.[47] Sonneberg's mayor, fed up with the bossy Border Police, openly declared he could no longer "speak with such people."[48] Pastors flouted the prohibition against services in the five-hundred-meter zone and condemned border brutality in their sermons. Churches attracted more and more congregants.[49]

Grievances mounted. In the wake of Stalin's death in March 1953, Moscow insisted that Berlin relax controls and improve living conditions throughout East

Germany. The Politburo announced its New Course on June 9, generating new hopefulness and greater public demands. In Sonneberg, the release of "economic" prisoners emboldened people to demand the return of Action Vermin and Werewolf deportees. Contrite party officials admitted "the regime had made mistakes" with these expulsions.[50] Some Sonnebergers also called for an end to the Prohibited Zone, arguing in town assemblies that government money would be better spent on more pressing material concerns. As rumors spread of the dismantling of security, residents took greater risks. By mid-June, the party agonized that "previously reserved and passive" frontier communities were acting up: "Even a certain brazenness can be ascertained . . . putting one's foot down and screaming at our Border Police."[51]

Throughout the country, on June 17, 1953, citizens revolted after the East German government increased work quotas.[52] Half a million people in 560 cities organized strikes and demonstrations before being defeated by Soviet tanks. The regime imposed martial law in three-quarters of all counties in East Germany.[53] The uprising made news around the world and was a major event in the early Cold War. Yet despite deep discontent in the borderland, in Sonneberg June 17 proved a nonevent.

The county had little to report. Someone broke a window at the state electronics store on Stalin Street.[54] People insulted party officials, sent them anonymous hate mail, and threatened to beat them up. One kindergarten teacher took down her picture of President Wilhelm Pieck.[55] A "large segment" of comrades openly criticized the party and resigned or stopped wearing their badges.[56] Around thirty farmers announced they were leaving their collective farms.[57] Though there had been talk of strikes, industrial workers did not organize. Only Erich Götz at the Neuhaus-Schierschnitz porcelain works publicly posted demands—to reduce work quotas, lower food prices, hold free elections, and abolish the border system.[58]

The regime had been nervous about the border zone. Officials (re)established emergency telephone service to the Protection Strip, stationed overseers at frontier factories, and held assemblies in border towns to "enlighten the population." But things were so tranquil that Sonneberg's party leadership fretted about the tranquility, reporting that "the calm behavior of all social classes gives us pause."[59]

Why Sonneberg's quiescence in June 1953? The border brutality of June 1952 was surely significant. Then, Sonneberg County had been especially rebellious, with high rates of deportation, resistance, and defection. A year later, many troublesome residents were gone, or loath to risk expulsion. Actually, the entire length of East Germany's southern borderland remained unusually quiet on June 17, 1953. This population was isolated by the Thuringian Forest, had fewer industrial workers (who propelled uprisings elsewhere in East Germany), and dreaded an outbreak of hostilities with the West.[60] Perhaps most of all, frontier repression had shown its effects. As one Berlin comrade quipped, Sonneberg stayed "peaceful" because it was effectively "a small Soviet republic."[61] For the borderland, June 1953 had already happened in June 1952.

That said, freer Neustadt was not much feistier. East German officials had feared a border breach by westerners, which would have been destabilizing. But on June 17, just thirty Neustadters gathered at Burned Bridge while extra Bavarian and American forces helped secure the boundary.[62] A few days later, at a Neustadt motorcycle race near the border, eighty East German "agitators" lined the frontier to prevent potential "disturbances" from West Germans. But "not a single citizen went in the proximity" of the boundary.[63] West Germany and the United States did little to assist East German protesters in June 1953 in general.[64] Westerners made calm gestures of solidarity. June 17 became a national holiday, the Day of German Unity, while Neustadt and other border towns held frontier demonstrations and minutes of silence for "bloody Soviet terror."[65] A choral concert in nearby Rottenbach brought two thousand western spectators to the boundary, but no unrest ensued. Communist leaders thought it "remarkable that calm prevailed on the western side of the border," and were relieved that westerners stayed out of the crisis.[66]

In June 1953, East German officials caused the greatest border unrest themselves. As part of its New Course, the government decided to win back citizens who had defected to the West, offering returnees amnesty, compensation for property, travel expenses, and a daily allowance of 10 East marks. Since Sonneberg County had lost over 3 percent of its total population in the past year, Sonneberg officials were particularly enthusiastic about the policy change, and embarked on a quixotic campaign for recruitment. They sent personal letters to Sonneberg business owners or doctors who had gone west, and set up an "information center" on the frontier to persuade people face-to-face. They also enlisted envoys such as ten-year-old Erich Eckardt; border guards simply "held up the barbed wire" for the child to cross, and he helped convince two families to return.[67]

The most peculiar initiative, though, was a series of large Sunday border gatherings. A handful of people in Heinersdorf had been meeting at the boundary each Sunday since June 1952 with loved ones who had fled to adjacent Welitsch. Such informal reunions were "tolerated to a certain point."[68] In June 1953, the party tried to leverage these gatherings into formal recruiting events at several points along Sonneberg's border. Things did not go as planned, however. In Heinersdorf especially, the People's Police "behaved obstinately" at the first meeting and held the crowd of more than 150 townspeople behind the ten-meter strip. They allowed just seven officials to talk over the barbed wire to forty Heinersdorfers who had fled. That day, no one was persuaded to return.[69]

After this public relations fiasco, the regime eased up. Sunday gatherings on June 21 and 28 were more jovial. The border police in Heinersdorf permitted hundreds to chat at the border for three hours. Eastern children were "allowed to crawl through the barbed wire," while westerners handed over food and chocolate. Sonneberg officials believed this border conviviality was reassuring to potential returnees, since "almost all wanted to come back, but they don't trust the regime enough."[70]

The party soon lost control over these Sunday reunions, however, as they spread to more communities and attracted more people each week. Easterners and westerners began meeting not just at designated spots but all along the border, especially around Burned Bridge and the Mountain Mill Tavern.[71] By July 19, more than a thousand people converged on the boundary. Sonnebergers living outside the Prohibited Zone "forced" their way to the frontier, their sheer numbers compelling border police to allow them at the barbed wire. Scenes of reunion

Talking through the barbed wire fence at a border meeting in Heinersdorf. Mitten in Deutschland: Mitten in 20. Jahrhundert.

were "staggering." Tearful relatives called out to one another, sometimes not recognizing grandchildren, nieces, and nephews who had grown up over the years.[72]

These border meetings were supposed to showcase East Germany's bright New Course, but the regime wound up looking fairly bad. Sunday openness only underscored the brutality of Monday through Saturday. Plus the dynamic suggested eastern inferiority. Sonnebergers kept outnumbering westerners at least two to one and, according to Neustadt reports, sought western charity. The *Neue Presse* described how "cigarettes, chocolate, etc. flew over the barbed wire to thankful hands," while "thick tears ran down the cheeks of the Thuringians, as their friends from West Germany threw over gift packages."[73] In the end, the Sunday reunions won few returnees. Out of Sonneberg's two thousand defectors over the previous twelve months, only fifty-seven returned during the summer of 1953.[74]

Meanwhile, Sonneberg officials worried about the "unsettled" border situation they had created. They combated rumors of mass crossings in the press, and called upon dozens of Soviet troops and local "agitators" to help the People's Police contain the Sunday meetings.[75] Although no breaches occurred, by the end of July nervous local leaders requested help from the Central Committee in Berlin "to suppress additional assemblies." The "wild border meetings" continued for another week or so, but then fizzled out as quickly as they had begun.[76]

It did not take much to ignite these gatherings, and it did not take much to halt them. As with the frontier breaches of 1949, it was the party that set off and then stopped the unorthodox border events. What began as East German propaganda transformed into displays of western munificence and eastern suffering, as people on both sides rapidly made them their own. The crowds' unexpected zeal rendered it all the more remarkable that the frontier closed again as peaceably as it opened, without reported unrest or violence.

The Sunday meetings exposed not the physical strength of the border in 1953 but its dependence on local observance. Emotional crowds massed on the border for seven Sundays in a row, separated by a few strands of barbed wire. In the context of mass uprisings elsewhere in East Germany, the collapse of border discipline loomed as a threat to the unsteady regime. The 1953 border gatherings, like the 1949 mass crossings, suggested the potential for collective action to render the boundary unworkable. But amid the greatest unrest in East Germany's history, the border endured, and expanded.

The Western Border Zone

Borderland restraint was even more notable among West Germans than East Germans because, after all, they had much less to fear. In Neustadt in the fifties, residents largely accepted the new border regime, benefiting directly and indirectly from its implementation. Of course, the dangers were real and the traumas were raw. Neustadters had their own wrenching experiences as bystanders to brutality and separation from loved ones. But emotional intensity was difficult to sustain, with insecurity breeding myopia, and public calamity devolving into mawkish opportunism. One local columnist recoiled at this strategic "kitsch," urging: "Let's protect our dignity as border residents. Let's not make business out of our distress, or God forbid anything that smacks of political or parliamentary favors."[77] Still, many did just that. Much as they had since the late forties, Neustadt leaders treated the border as a fait accompli and manipulated it to their political and economic advantage.

Border closure in 1952 raised the stakes of such tactics. National politicians and reporters now toured the barbed wire, giving Neustadt and other frontier towns an opportunity to influence the conversation. Material grievances predominated. Certainly the border fences of 1952 acquired nowhere near the emotive resonance of the Berlin Wall in 1961. There was little groundwork for a transcendent Kennedy moment, when the U.S. president's "I am a Berliner" statement in 1963 declared the barrier a human catastrophe.[78] Westerners' complaints of economic privation in the fifties rang hollow, especially in comparison to their neighbors' ordeal just across the border.

Neustadt leaders pursued state remuneration for an array of border injustices, lobbying for tax breaks, reduced freight rates, business subsidies, federal contracts, and road and housing construction. The problems were significant. East Germany's border measures severed transit routes, as well as sixteen electrical lines and water deliveries to Wildenheid.[79] The East German regime also halted natural gas deliveries to Sonneberg, which had consumed 80 percent of Neustadt's total production.[80] But western anger seems disproportionate. While Sonnebergers faced gas stoppages through the winter of 1952–53, for example, Neustadters preoccupied Bonn with finding new markets for their extra production capacity. They even issued an "urgent appeal" to end federal subsidies to a competing gas plant in Coburg, which was not a "real border town."[81] Western claims of victimization could be inventive. One small community that had done a brisk business with eastern border smugglers, boasting seventeen grocery stores for twenty-one hundred inhabitants, wanted compensation for the loss of its black-market profits.[82]

For all its rhetoric of "existential crisis," Neustadt was doing well by the early fifties. City revenue was growing at an average of 36 percent a year.[83] The influx of Sonneberg workers and businesses was paying off. The transplanted glass industry had grown from scratch to 40 percent of West Germany's Christmas ornament exports, and it still claimed federal subsidies.[84] Actually, Neustadt's greatest challenges stemmed not from the border but from its own structural insufficiencies. Fragmented artisanal workshops remained the norm, as "homeworkers," mostly women and children, made for cheap, flexible labor. They constituted up to a quarter of the workforce in both Neustadt and Sonneberg through the early 1960s.[85] Neustadt leaders wanted to modernize and diversify, but in many ways border lobbying stunted economic development, as city councilors and businesses owners wound up bickering with one another over federal handouts.[86]

Thus Neustadt leaders kept approaching Bonn with "wishes upon wishes," angry when state subcommittees responded with "promises, promises."[87] The West German government had, in fact, been conflicted over border towns' sweeping demands for economic, political, and cultural support. Federal offices had loosened the purse strings for short-term emergency funds in June 1952 and rhetorically supported the borderland as a "display window of the West" and defense against "Bolshevization." Yet it was the political watershed of June 1953 that solidified the creation of the official Zonal Peripheral Area. This thirty-to-sixty-kilometer-wide buffer zone was, in language recalling East German rhetoric, for the "spiritual and psychological strengthening of the border populace to defend against myriad communist influence attempts."[88]

Between federal subsidies and West Germany's famed "economic miracle," Neustadt grew increasingly prosperous in the fifties.[89] Its complacent borderland milieu was well portrayed in an unusual western movie, *Sky Without Stars*, filmed in the region. Anna, the sympathetic East German heroine, reproaches western self-absorption, materialism, and acceptance of border brutality. She cries that the border "will never disappear—because it is much too convenient for you in the West. You have simply written us off!"[90]

West German youths at Burned Bridge. Stadtarchiv Neustadt bei Coburg.

Westerners condemned the Iron Curtain even as they built upon it. Trifling events suggest how reflexively Neustadters defined the border from their privileged perspective. When one pub fashioned itself a border "lighthouse" with great fanfare, it was not to guide eastern refugees but to "warn" imbibing westerners that "grave dangers lurked only a few hundred meters away."[91] This western gaze both belittled and built up the border's frightfulness. The *Neue Presse* gaily reported how one night, "four merry revelers" illegally crossed into East Germany "in march formation" as "shock troops." The westerners captured a bottle of liquor as "proof" of their military "adventure," making their neighbors' captivity a humorous counterpoint.[92] Whether melodrama or comedy, the sense of battling totalitarianism in Neustadt infused everyday life.

The border also became an object of obsessive scrutiny. Eastern brigades' demolition of the railroad crossing and buildings inside the Control Strip in 1952 had appalled local sensibilities, and Neustadt newspapers began reporting frontier changes in indignant detail. The national and international press, too, disseminated images of East Germany's "puppet police" and "Death Strip," while even mundane border issues, such as signage for closed streets or inaccessible villages, became matters of considered federal policy.[93] At Burned Bridge, a western sign warned citizens to be vigilant and to "stop the smugglers! No supplies for Soviet armament!"—across from an eastern billboard that screamed, "Ami, go home!"[94] These visuals reinforced the Cold War's front line.

The barrier made a dramatic backdrop for flamboyant demonstrations in Neustadt. Torchlight parades, leaflet drops, and mass balloon releases spanned the political spectrum from right to left, from war veterans to youth groups. Speeches and articles condemned the frontier "dead zone" and sentimentalized the "feeling of togetherness between people of the same blood, language, and homeland."[95] These stylized rituals drew hundreds, yet usually were less about unifying Germany than about unifying the people that held them. The Wooden Church Crusade, an American charitable program to build forty-eight churches along the Iron Curtain (one for each of the forty-eight states), flew from its new church in Wildenheid a U.S. flag and rang bells loudly enough to be heard across the border, successfully blending religion, government, anticommunism, and local spirit.[96] Initiatives with real-life East Germans, however, drew less enthusiasm. When Lauscha yodelers visited Neustadt, the newspaper begged readers to go to the concert to "show our brothers from over there that they are not forgotten," but the concert was "only poorly attended."[97] For the most part, westerners embraced the plight of easterners without embracing actual easterners.

Neustadters' self-consciousness as a western bulwark shaped their economy, their sense of community, and ultimately their acceptance of a barrier in their midst.[98] A feeling of profound difference evolved with, and from, routines of border posturing and anticommunism. And in both East and West, the lived experience of the Iron Curtain intensified the sense of divergence. Already in 1955, one Sonneberg tradesman expressed the chasm he felt: "I can't imagine what a united Germany would look like. It is certainly impossible to reconcile both systems. With reunification, one system would have to disappear."[99]

East-West Contacts

Personal relations between East and West Germans grew more distant over the course of the fifties. Of course, many Neustadters and Sonnebergers maintained individual connections, exchanging letters, postcards, and limited visits with loved ones. As Neustadt's Mayor Ernst Bergmann put it in one radio interview, border residents retained a "good-neighborly spirit."[100] Moreover, a variety of cross-border ties survived 1952. More than one hundred farmers still crossed with commuter passes; Sonneberg workers still had temporary jobs at western toy and glass workshops; city officials still traded materials, medicines, and spare parts over the border unofficially. As one former Sonneberg functionary recalled, "Everything went in one pot."[101] Neustadt resumed gas deliveries to Sonneberg from 1955 to 1964, an important logistical and symbolic connection.[102]

But governmental policies increasingly strained East-West contacts. Since West Germany denied the legitimacy of the East German state, even low-level dealings assumed national significance. In their "shadowboxing" at home and around the globe, the two Germanys vied to control each interaction.[103] Wherever they could, western officials worked to circumvent the East German government, invoking freedom. By contrast, eastern officials worked to entangle West Germany in discussions wherever they could, invoking international harmony.

In such a context, cross-border contacts, no matter how minor, became both a threat and an opportunity. In the competition between communism and capitalism, Neustadters and Sonnebergers who had grown up together now found themselves surrogate ambassadors. Their exchanges in *gesamtdeutsch,* or "all-German," affairs were subject to vetting, preparation, and debriefing. These contact boundaries were not about halting interactions as much as manipulating interactions. As the two Germanys leveraged personal ties to strategic advantage, neither state intended to reduce travel per se. But since their strategies were mutually threatening, that was the net effect. The politicized crossings of the fifties further divided East and West.

The East German government aggressively sponsored collective crossings in the fifties. In September 1953, it illegally sent west more than seven thousand eastern "agitators" to disrupt West German parliamentary elections, a strategy reminiscent of the 1949 mass breaches that had aroused hostility in the borderland. Coburg County saw rioting, thirteen hundred arrests, and westerners pelting their eastern "captives" with garbage.[104] Such dramatic incidents justified western border force increases.[105] And westerners worried about East Germany's more peaceful cross-border ventures, too. Eastern summer camps for thousands of West German youths, for example, posed "dangers" to impressionable children.[106] Western authorities fretted that East Germany exploited the economically "disadvantaged borderland" for "political influence."[107] Near Neustadt, free buses took dozens of West German miners over the border each day for higher pay in East Germany's Lehesten quarry, as well as for subsidized spa vacations, shopping days, festivals, and health services. The western press rebuked the crossers as "traitors" and "activists for the East Zone."[108]

The main goal of East Germany's "all-German work" in the fifties, though, was less to provoke than to subsume cross-border interactions to the state. The "battle plan" to give East-West relations a public, "organized form" spanned multiple fronts, down to village officials sending letters and packages to designated counterparts in West Germany.[109] A flurry of athletic, cultural, and political events drew the most enthusiasm. Sonneberg held twenty-one East-West sports matches in the summer of 1954, from ping-pong to soccer.[110] These exchanges were usually light on the ideology, since "unfortunately" athletes failed to engage in much "political discussion," preferring movies, beer, and carousing.[111] But functionaries believed the events enhanced East Germany's stature. Everything counted, whether a small accordion concert or Sonneberg's Technical School toy exhibition in Neustadt, which drew twenty thousand visitors.[112] The regime poured resources into forging and tracking East-West ties. Over the summer of 1955, for example, Sonneberg sent twenty "delegations" to the West, received twelve "delegations" from the West, and wrote sixteen articles about it all for the newspaper.[113] Yet this charm offensive was so closely linked to the communist government that wary westerners often kept their distance. The campaign abated when East Germany tightened travel restrictions at the end of the decade.[114]

Eastern officials put more sustained effort into politicizing private trips. There were still frequent visits between the Germanys, ranging from more than three million a year between 1954 and 1957 to roughly one and a half million a year between 1958 and 1961, out of a combined East-West population of seventy-one million. In Sonneberg, with its strong ties to the West, the rate of travel was twice as great.[115] The county issued between four thousand and eleven thousand visas a year for westerners throughout the fifties, around a third from the Neustadt/Coburg border region.[116] Sonneberg's mayor and city councilors endeavored to propagandize the visitors, hosting "informal discussion evenings" at city hall or the House of German-Soviet Friendship once or twice a month between 1953 and 1961. These were rather awkward affairs, with two- to four-hour discussions of socialist development only slightly enlivened by modest offerings of drinks and cigarettes. Such events typically drew fewer than ten westerners each, leaving embarrassed local luminaries routinely outnumbering their guests.[117] Officials kept searching for a "totally new way" to impress travelers: slide shows, Soviet films, parties, and tours of the city and Toy Museum.[118] Functionaries also tried to talk to West Germans individually, setting up "enlightenment locales" in club rooms and cornering visitors as they registered for ration cards. By 1960, local officials reached over half of all western visitors in either formal events or one-on-one talks.[119] Repeat travelers, though, might have noticed a less friendly trend. Whereas welcome letters in 1953–54 had deplored the "unnatural" border, and in 1956 featured Sonneberg's "view toward Franconia" with a vista of Neustadt in the background, the brochure in 1960 showed Sonneberg from the reverse perspective, facing away from the West.[120]

West Germany likewise tried to control cross-border contacts.[121] Yet it was more circumspect in approach, so that "private meetings" between borderland residents would appear spontaneous and apolitical.[122] Guidelines remained "strictly confidential." Federal and American support was only for eastern travelers "willing and suitable to represent all-German interests in the West German sense," who would then foster a "liberal consciousness" upon their return to East Germany.[123] Rhetoric emphasized help to suffering easterners rather than explicit ideology; the tokens of magnanimity were material benefits instead of edification. But the West's intent to display its superiority was much the same. From 1953, American donations and federal funds gave East German visitors grocery coupons worth 20 DM each, food packages, and Christmas presents. West Germany also subsidized tickets for sporting and cultural events, movies, public transportation, and, after 1956, travel assistance and 10 DM "pocket money." With around four hundred "guests from the zone" claiming this cash in Coburg County each month (fifty in Neustadt), westerners accused easterners of abusing it for shopping ventures.[124] Then again, West Germany's main message was prosperity; its 1956 welcome brochure featured mopeds, refrigerators, and televisions, and invited easterners to "please compare."[125] Even as the West sought to impress, it did not want visitors to stay. The government offered travel money only to easterners "who intend to ultimately return to the Soviet zone." Coburg County purchased easterners' train tickets directly—wanting them to glimpse, but not sustain, life in consumer paradise.[126]

The travel of government officials was especially complicated. Since the two Germanys had no relations at the national level, dealings on the border served as proxy diplomacy.[127] Here officials had to interact and negotiate over railroad, gas, energy, waste, water, and travel matters. Each state tried to exploit contacts to opposite ends. Berlin saw local talks as a springboard for political recognition, exploiting logistical problems to win diplomatic ground. Bonn, however, eschewed "politics" and insisted that western officials stick to "technical" subjects because East Germany would use the "smallest opportunity" to declare a a propaganda "victory."[128] In effect, easterners could engage only politics, and westerners could engage only problems, leading to deadlock all along the Iron Curtain. Thus while Sonneberg barraged Neustadt with ideologically charged invitations for congresses and conferences, Neustadt barraged Sonneberg with practical grievances about utility payments and the filthy Röden River— neither side answering the other.

Local leaders were torn between their states' hard-line stances and enduring personal ties. After all, many had moved in the same circles or gone to school together. Some were related. Even their most stilted correspondence betrayed hints of these bonds, with nostalgia for "good, old relationships" palpable between the lines.[129] Working out frontier problems over beers, old friends would get in trouble for getting along, communicating, or conceding too much. As their respective governments groped for a more "unified approach" to cross-border contacts, policies progressively curbed connections.[130]

Neustadt and Sonneberg's protracted dealings about having dealings illustrates the extent to which state and media scrutiny affected local relationships. Part of East Germany's initiative for "western work," Sonneberg's Mayor Braun suggested in 1953 that the cities trade photograph albums with images of their development since the end of the war. Neustadt's Mayor Weppler initially declined the project as a propaganda ploy. He eventually relented in 1955, agreeing to send a delegation to Sonneberg for the exchange ceremony, though objections from Bavarian state offices resulted in the cancellation of both the trip and Neustadt's album. Sonnebergers came to Neustadt instead, handing over their album in a modest city council ceremony. When western state officials objected even to this display, Neustadt leaders called off a reciprocal trip to Sonneberg.[131]

Still, Sonneberg's exemplary "all-German work" tempted Neustadters into covert relations in the mid-fifties. Lower-level city and gas works employees sneaked into the East for meetings, "avoiding the press in order to avoid complications with the federal government."[132] Western negotiators described "a pleasant and intimate atmosphere without political tension," but they made little headway.[133] Neustadters would try to discuss practical problems, while Sonnebergers protested they could not enter into commitments without diplomatic recognition of East Germany. Neither Bonn nor Berlin budged, so local relations soon cooled. Then the only official "intermediary" between Neustadt and Sonneberg was a furtive individual called Captain Holm (westerners thought it was a code name), who popped up from time to time for talks on the boundary.[134] At a regional summit in 1958, the East German district chairman, Opitz, surprised everyone by addressing a range of border issues, even pledging to open a checkpoint at Rodach (Burned Bridge was too populated and difficult to monitor). Western newspapers breathlessly reported Opitz's concessions, but East German authorities in Berlin speedily sacked him.[135]

After this disappointment, Neustadt leaders decided to engage Sonneberg openly. Bavarian and federal offices worried the initiative would "look rather bad." Yet Neustadt's brash new thirty-two-year-old mayor, Ernst Bergmann, forced the issue, calling a town meeting at which residents overwhelmingly voted to revive ties and, after four years, to reciprocate a photograph album.[136] Bavarian authorities reluctantly acceded. Neustadt spent nine months crafting images of western progress, its album twice the length of Sonneberg's and five times the original cost. It featured elaborate calligraphy and images of the town's new diving board and garbage truck.[137] City leaders also tried to look good for the handoff ceremony in Sonneberg in 1959, strategizing Mayor Bergmann's dark suit and gray tie as well as the "generous" provisioning of all ten Neustadt representatives with quality cigarettes and cigars.[138]

Neustadt's unusual overture to East Germany backfired, though, notwithstanding positive feelings about the meeting itself. When the Sonneberg summit made headlines in both East and West, Bavarian officials pressured Neustadt to cool relations. The German Cities Parliament even voted unanimously to ban western cities from "semi-official delegation visits."[139] In October 1960, Neustadt hosted a Sonneberg delegation anyway. The media made political hay out of this, too, as each side portrayed the other as traitorous. The *Neue Presse* depicted the easterners on the brink of concession, quoting Sonneberg city councilor Lenk as ready to "open the border immediately." Meanwhile, the front page of East Germany's *Neues Deutschland* featured Neustadt leaders blithely flouting West Germany's "contact prohibition."[140] At the height of Cold War tensions, these low-level relations carried too much risk for each government and were ended by 1961. In both Germanys, it was irresponsible to flirt with undoing the East-West divide.

From photograph albums to logistical problems, state involvement in cross-border relations created frictions greater than the mundane matters ostensibly at issue. Frontier negotiations came to be about controlling the terms of conversation, with the appearance of interactions or political "imagineering" more important than substance.[141] As the two German governments fumbled along, neither won the concessions they sought. Their mutual response to the setbacks was to prune cross-border ties, all the while invoking the language of unity. Thus, within a few years, East and West reached a diplomatic impasse. They wrangled over the existence of talks, not even close to resolving their content.

The contact boundary between East and West, like the physical boundary, appears to have formed from a multitude of little actions, through trial and error. Rules governing travel and interactions were propelled by their own shortcomings, taking shape because of the problems they created. Here was another manifestation of the border's expanding authority.

While the experiences of Sonneberg and Neustadt suggest that people could maneuver around state strictures and even influence their development, this contact boundary seems more notable for adherence than for resistance. Ultimately, it was less important that neighbors continued to visit one another than that they submitted to such strange procedures to do so. Within a few years, people in adjacent towns were addressing each other with divergent rhetoric and divergent interests. For the most part, they saw each other how and when their states desired. Local leaders stopped meeting, stopped reaching agreements, and stopped showing up in each other's newspapers.

Today, Neustadters and Sonnebergers romanticize their "close, friendly relations" from the fifties, describing a straightforward neighborliness that was thwarted by communism.[142] But materials from the time portray a more complicated relationship, one of mutual frustrations, doubts, and self-censorship mediated through state policies. This interpersonal caution was part of the border, too. Locals laughed about the physical absurdities of cross-border contact— visiting someone a stone's throw away required a visa and a half day's journey (140 kilometers by rail through the checkpoint at Probstzella or 250 kilometers by car through Töpen/Juchhöh). Interpersonal contortions, however, were just as extreme. Renegotiated relationships likewise played a role in the creation of East and West.

The "Living Wall"

Germany's divide in the fifties was not a physical fortification as much as it was a "living wall": a product of the uneasy postwar society that endured, accepted, and entrenched it. After the East German regime's border escalations of 1952, frontier populations on both sides assimilated partition, creating in the process unforeseen economic, political, and social boundaries. By the end of the decade, many Sonnebergers and Neustadters felt that they lived in alternate realities, in divergent border zones with divergent rules, objectives, ideologies, and languages. Government and media hyperbole generated a Cold War barrier much stronger than the border's fragile reality.

The early frontier was actually quite porous. For all the menacing measures and rhetoric, there was no Iron Curtain in place. Borderland residents still crossed the primitive fences; this was especially true of children, who remained immune from prosecution. Notwithstanding grave risks, people continued to pick berries, smuggle, and shop over the border. A bottle of schnapps for the guards meant "you could go back and forth all day long," while sentries from East and West shared cigarettes, chocolate, and an occasional game of cards in the woods.[143] Nostalgia no doubt colors early tales, yet locals overwhelmingly remember the border of the fifties as only somewhat more systematic than the "green border" of the late forties.

East Germany's Prohibited Zone and Protection Strip remained porous, too. People sneaked in frequently, Sonneberg chairman Hildebrandt admitting in 1955 that "we don't know who's wandering around the 500-meter area anymore."[144] Rules for curfews, visits, assemblies, driving, farming, hunting, and fishing—even picking up the morning's milk deliveries—were consistently inconsistent. Overwhelmed officials misinterpreted, improvised, and enforced "false orders" ad hoc.[145]

The eastern border zone was a confusing blend of backwardness and militarization, exacerbated by a motley cast of new arrivals. Soviet soldiers helped farmers in frontier fields as "best friends," according to local newspapers.[146] Teenagers from the Free German Youth helped guard the boundary. Newcomers were often shocked by the unusual conditions of the Prohibited Zone but, in living there, "soon came to believe we had to protect the border." There emerged a strange frontier society of guards, youths, and farmers, who drank, danced, and caught border crossers together. One adolescent arrival wrote in his diary, "This insanity is simply inconceivable."[147]

At the same time, discontent may have run deeper in the borderland than in East Germany's general "grumble society" of the fifties.[148] In fact, pervasive hostility seemed to threaten the boundary's viability. Residents continued to battle border police over everyday ordinances, harassing and sometimes assaulting them. People also refused to serve as Voluntary Border Helpers, let alone show up for workplace "combat drills." Religious groups continued to buck frontier restrictions. Youths continued to draw swastikas and other public graffiti, even in the snow. Ordinary residents continued to grouse openly about frontier hardships: permits, closed taverns, abysmal television reception, "unjust" allocation of the 15 percent border bonus, travel prohibitions, and the closure of Burned Bridge.[149] Onerous security in the frontier zone jeopardized the economy and everyday well-being. In 1959, several people were knocked unconscious in Oberlind's long food lines.[150] Things reached a breaking point by mid-1960, when, as elsewhere in East Germany, farmers resisted a second wave of collectivization. Already irate at frontier bans that prohibited livestock, machinery, bicycles, and even their own children from fields inside the five-hundred-meter zone, farmers wrecked border markers, taunting the guards, "Go ahead, shoot us."[151] They also fled west.[152]

The border's permeability made for East-West confrontations. Westerners heckled eastern guards and damaged fortifications. Once, seven young men broke the Heinersdorf road barrier by sitting on it together.[153] Eastern People's Police cataloged such "provocations" and "serious territorial infractions," claiming up to 170 a month by the end of the fifties. Meanwhile, western officials protested that eastern guards themselves transgressed, pinching a mower for the ten-meter strip or lumber for fence repairs.[154] The atmosphere grew nastier. West

Germans avoided going too close to the border lest East German sentries harass, throw rocks, or even shoot at them. Talking over the boundary with loved ones, once a common custom, increasingly led to warning shots and arrests. People began to arrange viewings from a distance, sharing furtive hand signals on weekends from the terrace of the Mountain Mill Tavern.[155] Accidental crossing also brought hazards. After one Neustadter's puppy ran over the border, East Germany's Stasi interrogated the man for twelve hours.[156] Wayward horses, cattle, civilians, and soldiers required even lengthier negotiations. Most infamously, when American First Lieutenant Richard Mackin's liaison aircraft ran out of gas over Sonneberg, the East German government held him "hostage" for two months in its bid for diplomatic recognition.[157]

Thus, while the actual barrier of the fifties remained crude and porous, it came to feel like a Cold War divide. East Germany followed its crackdown of 1952–53 with some relaxation in the middle of the decade, yet further tightening in 1958–61 made the frontier seem like a different place altogether, with more guards, watchtowers, fences, roadblocks—and mines. The Sonneberg-Neustadt region was a "focal point" of escalations, particularly Burned Bridge, where searchlights in 1960 reached a mile.[158] Sonnebergers had grown so accustomed to the tense frontier that those traveling to Berlin, where the border remained open, were shocked by the city's easy atmosphere. Jörg Trautmann remembers walking into West Berlin flabbergasted, since he was not even allowed near the border back home.[159] At Burned Bridge, by the end of the decade "no one had contact anymore over the barrier. At most, a hasty greeting at harvest time."[160]

Rather quickly, East Germany's severe Prohibited Zone and West Germany's coddled Zonal Peripheral Area stabilized the previously unruly border and, as opposite microcosms of their respective new states, estranged former neighbors from each other. Everyday adaptations not only lent the fortifications an aura of inevitability but also suggested that further accommodations were possible. Sonnebergers and Neustadters feared East Germany's totalitarian aims for the border, even though the reality often fell short. To some extent, belief in the Iron Curtain helped solidify the Iron Curtain.

Germany's "living wall" became so daunting that easterners who opted to leave sought other means. In fact, most Sonnebergers who left East Germany during the fifties overstayed travel visas or went through West Berlin, not over the border in their backyards. To many, mass departure through Berlin suggested the essential weakness of the East German regime, unable to retain millions of citizens. But hidden behind this obvious failure was an unrecognized strength. After all, it was the authority of the much longer 1,393-kilometer frontier that channeled people through Berlin.

The unlikely effectiveness of the inter-German boundary not only intensified the Berlin Crisis, funneling the discontented through this hole in the Iron Curtain, but also portended the effectiveness of the Berlin Wall in 1961. East Germany had transformed the border, its greatest zone of instability, into a reliable bulwark, without the West objecting. This was a success story that made additional escalations seem possible. For all its problems, the fragile border worked well enough. So in the 1950s, the East German regime invested less in perfecting its physical border system than in controlling crossers one by one.

7

Surveillance: Individual Controls

East Germany faced a crisis of existence between 1952 and 1961. One in seven citizens left in these nine years. The exodus totaled around two and a half million people, half under the age of twenty-five. The vast majority went illegally: overstaying travel visas in West Germany, escaping over the inter-German border, or going through Berlin, which remained open. To prevent demographic catastrophe, the regime ultimately resorted, in 1961, to constructing stronger barriers on the border and to building the Berlin Wall.

A bird's-eye view of the population crisis, however, obscures profound changes in state power. Throughout the fifties, the East German government attempted to build a less obvious kind of boundary—one that bound people to the state individually. Unable to retain citizens through ideology or mass initiatives alone, the regime worked to secure them one by one. It laid invisible snares person by person, subtler than guns and watchtowers. Local functionaries were to "be careful and customized," keeping tabs on people who might travel, defect, or emigrate, and manipulating their families, careers, and everyday lives to get them to stay.[1]

State structures spiraled out, eastern officials spawning increasingly elaborate systems to track and thwart border crossings. Their ad hoc efforts to stem the population exodus expanded, over the 1950s, into systematized controls. Although East Germany's formidable surveillance apparatus can be seen from the top down, with the notorious Stasi, or Ministry for State Security, as the cornerstone of its construction, early measures against flight show how surveillance was also propelled from the bottom up, in multiple areas of government, with the Stasi as an outgrowth.

The struggle for citizens in the 1950s links East Germany's two most infamous peculiarities, its ominous boundary and ominous surveillance. The failure of everyday governance—and of ever more extreme measures—to halt East Germans' flight propelled the construction of the Berlin Wall as well as the development of the Stasi. Both emerged in the context of a demographic crisis that built over a decade.

East Germany's population battle in the fifties helped shape regime authority. Too unpopular to rely on either spontaneous loyalty or mass violence, the government retained people through entanglement. There was always the threat of physical force, but the state's greatest levers were intimidation, coercion, and persuasion at the level of the individual. Though the product of weakness, this customization created a mystique of omniscience, in the face of which East Germans felt vulnerable.

The nature of communism is still hotly debated, observers disagreeing on whether East Germany was a "niche society," a "thoroughly ruled society," a "participatory dictatorship," or a "welfare dictatorship," to name but a few.[2] Yet the primacy of population politics perhaps offers a frame that encompasses each of these perspectives. Individualized controls allowed for wide variation in the exercise of power. In fact, border problems spurred the East German government into multiple modes of rule. Thus while outcomes differed, it was the underlying knowledge and manipulation of personal lives that came to define the state, an ironic brand of individualism for the masses. After all, East Germany amassed not "mountains of corpses" but "mountains of files."[3]

Personal Flight

Flight was East Germany's central concern in the 1950s. Of the two hundred thousand to four hundred thousand people migrating between the two Germanys each year, more than 80 percent were heading from the East to the West (Appendices 1 and 2). Each day, more than six hundred easterners left; they were disproportionately young, skilled, and educated. Sonneberg County, which had lost nearly 4 percent of its population to flight and deportation in Action Vermin in 1952, continued to lose three hundred to eight hundred citizens a year. This exodus magnified the growing imbalance between the two states. While East Germany's population declined 7 percent in the fifties, West Germany's rose 12 percent in the course of its "economic miracle."[4]

Easterners left because of a variety of factors.[5] The disruptions of World War II had forced mobility; for millions who had lost homes, families, and livelihoods, the West seemed to offer greater opportunities. East Germany's political repressions and economic restructuring increased flight, as did the crushed uprisings of June 1953 and the continued emphasis on heavy industry at the expense of consumer goods.[6] Specific events also triggered defections. Migration spiked, for example, after West Germany's passage of the generous Equalization of Burdens Law in 1952, which redistributed wealth to expellees and others who could demonstrate war losses.[7] International tensions over the Geneva Conference in 1955 and the revolt in Hungary in 1956 also prompted migration. Different social groups left at different times, artisans and business owners fleeing production cooperatives in 1953 and farmers fleeing collectivization in 1953 and 1960–61. Defections were highly seasonal, with more people leaving during the summer and holiday periods. And geography mattered, with those living closest to the inter-German boundary, ironically, less likely to leave. After the imposition of the Prohibited Zone, border residents' rate of flight dropped from twice the national average before 1952 to half of it thereafter. This was, in part, because so many people had already left. In Sonneberg, flight decreased to 50 to 70 percent below the national average, 0.4 to 1 percent of citizens leaving Sonneberg each year in the 1950s, compared to the national rate of 0.8 to 1.8 percent.[8]

People did not experience these trends as impersonal factors, however. Rather, flight was felt to be a private choice that hinged upon individual well-being. One Sonneberg doll maker wanted to head west in 1958 not because he opposed socialism per se but because the "idiots" in his local production cooperative were not supplying him with doll heads. He was fed up and had begun selling off his possessions in preparation for leaving, yet still hoped things could improve.[9] It was a complex calculation. Sonnebergers with well-established businesses and farms were often reluctant to start over in the West, as were those who had gained higher-status positions under the new regime. In the words of one Sonneberg administrator: "I was, shall we say, well cared for. Maybe everything didn't go just so. But I adjusted."[10]

Going west meant walking away from an entire life, jettisoning home, community, and loved ones. Kurt Geis shook his head remembering the tempting job offers he had had across the border. "But we still had the business. My father was waiting for me. He was already getting older. My mind was racing: 'What will you do, what will you do?'" He decided to stay, imagining that he could always leave someday.[11] Those who did leave lost contact with friends and family for years, sometimes forever. Interviewees describe these disconnections haltingly, uncertain how to characterize parents or siblings they never saw again, even after reunification. Siegfried Tenner described the perpetual anxiety of the impossible choice: they "naturally wanted to" head west and "always, always" thought about it, but could not leave parents and grandparents behind. "No one thought to say outright that we should all just go now."[12]

It was difficult for a family to leave all at once. Often husbands or older children would leave first to find jobs and housing, letting others know to follow once they got established in the West. In fact, 17 percent of all East German asylum applicants in the fifties said they were joining relatives. For Sonnebergers, the ratio may have been as high as a quarter to a half.[13] To a point, eastern officials recognized family reunions as grounds for legal emigration, especially if they deemed the applicants to be a drain on the state. Even so, leaving home typically meant leaving someone else behind. Then again, for some, the finality of leaving was precisely its appeal. Going west was a good way to rid oneself of a domineering boss, spouse, or parent. Hundreds of Sonnebergers fled each year in the heat of love and anger—mid-affair, mid-argument, or both. These were impulsive, emotional crossings. When one unmarried teenage couple from Heubisch got pregnant, they fled to avoid their families' wrath.[14]

Youths, with less to lose, were most apt to leave. One-third of defectors in East Germany (and Sonneberg) were between the ages of fifteen and twenty-five, double their share of the population. Unencumbered by spouses or offspring, they left over lack of career prospects, denial of university placement, or avoidance of hard labor service. Their flight was not always meant to be permanent. Some left intending to come right back as returnees to East Germany, thereby avoiding military conscription and gaining priority for jobs and apartments. Or leaving could be a medium-term move that allowed young people to earn a degree, make money, or launch a career in the West before settling down back home. Stories of western success resonated. Four boys inspired emulation in Sonneberg, for instance, when they escaped one night through the basement window of their agricultural school dormitory. They wrote back to their friends with tales of western cars, motorcycles, and money: "One more year here, and we will have it made."[15]

Both the East and West German governments disliked youths' disruptive crossings. In the early fifties, western policy was to return those under eighteen to East Germany, but this became problematic as youths increasingly sought refugee status.[16] In the mid-fifties, Neustadt and Sonneberg's city administrations tried, together, to develop procedures to return adolescents "as quickly as possible to their parents' house."[17] But part of the problem was that sometimes there was no home to which the youths could return. The upheaval of the postwar years had filled institutions with abandoned children. When fourteen-year-old Jochen Seidler, after five years in a children's home, learned his mother was at a western refugee camp with his younger siblings, he tried to go find her, only to be caught between conflicting youth offices and border police in both the East and the West.[18]

For easterners in trouble with the law, leaving could seem the best option. In the East German police state, people feared the consequences of even petty infractions. Three soccer players fled after a drunken brawl at a game in Unterlind, lest they be charged with assault.[19] By 1959–60, Sonneberg County estimated that around forty people a year (12 percent of defectors) left either in anticipation of a police investigation or after one was launched. Since lives were easily ruined by insinuation and denunciation, local leaders began urging officials to "think seriously" before pressing charges.[20] Frightening someone into leaving was itself an offense. After one community policeman accused two workers of "sabotage" for a poor repair job, they fled in fear of prosecution; the policeman then found himself "disciplined" for scaring them away.[21]

East Germany's population exodus may have appeared a mass phenomenon, but it arose from a multiplicity of individual factors. The spiraling causes and consequences of flight were most visible at the local level. As certain neighborhoods, social cliques, or workplaces became hot spots of defection, flight wrought crisis on local governance and community life. Hospitals were going without doctors; schools were going without teachers. Everyone knew someone who had fled, and many Sonnebergers remain shaken by the memory of losing friends, coworkers, siblings, and children across the border. In the face of these pervasive, personal pulls, county functionaries worked harder and harder to hold on to people.

Proliferating Measures

Local officials were on the front line of the campaign against flight in the 1950s. Following a model of customized recruitment, they were to track and manipulate individual pressure points to retain citizens, "working for conviction."[22] Their files grew more expansive and intricate each year—classified by social status, age, political party, occupation, and motive—and by the end of the fifties, every community and workplace had its own flight commissions, resolutions, and "battle plans."[23] Population politics became East Germany's inquisition.[24] It fed off its own insufficiencies, manipulations, and paranoia. Dissent and surveillance yielded more dissent and surveillance, so the apparatus became self-perpetuating.

The regime, for example, individualized efforts to fend off western influence. The East German government limited cross-border commuting, farming, and visiting in 1952, and increasingly followed cross-border travel and relations in personal files. Western contact was a stain on citizens' standing. Having a relative who defected was even worse, a black mark that prevented party advancement, travel permits, apartments, and career and study opportunities for life. After Hannelore Reuther's father fled west, she said, she could not get an apprenticeship in Sonneberg as a seamstress: "They made it so bad for us, they did everything possible. We were so distressed; they put everything in our way."[25] Her entire family became suspect, and she wound up going west herself, part of the chain reaction of increasing tracking and increasing flight. Border behavior came to determine not only legal rights but also social status. Neighbors enforced the new border taxonomies, too—even when, or even because, they did not like them. Although his son had left for the West, Sonneberg officials granted one dentist in Schalkau multiple travel visas to West Germany because he was a member of the intelligentsia. Envious locals objected to the special allowance, and the community People's Choir threatened to boycott political events. The singers asserted that "every citizen has the same rights"—or lack thereof.[26]

Border transgression became a scarlet letter, exposed and reinforced by regime propaganda. Local newspapers were to portray "absconders" as cowardly, selfish degenerates who undermined socialism's virtues of public order, discipline, and honor, "publishing examples of particularly negative elements."[27] The press also vilified "respected" defectors. After one popular schoolteacher left, ostensible interviews with coworkers and students rebuked him for greed, laziness, and "sneak[ing] off in the night and fog."[28] Whether or not people believed or sympathized with such attacks, everyone recognized such shaming as a public consequence that implicated neighbors, associates, and loved ones.

Defamations snowballed, especially along the border, where neighboring western communities advanced their own counternarratives of heroic flight in the face of totalitarianism. In one war of words, Sonneberg's newspaper sneered at West German portrayals of escaped Klaus Elßman as a "persecutee" with a "halo" over his head, publishing details of his supposed unscrupulousness with work and women.[29] Cross-border spats could involve complicated webs of relations. When one western newspaper claimed the Klinger family had fled Neuenbau due to coercion on its collective farm, Sonneberg officials arranged for a westerner originally from Neuenbau to claim at a public meeting that Hans Klinger was actually a western spy.[30] Thus, managing not only flight but also its consequences—and its consequences' consequences—entailed extensive local knowledge and a lot of work.

This customized approach required ever more maneuvering. For example, to retain doctors, engineers, teachers, and business leaders, Sonneberg authorities kept detailed files on their susceptibilities and West German relatives. Continually refining leverage points, officials also hosted "roundtable" meetings for the intelligentsia to address personal concerns relating to the "problems of our time."[31] Yet individualization allowed people to carry out their own manipulations. As local functionaries bent over backward to prevent flight, preemptively resolving the gripes of disgruntled residents, citizens grew savvier. People would bluff about leaving to gain better apartments or working conditions. One weary Sonneberg functionary admitted, "Very often our citizens make unjustified demands as a bargaining chip."[32]

Although, taken individually, flight negotiations suggest citizens' potential power over the state as a useful "trump card," collectively they may have expanded East Germany's surveillance net.[33] Local officials got savvier, too. Not to be "threatened" by obstreperous citizens, they investigated each petitioner's sincerity.[34] This meant gathering more information. Administrators kept tabs on friends, relatives, and workplaces, following rumors and newspaper advertisements for used furniture and radios.[35] In an absurd inverse of population retention, resources were poured into people who did not plan to leave.

The regime also channeled resources toward people it wanted to see leave. On the flip side of border selection, those deemed detrimental to the state—the elderly, the disabled, and "people in need of care"—could legally emigrate west "out of purely material considerations."[36] Local officials were to appraise each emigration applicant, asking "the fundamental question, are they useful to our state or do they harm it?"[37] Fitness reviews became yet another escalating component of population management. By the period 1957–60, the number of Sonnebergers leaving with state permission was almost a quarter of the total leaving without it (13 percent in East Germany overall). They were a distinct group: 93 percent of Sonneberg's legal emigrants in the fifties were women, and 92 percent judged unable to work.

The East German government's intensifying efforts to classify and control its population frequently worked at cross-purposes, as different arms of the bureaucracy pursued different selection priorities. Eighteen-year-old Sonneberger Viktor Krueger was "one of the best" young musicians in East Germany, for instance, but his heart condition prevented admission to conservatories. He fled west to live with his sister, a doctor who had been denied university placement in the East. Only then did Sonneberg officials work to win them both back as members of the intelligentsia. They failed, and Krueger became a celebrated concert organist in West Germany in spite of his heart ailment.[38]

Central offices tended to blame retention failures not on the chaotic bureaucracy but on local functionaries' ineptitude and lack of seriousness. Certainly, tracking individuals could seem a low priority compared to the emergencies of daily administration during the 1950s. Stressed administrators often felt "there was nothing they could do" to stop people from leaving anyway. The regime made "far too many plans, programs, committees, etc. In the end nothing much comes of it."[39] Besides, flight sometimes made their jobs easier, relieving them of discontented citizens and opening up precious apartments in the process. Still, it appears from files and interviews that Sonneberg officials did worry about the population crisis. Only their tactical, practical approach contrasted with national, ideological strategy.

The East German government had proclaimed *Republikflucht*, or "flight from the republic," a treasonous act indicative not of state problems but of problem individuals. County officials were to root out "work-shy tendencies," "family degeneration," "lust for adventure," "political inadequacy," and "conspiratorial recruitment."[40] But such heavy-handedness tended to alienate citizens and distort potential solutions. Instead, flight committees in Sonneberg focused on redressing government failings and personal predicaments. By 1957–58, the county attributed no defections to fabled western "recruitment" and less than 1 percent to "oppositional attitudes." Rather, 36 percent of flight supposedly stemmed from "family reasons," with the majority a result of "other reasons."[41] This murkiness was at odds with Berlin's black-and-white vision of population control. But local functionaries were cultivating "the agility to handle things tactically, not mallet politics."[42]

This discrepancy between local and central approaches may well have propelled East Germany's bureaucratization of population control. Since central offices worried that lesser functionaries were not committed or ideological enough, they expanded the required volume and detail of county reports and committee work. Procedural nuance led to procedural overkill, as functionaries double-checked the double-checkers. In the battle for citizens, customized controls proliferated on multiple fronts.

Tracking Travel

Travel west was one central concern of East German population control, since easterners could defect simply by overstaying their visas. In fact, legal cross-border travel was the most common means of flight from East Germany by the mid-fifties. Passage was riskier through Berlin or over the newly fenced inter-German border—which, though it remained physically weak, saw a dramatic drop in crossings after 1952.[43] Travel, the safest method, was the choice of half of all easterners who left, with rates as high as 65 to 90 percent in Sonneberg.[44] Residents of the southern borderland, along with women and children, were East Germany's demographic groups most apt to flee using visas.[45]

Border residents' high share of defections through legal travel is notable. The borderland was far from Berlin, but the inter-German boundary was right there, after all, and remained permeable. The frontier population's caution *in* flight may suggest a general caution *toward* flight, since border residents fled at half the national rate after 1952. Plus, travelers from Sonneberg defected far less in the middle of the decade than those from other parts of East Germany (2 to 3 percent for Sonnebergers, compared to 4 to 7 percent of all East German travelers). Close ties in frontier regions led to an unusual dynamic of travel, and to officials' exhaustive efforts to contain it.

The challenge was considerable: one in four Sonnebergers traveled west each year in the mid-fifties, about double the national average. Many visited family, friends, and colleagues in Neustadt, while toy makers and glassblowers did intermittent jobs during peak holiday periods for extra cash. For Sonneberg officials, the problem of this constant exchange was twofold. First, travelers would be impressed with western material abundance; "already the difference was *very* big."[46] They would go home with tales of riches, samples of treasure, or, most embarrassingly, daily necessities. One Sonneberger was caught with forty pounds of cement in her backpack for chimney repairs.[47] Second, people decided not to return. Swayed by a loved one, or finding a foothold in the West, dozens of Sonneberg travelers each month simply stayed.[48]

To combat these risks, county officials were to prepare each traveler as an ambassador. According to instructions, "no one may travel to West Germany who has not been tasked as a conscious representative of our workers' and peasants' state."[49] In one-on-one "personal discussions," local functionaries vetted potential travelers for loyalty and outlined the political "dangers" of travel. Among them was that "recruiters," or *Abwerber*, supposedly enticed easterners either to stay in or to spy for the West.[50] Officials also admonished travelers' bosses, colleagues, and relatives to "ensure their associates come back." They debriefed travelers upon their return, asking the most "politically qualified" travelers to disparage their trips in town meetings and disabuse other Sonnebergers of illusions of a "golden West."[51]

Customizing travel allowed individuals to bargain back. Some visa applicants, if denied, would cease paying party and union dues, or threaten to not vote in the next state election, a problem for officials pressured to demonstrate full political participation. But if functionaries did trade privileges for compliance, other applicants learned of the exceptions and created "greater difficulties."[52] Given that Sonneberg issued more than fifteen thousand travel visas to West Germany a year in the mid-fifties, all this individualized handling became quite resource-intensive. Strapped administrations had glaring shortcomings. Sonneberg's Star Radio factory, for example, kept granting employees unpaid travel leaves to earn extra cash at a western radio factory. Each month, two to five of these skilled technicians decided to stay in the West. County officials had difficulty getting Star Radio supervisors to curb this, especially since the enterprise's trade union staff continued to give workers 30 marks for trips.[53]

What reduced travel defections most, though, was not local canvassing but East Germany's Pass Law of December 11, 1957. The national party leadership—increasingly concerned about travel and under continued pressure from the Central Command of the People's Police—tightened visa allowances, toughened the punishment for defection to three years in prison, and criminalized the preparation and assistance of flight. Within months, thousands of East Germans were arrested and prosecuted under the new policies.[54] To call "attention" to the law and to "warn the populace," Sonneberg leaders decided to prosecute one secretary because her boss wrote to her *after* his defection, asking her to handle his personal effects.[55]

The 1957 Pass Law was highly unpopular. It narrowed the categories of citizens allowed to travel, denying rights to state employees, relatives of defectors, or people otherwise considered at risk of defection. Complaints and petitions

Impact of the December 1957 Pass Law

Defection reduction in East Germany

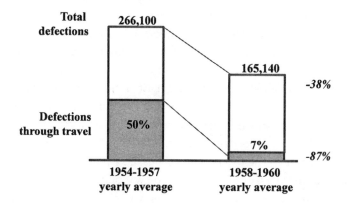

Defection reduction in Sonneberg

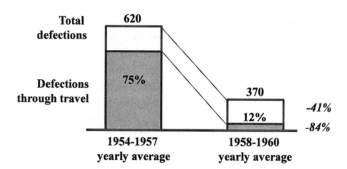

regarding travel skyrocketed throughout East Germany in early 1958.[56] The law was contentious even within Sonneberg's administration, and functionaries threatened to leave the party. Sonnebergers already traveling in West Germany became scared to return. They worried about imprisonment for having over-stayed their visas, and inundated local police with twenty extension requests a day, offering doctors' notes or other excuses.[57] Some Sonnebergers simply decided to stay in the West.

Notwithstanding widespread anger, the new Pass Law was extremely effective. Around 70 percent fewer East Germans traveled west between 1958 and 1961 compared to the period 1954–57—dropping from an average of 2.3 million a year to 712,300.[58] Officials turned down more visa applications, the formal rejection rate rising from 3 percent to 67 percent, in addition to issuing more verbal denials. The stricter selection process worked. Defections through travel went from being the most common mode of flight, at 50 percent in the middle of the decade, to just 7 percent after 1958. Plus fewer travelers defected, with just one in sixty opting to stay in the West, compared to one in seventeen previously.[59]

Most important, fewer people fled East Germany, period. The flight rate dropped 38 percent between 1958 and 1960 (41 percent in Sonneberg). On average, one hundred thousand fewer East Germans left each year. Since defections dropped half as much as did travel, it seems that many easterners who were determined to go still did; they just went through Berlin instead. The city saw up to around 90 percent of defections after 1958, up from 30 percent before then.[60] Other individuals (up to a hundred thousand a year) apparently decided not to leave once the safest option for defection was off the table.

Travel restrictions appear to have been a much bigger lever of population control than is customarily assumed.[61] Typically it is the Berlin Wall, not legislation, that is credited with halting East Germany's exodus. Yet East Germany managed to stem its most severe hemorrhaging of the mid-1950s with policy measures.[62]

The impact of the new law suggests a continuum of individual pressure points within the phenomenon of flight. Some people were willing to chance crossing the border, some went through Berlin, some went with travel visas, and some would not attempt it at all. The regime's task was to progressively fine-tune its citizens' risk profiles. This required, of course, ever more personal knowledge, and ever more personalized attention.

Moving East, More Complications

The East German regime also customized its efforts to recruit defectors back as "returnees," or *Rückkehrer*. Winning citizens from the West, in fact, was considered nothing less than a "test of existence for our administration."[63] The government had some success. The number of people heading east was significant demographically as well as politically. Statistics are slippery since the East German government exaggerated them; many returnees were repeat crossers, and some had not intended to leave home permanently in the first place. Yet it appears that at least one in ten people who went west in the fifties returned to East Germany for some length of time (Appendix 1).[64]

West Germany was uneasy about population movement east, which seemed to belie western claims of material and moral superiority. Government reports tended to portray returns as a product of personal predicaments, with over half (50 to 75 percent) due to family reasons, 15 to 30 percent due to economic problems (e.g., employment, housing), up to 20 percent due to denied asylum applications, and very small percentages due to study, jobs, or ideological conviction.[65] Western analyses tended to minimize easterners' negative experiences. Disliking the West suggested they had a problem, had "adventuresome natures," had "exaggerated expectations," or were suffering "psychosis" from refugee camps. These malcontents were also shifty, in "hopeless debt," or (up to a fifth) simply "criminal elements."[66]

By contrast, the East German government portrayed return as a political victory.[67] Officials pressured returnees to renounce their time in the West publicly, either in town assemblies or in the press. The newspaper ran testimonials of Sonnebergers fed up with the "lies and deception" of capitalism, crying out, "We want to come back!"[68] East German radio, films, novels, and posters contrasted the joys of socialism with the insecurity of western refugee camps and unemployment. The regime also organized returnee conferences, with mixed results. Sonneberg's 1956 meeting—headlined "There is no greater honor than working in the GDR"—drew just thirty of 150 expected attendees.[69] Discussions usually devolved into material complaints, hardly the message of the 1959 returnee conference: "Your life is worth living again."[70]

Sonneberg saw a sizable number of returnees, an average of 140 a year from 1954 to 1959. This was more than a quarter of the number heading west, and 7 percent higher than the national ratio.[71] It seems unlikely, however, that public outreach was the cause of success. Sonneberg officials even admitted their formal initiatives lacked traction, claiming credit in 1957 for less than a fifth of the year's total returns. East Germans had become skeptical of incessant party and newspaper admonitions.[72]

Rather, as with other population endeavors, functionaries increasingly customized their methods, with escalating effects. They recruited returnees with individual enticements, promising choice housing, work, salaries, and farms—so much so that some Sonnebergers gamed the system, defecting in order to gain perks, or even sending their demands in advance. Children of the intelligentsia required the greatest investment. Sonneberg officials tabulated lists of youths studying medicine, science, and engineering in the West, who were to be bribed back with spots at East German universities.[73] It was "not absolutely necessary to have first-class grades." If students declined such generous "offers," officials threatened to deny them travel permits to visit family in the future.[74]

Personal contacts were central to recruitment. Sonneberg functionaries pressured defectors' relatives, friends, and employers to write letters urging return, and summoned defectors' parents and spouses to committee meetings for further discussion. Officials also approached defectors already in the West. One day a Sonneberg delegation turned up unexpectedly at the Neustadt medical practice of the former head of Sonneberg's hospital. The doctor was "very nervous and jumpy," with nothing but praise for East Germany.[75] The Stasi, too, culti-vated individual ties, targeting people in Neustadt's refugee communities. After Sigmund Wolff fled west, denounced for slaughtering sheep without authoriza-tion, two Stasi operatives assured him he had nothing to fear back home and that he could even regain his property; he just needed to sign a false statement for the press. After returning to East Germany, though, Wolff soon found himself slated for deportation inland.[76]

The regime's false individualized promises entailed yet more individualized handling, especially in the borderland. Most Sonneberg returnees were from the Prohibited Zone, since it encompassed thirty of the county's thirty-seven mu-nicipalities in the 1950s. However, because returnees were explicitly barred from reentering the border area, officials relocated them to inland counties or housed them inside the city of Sonneberg, which at the time lay outside the Prohibited Zone. City housing, then, grew scarce, with at least twelve hundred people look-ing for apartments at any one time.[77] Returnees would face a catch-22. Rudi Arndt could not return to his wife and children in Heinersdorf, so he tried to move them to the city of Sonneberg, where they then were denied housing.[78] Many dislocated returnees simply fled west again, especially youths who could not get back home to their parents inside the Prohibited Zone. Some became troublesome. One man marched into county and district offices twenty times in six months before wresting permission to move back to his wife and elderly mother in Rottmar.[79] Others lived in the five-kilometer zone illegally and could not be persuaded to "leave voluntarily."[80]

For all of the resources the regime invested in recruiting returnees, it often alienated them and created more work for itself in the process. Different parts of East Germany's sprawling bureaucracy worked at cross-purposes. So while Re-turnee Committees were to increase the rate of return, border officials were to keep the border zone free of outside influences. Unwilling "to recruit at any price," the police, party, and Stasi vetted each returnee, interviewing former em-ployers and neighbors and weighing their costs and benefits to the community.[81]

In fact, the government may have expended as much effort selecting returnees *out* as it did recruiting them *in*. Upon reentering the country, people spent weeks under investigation at "reception centers," a rude welcome to those eager for a warm homecoming. The camps had strict security and poor provisions, and during long days of interrogations, returnees were pressured to incriminate friends or to collaborate with the Stasi.[82] The process weeded out unfit new-comers—as many as one in seven—and expelled them right back to the West, sometimes by force.[83] Sonneberg officials approved of the new admissions cen-ter near Meiningen precisely because it helped "immediately intercept criminal and asocial" returnees, thus making it easier to "smuggle them back again to West Germany."[84]

But the West did not want them, either. Western officials complained that East Germany sneaked "work-shy elements" back over the border, and that the practice was "scarcely controllable."[85] A few western cities even petitioned East Germany to take people back. Then again, West Germany also ousted people it deemed undesirable, especially "youthful strays." By one western estimate, East Germany deported fifty-four people to Bavaria in March 1957, while Bavarian border police deported twenty-five easterners back; most were judged to have "fled for baseless reasons."[86]

Local officials, too, could be vigilant in cross-border purges of riffraff from the other side. Feeling they had higher standards, Sonneberg functionaries protested that central administrators admitted returnees they had previously rejected: "It is simply scandalous what these reception centers allow."[87] To be rid of "completely unstable people" deemed likely to cause trouble and flee East Germany again, Sonneberg authorities resorted to kicking out returnees on their own—even against the wishes of higher offices.[88]

Sonneberg County also deported people long after their return. Officials kept files on returnees' social and economic worth, and cut their losses. When Klara Geiss returned to Sonneberg, leaving her husband and sixteen-year-old daughter in Neustadt, she worked only thirty-five days in seven months because of health problems. Her file, however, alleges that she was "seen often in taverns and on the dance floor" and "frequently change[d] her lovers, mostly much younger than she." After hospitalization for "a hysterical attack," Geiss was investigated for abuse of medical resources. The county decided to "smuggle" her back to Neustadt.[89]

Neighbors' suspicions created additional complications for returnees. People would remain cautious about befriending a potential enemy of the state. Some resented that these lawbreakers could waltz back from West Germany and claim Sonneberg housing, farms, and jobs. Those who had been targeted for banishment in Action Vermin were especially controversial. Why could slated deportees who defected return, whereas Sonnebergers who had complied with the deportations to Jena could not? Community animus could prevent new arrivals from settling in. When one master hairdresser returned to Neuenbau, officials gave him permission to open his own salon. But locals in the town's production cooperative shunned him, union hairstylists using "all means" to make his life miserable.[90] The intelligentsia, so coveted by the regime, also had a hard time reintegrating. Gert Friedrich, who had studied engineering in West Germany, was denied a position at all of the twenty-two eastern firms to which he applied. After six months, he went back west and immediately found a handsomely paying job.[91]

West German immigrants to East Germany had more difficult experiences than returnees because they lacked roots in the community. There were not very many newcomers.[92] Around 22,600 westerners moved to East Germany each year between 1954 and 1960. An annual average of sixty-seven went to Sonne-berg, less than 10 percent of the number going west. But West German immi-grants were important to propaganda, "fleeing in the fog of night" their grinding existence under capitalism.[93] The regime worried about their integration. West-ern newcomers knew little about how things worked in East Germany, let alone in a highly regulated border region such as Sonneberg. Plus locals were wary. Incredulous that West Germans "would be so dumb as to come over here," many "mistrusted" them as likely spies, deadbeats, or wanted criminals.[94] Stories circu-lated about "work-shy elements" abusing immigration handouts. Reportedly, some western immigrants bought furniture on state credit, sold it, and left again for the West; others "lost" their identification papers in order to receive addi-tional credit under another name.[95]

Certainly, material assistance was important to westerners' assimilation, or lack of it. Because eastern officials typically overpromised housing, jobs, and financial assistance during recruitment, westerners were dismayed to find them-selves on the lowest rung of East German society, with the lowest standard of living. A family of five would get a small one-room apartment, and they were lucky. The Kretschmers (with three children under three) had to live at the county's dingy nursing home.[96] To prevent mischief and flight, "young people" were "never to have their own furnished room," but were to be housed only with the "most politically conscious families."[97] Moreover, the vaunted 2,000 marks of immigration assistance was often withheld due to police processing delays and state requirements to prove an "occupational relationship." Then, because immi-grants had no money for rent, Sonneberg officials would put them up at the Cen-tral Hotel for weeks, which led to yet more alienation.

Recognizing the difficulties of integration, the government assigned both im-migrants and returnees individual overseers. Functionaries were to conduct "constant house and workplace visits," while designated "guardians" (colleagues or neighbors) were to conduct "constant personal discussions" on topics ranging from "reeducation" to loneliness.[98] Yet Sonneberg's harried handlers were not always sympathetic to whining westerners. When one immigrant went on a tirade about how "everything in our republic is just propaganda and shit," his guardian physically attacked him.[99] There were "huge deficiencies" in the "sup-port" of new arrivals.[100] Ingrid Schuster, who moved from West Germany in 1958 with her husband to Haselbach, his hometown, said that her family was discriminated against for decades: "I feel guilty I brought this on my children. A westerner was simply not a person in the GDR."[101]

Despite the resources spent on returnees and western immigrants, people who had moved east did not tend to stay long. By 1961, around two-thirds had already returned west. A quarter left the same year they arrived.[102] In one analysis of ten Sonneberg arrivals over three years, two had fled again, one was expelled to West Germany, and one was arrested. Most of the others wanted to return to the West and/or were deemed either "immoral" or "insane." Officials cited only one well-assimilated person in the group, a warehouse worker in Blechhammer who was often named in county reports as an exemplar.[103] Successes appear rarely in the files, however. In 1960, sixty-four defectors returned to Sonneberg, even as sixty-two returnees fled again.[104]

Since neither East nor West wanted this subclass of border transgressors, the states kept deporting them back to each other. Many crossers were young, ricocheting between siblings, parents, aunts, and uncles across the divided Germanys while they found work, fell in love, got homesick, and moved on. Twenty-year-old Tankred Ebeling, who had fled and returned to East Germany four times in three years, no longer had anywhere to call home.[105] An estimated 8 to 18 percent of all East German defectors were multiple crossers.[106] Increasingly, their border transgressions determined their legal rights and status—advancing new categories of citizenship.

A Stasi of One: Custom Collaborations

As the porous border led the East German regime to forge discrete ties between each person and the state, customized controls penetrated party and police operations. The template of population politics connected to the template for the surveillance state. This was an individualized, paranoid, and *Realpolitik* approach that had less to do with tapping into ideology or abstract allegiances than with leveraging family, personal circumstances, and incentives. In the 1950s, retaining citizens was not that different from handling collaborators, and efforts frequently overlapped. On the continuum of manipulation, ensnaring informants was of a piece with ensnaring residents.

Population retention and surveillance were mutually reinforcing. In the borderland, self-policing and individualized rewards suffused everyday life. Ordinary residents were to report outsiders traipsing through the five-hundred-meter zone, and "watchful" farmers, for example, got a medal, certificate, and front-page newspaper photograph for catching border crossers.[107] Voluntary Border Helpers earned special privileges, permits, and perks such as 200–300 marks a year for patrolling the border eight hours a month and for keeping watch on frontier communities. They, too, proliferated individualized controls. The civilian border helpers cultivated community subinformants, conducting routine chats with barkeepers, shopkeepers, truck drivers, bus drivers, farmers, and forest workers. The Stasi also solicited denunciations in newspapers and town meetings, assuring people of "confidential" handling.[108] All told, an estimated one in five of all border arrests arose from "direct tips from the populace."[109]

The Stasi became the primary institution of self-policing in the borderland. The Ministry for State Security had broadened its mandate after the June 1953 uprising from specific threats to everyday surveillance, and expanded its informant network from 20,000–30,000 in the mid-fifties to around 180,000 by the mid-seventies. The Stasi became East Germany's largest employer, enlisting 1.5 percent of the population at any given time, and achieving the highest surveillance rates in world history.[110]

Yet the Stasi was hardly the efficient, omniscient machine of popular imagination. Rather, it grew from its own weaknesses, escalating dynamically. The Stasi routinely recruited informers for the sake of having informers, not for discrete missions. In the early decades especially, enrollment was not terribly selective. Many recruits never became operational, and only a quarter of all informant reports were considered to be of any significance.[111] Still, saturation was the goal, and the borderland was a priority. Anecdotal evidence suggests that Stasi penetration in East Germany's Prohibited Zone was at least double the rate inland, ranging in the 1950s from one informant for every two hundred people to one in thirty, depending on a community's dependability and distance from the border.[112]

Recruiting informants became an individualized, snowballing process that mirrored population retention efforts. The Stasi's early tactics were clumsy. At least half of those it approached expressed outright qualms; up through the 1960s and 1970s, more than two-thirds of recruiting attempts failed.[113] Citizens simply refused, fled west, or sabotaged their suitability by deliberately breaking cover, missing meetings, claiming poor memory, or giving bad intelligence. The Stasi kept refining its approach. It emphasized positive inducements, such as material rewards, a sense of political purpose, and social privilege, over fear, blackmail, and coercion.[114] Caught up in the routine, flattery, and attention of handler meetings, informants rationalized their involvement, unaware of how the petty details they provided could cause harm. Accepting a new normalcy and set of perceived constraints, few informants tried to break with the Stasi, despite the actual ease of doing so. In later years, it was the Stasi that ended most collaborations.[115]

The Stasi's experiences in cross-border informing cast this evolution in particularly sharp relief. Because East and West Germany could easily sneak agents over the weak fortifications of the 1950s, the borderland was rife with intelligence activity. For the Stasi, the western "forefield," a thirty-kilometer belt of land along the border (expanded to fifty kilometers after 1960), was a priority. It is difficult to estimate the scope of Stasi activity in Neustadt. The state of Bavaria prosecuted as many as 148 defendants in the region for Stasi dealings between 1954 and 1970—a rate of more than nine people a year—and trials implicated numerous other uncaught accomplices.[116] High-profile shootings and abductions drew diplomatic and media attention, with ongoing spy games, suspicious figures, cars, and suitcases appearing along the western side of the boundary.[117] Yet the archival record suggests that most borderland snooping was rather mundane. State prosecutions in Neustadt tended to be petty or inconclusive. Half were discontinued, usually due to lack of evidence. Around 30 percent of defendants received sentences of less than a year in prison; 10 percent received more than a year, and the rest either were acquitted or got off with a warning.[118]

The Stasi targeted borderland informants from all walks of life. Much of the activity was compartmentalized, as separate police and Stasi units were responsible for infiltrating different segments of West German society. Handlers kept tabs on their charges through coded missives, dead letter drops, and clandestine meetings on the border or in "conspiratorial apartments."[119] Western border forces were, of course, a primary target. The Stasi planted informants among the Bavarian Border Police and BGS. It also interrogated returnees who had been processed by western agencies; Stasi files are replete with detailed conversations and diagrams from West German and U.S. border offices in the area, down to the racial backgrounds and license plate numbers of employees.[120] The Stasi also kept files on western border towns, gathering information on local mayors, parties, businesses, and clubs. Informants tracked public opinion, social events, product innovations, construction projects, "revanchist organizations," and the East German refugee community—recounting conversations verbatim from family gatherings, taverns, and chance encounters on the street.[121]

Most westerners did not know all of this was going on, but still feared communism's reach. From the early fifties, Neustadters whispered as Soviet and East German officials popped up mysteriously in borderland locales and newspapers ran stories about informants going back and forth.[122] "Naturally everyone knew" the telltale signs of agents spirited over the border: unfamiliar cars transporting men with caps pulled down over their faces.[123] In order to distinguish strangers, western border forces expressly enlisted local residents as guards. The head of Bavaria's Border Police, Karl Riedl, admonished sentries to be vigilant with the "smallest observances," warning of rampant "treasonous relations."[124] Neustadt police once investigated three men checking into the Train Station Hotel who, to their embarrassment, turned out to be Sonneberg's mayor and city councilors, in town for discussions about gas deliveries.[125]

Sonneberg refugees in Neustadt were particularly alert to cross-border spies. Some former easterners denounced westerners they had seen in Sonneberg dealing with eastern security officials, or named Sonnebergers who appeared in Neustadt suspiciously often. Locals noticed, for example, that Rudi Lackner, a fifty-year-old piano tuner, kept sneaking over the border quite easily. He would have feeble explanations: that he crossed on a dare, got caught in a storm, or had an overwhelming "longing" to see his mother at one o'clock in the morning. Upon arrest, Lackner admitted to gathering information on western border forces and recruiting Sonneberg defectors to return, saying that in exchange the Stasi granted him unlimited crossing privileges to see his family.[126]

Because of western watchfulness, the Stasi worked to recruit people with legitimate reasons to travel to the West, such as a Catholic priest code-named "Friedrich," who could travel ten times a year without arousing mistrust.[127] Avoiding leftists or other "progressive forces" already under western suspicion, operatives instead recruited opportunistically.[128] Easterners with built-in personal contacts with westerners were particularly useful. One informant in Sichelreuth (code-named "Lib") regularly chatted across the ten-meter strip with her neighbor of eighteen years.[129] Eastern officials and guards also approached West Germans who lived along the border, asking about western patrols. Minor detentions presented further opportunities. When one western woman mistakenly wandered over the border in a forest with her four-year-old granddaughter, she was held for thirty hours and questioned over tea and snacks about western forces and public opinion. Upon sending her back over the boundary, an eastern guard told her she was "welcome to come back anytime," an offer she said she refused. [130]

As the Stasi customized its recruitment and handling of cross-border informants in the fifties, it leveraged family ties. Officers targeted easterners from the Prohibited Zone who had relatives in the West—then tasked them to visit and enlist middle-aged male relations. Appraising his two West German brothers, one Sonneberger rated the elder one "an extremely ambitious and industrious worker" who did not drink, smoke, dance, or possess "special passions," while the other brother was "young and inexperienced," smoked, drank, played skat, and cursed the church.[131] Successful recruiting was well rewarded. Ernst Lochner earned 2,000 marks for enlisting both his western brother and brother-in-law.[132]

Such individual attachments played a critical role in western recruitment. Since West Germans were not as susceptible to regime privileges and punishments— they did not live in East Germany, after all—the Stasi worked to spin webs of personal and circumstantial entanglements. It was a slow, cumulative process. Udo Ungermann courted a relative in Neustadt, Gerd Schneider, for months. After visiting Brüx in the summer of 1957 to renew relations, Ungermann invited Schneider to meet him one day at the border and to survey his land in eastern Rückerswind. In initial border meetings, East German guards appeared and threatened to arrest Schneider (but never did). Then, knowing that Schneider was 6,000 DM in debt, Ungermann offered financial assistance, even giving Schneider a coat for his daughter. The first intelligence requests were small. Schneider was to start hanging out at a Neustadt tavern frequented by illegal crossers and western border guards, noting gossip. He was to watch for sentries who drank, played cards, or caroused with women and thus made themselves vulnerable to Stasi recruitment.

In time, Schneider provided operational details on western border posts and local life, reporting on a strike at the local porcelain factory and procuring a Philips tape recorder and brochure. Schneider received 20 or 50 DM at each border meeting with Ungermann (once 200 DM for outstanding work) and "reported very extensively." But his nervous wife told him to stop in 1962, which he apparently did, like many Stasi informants in this period, without incident.[133]

The Stasi had greater influence over East German informants it sent to West Germany as refugees. Officials typically targeted easterners who wanted to go west anyway, pressuring or tempting them into collaboration by manipulating their personal circumstances. Volker Adler, for instance, had inherited his parents' homestead in Wildenheid, but after nine months of waiting, Sonneberg County denied his family's application to emigrate west. A Stasi officer then questioned Adler about his siblings and connections in Neustadt, offering to help orchestrate a defection. So the very same week his wife and children traveled to Neustadt on a visa, Adler managed to "flee" over the border in an ox-drawn cart with his father-in-law and entire household in tow (including mattresses, three bicycles, and a sewing machine), drawing media attention in Neustadt as a heroic escape. Adler did not, it seems, repay the Stasi's favor. Although the Stasi officer allegedly warned him of the risk of arrest for noncompliance—there were agents "everywhere" in Neustadt—his former boss in Sonneberg advised him "not to be so tragic about it, write a couple of times, don't endanger anyone, and it will eventually die down." Sure enough, it did. Volker said he stopped responding to his Sonneberg Stasi handler's letters after eighteen months, without consequences.[134]

Certainly the Stasi had a hard time keeping informants who did not "remain true to their work" after they became personally secure in the West.[135] Within dense borderland personal networks, failures could cascade. In 1955, Sonneberg's Stasi reportedly gave Ingolf Lauer 80 marks and a travel visa (previously denied him because of a two-month incarceration) to convince his son-in-law in Neustadt, Paul Truemper, to return home and work for the Stasi. But Lauer decided to stay in Neustadt. Then the Stasi paid Lauer's wife to fetch both Lauer and Truemper back to East Germany. But she decided to stay in Neustadt, too.[136]

Compounding the Stasi's difficulties, the borderland of the 1950s was a murky mélange of intelligence interests. Locals slipped in and out of collaborations to pursue their own aims, creating work and worry for governments on both sides. Sonneberg's Stasi estimated that West Germany had dozens of informants in the region, and tracked refugee and cross-border relationships in detail.[137] West German authorities tried to keep tabs on eastern refugees also, especially those who had fled too easily, were "politically suspect," or maintained close "connections" to Sonneberg.[138] For example, the aforementioned Paul Truemper, who was working for U.S. intelligence, volunteered his father-in-law to the U.S. Counter

Intelligence Corps as a double agent in the Stasi, a suspicious proposal that then required Lauer to check in with Neustadt's Border Police station every other day.

East and West each had trouble keeping up with the tangled web of allegiances along the frontier—so much so that intelligence officials were sometimes unsure as to which team people were actually on.[139] When toy maker Bernhard Erhardt, an American agent inside Sonneberg, was arrested by the Stasi in 1957, he claimed he only had to sign a press report denouncing a fellow U.S. spy in Sonneberg in order to be let go after four days. Erhardt's lenient handling aroused western suspicions, as did the ease with which he'd always crossed the border. Perhaps he had been double-dealing with the Stasi all along, but there was no proof. Even more confusingly, Erhardt defected to Neustadt in 1960, staying with relatives and looking for work as a teddy bear stuffer.[140]

Cross-border snooping in the fifties was extremely fluid, and neither East nor West had a lot of confidence in their informants.[141] The files suggest that border residents collaborated, saw their activities as casual and inconsequential, and were hard to pin down. Officials feared that individuals were moving between assignments and states, playing them off each other, without either side knowing it. The extent to which people actually could or did maneuver is perhaps unknowable. But governmental uncertainty was itself significant, especially in East Germany, where it impelled the Stasi to ever greater penetration of tight-knit frontier communities.

The slipperiness of early borderland loyalties lends some credibility to the eastern regime's much-mocked paranoia of "spies"—its trumpeted rationale for border fortifications. Government propaganda surely exaggerated their prevalence, as unmasking "agents" became a consuming preoccupation of eastern newspapers. Upon the visit of Politburo member (and future head of state) Erich Honecker for the Border Police's tenth anniversary, Sonneberg sentenced seven men in a nefarious "spy ring."[142] Whatever the reality behind such sensational charges, the inquisitorial climate itself reflected and exacerbated confusion on the border. Citizens could be shifty and shifting, and eastern officials worked hard to cement their tenuous allegiances.

Although the efficacy of East Germany's personalized controls in the 1950s is debatable, since citizens continued to flee west in droves, the manipulative shift in governance left an enduring legacy. It swelled the regime's unwieldy bureaucracy in illogical and counterproductive ways. It also helped propel a dynamic of personal scrutiny that characterized the relationship between the East German government and its populace for the remainder of the state's history.

The border also became one organizing principle of citizenship in East Germany. Crossing history defined a new demographic category alongside class, religion, and party loyalty. Officials tracked people who passed between East and West—travelers, defectors, emigrants, returnees, immigrants, and spies—as threatening to the national community. In so doing, they created taxonomies of transgression that determined legal rights, employment, schooling, and family status. Correct border behavior established morality, worth, and reliability to the state, granting hierarchies of access and privilege. Wrong border behavior, especially contact with western heresy, marked one for life, and was to be eradicated.

Yet the East German government ultimately failed in its demographic inquisition. The regime could not keep up with the shifting complexity of its populace, which required ever more personalized cajoling and coercion. Thus it resorted, in 1961, to brute force in the population battle: constructing the Berlin Wall, mining the inter-German boundary, and deporting thousands from the Prohibited Zone. Border residents felt increasingly powerless before the state. Much had changed in the past decade, and much would change in the decades to come.

PART THREE

IRON CURTAIN, 1961–1989

8

Home: Life in the Prohibited Zone

Between 1961 and 1989, Germany's Iron Curtain grew from an incomplete stretch of barbed wire into a mined, multilayered, and military installation. It became notorious worldwide. During this period, only 16,348 East Germans reportedly escaped across the inter-German border, with the regime prosecuting an estimated 110,000 citizens and imprisoning more than 71,000 for attempted flight.[1] East German orders constituting a *Schießbefehl*, or a "license to kill" escapees, expanded. Hundreds died or sustained critical injuries within the fortifications.[2] Meanwhile, NATO and Warsaw Pact commands strategized for conventional warfare over the boundary. Their forces faced off, especially at the valley known as the Fulda Gap, which was considered the most likely site of Soviet invasion.[3] NATO's forward defense policy on the border in the 1960s even prepared for the use of nuclear land mines (or atomic demolition munitions) along the Iron Curtain.[4]

Germany's border apparatus was formidable and infamous. However, even at the height of the Cold War, the boundary comprised not just physical fortifications but also the accumulated actions of residents who lived along it. The Iron Curtain, far from being a technological monolith, was a living system that was inhabited by people. The human dimensions of this border expose how ordinary Germans in East and West both wittingly and unwittingly contributed to its sustainment and entrenchment.

This is not the same story as in 1945–61, when improvised local events played a role in shaping an as yet indeterminate barrier. In this later period, from the construction of the Berlin Wall on August 13, 1961, to its fall on November 9, 1989, the coercive border was firmly in place. Its existence was non-negotiable. But frontier populations were no less central to its history. Indeed, the border's permeation of everyday practices helps explain its remarkable stability over three decades.

A second generation of borderland residents, one that had been socialized and educated in divergent German states, increasingly saw life on the boundary as normal. So despite widespread dissent on the eastern side, daily activities buttressed the border regime, from patrolling to reporting transgressors. Despite widespread opprobrium on the western side, daily complacency and estrangement reinforced the divide, from border images and tourism to cross-border travel. In short, people in both East and West became enmeshed in the border apparatus in a variety of little ways, reflecting—and constituting—Cold War division.

By 1961, Germany's division seemed incontrovertible. Following the construction of the Berlin Wall, severance was a visible, physical reality. East Germany stabilized. Walter Ulbricht had successfully stemmed the mass exodus of citizens, repressed opposition, and revealed the West as unwilling to intervene. As East Germans stayed put and made do, the state saw an economic upswing, accompanied by a more decentralized New Economic System (NES) of 1963. Ulbricht allowed for somewhat greater freedoms and dialogue, at last following Soviet premier Nikita Khrushchev's precedent of destalinization in the USSR— though liberalization in East Germany did not approach Alexander Dubček's Prague Spring reforms of 1968. The subsequent Warsaw Pact invasion of Czechoslovakia and the Brezhnev Doctrine made clear the lengths to which the Soviet Union would go to enforce adherence in its bloc. Germany's division appeared increasingly permanent.

The two German states kept diverging. West Germany saw impressive material growth and prosperity, along with mounting political and generational frictions. These came to the fore in public controversy over the *Spiegel* Affair, a scandal in which the government was seen as restricting the freedom of the press that undermined the administration, and in growing student protests and clashes, part of an international trend that culminated in 1968. During the 1970s, the radical-left Red Army Faction (RAF), often called the Baader-Meinhof gang, rocked West Germany with terrorist bombings and assassinations, leading to state reactions that were criticized for endangering civil liberties. International oil crises threw West Germany's touted "social market economy" into recession, raising pressures for nuclear energy and, with it, protests over nuclear plants, nuclear armament, and environmental concerns in the seventies and eighties. Tensions grew over the migration of "guest workers" (*Gastarbeiter*) from Mediterranean countries, particularly Turkey, whom West Germany had recruited in the 1960s after the stream of East German labor ended with the construction of the Berlin Wall. While international recruitment ended in 1973, immigrants remained for decades without citizenship, and debate over their place in German society continues today.[5] Still, West Germany continued to liberalize. Among western nations it came to be seen as a model democracy, confronting its Nazi past and helping to lead the closer integration of western Europe in the European Community (EC).

West Germany also began engaging with its eastern neighbors. Social Democrat Willy Brandt became chancellor in 1969 and pursued a policy of *Ostpolitik*— against a backdrop of superpower détente between the governments of

American president Richard Nixon and Soviet general secretary Leonid Brezhnev.[6] Following treaties with the Soviet Union and Eastern bloc states, the Basic Treaty of December 1972 normalized relations between the two Germanys and ensured mutual recognition. Both East and West Germany became full members of the United Nations in 1973 and were signatories of the 1975 Helsinki Accords. There was fierce conservative resistance in West Germany to Brandt's de facto abandonment of the goal of reunification, and to compromising with what was seen as an illegitimate state. Yet Brandt's process of "small steps," offering financial incentives in exchange for East German humanitarian concessions such as greater cross-border contact and the release of political prisoners, opened East Germany to greater influence from the West. There remained fears of a nuclear "new Cold War" between the superpowers, with the Soviet invasion of Afghanistan in 1979 and the Reagan administration's military buildup, followed by the meltdown of Chernobyl's reactor in 1986, which made the stakes of nuclear disaster clear to all. Yet throughout, the two Germanys increased engagement with each other.

At the same time as East Germany began seeing more western involvement with détente, its new first secretary, Erich Honecker, initiated a policy of ideological and cultural *Abgrenzung*, or demarcation, from the capitalist West. Having replaced Ulbricht in 1971, Honecker shifted from striving toward ideal socialism, with its material privations, to working within "actually existing socialism." Even with the emphasis on improving living conditions through better consumer goods and housing, East Germany could not keep up with the West.[7] Its citizens could readily see the disparity in western television, western gift packages, visits with western relatives, and the spread of Intershops, Delikat, and Exquisit stores carrying western goods.[8] Notwithstanding the continued grumbling, however, East Germany appeared especially stable and prosperous within the Eastern bloc, a model socialist state.

The two Germanys developed different societies as different ideological and economic systems impacted daily life.[9] The imperative for political conformity in East Germany, versus democratic freedoms in the West, resulted in a censored, authoritarian system backed by the Ministry for State Security. Within limits, citizens could petition, maneuver, and negotiate concessions from the regime, and there were important niches of private life.[10] But open dissent was harshly repressed. Increasing state ownership of the means of production, as opposed to private ownership in West Germany, resulted in inefficient and unwieldy enterprises. East Germany had a broader health and social welfare net, with lower prices for food and housing, though many considered the quality of eastern services, products, and apartment blocks inferior to what was on offer in the West. Education diverged not only in ideological content but also in access—often limited by political background and adherence in the East and by socioeconomic status in the West. Socialization diverged as well.[11] East Germany organized citizens into mass organizations, from the comprehensive Free German Youth (FDJ) to the Free German Trade Union Federation (FDGB), while West Germany largely left associational life in community hands. Under Ulbricht, religion in East Germany had come under attack—the Christian confirmation ceremony, for example, was discriminated against in favor of the state's secular ceremony of *Jugendweihe*—though under Honecker the League of Protestant Churches played an important role in social work and in providing a space for citizens to voice dissent. The two Germanys even developed a different feel, palpable in the scent of brown coal combustion in the East or overflowing store shelves in the West, as well as in the look and sound of different kinds of cars in different kinds of streets.

What made these divergences—and East Germany—possible was the Iron Curtain. Without it, the eastern state would not have been viable, as suggested by mass flight in the fifties. But what made this border so powerful was not merely its physical fortifications. Less visible, though no less significant to its history, was the increasing militarization of life in East Germany's borderland. The East German government succeeded in creating a highly disciplined society to support the barrier. Through cumulative coercion and adaptation, the border regime became, over the decades, a fact on the ground. With the fortifications their home, frontier communities became both victims and perpetrators of their own captivity.

1961: Escalations and Expulsion

In 1961, East Germany faced demographic catastrophe. One in six citizens had gone west since 1949. The regime had tried to stem this exodus in the 1950s through border tightening, travel laws, and individual surveillance, each of which saw some success. But people continued to leave through Berlin, which remained open. International tensions escalated over the status of the city in the Berlin Crisis, beginning with Khrushchev's November 1958 ultimatum to western powers to end the military occupation of Berlin, and resulting in dissimilar negotiating tactics by the Eisenhower and Kennedy administrations.[12] As geopolitical relations worsened over conflicting proposals for the city, by the summer of 1961, 1,000–2,500 easterners left every day.[13]

Walter Ulbricht worried that restiveness could lead to uprising, and used mass flight as "indirect blackmail" to finally convince Khrushchev to do in Berlin what had been so effective along the rest of the border in 1952: construct a physical partition.[14] The world watched, horrified, as soldiers from the National People's Army began building barriers early on the morning of Sunday, August 13, 1961. East Berliners jumped out of buildings and ran through gunfire to escape, while anxious western crowds and politicians remained mostly nonconfrontational.

Peace was the highest priority. The passivity of western response surprised East German leaders.[15]

As the Berlin Wall grabbed international attention, East Germany also strengthened fortifications along the rest of its 1,393-kilometer border with West Germany. These escalations produced their own tensions at Burned Bridge, from water and territorial disputes to the "seizure" of one American soldier who strayed ten meters over the border.[16] On the whole, the atmosphere remained calm. A former BGS guard recalled that ten to fifteen westerners in Wildenheid threw stones and yelled "Ulbricht pigs!" at East German soldiers. But western sentries quickly put an end to "provoking" behavior for fear of incidents.[17]

This restraint was noteworthy because, as in Berlin, barrier construction drew large western crowds. Neustadt became the "destination of many visitors," whose "cars kept jamming" borderland roads. They gaped, "speechless," as hundreds of eastern civilians built fences under armed guard.[18] Neustadt newspapers carried daily photos of the spectacle, featuring brigades of Sonnebergers building their own prison.[19] In one western report, eastern workers demolishing a house were perhaps "enjoying it," "smirking" "triumphantly." The evicted occupant, portrayed as even more alien, did not dare acknowledge tearful shouts from his western siblings just across the border, though he had not seen them in ten years.[20] From Berlin to Burned Bridge, scenes of border construction themselves contributed to the East-West divide.

Western crowds gathered daily at the Mountain Mill Tavern to watch soldiers and civilians demolish Willy Schmidt's sawmill. As the proprietor described it, "So many sightseers, the place was packed!"[21] Western onlookers yelled insults at eastern border forces and, in solidarity, tossed over beer and cigarettes to Sonneberg workers who, at least at first, picked them up. East German soldiers crossed the border early one morning and "rather gruffly" awoke the owner of the Mountain Mill Tavern to warn patrons to be tidier.[22] To many westerners, the destruction of the sawmill was a crime; the escape of one eastern guard in front of the crowd heightened their sense of witnessing wrongdoing.[23] Sonnebergers drafted into demolition did not necessarily see it that way. One said that workers did not think twice about it. They talked most about laboring in the hot sun in front of the Mountain Mill's tantalizing flag advertising Schöller ice cream.[24]

For Neustadters, the escalations of 1961 were painful to witness but were not as shocking as border closure in 1952. Resignation prevailed. As the *Neustadter Tageblatt* put it, "One has gotten used to division."[25] Notwithstanding all the indignation about border construction, there was less community outreach than nine years earlier.[26] The East, and easterners, seemed further away.[27] However, city leaders were quick to spotlight western suffering and to draw parallels with beleaguered Berlin. A delegation drove to the divided metropolis in late August to present Mayor Willy Brandt with a giant Neustadt teddy bear.[28]

Meanwhile, in Sonneberg a "combat atmosphere" emerged.[29] The police launched a wave of arrests for "baiting," "opposition," and hostile comments, jokes, and songs.[30] Dozens of new checkpoints, controls, and roadblocks sprang up in the Prohibited Zone and Protection Strip, so quickly there were not enough resources to cover them.[31] Stricter border security interfered with already problematic food deliveries. When officials would not let one fish shipment pass, the cargo rotted for four days in Sonneberg, with odiferous consequences.[32] Sonnebergers began "hamstering" for food and "panic-buying" textiles, shoes, cameras, and valuable items. It felt "like the Dark Ages," a time of "pure randomness."[33]

Hardly anyone believed the regime's farcical propaganda that the new "antifascist protection barrier" was a defense against western provocateurs, agents, and "human traffickers."[34] Yet citizens were expected to show their support, arranging parades, assemblies, films, newspaper articles, banners, and music to celebrate the border escalations. Forty-six collective farms, factories, and villages formed Committees Against Human Trafficking.[35] Under the surface, though, many Sonnebergers were shaken by the "sin and shame" of the new fortifications.[36] When more than fifty women from the Clara Zetkin work brigade were to vote on an August 13 resolution, most left the room. Only six voted in favor, with one opposed.[37] Even people who officially endorsed the escalations seldom wanted to be open about it. Party functionaries were "reserved" in sparsely attended town meetings, and community and church leaders who signed supporting statements wanted to delay publication until someone else went first.[38] As one prominent businessman explained, "I would rather not have my name and picture published unless it's necessary."[39]

Still, there was nowhere near the level of opposition that either East or West German officials anticipated.[40] Some citizens shouted epithets and got into altercations with border guards and authorities. One Lindenberger poked out the eyes of government candidates on street posters. Dozens of Sonnebergers escaped to the West.[41] But most people had become accustomed to border escalations.

The expansion and intensification of Sonneberg's Prohibited Zone in late September 1961 drew more immediate resistance. As the regime blanketed each locality with police and party agitators, Sonnebergers spoke out hotly in "totally overflowing" town assemblies. They threatened to boycott work and community meetings over the new impositions on everyday life, particularly the tougher curfew and permit restrictions.[42] Actual Prohibited Zone registrations on September 22, though, reportedly went off "easily and without incident." People queued at seven o'clock in the morning to sign their names and "showed more understanding than expected."[43] In fact, party leaders worried that most "did not fully grasp the seriousness of the situation" and thought the measures "meant nothing new."[44] As in 1952, the 15 percent borderland salary bonus contributed to "broad acceptance."[45] Eventually local officials noted "great joy" among communities newly included in the five-kilometer area, "who saw just the material advantages" of life in the zone.[46] The only two Sonneberg municipalities *not* included in the enlarged Prohibited Zone, Steinach and Hüttengrund, repeatedly lobbied to join.[47]

Two weeks later, a wave of borderland deportations, code-named Aktion Festigung, or Action Consolidation, created the greatest alarm.[48] Drawing lessons from Action Vermin nine years earlier, it was far better organized and a fraction of the size. The night before it began, Sonnebergers knew something was up. There was elevated security status, increased police presence, and trucks waiting outside the city. Lights stayed on late inside the county administration building. Hundreds of local officials, police, firefighters, and volunteer helpers were summoned to special meetings.[49] One man wrote in his diary: "Uneasy night. Everything in motion and yet fully restrained silence. . . . People are looking out of their darkened windows onto the streets."[50]

The action began "promptly" at six o'clock the next morning, as paramilitary units of eight to twelve policemen, civilian helpers, Stasi operatives, and SED officials banged on the doors of fifty-four Sonneberg "targets" deemed too unreliable to live in the borderland. The occupants were to pack and leave immediately for homes further inland.[51] The units severed deportees' access to the outside world, prohibiting farewells, cutting their telephone lines, and blocking access to their streets and communities.[52]

Deportees did not have the opportunities for disobedience and escape they had in 1952, when victims were given twenty-four hours' advance notice and left unguarded. Supervision was much tighter in 1961. Some even had a "shadow" accompanying them to the toilet.[53] People did what they could, protesting their innocence or refusing to pack their things. Several tried bargaining. The Steubers denounced neighbors to be taken instead, while one man was ready to "divorce immediately" his politically problematic wife.[54] When one youth grabbed a kitchen knife to slit his wrists, police handcuffed him and took him downstairs. His mother cried, "You are doing what Hitler did to the Jews." His sister, who remembered the 1952 evacuations, "could not imagine that something like that could happen again. And all of a sudden I was sitting in this truck."[55]

Sonneberg officials were surprised by how well the operation went. Reportedly, "except for the Wittmanns and Gansels, no families showed resistance."[56] Unlike 1952, local paramilitary units were reliable and "faithfully fulfilled their tasks."[57] There were few of the tip-offs, rumors, and snafus that had created so much instability nine years before. One civilian helper, who was informed the night before that his parents-in-law were to be deported, did not tell them and still participated in the action. His wife wondered "how he could do such a thing," but he felt he "had to."[58] The stronger regime, and fear of it, made for awful choices.

While Sonnebergers were shaken by their neighbors' sudden deportation, the action seemed more rational and inexorable than Action Vermin. Officials had sent out fifteen hundred "agitators" in Sonneberg County and addressed more than twelve thousand citizens in sixty-one assemblies, explaining that residents vulnerable to western "extortion" faced a mere "change of domicile."[59] There was a sense that "this time the right ones were taken," as people had different sensibilities for troublemakers and upstanding citizens. "Of course wayward youths were expelled," one man wrote.[60] Some even incriminated additional Sonnebergers who deserved to go, naming suspicious neighbors or the "loose women" who lived behind the Hofburg Tavern.[61]

There was little unrest. Sonneberg police arrested "only" one nondeportee. He had yelled at civilian helpers that they ought to be ashamed of themselves and that there was no freedom in East Germany.[62] Church leaders were likewise much less vocal than expected. Everywhere, people "behaved cautiously and did not express their real opinions."[63] So Action Consolidation went "according to plan" and the last transport trucks were able to leave the county by three o'clock in the afternoon.[64] People watched them depart "from behind the curtains, only from behind the curtains."[65]

Thus, more than 95 percent of slated deportees in East Germany as a whole and Sonneberg in particular were successfully transported in 1961—compared to 81 percent and 38 percent, respectively, in 1952.[66] There was no mass flight west. In fact, not a single Sonneberg deportee was reported to have escaped over the border. Unlike 1952, when hundreds of Sonneberg refugees poured into Neustadt, westerners "had no clear picture" of events in October 1961.[67] The action was much more self-contained. This time "targets" were relocated with their families, making for less emotional strife. Also, the 1961 action had a scope less than 30 percent of that of the 1952 operation. In East Germany overall, 3,175 were moved in 1961, versus more than 10,300 slated to move in 1952.[68] The percentage was even smaller in Sonneberg: whereas the county had lost 1,260 people due to deportation and defection in 1952, it lost just 168 citizens in 1961.[69] In sum, Action Consolidation lived up to its name. With its better organization and stymied citizenry, it revealed how much stronger the state had become, as well as how much frontier residents had adjusted to ever more draconian controls.

The border escalation of 1961 in Sonneberg was not the radical break of 1952–53, when the rules of life fundamentally transformed. But it was a dramatic and frightening intensification. A "determined restraint and certain anxiety" followed in its aftermath, as waves of house searches and arrests continued throughout the fall, and "continual fear" became the new normalcy.[70]

Border Changes

After 1961, East Germany transformed the border into a military installation. Border police became border soldiers, and "border breaches" became classified as a form of terrorism. Potential penalties for attempted escape increased from three to five years in prison, plus severe repercussions for one's family and future.[71] Physically, the Iron Curtain widened from a partial strand of barbed wire fencing into a fortified martial zone. Two-thirds of all attempted "border violations" in East Germany reportedly occurred on the inter-German boundary, a quarter at the Berlin Wall, and 7 percent at the Baltic Sea.[72] With each phase of border escalation, it got harder to cross. The number of documented escapes over the inter-German border plummeted by more than 99 percent, from tens of thousands a year in the 1950s to under a hundred a year by the mid-1970s. The odds of successful flight dropped just as severely, from about even to less than 6 percent of all attempts.

Simply put, it became exponentially more difficult to escape over the frontier. The number of people documented to have fled East Germany over the inter-German border in its last fifteen years (1,222) was equivalent to the number who left in just one day before August 1961. By contrast, a reported 178,182 East Germans defected through third countries and other means from 1961 to 1988, and 383,114 emigrated legally (Appendix 3). More than thirty thousand were ransomed by West Germany as political prisoners, their freedom bought in secret negotiations for around 40,000 to 96,000 DM each; by the 1980s, some people deliberately invited incarceration in order to get to the West.[73] Thus the total number of escapes over the inter-German border in this period, 16,348, is less

Escapes over the Inter-German border, 1952–1989

Excluding defections through Berlin, transit routes, third countries, and travel to West Germany

< Estimates >

Border Fortifications		Border escapes per year, East Germany	Border escapes per year, Sonneberg	Percent of escape attempts that succeeded
	1952-1961	15,000-50,000	250-650	over 60%
1st generation	1962-1966	1,915	50-70	40-60%
2nd generation	1967-1973	550	20-30	7-30%
3rd generation	1974-1984	70	2-10	2-6%
Without mines	1985-1989	90	4-15	5-8%

Sources: StA-C BGS 145, "Flüchtlinge über die DDR-Grenzsperranlage," 1961–1989; Schmidt, BGS, 116; Ritter and Lapp, *Grenze*, 76–78, 173; BArch-B/SAPMO DY30 2507, 43–46, 353–54; Schultke, "Keiner," 108–9; Thoss, *Gesichert*, 195–206.

A western farmer crosses Burned Bridge in 1962, returning from his fields. Grenzerfahrungen Kompakt, Salier Verlag, Rainer Krebs collection.

Field work under the supervision of East German border guards in the 1960s. Archiv Klaus Bauer.

than 3 percent of all those who left East Germany by other means.[74] The modern border really worked.

At the same time, the border's physical evolution was not as smooth as these stark statistics suggest. Far from the monolithic force it appeared, the Iron Curtain was quite mutable. Its watchtowers, fences, booby traps, and mines changed form due to trial and error and eventually due to international pressure. The barriers were formidable, of course, yet still more fallible than people imagined.

There were a number of miscalculations during the first generation of border escalations from 1961 to 1966. Double and triple rows of barbed wire fencing grew weak and breakable with rust. They looked hideous and were widely criticized in the West as a "concentration camp wall." Wood-encased land mines also deteriorated quickly, especially in wetter areas, allowing people to cross rotting minefields unscathed. The bulk of enforcement fell to young soldiers who were hardly as reliable as the regime wished, and who themselves accounted for around 15 percent of escapes over the inter-German boundary.[75] In all, the fortifications of the early 1960s were still "not an effective obstacle for a border violator."[76]

The second phase of construction, launched in 1967, was more successful. Rows of tall mesh fencing were impervious to wire cutters and handholds, and required fewer troops to patrol. Set twenty to thirty meters back from the border, they looked more humane to the West and kept "embarrassing incidents" of border brutality out of western sight and earshot.[77] The regime also added durable plastic-encased mines, refined the alarm systems, and installed ever more trip wires that set off blank cartridges and signal flares to alert guards to intruders. These measures had an impact wherever they were implemented, but by 1971 only 38 percent of the border had what were considered "effective barriers."[78]

A third generation of escalations saw ongoing improvements in booby traps, bunkers, dog runs, communications systems, and night surveillance, as well as expanded use of electric signal fences and corrugated metal fences. Sonneberg County acquired two Berlin Wall–style concrete walls in 1982, in Heinersdorf and Görsdorf, to "negative morale."[79] Most controversially, border troops installed 60,000 highly lethal fence mines, or "self-firing devices," along almost a third of the border, in addition to the 1.3 million land mines planted between 1961 and 1983. West Germany had railed against the inhumanity of the mines for years, and finally bribed the East German government in 1983 into accepting hefty western credit agreements in exchange for removing all mines within two years. This was a blow to border security, since military resources were increasingly diverted to support the faltering economy. There were no significant additions to the Iron Curtain for the rest of the eighties.[80] Yet these cutbacks had relatively little impact on the flight rate. The number of documented escapes and attempts did go up somewhat, but still held to amazingly low levels, under 130 a year—a small fraction of the number before 1972. It appears that, by the late 1980s, the exact strength of the fortifications was rather beside the point.

So why did the border regime work? The technical apparatus, as powerful as it was, does not tell the whole story. After all, over time, fewer people were caught at the border itself. Whereas border guards had been responsible for more than half of all intercepted escapes in the fifties and sixties, by the late seventies less than a fifth of reported arrests were made by sentries in the fortifications. Most

Double layers of metal mesh fencing near Wildenheid in the 1980s. Johannes Seifert.

A section of concrete wall at Heinersdorf in the 1980s. Klaus Dietrich Zeutschel.

people were caught by transport and local police further inland, and up to a quarter were nabbed by frontier civilians.[81] The border regime was firmly entrenched in the practices and mentalities of the ordinary citizens who lived along it.

Negotiation

Behind the fortifications, the Prohibited Zone was to be a zone of total civilian control. It, too, wound up a product of trial and error that allowed for limited negotiations. But, arguably, its coercive compromises enhanced its resiliency.

Border zone rules were strict. Guards were present at all times, and access was limited. Westerners were forbidden, while nonresident East Germans had to apply weeks in advance for entry. The inner layer, or five-hundred-meter Protection Strip, was harshest. There virtually any activity besides sitting at home—from driving to swimming to social gatherings—required special authorization. The regime outlawed sporting events, photography, and camping outright. Farming and other work outside towns was allowed during daylight hours and under the watch of border troops, with curfews set inside Protection Strip villages themselves. This was to be a zone of martial law, cut off not only from the West but also from the rest of East Germany. People joked that they lived in a "prison."[82]

In 1961, the entire Prohibited Zone doubled in size in Sonneberg, encompassing 87 percent of the county's residents and 15 percent of East Germany's total Prohibited Zone population of 370,000. The whole city of Sonneberg was now included, East Germany's largest community and the only county seat in the zone. Within it, 7 percent of Sonneberg County fell into the five-hundred-meter Protection Strip; it would have been more, but economic and social considerations placed 10 percent under a third system, the Unterland, unique to Sonneberg, which had its own "quite complicated" set of requirements.[83] All told, the county had 121 entry barriers on routes to the five-kilometer and five-hundred-meter zones, though many forest and field paths remained unguarded.[84]

People pushed back against these encroachments. For example, when villagers protested the army's closure of the road between Heubisch and Unterlind, which necessitated a six-and-a-half-hour detour to Sonneberg, they successfully reversed the blockage.[85] Hönbachers voted unanimously against administrative isolation from Sonneberg in 1963 and prevented their severance from the city for two decades.[86] Easterners, and sometimes westerners, continued to sneak in and out of the Prohibited Zone in the 1960s, knowing tricks to evade bus and train controls or to get through on forest paths.[87] Residents commonly broke curfew, staying out late drinking. Authorities berated locals to be better behaved, but even guards and officials evidenced a "gradual dismantling of existing orders and tolerance of offenses."[88] Residents protested being treated like "chickens forced in their pens." Hönbachers got so angry about one curfew expansion that twenty-one Border Helpers threatened to strike.[89]

In 1972, East Germany shrank the unwieldy and expensive Prohibited Zone into a less ominous-sounding Border Area, or *Grenzgebiet*. This was part of a shift

Border Zones in Sonneberg County, 1967

Hasenthal

Sattelpaß

Haselbach

Steinach

Neuenbau

Hütten-
grund

Schalkau

Sonneberg

Almerswind

Rückerswind

Heinersdorf

Emstadt

Hönbach

Neuhaus-
Schnierschnitz

Heubisch

Mupperg

■ Protection Strip
    500 meter zone

▨ Unterland zone
    (Sonneberg only)

▥ Prohibited Area
    Five kilometer zone

□ Outside the border zone

Source: BStU BV Suhl, KD SON 3687, 37.

in border strategy, as détente and new travel agreements with the West spurred the East German government to greater openness. In the borderland, the regime yielded to community pressure and backtracked on several "unreasonable hardships" in private life, loosening curfew, permit, and visiting strictures.[90] Locals even successfully appealed some road closures and the placement of border fences near their homes.[91] Party officials claimed these diminutions were a testament to the border regime's strength, not weakness. The government could make concessions precisely because the borderland had become so stable.[92]

The 1972 relaxations reduced East Germany's border zone population by more than 40 percent. In Sonneberg County, it shrank 75 percent, from around fifty-five thousand to fourteen thousand residents.[93] The city of Sonneberg, like other larger towns, was released entirely. However, frontier residents were not as happy about their new freedoms as the regime expected—because they lost their 15 percent borderland bonus, an entitlement locals saw as regular salary and incorporated into the regional economy. Sonnebergers objected that without it, their incomes would be lower than in cities further inland. The issue remained contentious for months, until the regime agreed to compensate people with a lump-sum payment and ongoing salary adjustments.[94] Of all East Germany's rights abuses, property perhaps had the greatest currency of complaint on the socialist frontier.

Sonnebergers held "illusions" of "significant relaxations" in 1972 and hoped that as border technology improved, the security zone would dissolve. But inside the Border Area, fortifications increasingly enveloped border communities.[95] Villages in the Protection Strip were encircled by electric signal fences (allowed small openings so that rabbits and other small animals did not trigger alarms) and cut off from the rest of the county.[96] Residents worried Sonneberg was being turned into a military "deployment area" and left to die out. "Everything had come to a standstill," one remembered.[97]

The East German government did seek to halt development along the border, especially inside the five-hundred-meter zone. It prohibited new construction, making it exceedingly difficult to expand homes and businesses, even to put up a shed. It kept out new industries.[98] It restricted agriculture, allowing only low-growing crops such as potatoes near the frontier, requiring that equipment be stored outside the Protection Strip, and forbidding individuals to tend fields alone after 1972.[99] In all, Sonneberg's borderland population decreased more than 11 percent from 1960 to 1987, compared to a 3.4 percent decline nationally.[100]

Route closures, checkpoints, road erosion, and poor public transportation also froze local life. As road barriers sprang up everywhere, border towns typically had one or two points of entry with limited hours of operation. In 1972, the dilapidated road to Roth was open only eight hours on weekdays, two hours on Saturdays, and three hours on Sundays.[101] Troops observed routes from "hidden observation posts," and "one was checked constantly" on borderland buses, trains, and streets.[102] Being caught without a valid pass meant long detentions at the military command. One resident cautioned, "Without the thing, do not step a meter outside your house door!"[103]

The government exerted control over people's homes, as county officials juggled the twin priorities of improving buildings visible to the West and demolishing them for better security. Neither was popular, and it usually required "great efforts to convince" residents of any necessity. Many did not have the wherewithal for the repair work, or "beautification," especially the elderly, and state credit was hard to come by.[104] Contemporaries noted that several border towns did look better (from a distance). By 1989, Heubisch was rated among the one hundred "most beautiful" places in East Germany.[105] Still, people complained about the absurdity of pouring scarce resources into Potemkin villages that no one could visit.

After 1961, the government increasingly claimed land and demolished frontier buildings. As one pastor lamented, property was "not only ripped from the ground but from the heart."[106] Hundreds of Sonneberg residents lost their homes, and hundreds more lost gardens and orchards; dozens of deceased were even removed from their graves in the Hönbach cemetery.[107] While most property fell victim to the military's ever-expanding security requirements, the original impetus for demolitions in Sonneberg in 1961 actually came from local rather than central authorities. Sonneberg officials had lobbied for state funds to raze the Fischers' well-known house at Burned Bridge, and other buildings in the ten-meter strip, to prevent "sensation-seeking" western tourists from gaping at the abandoned "eyesores."[108]

The tenuousness of home and land created immense unease. Plus poor state compensation for property became an "extremely urgent" problem.[109] Tensions got so bad in "previously placid" Mupperg that thirty of thirty-six targeted owners "categorically refused" to sign transfer contracts.[110] Direct opposition could land Sonnebergers in jail, but some managed successfully to petition against, delay, and evade demolition of their houses. Elderly residents promised they would not live much longer, bargaining that the state could have their homes upon their demise.[111] Others turned the situation to their advantage, negotiating for larger houses before signing contracts—gaining ample room for their pigs, chickens, and beehives.[112] Under pressure to meet their quotas for border demolition, functionaries would accommodate these "constant new demands."[113] At least for a handful of particularly obstreperous locals, negotiations dragged on for years, the state eventually giving up in some instances.

Communities could likewise stymie demolition plans. Three of the four Sonneberg villages slated for destruction in the 1970s fended off the regime for years. Sattelpass residents vehemently protested the village's total "liquidation" in petitions and town meetings (the mayor had just completed "extensive renovations" on his house). Party officials backtracked, leveling instead eight of the village's seventeen houses.[114] Picturesque Korberoth took over a decade to raze. So, too, did Emstadt, which lost more than half its buildings as late as 1987–89.[115]

The one Sonneberg community efficiently destroyed had not put up a fight. Liebau's residents, fed up with life on the border, were mostly content to relocate further inland. Not native to the region, they had moved there after Liebau's original sixty-three inhabitants fled west in 1952. But the village's special security status suffocated local life, and people wanted out. Despite ongoing recruitment, the population grew from thirteen in the early 1960s to just eighteen by 1974.[116] Current residents kept applying to leave. One Liebauer even fled west and returned as a ploy, because he knew the punishment for returnees was relocation inland.[117] The village's decline was an ongoing embarrassment to the regime. All the empty houses became "more and more uneconomical" to maintain, and made a very "untidy and unclean impression" on western tourists—notwithstanding construction of a three-meter opaque fence in 1971 and a village-wide renovation campaign in 1972.[118] It took the county just one year to plan and demolish Liebau's thirty-five buildings, in 1975.[119]

Border demolitions appear to have been propelled by a self-perpetuating bureaucracy. Planning was complex, from relocating and compensating families to itemizing fruit trees to be purchased and destroyed. Since the military kept pressuring civil authorities to report constant activity, local offices kept lobbying central offices for frontier funds. Border budgeting assumed a logic all its own, with community administrators justifying requests for ever more money with ever more ambitious demolition plans.[120] If projected destructions did not happen in the designated year, funds could disappear the next.

Thus border budgets grew dramatically in the 1960s and early 1970s, by as much as 40 to 50 percent annually.[121] In 1972, district allocators protested that Sonneberg officials were getting greedy, using "tricks" like "hagglers at an auction," and joked that if the state claimed all the property county officials desired, it would "run out of money."[122] The county's frontier budgets shrank with the slowing of border fortification in the late 1970s and 1980s, though demolitions continued until the bitter end. This was certainly a rotten kind of pork, as bureaucrats wrangled over funds not for construction but for community destruction.

Although the border zone allowed for some give-and-take, citizens nevertheless lived according to its terms. Negotiating demolitions was a small victory in a world where demolitions were the norm. Small resistances were "like a liberation"—because residents tended to assume regime immutability. One woman remembered, "One took everything as it was, and didn't see a way to change it."[123] Paradoxically, however, wresting minor material concessions perhaps eased locals' forfeiture of the rest. Local maneuvering may have inadvertently contributed to the flexibility and durability of the border regime.

After all, daily defiance occurred within a context of daily compliance. Frontier controls were extraordinary, and most people grudgingly accommodated most measures. As one weary farmer explained his stance toward new curfew strictures, "I've already been in two world wars and am used to orders. I'd rather have peace and stay home after 9:00 p.m."[124]

Participation

Acceptance grew in part from everyday participation in the border regime. East Germany imposed dozens of quotidian obligations on residents that established habitual routines of compliance. Acts of participation were often insignificant in themselves, but their cumulative effects underpinned frontier stability.

From the outset, the regime drafted civilians to build and maintain the physical fortifications. In the second half of 1961, two hundred to four hundred

Sonnebergers a day labored on the fences, and for years locals were tasked with "voluntary" barrier construction, clearing land, and plowing the Control Strip.[125] The use of border brigades decreased by the end of the sixties, since installations became more complex and civilians posed too great a security risk—prone to drinking, talking to westerners, or fleeing on the job. Still, from a distance, local civilian officials oversaw frontier infrastructure, managing the upkeep of border buildings, signs, posts, tree stump removal, and swamp drainage.[126] County administrators became mired in the minutiae of the Iron Curtain. In 1969, for example, Sonneberg functionaries were responsible for installing 159 new road barriers and 842 border signs for East Germany's twentieth anniversary.[127]

Local officials had little power but performed an ensemble role in the theatrics of the border regime. One former administrator smirked as she remembered tedious meetings with border authorities, wryly pantomiming how people yawned through the scripted rhetoric and mechanically signed off on their to-do lists. Everyone knew these were empty gestures but went through the motions anyway.[128] Gerd Jahn, who was head of Sonneberg's Internal Affairs, conceded that community administrators did mostly make-work, with real security matters handled by the Stasi and military. But the goal was civilian participation, not efficiency.[129]

In order to "win every citizen for active cooperation with the border regime," officials pressured frontier residents into national organizations even more than elsewhere in East Germany.[130] Sonneberg's SED gained a reputation for being unusually persistent. After dramatic leadership purges in 1960–61, it counted, by 1963, a third of adult men, with higher enrollments than the national average.[131] East Germany's smorgasbord of state associations—including the Free German Trade Union, Democratic Women's Federation, German-Soviet Friendship League, Civil Defense Club, and People's Militias—mobilized the populace into border service.[132] These groups provided some recreation in dreary frontier towns, yet many people resented the "time tax" of the frontier's "forced volunteerism."[133] After working all day, residents "want[ed] to be left in peace after 8:00 p.m."[134]

There were more direct forms of border participation as well, from invasion drills and nighttime security watches to town meetings on the latest ordinances for mushroom picking.[135] At borderland workplaces, uniformed "combat groups" exercised with their "brothers in arms."[136] Every school in the Protection Strip was to sign "sponsorship agreements" with border soldiers. Older youths in the FDJ trained in "combat capabilities," and those who were nine to twelve years old joined Young Friends of the Border Soldiers to learn frontier orienteering, sleuthing, and footprint tracking.[137] Border training was a "nice and interesting experience," wrote one adolescent in his diary.[138]

Citizens also worked in Border Security Active Groups, or *Grenzsicherheitsaktive* (GSAs), that watched over community life. The mandate of Sonneberg's

A child at premilitary training in 1983. Grenzerfahrungen Kompakt, Salier Verlag, Hans-Jürgen Salier.

ninety-two GSAs, numbering more than seven hundred participants by 1988, ranged from barrier upkeep and trash disposal to tracking people undergoing divorce or "family problems" who might be a flight risk.[139] GSAs in schools even used children as "valuable information sources."[140] Border vigilance combined with small-town pettiness. One GSA for allotment gardeners expelled a member for leaving the door of his tool shed unlocked, creating a potential "hideaway for a border violator."[141]

Civilians served as Voluntary Border Helpers and Police Helpers as well. As visible agents of the state, they patrolled the frontier and wore red or green armbands in town, on the lookout for gossip and outsiders. While initial recruitment was "extremely problematic" in the late 1950s and 1960s, with people simply refusing to do the job, frontier collaboration became regularized over the years. In Sonneberg by the late 1980s, one in ten male borderland residents served as Voluntary Border Helpers or Police Helpers.[142] People had a range of motivations for signing up: real and perceived pressure, real and perceived benefits to career and family, and small stipends and perks such as free beer at local pubs. One woman remembered, "They were at dances, everywhere something was going on . . . and one was careful when they came by. It was known who did it voluntarily . . . these were the ones completely enthusiastic about it. Some even registered as soon as they turned eighteen, simply to have a certain kind of power."[143] Civilian helpers had an impact, reportedly accounting for one in five of all frontier arrests.[144]

Border soldiers, almost as numerous as civilian residents in Sonneberg's five-hundred-meter zone, likewise played a role in borderland life. Though their contacts with civilians were limited and regulated, they attended parades, social gatherings, and sporting events.[145] Local newspapers and community organizations feted the troops, and local women, charged with "mothering them a little," baked them cakes.[146] A scrapbook of one border soldier stationed in Mengers-gereuth-Hämmern in 1967 features snapshots of his buddies joking with a local woman, Elsa, next to his "favorite pub."[147] Some soldiers wound up marrying into communities, settling down, and continuing to serve on the frontier, consummating the regime's rhetorical marriage between the military and the populace.

But communal trust was strained, especially in the 1960s. As troops could detain residents for slight infractions, local youths, in turn, taunted, insulted, and challenged them. Most residents did not blame the young sentries for the border, yet it was still hard to feel comfortable with armed men standing guard in farms, taverns, and streets. In the fall of 1961, several farmers refused to work a field where "guns constantly followed" their movements. One group of women walked out "from fear and terror."[148] Soldiers went hunting, too, sometimes disobeying strictures and shooting animals outside the Protection Strip, even in the off-season.[149]

In "protecting the border together," civilians and sentries were to keep an eye on each other. On one hand, the Stasi tasked locals with forging "good personal relationships" with troops and asking them sensitive questions about the West and their duties, such as shooting border violators. Informants were to be especially watchful on paydays, when disproportionately more soldiers got drunk and fled.[150] On the other hand, the military monitored civilians' reliability. Since frontier residents were to report strangers and anyone headed to the fortifications, border forces sent outsiders into communities as tests to see who did not report the trespassers, and who reported residents who did not report the trespassers. Especially in the 1960s, a "certain segment of the population" kept showing people the way to the border, even offering "active help."[151] By the 1970s, though, people learned to report sightings in order to avoid trouble. They began to recognize border tests—young men in clean attire asking indiscreet questions in public locales—and resented these "posed situations."[152] But it was safer to play along. So when a high-ranking county official entered one village, an anxious villager reported him—even though he was there in order to inspect the fortifications.[153]

The delineation blurred between the guards and the guarded. Beginning in August 1961, "the entire populace" was to "defend the frontier," and was progressively militarized into a second line of defense.[154] The regime encouraged tip-offs. Newspapers reported model citizens catching crossers, one ten-year-old child supposedly doing so from his bicycle.[155] In 1963, when an average of five Sonnebergers fled over the border each month, the people who reported five people for arrest received medals and glowing press.[156] Through "discreet dealings," one fifteen-year-old boy handed over eight of his buddies trying to leave.[157] Emstadt was named "first border village" in East Germany because of its "exemplary" record of denunciation. The local pastor reportedly exhorted his flock in Sunday sermons to be watchful, and himself turned in a border violator.[158]

Over time, the regime channeled civilian vigilance further back from the frontier, to reporting people in the planning stages of escape. Such denunciations could be of dubious veracity, from anonymous letters to domestic calls (angry wives whose husbands had stormed out, threatening to head west), suggesting a certain privatization of state power.[159] They nevertheless led to arrests and made local law enforcement look good. By 1973, 35 percent of escape "preparation" charges in Sonneberg purportedly originated from the populace.[160] Some places generated so many "tips" that border troops considered them almost entirely self-policing.[161] While it is difficult to assess civilians' actual contributions from exaggerated government reports, the regime's mandate for denunciation was clear.

Border residents' motivation for reporting was less often conviction than simply avoiding trouble. Everyone in town paid when there was a border breach. The police clamped down on permits and controls, restricting access to ladders, tractors, or whatever had been the latest implement of escape, and generally making village life more miserable. One seventy-four-year-old grandmother reported the arrival of an outsider not because she supported the border regime (her own daughter was deported in 1961) but because she "wanted peace here, and we only have that when no one runs away."[162] Preemptive watchfulness became a mode of life, for oneself as well as others. When two men assembling a toy train set kept turning the room lamp off to test it, a village policeman knocked at the door and had them draw the blinds so as not to send inadvertent light signals to the West.[163] Locals shrugged off such incidents, chuckling in private. Cumulatively, however, caution and self-censorship were mutually reinforcing, and perhaps proved more insidious than the regime consequences they were meant to avoid.

East Germans viewed Stasi informing as the most odious form of surveillance. Stasi efforts, too, intensified after 1961, with the number of unofficial collaborators in Sonneberg doubling in a few years to one in every sixty-five Protection Strip residents. Stasi penetration appears to have remained at least twice the national average in the borderland, higher in many hot spots.[164] Sattelpass, a village of fifty-nine adults, had at least five "unofficial collaborators" (IMs) for the Stasi and five Border Helpers on active watch by the late sixties.[165] Yet informants were not always as dependable as the regime wished. Sonneberg MfS officials continually worried about Stasi "weaknesses." According to one estimate in 1964, 40 percent of informants showed signs of "two-timing with the enemy" and one in five was "not interested," producing "hardly anything" of value.[166] Recruiting and handling improved in later decades, though reliability remained an issue in close-knit border villages. Several IMs were caught failing to report escape attempts or even assisting them.[167] Yet many informants recounted conversations, scandals, and grumbles in exhaustive detail.[168] Nothing was too trivial. In a school essay on the theme "What would I show a new person in the village?" a ten-year-old's incorrect answer, "The road barrier and the barbed wire," caught one IM's attention.[169]

Regardless of how effective informants were, their sheer existence mattered most. Within the panopticon of the borderland, people knew they were under heavy scrutiny and censored themselves outside the company of close friends and family.[170] One woman recalled, "You really had no idea whom you could trust. . . . you could never say anything."[171] To some extent, borderland citizens became so watchful that surveillance became a victim of its own success. Sonneberg's Stasi officers complained they had a hard time infiltrating these careful communities, let alone arranging handler meetings, since it was so difficult to keep cover in a fishbowl.[172] But the MfS succeeded in the larger mission of inculcating frontier caution. It would seem the efficacy of surveillance did not mean as much as the simple fact, and act, of surveillance. This was the vicious cycle of self-policing systems: "People participated because everyone participated."[173]

Put another way, the substance of self-policing was its form. It was enough to go through the motions, and compliance counted most. In fact, the de-prioritization of conviction may have made it easier to comply, providing an outlet for small insubordinations. Sonnebergers could endure tedious border service believing they knew better, rolling their eyes and working halfheartedly. As they got used to separating inward belief from outward actions, cynical conformity proved a feasible way of life. In allowing an outlet for small insubordinations, however, it perhaps made the border regime all the more resilient.

Selection

The East German government increasingly selected border residents for compliance. Mass flight, mass arrests, and mass deportations in earlier decades had not only altered the demographics of the region but also intimidated those who remained. Sonnebergers well knew they were "allowed," not "entitled," to live in the borderland, an awareness that fostered anticipatory obedience.[174] Expulsion to inland counties was Sonnebergers' worst nightmare, the number one reason people said they kept their heads down. With many local families stretching back for generations, the loss of home meant the loss of everything. The October 1961 deportations had shocked residents anew, leading to rumors that the entire Protection Strip would be razed.[175] In 1962, the impending relocation of thirty-two Kleintettau residents, who escaped west with the help of West German border forces, did little to calm fears.[176] People worried their family or village could be next.

The regime relocated hundreds of border citizens individually between 1961 and 1989.[177] The process was not simple, especially in earlier years, as local constraints made it harder for the government to remove residents than most imagined. First people were able to delay, protest, and confound their removals with some success.[178] Then fear of community hostility prevented officials from initiating even more relocations.[179] Moreover, local administrators could stymie border authorities, preventing specific expulsions.[180] And finally, other counties could block Sonneberg administrators. Already short on housing and resources, they would balk at accepting Sonneberg's problematic people. In this way, the unwieldy twelve-member Graefe family, for instance, was not deported.[181]

For East German authorities, issuing official "residence restrictions" proved more workable than ad hoc family relocations. The former seemed more reasonable to the populace because they were punishments for breaking the law, unlike "evacuations," which designated "unreliable elements" without legal proceedings. Criteria for banishment, though, could be thin. Subjective transgressions such as criticizing the state, "idling at work," or being an "uncertain element" accounted for over a third of residence restrictions in the 1960s, while 5 percent were for "unknown reasons." Most of the rest were unruly youths who had broken frontier permit laws, tried to cross the border, or already crossed and returned.[182] By the 1970s, counties could officially declare residence restrictions "without criminal charges," relying purely on observations of "negative behavior."[183]

All told, Sonneberg exiled 194 residents from 1961 to 1971 and, notwith-standing the reduction of the Border Area after 1972, continued to expel citizens throughout the seventies and eighties.[184] Even if county officials eventually allowed people back in (only eleven in the 1960s), they carefully monitored those with criminal records.[185] Banished residents were often separated from their families forever. One man caught too near the border after a bar fight was relocated several hours away to a tiny apartment in Ilmenau. Without a car, his wife and young children could only visit intermittently on weekends, and the family fell apart.[186]

Sonneberg authorities likewise expelled people to West Germany. In the sixties, as in the fifties, the county "smuggled out" perhaps dozens of westerners who had lived in East Germany for years but proved more trouble, and cost, than they were worth.[187] Local officials had called in the Bredows, for example, for more than thirty scoldings in six years, haranguing them about their debts, af-fairs, drinking, and "immoral conduct." They were not found guilty of any crime in particular, but were deemed "a typical case of asocial elements who are a secu-rity risk in Sonneberg as a border county," and put on a train with their children to West Berlin in 1964. Western officials had a different response to the family, immediately finding severe child abuse and mental illness.[188]

The East German government not only selected out unwanted residents from the borderland but also selected East Germans wanting to move in. Applicants had to jump through formidable hoops. Beate Strassner was still vexed, decades later, by her six-month ordeal to join her husband in Neuhaus-Schierschnitz, and she was lucky.[189] After 1967, settlement in the Protection Strip was only for family reunification or specialists in desired professions. A new spouse did not count.[190] Even Sonnebergers who left temporarily, for study or career, could not go home again. Jörg Trautmann was incredulous that, after serving as a trusted border soldier on the Berlin Wall, he could not move back to his parents' house in Heubisch.[191] Thus the number of people moving into Sonneberg County (population 65,000) dropped from 550 to 600 a year in the early 1960s to just over 100 a year in the late 1980s, with extremely few allowed into the border zone.[192] Gerd Jahn, head of the Internal Affairs department that made the ver-dicts, said that although he was often sympathetic to petitioners, he was on the "front line," and the Stasi chewed him out if he was not "the bad guy."[193]

Visitors were also unwelcome along the frontier. During the sixties, when thirty-four of Sonneberg's thirty-six municipalities were in the Prohibited Zone, travel from West Germany all but stopped. The number of East German visitors dropped to around a thousand a month inside the Prohibited Zone and to five hundred inside the Protection Strip—mostly for work, deliveries, or family emergencies.[194] Sonnebergers got used to meeting with loved ones in Steinach, just outside the five-kilometer zone.[195] Travel opened up after Border

Area diminutions in 1972, particularly with the allowance of visitors for major family events. But entry permits in the mid-eighties still averaged only around 2,300 a month for Sonneberg's Border Area and 1,100 a month for the Protection Strip, 36 percent of which were for deliveries, repair work, or official business.[196] The border zone remained extremely restricted.

The regime, too, limited the movement of residents within the border area. Five-kilometer-zone residents were not allowed inside the five-hundred-meter zone without a permit, or even inside the five-kilometer zone of a neighboring county. Jakob Ziegler, who lived just beyond the Protection Strip, could not collect firewood right outside his house and was required to apply weeks in advance to visit adjacent towns, obtaining permission from the mayor, police, and local border commander, and then only for a few daylight hours.[197] The pass system confounded basic community functioning. Sonnebergers had trouble getting to their jobs, shopping for food, receiving house calls from doctors, and getting to the hospital.[198] When one ambulance rushing to Heubisch got lost (the regime falsified border zone maps), border troops in their winter-white uniforms jumped out to stop it, guns drawn.[199] The military and police kept shifting procedures, several villages had their own permit requirements, and there were always exceptions within the exceptions, particularly for the well-connected.[200]

Increasingly, East Germany's taxonomies of border reliability shaped not only rights but also physical territory. Selected citizens were sorted into ever more selective exclusion zones. There was even a hierarchy of harvesting, with more trusted residents such as government employees sent to collective crop "actions" closest to the border.[201] Borderland screening worked. All the deportations, applications, and rejections kept out potential troublemakers and constantly reminded locals their residence was conditional. With any infraction, they knew, they could be next to go. Decades later, Sonnebergers are still emotional remembering the trials and segregations of the border regime. Not only had they been trapped on "an island inside the GDR," but they had fought to be kept on that island, and to inhabit privileged gradations within it.[202]

A New Normalcy

Residents shuddered at the "gloom" that descended on border towns after 1961.[203] State officials had proclaimed that "the best must live there, for them we will also do the best," so those living on "the front" with the West would theoretically enjoy better food, equipment, and community life.[204] The reality fell far short of these rosy goals, however, and life on the frontier remained bleak. There were similar dislocations throughout East Germany, from poor consumer goods and television reception to oppositional youth and church movements.[205] But certain problems were pronounced in the borderland. East Germans who had moved to Sonneberg said they were struck by how "backward," "dilapidated," "isolated," and "repressed" the county was.[206]

There was not much for Protection Strip residents to do. Tough curfews, particularly in the sixties, made it difficult to get to the city of Sonneberg and back in time to go to the movies or to visit a friend. Inside towns, there was likewise little leeway. Once, two soldiers arrested twenty-five lingering patrons at Heinersdorf's Luzian Pub at 9:00 p.m. sharp and detained them for one and a half hours.[207] The regime tried to channel sociability into state-run organizations, tracking official club rooms, sewing circles, singing groups, and chess games in the borderland.[208] There was a lot happening on paper, but the reality was scarcely as lively, or as ideologically committed, as authorities envisioned. For youths, especially, there was "nothing going on in Sonneberg County."[209] State interference led to "reverse development" among Sonneberg hobbyists. In 1974, county officials could not muster up a musical group to play at community celebrations, even the May 1 parade.[210] Instead, many opted to drink, chat, and play cards on their own.

Taverns were in short supply due to security concerns.[211] Drinking was a symptom of disaffection in Eastern bloc countries in general, and Sonneberg, no exception, claimed the highest per capita beer consumption in East Germany by the mid-sixties.[212] Borderland officials worried that alcohol was a factor in 35 to 50 percent of the county's 270 to 330 "crimes" a year in the early seventies. Ten to 17 percent of these crimes were border crossing, plus people tended to flee after committing a punishable offense.[213] In other words, alcohol emboldened locals not only to cross but also to start bar fights and insult border soldiers that then led them to cross, escaping the consequences by going over the border the next day. To curb "crime," the regime typically allowed towns in the five-hundred-meter zone just one or two drab hangouts with restricted hours of operation, limited beverages, and unappealing food options such as "jarred bratwursts," if any.[214] In the early seventies, Heinersdorf's single pub, for its thousand residents, also doubled as the town hall, with drinkers having to vacate the place for civic meetings.[215]

Although frontier areas were supposed to be better-provisioned, this was often not the case. One report from 1987, for example, chronicles two-hour waits at Sonneberg's gas station, a "disagreeable smell" wafting from an "unclean" butcher shop, widespread shortages of underwear and shoes, and no beer in Mupperg's stores and pubs.[216] Meanwhile, county officials sometimes could not get permits inside the Protection Strip in order to actually investigate what was going wrong.[217] Even as frontier residents had so little to do or buy, they had disproportionately more money because of the 15 percent borderland bonus.[218] This was an expensive way to create discontentment, to be sure. Since thwarted consumers had little choice but to stash away their money, savings in the borderland outpaced East Germany's already high savings rate.[219]

Sonnebergers complained that their standard of living remained below the rest of East Germany's. While the regime spared nothing for high-tech fortifications, and spotlights kept the border "light as day," frontier communities remained dark, sometimes without electricity or running water up through the 1970s and 1980s.[220] Borderland towns also grew "very filthy and bedraggled," lacking investment in infrastructure.[221] Beautification campaigns improved the appearance of frontier communities from afar, but locals faced a landscape of debris and disrepair up close. Trash and animal dung littered frontier streets, manure pits proved "a center of contagion," and sewage remained a problem up through the 1980s.[222]

Border residents commonly said they lived at "the end of the world."[223] Inhabiting a "foggy gray zone" between the fortifications and the rest of East German society, people developed unique "border language," practices, and beliefs.[224] Locals described having a split kind of consciousness. On one hand, the border was part of everyday life and people got used to it. One resident said that although the restrictions were "humiliating," "I was shocked at how quickly I accepted the situation. One simply lived that way."[225] Some Sonnebergers supported the border regime. A number of interviewees defended the border as "necessary" to protect the East German state, and a quarter of Sonneberg survey respondents said its measures were "justified."[226] On the other hand, many Sonnebergers said they "always suffered emotionally."[227] Ursula Faber remembers how one day, while she was out berry picking, a border soldier questioned her and she suddenly began sobbing, hit by the "whole dilemma of our confinement."[228]

After 1961, a new generation was born into the militarized borderland, one that increasingly saw the border as "normal."[229] Its daily demands were par for the course: "It was simply so."[230] For this younger cohort, the boundary "was just there. It was there from the beginning, one didn't know anything else."[231] The restrictive border zone was home. Having little basis for comparison with life outside it, residents acclimated to the rituals, surveillance, and dreariness. People got used to the blasts of mines, the bursts of flares, and the long shouts and shots in the darkness. They got used to looking out their windows and seeing the frontier lit up with bright lights like a "beautiful pearl necklace."[232] It was possible to segment out the horrors of the border, keep one's head down, and make do.

Sonnebergers also found happiness. Even people who were sharply critical of the border regime became nostalgic reminiscing about communities and workplaces, remembering how the isolated frontier bred such a "very strong sense of kinship." Residents explained they had to rely on "neighborly help" for fixing furnaces or last-minute child care, creating a "positive" sense of "togetherness" that has since been lost.[233] In fact, many Sonnebergers said they "didn't have it that bad and lived contentedly."[234] Some proudly displayed East German memorabilia and commemorative booklets from their villages, schools, factories, clubs, and vacations—testaments to lives well lived.[235] They made the best out of what they had.

The Iron Curtain was simply a part of life, so integrated into the everyday that some experienced its loss as a loss of part of their identity. Beate Strassner hated border regime, but after 1989 she felt estranged from her former self: "I could, if I wanted to, pick up again exactly where I left off . . . it's like being in the middle of a film from this time; at least I feel it to be. I know that there is this reality, but the other one is still so strong!"[236]

The East German government succeeded in transforming not only the military landscape of the Iron Curtain but civilian life along it as well. Residents absorbed border controls into the fabric of daily life and began to see them as normal. Although the regime never achieved the complete control to which it aspired, and fell far short in winning ideological supporters, quotidian coercions and accommodations gave rise to an environment of anticipatory compliance.

East Germany's brutal border apparatus did allow limited room for local maneuver. Sonnebergers may not have been able to stop the Iron Curtain, but they were able to slow, speed, or affect the course of its expansion. In hindsight, some in the younger generation have suggested their forebears could have done more, criticizing how they "disappeared into their own homes and didn't come out again or resist. That was the disgrace here."[237] Sonnebergers who lived through the border regime, though, said they did their best. An elderly man stated quietly, "One shouldn't judge the people," for "one cannot imagine how it was."[238]

Like people everywhere, Sonnebergers had a range of responses to coercion as they retreated, resisted, and enlisted. The extent to which local actions did or could have altered the Iron Curtain is debatable. But no matter whether residents "tended their gardens," went to jail, volunteered for border service, or did all of the above, one thing is clear: the border became integrated into daily routines and mentalities.[239] The borderland was home. This assimilation helps explain how the border regime became as durable as it did, as East Germany managed to turn some of its most victimized inmates into willing and unwilling wardens.

‖ 9 ‖

Fault Line: Life in the Fortifications

One late November afternoon near Sonneberg in 1968, East German soldiers spied sixteen-year-old Günter Oppermann between the two outer fences of the border. They yelled for him to halt, ordering him at gunpoint to climb over the inner fence and to walk toward them through a minefield. The boy balked. A guard fired a shot near his feet, warning him to comply. As Günter took his first steps, he hit a mine. Severely injured, he started crawling. He then exploded another one. He could crawl no longer, but writhed and shouted on the cold ground. Western forces in Neustadt stood by, appalled, helplessly throwing bandages over the border. After nervous deliberation, eastern officers decided to retrieve the boy, and carefully detonated seven mines to clear a safe path for themselves.

Günter lay bleeding for almost four hours, crying under the bright border spotlights: "Help, you East Germans get me out! I'm just sixteen and don't want to die. Take me to a hospital, my legs are gone," and "Help, you West Germans get me out! Don't you hear me? In God's name get me out. I'm bleeding to death."[1] Western politicians immediately deplored the incident, and headlines screamed about the murder of an eastern boy escaping to liberty. The Federal Republic's Foreign Office planned to bring the case before the United Nations at once, as a prime example of East German inhumanity.

But the reality turned out to be more complicated. East German authorities revealed a couple days later that Günter had not died. He had lost his right leg below the knee and half of his left foot, but was otherwise well. He and his father publicly praised first-rate treatment in Sonneberg's County Hospital, surrounded by flowers, chocolate, oranges, and cigarettes. The regime also "announced with obvious relish" that Oppermann had not been fleeing west—he had been fleeing east.[2] The boy was a westerner from a broken family who was living in an abusive children's home near Coburg. He had escaped and was trying to get to his grandmother in East Germany.

In the end, both West and East Germany came out looking bad. The Sonneberg incident, as the *New York Times* put it, "fanned a two-decade-old propaganda war to new heights," though "subsided after both Germanys realized that the accident was unsuitable for propaganda purposes."[3] This was just one of many cases where what happened along the border did not match either side's clear-cut narrative of division.

Contrary to each Germany's projected image of a static barrier, the Iron Curtain remained a dynamic, uncertain space. Certainly its fortifications had grown formidable. But locals still crossed, interacted, and clashed over the boundary. Like other borders, to some extent, the Iron Curtain remained a porous zone of exchange and change. In both East and West, the residents of its borderland gave it culture, character, and life.

Border Jumpers

The Iron Curtain appeared impenetrable from afar, but it contained, and concealed, escalating escapades of crossers and their capturers. This liminal area between East and West Germany was tightly, yet not perfectly, controlled—and within its gaps chance events could have broader impact, assuming political significance and affecting the very form of the Iron Curtain.

The East German government, obsessed with security, was highly reactive to evolving flight tactics. Escapees and officials one-upped each other in ever more elaborate strategies. Some of the regime's early measures were straightforward, such as stopping the sale of wire cutters in the Prohibited Zone or placing decoy cardboard soldiers in watch towers.[4] Border forces also analyzed local flight patterns (Tuesday, Wednesday, and Thursday nights were peak times).[5] And they reinforced the fortifications where people escaped. The military added additional layers of fencing and mines where, for example, sixteen people had crossed at Liebau in 1966—and around Burned Bridge, which saw almost half of Sonneberg's flight.[6] Escape attempts met with massive response, up to several hundred troops drawn into a single search, their over-the-top tactics making "amusing theater" for bystanders.[7]

East German authorities were alert to western media coverage, so much so that it became West German policy to withhold flight details to prevent eastern forces from learning where the border was vulnerable.[8] Potential escapees also paid close attention to the western press, which both glorified those who made it across, making it seem like an attainable feat, and offered "instruction" on the dangers of the border. The West German government did not want to discourage flight, but was concerned that most easterners did not know what they were up against and would be surprised to discover the extent of the fortifications upon encounter.[9]

It is not known how many people were injured or killed at Germany's Iron Curtain, but the total number surely runs into the thousands. The death toll for the Berlin Wall is conservatively estimated at 136, and these figures do not include the many more who suffered devastating injuries and traumas.[10] For example, soldiers fired thirty-eight shots at one plumber from Hönbach who impulsively tried to cross in 1982. He was lucky to sustain only "light head injuries."[11] A former nurse at Sonneberg's County Hospital remembered many such terrified victims. The staff never quite got used to the trauma cases, but became expert at leg amputations and gunshot wounds.[12]

Crossing was extremely dangerous, and the number of guard dogs, signal fences, and trip wires grew spectacularly over the decades.[13] However, locals familiar with the terrain were much more successful than outsiders. Sonneberg-ers accounted for one-third to one-half of reported breaches in Sonneberg.[14] Officially, around fifty Sonnebergers fled over the border each year in the first half of the sixties, dropping to two to fifteen people a year by the seventies and eighties.[15]

Crossing the border was grueling, and it helped to know what you were doing. From outside the border area, one first had to get past East Germany's People's Police and Transport Police, who screened train and bus passengers up to thirty kilometers from the boundary. The police apprehended travelers for "intent to flee" if they did not have hotel reservations, looked "like hippies," or carried suspicious items such as compasses, maps, or pliers.[16] Then it was a multiple-hour hike from Sonneberg's train station to the fortifications, hilly areas requiring skis or snowshoes during winter. With two-thirds of Sonne-berg's ninety-three-kilometer border lying in forest and thicket, only one-third in open fields, it was hard to keep track of where one was going. Moreover, the East German government deliberately obscured the locations of frontier com-munities. Maps falsified their placement or excluded them; borderland road signs, if available, distorted their distances.[17] People who finally made it to the border also got lost, so disoriented by all the layers of fencing that they would give up, spend the night in the fortifications, or unwittingly climb back and forth between East and West a couple times.[18] Even when they got past all the booby traps and border troops, they still could be pulled off the fences at the last minute by a vigilant local farmer.[19]

East Germans found ingenious ways to circumvent these obstacles. Their famous tunnels, homemade air balloons, and freezing thirty-kilometer swims through the Baltic Sea were testaments to their determination and desperation. Subtler strategies were likewise daring. People bribed border soldiers, smuggled themselves out in vehicles, or improvised their own ladders, hooked shoes for fence climbing, and fogging agents to throw off the guard dogs.[20] Some Sonne-bergers managed to bulldoze through the barriers in a tractor or, most memorably in 1988, a potato delivery truck: "like in a gangster film."[21] While these dramatic escapes dominated western headlines, defining the border to the outside world, they were a minority of the crossings over the Iron Curtain.[22] Arguably, their over-emphasis has distorted understanding of the actual dynamic on the border.

The fortifications, in fact, could be vulnerable. Up close, locals saw a border riddled with malfunctions: rusted and breakable barbed wire, rotten minefields, and defunct trip wires. Contrary to popular memory, it appears that most crossings resulted not from the considered decisions of people trying to flee tyranny but from the impetuous exploits of frontier residents who were inebriated, young, fighting with a loved one, in trouble with the law—or a combination thereof. In the 1960s, Sonneberg officials estimated 90 percent were male, over three-quarters were under the age of twenty-five, at least a third had committed some form of offense against the state, and half were just plain drunk.[23] Certainly East German reports had a bias toward explaining flight as a product of individuals' erratic behavior, not state unpopularity, and emphasized the role of "arguments in the family" or "lust for adventure" in crossings. Still, local western sources, with easterners' statements to Neustadt's border police, corroborate a surprising degree of precipitate passages.

Border jumpers frequently returned to East Germany the next day and, registered as "illegal entrants" instead of refugees, were neither counted in official escape tallies nor publicized in the press. They were thus largely unknown to contemporaries and largely forgotten, save for their picaresque chronicling in local publications and interview collections. Certainly it was in neither side's interest to call attention to the haphazard to-and-fro over the border. East and West alike cultivated the narrative of an ominous Iron Curtain, East Germany portraying invulnerability and West Germany portraying totalitarianism. That so many locals, familiar with the terrain, could simply scramble across for petty or impetuous reasons did not fit either side's image of an inexorable border.

Although this unruly undercurrent of activity may, in retrospect, make the border seem less intimidating, it appeared to be a driver of its growth. Inebriated teenagers and young men inadvertently propelled barrier escalations. As the military chased after drunken crossers, fortifying the site of each breach, the more sober portion of the population gave them less reason for concern. Staid civilians paid for the capricious antics of their young.

Capricious they were. In the 1960s especially, Sonnebergers still crossed the border for sport and returned the same day, out of daring, from curiosity, and because it was something to do in dull frontier towns. Lured by adventure and the chocolate western guards tossed over the fences, kids threw rocks into the minefields to see if they would explode, and would sneak west to visit relatives and to buy gum and candy. It is difficult to say how many did so. But out of around two dozen children in Sattelpass, for example, seven were caught crossing within six months of each other in 1969.[24] Indeed, the prevalence of casual crossings in archival sources raises the question of how many more people were not caught—such as the five eastern border repairmen who, according to West German records, sampled western beer and sandwiches at a Neustadt pub in 1969, returned to East Germany across a minefield, and then went back later that afternoon for a second visit.[25]

Exploits became exceedingly more difficult in the 1970s and 1980s, but savvy locals still found ways across the border. In 1982, at the height of the fortifications, twenty-one-year-old Anton Witzke crossed twenty-three times in six months, with two friends accompanying him on several occasions. The three young men had fled from Neuhaus-Schierschnitz in 1981 and, from Neustadt, kept going back into East Germany for brief jaunts. They stole twelve mines to sell as souvenirs in the West, especially to American servicemen. They also made longer family visits out of "homesickness," staying up to four days at a time inside the border zone.[26] The youths' exploits revealed some amazing border weaknesses. Eastern officials did not realize the crossings were happening, or that any land mines were missing, until Witzke was arrested in *West* Germany for selling them. The young men had found numerous spots where the fortifications had deteriorated. Having scrutinized the landscape and troop patrols through binoculars, they called the border's technological bluff. On one of their trips, they did not even take the shortest route over the border, but traipsed for one to two kilometers inside the patrol area and another seven kilometers through the Protection Strip. Eventually all the young men were caught and sentenced to several years in prison. Witzke's family was banished to Leipzig because his sister and father, a Stasi informant, had aided their crossings. Notably, authorities decided not to expel the other two boys' families for fear of creating "unrest" in Sonneberg.[27] Still, this extraordinary case reveals gaping holes in the Iron Curtain, and the range of what could be possible up until the end.

Sonnebergers rashly crossed the border throughout its history. Alcohol often induced locals to jump the fences, border forces on both sides chronicling dozens of inebriated passages. Not everyone meant to leave. On New Year's Day in 1969, one Sonneberger woke up in Neustadt hungover, having somehow ambled over the border the night before. He immediately called home to return.[28] A number of local men crossed in the throes of anger, having fought with their wives and drowned their sorrows at a local tavern. After sobering up the next day at Neustadt's police station, they typically thought better of it and decided to go back.[29] Ralf Zieger twice stormed out on his wife over the border and returned, in 1965 and 1970.[30] If intercepted by eastern forces, the consequences for such inebriated crossings could be dire, resulting in prison or expulsion from the borderland, plus enduring hardships for one's family. One drunk lovelorn husband was shot and critically injured trying to cross near Meilschnitz in 1973. Another, who had fought with his wife after a skat tournament in 1989 (his teenage son having followed him to the fortifications, pleading with him not to flee), did not dare return to his family in East Germany.[31]

Youths particularly were prone to impulsive crossing—from the angst of love, avoiding military service, abuse at home, or fighting with parents.[32] One fifteen-year-old fled with her twenty-six-year-old lover in 1970 because her parents and her lover's wife all lived in the same house. The girl's uncle in Neustadt helped mediate, and the pair eventually returned.[33] A number of adolescents left because they did not pass into the tenth grade, due to either poor work or political discrimination. By one estimate, "weak achievement in school" accounted for around half of Sonneberg's youth flight in the midsixties, so eastern officials began to track teenagers' grades.[34] Other teenagers were simply anxious for a better future, restless in the border zone and chafing against its restrictions.[35] Western authorities typically sent these hopeful minors back home (provided they had not preemptively falsified their birth year), a practice that quickly became less tenable over the sixties because of East Germany's severe punishments.[36]

Many adolescents went west after falling afoul of eastern authorities, fearful of the consequences for even minor infractions. In 1962, two fled after stealing a rabbit. In 1971, inebriated Josef Werner got belligerent and fled when the police wanted to administer a blood test.[37] County officials recognized that "every punishable offense can lead to an attack on the state border," and that once teenagers got in trouble they tended to stay in trouble.[38] Sonneberg counted about a hundred boys in its "rowdy groups" in the sixties who, as in the fifties, regarded the frontier as their adventure playground.[39] Having grown up in the topsy-turvy borderland, these teenagers knew their way around, and had friends and relatives who had gone west. Dozens had already fled and returned, often two to four times, and kept stirring up trouble and planning future escapades.[40]

A subculture of border antics continued through the decades, from schoolkids improvising frontier hideaways and tree lookouts to cliques of adventurers.[41] Siegfried Tenner said he knew at least five young men who had crossed in the 1980s. His buddies swapped stories of "elegant tricks" at the factory where he worked, telling of homemade stepladders, walking backward over troops' footprints, or befriending border soldiers at bars. He said with a smile, "We knew everything."[42]

Loved ones were hardly so sanguine about border jumping, however. One mother said she was constantly terrified that her disaffected son would get drunk and try crossing.[43] Twenty-five years later, another mother still trembled recalling how her son "played with his life." In trouble with the law, he had crossed three times in the mid-eighties near Sattelpass—first westward, then eastward, then westward.[44] Today, some Sonnebergers grow irritated at the question of youth crossers, insisting either that such border escapades were not possible or that focusing on them diminishes the tragedy of all the East Germans who died trying to escape. Neither is the case. Impetuous crossings did happen, and their occurrence helps explain the regime's obsession with ever more brutal measures.

The East German government went to great lengths to curb youth "criminality." Sonneberg officials designated "overseers," infiltrated cliques, surveilled hangout spots, pressured parents, sent kids to group homes, and kept kids from these group homes out of the borderland.[45] However, police vigilance had spiraling repercussions, and prompted flight by teenagers who had not planned to leave. In 1965, Roland Doerner was sentenced to five months in prison because three of his friends fled west and he had not reported them; immediately Doerner made plans to leave with three additional friends from Sonneberg.[46]

What these crossing kids often did not realize were the consequences for those they left behind. One impetuous passage could affect the careers and prospects of parents, siblings, and friends forever. Leaving was also hurtful. Decades later, people remain conflicted when talking about their errant relatives. Many Sonnebergers did not leave precisely because of their sense of obligation. Edgar Pfisterer was the only remaining son after his brother fled; he always wanted to go west and "of course everyone thought about it," but "one still had parents and grandparents. And somehow those family ties really bound. It was a really tight grip."[47] When Beate Strassner's father found out she wanted to leave, "he didn't get very upset," but calmly told her that if she felt she had to, she should know he would lose his career as a judge. "And I thought, I can't do it. Poor Father. I felt so bad."[48]

The youths who did leave in the sixties often found themselves in a no-win situation. Upon arrival in the West, many wound up in dreary refugee camps and youth homes, became homesick, and decided to return a few months later. Yet if caught going home again, they typically faced a jail term or banishment from the border area for having fled. Given the unhappy choice between an institution outside Sonneberg County and an institution in the West, kids left again, sometimes doing several iterations of this lonely loop.[49]

East German officials tried, as they had in the fifties, to redress adolescent shiftiness through massive bureaucracy. They organized endless discussions, resolutions, and work plans, as well as kept close tabs on the roughly five hundred people who had been allowed back to Sonneberg over the years.[50] The regime clamped down on admittance to the borderland, the average number of entrants to Sonneberg County dropping from around 130 returnees and 65 western immigrants a year in 1954–60 to just 10 to 12 returnees and 2 to 4 westerners a year in 1961–65, with far fewer thereafter.[51] On the whole, returnees in the sixties were less troublesome than those allowed back the prior decade, but problems remained. At least one in six Sonnebergers allowed to return in the early sixties tried to or did leave again within a couple of years.[52] Given the growing difficulties of readmittance, homesick teenagers increasingly resigned themselves to staying in the West, occasionally sneaking back into Sonneberg illegally for short visits.

Westerners, too, crossed over the border—though at a small fraction of the rate of easterners.[53] Some sought new lives in East Germany, especially in the sixties. In 1967, a nineteen-year-old from Rottenbach went east because he was "fighting constantly" with his parents. In 1962, a fifteen-year-old from Wildenheid crossed to escape being sent to a children's home, because his mother was no longer able to care for him.[54] One twenty-two-year-old Neustadter, fed up with marital and family problems, crossed into Sonneberg in 1967 and visited relatives for a day before reporting his intention to stay.[55] Though immigrating westerners made for good propaganda in East Germany, they were, as in the fifties, often more trouble than they were worth. Many headed east to escape debts or criminal charges in West Germany, with fewer than 5 percent supposedly coming out of ideological conviction.[56] In fact, arriving westerners were such an unreliable lot that the Stasi had "few good experiences" recruiting collaborators among them.[57]

West German youths also crossed the frontier for brief jaunts. Some visited family. When three teenagers crossed for Easter in 1965, one of them lost his right forearm to a mine on the way back.[58] More often, western kids crossed the frontier for sport. As a local rite of passage, Neustadters would venture over the unfenced outer portion of the boundary for a few minutes at a time to tempt fate, taunt eastern soldiers, vandalize border posts, and steal frontier emblems. Though many got away with it, these juvenile antics could have serious consequences. When, for example, a group of friends carousing at the Mountain Mill Border Tavern in 1977 pooled 1,000 DM for someone to drink a bottle of beer on the other side of the fence, the young man who accepted the dare was quickly arrested by eastern troops and sentenced to ten months in jail, getting out after four.[59]

Most western crossings were momentary, as people deliberately or accidentally stepped over the unmarked boundary line, which lay several meters in front of the actual fence. The East German regime gladly arrested westerners for such slight "provocations"—up to five in Sonneberg and seventy-five in East Germany per month—because western ransom payments were a good source of hard currency. Eastern troops were vigilant, so much so that Neustadt's newspapers warned people where they had to be careful when out on a walk.[60] Western authorities even put up their own fences in some locations to prevent parked cars from rolling onto eastern territory or Neustadt kids from meandering over the line while playing.[61] The infirm were particularly vulnerable to frontier mishaps. Over the years, several elderly and mentally ill Neustadters lost their way; they could sustain injuries or lose consciousness, or they might be snagged by eastern soldiers, held at gunpoint, and subjected to lengthy ordeals before returning home.[62]

Crossing west to east was more perilous than heading east to west. East Germany's deadliest technologies were right on the border, so while eastern crossers often were caught before reaching them, stopped by signal fencing or trip wires, crossing westerners ran into land and fence mines first. Unlike eastern crossers, who might be familiar with the latest technologies and timing of patrols, westerners often did not fully realize the risks they undertook. After fighting with his girlfriend in 1984, one impulsive western seventeen-year-old tried to scramble over the fence at Burned Bridge and immediately detonated a self-firing device, losing both his feet.[63] Some of the most sensational border dramas in the region involved westerners, such as Günter Oppermann. In a case from 1969, a mentally ill fourteen-year-old, Isolde Beier of Neustadt, who had tried to run away across the border eleven times, got stranded one day in a minefield. She shouted to gathered onlookers that both eastern and western forces were "too cowardly to come get me." West Germany's BGS asked permission to rescue her with a helicopter, but East German authorities would not allow the infringement into their airspace. After three hours of wrangling, eastern soldiers went into the minefield and arrested the girl, returning her to Neustadt a few days later.[64]

The Iron Curtain's haphazard crossings contrast sharply with the tragedies of those who planned, suffered, and died trying to flee East Germany. Impetuous escapades were no less a part of the border's history, however, and their existence does not trivialize the very real dangers of the fortifications. Rather, uneventful crossings render stories of injuries and deaths all the more arbitrary and hideous, and shed light on an important factor propelling the border's brutality.

Border jumpers also suggest a central irony: frontier residents, the very same people who buttressed the border system, were also in a position to subvert it. Even as Anton Witzke, for example, crossed twenty-three times in 1982, his father continued to work for the Stasi and his mother continued to cook in the local border troops' canteen. Because frontier communities were part of the border system, they knew how it worked. So the fortifications were peculiarly porous for this special population, which had inside knowledge but kept the border strong for outsiders. The strength of the Iron Curtain depended not only on physical defenses but also upon the accommodations of residents themselves.

Border Encounters

The border remained active not only with east-west crossers but also with encounters between East and West. Especially in the 1960s, when the barbed wire fences were right at the boundary line, brigades, farmers, and guards had personal exchanges. Westerners photographed civilians at work, offered cigarettes or liquor, and yelled hello—"provocations" that East German sentries tracked in absurd detail, down to the friendly initiations of western "easy girls."[65] Moments of contact became meaningful, vividly recounted by Neustadters and Sonnebergers alike. As townspeople grew apart over the years, border interactions increasingly shaped how residents on each side saw those on the other side, and reveal the degree to which the Iron Curtain remained a zone of exchange between East and West.

Easterners and westerners had chilling memories of seeing family and friends on the frontier with whom they tried to communicate, neither sure people on the other side grasped their well-meaning intent. Neustadters said they would shout out greetings that Sonnebergers said they would pretend to ignore, fearful of getting caught or winding up on western television. Gerd Jahn, who later became responsible for border security in Sonneberg, recalled one painful 1964 encounter near Rotheul with a former playmate from kindergarten who had moved west. The man went up to the border to talk to him, calling out, "Old Gerd! It's me!" Jahn dared only tip his cap without looking at him. Decades later, he hoped his old friend understood.[66]

Cross-border contacts could escalate quickly into security problems for East Germany. When one brigade of twenty-nine women from Oerlsdorf was farming a potato field near the ten-meter strip in 1964, several western relatives came to see them. Five soldiers tried to prevent interactions through the fence—forbidding one woman from talking to her ill eighty-year-old mother—whereupon half the East German women threatened to stop work in protest. The lieutenant finally allowed two from the brigade to talk at the border for five minutes (which expanded to half an hour), though he stopped westerners from throwing over oranges and cigarettes. The rest of the women resumed work and, interestingly, there were few consequences for their insubordination. Community leaders, cowed by public opinion, did not plan to punish the women, except by barring them from future frontier service.[67] Soon East German officials grew wary of allowing civilians near the border at all. By the mid- to late sixties, locals lost even these fleeting opportunities for contact.

Heightened emotional dramas unfolded at Hönbach's cemetery, which lay right at the fortifications. Since westerners were not allowed to attend funeral services inside East Germany's border zone, grieving relatives watched from

Burned Bridge, 1964. Stadtarchiv Neustadt bei Coburg.

outside the fences, crying out to loved ones in the East. Divided memorials became legend in the region. One funeral in September 1962 drew twenty-four westerners. They waved tearfully from behind the barbed wire, though only Pastor Hendrik Richter dared wave back. They threw over wreaths and flowers, which easterners were not allowed to pick up, and many blooms got snagged on the fortifications.[68] Over time, the East German military isolated Hönbach's cemetery, planting taller hedges around it to make it less visible, leveling tombstones, and prohibiting further burials. By the late 1960s, even Sonnebergers were kept out.[69] Kurt Geis, who lived a kilometer away, had to jump through security hoops for allotted annual trips, and he had to enlist a "middleman" from Hönbach to tend his grandparents' graves. It was "like in a ghetto," he felt.[70]

East-West contacts decreased in the seventies and eighties, after East Germany moved the fortifications back from the boundary line. Yet Neustadters and Sonnebergers devised schemes to see each other from afar, relatives prearranging times for binocular viewings. Sonnebergers would stand atop the Schönberg mountain on Sundays, waving westward with a white towel, or would present themselves on certain city streets at an appointed time. East German authorities noted and punished even these minimal connections.[71]

Westerners' most frequent cross-border encounters were with East German troops. Some sentries became so familiar that Neustadters gave them nicknames ("the Gallows" or "the Fat One"), photographing them and noting their quirks and comical sunglasses like old friends.[72] In the sixties, eastern guards could have extensive interactions with Neustadters. In 1962, western revelers at the Mountain Mill Border Tavern even invited two soldiers to cross and have a beer. Everyone had a fine time until one of the troops, Reinhard Nagel, wanted to get back to East Germany before they were missed, while his partner, Emil Oberstedt, wanted to defect. The men drew their weapons inside the pub, Oberstedt shooting at Nagel twice and injuring him in his right thigh. Nagel limped back across the border and was promptly apprehended; Oberstedt stayed in the West and was charged with negligent criminal assault.[73]

Borderland residents witnessed up close the brutality of East Germany's guard system. The regime trained East German troops to make cruel choices, and continued to loosen rules of engagement after 1961 so that shooting was no longer a measure of last resort. Soldiers received pay bonuses, awards, special rations, and extra vacation days for catching and killing border violators, and faced disciplinary action for allowing successful escapes.[74] When a class of trainees was asked if they would shoot their own fathers, one soldier remembered that although everyone was shocked, "no one said anything."[75]

Frontier communities well knew what they were up against. In one pursuit in Unterlind in 1966, witnessed by a "large portion" of villagers, eastern soldiers fired several shots at two local boys trying to cross, and hit a fifteen-year-old in the lungs. The killing was "the topic of the day in all of Sonneberg," as people began calling the troops "child murderers." Though the local regiment distributed a leaflet celebrating the shooting as a "heroic deed" and claimed the youth was only injured, everyone knew about East Germany's medals for murder.[76]

East German border soldiers themselves lived in harsh conditions. Trapped in a paranoid military zone, the young men were subjected to even more scrutiny than the civilians they guarded. Up to one in twelve were Stasi informants reporting on one another.[77] Their lives were cheap, as dozens in the Sonneberg area fell victim to mine explosions and other accidents.[78] Morale was low. Soldiers felt their lives were "absurd" and "psychologically very taxing"; patrols in the "bush" were long and lonely; conditions in the barracks were poor; discipline and hazing were harsh.[79] Outside of a couple of bordellos and limited contact with the populace, troops had little to do for relaxation. Many drank, lazed about, snoozed on the job, doodled irreverent cartoons, got in fights with civilians, and took up with local girls—so that "one often forgot the macabre place one was in."[80]

A number of troops simply fled west. Soldiers accounted for around 15 percent of all escapes over the inter-German border (20 to 30 percent in the 1980s), not counting those who fled after their military service, having become familiar with frontier terrain.[81] Troop flight was a major concern in the early 1960s, when one to two defected from Sonneberg's regiment each month.[82] The regime got better at screening and training reliable soldiers, though local archives document a dizzying range of escapes through the years, from irrepressible young men in love to well-planned group escapes.[83] Legends lived long in the barracks. West Germany sent propaganda leaflets urging eastern soldiers to take the "big leap," signed by former comrades who were enjoying "the best cola" or watching "whatever television program" they wanted to.[84] Successful defectors also rubbed it in. In 1971, two escaped guards stood at the border near Heinersdorf and bragged over a loudspeaker that they were living it up in the West with cars, cigarettes, and girls: "Here you can have it all."[85]

The trickiest part about military defections was that soldiers were always paired with at least one partner, who could face severe repercussions for allowing an escape. Fleeing troops would hold their companions at gunpoint, take the bullets out of their weapons, or try to strike some kind of deal. When one soldier told his partner during a cigarette break that he wanted to leave, the guy kindly gave him fifteen meters' lead time before firing several shots in the air.[86] Not all were so fortunate. One escapee's partner fired at him six times after he was already in Bavarian territory, stopping only when a western guard issued two warning shots.[87] The western press sensationalized such internecine violence. After twenty-year-old Wolfgang Pommer's partner shot him in the back in 1972, newspapers ran photographs of the escape site, the western family who found him by their dung heap, the doctors tending him, and all the politicians who visited him. Pommer received letters from all over West Germany and collected over 1,000 DM in gifts.[88]

Civilians on both sides of the border felt conflicted about East German guards. On one hand, they were clearly just youths, scared, away from home, sneaking cigarettes from westerners on patrol, and getting away with what mischief they could. On the other hand, the young men also represented East Germany's police state, dutifully shooting at kids and comrades to keep their compatriots captive. Increasingly, the image of the stony soldier won out. As the primary figures westerners saw on the border, and the last obstacle to freedom for easterners, eerily unyielding troops became the face of the Iron Curtain. Stories of their coldness overshadowed any softening people saw one-on-one, and contributed to the inviolable image of the border.

Yet soldiers, like civilians, were a dynamic, unpredictable component of the border apparatus. Fleeting moments of East-West contact resonated disproportionately and had the potential to unsettle the system. It was precisely to contain the unpredictability of encounter that East Germany invested in the precautions it did. Even at the height of the fortifications, though, the East German regime still did not succeed in removing volatility from the Iron Curtain.

Border Volatility

While human interactions over the border diminished over the years, the border apparatus remained active. Residents said they saw or heard from it almost every day, from its signal flares to its guard dogs barking. The hungry, angry animals would keep people up all night, sometimes breaking free of their chains and running west.[89] The border also "destroyed all nature" it encountered. There was constant battle with the environment, whether it involved flooding, broken machinery, malfunctions, or upkeep. Something as simple as the ten-meter strip was "constantly tilled, constantly raked."[90] In short, the border was an actor in the frontier landscape, shaping—and ending—life on its own.

The western press featured the border's "death machine" in its heartrending accounts of easterners fighting their way toward freedom.[91] In one iconic case, newspapers recounted in excruciating detail how Sonneberg truck driver Fritz Gesell detonated a mine while escaping in March 1968, which exposed the bones in his leg up to the knee. He managed to crawl through five layers of fencing to get to the West, leaving a wide trail of blood. The city of Neustadt and private donations financed his lengthy hospitalization, and he eventually recovered, married a local girl, and settled in Neustadt.[92]

Mines were the most notorious—and unpredictable—feature of the border. East Germany's land mines were horribly indiscriminate, blowing up not just crossers but also East German soldiers and officials.[93] Worse, self-firing fence mines, or SM-70s, were activated by trip wires along the fence, and shot out 110 cube-shaped pellets that killed or severely injured anyone within twenty-five meters. These grisly devices were hypersensitive. In one twelve-month period in 1978–79, around 15 percent (ten thousand mines) detonated erroneously, triggered by animals, storms, or malfunctions. Border troops often turned off fence mines during bad weather, lest entire sections of fence explode.[94] Land mines could not be deactivated, however. An eight-inch snowfall caused three hundred to detonate near Neustadt.[95] Regional wildlife became "ever more decimated," with locals frequently finding blown-up deer and other animal carcasses.[96]

The mines also moved. Freezing, flooding, and heavy rains could bring them to the surface, washing them into communities or even across the border to West German territory. This was a major problem in the Sonneberg-Neustadt region, which was marshy and crisscrossed by overflowing streams. In January 1968, flooding of Steinach Creek dislodged eleven hundred mines and endangered more than twelve acres of inhabited land in Sonneberg County. Residents had to stay put until the East German military began clearing the area a week later. One detonating crawler vehicle became shredded from too many explosions. One tank got snowed in, embarrassingly visible to the West.[97] The shrapnel that flew during the clearings was dangerous; authorities on both sides warned civilians with alarms and megaphones to stay away from the frontier, but still a three-pound hunk of metal managed to fly through the window of Neustadt's Mountain Mill Border Tavern and hit an unsuspecting patron in the right thigh.[98]

Neustadters were "extremely unsettled" by ongoing mine explosions. They worried as their "windowpanes rattled," cows pulled on their chains, and children wandered toward the border during play.[99] Western officials protested and demanded compensation for property destruction. East Germany promised it would no longer mine areas in danger of flooding. But mines still swam their way west. In 1970, a western farmer stepped on one near Fürth am Berg and sustained severe facial injuries; a surgeon was able to save only one of his eyes.[100] Even after West Germany finally convinced East Germany with hard currency credits to remove all the mines, a final round of detonations in 1983–85 caused damage as well.[101] Despite additional clearances in the early 1990s, locals still find mines in the region today.[102]

The border provoked East-West dealings on several fronts, but Neustadters and Sonnebergers themselves had little say in the happenings in their backyards. After 1961, East Germany reversed its tack on promoting cross-border ties between local governments, and there was no meaningful contact between the cities for years.

Neustadt leaders wrote increasingly hostile letters about frontier problems, to which Sonneberg's responded first with generic propaganda and then with nothing at all. A former Sonneberg mayor explained that the "pure dictatorship" left him no choice.[103] Western officials tried approaching their eastern counterparts during personal travel to East Germany, telephoning or dropping in at their offices unannounced, only to be denied access.[104]

Border disputes in the 1960s largely became the province of the military and central offices. The East German regime tried to exploit frontier problems to gain diplomatic recognition, asserting the legitimacy of its "state border" with the West through obstinacy and harassment. Tiny events assumed international significance. Cleaning a frog pond or fighting a prairie fire caused complicated negotiations, as did the simple return of errant pets, livestock, and children.[105] In this proxy skirmishing, East Germany did not trust local authorities to deal directly with westerners. When sewage from Sonneberg, for example, flowed into ten of Neustadt's breeding ponds in May 1964 and killed off all the fish, it took ten hours to get anyone in Sonneberg on the phone. When a fire broke out the same year on the gas line at Burned Bridge, Neustadters had to wait until the next day to talk to eastern repair workers at the border.[106]

The lack of dialogue made for tense military confrontations. At the Double Water Mill in 1967, the East German army tried to move the border fifty meters out, undoing a 1946 agreement between Soviet and American troops (which had been decided in fifteen minutes). Eastern officials informed the thirteen surprised Bavarian occupants that they now resided in East Germany. The West German government got eastern officials to accede to the original boundary within a few months, but East Germany claimed victory by simply provoking East-West negotiations.[107] Soon after, western forces moved back two eastern border markers in Burggrub and Falkenstein that were slightly inside Bavaria (by fifty centimeters and two meters, respectively) with a massive show of force. The deployment of fifty-six BGS personnel, with NATO weapons and light machine guns, six armored vehicles, and a helicopter—flashing blue lights and sirens all around—was a disproportionate response that county leader Edgar Emmert said "terrified" border residents and aggravated relations. Tensions dissipated somewhat after détente in 1972 and the establishment of an East-West Border Commission to oversee larger territorial and logistical disputes.[108] Yet border reports from the seventies and eighties still reveal ongoing day-to-day nonsense over slivers of land. Infractions involved mowing, farmers' paths, wayward livestock, traffic accidents, and model airplanes.[109]

The chief problem in the region, however, was the sewage-laden Röden River, which flowed from Sonneberg to Neustadt. Because Sonneberg, as elsewhere in East Germany, lacked modern disposal infrastructure, its residents had dumped personal waste into the Röden. Also, the city's dairy and slaughterhouse, which supplied more than half a million people, used it as a direct outlet for offal.[110] The river's floating feces bred fungi, rats, and overpowering stenches, especially in the summer. Some days the "cesspool" turned red from animal blood; other days it became "black" and "almost viscous."[111]

The Röden was not the only source of waste coming over the border. A number of regional waterways lost their fish and wildlife from East German pollution. They even turned surprising colors from time to time. Ponds in Wildenheid and Meilschnitz become reddish brown, the stream at Autenhausen light blue, and the Tettau River "milky gray."[112] Springtime flooding of Steinach Creek also brought over an "unimaginable mass of refuse," with "entire mountains" of eastern sardine tins, beer cans, and plastic containers covered in a "layer of slime" that took weeks to clean and damaged "our fields."[113]

Neustadters became increasingly indignant about Sonneberg's waste and pollution. Western anger went beyond disdainful stereotypes of their neighbors as incompetent "Sonneberg sows" to create a sense of western victimization. One name suggestion for Neustadt in the 1960s was "Neustadt on the Stink-Röden," while Children's Festival floats from the seventies and eighties portrayed residents boating in hazmat suits and gas masks.[114] Sonnebergers expressed disgust, too. One annual church "Forest Sermon" took place, provocatively, on the anniversary of the June 17 uprising in 1984 at the Röden's source. It drew 250 people and called for greater environmental action, along with disarmament and travel freedoms.[115]

The Röden River, a symbol of political failure, also became the last diplomatic link between Sonneberg and Neustadt. As residents, farmers, and fisheries demanded compensation for property damage, western leaders tried to engage Sonneberg officials on the problem in different ways, from mailing newspaper clippings to sending Christmas cards.[116] Sonneberg leaders were embarrassed, but their hands were tied. Funding and border concerns had thwarted the construction of a much-promised wastewater treatment plant in Sonneberg in the early sixties.[117] Neustadt built its own purification plants in 1964 and 1974, with state subsidies, as a "bulwark against sewage from the GDR," though these proved insufficient.[118] Finally, Bavarian minister-president Franz Josef Strauss pledged 18 million DM to East Germany in 1983 for a treatment center in Sonneberg.[119] Neustadters rolled their eyes at the payoff (and called the Röden the "Strauss Canal") but were happy something was getting done.[120] At the opening of the plant in 1987, Sonneberg's mayor remembered sitting next to a Neustadt politician, to whom he was distantly related, and how he avoided eye contact and responded to the man's friendly conversation in monosyllables—East German protocol.[121] It was rather fitting that relations between the sister cities were reduced to a stream of sewage.

Much more than a military installation, the Iron Curtain was a dynamic space that shaped, and was shaped by, the lives of those who lived along it. The border's crossers, encounters, and volatile infrastructure reveal just how connected the border was to the borderland. The fortifications evolved with, not apart from, the land and people they divided. Enmeshed in everyday life, the barrier also mediated relationships between residents on either side.

10

Disconnect: East-West Relations

The Iron Curtain came to define contacts between East and West Germans. Allowing for only brief, selective interactions, partition framed public and personal ties for more than a generation. As easterners and westerners sought to overcome their growing separation, they tended to romanticize individual relationships while dissociating from the other culture as a whole. These imagined connections proved elusive, however, and propelled a cycle of alienation that pervades relations even today. Greater contact, ironically, often resulted in greater estrangement.

Border Images and Border Tourism

The Cold War barrier shaped how easterners and westerners saw and talked about each other. A lightning rod of contrasting representations, it spawned border cultures that distanced the other side, entrenching images of an unreachable West versus a captive East. The boundary not only divided people physically but also divided how people in each state regarded those in the other, its atmospherics as central to its legacy as the fortifications themselves.

While some Sonnebergers said they gazed wistfully at the Neustadt Gasworks or Coburg Fortress and imagined a life they would never live, some westerners said they shuddered at the fortifications or Sonneberg's high-rises and imagined a communism they would never want to endure. Without visiting the neighboring city, many locals created their own myths of a "poor East" and "golden West." They also internalized estrangement through the most quotidian of habits. Just as Elisabeth Dietzer stared out her window at Neustadt's Muppberg hill Mountain "with yearning" for twenty-five years, Thomas Friedrich imagined as a child that Sonnebergers "looked different."[1] These private vantage points, in turn, shaped people's public worldviews.

Official language also influenced people's mental maps of the Cold War. Though interviewees laughed off the crude propaganda, Sonnebergers chuckling at how teachers warned them the "class enemy lives in Neustadt," people employed old formulations unconsciously. Easterners and westerners continued to use different idioms when talking about each other. Neustadters would still refer to Sonneberg as the "East Zone" or across the "zonal border," invoking western rhetoric from the 1950s and 1960s that denigrated East Germany's legitimacy as a state.

Public images of the border likewise diverged. While West Germany scrutinized its horrors in newspaper photos, brochures, and coffee table books, East Germany hid its existence. East German travel books, for example, ignored, minimized, and misrepresented the region.[2] Sonneberg's cheerful pamphlets throughout the years never hint that there was anything unusual about the area, let alone that much of it was riddled with electric fencing and booby traps. On the rare occasions the border was portrayed—in state-orchestrated images, articles, and literature—it appears not as a prison wall but as an action zone with sporty soldiers in combat, defending against fascism in the West.[3] While postcards of Neustadt in the 1960s began featuring the barbed wire fences, postcards of Sonneberg turned away from the frontier, no longer showcasing its celebrated southern vistas of Upper Franconia but rather its two clunky socialist sites.[4] When one postcard of the countryside around Burned Bridge somehow made it into circulation in 1970, seeing "strong sales," the Stasi swiftly took action to eradicate it.[5]

A Neustadt postcard of the "zonal border" from the 1960s. Johannes Seifert.

In contrast to East Germany's censorship, West Germany brooded over the Iron Curtain's terrors.[6] Government diagrams overstated the scope of the fortifications, and newspapers chronicled the number of trees felled, smaller plants cleared, and watchtowers built, portraying the frontier as a ghoulish postapocalyptic landscape. Inside this "border of death," where "walls grow, shots crack, and mines explode," there was "nowhere a sign of life."[7] Neustadt's mayors were to alert the media when East Germany began house demolitions or border construction, and the city made several television appearances, featuring the latest escalations and territorial disputes in detail.[8]

Western representations, especially in the wake of 1961, contrasted the evil of the alleged "concentration camp wall" with local virtuousness. Depictions showed people on both sides as helpless victims—with a drawing of a Neustadt teddy bear gazing forlornly through the fence at a Sonneberg doll—or with a photograph of kids watching each other through the barbed wire.[9] Innocent children figured prominently in these images, the more complicated reality of their elders not part of the dominant narrative of "enslavement."[10]

The most famous border incidents involved youths caught in the border. Even decades later, locals animatedly recounted the "true miracle" of two-and-a-half-year-old Sonneberger Dieter Friedrich, who toddled west alone in 1963 through a minefield and four layers of fencing—only ripping his pants and losing a shoe.[11] It was a "Cold War Fairy Tale," proclaimed *Time* magazine.[12] After a Neustadt couple found him on their walk, he returned home by train two days later. Self-congratulatory western articles focused on the teddy bear, packages, and donations Neustadters gave "Peter" (the press got his name wrong). Western generosity was headlined: "Returning with New Shoes to the Zone."[13]

Then again, Neustadters often paid more attention to their own travails as a "doll paradise at the barbed wire" than to those of their neighbors caught on the wrong side of it.[14] Their pain would even be portrayed as more acute. Neustadt poems and articles belabored westerners' "bitter suffering" from the loss of family and home in Sonneberg, while portraying easterners as indifferent to their fates. One asked, "What is the use? The people have grown weary after many gray and monotonous years have passed."[15] Westerners sometimes projected the eerie externality of the Iron Curtain onto its eastern victims, characterizing the enigmatic inner lives of their neighbors.[16] All the while, though, westerners themselves were becoming inured to the border, the gory stories losing their shock value and tragedy becoming a tired trope.

Even as personal passions subsided, both states ratcheted up border propaganda efforts in the 1960s. East and West put up hostile billboards and dispatched thousands of propaganda flyers a month in air balloons (West Germany) and aluminum hand rockets (East Germany). Both sides also orchestrated imposing demonstrations. From opposite vantage points, they followed similar

The cover of a Bavarian borderland magazine in November 1961 features "the German doll paradise at the barbed wire." Stadtarchiv Neustadt bei Coburg.

sequences of scripted outrage, with busloads of westerners disembarking at the border to hear sanctimonious speeches and sing sentimental songs about their unlucky "brothers and sisters" in the East—typically amplified by megaphones and loudspeakers aimed at Sonneberg. Then East German officials would pipe over their own loud speeches and marching music to drown them out, in response to which westerners hurled indignant jeers and insults.[17]

Because early western rallies could turn tendentious, West Germany ultimately forbade demonstrations close to the boundary, and prohibited any assemblages of radical-right or other "extreme" political groups near the frontier.[18] Border theatrics still climaxed in spring showdowns between East and West Germany's rival May 1 and June 17 demonstrations. Sonneberg's May Day spectacle, widely watched and ridiculed by westerners, was moved back from the border after 1961, though Neustadt's commemorations of the June 17, 1953, uprisings in East Germany remained an ongoing source of anxiety. Eastern troops, on highest alert, would keep civilians away from the Protection Strip in mid-June, preventing farmers from going to their fields for an entire week, while sentries kept meticulous records of exactly how many western participants, buses, and cars showed up at border hot spots.[19]

Neustadters' fervor for June 17 demonstrations cooled over the years. Worried about the "slackening" of zeal and "weak involvement," West Germany's Trust for Indivisible Germany (Kuratorium Unteilbares Deutschland) "summoned" local leaders, schools, and organizations to display posters, banners, and flags.[20] But the Trust's heavy-handed exhibitions of "brainwashing in the Soviet zone" and torchlight relay races to a "burning border" of bonfires failed to drum up much enthusiasm.[21] With the rapprochement of *Ostpolitik* in the late sixties, angry Cold War performances increasingly seemed outmoded. By the seventies and eighties, frontier rallies were mostly the province of Christian Democrats and rightist political groups.[22]

After 1968, the city of Neustadt replaced its stilted June 17 demonstrations with a free-form "borderland walk." Promoting a more personal experience of the frontier, trails through the countryside directed participants' focus inward, to the western burden of division. Brochures featured an idyllic drawing of the (western) region surrounded by barbed wire, and urged hikers to "take the time today to let this border through our fatherland affect you."[23] The walks were successful, drawing more than three thousand participants by 1972, and were the largest West German demonstrations on the inter-German border. They also grew festive, offering bratwursts, beer, medals, and local toys for the walkers. Lost neighbors in Sonneberg became somewhat beside the point.[24]

The ceremonies that evoked the strongest emotions, though, were ones that linked division to individual lives. People on both sides best remember the simple things, the quiet gestures of connection that became integrated into private experiences. In Neustadt, the "cozy" wintertime candles in windows, the sending of Christmas packages east, and the lighted Christmas tree atop the Muppberg hill felt more personal—although these, too, were all government initiatives.[25] Homegrown rituals were also meaningful, such as church services in commemoration of loved ones in Sonneberg, or youths' letters launched in balloons at Neustadt's annual children's festival.[26] The ultimate irony of these "emotive" practices, however, was that decrying the horrors of the Iron Curtain rendered it a comfortable familiarity. All the "blazing bonfires, clangorous trumpet choruses, and impulsive speeches" only "bound the border to feelings of home."[27]

West German officials increasingly promoted border tourism. Frontier towns had long marketed themselves as triumphing over adversity, "isolated—but brave," with brochures and magazines juxtaposing the bleak border with gleaming new swimming pools, factories, and apartments.[28] From the late 1950s, Neustadt began hosting more school and cultural groups on the border, with the mayor and other city leaders personally ushering visitors to Burned Bridge.[29] The town was still ambivalent about defining itself by the frontier, its Beautification and Travel Committee unsure whether to mention the border in a 1959 city brochure for fear it might "turn off" visitors.[30] After the construction of the Berlin Wall in 1961, however, town leaders began advertising the Iron Curtain as an "interesting fact."[31]

Neustadt started talks with the Trust for Indivisible Germany in November 1965 to establish an "information center" for border tourists. Part of a nationwide initiative, the move toward museums was conceived as a shift away from confrontational anger with East Germany and toward understanding and reconciliation; border centers were to offer "information instead of polemics."[32] Neustadt's museum was delayed for years because its architects differed over just how nonconfrontational it should be. Local leaders wanted it to be at or near Burned Bridge, but state officials insisted it be at least five hundred meters from the border to avoid eastern incidents or scrutiny. The museum was to be tasteful—"small and nice"—unlike the "border carnival" with kiosks and souvenirs in Berlin.[33] After two and a half years of discussion, Neustadt's modest Information Center opened downtown, over a kilometer from Burned Bridge, at the former Café Teddy Bear.[34]

The diminutive museum still got its point across. Until 1987, its featured documentary compared the Iron Curtain to a "concentration camp wall." While one wall displayed the word "freedom" crossed out by barbed wire, there was no room for information on East Germans or East Germany in the exhibit.[35] Eastern officials regarded the Information Center as a "provocation" and protested its inauguration on June 17, 1968, through twenty-eight megaphones. In response, Bavarian minister-president Alfons Goppel gave his own impromptu speech through loudspeakers at Burned Bridge, to hundreds of assembled westerners.[36] The museum, though, attracted limited interest, and opened a couple of days a week for a few hours at a time. With around ten thousand visitors annually, mainly in prearranged school trips, its attendance over twenty years (1968–88), at 230,000, was equivalent to that of Sonneberg's Toy Museum in just one year.[37]

Certainly border tourism did not take off in the way that Neustadt leaders hoped. Locals were anxious to claim "money flowing into border regions," but travel on the Bavarian boundary continued to lag behind more populous areas of Hesse and Lower Saxony.[38] While West Germany marketed and subsidized border travel from the early 1960s on, overall interest in this form of "disaster tourism" (*Gruseltourismus*) remained low.[39] Only twenty thousand to sixty thousand tourists visited Neustadt's border each year, around half of whom came through BGS and Bavarian Border Police tours.[40] Travelers did not stay very long, with one hundred hotel beds sufficient for four thousand to thirteen thousand overnight stays a year.[41] The border was at best a long day trip or weekend destination.

Yet this macabre landscape maintained a steady niche appeal. In the late sixties, the frontier was "part of a fixed itinerary" in northern Bavaria, with "lines of traffic on holidays" jamming the roads around Neustadt.[42] The city got better at packaging tours of border highlights, shops, and lunch spots.[43] The Mountain Mill Border Tavern was a local "gold mine," its postcards touting an "unparalleled view of the Zone from a beautiful sunny terrace."[44] The clash with communism

Visitors to Burned Bridge in the 1960s. Archiv Klaus Bauer.

Neustadt's Mountain Mill Border Tavern in the 1960s. Stadtarchiv Neustadt bei Coburg.

was perhaps nowhere more apparent than here, as prosperous westerners sipped drinks under shiny commercial umbrellas next to minefields.[45]

The frontier with socialism became a capitalist commodity. Several sites turned themselves into border destinations.[46] Fürth am Berg's Border Inn expanded in the eighties to boast conference rooms, frontier coach rides, and festive pig slaughters followed by dancing.[47] Neustadt politicians raised over 5.5 million DM after 1986 for a modern "Thuringian-Franconian Meeting Hall" to house a revamped border museum, local clubs, and special events.[48] However, Neustadt never got the toilets or viewing platform at Burned Bridge that many wanted, as these additions were deemed too unseemly.[49]

Visitors' experiences of the Iron Curtain could be powerful—or superficial.[50] As busloads of schoolkids and outsiders shuttled to and from Burned Bridge, they often did not absorb the enormity of the border. Tourists rankled Neustadters by posing next to guards and barriers and writing "kitschy," overly sentimental poetry.[51] Visitors' brief comments in the BGS sign-in book convey this dichotomy, their clichéd remorse mingling with the hurried sense that this was not their immediate problem. Travelers from the German-Austrian borderland wrote, "At our border near Lindau, we can go back and forth without difficulty."[52]

Border tourists could also be unruly. They would heckle surly East German soldiers with insults and "Heil Hitlers," vandalize border posts, steal East German emblems, and throw stones and trash over the border.[53] Authorities on both sides warned visitors to conduct themselves better, while East Germany's military and Stasi watched and recorded western movements, from each "contact attempt" ("good morning") to the ages, nationalities, and license plates of visitors. The classic image from this time shows an expressionless eastern soldier and western tourist photographing each other in a silent standoff.[54]

Neustadters became increasingly cynical about how voyeuristic and unproductive frontier visits had become. In the late sixties, Neustadt's Mayor Bergmann, for one, tried to go beyond the "usual barbed wire tourism" to convey the human dimensions of division. He impressed upon travel groups that "the world did not end" at the fortifications, and that real families and neighbors lived beyond them.[55] The grandstanding of the 1950s and 1960s was toned down. Over time, the border featured less prominently in Neustadt's press articles and tourist itineraries, and the city promoted a wider range of events and attractions.[56] This deemphasis also reflected a loss of interest. For most westerners, the border and East Germany were no longer pressing concerns, the travails of their neighbors seeming ever more remote.

By the late sixties, western resignation and detachment replaced antagonism. The Iron Curtain, "as sad as it is, is an 'everyday' part of our lives," wrote one observer.[57] Border rituals assimilated into daily patterns: walking one's dog along the fences, chatting with border guards, reading the clock on Sonneberg's city hall through binoculars. One Neustadter reminisced that she and her friends roller-skated at Burned Bridge because they could be free of adults in the wide-open "play yard."[58] British writer Anthony Bailey portrayed Neustadt's border area as a tranquil site of weekend recreation, wedding celebrations, trim quiet homes, and young lovers seeking privacy. Residents lived there with "'unhesitating acceptance.'" Yet they saw the barrier, and East Germany, as "the edge of the Inferno, That is Hell."[59]

The border defined Neustadt's identity. Sensational incidents entered the canon of local lore, as cautionary tales or heroic legends. Neustadters delineated their history in the progression of fortifications and escape attempts, itemized in newspaper commemorations and local publications. Narratives of the Iron Curtain merged with the narratives of individuals and communities, in homages to the divided "fatherland" or to the suffering of lost brothers and sisters in the East. One woman explained, "The border belonged to my life, to my childhood and to my adult world. . . . it was permanently in my consciousness."[60] The Iron Curtain limited personal contacts to abbreviated visits, packages, and letters.[61] To feel in touch, Neustadters relied on the *Neue Presse*'s nostalgic reminiscences and brief listings of Sonneberg obituaries, birthdays, and anniversaries.[62] The East seemed otherworldly and even "dead" behind the barbed wire, local leaders and elders admonishing the younger generation not to "forget" their neighbors in the East, "people just like you and me."[63]

Burned Bridge in the 1980s. Archiv Klaus Bauer.

In the absence of regular relationships, Neustadters and Sonnebergers objecti-
fied each other. They collected, treasured, and displayed artifacts from the opposite
side, their gifts, postcards, leaflets, memorabilia, and even sugar wrappers serving
as emotional proxies for attachment. Isolated objects and utterances came to represent East and West more broadly. Locals deduced worldviews and ways of life
through the refracted lenses of cameras, binoculars, and television. Discomfort
could run deep at the distortions. Westerner Hedwig Gallert resented having to
"see her homeland through binoculars," while Sonneberger Margit Mertin felt "furious we were being inspected like 'monkeys in a cage.'"[64] All the while, people on
both sides were not fully aware of the estrangement they projected onto each other.

Images of easterners and westerners, filtered through the border, became increasingly depersonalized and one-dimensional. Projections were exaggerated,
then, by profound divergences in life in the two Germanys.

Divergence

Uneven development made for uneven relationships. For most, the growing gap
in the quality of life between East and West loomed largest. Neustadters had
much more freedom of choice than Sonnebergers in career, education, travel,

and residence, as well as broader options in consumption, entertainment, and recreation. Neustadters also enjoyed bigger homes, with cars, refrigerators, washing machines, televisions, and other amenities in far greater numbers.[65]

Sonneberg and Neustadt looked and felt quite different. East Germany saw regime-led change, with people's lives structured by the state in nationalized factories, collective farms, social organizations, and concrete slab housing projects. The tenor of life diverged from that in the West, where society, politics, industry, and daily culture became more fragmented. The landscape itself reflected the contrasts. Whereas state development in Sonneberg concentrated on a couple of massive residential and industrial projects and the rest of the city remained largely unchanged from the 1940s, citizens in Neustadt expanded their homes, businesses, and shops into shifting suburban sprawl.

The cities diverged economically.[66] Neustadt grew and shrank with market forces, the prosperity of its toy and glass industries in the 1950s slowing after the mid-1960s due to labor shortages, high labor and transportation costs, and international competition. One woman recalled, "We had to take even Turks, women from Turkey, because there wasn't anyone else, there was no more unemployment. None at all . . . then people discovered these cheap products from Hong Kong. And once a doll company started in Hong Kong, there was nothing here anymore. All the people were let go."[67] As local toy companies closed or moved operations to Asia, Neustadt became dependent on federal borderland support and the subsidized local Siemens cable plant that, from the late 1960s, employed the majority of Neustadt's workforce. By the 1970s and 1980s, the city had turned into a needy one-company town, hardly a shining model of capitalism on the Iron Curtain.[68]

Sonneberg's trajectory was the inverse: state economic and border policies enhanced the centrality of its toy industry. While the sector had suffered during the fifties from flight west, East Germany decided to reinvigorate it in 1959–60 as a source of hard currency and export growth. Sonneberg was designated the center of "revolutionary" toy restructuring, overseen by Erich Honecker himself, and was allowed to be unusually capitalist, industrialized, and autonomous for the borderland.[69] In 1972, to many Sonnebergers' dismay, East Germany finally placed producers "under control" in conglomerates. VEB Piko was a leading manufacturer of model trains in Europe, and VEB Kombinat Sonni, East Germany's largest toy company, employed ten thousand in Sonneberg.[70] These behemoths dominated Sonneberg's economy in much the same way as Siemens did Neustadt's.

Although the toy industry followed different courses in Neustadt and Sonneberg, locals experienced similar shifts in working life. Both cities moved from traditional independent craftsmanship to modern factory production. "Homeworkers" had been a source of cheap, seasonal labor and, in the 1950s and early 1960s, made up a quarter of Sonneberg's total workforce and over a third of

Neustadt's toy workforce.[71] Entire vocations went extinct as plastic, vinyl, and rubber technologies replaced individual expertise. While Neustadt producers trumpeted the "individualism of home production," international pressures won out. In 1955 the city even produced the first Barbie prototype, conceived of as a racy doll for adult men.[72] Sonneberg toy leaders disdained western dolls that resembled "barmaids," but were themselves under state directives to "transmit" a new modernity of "the new socialist person," embodied in synthetic materials and mechanization. [73]

The demographics of Neustadt and Sonneberg shifted with their toy industries. As production grew less specialized, low-paying, light factory work became the purview of women, who accounted for up to 80 percent of that workforce. A stock image in Sonneberg newspapers and brochures was an assembly line of uniformed women making toys, inspected by men in dark suits.[74] In both cities, female employment was much higher than their states' national averages, yet, commensurate with national trends, half as many women in Neustadt worked outside the home as in Sonneberg (44 percent versus 84 percent in the sixties).[75] This led to vastly different experiences of child rearing and family life. East Germany as a whole had the highest proportion of women in the workforce in the industrialized world, due in part to labor demands after population decline in the 1950s.[76] West Germany likewise saw labor pressures, but it turned to foreign "guest workers" to fill its needs. Neustadt's unemployment rate dropped to under 3 percent in the 1960s, while Neustadt's foreign population grew from 0.2 percent in 1959 to 7.1 percent in 1982.[77] At the same time, young people on both sides continued to leave. Sonneberg and Neustadt's populations declined by 6 and 8 percent, respectively, between 1961 and 1989. Though better off than other places on the border, the cities both shrank and aged—"soon we'll be a nursing home"—into remote, if very dissimilar, backwaters.[78]

Whereas East Germany sought to depopulate, deindustrialize, and demolish frontier towns, West Germany worked to bolster its borderland. In this Zonal Peripheral Area, or *Zonenrandgebiet*, state initiatives ranged from investment grants to tax breaks, freight, and energy subsidies.[79] Federal funds also paid for community harpsichords and the "beautification" of Muppberg's tavern and lookout tower, a "widely visible symbol of the West."[80] Yet state support for the *Zonenrandgebiet*, a belt of land encompassing a fifth of West Germany's area and 12 percent of its population, was too diffuse to truly revitalize Neustadt.[81] The city remained a relative "poorhouse" in "Bavarian Siberia."[82]

Neustadt leaders argued that West Germany should not allow such a "neglected area directly on the Iron Curtain" and were sensitive to comparisons with Sonneberg's development.[83] They kept an eye on Sonneberg's "extraordinarily active construction activity near the zonal border," especially the massive apartment complex at Wolkenrasen, which eventually housed ten thousand residents.[84] Wolkenrasen's dingy reality fell far short of its grandiose designs, but its rising gray apartments could be seen "extremely well" from Neustadt and "strongly impressed" western border tourists. Mayor Bergmann lobbied for Neustadt's own "demonstrational construction program" of high-rises in the mid-1960s to keep up appearances, desiring a "clearly visible location."[85] Like Sonneberg's, Neustadt's eventual "skyline" of "modern facades" contrasted sharply with the rest of the city, which remained underdeveloped relative to cities further inland.[86] To residents, though, these rival, quixotic high-rises on the Iron Curtain symbolized their states' divergent development.

Trips East, Tensions of Détente

While Neustadters and Sonnebergers gazed at each other from afar, it was, ironically, their intermittent encounters through travel that perhaps most enhanced the sense of East-West difference. People could project profound connections with lost brothers and sisters on the other side through letters, phone calls, and western gift packages. Yet actually seeing these relatives was much more awkward, bearing all the pressure of mini ambassadorial missions. Easterners and westerners alike derived—and magnified—mismatched meaning out of their limited contacts.

East Germany severely restricted cross-border travel in the 1960s. In 1967, for instance, Sonneberg allowed around fourteen westerners a month into the Prohibited Zone (including the city of Sonneberg), with five times that number into the sliver of county land outside the zone.[87] Easterners had even less opportunity to go west. Neustadt registered "not a single visitor from the East Zone" in the two years following the 1961 border escalations, compared to the 550 easterners who had come each year before.[88] East Germany eased conditions for traveling west somewhat in November 1964, allowing it in cases of serious family illness or death, and to all pensioners once a year. In reality these relaxations did not go very far, and regime pretexts for denial could be "such crap."[89] One Sonneberger given permission to visit her dying mother in West Germany one year was denied the next, based on the logic that her mother must not have been dying.[90] Border residents found it maddening to see the "other country" every day and not be able to visit, especially since four in five residents of Sonneberg's Prohibited Zone had relatives in the Neustadt region.[91] People openly called East Germany's travel policies "inhumane."[92]

Intense excitement greeted the opening of travel in the 1970s. West German chancellor Willy Brandt's policies of détente and *Ostpolitik*, building upon the foundation of the Moscow Treaty of August 1970, brought mutual recognition and the normalization of relations between the two Germanys in the Basic Treaty of December 1972, as well as agreements for additional checkpoints and more generous visitation allowances.[93] For Neustadt and Sonneberg, the allowance of *kleiner Grenzverkehr*, or "borderland travel," enabled residents of West Germany's fifty-six frontier counties to visit East Germany's fifty-four frontier counties for up to thirty days a year, nine times a quarter—in return for hard currency exchanges.[94] The travel relaxations raised expectations. Border residents envisioned joyous reunions, one float from Neustadt's Children's Festival in 1972 depicting local youths and teddy bears racing to embrace Sonnebergers over the fences.[95] Neustadt leaders lobbied hard to reopen Burned Bridge as one of the new checkpoints. However, East German officials deemed it too populous and opted for the more rural B4 route through Rottenbach instead, necessitating a winding forty-five-kilometer detour from Neustadt to Sonneberg.[96]

Westerners' initial enthusiasm for borderland travel to East Germany wore thin. Neustadters filed sixteen hundred daytrip applications (out of a population of around eighteen thousand) in the first nine months after the Rottenbach checkpoint opening in mid-1973, and Sonneberg saw a thirteenfold increase in western visitors, who arrived in buses that numbered 100 to 130 a week.[97] Yet borderland travel proved smaller than anticipated. Not only did the new rules fail to bring the "expected influx" of westerners, but their low numbers also "stagnated" and "disappointed."[98] In all, the Rottenbach checkpoint saw forty thousand to fifty thousand borderland travelers a year through the late 1970s (around 95 percent of whom were westerners), but that number halved by the early 1980s, even as national totals for West German travel to East Germany continued to rise.[99]

Westerners had a long list of travel complaints. East Germany doubled its minimum currency exchange requirement for borderland travel in November 1973 to 20 DM per person per day, dubbed "Honecker's boundary."[100] This "choked" travel from Neustadt, as did infrequent and inconvenient bus and rail connections.[101] Westerners were also put off by encounters with eastern officialdom, and harrowing checkpoint crossings became legendary—with surly soldiers, mirrors under the car, property confiscations, and full body searches. One Neustadter, who had fled Sonneberg over twenty years before, suffered a heart attack during her son's altercation with eastern authorities over damage to his car seats.[102] Decades later, checkpoint ordeals remain among people's most vivid and emotional memories of the border.

Sonnebergers, too, could be anxious about the cross-border visits. The county had been almost entirely closed off when 87 percent of it had been in the Prohibited Zone from 1961 to 1972, and locals were not accustomed to outsiders in their midst. Sonneberg officials worried about erosion of their authority, as the western "onrush" of tourists clogged traffic, appeared "arrogant and defiant," and threatened the established order.[103] Reportedly, some Sonnebergers resented the westerners, especially since many were former Sonnebergers who had fled. Now they had slick western cars and an overall "haughtiness," with more privileges than law-abiding citizens who had stayed behind. "They only want to show off to us," said one Sonneberger. [104]

The greatest East-West frictions revolved around material differences. While Sonneberg reports have a built-in bias toward negativity, the sheer volume of complaints, corroborated by interviews, suggests tensions from the outset of borderland travel in 1973. For starters, westerners had a lot more money. Since they were required to exchange large sums, they typically spent a great deal of it in Sonneberg shops. Easterners chafed as visitors "bought up our wares," especially luxury items that most locals could not hope to afford, such as silver, porcelain, and glass articles, as well as items in limited supply, such as cured sausage, shoes, and reference books. Some Neustadters also went on day trips to the East expressly for cheap haircuts, cheap lunches, and cheap gas.[105]

Uncomfortable exchanges were self-reinforcing. Neustadters could be "overbearing" in stores and restaurants, leading Sonnebergers to be ungenerous in return, resulting in more "snootiness" on both sides. According to one report, when a westerner cut the line to ask a Sonneberg shopkeeper if she had amber necklaces, she grumbled, "I wouldn't sell them to such people."[106] East-West disparities also affected encounters with youth. Sonneberg children would hang out near parked West German cars and ask for candy or tropical fruit when their owners returned.[107] Allegedly, two Sonneberg teenagers demanded a shirt off the back of one man, and another knocked out a westerner in an attempt to steal his suit.[108] These were the extremes of cross-border travel.

Travel within families was less contentious, as relatives were overjoyed to see one another. But people still had grown apart over the years, and even within the closest families, material differences could create awkwardness. As one westerner described it, "The first hour at their home is a little difficult. To be related without knowing one another is odd. . . . It is a bit embarrassing to play the rich relatives. Or should we have brought more?"[109] Sonnebergers sensed their discomfort. When one woman reminisced about how western relatives "brought such lovely things. Their visits were just one day," her husband interrupted her: "They also didn't want to stay longer. Only to look."[110] People on both sides said all the gifts seemed like compensation for estrangement, with the dynamic of patronage a ready structure for all too complicated human situations.

Material differences also dominated relations because it was difficult to talk about other things. Relatives divided for decades had little in common, and tended to avoid politics or weighty matters. They were trying to get along. Plus there was a sense the walls had ears, as the Stasi tracked western visits, and Sonneberg county employees had to report on their own meetings (though people varnished accounts).[111] Within this awkward interpersonal space, the language of comparison often prevailed. People found plenty to contrast in products, food, shops, pensions, rents, and housing, playing the universal sport of "prices for us and prices for you."[112] Moreover, westerners confronted visible disparities. Sonneberg was even more run-down than other parts of East Germany, having spent the 1960s in the developmental purgatory of the Prohibited Zone. Westerners were shocked that most of the city's hotels, restaurants, and stores were closed, with buildings crumbling and in disrepair: "It was almost surreal."[113] Sonneberg's celebrated Toy Museum remained an exception, but drab streets and frustrating waits at shops and eateries made a more lasting impression, leading to "annoyances and negative discussion."[114]

Western travelers brought tales of Sonneberg's dilapidation back home with them. Exposés of the city's decline appeared in Neustadt newspapers. Next to photographs of sewage in the streets or beloved buildings in "hopeless condition," articles portrayed Sonnebergers as incompetent, their "dead" surroundings "hardly bothering them at all."[115] Neustadters began referring to their kin over the Iron Curtain as "Sonneberg sows," a half-jocular, half-derisive term that is still invoked.[116]

With difference came a sense of distance. One Neustadter reminisced about her trips to Sonneberg as the "Near East."[117] Sonnebergers, uncomfortable being photographed, pitied, and exoticized, believed that even dear relatives came "for a bit of adventure."[118] Neustadt's press featured western explorers braving Sonneberg's alien landscape, fingering foreign wares and sampling strange cafés.[119] Even Neustadt's most well-intentioned representations portrayed Sonneberg as a far-off land, exhorting westerners to make day trips out of a sense of duty to eastern unfortunates "waiting for visits and personal contacts. Every visitor brings a breath of freedom over the border."[120] Westerners increasingly lost interest in East Germany. Relationships wore thin, division became less relevant, and the situation seemed stagnant. Some city elders tried to "preserve the memories" of the "'other' Germans," urging the younger generation to "still look 'over there.'"[121] But Neustadters grew resigned to a separate status quo. Volker Langer, perhaps Neustadt's staunchest advocate for close ties with Sonneberg, said he had accepted it. "The border was part of our lives. We couldn't drive in one direction, but otherwise we lived wonderfully here. We really did!"[122]

Still—beyond the awkward conversations, shallow stereotypes, and complacency—western travel to East Germany held individual, emotional significance. However strained, however limited, Neustadters and Sonnebergers remained touched by their infrequent interactions. Ephemeral memories often grew rosier over time and wound up feeding a sense of imagined connection, of human relationships triumphing over state barriers.

Some contacts did take on a life of their own. Notwithstanding East Germany's attempts to regulate them, personal relations proved impossible to control, snowballing into a multiplicity of unofficial communications that were unforeseen. Due to the lack of hotels in Sonneberg, for example, some easterners rented rooms privately to western visitors. Some exchanged currency and wares illicitly. Other easterners, who lived outside counties designated for borderland travel, illegally rendezvoused with westerners in Sonneberg, or illegally rendezvoused outside designated borderland counties altogether.[123] Party members, too, met up with West Germans in secret, creeping "under the fog of night" to prearranged locales, never their own apartments, for fear of losing their jobs.[124] The scope of cross-border interactions widened from individuals to include community organizations. Sonnebergers and Neustadters launched cultural exchanges through their toy museums, school reunions, ping-pong clubs, and dog breeders' meetings.[125]

Growing contact with the West worried East German officials. Sonneberg authorities complained that westerners were smuggling in pornography and drugs, and that their risqué fashions, music, "rowdy" behavior, and decadent lifestyles posed a "danger" to upstanding easterners.[126] Western men were supposedly seducing Sonneberg women, starting a "sex wave" of prostitution, semiprostitution, and "so-called love affairs." Like other transnational relationships born of unequal privilege, some western men did enjoy the perks of affluence, while some Sonneberg women were maneuvering for a marriage proposal to find a way out.[127] But eastern authorities were cynical about most emigration applications involving marriage, denying women who, "to satisfy their consumer interests," appeared to have gone on a "tramp tour" and ensnared men through "intimate relations."[128]

Western trips to East Germany after the travel relaxations of détente in 1972 had certainly expanded interactions between Neustadters and Sonnebergers. More contact, however, often made for more alienation, as state differences suffused personal ties. The cross-border operations of East Germany's secret police suffused East-West relations as well, more insidiously.

The Stasi in the West

East Germany's Stasi was especially active in the borderland, on both sides of the barrier.[129] Sonneberger Elisabeth Dietzer, familiar with the Stasi's frontier tactics for hiding agents in cars and nearby forests, explained how "it was a small village and people just knew. . . . there were a lot of agents smuggled over by us."[130] In fact, there were two "smuggling" tunnels in the region. Western border guards and civilians got used to noting suspicious packages and missives, as well as people near the border with suitcases or dark cars. After all, Neustadt "mushroom pickers who went to the border strip unusually often could have explosive espionage material on them."[131] For fear of eastern agents, western sentries controlled passersby they did not recognize.[132]

In the 1960s, as in the fifties, the borderland was rife with crossers and mistrust. Western border residents were watchful. One Sonneberg agent got lost in the fog and missed his Stasi contact; when he asked local westerners for a ride, they immediately reported him. The man wound up revealing a handful of other Stasi accomplices in Neustadt.[133] Officials were not always sure which side people were on. Sonnebergers and Neustadters fed interrogators fishy stories, claiming to work for the West, the East, or both, and reported other locals with similarly convoluted resumes.[134] Most suspicious were close networks of Sonnebergers who had moved to Neustadt, especially young men living alone, without family or ties in the West. Western officials, for instance, kept an eye out for "opaque" Gustav Schumacher, who alternated between youth homes and had twice fled and returned to East Germany. Frequently spotted near the border, he claimed to be "casting a look" at Sonneberg out of homesickness, but would mysteriously disappear in the wee hours of the morning.[135]

As it grew harder to cross the fortifications, western authorities became more cautious with people who claimed to have escaped East Germany. The BGS and Border Police interrogated them and retraced their flight routes, looking for footprints, dropped cigarettes, and other corroborating evidence.[136] Crossers who made it over too easily or looked too clean, without ripped clothing, were suspicious, and would be sent for further questioning in Coburg and Nuremberg. Western forces scrutinized defecting East German soldiers the most, to the point where the BGS kept a running tab at a local clothing store and tavern in Coburg to dress and feed them.[137] Of course, soldiers who chose to return to East Germany were suspect for potentially collaborating with western intelligence.[138]

With it being increasingly difficult to smuggle agents over the border, the Stasi focused on finding collaborators already in the West. It targeted Neustadters and former Sonnebergers who frequented public locales, such as bartenders, restaurant and hotel employees, patrons, and journalists. It also targeted locals who had reasons to go near the border regularly, such as forest workers, mailmen, bus and taxi drivers, and frontier property owners.[139] Travel to East Germany especially could leave westerners vulnerable to exploitation of "financial and character weaknesses." Westerners would get caught for minor violations in the East, such as speeding, that could be forgiven upon collaboration with the Stasi. One operative reportedly snapped an incriminating photograph of a married westerner conversing with a "charming lady" at an eastern bar, to be used as blackmail.[140] After the initial recruitment, it sometimes took little to retain agents in the West. One former Sonneberger living in West Germany spied for the Stasi for fourteen years. He showed up for forty handler meetings and forty-five indirect meetings, discussing western forces, checkpoint controls, border demonstrations, and political events for just 150–200 DM each time.[141]

The Stasi also targeted western border forces. While on patrol, East German guards would build rapport with western guards through casual conversations. The eastern sentries would try to fish out "small careless tips" or get western sentries drunk so that they could plant listening devices on the western side or photograph western guards in compromising behavior, such as putting down weapons or crossing the border to chat, in order to pressure them into collaboration.[142] A former BGS guard in Neustadt said his unit swirled with Stasi suspicions: "The other side always knew when we had operations before we knew ourselves." A number of the unit's Stasi files remain curiously unavailable today.[143]

Stasi coverage in the Neustadt region appears to have grown considerably over the years. Whereas Sonneberg's headquarters worried in the 1960s that "there is basically no effective IM network in the western forefield," by 1973 it claimed at least thirty agents. There were three informants covering Burned Bridge, six in Wildenheid, eleven in Neustadt, and ten in Coburg.[144]

Westerners did not know the full extent of Stasi activity in Neustadt but had a selective wariness. They tended to trust one another while remaining suspicious of former easterners, frequent crossers, leftists, and "people with long hair of both genders."[145] People spotted obvious signs of snooping, such as cars and trucks from Warsaw Pact countries near NATO installations. They also denounced suspicious border sightings—such as a toupee-wearing Neustadt shopkeeper (a former easterner) who handed a briefcase to eastern troops at the border.[146] Still, there was a sense that ordinary citizens were unaffected. As in East Germany, Neustadters were surprised to discover after 1989 the true breadth of Stasi activity in the western borderland, raising doubts and accusations among former neighbors and colleagues.[147]

Stasi informants kept thorough records on Neustadt. They tracked local institutions, businesses, politicians, and ordinary residents, from school principals to railroad workers. At least nine Stasi informants spied on local volunteer organizations in the 1980s.[148] Agents watched the border most carefully. They itemized the movement of patrols and tourists to each locale, as well as the varied offerings of Neustadt's border museum and establishments, down to the precise dimensions of the Border Inn Fürth am Berg's "attractive" curtains, cut glass doors, and buffet table.[149]

The western clubs of greatest concern were "homeland" groups of easterners who had fled to the West. Former Sonnebergers living throughout West Germany met up at annual meetings in Neustadt, their "substitute home." They shared reminiscences, ate local dumplings, danced, sang, heard poetry in dialect, and, at the border, literally "spat on" East German territory.[150] The Stasi targeted the rightist German Alpine Association's Sonneberg Section (DAV) as well as the less ideological Sonneberg Homeland Circle, both of which had annual gatherings that by the eighties attracted 150 to 400 participants.[151] The Sonneberg Homeland Circle was particularly active. It published its own newspaper, sent gift packages to Sonnebergers, funded all-expenses-paid vacations for Sonnebergers, and covered the costs of travel for Sonnebergers coming to its yearly meetings. The Stasi debriefed dozens of Sonneberg beneficiaries and sent at least two to five IMs to each major Homeland Circle gathering. There were also allegations that the group's leadership was on the take.[152] Stasi overvigilance became self-defeating, however, because the Homeland Circle became more careful. The organization ratcheted down its political rhetoric, was more selective in issuing invitations to Sonnebergers and did so verbally, and outright forbade some easterners from entering its conference hotel. The group's participation dwindled.

The most subtle form of Stasi infiltration in Neustadt occurred in cross-border families. Sonneberg's Stasi kept tabs on residents who had western relatives, granting travel privileges in exchange for reports on their trips to the West.[153] The price of these trips was often known. One resident shrugged, saying, "Naturally they brought intelligence back with them!"[154] Some Neustadt families accused relatives of being "spies" during their visits.[155]

The gossip, maps, brochures, and newspapers that eastern travelers brought back appear to have been of little operational value. At least "Thomas," Sonneberg's Stasi coordinator for travel from 1968 to 1982, thought so. His reports perpetually complained of travelers' "reticence and reserve" in debriefings. Some offered exhaustive information, such as the inscriptions on banners at the Neustadt Children's Festival; some volunteered for additional assignments in the hope of winning more perks. Yet most of the Sonnebergers summoned to "Thomas'" office claimed to have "forgotten" the details of their journeys or not to have left their relatives' houses, and would be dismissed as "not a good source of information."[156]

The Stasi was pervasive in the borderland, infiltrating western neighborhoods, border forces, clubs, and families. The East German government did its best to manipulate cross-border interactions, but its pervasive controls did not squelch cross-border ties. Relationships between easterners and westerners were distorted in myriad ways by state measures, but they nevertheless endured. Persistent connections underlay imagined connections as well as the erosion of East Germany's border controls in the late 1980s.

Trips West, Border Erosion

Sonnebergers who traveled to Neustadt were often overcome by western prosperity. Even Stasi informants convey breathless impressions of shops and affluence, down to neighborhoods' fresh paint, tidy gardens, and clean streets.[157]
Easterners were often stunned by westerners' freedoms. Greta Geis was incredulous her first time on the western side of Burned Bridge, in 1987: "I was totally
excited that they could get so close to the border; we were only allowed far away,
you know? They could go right up to it."[158] West Germany seemed so incredibly
open. In a thank-you note to her Neustadt aunt and uncle for hosting her "dream
trip to the West," another woman marveled "not only at the department stores,
but also the love of home, hospitality, and personal warmth" she encountered.
"It will remain an unforgettable experience for me. Enjoy the fruits of your labor
and be thankful you are allowed to live here."[159]

Travel west, like travel east, laid bare divergences and made for interpersonal tensions. Interviews and contemporary reports suggest that envy or disdain could taint family relations, with wares and façades bandied back and
forth as symbols of civilizations. Just as Neustadt travelers conflated the unpleasantness of East German checkpoint controls and shabby streets with the
plight of their woebegone relatives, Sonneberg travelers would stare at overflowing store windows and wondered whether everyone in Neustadt had it
easy.

Moreover, people on both sides magnified others' misconceptions. Inge Mulzer, like many Neustadters, laughingly itemized her Sonneberg relatives' false
impressions. Since the main obstacle to goods in East Germany was shortages,
not money, she said, "They thought you could buy everything simply because it
was available," be it a Mercedes or a pot. "They had such funny ideas."[160] Some
Sonnebergers complained their Neustadt relations affected "arrogance," treating
them like "a piece of dirt."[161] Some westerners got "annoyed" by easterners pre-
senting themselves as "beggars from the GDR," who "used" guilt trips to gain
presents and assistance from their western relatives.[162]

But glimpses of the West were often a watershed experience for Sonnebergers, shocked by just how different it was. Jakob Ziegler said western abundance
threw the poverty of his home country into sharper relief, so East Germany's
failings seemed a personal humiliation. Travel west was "depressing" and "embarrassing."[163] Going back home was alienating, too, since "it took a long time to get
used to everyday life here again." As returning easterners showed off their wares
and stories of western "perfection" in Sonneberg, western trips led to "more
unrest and dissatisfaction."[164] Travel offered a vision of an entirely different
world. One woman remembered how "the bright offerings almost took our
breath away. We let ourselves drift along and just looked and looked, enchanted

by each dreamy corner.... We felt a hopeless sadness. And we well knew that in the evening the bus would bring us back to our usual everyday life."[165] This clash of awareness then bred further impetus for change back at home. Some believed the increasing "stream of visitors" to the West directly led to protest in 1989, as "the envy in people's hearts grew into frustration that was later carried by burning candles in their hands," and eventual street demonstrations.[166]

Due to mounting domestic and international pressure, and the promise of additional western bank loans, East Germany relaxed western travel and emigration in the late 1980s, most notably for people below retirement age. These concessions were a "small miracle" for East Germany's 16.7 million citizens, who racked up five million trips to West Germany in 1987.[167] Greater freedoms, however, had the opposite effect from what was intended.[168] Far from releasing tensions, as the regime had hoped, the mobility of younger people aggravated discontent. Going west could make conditions at home seem even worse—and the more people traveled, the more wanted to go. What was once forbidden began to seem like an entitlement. Sonnebergers "increasingly" inundated county offices with travel applications, protesting rejections as "state inhumanity."[169]

Easterners' day trips over the border became a phenomenon in the Neustadt-Sonneberg region. Local eastern travel more than doubled in 1987, with 12,500 easterners visiting Coburg and 2,400 going to Neustadt.[170] The "storm" of Sonnebergers was initially celebrated, but then led to greater frictions.[171] In 1987, westerners grew annoyed as each morning up to 100 to 150 easterners piled onto the "begging bus" from the Rottenbach checkpoint to Coburg, leaving "no space" for western commuters. Despite extra buses at Christmastime, western border police directed eastern visitors off the vehicles to make room.[172] Westerners also resented the "column" of Sonnebergers who queued for 160 DM in "welcome money," long-standing federal, state, and local government payouts to East German visitors that increased in the late 1980s. Day-trippers could enjoy "free Christmas shopping" at Coburg's finest department stores and return home after a few hours "with overflowing bags."[173] The western press played up easterners' material motivations, reporting abuses of the western handouts and fraudulent claims of extra payments. One article estimated that two-thirds were "shopping retirees," and quoted an elderly man quipping, "We wouldn't come if it weren't for the welcome money."[174] Borderland frictions were an extension of misunderstandings in earlier travel between East and West.

Alongside public frictions, however, Neustadters and Sonnebergers cultivated an array of personal contacts, developing individual ties in the face of broader estrangement. There was a burst of cross-border outreach, from pen pals to love affairs to bonsai clubs. Black-market dealings also increased.[175] Borderland leaders sought to forge links between city governments. Official partnership between Neustadt and Sonneberg remained a "utopia," despite both sides lobbying Berlin.

But politicians worked behind the scenes on other initiatives, such as reinstating gas deliveries or organizing western school trips to Sonneberg.[176] Borderland pastors hosted East-West meetings and services. It was "unforgettable" when one Sonneberg pastor assured his western counterpart, "The walls here don't have ears."[177] Some clerics even synchronized their services verbatim during the holidays, churchgoers on both sides "bringing the exact same prayers before God and singing the exact same songs" at the same time, a "profound and invigorating experience."[178]

In many ways, borderland interactions in the late eighties constituted a border opening before the opening of November 1989. They foreshadowed both the elations and frustrations of reunification, the bittersweet mix of intense personal connections and broader disparity. Growing contact with the West also contributed to East Germany's demise. As people demanded greater rights and freedom of movement, transformation became self-propelling, so much so that Germany's *Wende* (change) began before the fall of the Berlin Wall.[179]

The number of people trying to leave East Germany legally, for example, skyrocketed at the end of the 1980s—and eroded bureaucratic authority.[180] Previously, applying to emigrate had been a form of political suicide. Petitions were seldom granted, and applicants faced repercussions for even trying. Disgruntled citizens seized on East Germany's policy relaxations of December 1988, however, and found power in numbers.[181] Applicants became "doggedly intractable, incorrigible, and increasingly aggressive," showing up at state offices "more and more without an appointment."[182] The number of emigration applications in Sonneberg quintupled from around twenty in the late 1970s to well over a hundred by 1988 and 1989, and the number of departures increased ten-fold in East Germany overall, to thirty-four thousand in the first half of 1989.[183] Inundated functionaries wound up granting petitions against the wishes of central offices. But concessions only invited more attempts and, as people met up in apartments, restaurants, and church groups to discuss strategies, emigration emerged as a point of open protest. Thirty-one people occupied Eisfeld's city church to force the issue in September 1988, vacating the premises only after being guaranteed immunity and access to Suhl's district chairman.[184] By late October 1989, county officials were basically granting all emigration applications.

As the East German regime weakened, citizens preyed upon officials' desperation to maintain order.[185] Increasingly, people threatened to file emigration applications or to abstain from voting, acts of bureaucratic insolence, in order to "extort" the apartment, job, or rights they wanted. The strategy worked. Nervous local functionaries met angry demands, fearful of rising petition rates and declining voter turnout (some Sonneberg communities registered 100 percent election returns until the very end).[186] This fed a spiral of appeasement: the more ground the regime ceded, the more people raised the stakes, and won.[187] In December 1988, the Glöckners heralded what was to come by openly demonstrating against bureaucratic injustices in Sonneberg's busy Karl-Marx Street, waving placards for twenty minutes before getting arrested.[188]

The East German government, however, maintained a hard line. The Honecker regime had remained cool to Mikhail Gorbachev's reforms of glasnost and perestroika in the late eighties and, compared to reforms in the Soviet Union and liberalization in other Eastern bloc countries, relatively little changed in East Germany. When Gorbachev abandoned the Brezhnev Doctrine in 1988, allowing states to follow their own "way" in what was subsequently dubbed the "Sinatra Doctrine," noncommunist parties ascended in the governments of Poland and Hungary in 1989. But the East German regime held fast. Honecker's government even praised the Chinese leadership for its massacre of pro-democracy demonstrators in Tiananmen Square.

Dissent in East Germany was significant, especially that expressed under the aegis of the church in activism for peace and environmental reform. Yet internal opposition aimed at reform did not appear to threaten the state's fundamental viability. Once East Germany's external boundaries began crumbling, however, the state was thrown into crisis. Hungary began removing its border fortifications with Austria in May 1989, opening the way for thousands of East Germans to escape west that summer and fall. Thousands more easterners camped out at West German embassies in Prague, Warsaw, and Budapest in the hopes of getting out. There was widespread, emotional media coverage of the exodus. West Germany's *Welt am Sonntag* profiled one of dozens of Sonneberg families that had defected, stressing that although they owned a large house, two cars, and a motorboat, they just "wanted to be free, only free."[189] Mass flight from East Germany provided dramatic footage that all the world could see.

The erosion of state boundaries was followed, on October 7, 1989, by the erosion of state authority during East Germany's hollow celebrations of its fortieth anniversary.[190] In Berlin, crowds greeted Gorbachev with notably more enthusiasm than they did Honecker, some shouting, "Gorby, help us!"[191] As the regime forcibly suppressed and arrested more than a thousand protesters, Gorbachev told the East German leadership that reform was essential. Two days later, when attendees at Leipzig's Monday night service at St. Nicholas Church and demonstration feared violent repression, the Honecker regime unexpectedly allowed seventy thousand people to march peacefully in the streets. The October 9 demonstration in Leipzig was a turning point after which East Germans took ever more public action. Fed up with the "crass contradiction" between the government's empty promises and the grim reality of "everyday life," people turned socialist symbols into ironic signs of opposition, such as wearing Gorbachev emblems in support of reform or singing lines on human rights from "The Internationale."[192] The replacement of Honecker by Egon Krenz on October 18 signaled greater changes to come.

In Sonneberg, organized political opposition began in late October 1989. A demonstration of at least 250 people took place on October 27, citizens' forums met in the following days, and a New Forum opposition group formed on November 8.[193] Sonnebergers also spoke out in church and church groups that provided institutional and ideological backing to popular disaffection.[194] Monday night "prayers for peace" (*Friedensgebete*) and demonstrations, already taking off throughout East Germany, started in Sonneberg on October 30, 1989. Congregants shared their "drive for renewal" on issues ranging from consumer goods to the border regime.[195] Afterward, five thousand people marched from the church holding candles and placards—"for free elections and opposition"—and planted them in front of the county administration building.[196] By the following week, up to fifteen thousand citizens gathered at the church with banners reading, "Down with the SED!"[197] Citizens voiced demands and grievances before local officials, and spoke of their hopes for political reform and civic freedom. Their emotional dialogue was broadcast over ten speakers to crowds outside.[198] Then thousands marched peacefully through Sonneberg's streets.

A "Peace Prayer" for reform in Sonneberg, November 6, 1989. Klaus Dietrich Zeutschel.

Sonneberg demonstrators place candles in front of the county administration building.
Klaus Dietrich Zeutschel.

All of this activism, however, had little effect on the inter-German border. East Germans were taking ever greater risks in 1989, puncturing holes in other regime boundaries through emigration and defecting through Eastern bloc nations. But the East-West frontier, and the Berlin Wall, stayed strong throughout, continuing to see relatively little erosion of discipline and extraordinarily low rates of flight. Attempts increased somewhat, but there remained fewer than 130 escapes over the entire inter-German border in 1988 and 1989.[199] In the district of Suhl, which encompassed Sonneberg, the border was the source of just 19 of 1,107 total defections between January and September 1989.[200] While East Germany was brought down by boundary relaxations elsewhere, the border regime held until the very end. Its power is all the more remarkable given how easily the Iron Curtain ultimately fell—almost as if the emperor had no clothes all along.

Not until the fumbled announcement of new travel regulations on November 9, 1989, did the Iron Curtain collapse in Berlin and, shortly thereafter, on the inter-German boundary. This was due entirely to administrative floundering. The border regime itself was stable and could have held much longer. It was perhaps because people felt the Iron Curtain's inherent sustainability that they seized on the demise of the physical border as marking the end of the East German dictatorship as a whole. That was the central irony: after decades of extraordinary effort to build an impenetrable border, it was legalizing exit that brought down East Germany. The state proved weaker than its border.

But physical division proved weaker than social division. A generation of partition had estranged East and West Germans, reshaping an array of public and personal relationships. At Burned Bridge, the disconnect between easterners and westerners before 1989 produced new disconnects after 1989.

Epilogue: New Divides

Burned Bridge reopened in 1989 to euphoria and mass celebration. Barely a week later, Neustadt leaders considered closing it again, and tensions arose on both sides.[1] How did mass excitement so quickly become mass disappointment? The Iron Curtain was gone, but the way Germany's *Wende*, or "change," unfolded created new divisions between East and West. Changed circumstances changed relationships. Just as, four decades prior, the construction of the border brought swift realignment of identities and everyday practices, so too did its dissolution.

On November 9, 1989, East German Politburo spokesperson Günter Schabowski prematurely announced that relaxations on travel west would take effect "immediately, without delay!" Berliners rushed to checkpoints along the Berlin Wall. The growing crowd at Bornholmer Strasse pressured the guards to open the gate. To everyone's astonishment, officials there decided, without instructions, to do so.[2] As East and West Germans massed at other locations, too, the Berlin Wall fell peacefully, without a single shot fired, to international elation.

It seemed Burned Bridge would soon follow. In Sonneberg, it was "unclear" even to local leaders whether the border zone still held.[3] In Neustadt, people began gathering at Burned Bridge on November 11, shouting for the gate to open.[4] Around a hundred stayed through the night. Some westerners pushed into East German territory, shaking the fence, but were held back by western police. Then, at 4:48 a.m. on November 12, eastern border officials finally opened the gate to "jubilant cries and popping champagne corks," an "unbelievable scene."[5]

There was euphoric celebration at Burned Bridge. More than twenty thousand easterners "surged" across the border that day, welcomed by western crowds' cheers and victory gestures.[6] Strangers embraced; children held handmade signs; volunteers gave out hot tea. People were amazed they shared the same dialect: "They speak just like we do!"[7] Most still recall exactly where they were and what they did when Burned Bridge opened, and cry with joy at the memory.

Burned Bridge opening, November 1989. Stadtarchiv Neustadt bei Coburg.

West Germans greeting East Germans. Stadtarchiv Neustadt bei Coburg.

Celebration spread in the following days and weeks. Incredulous East Germans walked, biked, and drove west, overflowing Neustadt's streets and shops.[8] West Germans set up warming stations and provided hot meals; they offered spontaneous musical performances in the town square as well as free entrance to cultural events. Thousands of Sonnebergers joined in the Monday night "prayers for peace" and candlelight marches, voicing increasingly outspoken opinions.[9]

The border regime collapsed. Not only was "security in border localities no longer guaranteed," but Sonneberg communities organized petitions and protests to unlock checkpoints in ever more locations. Placards read, "Open hearts, open borders!"[10] Each village's gate opening re-created the opening of the wall. Locals from the East and the West came together with tears, food, drink, and music, commemorating the moment of encounter in countless photographs and home videos.[11] There were still perfunctory checkpoint controls at Burned Bridge and elsewhere, but Neustadt and Sonneberg forged ever more linkages. City leaders rushed to build a bicycle path between the cities, as well as to enter discussions for a formal city partnership and roundtable meetings about administration and reform.[12]

The fall of the Iron Curtain was a surreal, fantastic realization of people's dearest dreams. The profoundly emotional event left its mark on Germany and the world. Two decades later, Sonnebergers and Neustadters say it was the happiest moment in German history, in Europe's twentieth century, and in their own lives.

Alongside great hopes, however, the fall of the wall quickly, very quickly, created new tensions between East and West. Differences were especially apparent in the borderland, where two worlds intersected and had to coexist. Just five days after Burned Bridge opened, the western *Coburger Tageblatt* reported that "high spirits" had given way to "daily problems," and that even westerners with eastern relatives "barricaded themselves and hoped their visitors would leave."[13] Western border residents publicly complained about disruptive Sonneberg crowds and the polluting "stink bombs" of East German cars, or Trabis. The eastern influx was violating western environmental laws, traffic laws, store hour laws, and labor laws.[14] By the time 150 easterners demonstrated at the border to create a new checkpoint in Heubisch, shouting, "Open it!" one Neustadter said his son yelled, "Leave it!" "It would have been better that way . . . they are true Russians."[15] Actually, some Neustadt city councilors did try to close Burned Bridge. After eight days of togetherness, they reasoned, westerners' "aversion" to the throngs of eager easterners was "already apparent," and it was necessary to reroute the "danger" of their Trabi traffic around the city.[16]

While long romanticized visions of a generous West aiding a grateful East reached their climax with the fall of the wall, these mutual idealizations dissolved in the immediate aftermath. Neustadters were surprised that Sonnebergers were not behaving like freed prisoners. Few fled. The region had expected thousands of refugees, but of the 700,000 easterners who crossed there in the first few weeks, only 310, or 0.5 percent, stayed in the West.[17] Civic opposition in Sonneberg also appeared weak. Attendance at peace prayers for reform dwindled from around fifteen thousand on November 6 to twenty-five hundred a couple of weeks later, with people "skeptical" about the New Forum.[18] Some Sonne-bergers were even skeptical about the border opening and did not visit the West for several months. A few feared also the loss of their 15 percent border bonus, demanding and striking for compensation.[19]

Western articles increasingly portrayed easterners not as liberated captives but as materialistic tourists. The fall of the Iron Curtain went from being about freedom to being about free spending. A major focus of reporting was the federal government's bestowal of 100 DM per East German visitor as "welcome money." Newspapers ran photos of long lines at disbursement points and updates on ex-actly how much was given out. Neustadt registered 212,894 recipients between November 12 and December 31 1989.[20] There were exhaustive lists of how east-erners spent the cash, itemizing fruits and vegetables, cosmetics, deodorants, tampons, jeans, Walkmans, and clock radios.[21] The West was portrayed as a "shopping paradise."[22] Also, East Germans' lack of sophistication bemused west-erners. Reportedly, easterners kept plastic bags as souvenirs and did not know how to eat bananas properly; they gaped with "disbelieving stares" in their "con-sumer confusion," entranced by the "glittering world" of western products, and one woman in a store aisle simply burst into tears.[23]

Many Sonnebergers remembered the border opening as a bewildering time, describing the simultaneous "euphoria and shame" of their journeys into a dif-ferent world.[24] It was a "shock" that the West was so much better off; the contrast "was really painful" and "embarrassing."[25] It was also "depressing, shattering" to realize that easterners had invested their lives in a failed system.[26] Out of "humil-iation," some people said, they stopped crossing—"to me it felt too stupid, shop-ping in the West as a beggar."[27]

It did not help that westerners portrayed them as beggars. Articles stressed western charity, "helpfulness without limits" on the "front" at Burned Bridge, as well as sacrifices in staffing welcome-money offices, in opening shops on Sundays, and in tolerating store lines, jammed buses, full parking lots, and increased litter.[28] Reports also stressed rumors of easterners' abuses, claiming that they "used every trick" to get extra welcome money, work illegally, smuggle goods, or falsely claim refugee benefits.[29] There were also "horror stories" of "guests with sticky fingers" crossing to steal. Despite low rates of recorded theft (sixteen incidents among Coburg's 120,000 eastern weekend visitors), depart-ment stores were on "high alert."[30]

Neustadters soon began shutting down the welcome wagon. Two weeks after Burned Bridge opened, the city stopped providing welcome money and closed local shops on weekends, an impediment for East Germans who worked during the week.[31] Some westerners took advantage of visitors, raising store prices, striking shady deals, or buying up easterners' antiques and family heirlooms for a song.[32] There was also growing antipathy toward the continued crowds, as more than twenty thousand people crossed Burned Bridge every day.[33] When too many Sonnebergers swam at Neustadt's indoor pool, making it difficult to do laps, the town raised prices and reduced access times for them.[34] Still, the narrative of eastern gratitude was set. To great fanfare, the city of Sonneberg staged a variety show in Neustadt called *Sonneberg Says Thank You.*[35]

For many East Germans, this was an embarrassing dynamic. A week after the border opened, one woman apologized in the western *Coburger Tageblatt* for easterners' long lines and Trabi "stink clouds," thanking westerners for their patience with the "trouble."[36] Sonnebergers also admonished each other to be better behaved in the West. In *Freies Wort* and at peace prayers, easterners cautioned against appearing "undignified," as "needy," or as "beggars"; some worried they were "annoying" westerners, "just like the Poles annoyed us."[37]

Humiliation was compounded by westerners' adventuring in the East. Notwithstanding a preponderance of genuinely joyous encounters between Neustadters and Sonnebergers over the winter of 1989–90, some westerners strutted down eastern streets, "openly swearing about the stench" and how "dreary, gray, and filthy" things were.[38] Some filmed and photographed Sonnebergers' strange ways and strange stores, "dying with laughter"—"like we were in the Third World."[39] When Sonnebergers chose to stay home, watching from behind their curtains, this was filmed, too.[40] Western public images even portrayed easterners as not quite human. Newspaper exposes of Sonneberg's border zone likened it to a "science fiction film," ridden with "lagoons" of trash and feces, where border residents were awakening from a "deep sleep" and "seemed to feel a little uneasy (like animals in a zoo)."[41]

A colonial dynamic, emerging throughout East Germany, appeared quickly in the borderland. Neustadt men bragged about playing a "pasha role" in the East, "living like kings" and drinking and eating out for pennies.[42] They enjoyed the Sonneberg discos that sprouted up, as well as the fabled sexual freedom of eastern women.[43] People still snigger about all the men who divorced their staid western wives for new Sonneberg brides. Westerners seemed to be "greedy" and "buying up everything."[44] By early 1990, Sonnebergers complained that they crossed the border to shop, abusing low prices and exchange rates to purchase twenty bags of sugar or one hundred lightbulbs at a time, depleting borderland stores; they cut in line and treated East Germans like "third-class citizens" in their own country.[45]

The estrangement from one's own home and one's own life was perhaps what hurt most of all. For easterners, the fall of the Iron Curtain meant the fall of the familiar, plus massive uncertainty. It was unclear whether the two Germanys would reunify, and whether their Cold War patrons would allow it. While West German chancellor Helmut Kohl advocated confederation, the Two Plus Four Talks from May to September 1990 opened the question to the Soviet Union, the United States, Britain, and France. Leaders Mikhail Gorbachev, George Bush, Margaret Thatcher, and François Mitterrand had differing opinions.[46] In Sonneberg, it was a confusing, chaotic, "lawless," and "difficult" time.[47] County and city governments were in disarray; new political organizations were taking shape; accusations and insults swirled; household security was uncertain; petty crime increased; street names were changed; everyday language lost, and gained, words and expressions.[48] There was great excitement as well as "great fear about the future."[49] One woman shook her head, saying it was "completely mind-boggling."[50]

Hidden aspects of the East German regime became increasingly visible. Suddenly Sonnebergers could visit border zone villages they had never seen before, whose names they did not know. They could see the border fortifications up close, stunned at how elaborate they had been. They photographed, posed before, and mocked the watchtowers and electric fences, pilfering and vandalizing border installations.[51]

As East Germans demanded transparency and access to Stasi files, regime crimes made headlines and wrought nationwide controversy over adjudication.[52] The exposure of Stasi informants—public figures, neighbors, coworkers, and loved ones—rocked communities and individual lives for years.[53] People whispered the names of those who they believed had watched them, or who they worried continued to watch them. Some chose not to see their Stasi files because they did not want to know. Some who could not locate their Stasi files suspected they had been destroyed. Others who photocopied theirs still tear up as they read them. One woman sends postcards to her denouncers every year on the anniversary of her deportation in 1961: "Hello informer . . . because of your unconscionable action we were expelled from our homeland. Have a happy October 3!"[54] The traumas of the past are far from past.

Sonnebergers came forward to share stories of their victimization by the regime, gathering courage to discuss events long stigmatized and unmentionable. In haunting conversations and newspaper articles, Sonnebergers recounted "inhuman," Kafkaesque sagas of imprisonment and persecution, with minute details remembered, told, and retold.[55] Many continued to have difficulty. Twenty years later, one woman was embarrassed to see a therapist about her memories. At the same time, a certain politics of suffering emerged, in which victimization was seen to confer virtue. A few complained that people were brandishing their Stasi files as though they had been morally superior resisters. Even former high-ranking officials portrayed themselves as victims of pure dictatorship.[56] Battles waged over who should be allowed to continue in public office and public life, as well as over the trials of former border authorities.[57] When the major formerly in charge of Sonneberg's border troops showed up with flowers at the unveiling of a commemorative plaque for the city's deportees in 2001, one attendee yelled before the crowd of two hundred, "Go away, go away!" And he did.[58] No one was neutral about the past. Whatever one's position in East Germany, its history elicited strong emotions.

During the *Wende*, the rush to repudiate the East German regime brought with it a rush to reform everything at once. Nationally and locally, an explosion of proposals abounded involving politics, government, business, pollution, roads, housing, public buildings, sewage systems, trash collecting, consumer goods, swimming pool hygiene, and playground renovation.[59] "All of life" was to change, with West Germans "providing the know-how."[60] On March 18, 1990, East Germans voted in favor of Chancellor Helmut Kohl's plans for extending the West German deutsche mark and swift unification. Kohl's promises of capitalist "blossoming landscapes" in "new federal states" appealed more than a potential "third way" of reforming democratic socialism in a separate East German nation. So when East and West Germany officially reunified on October 3, 1990, it marked not a merger of two systems but rather the absorption of the East into the existing Federal Republic.

As "liberators" or as "colonizers"—depending upon the perspective— westerners headed East to advise and supervise the integration. At Burned Bridge, Neustadters became enmeshed in Sonneberg's daily functioning.[61] There was mutual coordination, cultural exchange, and sociability in organizations such as SonNec or "Peace in Microcosm," or in individual initiatives such as stamp clubs or volunteer church renovation.[62] There was patronage, too. To great publicity, Neustadt's city government gave Sonneberg's a photocopier, two desk calculators, a used telephone system, library books, and other goods worth 19,526 DM.[63] From politics to businesses to schools, westerners lectured and led. Not only did Neustadt police instruct Sonneberg police on how to write police reports, with one Neustadter eventually heading the eastern office, but some Sonnebergers even appealed to Neustadt authorities to adjudicate their arrests in Sonneberg.[64]

The fall of the Iron Curtain seemed proof that West Germans had been doing things better for forty years. It "really hurt," said one Sonneberger.[65] As the "two worlds collided," it was hard to "deal with" the other side because everyday practices were so foreign.[66] Many felt that easterners and westerners were even distinct peoples. They seemed to look different—in clothes, hairstyles, and even body postures—and to have different characters, ways of speaking, and modes of thinking.[67] Among easterners, "self-image suffered. One assumed that the people were cleverer than you with your experiences. . . . One abased oneself"; it was embarrassing, even "devastating," to realize you had been "completely satisfied" living in "a cage."[68] The intensity of many East Germans' experiences gave rise to elaborate (western) psychological theorizing, ranging from "emotional liberation" to "posttraumatic embitterment disorder."[69] However, East Germans'

reactions speak not to pathology but to the hugeness of the *Wende*'s dislocations. One Sonneberger sighed at her childhood vision of "unity" as a hero in
physical form. Her father had said that when unity came they could go West and
reconnect with lost relatives, so she thought one day Unity would simply knock
on the door and escort them to East-West harmony.[70] How devastating the
reality was.

Many had hoped that once the yoke of communism was lifted, Germans'
inherent affinities as "one *Volk*" would naturally come forth. But the realities of
living together dashed mutual fantasies of togetherness. The West was neither as
golden nor as charitable as many easterners had imagined, and the East was neither as enthusiastic nor as thankful as many westerners had expected. In time,
daily frictions expanded into broad resentments. Sonnebergers and Neustadters
demonized in each other the very same qualities they had previously romanticized. Stereotypes were inverted. The prosperity of *Wessis*, westerners, was
derided as a materialistic and selfish "elbow society," and the resilience of *Ossis*,
easterners, was scorned as passivity and laziness. Each asserted greater virtue.
Westerners claimed they were more capable because their material conditions
were better, whereas easterners claimed they were more capable because their
material conditions were worse; they had made "bonbons out of shit."[71] Images
of the other became worse after the border fell, and these inversions created a
different German divide.

This "wall in the head" found expression in new border practices. In Sonneberg, some no-longer-victimized border residents staged a nostalgic "Prohibited
Zone Party" with faux security controls and uniformed border troops.[72] In Neustadt, some no-longer-generous westerners refused to shop in Sonneberg stores.
The cities reversed their views over the fate of the barrier itself. Whereas Neustadt leaders who had decried it for decades wanted to preserve a section as a
museum, Sonneberg leaders who had upheld it for decades wanted it all gone.[73]
There were inversions of wealth, too, overturning previously "clear relationships." For example, when currency union proved a windfall for Sonnebergers
who had saved their 15 percent border zone bonuses, Neustadters grumbled
that people who had sustained the Iron Curtain were now driving around in
"huge Mercedes."[74] Not that they preferred eastern cars. To close Burned Bridge
to the eastern "invasion of Trabis," 30 percent of Neustadt voters signed a citizens' petition to "get through-traffic out of Neustadt" in 1990.[75] One sign in their
poster campaign fumed:

> From two-stroke engine exhaust and stench
> since '89 I've had to retch.
> I've had enough of this air like rot,
> and I want it out of downtown Neustadt.[76]

Federal policies exacerbated tensions. By law, easterners received lower salaries but greater development subsidies than westerners, with contrasts and consternations especially pronounced in the borderland. As thousands of Sonneberg workers commuted west, just across the border, and a number of western business relocated east, just across the border, Sonneberg came to see lower unemployment and greater growth than Neustadt.[77] Meanwhile, both cities lost their primary employers. Siemens closed after the end of Neustadt's federal Zonal Peripheral Area subventions, and Sonni closed after Germany's Treuhand restructuring of eastern state-owned enterprises.

As elsewhere in Germany, easterners experienced profound changes in social, professional, and economic status, while westerners perceived ingratitude and a loss of former wealth and income. Each side felt it lost under reunification. Bitterness over unequal policies as well as economic dislocations infused daily grumbles and deeper worries. Sonnebergers mourn the decimation of their toy and crafts industry, the source of city fame, and Neustadters fear that Sonneberg is regaining its pre-1945 dominance, with Neustadt its "lesser suburb."[78]

Although locals did not devise the laws that divided them, they became increasingly invested in their cities' economic competition. The fate of Burned Bridge, once cleared of border fortifications, was particularly controversial. Beginning in 1991, Neustadt initiated legal proceedings against Sonneberg's unilateral plans to build a massive shopping complex there, claiming the eastern city was flouting "the rules of democracy"; Sonneberg leaders saw the "construction embargo" as "an effrontery."[79] Each town then built its own mall on Burned Bridge. Sonneberg's proved larger and more successful, but Neustadt won the contest for a McDonald's on its side. In the early 2000s, plans for a joint recreational center and swimming pool came to naught. City officials, facing different state and federal incentives, could not reach agreement. Today people still grow emotional as they retell details of these municipal conflicts and allocate blame to the opposite town. Stereotypes of each other's mayors are personal and unflattering.

Frictions expanded in numerous areas of life. Development projects, clubs, and organizations between the cities collapsed for lack of "trust."[80] Many tensions stemmed directly from state policies. Due to lower housing costs in Bavaria than in Thuringia, for example, hundreds of Sonnebergers moved to Neustadt. Because of different Bavarian and Thuringian education guidelines, the caliber of the cities' schools and which school a child could attend became hot-button issues.[81] Differences affected core identities. In Neustadt, several people with German heritage said they felt more affinity with the city's Turkish community (around 7 percent of the population) than with Sonnebergers. Meanwhile, in Sonneberg, home before 1989 to just seventeen international workers from Vietnam, several people said they did not feel comfortable with their new multicultural society at all.[82] Among many Sonnebergers, the sense of *Ostalgie*, or nostalgia for East Germany, was palpable.[83]

Sonnebergers and Neustadters seemed readier to posit a yawning gulf between East and West *after* reunification, often speaking as if the differences between them were insurmountable. In a 2003 survey, the stereotyping labels of *Ossi* and *Wessi* still had currency.[84] Of 259 respondents, 53 percent of former East Germans and 46 percent of former West Germans agreed that they "saw themselves" as *Ossis* and *Wessis*, with just one-third rejecting these categories. While easterners identified with the label more deeply, westerners consistently admitted to greater prejudice. Only 59 percent of former westerners said they would be "fine" with their children marrying someone whose family was from the opposite side, compared to 81 percent of former easterners—as though the categories of *Ossi* and *Wessi* were heritable ethnicities. Around half of all respondents from both sides stated that easterners and westerners were simply "different types of people."[85]

At the same time, survey respondents conceded that they themselves could have been different had they lived on the other side. More than three-quarters said that "people adapt to the system in which they live," implying that differences were constructed, rather than fundamental. Furthermore, respondents were in complete agreement about how quickly division happened and how impermanent it was. The majority said Neustadters and Sonnebergers were "similar" before 1945, became progressively "dissimilar" between 1945 and 1989, and would converge again within a generation, albeit more slowly than they had come apart.[86] This sense of contingency, though, did not mitigate the raw animus that many still felt.

This sense of contingency did not mitigate divergent political opinions, either. Former westerners judged the East German regime quite harshly, ranking it on par with the Third Reich, while former easterners were far more critical of the Federal Republic and the course of reunification.[87] Respondents also assessed the Iron Curtain differently. Former easterners tended to see the border as a product of superpower politics. They blamed the United States, the Soviet Union, West Germany, and East Germany alike, and downplayed local actions, 90 percent saying Sonnebergers bore "no responsibility at all." Former westerners blamed the border squarely on the East, the East German government, the Soviet Union, and to some extent Sonnebergers themselves.[88] A quarter of former East Germans stated the border was at least somewhat "justified," as opposed to only 9 percent of former West Germans.

Ironically, Sonnebergers and Neustadters appeared most at odds when the border was open and felt closest when it was closed. During partial partition (1945–52) and reunification (post-1990), a permeable boundary allowed disparate infrastructures to clash, fueling oppositional interests and animosities. During severance (1952–89), limited contact enhanced rosy fantasies of generous, bighearted westerners and virtuous, grateful easterners, leading to underestimation of differences between the two sides.

The tensions that underlay division were exacerbated, and transformed, by the way the *Wende* unfolded, which was especially tumultuous in Berlin and the borderland. Although many feel it "astonishing that a certain border in the head still exists" and believe it will "die out in the next generation," such sentiments presuppose that the rifts of today stem mostly from the experiences of yesterday.[89] But Germany's current mental divide is not the same as that of 1989. Policies and dislocations since reunification created their own frictions.

While East-West resentments are attenuating in many places in Germany, they can still run strong. At Burned Bridge, they are apparent even among youths who have no recollection of life before 1989. In one 2005 survey, Neustadt and Sonneberg teenagers voiced stereotypes of "arrogant" westerners and "dumb" easterners that were just as vituperative, if not more so, than those held by their elders.[90] Only four of fifty-four Neustadt adolescents said they would be willing to take a job in Sonneberg. More Sonnebergers said they would work in Neustadt for its higher pay and greater perks; however, thirty-eight of the fifty-five Sonnebergers refused, reportedly "because of the Turks and foreigners." Perhaps most telling, only 35 percent of all the teenagers said they would readily date someone from the opposite side.[91]

As people of all ages can project intractable differences between former easterners and westerners—and between the *children* of former easterners and westerners—contingent and material frictions are often seen as immutable cultural distinctions. Yet the current animus says less about Germany's forty years of division than about Germany's course of reunification. More so than is commonly believed, the problems of today have to do with the problems of today.

Put another way: the long-distance romance of division culminated in the hopeful elopement of East and West Germans after the fall of the Iron Curtain. Their rocky honeymoon, however, created a new pattern of conflict that became a template for the rest of the marriage. Disappointment and anger went beyond preexisting differences, though these feelings were often attributed to those preexisting differences. The emotional whiplash of the *Wende*, with its mutual hurt and alienation, made for ongoing aftershock.

In November 2009, the world commemorated the twentieth anniversary of the fall of the Iron Curtain. From Berlin to American college campuses, excited crowds gathered to celebrate with speeches and symbolic wall demolitions. Yet the anniversary was muted at Burned Bridge. Sonneberg and Neustadt each hosted their own, limited events. Both town halls held photograph exhibits, with sparsely attended openings that drew just a handful of people from the other city. Scattered concerts, church services, and tributes by individual associations attracted somewhat more.[92] The towns' main events occurred apart. In contrast to the tenth anniversary in 1999, when Neustadt and Sonneberg had jointly hosted a celebration at Burned Bridge, Neustadt held a simple church service with former Bavarian minister-president Günther Beckstein that received little advance notice or publicity, and Sonneberg held a ticketed, opulent gala that Neustadt's mayor elected not to attend. Many locals expressed surprise that there was not more happening and more in common.

Instead, a number of people marked the twentieth anniversary of the border opening by themselves, at home or with a walk along the former boundary in the rain. They felt their intensely individual, emotional experiences of the Iron Curtain and its fall were best honored in private remembrances. It seemed unbelievable that two decades had passed. One Neustadter said that he could not get the border "out of his head at all."[93] One Sonneberger shuddered to note that twenty years had gone by as though it had been "nothing—and what is there to show for it?"[94] Locals still focused on East-West frictions, clipping newspaper articles about the latest insults from the other city. In people's long lists of grievances, what stood out most was the profound emotion behind their disappointments, and their desire to talk and talk and talk about them. Former easterners and westerners still cared deeply about their relationship. They had not let go of their shared history, nor of each other. Past politics was profoundly personal.

The popular understanding of severance—a belief in early unity versus a now unbridgeable gap between East and West Germans—posits that societies are slow to change and underestimates the magnitude of short-term shifts. Events at Burned Bridge, however, suggest that people adjusted their allegiances rather quickly. East-West divisions emerged in the tumult of the early postwar period, and new East-West divisions emerged in the tumult of the *Wende*. The dynamic of difference was, and is, far more interactive than Neustadters and Sonnebergers today would like to believe. Many hold to a vision of citizens without agency and a wall without foundations.

How did a line on the ground become a "wall in the head"? A perceptual barrier between East and West is still felt today, more than two decades after the end of communism in eastern Europe. In the turbulent aftermath of National Socialism and World War II, the mental boundary between the two Germanys evolved surprisingly quickly and proved remarkably powerful, not just reflecting the growth of the physical border but propelling it. At Burned Bridge, the Iron Curtain was not a static periphery of two dissociated states but a troubled contact zone through the geographical and symbolic heart of a nation that was central to Europe's Cold War.[95]

Winston Churchill had famously envisioned an iron curtain already "descended" across Europe in 1946. Yet an iron barrier between the two

Germanys was not a fait accompli, nor a product of cold, static detachment. Rather, it was forged in a crucible of protracted postwar confusion. As the victors of World War II clashed for years over Germany's fate, the border became a by-product of their differences. Austria and Korea likewise were partitioned into Soviet and western zones at the end of World War II, but the strategic position of each, as well as the willingness of national leaders to unify, led to opposite results. Austria peaceably reunified in 1955, whereas Korea saw war, division, and the most fortified border in the world in the demilitarized zone (DMZ).[96] Germany charted a path between these two extremes, reflected in the evolving forms of its divide.

Indeed, the inter-German border changed dramatically over time. For the East, it transformed from an outlet for excess population in the late 1940s into an instrument of propaganda and assertion of state legitimacy. Over time, it became a site of social engineering, surveillance, and, finally, one of the longest demographic controls on earth. For the West, the border progressed in the 1940s and 1950s from a postwar security measure to a barrier against smuggling and immigration and then to a bulwark against communist infiltration and a politically advantageous symbol of totalitarian oppression; by the 1970s and 1980s, it had become an unfortunate but accepted geopolitical arrangement.

The border's variability underscores the Cold War as a time of transition and undercuts any easy picture of it as a frozen standoff between bipolar blocs. Its history adds to a growing body of scholarship that sees the period 1945–89 not as the dawning of a bright new era on the western side of the continent but as an unsettling aftershock to the butchery of the first half of the century that encompassed all of Europe. Peaceable postnational cooperation, far from arising straightforwardly, took a darker journey through the postwar period, in which reforms and institutions developed as anxious safeguards against continued bloodshed.[97]

The Iron Curtain between East and West may have evolved as one such safeguard. While Cold War powers clashed violently around the globe, in Europe a continental barrier cordoned off spheres of influence, perhaps redirecting economic, political, demographic, and military tensions that could have led to greater violence into one colossal barricade instead—channeling war into a wall. The Iron Curtain was brutal, but it was less ferocious than the Armageddon that preceded it. As nuclear weapons tempered decision making, and as Germany became the lightning rod for superpower conflict, the Cold War stabilized postwar antagonisms in Europe; hot wars were waged elsewhere. Yet the continent itself underwent the most pivotal transformation in its history, toward the elimination of war: a shift from states built around war to states built around peace.[98] Arguably, the Iron Curtain was a way of managing conflict, one that played a central role in Europe's transition from militarism to pacifism. In this light, the

Cold War, with its iron borders, appears as something truly *post*war, securing the end of all-out warfare in Europe.

Of course, walls create their own problems. They are nothing new, from the Great Wall of China to Hadrian's Wall, the Maginot Line, and walled cities around the world. Barriers tend to enlarge during a crisis. Concrete answers to instability, they are symbols of government authority and bulwarks against security threats. As a modernizing Europe increasingly organized around distinct territories, states' imperative for spatial control expanded.[99] The drawing and redrawing of borders was central to peace settlements among great powers and to imperial command around the globe. According to one nineteenth-century British demarcation commissioner in West Africa, "It is a question if a wrong line is not better than no line."[100] Then, in the context of twentieth-century decolonization and conflict, the strategy of "divide and rule" became one of "divide and quit" in the convulsive partitions of Ireland, India, Palestine, and Cyprus.[101] Cold War partitions of Korea and Vietnam at the thirty-eighth and seventeenth parallels, also attempts at containment, likewise saw massive insecurity and violence.

Germany's Iron Curtain shared features with these other demarcations, partitions, and walls. A product of great-power treaties and military insecurity, it at first looked like other "unruly borderlands."[102] Smuggling, illegal crossing, and violence prevailed, with frontier residents subverting and appropriating border measures. Germany's divide then came to resemble other national partitions. Intended to contain domestic and international tensions, it led instead to the migration of millions and to lasting frictions, though with considerably less violence than in other cases.[103] Its mechanization also had international counterparts, most notably in Soviet and Soviet bloc borders, and in Korea's DMZ.[104]

What made Germany's Iron Curtain so distinctive was the visibility of its human costs. Divided communities, from Berlin to Burned Bridge, transformed rapidly from "integrated," cohesive borderlands into "alienated," bifurcated borderlands.[105] Most of all, the entire world could see that East Germany directed the bulk of its fortifications not outward, at armies, but inward, at individual citizens. This bid for barricaded demographic control is perhaps the Iron Curtain's most significant legacy—and signifies a development in global relations.

Since the fall of the Berlin Wall, walls have proliferated around the world. Most are meant to keep people out, not in, but likewise serve as instruments of social engineering, less about protecting against militaries than about restraining the movement of problematic people.[106] Contrary to the promises of globalization enthusiasts, the flow of individuals, communication, and information has made many borders starker than ever, since people deemed economic, cultural, or security threats have become more mobile.[107] The larger the perceived threats, the tougher the border controls.

Tellingly, today's metal and concrete installations look a lot like the Iron Curtain. These walls symbolize state power, but their existence reveals a central paradox. Even as they appear to affirm a state's sovereignty and control, they are themselves evidence of its weakness.[108] Within state aims to monopolize movement, barriers expose state failures to manage by other means the people they are intended to restrain.[109] The extreme disproportion between walls' hulking physicality and the mobility of individual crossings is further testament to state desperation.[110]

A "wall around the West" is growing stronger.[111] The countries of the European Union and the United States, in addition to controls inland, use separation barriers against their poorer neighbors to reduce smuggling and immigration. While the European Union dissolved internal border restrictions in the Schengen Agreement, it is hardening external boundaries. A "new Iron Curtain" stands on its eastern boundary with Russia, Belarus, and Ukraine.[112] Measures at Ceuta and Melilla in the south are even firmer. Double rows of metal fencing—up to six meters high, topped with razor wire, and reinforced with watchtowers, infrared cameras, and motion sensors—keep Africa out of Europe.[113] The United States' border with Mexico has also toughened. Increased Mexican migration after passage of the North American Free Trade Agreement (NAFTA) met with ever stronger walls, patrols, technologies, and rhetoric.[114] Now, online streaming video from the border allows Americans inland to report crossers from their home computers.[115] More than four thousand people have died from dehydration, exposure, drowning, and violence as they tried to cross the U.S.-Mexico border in the past decade—a number that far exceeds the estimated 136 deaths at the Berlin Wall.[116] As fences cut across the Pacific coast's beach and the Rio Grande, Lithuania and Spain, controversy festers over these abrasions where, in the words of writer Gloria Anzaldúa, "the Third World grates against the First and bleeds."[117]

Separation barriers have arisen elsewhere around the world, too, to control the movement of undesirable individuals. Military lines such as Korea's DMZ and Cyprus's "Green Line" still halt armies. But, increasingly, walls are intended for demographic control. Conflict barriers seek to prevent individual acts of violence, most notably Israel's "security fence" with Palestine and Northern Ireland's "Peace Lines" in Belfast. Beyond stopping militants, other walls target migrants and smugglers, such as barriers in various stages of planning and development in Botswana, Brazil, Brunei, China, Egypt, Greece, India, Iran, Kazakhstan, Malaysia, Mongolia, Morocco, North Korea, Pakistan, Russia, Saudi Arabia, South Africa, Thailand, Turkmenistan, United Arab Emirates, and Uzbekistan.[118] Fences can reduce crossings, especially at certain sites. Indeed, the rise of the inter-German border reduced migration, smuggling, and daily violence. However, no matter how severe, barriers fail to stop unwanted movement and influence completely. They often just displace, or cement, the dislocations they are meant to suppress.

Today's walls are frequently compared to the Iron Curtain, an enduring archetype against which they are measured. Germany's barrier demonstrated the power and perils of barricaded population control. In spite of its iconic status, though, its human causes and consequences remain misunderstood. The Iron Curtain penetrated society deeply. Ordinary people became part of, and perpetuated, the fortifications that divided them.

Like current separation barriers, Germany's wall was a rushed response to structural conflict that failed to solve underlying problems, and wound up creating different ones of its own. Not least, the Iron Curtain institutionalized new forms of violence and magnified divisions, incarnating and reinforcing unequal development between its two sides. Two decades after its fall, it lives on as a "wall in the head" and pervades popular memory. It remains to be seen what the ultimate effect of today's demographic barriers will be, as they aim to contain threats that could lead to greater conflict. Their relationship not just to states but also to societies is at stake. If walls are the new war, they demand comprehensive scrutiny. Burned Bridge provides a cautionary tale about their potential.

On the heels of Hitler's "Thousand-Year Reich," the quiet road at Burned Bridge seemed an unlikely site of severance. Sister cities Neustadt and Sonneberg had no preexisting religious, cultural, or ideological differences. Within a few years, however, Germany's new demarcation line fueled oppositional identities and became a mind-set and a way of life. Borderland mentalities, in turn, shaped the border. Amid postwar chaos, citizens and officials used the boundary to address a range of problems in both East and West.

While the geopolitical terms of Germany's partition were set from afar, the Cold War's actual front line formed on the ground. For its first sixteen years, the border was improvised, revealing contingency within Cold War structures. There was ongoing confusion, discontent, and disobedience. But increasingly, everyday practices of state coercion and individual accommodation expanded anticipatory compliance. An Iron Curtain grew, culminating in the construction of the Berlin Wall in 1961.

The mechanized barrier was central to the two postwar Germanys and Europe's Cold War. For the East, stemming the flight of millions was crucial to survival. The regime had succeeded in transforming its weakest fault line into its sturdiest foundation, and collapsed as soon as the border fell. For the West, the Iron Curtain enhanced global legitimacy and support, helping to solidify an unanticipated degree of economic, military, and political backing from the United States and western Europe. East and West Germany came to be the societies they were, in part, because of their common barrier.

The Iron Curtain drew a line not only between East and West but also between past and present. Both sides endeavored to represent it as a break with the Third Reich. The West condemned it as an eastern "concentration camp wall" that bore the legacy of "totalitarianism," and the East blamed the necessity of its "antifascist defensive wall" on western dangers of Nazism and capitalism. Each state effectively used the barrier to call the other the inheritor of National Socialism, offering its own citizens a kind of collective redemption.

At a crossroads of Cold War tensions, Burned Bridge cast postwar development in particularly sharp relief. Relations here frequently presaged and amplified national East-West relations. Here were early oppositional identities, early concerns about eastern migration, early border closure, early hopes for cross-border détente and travel, and early animosities from these contacts. The joys and frustrations of the border opening in 1989 likewise emerged first and perhaps most intensely in the borderland. This space of abrasion exposed much about the frictions between its two sides, as well as the growth of the scar between them.

The physical and imagined barriers of East and West arose together. An anxious cycle of severance emerged from the fears and rubble of postwar life, as haphazard border escalations gave rise to tensions and identities that propelled more border escalations. Circumstances reinforced each other, so the act of

Burned Bridge after reunification.

division furthered the fact of division. The "wall in the head" shaped the wall on the ground. Burned Bridge depicts this process of disconnection. Here, for almost half a century, a brutal borderland cut through the core of Cold War Germany—and an Iron Curtain became part of the troubled society it divided.

The Iron Curtain continues to haunt its former residents, but the edifice itself has all but vanished. It now constitutes a "green belt" through Germany, with scattered memorials where a few fences still stand.[119] Between Neustadt and Sonneberg, there are only walking paths and an occasional sign warning about the "residual risk" of mines.[120] There is no visitor information at the site; Neustadt's border museum was downsized and moved to an office park in the outskirts of the city.[121] It is even hard to tell where the border lay. Traces of electric fences, dog runs, and minefields are overgrown in the marshy lowlands.

At Burned Bridge, the commemorative stone between the cities' two shopping centers is scarcely visible from the busy road. It is best seen from the McDonald's parking lot. Though obscured by the shiny commercialism of post-wall development, Burned Bridge is still a contentious contact zone between East and West. Here the processes of division and reunification remain heightened and laid bare—and relations continue to evolve. Perhaps in time, in the course of ever-shifting interactions, this dynamic place may well reconstitute a bridge linking its two sides.

Appendix 1

Population Movement, East Germany

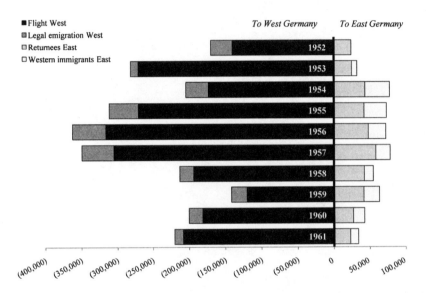

	Flight West	Flight West West German records*	Legal emigration West	Returnees East	Western immigrants East	Population change from 1950
1952	140,131	182,393	29,560	24,012	-	-0.50%
1953	270,440	331,390	10,789	24,665	7,536	-1.50%
1954	173,279	184,198	30,857	43,277	33,962	-2.10%
1955	270,115	252,870	41,185	41,937	30,991	-3.00%
1956	316,028	279,189	46,313	47,819	24,305	-4.30%
1957	304,957	261,622	44,331	58,247	19,680	-5.30%
1958	193,714	204,092	19,115	42,203	12,397	-5.90%
1959	120,226	143,917	21,439	41,580	21,503	-6.00%
1960	181,473	199,188	18,695	26,850	15,629	-6.50%
1961	208,254	207,026	12,060	22,653	11,050	-7.10%
Total	2,178,617	2,245,885	274,344	373,243	177,053	

Source: East German People's Police records synthesized by Professor Patrick Major, of the University of Reading, at the Federal Archives in Berlin. Graphed: Major, *Behind the Berlin Wall*, 64. Available: Chronik der Mauer, http://www.chronik-der-mauer.de/index.php/de/Start/Detail/id/593791/page/2, accessed January 2011.

Appendix 2

Population Movement, Sonneberg

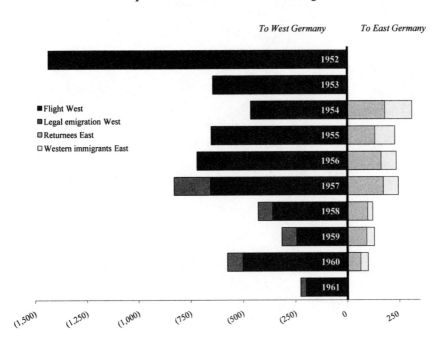

	Flight West	Legal emigration West	Returnees East	Western immigrants East	Population change from 1950
1952	1,434	-	-	-	-
1953	643	-	-	-	-
1954	462	-	181	131	-
1955	651	-	133	95	-4.30%
1956	719	-	163	72	-4.60%
1957	655	174	173	72	-
1958	359	69	98	24	-6.00%
1959	244	71	93	37	-5.60%
Total	**5,167**	*314*	**841**	**431**	-

Sources: KrA-S: In. 106-39, 144-51, 438-128, 439-129; Vors. 31-10; *Statistisches Taschenbuch—Kreis Sonneberg*, 1966.

Appendix 3

Escapees, Refugees, and Legal Emigrants from East Germany, 1961–1990

	Escapees over the inter-German border (BGS)*	Escapes through transit routes, border fortifications, or the Baltic Sea	Refugees via third countries, etc.	Legal emigrants	Ransomed political prisoners
1961	1,709	8,507	43,117	700	
1962	2,656	5,761	10,980	4,615	
1963	2,300	3,692	9,275	29,665	
1964	1,811	3,155	8,709	30,012	884
1965	1,652	2,329	9,557	17,666	1,555
1966	1,155	1,736	6,720	15,675	407
1967	827	1,203	5,182	13,188	554
1968	587	1,135	3,767	11,134	693
1969	651	1,193	4,080	11,702	880
1970	517	901	4,146	12,472	888
1971	452	832	5,011	11,565	1,375
1972	401	1,245	4,292	11,627	731
1973	408	1,842	4,680	8,667	631
1974	116	969	4,355	7,928	1,053
1975	79	673	5,338	10,274	1,158
1976	74	610	4,500	10,058	1,439
1977	85	721	3,316	8,041	1,475
1978	48	461	3,385	8,271	1,452
1979	86	463	1,768	9,003	890
1980	51	424	2,552	8,775	1,036
1981	61	298	2,599	11,093	1,584
1982	72	283	2,282	9,113	1,491
1983	51	228	2,259	7,729	1,105
1984	54	192	3,459	34,982	2,236

(Table continued)

Appendix 3

Escapees, Refugees, and Legal Emigrants from East Germany, 1961–1990

	Escapees over the inter-German border (BGS)*	Escapes through transit routes, border fortifications, or the Baltic Sea	Refugees via third countries, etc.	Legal emigrants	Ransomed political prisoners
1985	30	160	3,324	18,752	2,669
1986	64	210	4,450	19,982	1,450
1987	98	288	5,964	11,459	1,209
1988	125	590	9,115	29,033	1,094
1989	128				1,175
TOTAL	16,348	40,101	178,182	383,181	31,114

Sources: Ritter and Lapp, *Grenze*, 176. Available: German History in Documents and Images, http://germanhistorydocs.ghi-dc.org/sub_document.cfm?document_id=824, accessed January 2011. StA-C BGS 145, "Flüchtlinge über die DDR-Grenzsperranlage," 1961–1989. Similar: BGS, 116; Ritter and Lapp, *Grenze*, 173; BArch-B/SAPMO DY30 2507, 43–46, 353–54.

ABBREVIATIONS

AHR	Annual Historical Report
BBP/BGP	Bavarian Border Police
BBP-Dir	Bavarian Border Police Directorate
BGS	Federal Border Security, West Germany
BL	District Leadership
BMiB	Federal Ministry of Intra-German Relations
B-MInn	Bavarian Interior Ministry
BPO	District Party Organization
Cbg	Coburg
CT	*Coburger Tageblatt*
CYH	Cumulative Yearly History
DfW	*Das freie Wort*
DM	Deutsche mark
DV	*Das Volk*
DW	*Die Welt*
DWg	*Der Wühlpflug*
DZ	*Die Zeit*
EURCOM	U.S. European Command
FDJ	Free German Youth
FW	*Freies Wort*
GDR	German Democratic Republic
GT	Border Troops, East Germany
FRG	Federal Republic of Germany
HICOG	U.S. High Commissioner for Germany
HICOG-LCB-ID EEI	HICOG, Land Commissioner Bavaria, Intelligence Division, Essential Elements of Information
HICOG-ID-Brd	HICOG, Intelligence Division, Border Reports
IM	Informal collaborator, Stasi

KD SON	County Service Office Sonneberg
KL	County Leadership
KPD	Communist Party of Germany
KR	County Council
MfS	Ministry for State Security, East Germany (Stasi)
MHR	Monthly Historical Report
MInn	Interior Ministry
MR	Monthly Report
ND	*Neues Deutschland*
Nec	Neustadt bei Coburg
NecSR	Neustadt bei Coburg City Council
NN	*Nürnberger Nachrichten*
NP	*Neue Presse*
NT	*Neustadter Tageblatt*
NVA	National People's Army, East Germany
NYT	*New York Times*
OMGB-B	U.S. Office of the Military Government for Bavaria
OMGB-Cbg	OMGB Coburg Office
OMGB-ID	OMGB Intelligence Division
OMGUS	Office of the Military Government of the United States
OMGUS-CAD-PS	OMGUS Civil Administration Division, Public Safety Branch
OMGUS-Decart.	OMGUS Decartelization Branch
OMGUS-Exec.	OMGUS Executive Office of the Office of Military Government
OMGUS-POW&DP	OMGUS Prisoner of War and Displaced Persons
QHR	Quarterly Historical Report
RdBz-Su	District Council, Suhl
RM	Reichsmark
SB	*Sonneberger Bauernzeitung*
Sbg	Sonneberg
SbgSR	Sonneberg City Council
SBZ	Soviet Occupied Zone
SED	Socialist Unity Party
SED-BL-Suhl	SED District Leadership Suhl
SED-KL-Sbg	SED County Leadership Sonneberg
SED-ZK	SED Central Committee
SPD	Social Democratic Party
SR	*Sonneberger Rundschau*
ST	*Südthüringer Tageblatt*

Stasi	State Security Service, East Germany
SZ	*Sonneberger Zeitung,* West Germany
TBP	Thuringian Border Police
ThT	*Thüringer Tageszeitung*
TV	*Thüringer Volk*
TVz	*Thüringer Volkszeitung*
USAREUR	U.S. Army, Europe
VP	People's Police
VPKA	People's Police County Office
WP	*Washington Post*
WPS	Weekly Public Safety Report
WR	Weekly Report

NOTES

Introduction

1. Interview, Frieda Gansel, Neustadt/Ketschenbach, 17 Jun. 2002.
2. As Peter Schneider foretold in 1982, "It will take us longer to tear down the Wall in our heads than any wrecking company will need for the Wall we can see." Schneider, *Wall Jumper*, 119.
3. New approaches to Cold War history: e.g., Gaddis, *Cold War*; Westad, *Global Cold War*; Engel, ed., *Local Consequences*; Sheehan, *Soldiers*, 147–197. Germany: Gray, *Cold War*.
4. Wright, *Iron Curtain*, 375–382.
5. Churchill, "The Sinews of Peace," Westminster College, Fulton, Missouri, 5 Mar. 1946; Wright, *Iron Curtain*, esp. 42–50.
6. Chandler, *Institutions*, 38–40; 63–66; 77–78.
7. Origins: Harrison, *Driving the Soviets*; Hertle, Jarausch, and Kleßmann, *Mauerbau*; Gearson and Schake, eds., *Berlin Wall Crisis*.
8. Hertle and Nooke, *Todesopfer*, 18 (English: www.berliner-mauer-gedenkstaette.de/en/todesopfer-240.html). An estimated 98 intended to flee, 30 had not intended to flee, and 8 were border guards.
9. Daum, *Kennedy*, 153–156; Hacke, "United States," 24–25.
10. StA-C BGS 145, "Flüchtlinge über die DDR-Grenzsperranlage," 1961–1989; Schmidt, *BGS*, 116; Ritter and Lapp, *Grenze*, 173; BArch-B/SAPMO DY30 2507, 43–46, 353–354. The number of fatalities on the inter-German border is unknown, and remains difficult to approximate: Hertle and Sälter, "Todesopfer," 669, 672. A disputed uppermost range, given by the August 13 Working Group, estimates 275 border deaths after 1961 and 319 deaths from 1945 to 1961; Hildebrandt, *Wall*, 75.
11. Marx, *Eighteenth Brumaire*, 9.
12. Emphasizing the local effects of Cold War diplomacy: Engel and Engel, "Introduction," in Engel, ed., *Local Consequences*, 1–30.
13. E.g., Judt, *Postwar*; Mazower, *Dark Continent*, 212–394; Biess and Moeller, eds., *Aftermath*.
14. E.g., a similar vantage point for the Berlin blockade: Steege, *Black Market*.
15. Historiographical overviews: Jarausch and Geyer, *Shattered Past*; Kleßmann, *Divided Past*; Schissler, ed., *Miracle Years*; Ross, *Dictatorship*.
16. East-West comparisons: Hochscherf, Laucht, and Plowman, eds., *Divided*; Borneman, *Belonging*; Herf, *Divided Memory*; Heinemann, *What Difference*; Poiger, *Jazz*; Biess, *Homecomings*; Black, *Death*; Crew, ed., *Consuming*; Wierling, "Mission." East-West cultures: Pence and Betts, eds., *Socialist Modern*; Fulbrook, ed., *Power*; Major and Osmond, eds., *Workers'*; Moeller, ed., *West Germany*. East-West politics: Patton, *Cold War*; Smyser, *Yalta*. East-West relationships: Pence, *Rations*; Stiftung Haus der Geschichte, *Drüben*; Härtel and Kabus, eds., *Westpaket*; Dietzsch, *Grenzen Überschreiben?*
17. Differing seminal analyses: Blackbourn and Eley, *Peculiarities*; Smith, *Continuities*.
18. Eckert, "Greetings," 9; Ahonen, "Werner Weinhold" (3–4). Victimization in public remembrance: Moeller, *War Stories*.
19. The term "Third Germany" has been used by scholars to describe German states apart from Prussia and Austria in the late eighteenth and nineteenth centuries; Burg, *Deutsche Trias*.

20. Trachtenberg, *Constructed Peace*; Eisenberg, 363–493; McAllister, *No Exit*, 72–120; Schwartz, "No Harder"; Spevack, "Allied Council"; Naimark, *Russians*, 318–352; Laufer, *Pax Sovietica*, 379–603; Uhl, *Teilung*. Overview of extensive scholarship and debates over Germany's diplomatic division, Leffler and Westad, eds., *Cold War*, 520–521; Spilker, *Leadership*, 1–6.

21. E.g., Ritter and Lapp, *Grenze*; Lapp, *Gefechtsdienst*; Hermann, *Deutsch-Deutsche Grenze*; Lebegern, *Mauer.*

22. Thoß, ed., *Eiserner Vorhang*; Thoß, *Gesichert*. From the former head of East Germany's Border Troops: Baumgarten and Freitag, *Grenzen*. A bibliography including several volumes from a similar perspective: http://grenztruppen-der-ddr.org/00008.html.

23. Berdahl, *Where the World Ended*; Ullrich, *Geteilte Ansichten.*

24. E.g., Schätzlein, Albert, Rösch, and Salier, *Grenzerfahrungen*, vols. 1–3; Grafe, *Grenze*; Hermann, *Grenze*; Schultke, *Grenze*; Hartmann and Doering-Manteuffel, eds., *Grenzgeschichten*; Kleindienst, ed., *Von hier*; Kleindienst, ed., *Mauer-Passagen*; Scherzer, *Grenz-Gänger*; Bailey, *Along*; Witzel, *Disturbed Ground*. Additional: www.grenzerinnerungen.de/seite16.htm.

25. Berdahl, *Where the World Ended*; Bennewitz and Potratz, eds., *Zwangsaussiedlungen*; Weisbrod, ed., *Grenzland*; Bessel, "Making." Social dimensions of the Berlin Wall: Major, *Berlin Wall*; Ross, "East Germans" and "Before the Wall"; Roggenbuch, *Berliner Grenzgängerproblem.*

26. The Berlin Wall Memorial at Bernauer Street and the Center for Research on Contemporary History (ZZF) are coordinating a number of Berlin Wall–and border-related projects; most notably, Hans-Hermann Hertle and Gerhard Sälter have established the number of deaths at the Berlin Wall (at least 136). The Institute for Contemporary History (IfZ) and the Federal Institute for Military History (MGFA) are collaborating on a project about the dynamic interaction between governmental policy, military developments, and construction at the Berlin Wall. Recent conferences have showcased forthcoming work: panels at the Deutscher Historikertag, "Grenzräume," and "Die innerdeutsche Grenze," Berlin, Sep. 2010; the conference "Grenze—Konstruktion Realität Narrative," Hanover, Jun. 2010, organized by Carl-Hans Hauptmeyer, Detlef Schmiechen-Ackermann, Thomas Schwark, Astrid Eckert, Rainer Potratz, and Hedwig Wagner; panels at the German Studies Association, "Border Regimes as Political Governance," "The Iron Curtain in East and West Germany," "Die Berliner Mauer," and "Grenzregime und Grenzbevölkerung," Washington, D.C., Oct. 2009.

27. Respectively, Sälter, *Grenzpolizisten*; Schaefer, "Ironing the Curtain"; Johnson, "Dividing Mödlareuth"; Eckert, *West Germany*; Ahonen, *Death.*

28. E.g., Glassheim, "Ethnic Cleansing," Blaive and Molden, *Grenzfälle*; Pittaway, "Making Peace"; Ballinger, *History*; Pelkmans, *Defending*. Additional scholarship on European "border communities," including those divided by the Iron Curtain, is coordinated by the Ludwig Boltzmann Institute in Vienna under the direction of Thomas Lindenberger.

29. Port, *Conflict*, 10; Port argues that "horizontal relations *among* East Germans" are vital to explaining East Germany's stability, as social divisions precluded citizens' ability to oppose the regime.

30. Kocka, "Durchherrschte Gesellschaft," 547–553; Bessel and Jessen, eds., *Grenzen der Diktatur*. Historiographical overview: Ross, *Dictatorship*, 46–68.

31. Jarausch, "Care and Coercion," 47–69; Fulbrook, *People's State*, 10–17.

32. Translation by the originator of the concept, Alf Luedtke, in "People Working," 83 (see Rubin, "Trabant," 28). Seminal essay on its application to East Germany: Lindenberger, "Diktatur der Grenzen," esp. 23–26.

33. For this and additional discussion of border effects, see Wilson and Donnan, "Nation," 12–26; Ganster and Lorey, *Borders*; Anderson, *Frontiers*; Baud and Schendel, "Comparative History." The contingency of group identities: Brubaker, *Ethnicity Without Groups*; Zahra, "Imagined Non-Communities." In European borderlands: Judson, *Guardians*; Murdock, *Changing*; Brown, *Biography.*

34. Peter Sahlins' pathbreaking study argued that different identities form from a "dialectic of local and national interests" in which "frontier regions are privileged sites for the articulation of national distinctions": Sahlins, *Boundaries*, 8, 271. See also Berdahl, *Where the World Ended*, 3–9; Driessen, "New Immigration," 96–116. The especial significance of local identities in Germany: Confino, *Nation*; Applegate, *Provincials*; Blackbourn and Retallack, eds., *Localism*; Palmowski, *Inventing.*

35. Sahlins, *Boundaries*; Elton, "Jivaro"; Miles, *Hausaland.*

36. Martínez, *Troublesome Border*, 4.

37. Donnan and Wilson, *Borders*, 13. E.g., Pelkmans, *Defending*, 216–217. Pelkmans' argument about the incremental formation of the Turkish-Soviet border is similar to the one advanced in this book, yet he reaches an opposite conclusion about its essential impermeability.

38. Since the East and West German states were declared in 1949, Part One uses the terms "East" and "West," where appropriate, as shorthand for the more awkward formulations of the Soviet zone/East Germany and the western zones/West Germany.

39. Summary: Sheffer, "On Edge."

40. Additional details and citations regarding events described in this book can be found in the longer dissertation: Sheffer, "Burned Bridge."

41. Eastern and western archival sources were asymmetrical throughout the study. American and western German documents from 1945 to 1952 were both more suggestive and expansive than eastern records from this period. Moreover, Soviet occupation records on Sonneberg were unavailable at the time of this field work. In later decades, the masses of party and administration reports produced in East Germany not only dwarfed the sparse local records for the West, but were also available for the entire lifetime of the state, versus embargoed western records. Although access to some western sources was granted, glaring disparities remain. For example, in intelligence, extensive Stasi sources remain unaccompanied by any from the western Federal Intelligence Service, or Bundesnachrichtendienst.

42. Research was conducted in accordance with protocol of the Office for the Protection of Human Subjects at the University of California, Berkeley. Names remain unchanged for public officials cited in archival sources, as well as for people discussed in already published works, when they are not accompanied by additional archival material.

43. Löffler, "Ein durch und durch menschliches Problem. US-amerikanerische Historikerin Edith Sheffer untersucht die Entwicklung des Verhältnisses Neustadt-Sonneberg seit 1945," *FW*, 14 Feb. 2003.

Chapter 1: Foundations

1. "Die 'Gebrannte Brücke' lüftet ihr Geheimnis," *CT*, 20 Jan. 1990. Local historians speculate that Charlemagne built Burned Bridge in the 800s as a troop road, or that it was once an actual bridge over the Röden. Burned Bridge was first documented in 1162 as the subject of a border dispute when its river ford became the site of a customs office. Schwämmlein, "Sonneberg und Neustadt"; Eichhorn, *Blick nach drüben*, 82–90.

2. From 1353 until 1735, both cities belonged to the Thuringian House of Wettin in the Coburg territories. They were designated as a borderland for four hundred years and were of ambiguous status as the dynasty's "local estates in Franconia" (*Ortlande in Franken*). Neustadt was designated a market town in 1248, attained city status in 1316, and was granted a fair in 1343. Neustadt auf der Heide was renamed Neustadt (Herzogtum Coburg) in 1892 and Neustadt bei Coburg in 1921. The knights of the Sonneberg family were first documented occupying the Schlossburg hill in 1207, with the small Röthen settlement along the river below in 1225; Luthardt, *Geschichte*, ii.

3. Bretschneider, *Grenzen*, 16.

4. Fugmann, *Wirtschaftsraum*, 248–266; Meyfarth, *Spielzeugmacher*, 7–19.

5. Kalter, "Neustadts Weg," 4–6; Wirth, *"Dreschflegelkrieg."*

6. Schwämmlein, "Stadtgrenze," 8–9.

7. Greiner, *Neustadt*, 60–64; Neumann, *Spielzeugland*, 38–39; Sperschneider, "Spielwarenindustrie," 42–49, 113–118.

8. Bretschneider, "Es brennt," 54–55; Schwarzkopf, "Stadterweiterung," 133; Hoßfeld, *Strassen*, 16.

9. Schwämmlein, "Sonneberg und Neustadt," 135.

10. Fugmann, *Wirtschaftsraum*, 265–266; Meyfarth, "Spielzeugindustrie," 222–223. Overview: Hamlin, *Work*, 86–92.

11. Löffler, "Auf in's Gelobte Land," 33, 73. The U.S. consulate in Sonneberg (1851–1916) was the third in central Germany, before Chemnitz, Magdeburg, Erfurt, and Weimar; Gerhard Stier, "Ein Konsulat der USA in der Spielzeugstadt," *Südthüringer Heimatblätter* 1, no. 5 (96): 20. Ernst Thauer worked his way up from warehouse worker to president of FAO Schwarz; "Ein Sonneberger war Boß des weltgrößten Spielwarenladens," *FW*, 12 Feb. 1999.

12. Fromm, *Eingliederung*, 16; Sperrschneider, "Spielwarenindustrie," 18.

13. Rausch, *Spielwaren-Industrie*, 84–86.

14. Fugmann, *Wirtschaftsraum*, 410; Franz Förster, "Kleine Industriestadt mit großer Zukunft," *NP*, 11 Dec. 1948.

15. Scheuerich, *Geschichte*, 1:394; Schwarzkopf, "Stadterweiterung," 133. Precise population comparisons are difficult since the cities incorporated surrounding municipalities at different rates. Overview: Hoßfeld, ed., *Sonneberg*.

16. Cleavages stemmed from Sonneberg's trade privileges of 1789, which limited trading rights to thirty firms and legally separated trade from manufacturing. These were reversed in 1862 and smaller exporters grew, but divisions were already pronounced. Lischewsky, *Puppen*, 47–51, 57–58.

17. Stenbock-Fermor, *Deutschland*, 89 (Lischewsky, *Puppen*, 47), regional poverty: 89–102.

18. Meyfarth, "Spielzeugindustrie," 222–223; Sperschneider, "Spielwarenindustrie," 107.

19. Fugmann, *Wirtschaftsraum*, 274; Hoßfeld, "Zwanziger Jahren,'" 33; Bierer, "Kinderarbeit," 22–23, 32, 154–155; Scheuerich, *Geschichte*, 1:35; Schwämmlein, "Sonneberg und Neustadt," 81.

20. Scheuerich, *Geschichte*, 2:347. E.g., available online: Viktor Walther, "Diary," 1916–32. www.familientagebuch.de/viktor.

21. Hofmann, "'Gewerbemuseum,'" 84–85; Schwämmlein, "Industrieschulen," 28–41; e.g., Hofmann, "Einwohner der Puppenstadt von 'draußen' gesehen," *NP*, 7 Oct. 1949; Wenzel, "Warum sind die Sonneberger so und nicht anders?" *TV*, 15 Jul. 1946.

22. Herold, "Puppenstadt," 5.

23. Zogbaum, *Weltspielwarenstadt*, 12.

24. Overview: BayHStA B-StK-10277, "Union of Southern Thuringia with Bavaria," 1946. Dialect: Schindhelm, *Ortsnamen*, 114–121.

25. BayHStA B-StK-5870, B-StK, 25 Oct. 1935.

26. "Grenzbesichtigungen vor 100 Jahren," *NP*, 5 Oct. 1948.

27. Bachmann, "Anschluß," 114.

28. "Coburger entschieden sich für Bayern," *ThT*, Oct. 1980; Schmehle, "Coburg," 132. Pro-Thuringian opinion: Schwämmlein, "Sonnebergs Reaktionen," 29–33.

29. Bachmann, "Coburgs Anschluß," 113; Erdmann, "Anschluss," 16–23.

30. Scheuerich, *Geschichte*, 1:4; Hambrecht, "Krieg," 144–145.

31. Hambrecht, "Krieg," 192; Scheuerich, *Geschichte*, 2:2.

32. Schmehle, "Coburg," 154, 180; Schwämmlein, "Sonneberg, 1918–1945," 79–80; Scheuerich, *Geschichte*, 1:79–85.

33. Scheuerich, *Geschichte*, 2:416; Hoßfeld, "Sonneberg, 1932–1939," 6; Schwämmlein, "Sonneberg, 1918–1945," 81. Background: Schmehle, "Coburg," 55–58; Gretzbach, *SPD*, 8–12.

34. Hayward and Morris, *First Nazi*, 58–59, 113–119.

35. SA-N 2111, Schubart, 23 Mar. 1935; *Völkischer Beobachter*, "Eine neue soziale Tat," 15 Apr. 1935.

36. Hoßfeld, "Zwanziger Jahren," 25–29, Hoßfeld, "Sonneberg, 1929–1932," 13; Scheuerich, *Geschichte*, 2:361.

37. E.g., Müller, *Mein Deutschland!*; Heß, *Heimat*; Sonneberger Beobachter, *Kommunalpolitik*.

38. Schwede, *Kampf*, 101.

39. SA-N 2111, Schubart, 23 Mar. 1935; Hoßfeld, "Sonneberg, 1929–1932," 7–8. Notwithstanding a mini-boom in the late 1920s, the toy industry never returned to prewar levels. Seventy percent of production had been exported (four-fifths to the United States); by 1925 the region claimed only 13 percent of European and 7 percent of global toy production (down from 24 percent and 20 percent in 1913). Grünspan, "Die Deutsche Spielwarenindustrie," 82–85; Meyfarth, *Spielzeugmacher*, 10; Hoßfeld, "Sonneberg, 1932–1939," 11.

40. Grund, "Arbeiterbewegung," 109–111; Hoßfeld, "Sonneberg, 1929–1932," 21–27; Scheuerich, *Geschichte*, 1:93–99.

41. Votes, 1920–32: Sheffer, "Burned Bridge," 34–35. Synthesized from: Scheuerich, *Geschichte*, 1:101–108; Hoßfeld, "Sonneberg, 1932–1939," 7–8; SA-S C3-1.

42. BayHStA B-StK-5870, B-StK, 25 Oct. 1935.

43. Participation: Hoßfeld, "Sonneberg, 1932–1939," 8; BayHStA MWi-7275, Schubart to Ley, 9 Nov. 1934. Arrests: Grund, "Arbeiterbewegung," 109–111; Schwämmlein, "Sonneberg, 1918–1945," 83–85.

44. Schwämmlein, "Jüdische Bürger," 351–352. Schoenau, *Sonneberg*, 265–266; Reich, *Erinnerung*, 17–24. Region: Fromm, *Die Coberger Juden*.

45. Maslowski, "Stoff zu einem Gesellschafts-Roman," *NP*, 19 Apr. 1947. Because of his opposition to Nazism, Kiesewetter was sent to Dachau in 1941—and appointed Neustadt's first postwar mayor by the Americans, April–September 1945.

46. "Sechs Jahre Gefängnis für Denunzianten," *TV*, 13 Mar. 1948; Hoßfeld, "Sonneberg, 1932–1939," 10–11; Luthardt, *Geschichte*, 126.

47. SA-S C3-4, Geyer, 15 Sep. 1945. Individuals: Reich, *Erinnerung*, 18–24.

48. "Ganz Neustadt im Zeichen des Ministerpräsidentenbesuches," *Tageblatt Neustadt*, 24 Mar. 1936; Scheuerich, *Geschichte*, 1:135–138; "Über eine geheime Fabrik und KZ-Lager," *FW*, 26 Aug. 2003;

"Geheimes Zahnradwerk," *FW*, 3 Sep. 2003. Toy industry: BayHStA MWi-7275, Correspondence, Hausser-Siemens, 1937.

49. Hoßfeld, "Sonneberg 1932–1939," 14.
50. Stier, *Zwangsarbeit*, 6, 31–37; Hoßfeld, "Sonneberg, 1939–1944/45," 11.
51. NACP RG338, USAREUR-War Crimes 266, "United States v. Heinrich Buuck," 19 Apr. 1951; NACP RG226, OSS-Jewish Desk: 1–8, Egon Fleck, "Buchenwald: A Preliminary Report," 24 Apr. 1945. Historical awareness of the camps is greater in Sonneberg than Neustadt because East German publications publicized (and distorted) local Nazis' misdeeds. "Divided memory" became an issue in the cities' Cold War rivalry, one Sonneberg pamphlet (which neglects to mention that Sonneberg's inmates were Jewish) protesting the past was "hushed up in Neustadt/Coburg." Cremer: SED-KL-Sbg, "Todesmarsch," May 1985, private possession. Cold War context: Herf, *Divided Memory*, esp. 390–391. Minimizing Neustadt accounts: e.g., Scheuerich, *Gechichte*, 1:138–139, 2:305; Rauer, "'Nach Auschwitz war hier das Paradies,'" *NP*, 11 May 2005.
52. The American War Crimes Branch prosecuted Heinrich Buuck, a guard at Sonneberg's camp, for killing "approximately" ten Jews. NACP RG338, USAREUR-War Crimes 266; ThHStAW LBdVP-365 Bd. 1:51. The U.S. Holocaust Memorial Museum holds sixty-four interviews with survivors of Neustadt's and Sonneberg's concentration camps.
53. From, *Eingliederung*, 51; Luthardt, *Geschichte*, 135. Bombing: Scheuerich, *Geschichte*, 1:167–175; NACP RG243: G2-Survey: 34–589, 21 Jul. 1944; G2-Survey: 149–2677, 14 and 16 Feb. 1945; Stier, *Letzten Tage*, 31; Bretschneider, "11. April 1945," 81–84. Military casualties, around 5 percent of the population: Scheuerich, *Geschichte*, 1:58–63; Hoßfeld, "Sonneberg, 1939–1944/45," 4, 13–14. Meanwhile, the Volkssturm dynamited Sonneberg's Woolworth's distribution center and planned to destroy the military clothing warehouse and county offices. Stammberger, 26 May 1945, StA-M Bib-7827.
54. E.g., Judt, *Postwar*, 21.
55. While historians have argued that the term "zero hour" implies more of a break with the National Socialists than was the case, Richard Bessel contends Germans' use of the term is itself significant: Bessel, *Germany 1945*, 395–396. Upheaval across Europe: Hitchcock, *Bitter Road*.
56. Details: Sheffer, "Burned Bridge," 39–41. NACP RG407, 26th Inf-Div: 8276–1, 101st Inf-Regt, 16 Sep. 1946; 8717–1, 8222–1, 8282–2; Stier, *Letzten Tage*, 18–20; SA-S C2-201 (StAM Bib-7827), Dietzler, "Kampflose Übergabe," Jun. 1945; ThHStAW LBdVP-365 Bd. 1, 1–5. Neustadt's capitulation: NACP RG407: 11th Arm-Div CCA: 16087–1, 2, 16, 17; 71st Inf-Div: 11397–1, 2; 90th Inf-Div: 13396–2; Scheuerich, *Geschichte*, 1:153–154; Schmidt, *Coburg*, 8–22; Schubert, *Ende*, 166–183. American shooting of one eleven-year-old: StA-C LRA-14788, H., 14 Aug. 1945.
57. Interviews: Günter Oppinger, Neustadt/Ebersdorf, 2 May 2003, and Heinz Thormann, Neustadt, 14 Jan. 2003. "Vor einem Jahr wurde Neustadt besetzt," *NP*, 17 Apr. 1946.
58. Klein, AHR, 23 Jun. 1946, NACP RG260, OMGB-Cbg 1200–3.
59. Schubert, *Ende*, 299–300; SA-S C2-201, Glöckner, "Sonnebergs schwärzestes Vierteljahr," Jun. 1945. E.g., ThHStAW LBdVP-365 Bd. 1, 308.
60. Hoßfeld, "Sonneberg 1939–1944/45," 4, 11; SA-S C3-57, Geyer, 13 Jul. 1947; NACP RG260, OMGB-Cbg 1203–6; Sussell, 23 Aug. 1947.
61. "Rechenschaftsbericht," *TVz*, 14 Dec 1945.
62. SA-S C2-201, Glöckner, Jun. 1945.
63. SA-S C2-201, Ortelli, 4 Jun. 1945. Ortelli stepped down within days; Herman Am-Ende became mayor, who had had set up a local *Antifa* of ten anti-fascists who planned for the transfer of power after surrender. SA-S C2-201 and StA-M Bib-7827, Am-Ende, "Übergabe," Jun. 1945.
64. NACP RG407, 6th Const-Regt-6th Sqdn: 18423, 2 Aug. 1946; SA-S C16-172, Weinland, 16, 19, and 23 May 1945. Though curfews were lifted in April 1946, some locals requested the U.S. Coburg Office reimpose it due to increased theft after dark. StA-C LRA-15131, Lockland, 11 Sep. 1945; Klein, 2 Apr. 1946.
65. StA-M KR-S S5/11 1/79, Weinland, 22 May 1945; StA-C LRA-15132, Klein, 30 Jun. 1945.
66. SA-S C2-201, Glöckner, Jun. 1945.
67. Scheuerich, *Geschichte*, 1:154. Non-fraternization policy was often ignored, and it ended by May 1945.
68. Interview, Norm Greendel, telephone, 27 Jan. 2001.
69. E.g., StA-M SED-BL-Suhl V/1/1/072, Ludwig and Zetzmann, "Parteiarbeit."
70. E.g., Stier, *Letzten Tage*, 22, 29.
71. Interview, Elisabeth Dietzer, Sonneberg/Wolkenrasen, 18 Dec. 2002; Stier, *Letzten Tage*, 36. American distributions of candy for children: "Weihnachtsfeiern in Neustadt," *NP*, 11 Sep. 1946, "Deutsche Kinder beim 'Santa Claus,'" *NP*, 31 Dec. 1947.

72. Interviews, Johann Thull, Coburg, 10 Jul. 2002, Günter Oppinger; Survey Respondent #10260. Details: Schmidt, "Sowjets hatten alte Landkarte," *NP*, 20 Aug. 1996; Bachmann, "45 Jahre," 111.
73. Private possession, Mulzer: Greiner, "Errinnerungen."
74. SA-S: C2–201, Ortelli, 4 Jun. 1945; C3–23, E., 12 Sep. 1946; C3–24, "Geschäftsbericht," Oct. 1945.
75 ., "Mich ärgert schon lange," *TVz*, 19 Oct. 1945; "Ein umstrittenes Kapitel," *TVz*, 26 Oct. 1945; "Strassenumbenennungen in Sonneberg," *TVz*, 30 Oct. 1945; SA-S C3–23, Geyer, 15 Aug. 1946.
76. Grams, *Grenze*, 11; ThHStAW LBdVP-365 Bd. 1–3, Sonneberg Police Reports, Aug.–Dec. 1945; styling: 3:152. Confiscations: SA-S: C3–17, -18, -21, -22. The Soviet army claimed fifteen houses and nine buildings, plus four houses near Burned Bridge for checkpoint administration. Hoßfeld, "Was kostete den Sonnebergern die Besatzung?" *NP*, 30 Oct. 1993; "Schwere Zeiten im zweiten Halbjahr 1945," *NP*, 18 Dec. 1993.
77. Hoßfeld, "Die Demontage der Sonneberger Betriebe," *NP*, 31 Dec. 1993; StA-M KR-S S5/19 1/79, Weinland, 22 Jun. 1946; "Fabrik und KZ-Lager," *FW*, 26 Aug. 2003; "Arbeit unser wertvollstes Kapital," *TVz*, 8 Oct. 1945; Stier, "Zwangsarbeit," 40–43. Zone overview: Laufer, "Dismantling."
78. Expropriation affected four estates in the county, all near the border; in total, 1,022 hectares were redistributed to 2,907 small farmers and refugees. Matthäi, *Anfänge*, 56–57; Schwämmlein, "Landwirtschaft"; "Rechenschaftsbericht," *TVz*, 14 Dec. 1945. "Lively debate": "Die Bodenreform im Kreis Sonneberg," *TVz*, 29 Sep. 1945; "243 Hektar für landarme Bauern," *TVz*, 11 Oct. 1945. Oerlsdorf as the "first model New Farm in Thuringia": ThHStAW Th-MInn 130.
79. NACP RG260, OMGB-Cbg 1200–3, Klein, AHR, 23 Jun. 1946. Police reports: NACP RG260, OMGB-Cbg 1208–1. Shooting: StA-C StAnw-18, District Attorney, 1945. U.S. criminality: Willoughby, *Conquering*, 16–28; Fraternization policy: Kleinschmidt, "*Do Not Fraternize*."
80. Private possession, Mulzer; Greiner, "Errinnerungen"; Grams, *Grenze*, 9–11.
81. BayHStA B-StK-10277, "Lage im russisch besetzten Teil Deutschlands," 20 Aug. 1945.
82. Naimark, *Russians*, 381–382; von Plato, Mironenko, and Niethammer, *Speziallager*. U.S. troops also made "numerous unjustified arrests" in the region, though on nowhere near the same scale. NACP RG260, OMGUS-Exec. 310–9, MG DetG-225 Coburg, "War Diary," 21 Aug. 1945.
83. Schleevoigt, "Heubisch," 16. Initial arrest and surveillance lists: SA-S C3–2, Weinland, 13 Jul. 1945.
84. StA-C StAnw-403, 74–79, Coburg Regional Court, 19 May 1955. Lists: Prieß, *Erschossen*, 122–124.
85. Schoenau, *Sonneberg*, 61.
86. "Ohnmächtig geprügelt," *NP*, Series: 1–33, 3; May 1990.
87. Private possession, Mulzer; Greiner, "Errinnerungen"; "Vom Bett weg verhaftet," *NP*, 9 May 1990.
88. Neustadt City Councilor Erich Czapiewsky and the four policemen were sentenced to two and a half years in prison in 1952; the instigator was sentenced to four years in 1954. StA-C: StAnw-403; StAnw-54, 1, 8–10; "Bundesgerichtshof bestätigt Urteil," *NP*, 14 Mar. 1953.
89. Interview, Jakob Ziegler, Sonneberg/Steinbach, 7 Feb. 2003; Günther, "Die Hilflosen Opfer Der Geheimpolizei," *NP*, 9 May 1990.
90. Prieß, *Erschossen*, 122–124.
91. Naimark, *Russians*, 69–140; Grossman, *Jews, Germans*, 48–68. U.S. rapes in the area: NACP RG260, OMGB-Cbg: 1200–2, WPS, 30 Aug. 1946; 1208–1, Müller, 7 Sep. 1948.
92. StA-M SED-KL-Sbg: 276, Minutes, Dec. 1948; 287, 19 Jul. 1949.
93. SA-S C3–57, Geyer, 13 Jul. 1947; ThHStAW LBdVP-365 Bd. 1, 50, 52; NACP RG260, OMGB-Cbg 1202–5, Walston, 7 Sep. 1948; "Hat unsere Stadt einen großen Frauen-Überschuß?" *NP*, 18 Aug. 1949.
94. Interview, Ray Davis, telephone, 14 Apr. 2001; Kaufmann, *Schicksalsjahre*, 29.
95. Interview, Stan Witkowski, telephone, 27 Jan. 2001.
96. Interview, Jack Gunderson, telephone, 27 Jan. 2001.
97. NACP, RG260, OMGB-Cbg: 1208–1, Security Police 187/48, 5 Aug. 1948.
98. Heineman, *What Difference*, 105–106. Grossmann, *Jews, Germans*, 48–86; Goedde, *GIs and Germans*, 80–126; Fehrenbach, *Race*, 46–52.
99. BayHStA OMGB-CO 438/3, "An die Schokoladen-weiber!" 21, 27 Nov. 1945.
100. "Sind Geschlechtskrankheiten heilbar?" *NP*, 3 Aug. 1946; "Ernste Fragen für unsere Frauen," *TVz*, 25 Feb. 1946; "Frauen, die keine sind," *TV*, 2 May 1946. E.g., "Gefängnis für Abtreibung," *TV*, 26 Apr. 1948; "Verhandlungen vor dem Militärgericht," *NP*, 2 Feb. 1946; "Wegen gewerbsmäßiger Abtreibung," *NP*, 14 Aug. 1945; "Betrunkenes Mädchen," *NP*, 31 Aug. 1946.
101. NACP RG260, OMGB-Cbg: 1208–1, Müller, 11, 17 Aug. 1948. Similar: 1201–4, Police statements, 2 Feb 1949.
102. E.g., four-Power Berlin: Timm, *Politics*, 187–226.

103. ThHStAW Th-MInn 1581, 315–316; similar: SA-N StRPr 024–10/1, NecSR, 6 Nov. 1945; reports: NACP RG407, 6th Const-Regt-6th Sqdn: 18423.
104. FDJ-KL-Sbg, "Senkt die Zahl der Geschlechts-Krankheiten," *TV,* 3 Dec. 1946.
105. NACP RG260, OMGB-Cbg 1202–9, MHR, 5 Sep. 1946; 1200–2, 6th Const-Sqdn, 2 Aug., 4 Sep. 1946; *NP,* "Deutsche Mädchen in amerikanischen Clubs," 15 Jun. 1946.
106. NACP RG260, OMGB-Cbg 1200–2, 14 Sep. 1946; e.g., OMGB-CAD-PS: 67–3, PSR, 1946; ThH-StAW LBdVP-365 Bd. 3, 184–186. American censure of women's confinement: BayHStA B-StK-13540, Correspondence, Oct.–Dec. 1947. Naimark, *Russians,* 100.
107. StA-M KR-S S5/22 1/79, Behandlungstelle für Geschlechtskranke, MR, 1946–1947; SA-S C3–16, Sonneberg County Chairman, 11 Aug. 1945; Orders: ThHStAW LBdVP-365 Bds. 1, 2, and 3.
108. NACP RG260, OMGB-Cbg 1204–2, Sussell, "V.D. Suspect Sheets," 9 Oct. 1947. Suspect lists were drawn up collaboratively by the German police, U.S. Army, and U.S. Coburg Office.
109. Interview, Jim Nolan, Sacramento, CA, 26 Feb. 2001.
110. NACP RG260, OMGB-Cbg 1204–1: Totenhaupt, "Moral-Control on 21 April 1947"; plus file. Thereafter, U.S. officials directed that Moral Controls be "conducted in a democratic manner" and only collect women "infected . . . beyond a reasonable doubt." But American soldiers would still get "somewhat out of hand" and stage their own "every now and again." Anecdotal reports suggest 2 to 25 percent of women seized in weekly raids tested positive for venereal disease. NACP RG260: OMGB-Cbg 1204–1: Totenhaupt, 22 Apr. 1947; Maddox, 19 May 1947; OMGB-ID: 158–6, OMGB-IA (and Rohan) 4 Feb. 1948; OMGB-ID: 153–9, Stearns, 7 May 1947.
111. Beyersdorf, "Militärregierung," 19. Culture of denunciation in the Third Reich: Gellately, *Gestapo.*
112. *NP,* "Anonyme Zuschriften zwecklos," 24 Jan. 1948.
113. Overviews: Ermarth, ed., *America*; Pommerin, ed., *American*; Naimark, *Russians.*
114. NACP RG260: OMGB-Cbg 1200–3, Robie, CYH, 20 Jul. 1947. Detachment details: OMGB-B 1062–1, "Ober and Mittelfranken," 20 Jun. 1946.
115. SA-S C3–68, Geyer, 13 Sep. 1947; Hess, 16 Sep. 1947. Though Sonneberg's Soviet documents were not accessible at the time of this research, German records suggest significant organizational difficulty.
116. E.g., "Blick," *NP,* 6 Aug. 1947; "'Absolute Objektivität und Sachlichkeit . . . ,'" *TV,* 24 Dec. 1947. Sonneberg's was far more critical of its neighbor, while reporting little on its own tribunals.
117. "Der Befehl 201 wird durchgeführt!" *TV,* 8 Oct. 1947. Soviet Zone: Welsh, *Wandel,* 167; Classifications: SA-S C3–41, Labor Office of Thuringia, 24 Sep. 1945.
118. "Abschluß der Entnazifizierungsverfahren," *TV,* 19 May 1948; ThHStAW LBdVP-365 Bd. 1, 44; SA-S C2–2, C3–3. There were eighty-five dismissals, forty-three demotions, and 106 trade license removals, while the sequestering of Nazi-owned companies was uneven. Meanwhile, 111 people faced property seizures, bank account blockages, or loss of the right to vote in the 1946 elections. "Blick nach Sonneberg," *NP,* 21 Apr. 1948; Hoßfeld, "Entnazifizierung in Sonneberg," *NP,* 4 Dec. 1993; SA-S C3–24, Sonneberg City, "Geschäftsbericht," Oct. 1945; ThHStAW Th-MInn 716/2, 15, 75; "Wie arbeiten die sequestrierten Betriebe?" *TV,* 8 Feb. 1946, "24 Sequestierte Betriebe zurückgegeben," 10 Sep. 1946.
119. Boehling, *Question,* 234. Seminal: Niethammer, *Mitläuferfabrik.*
120. NACP RG260, OMGB-Cbg 1202–9, Klein, MHR, 5 Apr. 1946; BayHStA MSo859, OMGB, 14 Aug. 1946. Excusatory certificates, or *Persilscheine*: StA-C LRA-15134, -15135.
121. NACP RG260, OMGB-Cbg 1202–9, Lockland, MHR, 30 Oct. 1945. "Decartelization" at Siemens: NACP RG260, OMGUS-Decart. 140–5. Legacy of National Socialism in Western business: Wiesen, *West German.*
122. Neustadt's tribunal processed 10,256 Meldebogen, or individual questionnaires, and held 1,031 hearings; it deemed no one a "major offender," nineteen "offenders," 102 "lesser offenders," and 519 "fellow travelers." Operations: BayHStA: MSo549, Neustadt Arbitration Board, 26 Aug. 1946; MSo249, Hertle, 10 Sep. 1948; StA-C LRA-15133, Lockland, 23 Oct. 1945; Beyersdorf, "Militärregierung," 140–163, 183–186.
123. "Als *Mitläufer* mit der Mitglieds-Nr. 10 653," *NP,* 10 Apr. 1948.
124. Vice-mayor Wilhelm Plitz, deemed a "fellow-traveler," had to resign by law. Coburg County saw forty-four ex-Nazis elected mayor, and fifteen County Councilors. SA-N StRPr 024–10/1, NecSR-6, 12 Oct. 1948; NACP RG260, OMGB-Cbg 1199–2, Tadross, AHR, 9 Aug. 1948; "Friedrich Schubart—Belasteter," *NP,* 7 Jul. 1948.
125. SA-S: C6–31, Hess, 8 Dec. 1947; C3–99, 5 Nov. 1948.
126. NACP RG260, OMGB-Cbg 1199–8, Sussell, QHR, 7 Oct. 1947.
127. Neustadt weekly reports: SA-N S697 and NACP RG260, OMGB-Cbg 1207–4. Coburg Office: Beyersdorf, "Militärregierung," 25–59.

128. NACP, RG260, OMGB-Cbg 1203–5, R., 3 Jan. 1948; 1203–6, Sussell, 11 Oct. 1947 and 21 Jan. 1948; StA-C LRA-15131, Lockland, 3 Nov. 1945. Third Reich petition strategies: Connelly, "Volksgemeinschaft," 928–930.

129. NACP RG260, OMGB-Cbg 1202–3, Sussell, 28 Sep. 1948. Correspondence: OMGB-Cbg 1202–1/2/3, 1203–5/6, 1204–2.

130. NACP RG260, OMGB-Cbg 1202–3, Sussell, 28 Sep. 1948.

131. "Acht Tage Spiel in Luft und Sonne," *NP*, 3 Aug. 1946. Weekly updates: SA-N 5697. FDJ: Matthäi, *Anfänge*, 46–48.

132. "Unser Bürgermeister berichtet," *TV*, 14 Jun. 1947.

133. SA-N 5697, Woltz, 21 Oct. 1947; SA-N StRPr 024–10/1, NecSR-28," 24 Nov. 1947. Overview: Beyersdorf, "Militärregierung," 99–101. "Reorientation": NACP RG260, OMGB-B 333–346.

134. SA-S C3–23, Geyer, 15 Aug. 1946.

135. NACP RG260, OMGB-Cbg 1202–5, Walston, 7 Sep. 1948.

136. Teßmer, *Geschichten*, 16.

137. Popular support for socialism: Pritchard, *Making*. Public opinion: Allinson, *Politics*, 21–44. Evolution within the East German leadership: Epstein, *Revolutionaries*.

138. SA-S C2–4, KPD-KL-Sbg, Circular-18, 11 Nov. 1945.

139. SA-S C2–4, KPD-KL-Sbg, Circular-20, 30 Nov. 1945. Representations and relations between German woman and African American soldiers: Fehrenbach, *Race*; Höhn, *GIs*.

140. Sonneberg County's KPD and SPD merged 12 April 1946 with 3,685 members, growing to 10,739 in 1947. "Erste gemeinsame Mitgliederversammlung," *TVz*, 30 Jan. 1946; "Start der SED in Sonneberg," *TV*, 16 Apr. 1946; "Mit der SED in eine bessere Zukunft!" *TV*, 26 Aug. 1947; Matthäi, *Anfänge*, 72–75, 91.

141. Votes: Sheffer, "Burned Bridge," 70–71. However, the SED did fail to get a majority in the City Council in 1946 and claimed only 56 percent of factory council representatives. Schoenau, *Sonneberg*, 62; Schwämmlein, "Sonneberg 1945–1990," 89. "Durchschlagender Erfolg der SED," *TV*, 13 Jul. 1946; "Wahlsieg der Sozialistichen Einheitspartei," *TV*, 10 Sep. 1946; "Wilhelm Pieck zeigt uns den Weg in die Zukunft!" *TV*, 19 Oct. 1946; SED die stärkste der Parteien," 22 Oct. 1946. Soviet Zone: Welsh, *Wandel*, 16.

142. ThHStAW LBdVP-365 Bd. 3, 184–186; SA-S C2–8, SbgSR-76, 11 Jun. 1948.

143. Interview, Elisabeth Dietzer.

144. Votes: Sheffer, "Burned Bridge," 68–69. Synthesized: "Kreistagswahlen bei geringerer Wahlbeteiligung," *NP*, 1 May 1946; "Wahlergebnisse der amerikansichen Zone," *NP*, 3 Jul. 1946; "Neustadt stimmte mit 'Nein,'" 4 Dec. 1946; NACP RG260, OMGB-Cbg 1201–1, "Landtag Election on 1 December 1946." Overview: Adam, *Volk*, 17–29. Resistance groups in Coburg County: NACP RG260, OMGB-Cbg 1202–9, MR, Dec. 1945, Jan. 1946; 1200–3, Klein, AHR, 23 Jun. 1946; "Sprengstoffvergehen 'christlicher Pfadfinder," *NP*, 6 Feb. 1946; BayHStA PrBGP-116, Heppner, 22 Jun. 1946.

145. Interview, Günter Oppinger.

146. BArch BY1–290, District Leadership Meeting, 14 Oct. 1945.

147. Elections: Scheuerich, *Geschichte*, 1:174–184. Early socialist organization: Gretzbach, *SPD*, 12–13; Grund, "Arbeiterbewegung," 113; Döbrich, "Aufruf"; Karl and Zetzmann, "Parteiarbeit"; Major, *KPD*. Protocols: Matthäi, *Anfänge*, 30–32. Monthly reports: NACP RG260, OMGUS-Exec.: 310–9 and 658–4. U.S. informants' reports: NACP RG260, OMGB-Cbg 1202–1205. Trade union monitoring: StA-C LRA-15131, Lockland, 30 Jul. 1945. Party licensing: Beyersdorf, "Militärregierung," 63–70, and Adam, *Volk*, 9–14.

Chapter 2: Insecurity

1. Strang, *Home*, 213 (Witzel, *Disturbed Ground*, 17).

2. NACP RG260, OMGUS-CAD-PS 326–9, Critchfield, 3 Oct. 1946.

3. Stacy, *Operations*, 4–8.

4. "Mich ärgert schon lange," *TVz*, 19 Oct. 1945; "Gegen die Gerüchtemacher," *TV*, 27 Jun. 1946, StA-C LRA-15131, US MG #40, 16 Jul. 1945.

5. "Bürgermeister Edgar Müller," *NP*, 28 Aug. 1973; "27 Jahre Gemeindeoberhaupt," *CT*, 29 Aug. 1973. Incidents: NACP RG260, OMGB-Cbg 1200–2, WPS; ThHStAW Th-MInn 3033 (1, 47).

6. BayHStA B-StK-10277, Hacht, 14 Jul. 1945; Schäffer, 18 Jun. 1945.

7. BayHStA B-StK-10859, Heppner, 26 Oct. 1945; BayHStA B-StK-10277, Correspondence, 1945–1946; Schmidt, *Freiheit*, 36.

8. StA-C LRA-15269, Coburg County Chairman, 6 Aug. 1945.
9. E.g., "Ernährungslage und deutsche Einheit," *TV*, 20 Feb. 1948; SA-S C3–15, Lohau School, 10 Nov. 1945.
10. NACP RG260, OMGB-Cbg 1200–3, Klein, AHR, 23 Jun. 1946; NACP RG260, OMGB-Cbg 1207–3, Weppler, 16 Aug. 1949; "Interzonale Gasversorgung," *NP*, 21 Aug. 1946; SA-S C3–13, Reconstruction Director, 6 Sep. 1945.
11. NACP RG260 OMGB-Cbg 1200–3, Klein, AHR, 23 Jun. 1946.
12. ThHStAW Th-MInn 716/2, 104.
13. SA-S C2–201 (StA-M Bib-7827), Glöckner, Jun. 1945.
14. ThHStAW Th-MInn 3969, 3.
15. ThHStAW Th-MInn 3969, 1–3; ThHStAW Th-MInn 3970, Sonneberg Red Cross, 3 Sep. 1945.
16. NACP RG260: OMGB-Cbg 1200–3, Klein, AHR, 23 Jun. 1946; OMGUS-Exec. 310–9, MG-I2B3-Cbg, 20 Jul. 1945.
17. Stacy, *Operations*, 6; Schmidt, *Coburg*, 34.
18. Chandler, *Institutions*, 63 (55–79).
19. SA-S C16–172, Weinland, 9 Jul. 1945.
20. SA-S C16–172, file; SA-S C3–24, Sonneberg Welfare Office, Sep. 1945; e.g., "Neue Ausgehzeit," *TVz*, 8 Sep. 1945.
21. NACP RG260, OMGUS-CAD-PS 326–8, McCraw, 3 Jul. 1946; Milburn, 9 Jul. 1946. Overviews: Stacy, *Operations*, 5–6; Schmidt, *Grenze*, 57.
22. NACP RG407, 6th-CRgt 18400, "Survey," 16 Jul. 1946; NACP RG260, OMGB-CAD-PS: 67–3, OMGB-Cbg, 3 and 23 Aug. 1946; 356–4, Heppner, Jul.–Aug. 1946.
23. American Zone: NACP RG407, 6th-Const-Regt, 6th Sqdn 18423, "Operations," 1 Jul., 2 Aug. 1946. Ebersdorf: StA-C LRA-14659–14660. Meilschnitz: SA-N MB-117, Müller, 17 Sep., 18 Nov. 1946. Soviet Zone: e.g., ThHStAW Th-MInn 3969, 1; NACP RG260: OMGB-Cbg 1200–2, WPS, 3 Aug. 1946; OMGB-ID: 153–8, Rodes, 14 Oct. 1947.
24. NACP RG260, OMGB-Cbg 1200–3; Robie, CYH, 20 Jul. 1947.
25. Interview, Stefan Taubert, Neustadt, 15 Jul. 2001.
26. Greendel to Sheffer, 25 Jan. 2001.
27. Interviews, Jack Gunderson, Stan Witkowski.
28. Private possession, Thull; N., 23 Aug. 1999; interview, Berthold Thiel, Neustadt, 17 Feb. 2003.
29. BayHStA PrBGP 118, Riedl, 16 Apr. 1949.
30. E.g., ThHStAW Th-MInn 1130, TBP Weimar, 26 Apr. 1948; BayHStA PrBGP 118, Riedl, 20 May 1949.
31. NACP RG260: OMGB-Cbg 1200–3, Robie, CYH, 20 Jul. 1947; Schultke, *"Keiner,"* 19; NACP RG260: OMGUS-CAD-PS 326–8, BBP Commissariats; OMGB-B 129–1, BBP-Nec, 2 Feb. 1949; OMGB-ID 158–6, OMGB-IA, 4 Feb. 1948. American Zone operations: OMGUS-CAD-PS 326–9; Stacy, *Operations*, 9–24, 33–35; Schmidt, *Grenze*, 55–63.
32. BayHStA B-StK-10859, Heppner, 9 Apr. 1946.
33. Schmidt, *Coburg*, 38–39.
34. NACP RG260: OMGB-Cbg 1200–2, WPS, 29 Nov. 1946; OMGUS-CAD-PS 275–9, "Intelligence Report No. 78," 14 Nov. 1947. Files: BayHStA PrBGP-116–117.
35. NACP RG260: OMGB-ID 158–5, Larned, 13 Aug. 1947; OMGB-ID 158–6, Sims, 24. Nov 1947.
36. NACP RG260 OMGB-Cbg 1200–2, WPS, 1 Nov. 1946; BayHStA B-StK-10859, Heppner, 9 Apr. 1946.
37. NACP RG260, OMGB-ID: 170–3, 5; OMGB-Cbg 1200–2, WPS, 29 Jun. and 27 Jul. 1946; OMGB-ID158–6, correspondence. "Nazified" sentries: OMGUS-CAD-PS: 326–9, Balthis, 31 Jan. 1947; OMGUS IA&C, 13 Feb. 1947; OMGB-ID:158–6, Rogers, 24 Jun. 1948.
38. Divergent East German accounts: Beth and Ehlert, *Militär- und Sicherheitspolitik*, 367–373.
39. Schultke, *"Keiner"*, 19; Bessel, "Making," 205–213.
40. SA-S: C2–7, SbgSR-42, 10 Dec. 1947; C3–99, SbgSR-109, 13 Nov. 1948; File: C6–31; e.g., C2–2, Sonneberg Office of the Mayor, 23 Aug. 1946; StA-M KR-S S5/11 1/79, Baumann, 5 Feb. 1946. Overview: Bessel, "Making," 205–208.
41. ThHStAW LBdVP-166, 57, Ripperger, 24 Jul. 1948.
42. Grams, *Grenze*, 14.
43. ThHStA: BMPr 1144, Film 102, 164–166; Th-MInn 1135, 64–69. E.g., "Beschlagnahmte Waren wurden verteilt," *TV*, 10 Sep. 1946; "Er hatte es selbst aufgegessen!" *TV*, 12 Jan. 1948. Eastern confiscations: Bessel, "Making," 211–212.
44. E.g., Interviews, Elisabeth Dietzer, Berthold Thiel, and Jakob Ziegler.

45. ThHStAW Th-MInn 1193, 36–39. History of the *Schießbefehl*: Sälter, *Grenzpolizisten*, 162–176. People's Police: Lindenberger, *Volkspolizei*, 37–49; Bessel, "Policing."

46. E.g., ThHStAW: LBdVP 166, 26; Th-MInn 1193, 36–39. U.S. interrogations: NACP RG260, OMGUS-CAD-PS 302–4.

47. NACP RG260, OMGUS-CAD-PS 459–12, Clay to Sokolovsky, 29 Feb. 1948; plus correspondence. Overview: "Raids by Russians Arouse Bavarians," *NYT*, 27 Feb. 1948. Soviet incursions over Austrian and Czechoslovak borders do not appear to have been as numerous; e.g., OMGUS-CAD-PS 275–9.

48. E.g., BayHStA PrBGP 116, BBP-Nec, 26 Aug. 1946; BayHStA PrBGP 117, Zanker, 8 Jun. 1948; Teßmer, *Geschichten*, 88–89.

49. Summary: NACP RG260, OMGB-ID 7–1, OMGB-PS to Muller, 11 Mar. 1946. E.g., NACP RG260, OMGUS-Exec. 310–9, Klein, 19 Jan. 1946.

50. NACP RG260 OMGB-Cbg 1200–2, WPS, 18 Oct. 1946.

51. Overview: NACP RG260, OMGB-Cbg 1200–3, Klein, AHR, 23 Jun. 1946.

52. BayHStA PrBGP-118, Mulzer, 17 Jun. 1949.

53. NACP RG260, OMGUS-CAD-PS 335–2, Riedl, 11 May 1949.

54. Interview, Norm Greendel. E.g., NACP RG260: OMGB-ID 7–1, Urton, 27 Mar. 1946; OMGUS-CAD-PS 323–6, BBP-Dir, 6 Jun. 1946.

55. E.g., BayHStA PrBGP-117, Heppner, 3 Jan. 1948; Schmidt, *Coburg*, 43.

56. Unusual trial publication: BayHStA PrBGP-117, Rohan, 24 Aug. 1948; "Amerikanisches Militärgericht verurteilt Ostzonenpolizisten," *Neue Zeitung*, 28 Sep. 1948.

57. StA-C StAnw-54, 1, 8–10; NACP, RG260, OMGUS-CAD-PS 291–8, EUCOM-27, 12 Feb. 1948.

58. RG260, OMGB-Cbg 1200–3, Robie, CYH, 20 Jul. 1947. Thirteen involved the U.S. Constabulary, twenty the Bavarian Border Police, and thirty-two German civilians. Incidence was likely higher the prior year, some suggesting shootings daily: Schmidt, "Spähpanzer lief mit Jauche voll," *NP*, 29 Aug. 1996; Scheuerich, *Neustadt*, 1:249–261. The relative rarity of American-instigated shootings is suggested by the considerable attention they received: e.g., "U.S. Officer Slays Russian in German Border Incident," *WP*, 10 Jul. 1949.

59. NACP RG260 OMGB-Cbg 1200–2, WPS, 8 Feb. 1946.

60. BayHStA PrBGP 116, BBP-Cbg, 16 Dec. 1947. Similar: NACP RG260, OMGB-Cbg 1202–9, Klein, MR, 5 Sep. 1946.

61. StA-C StAnw: case holdings; -54, BLP, "Tötungsdelikte," 20–26, (44–46); "Zwanzig Jahre Zonengrenze," *NT*, 21 Sep. 1964.

62. NACP RG260 OMGB-Cbg 1200–2, WPS, 22 Jun. 1946; StA-C StAnw-29, District Attorney, 1946.

63. SA-S C2–23, Christmas skit, Dec. 1948.

64. StA-C StAnw-31, District Attorney, 1946.

65. NACP RG260, OMGB-Cbg 1202–9, Klein, MHR, 5 Mar. 1946.

66. BayHStA PrBGP-116, State Police Criminal Office-Cbg, 6 and 14 Sep. 1946.

67. "Notzuchtverbrechen?" *NP*, 26 Apr. 1949 (name changed). BayHStA PrBGP-118, State Police Criminal Office-Cbg, Deposition, 1 Apr. 1949; NACP RG260, OMGB-B 1128–2, Kampmann, 10 Mar. 1949; Weisel, 23 Mar. 1949.

68. NACP RG260, OMGUS-CAD-PS 356–4, Heppner, 5 Jul. 1946.

69. ThHStAW Th-MInn 1126–1133, TBP Reports, Köppelsdorf/Thuringia, 1947–1948.

70. NACP RG260, OMGB-Cbg 1200–3, Klein, AHR, 23 Jun. 1946. Violence diminished as the Soviet Army became stricter over time, but did not disappear; Naimark, *Russians*, 90–97.

71. In addition to five cases of Soviet shootings, four abductions, and one American shooting; StA-C StAnw: case holdings; -54, BLP, "Tötungsdelikte," 20–26. Inquiries: e.g., NACP RG260, OMGUS-CAD-PS 275–9, ODI-78, 14 Nov. 1947.

72. NACP RG260, OMGB-Cbg 1200–2, WPS, 8 Feb. 1946.

73. StA-C LRA-15131, Rodach Mayor, 2 May 1947; NACP RG260, OMGB-Cbg 1200–2, WPS, 9 Mar. 1946; OMGB-ID 7–1, Reese, 8 Mar. 1946. Additional: OMGUS-CAD-PS 323–8, Heppner, 29 Apr. 1946.

74. NACP RG260, OMGUS-CAD-PS 276–23, Klein, 29 Aug. 1946.

75. StA-C LRA-15269, Coburg County Chairman, 6 Aug. 1945.

76. NACP RG407, 6th-CRgt 18400, "Survey," 16 Jul. 1946.

77. SA-S C3–102, Sonneberg County Chairman, 27 Nov. 1946.

78. NACP RG260, OMGB-ID 170–3, HQ Third U.S. Army, 24 Oct. 1946.

79. StA-C LRA-14671, 4 Feb. 1946. Provisional arrangements: NACP RG407, 6th-CRgt 18400, "Survey," 16 Jul. 1946; SA-N MB-254; ThHStAW Th-MInn 3035, 49.

80. The number of Meilschnitzers granted field passes for the Soviet Zone fluctuated greatly: SA-N MB-117.

81. SA-S C16–172, Sonneberg Office of the Mayor, 2, 14 Aug. 1945; StA-C LRA-15269, Coburg County Chairman, 6 Aug. 1945; ThHStAW Th-MInn 3969, 1.

82. Private possession, Mulzer: Greiner, "Errinnerungen," date unknown.

83. NACP RG407, 6th-CRgt 18400, "Survey," 16 Jul. 1946.

84. Compiled PS and BBP reports, 1946–1951. Between Bavaria and the Soviet Zone in 1948, 800–1,500 people a day crossed each direction with an interzonal pass, and 150 per day with frontier passes: OMGUS-CAD-PS 335–2, "Traffic between Bavaria and the Soviet Zone"; OMGB-ID 158–6, Rohan, 4 Feb. 1948. In the early 1950s, travel through Burned Bridge was less than 10 percent of total legal traffic between Bavaria and East Germany.

85. ThHStAW LBdVP-175, 191–195, 231–232. Around 1,500–2,800 Neustadters traveled to the Soviet Zone each year with an interzonal pass; SA-N 5698, 52; SA-S C3–69–70, "Register," Jan. 1947–Jun. 1948. Sonneberg registered an average of 230 western visitors a month, 30 percent of whom were from the Coburg region, including 10 percent from Neustadt.

86. Application processes: SA-S C16–172; St-N 3021; ThHStAW Th-MInn 3035, 3; ThHStAW Th-MInn 1581, 5.

87. NACP RG260, OMGB-Cbg 1208–1, "Border Crossing," 18 Apr. 1949; Hartmann, 13 Apr. 1949. Allocations: StA-C LRA-15269; SA-N MB-117.

88. NACP RG260: OMGUS-CAD-PS 275–9, EUCOM-14, 18 Aug. 1947. E.g., checkpoint negotiations: OMGUS-CAD-PS 291–9, Oct.–Nov. 1947.

89. Crossing estimates vary widely according to reporting agency, variance in force strength, and patrol distances. In the American zone, Coburg's Border Police typically apprehended 40 to 180 people per day and made fewer than four formal arrests, while the Soviet zone People's Police arrested an average of 50 to 100 people per day. Ranges derived from numerous reports: e.g., NACP RG260, OMGB-Cbg 1200–2; 1205–2/3; BayHStA LFlüV 1120, 19–26; ThHStAW Th-MInn 1126–1133.

90. ThHStAW Th-MInn 1126–1133; NACP RG260, OMGB-ID 158–6, Rohan, Jan.–Feb. 1948; OMGUS-POW&DP 198–2, OMGUS, Aug. 1947. More densely populated regions to the west and north posed greater problems for border forces. Additional: Bessel, "Making," 210–211.

91. "Der Grenzgänger auf dem Weg von Fürth am Berg," *FW*, 29 Dec. 2004.

92. While the skewed proportion could reflect police bias rather than actual crossings, the ratio is remarkably consistent across all border reports.

93. NACP RG260, OMGUS-CAD-PS 335–2, "Traffic between Bavaria-Soviet Zone," 1949; 275–9, "BBP Arrests and Rejections," EUCOM Intel.

94. NACP RG260: OMGUS-CAD-PS 291–8, EUCOM Intel—21, 24 Nov. 1947; Reeves, 11 Feb. 1949; NACP RG260, OMGB-Cbg 1199–8, Klein, CQH, 14 Jan. 1947; MR, 5 Sep. 1946; QHR, 19 Apr. 1947; "Über 3000 Grenzübertritte seit Mai 1945," *NP*, 1 Feb. 1947. Local courts became the primary venue for border prosecutions after 1948.

95. Hoßfeld, "Grenzschließung," *NP*, 22 Jan 1994. Of the 3,085 people arrested by the Sonneberg People's Police prior to currency reform (7 May–23 Jun. 1948), 94 percent were Soviet Zone residents; 86 percent were released, 3 percent held for questioning, 10 percent handed to the Soviet command, and the rest handed directly to the Criminal Police; ThHStAW Th-MInn 1126–1133, TBP Reports, Köppelsdorf, 1948. Arrest procedures: Lapp, *Gefechtsdienst*, 14–15.

96. Interview, Elisabeth Dietzer.

97. "Der Grenzgänger auf dem Weg von Fürth am Berg," *FW*, 29 Dec. 2004.

98. Schleevoigt, "Heubisch," 25.

99. Sheffer, survey, "Gebrannte Brücke." Some may have been unwilling to confess to illegal crossings in their (anonymous) answers, but locals commonly boast of early border adventures.

100. Schleevoigt, "Heubisch," 21.

101. Grams, *Grenze*, 17–18. Unhunted wild boars: NACP RG260, OMGB-Cbg 1199–8, Sussell, QHR, 16 Jan. 1948.

102. "Der entfleuchte Braten," *NP*, 31 Aug. 1948.

103. "Ein Weg Mit 'Hindernissen' Zur Bergmühle," *NP*, 20 Aug. 1949.

104. "Die 'zergrenzte' Bergmühle," *NP*, 25 Aug. 1948. Abduction of building resident: BayHStA PrBGP 116, Heppner, 22, 27 Oct. 1947.

105. Interview, Günter Oppinger.

106. Interview, Inge Mulzer, Brigitte Laub, Neustadt, 13 Dec. 2002.

107. NACP RG260, OMGB-Cbg 1202–1, Schweiger, 17 Feb. 1948. E.g., BayHStA PrBGP-116, BBP-Cbg, 10 Oct. 1947.

108. Interview, Günter Oppinger; Schleevoigt, "Heubisch," 19.
109. Interview, Kurt Geis, Sonneberg, 1 Jul. 2002.
110. Interview, Mathilde Schuster, Neustadt, 25 Feb. 2003.
111. Interview, Elisabeth Dietzer.
112. Grams, *Grenze*, 11.
113. Unusual defense of western guards, who appreciated "purely human and noble arguments" for crossing yet still had to enforce the law: "Zerstörte Bahnverbindungen hergestellt," *NP*, 11 Sep. 1946.
114. Interview, Berthold Thiel.
115. "Bajuwarische Grenzen," *NP*, 8 Oct. 1947.
116. "Früher gab es kein 'hüben' und 'drüben'!" *TV*, 19 May 1948.
117. F., "Blick über die Grenze," *NP*, 17 Aug. 1946.
118. Stegemann, "Zonengrenzen," *NP*, 29 May 1948.
119. Schüler, "Blick von der Linder-Ruh," *NP*, 23 Sep. 1948.
120. Public opinion: e.g., NACP RG260, OMGB-Cbg 1205–2: Quick, "Interview of Border-Crossers," Dec. 1947; OMGB-ID 112–9, U.S. Civil Censorship, 30 Sep. 1946; SA-S C2–4, KPD-KL-Sbg, Circular-11, 23 Aug. 1945; BArch-K B106–15424.
121. Dorst, *Deutsche Stücke*, 382 (Erken, 605). Born in Oberlind in 1925, Dorst has written more than thirty plays and received several awards, including the Gerhart Hauptmann Prize, the Georg Büchner Prize, and the ETA Hoffmann Prize.
122. "Wirtschaftliche Folgen durch illegale Grenzgänger," *NP*, 16 Dec. 1948, "'Späte Mädchen' im Scheinwerferlicht," *NP*, 12 Sep. 1950. Wricke, "Große und kleine Sünder an der 'Grenze,'" *TV*, 21 Aug. 1948.
123. "Wirtschaftliche," *NP*, 16 Dec 1948; "'Späte Mädchen,'" *NP*, 12 Sep. 1950. Wricke, "Große und kleine Sünder," *TV*, 21 Aug. 1948. Neustadt District Court, StA-C AG-N, cases 34 and 151 (self-cataloged).
124. "Penicillin und Insulin für Coburg," *NP*, 6 Mar, 1946. As border cities, both Neustadt and Sonneberg took additional public health precautions (i.e., frontier quarantine stations); e.g., SA-N MB-254, Mayors' Conference, 6 Nov. 1945.
125. "Heinersdorf, die Grenzgemeinde," *TV*, 13 Aug. 1946.
126. StA-C StAnw-30, District Attorney Records, Apr.–Aug. 1951. Due to lack of zonal cooperation, "information on previous convictions [was] almost impossible to ascertain," and criminals could flee over the border with relative impunity; NACP RG260, OMGB-Cbg 1200–3, Robie, CYH, 20 Jul. 1947. Elsewhere: Bailey, *Iron Curtain*, 79.
127. "In Coburg lauert die Reaktion," *TV*, 14 Dec. 1946. Later training materials for East Germany's border guards taught that smuggling, "organized from the western zones," necessitated the early "struggle against speculators and saboteurs" and was to blame for border escalations: Reisenweber, *Reihe*, 1:9–10; Hanisch, *Anfang*, 1:5.
128. Interview, Kurt Geis.
129. Merritt, *Democracy*, 319, 332.
130. E.g., SA-N 4403, Gindele, MR, 1946; BayHStA PrBGP-116, BBP-Cbg, 26 Nov. 1946; SA-S C3–106, TH-MInn, 22 Mar. 1947; Sonneberg Chairman, 16 Apr. 1947; "Eine Kartoffelaktion," *TV*, 1 Dec. 1947.
131. "Unser Bürgermeister gab Rechenschaft," *TV*, 21 Aug. 1946, "So sieht es im 'goldenen Westen' aus!" *TV*, 26 May 1948.
132. "Die Fleischversorgung," *NP*, 21 Oct. 1948. Food protests: NACP RG260, OMGB-Cbg 1207–4, Woltz, 21 Apr. 1948; SA-N 5697, Woltz, WR, 28 Jan. 1948; "Machtvolle Streikkundgebung," *NP*, 28 Jan. 1948.
133. E.g., SA-S C2–1, E., 12 Jul. 1945; SA-S C2–2, M., 30 Sep. 1946; SA-N 5697, Woltz, WR, 5 Nov. 1947; StRPr 024–10/1, "NecSR-28," 18 Dec. 1947.

Chapter 3: Inequality

1. The Eichsfeld: Schaefer, "Ironing," chs. 1 and 4.
2. E.g., Greiner-Vetter, "Hochzeitsreise," 146–153.
3. "Zu Besuch bei einem 'diamantenen' Ehepaar," *NP*, 11 Sep. 1948.
4. E.g., Story collections: Grafe, *Grenze*; Hartmann and Doering-Manteuffel, eds., *Grenzgeschichten*.
5. NACP RG260: OMGB-Cbg 1200–2, WPS, 20 Jul. 1946; OMGB-ID 158–5, Larned, 13 Aug. 1947.
6. Interviews, Jack Gunderson, Ray Davis, and Berthold Thiel.

7. NACP RG260, OMGB-Cbg 1199–8, Sussell, QHR, 16 Jan., Apr. 1948; 1202–5, "Agricultural situation," 10 Jun. 1948; "Machtvolle Streikkundgebung," *NP*, 28 Jan. 1948. Legal register, Burned Bridge imports/exports: OMGB-Cbg 1208–4.

8. Interviews, Norm Greendel, Jim Nolan. Values fluctuated, but in Neustadt in 1946, average wages were around 35 RM a week, American cigarettes were 8 RM, and a pound of flour was 50 RM; SA-N 5697, Woltz, WR, 8 Nov. 1946; Grams, *Grenze*, 5.

9. Interview, Mathilde Schuster.

10. Interview, Günter Oppinger.

11. Interview, Kurt Geis.

12. StA-C LRA-14709, esp. Langer, 17 Jul. 1946.

13. E.g., "Mit falschem Registrierschein," *NP*, 17 Aug. 1946, "Kennkarten auf Vorrat," *NP*, 9 Oct. 1946; SA-S: C2–7, SbgSR-55, 2 Mar. 1948; C6–25, R., 4 Jul. 1947.

14. "50 RM für eine Handwagen-Fahrt," *NP*, 7, 14. Jan 1948, "Kinder im Dienste der Grenzgänger," *NP*, 11 Oct. 1947.

15. "Im Fieber der Erwartung," *NP*, 19 Jun. 1948.

16. "'Ich will mein Geld los werden . . .'" *TV*, 23 Jun. 1948.

17. NACP RG260, OMGUS-CAD-PS 335–1, Hays, 16 Jun. 1948; SA-S C2–8, SbgSR-79, 18 Jun. 1948; "Am Schlagbaum zwischen Ost- und West," *NP*, 26 Jun 1948; e.g., "U.S. Zonal Border Closed by Soviet," *NYT*, 18 Jun 1948.

18. "Thüringens Sicherheitsmaßnahmen," *TV*, 23 Jun. 1948.

19. "Am Stichtag der Währungsreform," *NP*, 23 Jun. 1948; NACP RG260, OMGB-Cbg 1207–4, Woltz, 30 Jun. 1948; ThHStAW Th-MInn 1126–1133, TBP Reports, Köppelsdorf/Thuringia, 1947–1948.

20. SA-S C3–108, Daily County Police Reports, 1948–1949; "Herr Kritikus ist natürlich wieder nicht zufrieden!" *TV*, 28 Jun., 1948; "Fünfzig Millionen Mark umgetauscht," *TV*, 2 Jul. 1948.

21. "D-Mark als Magnet an der Zonengrenze," *NP*, 12 Oct. 1948.

22. Apprehending an average of 1,330 people and 10,000 East marks per day; Glaser, "*Reorganisation*," 303. In Coburg County, an average of 70 border-goers per month claimed to be political refugees; of these, around six per month were eastern People's Police. Crossing statistics: NACP RG466, HICOG-ID-Brd 1–2 and RG260, OMGB-B 1129–1, BBP-Dir, Monthly Reports. Published weekly BBP reports, *NP*, 1951–52. Tadross to OMGB-ID, 2 Nov. 1948. NACP RG260, OMGB-Cbg 1202–5. BArch-K B106–15423, Ankermüller, 14 Nov. 1949.

23. E.g., BayHStA B-MInn 91695, Riedl, 25 Jan. 1950.

24. Grams, *Grenze*, 30.

25. SA-S C2–23, Sonneberg Post Office Staff, Christmas skit, Dec. 1948.

26. "Was gibt es heute im Kaufhaus Konsum?" *TV*, 17 Dec. 1949.

27. Sonneberg Police reports, e.g., ThHStAW LBdVP 365 Bd. 1, 151–152, 162; StA-M SED-KL-Sbg 307, SED-KL-Sbg, Minutes, 16 Nov. 1949.

28. Small-scale smuggling in the Eichsfeld: Schaefer, "Ironing," ch. 1.

29. "'Fabrikanten lachen über Jedermann-Waren,'" *NP*, 16 Sep. 1948; "Preise klettern in die Höhe," *NP*, 2 Nov. 1948.

30. Term origination: Thompson, *Making*.

31. SA-N 2050, Weppler to Ehard, 18 Nov. 1948.

32. "Geht nicht schwarz über die Zonengrenze," *TV*, 11 Jul. 1946, "Unterstützt die Volkskontrollausschüsse!" *TV*, 26 Nov. 1947. E.g., ThHStAW Th-MInn 716/2, 25.

33. "Spielwarenindustrie erlebt Hochkonjunktur," *NP*, 2 Oct. 1948.

34. "Kalorien wandern über die Grenze," *NP*, 7 Feb. 1948; e.g., "Eine 'schwarze' Ochsengeschichte," *NP*, 29 Nov. 1947.

35. "Coburger Hamsternest ausgehoben," *TV*, 2 May 1946; "Eine Pestbeule wurde aufgestochen!" *TV*, 14 Dec. 1946; "Warenverteiler, wie sie nicht sein sollen!" *TV*, 12 Jul. 1946; Walter, "Interview mit Herrn Schieber," 18. Dec 1946.

36. Cohen, *Moral Panics*.

37. Broader conflicts over displaced children in Europe: Zahra, *Lost Children*.

38. ThHStAW BMPr 1854, 4, Film 151, Stempel, 10 Nov. 1949; "Kinder kommen über die Grenze," *NP*, 23 Oct. 1948.

39. SA-S C2–17, Hess, "Stadtratsprotokollen, 1946–1950," 1952. E.g., Teßmer, *Geschichten*, 65; SA-N 2050, Seifert, 6 Dec. 1948. Schooling in the Soviet Zone: Blessing, *Classroom*; Lansing, *Schoolteachers*, 129–215.

40. Interview, Götz Emrich, Sonneberg, 1 Jul. 2002.

41. Interview, Hannelore Reuther, Neustadt/Wildenheid, 27 Jun. 2002.

42. "Kinder kommen über die Grenze," *NP*, 23 Oct. 1948; SA-S C10–3, Minutes, "Schulschwänzerei-Grenzgängerei," 19 Oct. 1949.

43. "Kinder als Sendboten des Hungers," *NP*, 11 Sep. 1948; "Jugendliche Langfinger," *NP*, 12 May 1948; "Werden die Erwachsenen darüber lächeln?" *NP*, Feb. 1948; "Kinder beraubt," *NP*, 23 Jul. 1947.

44. SA-N 2050, Weppler to Ehard, 18 Nov. 1948. The term "plague" is also used in Sonneberg sources.

45. "Kinder kommen über die Grenze," *NP*, 23 Oct. 1948; SA-S C10–3, Munich Youth Office, 23 Oct. 1947.

46. SA-S C10–3, Bamberg Catholic Travellers' Aid Society, 8 May 1948; NACP RG466, HICOG-ID-Brd 1–2, Riedel, MR, 16 Aug. 1950.

47. SA-S C10–3, Bamberg City Council, 13 Oct. 1947; correspondence, 1947–1949. Publicized: "Grenzübertritte," *TV*, 22 Nov. 1947.

48. SA-S C10–3, Bamberg Diocese Caritas Union, 7 Nov. 1947.

49. "Öffentliche Elternabende der SED," *TV*, 26 Jan. 1948.

50. SA-S: C10–3, SbgSR-77, 14 Jun. 1948; City Council, parent form letter, 27 Nov. 1947; Minutes, "Schulschwänzerei-Grenzgängerei," 19 Oct. 1949; C2–7, SbgSR-41, 15 Nov. 1947; "Jeder ehrliche Friedenskämpfer," *TV*, 22 Sep. 1949. The City Youth Office advocated softer solutions such as providing lunch and milk in schools; SA-S: C10–3, Böhme, 11 Oct. 1948; C3–97, SbgSR-115, 18 Dec. 1948.

51. "Öffentliche Elternabende der SED," *TV*, 26 Jan. 1948; "Noch einmal: Schule und Elternschaft," *TV*, 27 Jan. 1948; "Wir sprechen mit Schulleiter Schöntag . . ." *TV*, 30 Jan. 1948.

52. "Ernste Aufgaben für das Arbeitsamt," *TV*, 12 Oct. 1949.

53. SA-S C3–97, Sonneberg Community Councils, 24 Jan. 1949; Hess, 11 Jan. 1949.

54. "Ernste Aufgaben für das Arbeitsamt," *TV*, 12 Oct. 1949; SA-S C2–7, SbgSR-74, 3 Jun. 1948.

55. SA-S: C10–3, Sonneberg Social Committee—8, 20 Dec. 1948; Coburg Youth Office, 3 Dec. 1948; C3–97, SbgSR-115, 18 Dec. 1948; "Grenzgängerei eine ernste Gefahr!" *TV*, 11 Oct. 1949.

56. BArch-B DE1 5303, 41–46; BayHStA LFlüV 1152, 37–46.

57. "Ein Kind wird zum Verbrecher," *TV*, 20 May 1949; "Bahnfahrgespräch," *TV*, 20 Aug. 1949; "Wir wollen Lehren daraus ziehen!" 12 Nov. 1949.

58. SA-N 5697, Woltz, WR, 22 Aug. 1946 and 29 Oct. 1947. E.g., "'Ihren Ausweis, bitte!'" *TV*, 7 Jun. 1948; "Wenn man illegal die Grenze passiert," *NP*, 15 Oct. 1947. Reinforcements: e.g., SA-N StRPr 024–10/1, NecSR-16 and 24, 10 Feb., 25 Jul. 1947. Rein ThHStAW LBdVP 365 Bd. 1, 44.

59. "Machtvolle Streikkundgebung," *NP*, 28 Jan. 1948.

60. "Wenn man illegal die Grenze passiert," *NP*, 15 Oct. 1947.

61. Overview: Sälter, *Grenzpolizisten*, 61–69.

62. "Entschlossene Kampfansage gegen den Schwarzhandel," *DV*, 13 Nov. 1951. Border trial records were not found in Sonneberg's city or county archives, nor in Thuringia's state archives at Meiningen or Weimar. Select 1948 titles: "Einbrecherbande unschädlich gemacht," *TV*, 8 Jun. 1948; "Diebe und Betrüger," *TV*, 26 Jul. 1948; "Ein warnendes Beispiel!" *TV*, 30 Aug. 1948; "Im Schnellverfahren abgeurteilt," *TV*, 7 Sep. 1948. From June 1948 to July 1949, eastern border police apprehended 490,634 people, 2,783 of whom were charged with smuggling (215 for spying and sabotage, and 2,418 for "criminal acts"). Ritter and Lapp, *Grenze*, 18; Hanisch, *Anfang*, 57.

63. "Illegale Grenzgängerei wird zur Landplage," *NP*, 27 Nov. 1948.

64. SA-N 2050, Weppler, 18 Nov. 1948.

65. NACP RG260, OMGB-Cbg 1207–2, Weppler, 8 Nov. 1948; NACP RG260, OMGB-Cbg 1202–5, Tadross, 2 Nov. 1948; SA-N 2050, Weppler, 18 Nov. 1948. Weppler also urged the replacement of native policemen with sentries not familiar with the local population.

66. BayHStA B-MInn 91695, Seifert, 6 Dec. 1948; Resch, 28 Apr. 1949; SA-N 2050, Kääb, 2 Dec. 1948.

67. "Woran erkennt man Falschgeld?" *NP*, 2 Mar. 1950; "Sieben Mann einer Insulin-Schmugglerbande gefaßt," *NP*, 13 Jun. 1950.

68. "'Welt im Film' in Neustadt," *NP*, 14 Oct. 1948; "Illegale Grenzgängerei wird zur Landplage," *NP*, 27 Nov. 1948; "Illegaler Grenzübertritt bestraft," *TV*, 19 Nov. 1948.

69. Compiled: StA-C AG-N, Neustadt District Court, 1949–1952. Coburg's State Archive contains records for approximately 1,080 Neustadt defendants in 550 cases. Because the cases shifted abruptly from economic to political, the data from these files has been divided into Jan. 1949–Oct. 1950 (650 defendants, 410 incidents) and Nov. 1950–Jun. 1952 (430 defendants, 140 incidents).

70. Forty percent were headed westward, and 11 percent eastward.

71. StA-C AG-N, 269.

72. Unusual critique: "Eine 'gerechtfertigte' Denunziation," *NP*, 4 Sep. 1948. Of the other border-goers caught in Neustadt, 47 percent were outside (in streets or nearby fields) and 22 percent were at the train station.

73. E.g., StA-C AG-N 461; NACP RG466, HICOG-ID-Brd 2–1, Thomsen, 5 Feb. 1951; ThHStAW LBdVP-365 Bd. 1, 156.

74. StA-C AG-N, 168.

75. Charges were brought under U.S. Military Government Laws 53 and 161 for the "prohibited import of wares" and "illegal border crossing." In 1949 probationary sentences ran four to six weeks, and were shortened in 1950 to only a few weeks or days.

76. NACP RG260, OMGB-Cbg 1202–5, Tadross, 2 Nov. 1948; "Unerlaubter Grenzübertritt und seine Auswirkungen," *TV*, 5 Jan. 1950.

77. Notable case: StA-C StAnw-33, "Strafanzeige," 28 Mar. 1954. Resolution to prosecute western purchasers: SA-N 2050, Seifert, 6 Dec. 1948.

78. StA-C AG-N, 308–312, to Neustadt Customs Office, 4 Apr. 1950; Neustadt District Court Minutes, 12 Oct. 1950; "Ostzonale Schäfchen führen zum Gericht," *NP*, 14 Oct. 1950 (name changed).

79. StA-C AG-N, 265, VBSCH, 9 Sep. 1950; plus file.

80. StA-C AG-N, 285; also 59, 467–469; "Waren für 9000 DM illegal eingeführt," *NP*, 5 Dec. 1950; "Freispruch in Sachen 'Christbaumschmuck,'" *NP*, 3 Apr. 1951.

81. "D-Mark als Magnet an der Zonengrenze," *NP*, 12 Oct. 1948.

82. Scheuerich, *Geschichte*, 1:246. Sales and auctions waned over time, but continued until 1952; in all of Coburg County, border police confiscated an average of 20,000 DM worth of goods per month from 1948 to 1951; NACP RG466, HICOG-ID-Brd 1–2 and RG260, OMGB-B 1129–1, BBP-Dir, Monthly Reports. Sale of captured textiles in the Eichsfeld: Schaefer, "Ironing," ch. 1.

83. NACP RG260, OMGB-B 1129–1, Riedl, "Verstärkung der Bayer. Landesgrenzpolizei," 9 Apr. 1949; "800 Millionen DM Jahresverlust durch Schmuggel," *NP*, 11 May 1950. Other border communities: e.g., BArch-K B137–691, Hartmann, 24 Mar. 1950; BayHStA PrBGP-118, Brown-OMGB-B, Aug. 1949.

84. BArch-K: B106–15423, FRG Ministry of the Interior, Press Release, 12 May 1950; B137–691, National Union for Peace and Liberty, 19 Jul. 1951.

85. Sagi Schaefer argues the development of the customs police as a federal force was a central factor in the transformation of the border after currency reform; Schaefer, "Ironing," ch. 1.

86. "Zonengrenze und Zollgrenze," *NP*, 29 Sep. 1949; "Zollkommissariat: Keine Panzersperren an der Zonengrenze," *NP*, 21 Jul. 1951; BayHStA B-StK 14182, Ankermüller, 30 May 1949; BArch-K, B106–15423, B-MInn, "Übernahme der Grenzpolizei," 1950.

87. "Die 'zergrenzte' Bergmühle," *NP*, 25 Aug. 1948; "Wo bleibt da die Polizei . . . ?" *NP*, 9 Aug. 1951. Other police expansions: NACP RG260, OMGB-Cbg 1208–1, Seifert, 28 Jun. 1949.

88. Overview: Sperschneider, "Spielzeugindustrie," 126–131, 152–153; Hamlin, *Work*, 61–62.

89. SA-N 4343, 110–123; NACP RG466, HICOG-B-ID-Brd: 1–2, Riedl, MR, Sep. 1949, Dec. 1950.

90. BArch-B DE1–11288, 1, 5–19.

91. BArch-B DE1–11288, 1, 5–19.

92. BArch-B DE1–11425, 1–9.

93. Rau, "Bündnispolitik."

94. BArch-Filmarchiv AZ 31/1949, DEFA Deutsche Film AG, "600-jähriges Jubiläum der Stadt Sonneberg," 1949: wochenschau-archiv.de; SA-S C2–14, SbgSR-81, 13 May 1952. In September 1948, one fifth of Sonneberg artisans belonged to unions; six months later it was over half. BArch-B DE: 1–11425, 1–9; 1–11288, 22, (24–30), 34.

95. BArch-B DO1–8.0.296, 33.

96. SA-N 3021, Wagner, 4 Oct. 1951.

97. SA-N 3021, Wagner, 4 Oct. 1951; BArch-B DE1–11288, 5–19. More pressingly, he worried that crossing workers were vulnerable to intelligence abductions.

98. "'Furcht vor Zonengrenze Hemmt Niederlassung Von Betrieben,'" *NP*, 11 Mar. 1950.

99. NACP RG260, OMGB-Cbg 1199–1, Tadross, 15 Jul., 3 Aug. 1948; "Die Situation auf dem Arbeitsmarkt," *NP*, 28 Jul. 1948; "Die Tore zur Welt erst halb geöffnet," *NP*, 31 Aug. 1948.

100. "Keine Aufenthaltsbewilligung für illegale Grenzgänger," *NP*, 10 Jul. 1948. Measures: SA-N 4403, e.g., 45.

101. SA-N 4404, Handwerkskammer Coburg, 23 Dec. 1949; "Auswirkungen des Grenzverkehrs erfordern Sonderregelung," *NP*, 18 Oct. 1949.

102. SA-N: 2050, Weppler, 11 Nov. 1949; Weppler, 27 Dec. 1949; 4404, Coburg Chamber of Crafts, 23 Dec. 1949; Wagner, 2 Oct. 1949; "Auswirkungen des Grenzverkehrs erfordern Sonderregelung," *NP,* 18 Oct. 1949.

103. SA-N 4343, 65–72, Weppler, "Besprechungspunkte," 12 Jul. 1950.

104. SA-N 2050, Weppler, 20 Jan. 1950; "Berücksichtigung Neustadter Wünsche zugesagt," *NP,* 6 Mar. 1951; BayHStA LFlüV-1120, 184. Application screenings: SA-N 2191. Policy in Bavaria: BayHStA LFlüV-1152, esp. 1, 18.

105. ThHStAW LBdVP-175, 28–29, 109–129. Disproportionately more businesses left from border regions; of seventy-one Thuringian firms that moved permanently to Upper Franconia, three-quarters relocated within thirty kilometers of the border. In all, 9 to 13 percent of all eastern firms resettled in the West. Meanwhile, some western businesses established collection warehouses in Sonneberg for purchasing cheaper eastern wares; Hefele, *Verlagerung,* 54–55, 66, 116–117, 176; ThHStAW LBdVP:-365 Bd. 1, 50–52; -175, 28–29, 109 (110–129); SA-N 4404, "Liste—Firmen der Ostzone," Mar. 1950.

106. "Werbemöglichkeiten für die Spielwarenindustrie," *NP,* 7 Oct. 1949; "Dr. Weppler rügt Vernachlässigung Neustadts," *NP,* 25 Mar. 1950.

107. SA-N: StRPr 024–10/1, NecSR, 10 Nov. 1949; 4404, esp. "Stellungnahme des Wirtschaftsaufsichtsamtes," 14 Oct. 1949; Minutes, 19 Oct., 7 Dec. 1949; Weppler, 17 Nov. 1949; 4403, 38.

108. SA-N 4404, BBP-Nec, 21 Jan. 1950; NACP RG466, HICOG-LCB-ID EEI-2-2, Lindaman, 13 Jul. 1950; "Kalter Krieg auch gegen die Weihnachtsengel," *DV,* 18 Mar. 1952. SA-N: 4403/4404, 6–9; 4343, esp. 98–99; Weppler, 8 Jun. 1951. On the flip side, recruiting eastern companies to relieve unemployment in Mellrichtstadt: BayHStA LFlüV-1152, Bavarian Economics Ministry, 6 Aug. 1951.

109. Inauguration "Glasindustrie muss gesunden," *TV,* 6 Nov. 1948; "Glasbläser beschliessen Genossenschaftsgründung," *TV,* 11 Nov. 1948.

110. ThHStAW Th-MInn 1583, 135–136; StA-M KR-S 29, Wagner, 14 Feb. 1951. Sonneberg estimated that 600,000 DM a year was smuggled in doll and animal eyes; and three-quarters of Lauscha's home workshops closed, either through centralization or the loss of skilled workers to the West. Files: StA-M KR-S 29, 276; ThHStAW Th-MInn 1127; Neustadt Christmas Museum, permanent exhibition.

111. SA-N 4404, Weppler-Upper Franconian Glass and Toys, 1949–1950; BBP-Nec, 21 Jan. 1950; NACP RG466, HICOG-ID-Brd 1–3, Riedl, 17 Jul. 1951; SA-N 4343, 88.

112. SA-N 4343, 85, 79–84.

113. SA-N 4404: Pollack-Weppler, Mar.–Jun. 1951; 4343, 110–123; "Ankurbelung der Spielwaren- und Christbaumschmuck-Industrie," *NP,* 27 Sep. 1951. GDR measures: StA-M KR-S 29, Braun, 22 Dec. 1950; Böhm, 10, 12 Feb. 1951.

114. SA-N 4343, 110–123.

115. "'Haus der Oberfränkischen Spielzeugindustrie,'" *NP,* 3 Nov. 1951; "Gründung einer 'Christbaumschmuck-Verkaufsgenossenschaft?'" *NP,* 29 Apr. 1952; "Häuser der Glasbläser-Siedlung gerichtet," *NP,* 14 Sep. 1956; Sperschneider, *Spielzeugindustrie,* 164–165. File: SA-N Obgm. 80.

116. Sheffer, survey, "Gebrannte Brücke." Data: Sheffer, "Burned Bridge," 189.

117. "1004 Arbeitsplätze mehr in Neustadt," *NP,* 13 Dec. 1951.

118. Neustadt's tax revenue grew 50 percent and commercial founder tax grew from 1,200 DM to 70,000 DM. The city ranked twelfth out of Bavaria's forty-seven municipal counties in employment creation, and was prosperous compared to neighboring border regions such as Kronach, where unemployment was over 30 percent. Despite rhetoric about the flight of industry, from 1948 to 1951 twice as many firms settled in Neustadt as left (658 to 337); SA-N: 5698, 7–8, 28; 4343, Weppler, 22 Oct. 1951; 4403, 59–61. Borderland economy: Altrichter, "Schatten."

119. SA-N 4343, 110–123. Originally, federal Borderland Assistance was an economic program for severely depressed communities, particularly along the Bavarian-Czech border. In 1950 Neustadt qualified as one of sixty Bavarian "depressed areas," but by 1951 was upgraded to a lesser subsidized "redevelopment area." BayHStA B-StK 14466; BArch-K B137–579; "'Furcht vor Zonengrenze hemmt Niederlassung von Betrieben,'" *NP,* 11 Mar. 1950; SA-N 4343, Weppler, 23 Mar. 1951. Overview: Offer, *Zonenrandgebiet,* 24–26.

120. "Spiegel der Woche," *NP,* 1 Apr.1950; "Dr. Weppler rügt Vernachlässigung Neustadts," *NP,* 25 Mar. 1950.

121. "'Wir kämpfen um die baldige Aufhebung der Zonengrenzen,'" *NP,* 6 Apr. 1950.

122. "Kultusminister Dr. Hundhammer in der Puppenstadt," *NP,* 29 Apr. 1950; "'Dem Coburger Land gilt unsere Sorge,'" *NP,* 4 Jul. 1950; "'Deutschlands Grenze ist auch unsere Grenze,'" *NP,* 10 Feb. 1951; "'Gestern Nacht kam ich über die Grenze...,'" *NP,* 19 May 1951. State visits: BayHStA B-StK 13077; SA-N 5823.

123. Vieth, "Oberfranken das Aschenbrödel Westdeutschlands," *NP,* 24 Mar. 1951; BayHStA B-StK 14466, Krazer, 26 Oct. 1949.

124. BayHStA B-StK 14466/67, esp. B-StK, 2 Mar. 1950; BArch-K B137–579. The concept of cultural endangerment along the inter-German boundary was advanced by the Bavarian Party in 1949 and met with initial resistance; cultural funds were for regions bordering foreign states (e.g., the "Danish danger").

125. Ahonen, *Expulsion.* Refugee crisis in Wildflecken, near the inter-German border in Lower Franconia: Seipp, "Refugee Town."

126. NACP RG260, OMGB-Cbg 1207–4, Weppler, MR, May 1948. 1199–8, Klein, CQH, 14 Jan. 1947; 1200–3, Klein, AHR, 23 Jun. 1946; "Flüchtlinge erhalten Wohnungen," *NP,* 10 Jul. 1946; "Amerikanische Polizei muß eingreifen," *NP,* 27 Sep. 1947.

 Larger Sonneberg was likewise assigned 2,500–3,000 expellees, 10 to 14 percent of its population (Soviet zone and Bavarian averages ranged over 20 percent). But expellee concentration in the city was actually rather high, since although the Soviet Zone allocated border counties fewer refugees, they were forbidden to live in the Prohibited Zone; this was relaxed in 1948. ThHStAW LBdVP-365 Bd. 1, 50–52; SA-S: C3–23, Geyer, 15 Aug. 1946; C6–26, New Citizens' Commission—1, 18 Aug. 1948, Minutes, "Überprüfung," 29 Oct. 1948; C6–9, Sonneberg Housing Office, 12 Jan. 1948; Fromm, *Eingliederung,* 20–24, 61–62.

127. NACP RG260, OMGB-Cbg 1207–4, Weppler, MR, Nov. 1946. Ansbach investigation: "'Der krasse Fall,'" *NP,* 12 May 1948; "Neustadt braucht 2000 Wohnungen," *NP,* 7 Sep. 1948. Censure of Fürth am Berg: StA-C LRA-14671, 1948–1949. In Neustadt forty-five homes were constructed from January-June 1948 (compared to thirty-one in Coburg County and forty-one in Coburg itself) thanks to ongoing fundraising efforts.

128. SA-N 2189, Seifert, 8 Feb. 1949; Fromm, *Eingliederung,* 61–62; NACP RG260, OMGB-Cbg 1208–03, Coburg County Office for Refugees, 22 Mar. 1948, 1 Apr. 1949 (OMGB-B 1127–1).

129. SA-N 2192, Weppler, 16 Feb 1949. Administration: SA-N 2188–2193.

130. The rates of this eastern exodus fluctuated: 290,000 in 1945, dropping to under 200,000 from 1946 to 1949, then increasing dramatically to 337,300 in 1950 and 287,800 in 1951. In Bavaria, which housed a disproportionate number of expellees, easterners comprised less than 30 percent of the German refugee population. Meanwhile, an average of 50,000 westerners each year resettled in the East. Heidemeyer, *Flucht,* 43–45; AA B10 Abt. 2 Bd. 333, Nr. A 6940, 18; BArch-K B106–15423.

131. Interview, Elisabeth Dietzer.

132. Dorst, "Die Villa," 403.

133. van Melis and Bispink, *Republikflucht,* 20–29; Heidemeyer, *Flucht,* 62–63.

134. SA-S C2–7, SbgSR-55, 2 Mar. 1948.

135. SA-S C6–25, D., 8 Jul. 1947.

136. Authorizations were granted mostly for reuniting family. Logistics: SA-S C16–66, 84–95.

137. SA-S C2–8, SbgSR-76, 11 Jun. 1948; "Rückkehr in die russische Zone," *NP,* 15 Jun. 1946.

138. "Zuzug nach Sonneberg," *TV,* 26 Nov. 1946; ThHStAW Th-MInn 3969, 7.

139. Short-term western policy: Heidemeyer, *Flucht,* 8–32; Ackermann, *Flüchtling,* 76–85.

140. NACP RG260, OMGUS-POW&DP 198–2: EUCOM-26, 2 Feb. 1948; OMGUS to AGWAR, Aug. 1947. Surveys of border crossers did suggest that personal and material considerations did rank above concerns of physical harm; e.g., EUCOM—14, 20, 22, 18 Aug., 20 Nov., 8 Dec. 1947; Seppner, 16 Jun. 1947.

141. Knop, *Prowling,* 157.

142. NACP RG466, HICOG-ID-Brd: 1–2, Mulzer, MR, 12 Apr. 1950.

143. BayHStA LFlüV-1120, 49–50.

144. NACP RG466, HICOG-ID-Brd 2–2, Riedl, 24 May 1950; "Refugee Massing Seen," *NYT,* 16 Mar. 1950.

145. BayHStA LFlüV-1120, 49–50, 32–36; English: NACP RG260, OMGB-ID 153–8, Jaenicke, 8 Jul. 1947.

146. NACP RG260, OMGB-ID 170–3, HQ Third US Army, 26 Nov. 1946; BayHStA B-MInn 91695, Seifried, 20 Aug. 1947. Although Bavaria negotiated the return of around 2,000 border crossers per week, actual returns ran around 350 per week in the first half of 1948. The Soviet Zone's forcible returning of western illegal crossers was likewise problematic, but much smaller; NACP RG260, OMGUS-CAD-PS: 335–2, "Traffic between Bavaria-Soviet Zone," 1949; e.g., ThHStAW Th-MInn 3970, 44, 48, 56; BayHStA LFlüV-1120; SA-N 4404, Riedel, 7 Jun. 1950. In late 1946, the Soviet Zone began denying readmittance to illegal crossers who had destroyed their identification papers and thus had no proof of

former residence; as people adopted this strategy, the West determined German court authorization would be "sufficient evidence to return border violators"; 275–9, Third U.S. Army, 24 Oct. 1946; ODI-78, 14 Nov. 1947.

147. Knop, *Prowling*, 166, 168.

148. Krüger, "Unter Illegalen hinter dem Stacheldraht," *NP*, 3 Mar. 1948; "Stationen auf dem Weg zur Heimat," *NP*, 10 Aug. 1946. Account: Greiner-Vetter, 148–149.

149. BayHStA LFlüV-1120, 19–26. Discussion: BayHStA B-MInn 91695.

150. NACP RG260, OMGB-ID 153–8, Jaenicke, 8 Jul. 1947. Deliberations: BayHStA PrBLP-110.

151. In federal parliament debate on November 18, 1949, Bavaria urged the continuation of the forcible refugee return, while most states believed the policy had failed. Around half of easterners at the Moschendorf camp received asylum; of those who did not, 25 percent chose to return to the East on state transports, the remainder "disappearing" illegally into Bavaria. Heidemeyer, *Flucht*, 99–100; "Verbrecher strömen nach Bayern," *Frankenpost*, 4 Apr. 1949; BArch-K B106–15423, Ankermüller, 14 Nov. 1949.

152. After 1949, around 165,000 easterners a year sought official admission into West Germany, and 35 to 39 percent of applicants were accepted. Attitudes changed abruptly after border closure in 1952, however, and almost all applicants were admitted throughout the 1950s; Heidemeyer, *Flucht*, 43–46.

153. StA-C StAnw-2, Schwarz, 3 and 28 Jun. 1952. In the Neustadt region an average of seventy crossers apprehended a month claimed to be political refugees and were transferred to Moschendorf camp. BBP Monthly Reports, 1948–1951; published weekly BBP reports, *NP*, 1951–52.

154. West German debate came a head in the autumn of 1949; the headlines speak for themselves: e.g., "Flüchtlingsstrom Kritisch, Bonner Kabinett sucht nach Lösungen,'" *DW*, 19 Oct. 1949; "Dunkle Wege führen nach Westdeutschland," *Süddeutsche Zeitung*, 3 Nov. 1949; "Ostflüchtlinge werden zum Problem. Pro Monat 4000. Strengere Grenzsperre?" *NN*, 18 Nov. 1949. Scams: e.g., BayHStA LFlüV 1108, Krömer, 19 Jul. 1950.

155. BArch-K: B137–28, Firgau, 1951; B106–15423, Ankermüller, 14 Nov. 1949.

156. "Die gegenwärtige Bevölkerungsstruktur," *NP*, 7 Jan. 1950; Scheuerich, *Geschichte*, 1:394; SA-N: 2190, esp. Weppler, 2 Oct. 1948; 2191, Weppler, 22 May 1950.

157. For example, in his daily maintenance trips the technician from Neustadt's gas works brought food from the Würzburg Bishopric to Sonneberg border communities; and small companies like Firma Eisenhandlung Dehler helped eastern partners by sending materials and supplies. Interview, Brigitte Laub; private possession, Firma Eisenhandlung Dehler: correspondence 1945–52.

158. NACP RG260, OMGB-Cbg 1203–5, Sussell, 11 Dec. 1947, 3, 12 Jan. 1948.

159. Interview, Jens Reichert, Sonneberg/Hönbach, 17 Jan. 2003.

160. Interview, Inge Mulzer; Greiner, "Errinnerungen."

161. "'Amerikanische Deutschland-Politik grundlegend geändert,'" *NP*, 22 Jul. 1949.

Chapter 4: Kickoff

1. NACP RG260, OMGB-Cbg 1205-3, Kleindienst, 27 Jul. 1949.

2. City competition to provide bratwursts at festivals: Roß, "Traditionsreiche Feiern," 123–129; SA-N StRPr 024-10/1, NecSR-20, 22 May 1947.

3. NACP RG260: OMGB-Cbg 1205-3, Kleindienst, 27 Jul. 1949; OMGUS-CAD-PS 335-2, Riedl, 5 Aug. 1949. "Nur ein Wille," *TV*, 1 Aug. 1949. Photographs: SA-S BII-2-46. Neustadt's major players did not participate in the 1949 interzonal games.

4. "Ein Volksfest Deutscher Einheit," *NP*, 2 Aug. 1949.

5. "10 000 kamen herüber," *NP*, 2 Aug. 1949.

6. Interview, Gerd Jahn, Sonneberg, 26 Jun. 2002.

7. Franz Förster, "1949—ein denkwürdiges Jahr." In *SPD im Land zwischen Main und Saale*, 1959, 18–19.

8. Interview, Hermann Volker, Neustadt/Wildenheid, 10 Nov. 2009.

9. NACP RG260, OMGUS-CAD-PS 335-2, Riedl, 5 Aug. 1949.

10. Interview, Inge Mulzer.

11. Political role of sporting events: Johnson, *Training*.

12. SA-S C2-9, SbgSR-157, 25 Jul. 1949; "Grenztreffen geplant," *TV*, 26 Jul. 1949; SA-S C3-104, Administrative/Financial Committee—32, 27 Jul. 1949.

13. SA-S C2-9, SbgSR-157, 25 Jul. 1949; StA-M SED-KL-Sbg 287, Minutes, 19 Jul. 1949. Sonneberg's SED leadership knew of plans for the game a week before the Congressional County Committee unanimously approved it.

14. SA-S C2-9, SbgSR-157, 25 Jul. 1949.
15. Amos, *Westpolitik*, 26.
16. NACP RG260 OMGUS-CAD-PS 335-2, Riedl, 5 Aug. 1949; *TV*, Reports, 26–31 Jul. 1949; e.g., Schnackenburg: Welt im Film, "Treffen an der Zonengrenze," 1949, Deutsche Wochenschau GmbH, WIF 218 (wochenschau-archiv.de); Adelhausen: NACP RG260, OMGB-B 1129-1, BBP, 15 May 1949.
17. E.g., "Ein schöner Tag ging zu Ende," *NP*, 16 Jun. 1949; "Ein würdiger Auftakt zum Schützenfest," *NP*, 19 Jul. 1949; NACP RG260, OMGB-ID: 20-4, Vögele, 28 Jul. 1949.
18. SA-N 2050, Weppler, 8 Aug. 1949.
19. NACP RG260, OMGB-Cbg 1205-3, Kleindienst, 28 Jul. 1949;
20. SA-N 2050, Weppler, 8 Aug. 1949. E.g., NACP RG260 OMGB-ID 158-5, Larned, 9 Aug. 1949. E.g., "'Ost gegen West' im Fußballsport," *NP*, 2 Aug. 1949; "Thüringer Fußballer in Wildenheid siegreich," *NP*, 4 Aug. 1949; "Ostzonenfußballer in Neustadt und Wildenheid," *NP*, 6 Aug. 1949. "Sportler ohne Zonengrenzen," *ThT*, 20 Aug. 1949; "Sport kennt keine Zonengrenzen," *TV*, 30 Aug. 1949.
21. NACP RG260: OMGB-Cbg 1205-3, BBP-Cbg, 8 Aug. 1949; OMGB-ID 39-5, Riedl, 9 Aug. 1949;
22. "Neustadt-Sonneberg 3:3 (1:1)," *TV*, 9 Aug. 1949.
23. "Alle Betriebe rüsten zum Friedenstag!" *TV*, 27 Aug. 1949; "Zum Friedenstag," *TV*, 31 Aug. 1949; "Die Völker können den Frieden erzwingen," *TV*, 2 Sep. 1949.
24. "Friedensdemonstrationen entlang der Zonengrenze," *TV*, 2 Sep. 1949.
25. "Fließende Zonengrenze," *NP*, 3 Sep. 1949; NACP RG260, OMGB-Cbg 1205-3, Kleindienst, 3 Sep. 1949.
26. NACP RG260: OMGB-Cbg 1205-3, Kleindienst, 3 Sep. 1949; thirty were formally arrested, and 6,000 DM worth of wares confiscated.
27. NACP RG260: OMGB-Cbg 1205-3, Kleindienst, 3 Sep. 1949; OMGB-ID: 4–11, Feiler, 2 Sep. 1949; BayHStA PrBGP-118, Mulzer, 1 Sep. 1949.
28. "Fließende Zonengrenze," *NP*, 3 Sep. 1949.
29. "Swarm into U.S. Zone," *NYT*, 2 Sep. 1949; Peace Day crossings at Bad Steben (2,500–3,000), Hirschberg (1,500), Weissenbrunn (2,000), and Ellrich-Walkenried were less than a tenth the size; NACP: RG466, HICOG-ID-Brd 2-4, BBP-Dir, 7 Sep. 1949; RG260, OMGUS-CAD-PS: 335-2, Mulzer, 7 Sep. 1949; "Einheitsgedanke ist starker als Willkür," *TV*, 3 Sep. 1949.
30. "Fließende Zonengrenze," *NP*, 3 Sep. 1949.
31. "Straßen wurden zu Boulevards," *NP*, 3 Sep. 1949.
32. ThHStAW Th-MInn 1133, 67. Propaganda: e.g., "Großkundgebung vor amerikanischen Maschinengewehren," *ND*, 2 Sep. 1949; "Zwei Welten begegnen sich," *Berliner Illustrierte*, 3 Sep. 1949. Openings downplayed on newsreel: DEFA Deutsche Film AG, "Deutscher Friedenstag wird begangen," 1949, wochenschau-archiv.de.
33. NACP: RG260, OMGB-Cbg 1205-3, Kleindienst, 3 Sep. 1949; RG466, HICOG-ID-Brd 2-4, BBP-Dir, 7 Sep. 1949.
34. SA-N 5821, "Erntedankfest am 1–2 October 1949," 17 Sep. 1949, plus file; "Für einige Stunden keine Zonengrenze," *NP*, 4 Oct. 1949.
35. NACP RG466, HICOG-ID-Brd 2-4, BBP-Dir, 6 Oct. 1949.
36. "Für einige Stunden keine Zonengrenze," *NP*, 4 Oct. 1949; BayHStA PrBLP-110, Riedl to Bavarian State Police Directorate, 29 Sep. 1949, BayHStA PrBLP 110. Meanwhile, crossings elsewhere had grown—up to 12,000 near Lübeck, for example, on October 1. "Eastern Germans Flock into West," *NYT*, 2 Oct. 1949. Planning: BArch-B/SAPMO DY30/IV 2/2-42, Anlage 2, f, Politburo–42, 6 Sep. 1949.
37. "Mit Rädern, Kinderwagen und Kisten," *NP*, 4 Oct. 1949.
38. "Christbaumschmuck, Heringe und Damenstrümpfe," *NP*, 4 Oct. 1949.
39. "Mit Rädern, Kinderwagen und Kisten," "Erntedankfest ohne Zonengrenze," *NP*, 4 Oct. 1949.
40. "20 000 Bratwürste und 10 000 Liter Bier," *NP*, 6 Oct. 1949
41. "Mit Rädern, Kinderwagen und Kisten," *NP*, 4 Oct. 1949.
42. Teßmer and Zien, *Geschichten*, 38.
43. SA-N MB-772, Thalmeyer, "Damals," Jan. 2000.
44. NACP RG466, HICOG-ID-Brd 2-4, BBP-Dir, 16 Nov. 1949; ThHStAW Th-MInn 1133, 44; James, "East Germans Throng U.S. Zone Stores," *NYT*, 10 Nov. 1949; "Russ Border Bars Lifted," *Los Angeles Times*, 10 Nov. 1949. Both American newspapers mistakenly reported that eastern forces promoted the opening.
45. "Wieder geöffnete Zonengrenze," *NP*, 6 Nov. 1949.
46. "Streiflichter von der gestrigen Grenzöffnung," *NP*, 10 Nov. 1949.

47. Ibid.
48. James, "East Germans Throng U.S. Zone Stores," *NYT,* 10 Nov. 1949.
49. NACP RG466, HICOG-ID-Brd 2-4, BBP-Dir, 16 Nov. 1949; "Zollschutz oder Grenzpolizei?" *NP,* 12 Nov. 1949.
50. Scheuerich, *Geschichte,* 1:251; interview, Helmut Traub, Sonneberg, 23 Jul. 2001; Stier, "1949: Fußball für Deutsche Einheit," *FW,* 31 Jul. 1999.
51. Sheffer, Survey, "Gebrannte Brücke."
52. *Thüringen Journal,* MDR-Fernsehen, "Denkwürdiges Spiel zwischen Sonneberg und Neustadt," 1 Aug. 2009; MDR-1, MDR-Figaro, 31 Jul. 2009. Also: NecTV, "Magazinsendung," 16–22 Feb. 2003.
53. By comparison, of the 112 respondents born before 1945 who answered this question, 67 percent knew of the mass crossings and 93 percent knew of the forced evacuations.
54. "Erkennt die Methoden feindlicher Agenten!" "Das Volkspolizeiamt Sonneberg," *TV,* 10 Nov. 1949.
55. BayHStA B-MInn 91695, Riedl, Jan. 1950. Western offices strained to decipher the new signals from across the border: NACP RG466, HICOG-ID-Brd 2-4, BBP-Dir, 23 Nov. 1949; "Öffnen der Zonengrenze von drüben gesehen," *NT,* 12 Nov. 1949; "Spiegel der Woche," *NP,* 12 Nov. 1949.
56. "Durch sachliche Diskussion zur Klarheit," *TV,* 19 Nov. 1949.
57. E.g., StA-M SED-KL-Sbg 307, Minutes, 16 Nov. 1949; SA-S C6-153, Sonneberg Construction Office, 18 Nov. 1949; Geyer, 16 Jan. 1950.
58. StA-M SED-KL-Sbg 303, Minutes, 1 Dec. 1949; ThHStAW Th-MInn 1133, 29–33.
59. ThHStAW Th-MInn 1133, 34–37.
60. Ibid.
61. ThHStAW Th-MInn 1133, 38.
62. BArch-K B106-15423, Ankermüller, 14 Nov. 1949 (BayHStA B-StK 10860; BayHStA LFlüV-1120, 528–532). Further discussion: NACP RG466, HICOG-ID-Brd 2-4, BBP-Dir, 16 Nov. 1949; Lindaman, 10 Nov. 1949.
63. SA-N 2050, Weppler, 9 Sep., 11, 14 Nov. 1949.
64. SA-N: 6564, Neustadt Food Office, 9 Nov. 1949; 4404, 2.
65. "Auswirkungen des Grenzverkehrs erfordern Sonderregelung," *NP,* 18 Oct. 1949.
66. NACP RG466, HICOG-ID-Brd 2-4, BBP-Dir, 16 Nov. 1949.
67. SA-N 2050, Weppler, 9 Sep. 1949. English: NACP RG466, HICOG-ID-Brd 2-4.
68. SA-N: 2050, Weppler, 11 and 14 Nov. 1949; 6564, Neustadt Food Office, 9 Nov. 1949; plus file; 4404, 4–5; Minutes, 30 Sep. 1949; "Ambulanter Handel," 9–28 Nov. 1949.
69. BayHStA, B-MInn 91695, Riedl, Jan. 1950.
70. SA-N 2050, BBP-Cbg, 17 Dec. 1949; BayHStA B-Minn 91695, Clark, 19 Dec. 1949; PrBLP-110, Riedl, 21 Dec. 1949; NACP: RG260 OMGUS-CAD-PS 335-2, Clark, 14 Dec. 1949; RG466, HICOG-ID-Brd 2-4, BBP-Dir, 30 Dec. 1949. Combatting rumors: e.g., "Die Bevölkerung wird gewarnt," *TV,* 17 Dec. 1949; "Glaubt nicht dem Lügensender 'Rias,'" *TV,* 19 Dec. 1949.
71. SA-N 2050, BBP, 21 Dec. 1949; BayHStA PrBLP-110, Riedl, 21 Dec. 1949.
72. Because of continued rumors of openings, East Germany took extra border precautions on major holidays, especially May 1 and September 1.
73. Interview, Hilda Schwartz, Neustadt, 10 Nov. 2009.
74. SA-S C2-1, 5, 10 Dec. 1949. The skit was to be performed at Sonneberg's Friedel & Co., and was approved by Vice-Mayor Blechschmidt, who censored out only an exchange about American cigarettes.
75. NACP RG466, HICOG-ID-Brd 1-2, Riedl, 15 May 1951.
76. "Am 23. Juni große Freiheitsfeuer," *NP,* 26 May 1951.
77. "10 000 Flugblätter per Luftpost über die Zonengrenze," *NP,* 3 Apr. 1951.
78. "Der erste Wahltag für den Dritten Deutschen Volkskongreß," *TV,* 16 May 1949.
79. NACP RG466, HICOG-ID-Brd 2-3, Mulzer, 21 Oct. 1950.
80. NACP RG260, OMGB-ID 14-7, Miedrich, "Neue Presse in der East Zone," May 1949; BayHStA PrBGP-119, Riedl-Hugunin, 6, 27 Jun. 1951.
81. NACP: RG466, HICOG-ID-Brd 2-1, Thomsen, 7, 20 Mar. 1951; RG260 OMGB-ID: 23-21, Walston, 22 Apr. 1949; Joublanc, 7 Apr. 1949; "Ruf nach dem Westen," *DV,* 2 Feb. 1951; "Kreistag Sonneberg ruft den Kreistag Coburg," *DV,* 18 Feb. 1952; ThHStAW Th-MInn 1583, 40–42.
82. NACP RG466, HICOG-B-ID: EEI 1-4, Thomsen, 13 Jul. 1951.
83. The U.S. Coburg Office estimated that western police seized 40 percent of all GDR propaganda, and that 10 percent was sent by mail. NACP: RG466, Lindaman, 13 Jul. 1950; RG260, OMGB-Cbg 1202-8, 6th Const-Sqdn, WIS, 6 May 1948; 1202-2, Sussell, 26 May 1948.

84. SA-N: 4343, 94–97; 2050, Weppler, 14 Dec. 1948; 4404, "Besprechung," 7 Dec. 1949; "Grenzgänger der SEP," *Echo Der Woche*, 3 Feb. 1950; "Furcht vor der Zonengrenze," *NP*, 1 Jul. 1950; "Verteidigungsbeitrag zugunsten der Grenzgebiete kürzen," *NP*, 19 May 1951.

85. "Wie es im Westen 'aufwärts' geht!" *TV*, 29 Dec. 1949; "Die Wahrheit über die USA Kolonie Westdeutschland," *TV*, 3 Jan. 1950; "Wildwest in Coburg," *TV*, 4 Jan. 1950; "Die Bevölkerung fordert: 'Ami, go home!'" *DV*, 25 Nov. 1950; "USA-Gangster bei der Arbeit," *DV*, 29 Nov. 1950.

86. Governmental relations: Chapter 5. E.g., "600-Jahr-Feier in Sonneberg," *NP*, 13 Jan. 1949; SA-N StRPr 024-10/1, NecSR-10, 13 Jan. 1949; SA-S C2-9/14, SbgSR-183, 43, 61, 64, 65, 68, 75, 1950–1952.

87. SA-S C3-210, Langer, 4 Jun. 1951.

88. ThHStAW BMPr-1154, Film 102, 12–13. "Political awareness" and rules of conduct at Berlin checkpoints: Steege, "Ordinary Violence."

89. SA-S C3-99, Hess, 11 May 1949; "Der Kreis Sonneberg für die Einheit Deutschlands," *TV*, 11 May 1949. Operations and improvements: SA-S 16: 153–153a, "Ausgaben der Zollkontrollstelle Hönbach"; SA-S: C2-10/13, SbgSR-224, 233, 21 Aug., 23 Sep. 1950; C6-153, Barthelmes, 25 May 1949; file: C16-170.

90. "Eine historische Fahrt nach 'drüben,'" *NP*, 14 May 1949.

91. NACP RG466, HICOG-ID-Brd 2-3 and 2-2, BBP-Dir, MR; Riedl, 7 Jul. 1950, 12 Jun. 1951; "Die Remilitarisierung bedeutet für unser Volk Not und Elend," *DV*, 7 Jun. 1951; SA-S C2-13, SbgSR-13, 26 Jan. 1951.

92. "Interzonen-Autobusfahrt nach Sonneberg mit Leibesvisitation," *NP*, 7 Jan. 1950; "2027 'Legale' schauten hinter den Eisernen Vorhang," *NP*, 17 Jan. 1950; "Am Grenzpfahl zwischen Ost und West," *NP*, 4 Feb. 1950; "Oberleitungs-Omnibuslinie Sonneberg-Neustadt," *NP*, 1 Apr. 1950.

93. NACP RG466, HICOG-LCB-ID EEI-3-1, Thomsen, 6 Nov. 1950.

94. Amos, *Westpolitik*, 62–63.

95. NACP RG466, HICOG-ID-Brd 2-2, Schaumberger, 4 Jun. 1951.

96. "FDJ-Aufruf: 'Meidet das Neustadter Grenzgebiet!'" *NP*, 27 May 1950; "Besprechung der Sacharbeiter der Paßwesen Coburg-Neustadt," *NP*, 8 Mar. 1951; e.g., StA-C AG-N, cases 278–279, 340, 346.

97. "Red Youths Defy Inspection, Stage Sitdown at Border," *WP*, 1 Jun. 1950. Neustadt was spared the 4,000 western FDJ members (150 from Neustadt) who had been expected to cross there May 22–25, 1950; NACP RG466: HICOG-ID-Brd 2-1, Lindaman, 22 May 1950; HICOG-LCB-ID EEI-3-1, Thomsen, 6 Nov. 1950; Amos, *Westpolitik*, 62.

98. "Alarmstufe III bei den Polizeieinheiten an der Zonengrenze," *NP*, 2 Aug. 1951.

99. StA-M: KR-S 6, Rost, 30 Jun. 1951; SED-KL-Sbg IV/4.07/152; SA-S C2-14, SbgSR-43, 16 Aug. 1951; Hanisch, *Schutz*, 18–21; SA-N 2050, Weppler, 23 Jul. 1951; "1000 versuchten gewaltsamen Grenzübertritt," *NP*, 9 Aug. 1951; "Noch immer unruhige Zonengrenze," *NP*, 11 Aug. 1951; "Der erwartete Ansturm blieb aus," *NP*, 23 Aug. 1951; "Border Guards Increased," *NYT*, 29 Jul. 1951. Similar, May 1950: NACP RG466: HICOG-ID-Brd 2-1, Lindaman, 22 May 1950; StA-M: KR-S 6; SED-KL-Sbg IV/4.07/152.

100. "Söldnertruppen an der Demarkationslinie," *DV*, 24 Jul. 1951.

101. NACP RG466, HICOG-ID Brd 2-1, Thomsen, 7 Mar. 1951; BayHStA PrBGP-119 (SA-N 3021), Kleindienst, 2 Mar. 1951; "Zonengrenze forderte ein neues Todesopfer," *NP*, 27 Feb. 1951; "Gedenkstein," 2 Aug. 2003; Survey #10468; Private possession: Treichel, scrapbook; and Mulzer, memoir.

102. StA-C AG-N, Nov. 1950–Jun 1952. In this second data set of 430 defendants, 5 percent claimed they crossed to visit loved ones, 4 percent to leave the GDR, and 3 percent to find employment. Twenty-eight percent of cases involved westerners from the Coburg region (20 percent from Neustadt proper), with the majority against non-local westerners; 6 percent were from Sonneberg County, with 3 percent from the immediate Sonneberg border region, compared to previous proportions of 84 and 51 percent, respectively. Political defendants were also younger (with an average age of twenty-four, compared to thirty-two previously) and more heavily male (82 percent, versus 74 percent previously).

103. StA-C AG-N, 339, Deposition, Ruschke, 14 Feb. 1951.

104. StA-C AG-N, 278–279.

105. StA-C AG-N, 345.

106. StA-C AG-N, 372. Similar: "Grenzübertritt?" *NP*, 28 Jun. 1951.

107. BayHStA B-MInn 91700, Hoegner, 11 Dec. 1951.

108. StA-C AG-N, 346, E., 19 Mar. 1951; StA-C AG-N, 372, J., 6 Sep. 1951.

109. StA-C AG-N, 353, J., 30 Mar. 1951. Such rhetoric was common in East German propaganda, but also appeared in various guises across the political spectrum.

110. "20 Red Agents a Day Reported Slipping Across Line into West," *WP*, 8 Jul. 1950; "Moscow hat einen langen Arm," *NP*, 13 Oct. 1951; StA-C AG-N, 377. Neustadt's court sentenced KPD member Rudolf Ahr, who had spent five and a half years in a Nazi concentration camp, to two months in prison for illegal border crossing and "intimidating" a border policeman with this "threat."

111. NACP: RG466, HICOG-LCB-ID EEI-3-1, Thomsen, 6 Nov. 1950; RG260, OMGB-Cbg 1205-3, Zenkel, 3 Sep. 1949. Neustadt's KPD had been fractious and disorganized, with early eastern intelligence in the region "sloppy and confused." BArch BY1-290; NACP RG260, OMGUS-Exec 795-3, "Russian Intelligence," 15 Mar. 1948.

112. StA-C AG-N, 226, Minutes, 8 Jul. 1950; E., 20 Oct. 1950.

113. Major, *Death of the KPD*. E.g., "Ein Kampfgruß aus Neustadt bei Coburg," *DV*, 29 Apr. 1950; "Die Bürger von Ketschenbach sagen 'Nein,'" *DV*, 21 Apr. 1952; "Jugendorganisation warb neue Mitglieder," *ThT*, 25 Feb. 1950; "FDJ-Aufruf," *NP*, 27 May 1950; "Illegale Einfuhr kommunistische Schriften," *NP*, 28 Nov. 1950.

114. NACP RG466, HICOG-LCB-ID EEI-2-2, Lindaman, 13 Jul. 1950.

115. In 1950 the neo-Nazi Deutsche Block (DB) split the FDP vote in Neustadt, which, together with the SPD, had dominated postwar politics. FDP leaders pledged to form a coalition government with the DB in the 1952 election, and endorsed Schubart in the runoff. In the first round of voting, Schubart won 38 percent to Weppler's 45 percent, and the DB claimed six of Neustadt's twenty-one city council seats. "Neustadt im Zwielicht," *NP*, 1 Apr. 1952; "Wiederwahl Dr. Wepplers," *NP*, 8 Apr. 1952. Additional: Sheffer, "Burned Bridge," 196–197.

116. "Söldnertruppen an der Demarkationslinie," *DV*, 24 Jul. 1951.

117. "Moscow hat einen langen Arm," *NP*, 13 Oct. 1951. E.g., "Ein paar Schritte vom Wege und verhaftet," *NP*, 15 Nov. 1951.

118. Overview: Glaser, "*Reorganisation*," esp. 23–27, 298–299; Lindenberger, *Volkspolizei*, 40–42, 462; ThHStAW Th-MInn 1138, 21–23(-37); Stubler, 8 Aug. 1949. Thuringia: SA-S C16-97, SMA-Th Order Nr. 52, 27 Mar. 1948; ThHStAW Th-MInn 1129, 2–3.

119. ThHStAW: Th-MInn 1127, 53; LBdVP-166, 5; SA-S C6-31, SMA-Th Order Nr. 253, 5 Apr. 1948.

120. ThHStAW Th-MInn 1052, 2–5. The border police reported an average of twenty-five warning shots per day from July 1948 to June 1949, 79 percent of which were "successful" in halting violators, with improbably few injured (thirty-two) or killed (sixteen) by such shots; Glaser, "*Reorganisation*," 303.

121. SA-S: C2-7, SbgSR-68, 24 Apr. 1948; C16-170, Meiningen City Construction, 20 May 1948.

122. ThHStAW Th-MInn 1129, 9; "Verbrecherische Umtriebe an den Zonengrenzen," *TV*, 27 Mar. 1948.

123. "Gegen verbrecherische Umtriebe in den Grenzkreisen," *TV*, 24 Mar. 1948; "Verbrecherische Umtriebe an den Zonengrenzen," *TV*, 27 Mar. 1948; "Zu den Grenzübertritten aus der Bizone, *TV*, 7 Apr. 1948.

124. Cargo traffic resumed in April 1949, but not passenger rail; an interzonal bus was established instead, after long negotiations, SA-S C2-7, SbgSR-127-129, 14, 15, 25 Feb. 1949; ThHStAW Th-MInn 1581, 70, 87, 224, 259.

125. Traffic at Burned Bridge represented only around 10 percent of total legal traffic between Bavaria and East Germany. Authorized crossing points in 1949 also included Hof-Gutenfurst, Probstzella, Untersuhl-Wartha, and Phillipsthal-Vacha. Statistics: Sheffer, "Burned Bridge," 166–167; NACP RG260: OMGB-ID 158-5, Rohan, 4 Feb. 1948; OMGUS-CAD-PS 335-2, McCraw, 29 Nov. 1949; BayHStA PrBGP-1629, Martin, 9 Nov. 1954; *NP*, BBP reports, 1951–1952.

126. SA-N: 3021, Neustadt Pass Office, 3 Jan. 1951; plus file; 5698, 52; NACP RG466, HICOG-B-ID-Brd: 1–2, Riedl, MR, 1949–1951; HICOG-LCB-ID: EEI: 3-1, Thomsen, "EEI-Travel," 6 Nov. 1950; RG260, OMGB-Cbg 1207-3, Weppler, 31 Aug. 1949; "Interzonenpässe nach Gebrauch zurück!" *NP*, 19 May 1948; SA-N 2050, "Besprechung—Paßwesen," 8 Mar. 1951.

127. ThHStAW LBdVP-175, 191–195 and 231–232.

128. *NP*, BBP reports, 1951–1952. Around one thousand farmers and workers in both Sonneberg and Coburg Counties had frontier permits, increasingly restricted for Sonnebergers after 1950: NACP RG466, HICOG-LCB-ID EEI-3-1, Thomsen, 6 Nov. 1950; ThHStAW Th-MInn 1133, 29–33; BArch-B: DE1-11288, 5–19; DO1-8.0.296, 33; DO1-3911, Brückner, 7 May 1952; BayHStA PrBGP-1629, Martin, 9 Nov. 1954; SA-N EAP 001–008(2), Bergmann, 20 Sep. 1971. Centralizing: ThHStAW Th-MInn 232, 27; ThHStAW Th-MInn 3038, 11; ThHStAW Th-MInn 1583, 50–55.

129. ThHStAW Th-MInn 3038, 33 (43–57); BArch-B DO1-8.0.296, esp. 15–33. Lehesten workers: BayHStA B-MInn 91700, Heilmann, 6 Sep. 1951; ThHStAW LBdVP-175, 215.

130. AA B10 Abt.2 Bd. 451, Nr. A 7334, 29 (16–19); BArch-K B106-15423, Thiedick query, Feb.-Mar. 1950 (BayHStA B-MInn 91699). Regulation difficulties: BayHStA B-MInn 91700, Riedl, 22 Sep.

1951; NACP RG466, HICOG-ID-Brd 1–2, Riedl, 15 May 1951, ThHStAW Th-MInn 3038, 33–57; BArch-B DO1-8.0.296, 15–33.

131. ThHStAW Th-MInn 1133, 77–78; "Güteraustausch auf der Strecke Neustadt-Sonneberg," *NP*, 19 Nov. 1949; Greiner, "Wird Expreßgut spazieren gefahren?" *DV*, 16 Aug. 1950; SA-S: C3-155, State of Thuringia, 12 Nov. 1949; C3-166, "Schriftverkehr über das Kreisamt mit dem Westen."

132. ThHStAW Th-MInn: -1581, 306; - 1582, 48.

133. ThHStAW Th-MInn: Th-MInn 3038, 25–26; - 1583, "4. ordentliche Kreistagssitzung," 4 Apr. 1951. When Heinersdorfers issued a "protest resolution" against border measures, they gained temporary concessions: Th-MInn: -232, 30–34; -3038, 25–27.

134. SA-S: C3-155, Sonneberg County Chairman, 28 Apr. 1950, SA-S C3-155, C2-9. C2-9; C3-99, Hess, 31 Mar. 1949.

135. StA-M KR-S S5/15 1/79, Stubler, 14 Jul. 1949. Major frictions: ThHStAW Th-MInn 1181, 44; LBdVP-365 Bd. 1; Klemke, 14 Feb. 1950; SA-S: C6-31, Hess, 2 Nov. 1948; C2-14, SbgSR-73, 77, 18 Mar., 16 Apr. 1952.

136. Borderland curfews extended from 6:00 p.m. to 7:00 a.m. within 200 meters of the border, and sentries were authorized to shoot without warning up to 300 meters from the border: NACP RG260, OMGUS-CAD-PS 335-1, Riedl, 21–22 Nov. 1948. Expansion of *Schießbefehl*: Order Nr. 14, 19 Nov. 1948, Glaser, "*Reorganisation*," 209–211 (civilian assault: 22–23). Sonneberg incident: "Überfall auf Grenzpolizisten," *TV*, 14 May 1949.

137. Glaser, "*Reorganisation*," 194.

138. NACP RG466, HICOG-ID-Brd 2-3, 1-2, 2-2, Riedl, 21 Oct. 1950, 15 May 1951, 12 Jun. 1951.

139. ThHStAW LBdVP-365 Bd. 1, 163. E.g., "Schütze Dich selbst!" *TV*, 17 Dec. 1948; "Die Volkspolizei im Kampf um eine geordnete Wirtschaft," *TV*, 7 Jan. 1949.

140. BayHStA PrBGP-118, Riedl, 19 Feb., 31 Mar. 1948.

141. BayHStA PrBGP-119, Riedl-Hugunin, 6, 27 Jun. 1951.

142. StA-C StAnw-23, "Verschleppung des Dr. med. O.A.," 31 Aug. 1955, BayHStA PrBGP-118, Riedl, 11 Oct. 1949; NACP RG260, OMGB-Cbg 1205-3, BBP-Wildenheid, 11 Oct. 1949; RG466, HICOG-ID-Brd 2-4, Riedl, 22 Nov. 1949. Albrecht returned west after seventeen days.

143. E.g., StA-C StAnw-54, 44–46.

144. "Das Deutsche Gespräch wird von Sportlern vorgesehen," *DV*, 21 Mar. 1951; "Gute turnerische Leistungen im Interzonenkampf," *NP*, 20 Mar. 1951; NACP RG466, HICOG-B-ID-Brd: 2-2, Schaumberger, 27 Apr. 1951; Mulzer, 12 Apr. 1950; Zanker, 19 May 1950; 1–2, Thomsen, 7 Mar. 1951. In one well-known incident, fifty Thuringian athletes from Hildburghausen illegally crossed in March 1950 to play a handball game in Coburg, having been forbidden interzonal passes by eastern police. The players were arrested upon their return, but released when local authorities learned the team had won the match. Instead, the County Police were called to task for having denied the passes and thereby "sabotaging German unity." Schätzlein, Rösch, and Albert, *Grenzerfahrungen*, 1:61; Sandner, *Coburg*, 203.

145. BayHStA PrBGP-119, Riedl, 15 May 1951.

146. The eastern police invited westerners to speeches, but these were "sparsely attended." NACP RG466, HICOG-ID-Brd 2-2, Riedl, 15 May 1951; BayHStA PrBGP-119, Riedl, 15 May 1951.

147. BayHStA PrBGP-119, BBP-Cbg, 21 May 1951; "Die Wildenheider Sänger dürfen nicht kommen," *DV*, 19 May 1951; NACP RG466, HICOG-ID-Brd 2-2, Thomsen, 22 May 1951; ThHStAW LBdVP 027, 24-28.

148. BayHStA PrBGP-119, Riedl, 21 May 1951.

149. "4000 Germans Crash Police Lines for Beer," *WP*, 21 May 1951; "'Sängerkrieg' an der Zonengrenze," *SdZ*, 21 May 1951; "4000 Personen erzwangen Grenzübertritt bei Wildenheid," *NP*, 22 May 1951.

150. Interview, Jakob Ziegler.

151. ThHStAW LBdVP-027, 24–28. However, eastern forces registered more than 500 illegal crossers and confiscated illicit wares.

152. ThHStAW BMPr 1159, 20-25, Film 103; NACP RG466, HICOG-ID-Brd 2-2, Schäffer, 31 May 1951; SA-S: C2-13, -14, SbgSR-33, 39, 7 Jun., 13 Jul. 1951.

153. NACP RG260, OMGB-B 1129-1, BBP-Dir, MR, Jun. 1951.

154. NACP RG466, HICOG-ID-Brd 2-2, Riedl, 18 Jun. 1951; Teßmer and Zien, *Geschichten*, 69. Sonneberg's Party Leadership resolved to combat further attempts through public meetings and newspaper articles that featured "known personalities," urging against "clamor and commotion on the demarcation line"; StA-M SED-KL-Sbg 312, Minutes, 18 Jun. 1951. E.g., "Den Kampf um die Einheit und den Frieden Deutschlands verstärken," "Wir lehnen jegliche Provokationen ab," and "Tretet Gerüchten energisch entgegen," *DV*, 21, 22 Jun. 1951.

155. "In Freud und Leid zum Lied bereit," *NP*, 19 Jun. 1951; BayHStA PrBGP 119, Adam, 9 Jul. 1951.
156. "Die amerikanischen Kriegstreiber wünschten es nicht," "Mit Lügen und Verleumdungen wollen sie die Einheit Deutschlands verhindern," and Chirbod, letter, *DV*, 27, 29 Sep. 1951.
157. East and West Germany signed an Agreement on Interzonal Trade on September 20, 1951: SA-N 3021, Martin, 1 Oct. 1951; Weppler, 28 Sep. 1951; Hagen, 10 Oct. 1951; "Einige tausend Sonneberger warteten vergebens," *NP*, 27 Sep. 1951; "Grenzübergänge Neustadt und Falkenstein geschlossen," *NP*, 2 Oct. 1951.
158. "Spielabbruch in Neustadt," *DV*, 13 Apr. 1952.
159. StA-M SED-KL-Sbg 366, Minutes, 2 May 1952; Heinersdorf: Bennewitz and Potratz, *Zwangsaussied-lungen*, 220; BArch-B DO1-3911, Brückner, 7 May 1952.
160. StA-M SED-KL-Sbg 366, Minutes, 2 May 1952.
161. StA-M SED-KL-Sbg 366, Minutes, 2 May 1952; BArch-B DO1-3911, Brückner, 7 May 1952.
162. KrA-S Vors. 17, 6, Schubert, 7 Jun. 1952.

Chapter 5: Shock

1. E.g., blaming western inflexibility: Loth, *Sowjetunion*; Eisenberg, *Drawing*. Contra: Ruggenthaler, *Stalins grosser Bluff*; Spilker, *Leadership*.
2. Weitz, *German Communism*, 365–366. Evolution of state planning: Caldwell, *Dictatorship*.
3. Ostermann, *Uprising*, 34–35.
4. Potratz, "Stigmatisierung der Opfer." Overview, 1950–1952: Stacy, *Operations*, 48–50. Resolutions: BArch-B: DY30/IV 2-2-210, SED-ZK, "Schließung der Thüringer Grenze," 6 May 1952; DY30/IV 2-2-211, 38–40, "Maßnahmen zur Errichtung eines besonderen Regimes an der Demarkationslinie," 13 May 1952.
5. "Verordnung über Maßnahmen an der Demarkationslinie," 26 May 1952, available: www.document-archiv.de/ddr/1952/demarkationslinie-schutz_vo.html.
6. Van Melis and Bispink, "*Republikflucht*," 36–37.
7. The goals of earlier Soviet border fortifications: Chandler, *Institutions*, 3–5.
8. BArch-K B285-220, 224/143–144.
9. "Wiederholt sich die Berliner Blockade?" *NP*, 20 May 1952; BArch-B: DO1-3911, Brückner, 7 May 1952; DO1 8.0-307, 1–3.
10. "Wie Sonneberg künftig aussehen wird," "Der Handel mit dem Osten könnte helfen," *DV*, 24 May 1952.
11. "Befestigen die Russen die Zonengrenze!" *NP*, 22 May 1952; "Wir fordern Schutz gegen Saboteure und Agenten," *DV*, 23 May 1952. Headlines throughout East Germany: BArch-K B285-220, May 1952.
12. E.g., BArch-B DO1 8.0-304, 6, Eggerath, 27 May 1952.
13. StA-M SED-KL-Sbg 371, Minutes, 30 May 1952.
14. Ibid.
15. KrA-S Vors. 17-6, Brückner, 29 May 1952; BArch-K B285-220, 224/143–144.
16. KrA-S Vors. 17-6, Brückner, 29 May 1952.
17. BArch-B DE1-6084, 178.
18. KrA-S Vors. 17-6, 20–24; BArch-B DO1-3911, 18 Jun. 1952; BArch-K B285-220 224/309–314.
19. ThHStAW BMPr 243, 268–84, Film 20, 26 May 1952; BArch-B DO1 8.0-307, 5–8.
20. KrA-S Vors. 14-5, VP Köppelsdorf, 23 May 1952; ThHStAW BMPr 244, 122, Film 20, 23 May 1952.
21. "Behörden der Ostzone wollen Zonengrenze mit Stacheldraht und Minen befestigen," *NP*, 1 Jun. 1952.
22. Schleevoigt, "Heubisch," 30.
23. BArch-K B285-220, 224/86–87, emphasis in original.
24. KrA-S Vors. 17-6, "Situationsbericht," 6 Jun. 1952. "Action Vermin" was the Stasi's name for the measure; police heads in Thuringia dubbed it "Aktion X"; Wagner, "Zwangsaussiedlungen," 12. Administrative overview: Bennewitz and Potratz, *Zwangsaussiedlungen*, 26–36. Elbe: Wolter, *Aktion Ungeziefer*.
25. "Blick hinter den Eisernen Vorhang," *NP*, 7 Jun. 1952.
26. KrA-S Vors. 12-4, Report, 5 Jun. 1952.
27. KrA-S Vors. 12-4, VP Sonneberg, 4 Jun. 1952.

28. KrA-S Vors. 12-4, "Beobachtungen," 5 Jun. 1952.
29. KrA-S Vors. 12-4 and 15-5, Reports, 5 Jun. 1952; BArch-K B106-15424, Mulzer, 9 Jun. 1952.
30. Accounts differ slightly: BArch-B DE1-6084, 233; BArch-K B285-225, 229/44, 7 Jul. 1952; Grafe, *Grenze*, 50. There were additional mentions of suicide and attempts not mentioned in official reports, e.g., "Volkspolizei setzt den Terror an der Grenze fort," *NP*, 11 Jun. 1952.
31. E.g., KrA-S Vors. 17-6, 2 and 9–10; BArch-K B106-15424, Mulzer, 9 Jun. 1952.
32. KrA-S Vors. 17-6, "Situationsbericht," 6 Jun. 1952. Procedure: KrA-S Vors. 14-5, "Instruktion," Jun. 1952. The regime had scheduled the deportations around Pentecost so as to not to disturb holiday traffic.
33. "Zerschlagt die Lügen der Volksfeinde," *DV*, 5 Jun. 1952. Emphasis in original.
34. Interview, Jörg Trautmann, Sonneberg, 16 Dec. 2002.
35. Interview, Waltraud Wagner, Haselbach (Sonneberg), 13 Nov. 2009.
36. KrA-S Vors. 17-6, "Situationsbericht," 6 Jun. 1952; BArch-B DO1-3912, Th-VP, 21 Jun. 1952.
37. KrA-S Vors. 15-5, 6 Jun. 1952.
38. LBdVP Th-Weimar, 23 May 1952, in Wagner, "Beseitigung," 16–17.
39. Directives: BArch-B DO1-0.1.2-55074, 31–32, 38–40; BArch-B DO1 8.0-304, 10; western accounts: BArch-K B285-850. The Politburo devised deportation plans in tandem with border closure on May 13, 1952. Earlier sentencing of Jehovah's Witnesses: ThHStAW GStAnw-E 270, 33–36.
40. KrA-S Vors. 10-4, "Listen der Umsiedlungen," "Transport nach Jena," 7 Jun. 1952.
41. BArch-B DO1-3912, Th-VP, 22 Jun. 1952.
42. KrA-S Vors. 17-6, "Situationsbericht," 6 Jun. 1952; Bennewitz and Potratz, *Zwangsaussiedlungen*, 40.
43. E.g, "1952: Aus dem Kreis sollten 850 Leute verschwinden," *FW*, 6 Jun. 2002.
44. BArch-B DO1-3912, Th-VP, 22 Jun. 1952; KrA-S Vors. 17-6, "Situationsbericht," 6 Jun. 1952; BArch-K B285-220, 224/86–87. Local officials may have made mistakes deliberately, as an exculpatory strategy, though this possibility is not mentioned in reports on either side of the border.
45. KrA-S Vors. 15-5, Neuhaus-Schierschnitz mayor, 5 Jun. 1952.
46. "Anerkennung für tatkräftige Hilfe bei Flucht vor dem Terror," *NT*, 7 Jun. 1952.
47. KrA-S Vors. 14-5, Th-MInn, 12 Jun. 1952.
48. Compiled: KrA-S Vors. 10-4 and 17-6; BArch-B: DE1-6084, 3; DO1 8.0-307, 63–80; DO1-3912; NY4090-446, 121–122; Bennewitz and Potratz, *Zwangsaussiedlungen*, 83, 246.
49. BArch-K: B137-6, BMG, "Schließung der Zonengrenze"; B285-220, 224/151–156. Southern borderland: Moczarski, "Archivalische Quellen"; Wagner, "Beseitigung." Also, much of the southern borderland was separated from the rest of East Germany by the hilly terrain of the Thuringian forest.
50. The whereabouts for dozens more remained "unknown," and western estimates placed the number of Sonneberg refugees closer to one thousand.
51. Prohibited Zone population loss in Sonneberg, Thuringia, and East Germany, respectively, was 4.0 percent, 3.9 percent, and 3.6 percent. Figures: Sheffer, "Burned Bridge," 229.
52. DO1-3912, Th-VP, 21 Jun. 1952.
53. Schleevoigt, "Heubisch," 31.
54. BArch-B DO1-3912, Th-VP, 22 Jun. 1952.
55. KrA-S Vors. 12-4, Report, 5 Jun. 1952.
56. E.g., BArch-B DO1 8.0-306, 100; StA-C StAnw-4, 6 Mar. 1954.
57. BArch-B: DO1 8.0-305, 116–117; DO1 8.0-306, 54–61; DE1-6084, 239–244; "Turbine in der Bergmühle ausgebaut," *NT*, 9 Jun. 1952.
58. "Anerkennung für tatkräftige Hilfe bei Flucht vor dem Terror," *NT*, 7 Jun. 1952.
59. With the important exception of Bennewitz and Potratz's *Zwangsaussiedlungen*.
60. E.g., KrA-S Vors. 17-6: Schubert, 7 Jun. 1952; Brückner, 7 Jun. 1952.
61. KrA-S Vors. 15-5, "Situationsbericht—Heinersdorf," 5 Jun. 1952; Grafe, *Grenze*, 48.
62. KrA-S Vors. 17-6, 2.
63. BArch-B DE1-6084, 230; BArch-B: DO1 8.0-306, 54–61; DO1-3912: "Abschlussbericht" and Th-VP, 22 Jun. 1952; Ziereis, "Flucht," 20; BArch-K B285-220, 224/86–87.
64. "Die Massenflucht von 1952," *FW*, 8 Jun. 2009.
65. KrA-S Vors. 17-6, Brückner, 29 May 1952; BArch-B DE1-6084, 213–214; Private possession, Gansel: "Flucht vor der Zwangsverschleppung."
66. Interview, Gerd Jahn, Sonneberg, 27 Jun. 2002; rumors also published: "Eiserner Vorhang im Scheinwerfer," *NP*, 5 Jun. 1952.
67. "Das 'Niemandsland' wird evakuiert," *NP*, 7 Jun. 1952. Similar events elsewhere: "Four Mayors Lead Mass Flight," *NYT*, 7 Jun. 1952.

68. Straeten, "Das verlassene Dorf im Niemandsland," *NP*, 21 Jun. 1952. Western attempts to clarify Liebau's status: AA B10 Abt. 2 Bd. 450, Nr. A 7332, 126 and 133; BayHStA B-StK-10278, Kaemmerer, 4 Jun. 1952; Vogel, 10 Jun. 1952.

69. E.g., Dorndorf, 130 kilometers from Sonneberg: BArch-K B285-220, 224/346–349; BArch-B DO1-3912, Th-VP, 22 Jun. 1952; "Abschlussbericht," 22 Jun. 1952; BArch-B DO1 8.0-306, 54–61; Bennewitz and Potratz, *Zwangsaussiedlungen*, 51. Saalfeld and Grevesmuehlen revolts: "East German Revolt Reported Put Down," *NYT*, 22 Jun. 1952.

70. *Das verurteilte Dorf*, directed by Martin Hellberg, 1952. Film context: Lindenberger, "Home Sweet Home."

71. Bennewitz, "Das verurteilte Dorf"; Schätzlein, Rösch, and Albert, *Grenzerfahrungen*, 1:87–92.

72. BArch-K B285-220, 224/346–349.

73. Reports: BArch-B: DE1-6084: 235, 239–244; BArch-B DO1 8.0-305, 116–117; DO1-3912, Th-VP, 22 Jun. 1952; BArch-K B285-225, 229/135, Informationsbüro West, 14 Aug. 1952; Ritter and Lapp, *Grenze*, 22–23; Rothe, *Verraten*, 38–44. When the Stasi could not locate one of the men involved in the fighting, whose identity was unknown, they arrested Egon Altmann instead, the only Streufdorfer who matched the description of having a prosthetic left arm. Altmann was sentenced to eight years in prison while the real "ringleader," Manfred Engelhardt, fled west. Two years later, Engelhardt came forward to the district attorney in Coburg, confessing his "conflicted conscience" and wanting to help free the man who had been arrested in his place: StA-C StAnw-4, "Selbstanzeige wegen Aufruhrs in Streufdorf," 1954.

74. Schleevoigt, "Heubisch," 32.

75. BArch-K B285-220, 224/70–74.

76. BArch-K: B106-15424, Mulzer, 9 Jun. 1952; B285-220, 224/151–156.

77. Schätzlein, Rösch, and Albert, *Grenzerfahrungen*, 1:90–92.

78. "Der 'RIAS' hetzt Deutsche auf Deutsche," *DV*, 7 Jun. 1952.

79. BArch-B DE1-6084, 213–214.

80. "Wer auf die Hetzsender hört, unterstützt die Kriegsbrandstifter," *DV*, 9 Jun. 1952; ThHStAW BMPr 244, 78–79, Film 20, 24 Jun. 1952.

81. BArch-B/SAPMO DY30/IV 2-2-217, 2, SED-ZK, 24 Jun. 1952.

82. "Sie hatten es satt, noch länger dem RIAS zu glauben," *DV*, 10 Jun. 1952; "Die Schuld trägt der RIAS," *DV*, 11 Jun. 1952.

83. BArch-B DO1-3911, "Kreis Sonneberg," 18 Jun. 1952. Heinersdorf: KrA-S Vors. 17-6, 3–4 and 16–17.

84. BArch-B DO1 8.0-305, 116–117; Bennewitz and Potratz, *Zwangsaussiedlungen*, 77.

85. "Flüchtlingstreck aus Billmuthhausen," "FdJ beschlagnahmt die Ernte," *NT*, 21 Jun. 1952; Fuchs, *Billmuthausen*, 50.

86. BArch-K B285-225, 229/118–119.

87. KrA-S Vors. 17-6, Kain, 7 Jun. 1952. Schleevoigt, "Heubisch," 34.

88. ThHStAW Th-MInn 257, 2–3.

89. ThHStAW BMPr 244, 48, Film 20, 2 Jul. 1952.

90. ThHStAW BMPr 244, 78–79, Film 20, 24 Jun. 1952.

91. KrA-S Vors. 13-5, Barnikol, 11 Aug. 1952; files KrA-S Vors. 13-5, 16-6.

92. "Protokollauswertung," 8 Oct. 1952, in Rothe and Jödicke, *Zwangsaussiedlungen*, 23.

93. StA-M RdBz-Su, 903, 35.

94. BArch-B DO1 8.0-306, 22–23.

95. H. H. to Pieck, 17 May 1958, in Rothe, *Verraten*, 139–144.

96. KrA-S Vors. 13-5, O. M., 14 Sep. 1952.

97. Moczarski, "Archivalische Quellen," 345.

98. BArch-B DO1 8.0-304, 168–169, Eggerath, 24 Sep. 1952.

99. KrA-S Vors. 13-5, Bucha-Jena Mayor, 15 Jan. 1953.

100. KrA-S Vors. 16-6, Beier, 13 May and 1 Aug. 1953.

101. H. H. to Pieck, 17 May 1958, in Rothe, *Verraten*, 139–144.

102. KrA-S Vors. 14-5, Th-MInn, 12 Jun. 1952.

103. KrA-S Vors. 13-5, Correspondence Matthai-KrS, Sep. 1952–Feb. 1953; StA-M: RdBz-Su, Sek., 539, Söllner, 7 Aug. 1953; RdBz-Su, 903, 3–5, 88–89.

104. KrA-S Vors. 13-5, Brückner, 2 Oct. and 5 Dec. 1952; StA-M RdBz-Su, 903, 13-17 and 28.

105. KrA-S Vors. 10-4, Schubert, 6 Sep. 1956. Decisions: StA-M: RdBz-Su, In. 903, List, 1953; RdBz-Su, 42, Protocols, 12 and 19 Aug. 1952.

106. Schleevoigt, "Heubisch," 39.

107. Interview, Anna Emrich.

108. Events reported along the entire border: BMiB, *Sperrmassnahmen.*

109. BArch-K B106-15424, Mulzer, 9 Jun. 1952; "Turbine in der Bergmühle ausgebaut," *NT*, 9 Jun. 1952; "Husarenstück an der Zonengrenze," *NT*, 10 Jun. 1952.

110. "Flucht aus dem ostzonalen Sperrgebiet," *NP*, 7 Jun. 1952; "Willkür und Terror an der Zonengrenze," *NT*, 7 Jun. 1952; BArch-K B106-15424, Mulzer, 9 Jun. 1952, BayHStA PrBGP 119, Mulzer, 9 Jun. 1952.

111. E.g., "Volkspolizei spionierte im Landkreis Coburg," *NT*, 14 Jun. 1952. Discussion: BArch-K B285-220, 224/151-156.

112. "Das 'Niemandsland' wird evakuiert," *NP*, 7 Jun. 1952.

113. "Anerkennung für tatkräftige Hilfe bei Flucht vor dem Terror," *NT*, 7 Jun. 1952.

114. "Mit Vieh und Hausrat über die Grenze," *NP*, 7 Jun. 1952; "Die Massenflucht von 1952," *FW*, 8 Jun. 2009.

115. "Mit Vieh und Hausrat über die Grenze," *NP*, 7 Jun. 1952.

116. SA-N 4343, 166.

117. Refugee estimates vary considerably, even ranging up to 2,000 for Coburg. E.g., BArch-K B285-225, 229/43–46; BArch-K B137-6, Heilmann, 16 Jun. 1952, and contemporary newspaper reports.

118. Interview, Hannelore Reuther.

119. Straeten, "Das verlassene Dorf," *NP*, 21 Jun. 1952; Heidemeyer, *Flucht*, 190, 331.

120. Interview, Mathilde Schuster.

121. For this, Neustadt leaders requested 390,000 DM compensation from the government: "25 Wohnungen zur Unterbringung von Ostzonenflüchtlingen?" *NP*, 19 Jun. 1952.

122. In 1952, Neustadt's proportion of expellees, at 18 percent of the population, was in line with the West German and Bavarian averages (17 and 21 percent, respectively). "3230 Vertriebene u. Flüchtlinge fanden in Neustadt eine Heimat," *NP*, 14 Feb. 1953; Förster, "Grenzlandschicksal—wie lange noch?" *NP*, 13 Sep. 1952.

123. Refugee assistance: BayHStA: B-StK-10278; B-MInn 80870. Local summary: "Arbeiterwohlfahrt will Ostzonen-Flüchtlingen helfen," *NP*, 26 Jul. 1952.

124. "Was wird aus den Flüchtlingen?" *NP*, 12 Jun. 1952; Straeten, "Das verlassene Dorf im Niemandsland," *NP*, 21 Jun. 1952.

125. KrA-S 13-5, VP-Sbg, 7 Nov. 1952; StA-M RdBz-Su, Sek., 563, Suhl District Council, 28 May 1953.

126. StA-C AG-N, 1953. The rate of acceptance remained high throughout the mid-1950s and stayed at 99 percent after 1957: Heidemeyer, *Flucht*, 45, 133–142, 300.

127. BayHStA B-MInn 91695, Gumppenberg, 6 Aug. 1952.

128. "Volkspolizisten und Russen plötzlich freundlich," *NP*, 9 Mar. 1953.

129. "Illegaler Grenzgänger besonderer Art," *NP*, 2 Oct. 1952.

130. E.g., SA-N 2050, Weppler, 3 Nov. 1955.

131. BayHStA B-MInn 91695, Riedl, 22 Oct. 1952.

132. Ibid.

133. BayHStA LFlüV 1121, Senteck, 9 Oct. 1952; StA-M RdBz-Su, Vors. 49.

134. Scheuch, "Was erwartet das Handwerk von dem neuen Bundestag?" *NT*, 14 Nov. 1953.

135. "Versammlung der Sowjetzonenflüchtlinge," *NP*, 19 Dec. 1953.

136. SA-N 2050 (3021), Weppler, 7 Jul. 1953.

137. E.g., "Betrüger gab sich als Spätheimkehrer aus," *NP*, 14 Jan. 1954; BayHStA B-StK-14883, Reichenbecher, 15 Nov. 1956. File: SA-N 024-10/1.

138. SA-N 2050, Altenfelder-Weppler correspondence, Mar. 1953; "Politische Aufgabe der Sowjetzonen-Flüchtlinge," *NP*, 5 Mar. 1952; "Deutsche kämpfen und sterben für unsere Freiheit," *NP*, 30 Jun 1953.

139. "Sowjetzonen-Flüchtlinge jetzt gleichgestellt," *NP*, 21 Apr. 1952; "Versammlung der Sowjetzonenflüchtlinge," *NP*, 19 Dec. 1953; SA-N 024-10/1, NecSR, 10 May 1961; plus file.

140. SA-N 2111, M.G., 14 Apr. 1960; Bergmann, 10 May 1960.

141. A moving account of the challenges confronting this "new class in German society": Olsen, "German Refugees Face Weary Road," *NYT*, 31 Mar. 1957.

142. Weiner, ed., *Landscaping.*

143. KrA-S Vors. 17-6, 16-17, 9–10.

144. Interview, Wolfgang Mayerhofer, Sonneberg, 11 Dec. 2002.

145. Fuchs, *Billmuthausen*, 52.

146. Gross, *Revolution*, 122.

147. Havel, *Power of the Powerless.*

Chapter 6: Shift

1. BayHStA PrBGP 120, Riedl to B-MInn, 3 Feb. 1953; BBP-Nec to B-MInn, 23 Jan. 1953.

2. "'Friedenskämpfer' Dr. Peltzer setzte sich für Deutschen Block ein," *NP*, 22 Jan. 1953.

3. "Die Kundgebung an der Zonengrenze," *CT*, 21 Jan. 1953.

4. "Die Stimme der Parteien," *NT*, 21 Jan. 1953; BayHStA PrBGP 120. The men earned reduced sentences for their "idealistic reasons" and status as injured veterans, from a 530-DM fine (or fifty-three days in jail) for Jungnickel to a 20-DM fine for Peltzer.

5. Evolution: Geyer, "Cold War."

6. Schultke, *"Keiner,"* 45.

7. Naming and map representations in East and West: Herb, "Double Vision."

8. BArch-K B137-591, Kaiser, 27 Nov. 1952.

9. BArch-K B106-15424, "Dekadenmeldung," 4 Jul. 1952; Stacy, *Operations*, 57 (51–59); AA B10 Abt.2 Bd. 450-A7332, 130–133.

10. Daily border reports, esp. AA B10 Abt.2: Bd. 450-A7332, 182, 187; Bd. 446-7333; Bd. 446-A7312, 38; BayHStA PrBGP 120; BArch-K B137-6; BArch-K: B106-15424; B285-225, 229/226–232. Chronology: Schätzlein, Rösch, and Albert, *Grenzerfahrungen*, 1:81–92. Only a handful of incidents made it into the local newspapers.

11. BArch-K B285-220, 224/133–134, Rahner, 13 Jun. 1952; "Volkspolizei spionierte im Landkreis Coburg," *NT*, 14 Jun. 1952; "Volkspolizei setzt den Terror an der Grenze fort," *NP*, 11 Jun. 1952. East German accounts: KrA-S Vors. 17-6, 16–17; BArch-B: DE1-6084, 205; DO1-3912, Th-VP, 22 Jun. 1952.

12. "Unerträglicher Kleinkrieg an der Grenze," *NP*, 14 Aug. 1952.

13. "Ein Blick hinter den Vorhang," *NP*, 17 Jun. 1952; BArch-K B285-225, 229/43–46.

14. Sonneberg buildings slated for destruction: KrA-S Vors. 14-5, "Beschluss der op. Kommission," May 1952; BArch-B DO1 8.0-305, 118.

15. "Behörden der Ostzone wollen Zonengrenze mit Stacheldraht und Minen befestigen," *NP*, 1 Jun. 1952; KrA-S Vors. 17-6, 1; Grafe, *Grenze*, 40.

16. BArch-B DO1-3912, Th-VP, 21 Jun. 1952; BArch-K B106-15424, 30 Jun. 1952. Control Strip construction: KrA-S: Vors. 12-4; Vors. 17-6, StA-M RdBz-Su: Vors. 8; Vors. 9; Sek. 529.

17. Violators faced up to two years in prison and 2,000 DM in fines (two-thirds the punishment for escaping West), though one or two days' detention was the most common penalty. "Unkenntnis schützt nicht vor Strafe," *DfW*, 5 Dec. 1952.

18. BArch-B/SAPMO DY30/IV 2-2-218, 2, SED-ZK, 1 Jul. 1952. Overview, restrictions: Ritter and Lapp, *Grenze*, 19–22. Sonneberg ordinances: KrA-S Vors. 17-6; SA-S C2-258.

19. E.g., StA-M RdBz-Su, 903, 24–29. Phone service was reinstated in early 1954.

20. StA-M SED-KL-Sbg 371, Minutes, 30 May 1952.

21. StA-M SED-KL-Sbg IV/4.07/153, "Monatsbericht," 25 Feb. 1953.

22. StA-M RdBz-Su, Vors. 32, esp. Schwindack, 23 Oct. 1952.

23. KrA-S Vors. 12-4, Evaluation Commission, 9 Jul. 1952; StA-C AG-N, 186, Neustadt Court to district attorney, Thuringia, 11 Nov. 1952; "'Heldenscherz' an der Zonengrenze," *NP*, 10 Nov. 1956.

24. Compensation was negligible, summary: KrA-S Vors. 17-6, Gruhn to GDR Ministry of Finance, 30 Oct. 1952.

25. Coburg County had the highest number of severed farms in West Germany, representing 10 percent of all land lost by westerners. Details: Sheffer, "Burned Bridge," 283–285. Compiled from: BArch-K B137-582, Sonnemann, 1 Aug. 1952; AA B10 Abt.2 Bd. 452-A7342, 271–275; KrA-S Vors. 17-6, 7, 19–24; BArch-B DO1-3911, Brückner, 7 May 1952; BArch-B DO1 8.0-303, 31–35. Property inventory: KrA-S Vors. 12-4, Brückner, 16 Aug. 1952.

26. SA-N 2050, "Vorsorgliche Maßnahme," 3 Jul. 1952; SA-N 024-10/1, NecSR, 19 Jun. 1952; SA-N MB-117, May–Dec. 1952. Differences among Catholics and Protestants in the Eichsfeld: Schaefer, "Border-Land."

27. SA-N 4403, Neustadt Trade Office, 24 Jun. 1952. Nagel: KrA-S Vors. 13-5, Brückner, 2 Jan. 1953.

28. Interview, Ingeborg Friedrich, Sonneberg/Muppberg, 22 Jan. 2003.

29. BArch-K B285-220, 224/343–344.

30. "Die Oerlsdorfer Bauern machten den Anfang," *DfW*, 6 Sep. 1952, and "Liebau schafft sich eine neue Zukunft," *DfW*, 1 Nov. 1952. Road decision: StA-M RdBz-Su, 42: Protocols, 19 and 20 Aug. 1952; Söllner, 6 Sep. 1952. For months, the newspaper called all Sonnebergers to volunteer work, but the new access road turned out to be well-nigh impassable. Albert and Salier, *Grenzerfahrungen Kompakt*, 347.

31. KrA-S Vors. 16-6: Suhl District Chairman, 13 Dec. 1952; Dötsch, 18 Oct. 1952, SED-BPO Consumer Cooperative, 12 Nov. 1952. Westerners continued to petition for Liebau to be incorporated into West Germany: AA B10 Abt.2 Bd.446- A7312, 33–34.

32. Border Police escalations: Sälter, *Grenzpolizisten*, 70–85.

33. StA-M SED-KL-Sbg IV/4.07/152, "10-tägige Berichterstattung," 18 Nov. 1952. Borderland purge order: BArch-B/SAPMO NY4090-446, 123–127. Implementation: BArch-B DO1: 8.0-303, 121–127; 8.0-307, 1–3, 63–80.

34. ThHStAW Th-MInn 257, 22, Dose, 5 Jun. 1952. KrA-S Vors. 16-6, "Abhaltung kirchlicher Handlungen," 28 Jan. 1953; BArch-B DO1 8.0-304, 143–144.

35. "Da-da-das . . . ein Kulturraum?" *DfW*, 19 Aug. 1952; KrA-S Vors. 17-6, 17–27; BArch-B DO1 8.0-304, 147–148.

36. E.g., BArch-B DO1 8.0-305, 150–152.

37. Schleevoigt, "Heubisch," 29.

38. StA-M RdBz-Su, 42, Sattler, Brückner, Eckardt, and Wolff correspondence, Nov. 1952–Jan. 1953; private firms agreed to participate for a "limited time."

39. StA-M SED-KL-Sbg IV/4.07/152, 11 Jul. 1952; BArch-B DO1 8.0-304, 164; KrA-S Vors. 12-4, Correspondence—Jun 1952. East Germany's reduction in agricultural quotas for the borderland did not engender as much enthusiasm; that seemed "a matter of course." KrA-S Vors. 17-6, Office of Information, 11 Jul. 1952.

40. StA-M SED-KL-Sbg IV/4.07/153, "Monatsbericht," 25 Feb. 1953; StA-M RdBz-Su, Vors. 32, Sattler, 6 Jul. 1953.

41. BArch-B DO1-3912, Th-VP, 22 Jun. 1952; SA-S C2-15, SbgSR-85, 3 Jul. 1952; KrA-S Vors. 13-5, Flurschütz, "Sperrzonenermässigung für Sbg-West," 1952.

42. "Ein Tag beim Bürgermeister in Mupperg," *DfW*, 20 Sep. 1952.

43. BArch-B/SAPMO NY4090-449, 15.

44. van Melis and Bispink, *"Republikflucht,"* 255.

45. StA-M SED-KL-Sbg IV/4.07/152, Reports, 8 Apr. and Dec. 1952. Additional incidents in files 4.07/152, 153, 167, and Sheffer, "Burned Bridge," 295–312.

46. SED-BL Protocol, 27 Nov. 1952, in Moczarski, *Protokolle*, 261–262. The boys were sentenced to two to six years in prison.

47. KrA-S Vors. 13-5, Appeals—Jun 1952.

48. SA-S C2-42, Braun, 9 Jun. 1952.

49. State Bishop Mitzenheim denounced the Jun. 1952 deportations in an open letter, leading church support of affected border villages. BArch-B DO1 8.0-304, 194–197; ThHStAW BMPr 245, 37–38, Film 20; Bennewitz and Potratz, *Zwangsaussiedlungen*, 68–69. Exhaustive Stasi reports on Sonneberg pastors and religious groups: BStU BV Suhl XI/212/76 I and II: "Kirchen und Sekten," 1953, esp. overview: II-188–191; explosion of religious activity after the New Course: II-199.

50. StA-M SED-KL-Sbg IV/4.07/153, "Informationsbericht," 16 Jun. 1953.

51. StA-M SED-KL-Sbg IV/4.07/153, "Analyse," 16 Jun. 1953.

52. Overview: Sperber, "17 June."

53. Ostermann, *Uprising*, 165; Diedrich, *Waffen*, 169.

54. StA-M SED-KL-Sbg IV/4.07/153, "Informationsbericht," 20 Jun. 1953. *Das freie Wort* cited this as Sonneberg's noteworthy incident: "Die Werktätigen des Kreises Sonneberg ließen sich nicht provozieren," 29 Jun. 1953.

55. StA-M SED-KL-Sbg IV/4.07/153, "Analyse," 16 Jun. 1953.

56. StA-M SED-KL-Sbg IV/4.07/153, "Informationsbericht," 20 Jun. 1953.

57. StA-M SED-KL-Sbg IV/4.07/167, "Telefonische Durchsage," 18 Jun. 1953; StA-M RdBz-Su, Sek., 559, Brückner, 18 Jun. 1953. Collectivization of agriculture in Sonneberg was never popular: Schwämmlein, "Landwirtschaft," 255–261.

58. Erich Götz, 17 Jun. 1953, in Moczarski, *Protokolle*, 1023–1024.

59. StA-M SED-KL-Sbg IV/4.07/167, "Telefonische Durchsage," 18 Jun. 1953, StA-M SED-KL-Sbg IV/4.07/153, "Informationsbericht," 18 Jun. 1953; District Suhl: BArch: DO1 11.0-306, 347–354 and NY 4062-94, 388–394, both available: www.17juni53.de/karte/suhl.html.

60. Moczarski, *17. Juni*, 8–11, 17, 20, 26–33. Regional summaries: Schätzlein, Rösch, and Albert, *Grenzerfahrungen*, 1:103–106; "Vor 50 Jahren war der Bezirk Suhl der einzige ohne Ausnahmezustand," *NP* and *FW*, 17 Jun. 2003.

61. StA-M SED-KL-Sbg IV/4.07/153, "Informationsbericht," 20 Jul. 1953.

62. StA-M SED-KL-Sbg IV/4.07/167, "Telefonische Durchsage," (17) Jun. 1953.

63. StA-M SED-KL-Sbg IV/4.07/153, "Analyse," 21 and 22 Jun. 1953. Neustadt newspaper accounts made no mention of the border.
64. US policy: Buckow, *Zwischen*, 360–374.
65. "Deutsche kämpfen und sterben für unsere Freiheit," *NP*, 30 Jun. 1953.
66. SED-BL-Suhl, "Tagesmeldung," 18 Jun. 1953, in Voigt, "Der 17. Juni Im Landkreis Sonneberg," *NP*, 17 Jul. 2003. Rottenbach: StA-M RdBz-Su, Sek., 539, Rüdiger, 6 Jul. 1953; BayHStA PrBGP 120, Riedl, 8 Jul. 1953.
67. Eckardt, "Augenzeuge," 10. Similar to Jun. 1952: BArch-K B106-15424, Mulzer, 9 Jun. 1952.
68. KrA-S Vors. 13-5 (and StA-M RdBz-Su, In. 903), Heinersdorf Council, 2 Jan. 1953. Problematic New Year's Eve gathering: BayHStA PrBGP 120, Riedl, 3 Jan. 1953; BArch-K B285-225, 229/339–340; "Deutsche aus Ost und West knieten im Schnee zum Gebet nieder," *NP*, 3 Jan. 1953.
69. StA-M SED-KL-Sbg IV/4.07/153, "Telefonische Durchsage," 14 Jun. 1953. Burned Bridge: BayHStA PrBGP 1629, Riedl, 18 Jun. 1953.
70. "'Todesstreifen' war Treffpunkt deutscher Menschen," *NP*, 23 Jun. 1953; StA-M SED-KL-Sbg IV/4.07/167, "Durchsage," Jun. 1953.
71. BayHStA PrBGP 120, Riedl, 30 Jun., 8 Jul. 1953.
72. "Nur noch der 10-Meter-Streifen lag dazwischen," *NP*, 13 Jul. 1953, "Erneutes Ost-West-Treffen am Stacheldraht," 20 Jul. 1953.
73. "10-Meter-Streifen" *NP*, 13 Jul. 1953; "Ost-West-Treffen," *NP*, 20 Jul. 1953.
74. Weekly Sonneberg statistics: KrA-S In. 106-39. Suhl: RdBz-Su, Sek. 559. Coburg County: BayHStA PrBGP-123.
75. StA-M SED-KL-Sbg IV/4.07/153, "Informationsbericht," 20 and 23 Jul. 1953; "Anneliese ärgert sich," *DfW*, 24 Jul. 1953. Sonneberg's official border regiment history claims 300 West German "counterrevolutionary elements" were trying to cross; the "German-Soviet brotherhood-in-arms" thwarted their "revanchist spooking." Reisenweber, *Reihe*, 1:25.
76. StA-M SED-KL-Sbg IV/4.07/153, SED-KL-Sbg, 30 Jul. 1953; StA-M RdBz-Su, Sek., 539, Söllner, "Situationsbericht," 6 Aug. 1953. Border meetings died out sooner in Bad Salzungen County: StA-M RdBz-Su, Vors. 32, Sattler-Salden, 2–6 Jul. 1953.
77. K., "Eingedostes Grenzland-Elend," *NP*, 11 Sep. 1952.
78. Daum, *Kennedy*, 147–156.
79. Overview: BArch-K B137-593: "Memorandum des Landkreises Coburg und der Stadt Neustadt b. Coburg," 1952; Coburg, "Grenzland in Not"; Muth, *Wirtschaft*. Main projects included a new road from Wörlsdorf to Fürth am Berg, a new three-hundred-meter route to the Mountain Mill Tavern, and apartment buildings for eastern refugees. Severance in the nearby border region Tettau/Lehesten was particularly difficult; around 250 people still worked on either side of the border (at the Lehesten slate quarry and Tettau's porcelain works), while the rail line meandered over the border fourteen times: BArch-K B137-6, B137-586.
80. Overview: BArch-K B137-6 (B137-579), Heilmann, 23 Jul. 1952.
81. "Resolution—Sofortige Hilfsmaßnahmen für das Ferngaswerk Neustadt b. Coburg," *NP*, 12 Jul. 1952, "Coburger Lokal-Egoismus schädigt Neustadt Interessen," 28 Jun. 1952. Border programs often conflicted; subsidized Neustadt glassblowers won a 13 percent price reduction by threatening to switch to Coburg's subsidized new plant: SA-N 024-10/1; SA-N 4343, 190–192. Neustadt eventually planned to build a pipeline expansion to Kronach-Tettau with federal help: BArch-K B137-590, -591, -593. Sonneberg officials worked to reopen the pipeline: SA-S C2-15.
82. SA-N 4403, 202–212; *Der Lebensmittelgroßhandel*, "Probleme Des Lebensmittel-Großhandels im Zonen-Grenzgebiet," 11 Mar. 1955.
83. *Bayerisches Volks-Echo*, "Existenzkrise der Spielwarenindustrie," Oct. 1952; SA-N 5698, 7–8.
84. "Ausgezeichnete Weihnachtssaison der Spielwaren-Industrie," *NP*, 10 Dec. 1953.
85. Lischewsky, *Puppen*, 66–78; Sperschneider, "Spielwarenindustrie," 140–150. Sonneberg child labor: BArch-B DE1-27174, Volkmar, 20 Nov. 1958. Homeworkers: BArch-B/SAPMO DY47-27, Hartig, 28 Mar. 1956; "Lage der Heimarbeiter," 23 Mar. 1956; BArch-B/SAPMO DY47-111.
86. File: SA-N 4343, esp. 171–189; *Fränkischen Presse*, "Auch die 'Puppenstadt' sucht neue Industriebetriebe," 7 Oct. 1952. Toy industry: SA-N 024-10/1; SA-N Obgm. 80. The relatively small economic impact of the border: Altrichter, "Schatten."
87. "Bonner Ausschuß studierte Zonengrenz-Probleme," *NP*, 18 Oct. 1952; Förster, "Versprechen, Versprechen … dabei bleibt's!" *NP*, 22 Apr. 1953.
88. BArch-K: B137-591, Kaiser, 27 Nov. 1952; B137-580, Henn, "Entwurf—Förderungsmaßnahmen," 5 Jun. 1953, plus file. Overview, 1952: BArch-K B137-582, Thedieck, "Bereitstellung von Bundesmit-

teln," 21 Aug. 1952; AA B10 Abt.2 Bd.452-A7338 and A7339. Neustadt efforts: SA-N 2111. Federal
debate: BArch-K B106-5151. Offer, *Zonenrandgebiet*, 24–26.
89. Bourgeois evolution: Berghahn, "Recasting."
90. *Himmel ohne Sterne*, directed by Helmut Käutner, 1955; "Aufnahmen für 'Himmel ohne Sterne' auch
in Neustadt," *NP*, 29 Jul. 1955.
91. "Stopp—Kap zur Zonengrenze," *NP*, 11 Aug. 1953.
92. "Vier lustige Zecher durchbrachen 'in Marschordnung' die Grenze," *NP*, 8 Aug. 1953.
93. E.g., "Through the Iron Curtain," *NYT*, 27 Jul. 1952. Signage: BArch-K B137-1059.
94. Zöller, "Grenze der hundert Gemeinheiten," *Rheinischer Merkur*, 19 Sep. 1952.
95. Förster, "Grenzlandschicksal—wie lange noch?" *NP*, 13 Sep. 1952. Western images of the border:
Ullrich, *Geteilte Ansichten*, 41–84.
96. StA-C LRA 14788, Correspondence, Jul.–Oct. 1956; "Stützpunkt des Glaubens, der Freiheit und des
Friedens," *NT*, Aug. 1955; private possession, Treichel.
97. "Wildenheids Wasserversorgung gesichert," *NP*, 17 Sep. 1953; "Sang und Spott vom Thüringer Wald,"
NP, 24 Sep. 1953.
98. The role of public fear in civil defence: Biess, "Everybody."
99. StA-M SED-KL-Sbg IV/4.07/154, "Politische Lage," 8 Oct. 1955.
100. SA-N, Bergmann, "Stadtratsbesuch—Tonband," Aug. 1959. East-West correspondence: Dietzsch,
24–29.
101. Interview, Konrad Rademacher, Sonneberg, 1 Jul. 2002; KrA-S Vors. 17-6, 17–27.
102. Petzold, "Entwicklung," 302.
103. Gray, *Cold War*, 6.
104. "West Germans Fight Bands Sent by East to Disrupt Vote," *NYT*, 3 Sep. 1953; "Die meisten Ver-
hafteten sind Fanatiker," *NP*, 3 Sep. 1953. Attempt, 1957: BayHStA B-StK-14184, 16 Sep. and 21 Oct.
1957.
105. Dierske, *Bundesgrenzschutz*, 56–57.
106. BayHStA B-StK-14184, Riedl, 24 Sep. 1956.
107. Böhm, "SED lockt unsere Kinder in die Sowjetzone," *Bayerische Staatszeitung*, 28 May 1955.
108. *Kronacher Volksblatt*, "Verräter sind unter uns!" 1 Apr. 1959; BArch-K B137-1498, Herbert, 19 Jan.
1960, plus reports, 1955–1961.
109. StA-M SED-KL-Sbg IV/4.07/212, "Protokoll," 23 Nov. 1955; Amos, *Westpolitik*, 115–121.
110. Political import of sporting events in East Germany: Johnson, *Training*, 31–64.
111. KrA-S In. 144-51, "Bericht—gesamtdeutsche Arbeit," 8 Nov. 1954. Voluminous files: KrA-S: In. 106–
39, 144–51; Vors. 31-10; StA-M RdBz-Su, KmAbz., 691.
112. Döbrich, "Das Sonneberger Reiterlein sprang über die Zonengrenze!" *Sonneberger Kulturspiegel*, Mar.
1955; interview, Dietmar Huber, Sonneberg/Wolkenrasen, 11 Dec. 2002; plus private papers.
113. KrA-S Vors. 31-10, "Bericht—gesamtdeutsche Arbeit," 24 Oct. 1955.
114. "Gewachsene Beziehungen jäh unterbrochen," *NP*, 14 Jan. 1995.
115. Figures: Sheffer, "Burned Bridge," 348.
116. Compiled: SA-S C2-33/169–172/249–250. Travel ordinances: BMiB, *Bau der Mauer*, 84–94; File:
SA-N 3021.
117. SA-S C2-170-172/215/249–250, "Aussprache mit Westdeutschenbesucher," Aug. 1957–Mar. 1961.
Beginning: KrA-S Vors. 31-10, Stier, 31 Dec. 1954. National policy: Amos, *Westpolitik*, 120–121.
118. SA-S C2-33, Stier, 14 Apr. 1954. Sonneberg's Toy Museum averaged over 100,000 visitors a year
during the fifties, 233,000 by 1960. Overview: Hofmann, "Deutsche Spielzeugmuseum," 367.
119. KrA-S In. 144-51, "Bericht—Bevölkerungspolitik," 4 Jan. 1961.
120. SA-S: C2-33; C3-210; C3-249.
121. Bureaucratic apparatus: Creuzberger, *Kampf*.
122. BayHStA B-StK-10281, esp. B-MInn, 15 Apr. 1957.
123. SA-N 2050, German County Association, "Rundschreiben Nr.58/56," 27 Mar. 1956; BArch-K B137-
2507, Thedieck, "Auswirken der nachbarschaftlichen Beziehungen," 19 Aug. 1957. American funding:
BArch-K B137-4724.
124. Averages, Jul. 1958–Sep. 1960: BArch-K B137-1487; SA-N, "Verwaltungs- und Tätigkeitsbericht
1958–1962," 31 Mar. 1963; DW, "Wenn Gäste aus der Zone kommen ...," 6 Feb. 1957.
125. StA-C LRA 15433: "Lieber Landsmann von drüben," 1956.
126. German County Association, "Rundschreiben Nr.6/55," 20 Feb. 1955; Gröbe, 8 Jan. 1957.
127. Sonneberg-Neustadt details: Sheffer, "Burned Bridge," 560–568. Eichsfeld: Schaefer, "Hidden."
128. SA-N 2050, Thedieck, 27 Jan. 1954. Discussion and guidelines on East-West contacts: BArch-K B137:
-1470, -1471, -1553. Summary, cross-border logistical issues: BArch-B DE1-1235, 15–18.

129. SA-N 2050, Weppler, 7 Sep. 1953.
130. SA-N 2050, Günder, 15 Nov. 1955.
131. SA-N 2051, Platz, 14 Jun. 1956. Sonneberg's "all-German work": SA-S: C3-210, C2-33.
132. StA-M RdBz-Su, 965, Hess, 24 Nov. 1955; StA-M RdBz-Su, 6679, Hess, Jun. 1956.
133. SA-N EAP 001-10, 42-48, Lange, 23 Nov. 1956.
134. BayHStA PrBGP 1629, Martin, 15 Jan. 1958, file. BArch-K B137-2507; SA-N EAP 001-10; StA-M RdBz-Su, Vors. 210.
135. E.g., "Kleine Ost-West-Konferenz," *Bild*, 12 Feb. 1958. Oberhof: BArch-B DO1 9231.
136. BArch-K B137-1470, Plück, 18 Dec. 1958.
137. SA-N: 5824; EAP 001-10. Protracted meeting planning: SA-S: C2-111; C2-170.
138. SA-N EAP 001-10, 104, Bergmann, 27 Aug. 1959.
139. SA-N 2051, Ziebill, 19 Sep. 1960; SA-N EAP 001-117. Press reports: BArch-K B137-2508.
140. "Mit den Sonnebergern an der Zonengrenze," *NP*, 24 Oct. 1960; "Neustädter Stadtrat: Kontaktverbot gilt nicht für uns," *ND*, 25 Oct. 1960.
141. Holert, *Imagineering*, in Derix, "Emotional," 118.
142. Interview, Helmut Traub.
143. Interviews, Götz Emrich, Jörg Trautmann, and Elisabeth Dietzer. Krause, "Die 'grüne Grenze in den 50er Jahren,'" in Schugg-Reheis, ed., *Grenzenlos*, 22.
144. StA-M SED-KL-Sbg IV/4.07/172/1,"Protokoll—BPO SED-Kreisleitung," 16 Nov. 1955.
145. StA-M SED-KL-Sbg IV/4.07/207, "Bemerkungen zum Verhalten des Genossen B.," Oct. 1961. Disorder in Hagenow: Kufeke, "Unzufriedenheit."
146. *DWg*, "Neue Entwicklungsphase der LPG Begann," 7 Oct. 1959, Schwarze, "Sowjetische Soldaten packten mit an," 12 Nov. 1957.
147. Cerny, "Die Westgrenze in DDR-Sicht," in Weisbrod, ed., *Grenzland*, 141; Fuchs, *Billmuthausen*, 90; StA-M SED-KL-Sbg IV/4.07/155, "Politische Lage," 27 Aug. 1956.
148. "Grumble Gesellschaft": Port, *Conflict*, 115–120; Johnson, "Dividing Mödlereuth."
149. Prohibited Zone Reports, 1951–1960: SED-KL-Sbg IV/4.07/154-162; 167; 207; BStU BV Suhl XI/212/76 I and II. East German radio and television signals were poor south of the Thuringian Forest; several Sonneberg communities received only West German programming, a political problem. Reception maps: BArch-B DE1-1235, 15–18.
150. BStU BV Suhl XI/196/76, 210, Dubian, 14 Nov. 1959.
151. StA-M SED-KL-Sbg IV/4.07/212, Modes, 28 Jun. 1961. Files, 1960: StA-M SED-KL-Sbg IV/4.07/161–162, 172; BayHStA PrBGP 121. Frontier communities were among the first in Sonneberg County to form Agricultural Production Cooperatives (LPGs) for "defense of our republic" (and because of all the vacated farmland). The County was proclaimed fully collectivized in the summer of 1960, the first in the district of Suhl. Summary: Hoffmann, "Landwirtschaft," 689–695.
152. Last, *After*, 39–44.
153. BayHStA PrBGP 120, Martin, 28 Jun. 1954.
154. Hanisch, *Schutz*, 35–36; BArch-B/SAPMO DY30-3682, 113–124. Sonneberg: Reisenweber, *Reihe*, 1:81. GDR infractions: BayHStA PrBGP 120; 121.
155. Interview, Inge Treichel, Neustadt/Wildenheid, 14 Nov. 2009.
156. BStU BV Suhl XI/196/76, 260–261.
157. Topping, "Flier's Use as Berlin Pawn Seen," *WP*, 6 Dec. 1958; Mackin's plight made headlines in U.S. newspapers until his release on February 5, 1959.
158. Dierske, *Bundesgrenzschutz*, 23; BArch-K B137-1474, "Daten von der Zonengrenze—1959 und 1960."
159. Interview, Jörg Trautmann.
160. Wachter, "Umständliche Reise," 106.

Chapter 7: Surveillance

1. SA-S C2-38, SbgSR-375, 4 Feb. 1958.
2. Gauss, *Wo Deutschland liegt*, 117 (see Betts, *Within Walls*, esp. 9–12); Kocka, "Durchherrschte Gesellschaft," 547–553; Fulbrook, *People's State*, 10–17; Jarausch, "Care and Coercion," 47–69. Overview: Port, *Conflict*, 2–10.
3. Brentano, "So bescheiden," *DZ*, 16 Aug. 1991.
4. All population figures in this chapter, unless otherwise specified, are compiled from Sonneberg's County Archive (KrA-S: In. 106-39, 144-51, 438-128, 439-129; Vors. 31-10), *Statistisches Taschenbuch—Kreis Sonneberg*, 1966, and People's Police records synthesized by Professor Patrick Major, of

the University of Reading, at the Federal Archives in Berlin. While there are inaccuracies in both East and West German statistics (which should be viewed as broad indicators, not exact data), this chapter utilizes East German figures as the most consistent approximation of population movement in the 1950s. Heidemeyer, *Flucht*, 37–48; Effner and Heidemeyer, *Flucht*, 27–32. Federal Republic figures available: Chronik der Mauer, www.chronik-der-mauer.de/index.php/de/Start/Detail/id/593791/page/2, accessed Jan. 2011. Alternative migration figures based on East German records: van Melis and Bispink, *"Republikflucht,"* 255–259.

5. On flight in the 1950s: Major, *Berlin Wall*, 56–116; van Melis and Bispink, *"Republikflucht,"* 73–111; Ross, "East Germans," 25–43.

6. The politics of economic priorities: Landsman, *Dictatorship*.

7. Policy evolution: Hughes, *Shouldering*.

8. However, rates of flight varied considerably among towns in Sonneberg County. Flight maps: BArch-B/SAPMO NY4090-448, 348, 359, 363; Major, *Berlin Wall*, 60–61.

9. BStU BV Suhl XI/212/76 II, 440–441, GI "Brot," 5 Dec. 1958.

10. Interview, Konrad Rademacher.

11. Interview, Kurt Geis.

12. Interview, Siegfried Tenner, Sonneberg, 3 Feb. 2003.

13. Heidemeyer, *Flucht*, 47; KrA-S Vors. 31-10, Report, Sep. 1955.

14. KrA-S In. 144-51, Schubert, Apr. 1957.

15. KrA-S In. 106-39 and StA-M RdBz-Su, 965, 2 May 1955; also Schilling, 6 Apr. 1955; StA-M SED-KL-Sbg IV/4.07/212, "Bürositzung," 24 May 1955.

16. BayHStA B-StK-14184, Riedl, Mar. 1957; KrA-S In. 438-128, "Protokoll—Passgesetz," 19 Mar. 1958.

17. SA-N 2050, Weppler, 3 Nov. 1955.

18. NP-A 564-8 I, Weiland, 8 Jan. 1956.

19. KrA-S In. 106-39, Schubert, 9 Nov. 1956.

20. KrA-S In. 144-51, Heublein to Heiliger, Mar. 1961. List: StA-M SED-KL-Sbg IV/4.07/212, "Republikflucht, Rückkehrer u. Zuwanderer," 1955.

21. KrA-S In. 144-51, Schubert, Nov. 1956.

22. StA-M SED-KL-Sbg IV/4.07/212, "Protokoll—Arbeitstagung," 23 Nov. 1955.

23. Directives: KrA-S In. 296-81; SA-S C2-95.

24. On the inquisitorial dynamic propelling Soviet terror, see Kotkin, *Magnetic Mountain*, 280–354.

25. Interview, Hannelore Reuther. Lists: SA-S C2-95.

26. StA-M SED-KL-Sbg IV/4.07/171, Thiele, 17 Sep. 1959.

27. StA-M SED-KL-Sbg IV/4.07/212, "Bürositzung—Bezirksleitung," 24 May 1955.

28. "Mußte Linne türmen?" *FW*, Jul. 1958, in KrA-S In. 106-39.

29. "Der Verrat des Klaus Elßman," *FW*, 16 Aug. 1958. Internal version: KrA-S In. 106-39, Schubert, 5 Jul. 1957.

30. KrA-S In. 106-39, Report, 5 Jul. 1956.

31. Frenkel, "Zu den bevorstehenden Jahreshauptversammlungen," *Sonneberger Kulturspiegel*, Mar. 1956. Lists: KrA-S In. 144-51, Sommer, 3 Aug. 1961.

32. SA-S C3-214, Grüning, 30 Oct. 1957. Negotiations: SA-S C2-95.

33. Empowering individuals: Ross, *Socialism*, 143.

34. BArch-B DO1-9084, Opitz, 8 Feb. 1957.

35. StA-M SED-KL-Sbg IV/4.07/212, "Protokoll—Arbeitstagung," 23 Nov. 1955.

36. SA-S C3-214, Grüning, 20 Sep. 1957.

37. SA-S C3-214, Stier, 16 Oct. 1957.

38. KrA-S In. 144-51: Schubert, 30 Oct. 1956; "Analyse—illegale Abwanderung," Nov. 1956; KrA-S In. 106-39, Schubert, 9 Oct. 1956; BArch-B DO1-9084, Engelmann, 15 Nov. 1956 (name changed).

39. StA-M SED-KL-Sbg IV/4.07/212 (and KrA-S Vors. 31-10), Schubert, "Verhinderung der Republikflucht," May 1955, and "Protokoll—Arbeitstagung," 23 Nov. 1955.

40. On the limits of official vocabulary: Ross, *Socialism*, 144–145.

41. KrA-S: In. 106-39; 144-51; and Vors. 31-10.

42. BArch-B DO1-8012, "Arbeitstagung," 30 Sep. 1954.

43. Though available statistics are inconsistent, border police on both sides reported an abrupt decrease in illegal border traffic. In the Neustadt-Sonneberg region, eastern and western forces apprehended 1 to 3 people per day after 1952, compared to 50 to 300 before. Over the entire boundary, West Germany registered a 99 percent decrease in illegal crossings, from an average of 110,000 a month in 1951 to just 550 a month in 1953. Behrens, "Schicksale Unserer Zeit," *NT*, 28 Dec. 1963; BArch-K B137-4,

"Personenverkehr über die Zonengrenze," Jan., Jun. 1953; BArch-K B137-5, "Monatslisten und Vernehmungsprotokolle," Nov. 1955.

44. StA-M SED-KL-Sbg IV/4.07/212, 29 Apr. 1955, and "Protokoll—Arbeitstagung," 23 Nov. 1955.
45. Major, *Berlin Wall*, 102.
46. Interview, Kurt Geis.
47. StA-M SED-KL-Sbg IV/4.07/155, "Politische Lage im Kreis," Sep. 1956.
48. KrA-S 144-51, VPKA Abt. PM, 1 Jan. 1959.
49. StA-M SED-KL-Sbg IV/4.07/212, "Protokoll—Arbeitstagung," 23 Nov. 1955.
50. SA-S C2-170, "Bezirksvorsteherbesprechung," 8 Jul. 1958.
51. SA-S C2-87, "Schlussfolgerungen," 8 Jul. 1957.
52. StA-M SED-KL-Sbg IV/4.07/162, "Berichterstattung—Grenzgebiet," 8 Dec. 1960.
53. StA-M SED-KL-Sbg 526, minutes, 8 Feb. 1957; KrA-S In. 106-39, Schubert, 2 Oct. 1957; BArch-B DO1-9084, "Erfahrungsaustausch," 8 Nov. 1957.
54. van Melis and Bispink, *"Republikflucht,"* 49.
55. KrA-S In. 438-128, "Protokoll—Passgesetz," 19 Mar. 1958.
56. Major, *Berlin Wall*, 104.
57. StA-M SED-KL-Sbg IV/4.07/156, Maaser to SED-BL-Suhl, Dec. 1957. Travel strictures were long contentious in local government, Sonneberg's more liberal city council typically battling against the stricter county and border police administrations.
58. In Sonneberg, the average number of visas issued dropped from 16,700 in 1954–57 to around 5,000 in 1958–60.
59. In East Germany, the percentage of travelers defecting dropped from 5.8 percent to 1.7 percent. In Sonneberg, the number of travel visas issued to West Germany dropped from 16,700 in 1954–57 to 4,940 in 1958–60, with the percentage of travelers defecting decreasing from 2.6 percent to 1 percent.
60. Major, *Berlin Wall*, 105.
61. Ross, *Socialism*, 151.
62. East Germany also strengthened security on the inter-German border in 1958, but this did not have nearly the impact of the new travel strictures. The 1957 Pass Law likewise reduced the number of western travelers to East Germany, down almost a quarter from 1.1 million a year 1954–57 to an average of 850,000 in 1958–60; Sonneberg County saw a 43 percent drop in permit approvals, from 9,550 a year to 5,480.
63. BArch-B DO1-8012, "Arbeitstagung," 9 Sep. 1954. Overview: Schmelz, *Migration*; district of Suhl, 1961–72: Neumeier, "Rückkehrer."
64. BArch-K B137-5, "Rückkehr in die SBZ," 25 Nov. 1958; Ross, *Socialism*, 147.
65. BArch-K: B137-5, "Bevölkerungsbewegung," 16 May 1955, "Monatslisten und Vernehmungsproto-kolle," Nov. 1955; B137-6, "SBZ-Flüchtlinge kehren in die Zone zurück," 1959.
66. BArch-K: B137-3, "West-Ost Wanderung," 27 Apr. 1959; B137-4, "Abwanderung," 10 Dec. 1952.
67. Stoll, *Einmal*, 14–15.
68. "Wir wollen zurück!" *DfW*, 19 Dec. 1958.
69. KrA-S In. 144-51, Neiken, 17 Jul. 1956; "Protokoll," 9 Aug. 1956; "Bei uns seid ihr jederzeit willkom-men!" *DfW*, 30 Aug. 1956. Conferences: Amos, *Westpolitik*, 261.
70. KrA-S In. 144-51, Kessel, "Ihr Leben ist wieder lebenswert!" 1959.
71. Figures: Sheffer, "Burned Bridge," 372.
72. KrA-S In. 106-39, Schubert, 6 Jan. 1958.
73. University sovietization: Connelly, *Captive University.*
74. SA-S C2-87, Schubert, 11 Feb. 1958; KrA-S In. 106-39, "Studenten," 5 May 1955; SA-S C2-38, SbgSR-409, 30 Dec. 1958.
75. SA-S C3-210, Bunzel, 1 Dec. 1955; StA-M SED-KL-Sbg IV/4.07/212, "Meldung," 7 Nov. 1955. Others: KrA-S In. 144-51.
76. BayHStA BayObLG 103/1961, BBP-Cbg, 4 Feb. 1954.
77. KrA-S In. 106-39, Schubert, "Analyse," Sep. 1954. The housing shortage was somewhat puzzling, since the rate of flight far outstripped the rate of return, and the overall city population had declined more than 4 percent by 1961. Logistics: SA-S C2-71, SbgSR-441, 8 Sep. 1959. Files: SA-S C6-65 and -68; KrA-S In. 296-81.
78. KrA-S: Vors. 31-10, Schubert, 26 Oct. 1954; In. 144-51, Schubert, 8 Nov. 1954.
79. KrA-S: Vors. 31-10, Schubert, 26 Oct. 1954.
80. KrA-S In. 106-39, Report, 5 Jul. 1956.
81. SA-S C2-95, Müller, 26 Nov. 1959.

82. File: KrA-S In. 442-131; BArch-K B137-5, zur Mühlen, 17 May 1957, and "Rückkehr in die SBZ," 25 Nov. 1958.
83. Major, *Berlin Wall*, 93; BayHStA B-StK-14184, Riedl, Monthly Report, Mar. 1957.
84. StA-M SED-KL-Sbg IV/4.07/212, "Protokoll—Arbeitstagung," 23 Nov. 1955; BArch-B DO1-9084, "Analyse," Jan. 1956.
85. BArch-K B137-5, zur Mühlen, 17 May 1957.
86. BayHStA B-StK-14184, Riedl, Monthly Reports, Mar. and 16 Sep. 1957.
87. StA-M SED-BL-Suhl IV/2/12 1140, Prochazka, 9 Mar. 1960.
88. KrA-S In. 442-131, Schilling, 4 Apr. 1961; correspondence, 1959–60.
89. KrA-S In. 442-131, "Protokoll—Zurückschleusung K.G.," 28 Jun. 1960; "Antrag der K.G.," 9 Jan. 1960.
90. KrA-S In. 144-51, Schubert, Apr. 1957.
91. BArch-B DO1-8012, Opitz, 5 Jan. 1955; KrA-S In. 106-39, Schubert, 22 Dec. 1954.
92. Overview: Stöver, *Zuflucht*.
93. "Ebersdorfer Bauer kam in die DDR," *SB*, 9 Feb. 1961. East Germany used "statistical tricks" to make western immigration appear greater, often including returns, which were twice as numerous. West Germany worried about how this "so-called West-East migration" appeared and, as with returnees, insisted that western immigration did not signify a rejection of state: people went east for personal and family considerations, economic worries (work, debt, housing), and escaping criminal prosecution—with less than 2 percent supposedly relocating out of ideological conviction. BArch-K B137-2078, Haack, 3 May 1966. Files: BArch-K B137-3, B137-5, B137-6.
94. KrA-S In. 144-51, "Protokoll—Konferenz der Zuwanderer und Rückkehrer," 27 Aug. 1956.
95. BArch-K B137-5, zur Mühlen, 17 May 1957.
96. KrA-S In. 106-39, Schubert, 2 Apr. 1959.
97. KrA-S Vors. 31-10, Schubert, May 1955.
98. SA-S C2-95, Müller, 26 Nov. 1959; BArch-B DO1-9084, "Erfahrungsaustausch," 8 Feb. 1957. File: KrA-S In. 296-81.
99. KrA-S In. 106-39, Schubert, 3 Apr. 1957.
100. BArch-B DO1-9084, "Analyse," Jan. 1956.
101. Interview, Kurt and Waltraud Wagner.
102. Heidemeyer, *Flucht*, 281. Sonneberg: KrA-S In. 144-51, "Bericht—Betreuung der Rückkehrer und Zuwanderer," 1960.
103. KrA-S In. 106-39, Schubert, 1 Feb. 1957.
104. KrA-S In. 144-51, "Bericht—Bevölkerungspolitik," 4 Jan. 1961.
105. KrA-S In. 442-131, Schilling, 4 Apr. 1961.
106. BArch-K B137-3, "Abwanderung von Personen aus der Bundesrepublik," 1959.
107. *DWg*, "Für gute Mitarbeit," 29 Jun. 1960.
108. *DWg*, "Für Agenten kein Platz," 16 and 30 Apr. 1957.
109. StA-M SED-KL-Sbg IV/4.07/162 and 207, "Berichterstattung," 3 Nov. 1960; Schätzlein, Rösch, and Albert, *Grenzerfahrungen*, 1:158.
110. Bruce, "Surveillance"; Gieseke, *Mielke-Konzern*, 112–122. Comparison of the Gestapo and the Stasi: Gellately, "Denunciations."
111. Dennis, *Stasi*, 103. In 1968, according to one estimate, more than three-quarters of active informants were not tasked with specific cases, and a quarter never had been. Miller, *Stasi Files*, 53.
112. BStU BV Suhl XI/196/76, 237–238, 266.
113. Dennis, *Stasi*, 96, 101–104; Miller, *Stasi Files*, 38.
114. Miller, *Stasi Files*, 41–74; Gieseke, *Mielke-Konzern*, 125–127.
115. Informant motivation: Bruce, *Firm*.
116. BayHStA BayObLG, Case index, 1952–73. Records are still sealed on the majority of cases, but available files suggest the Stasi's chaotic range of pursuits in the borderland.
117. In one high-profile case in the region, eastern forces shot western border guard Albin Weigelt in the leg as he was walking to investigate a suspected dead letter drop. In another instance, the Stasi tricked an East German soldier who had defected, Manfred Smolka, by using his wife as bait, abducting him back over the border and later executing him. BArch-K B136-6641, Correspondence, Jun.–Aug. 1960; Grafe, *Grenze*, 54, 91–93; Schätzlein, Rösch, and Albert, *Grenzerfahrungen*, 1:147–148.
118. BayHStA BayObLG, Case index, 1952–73.
119. Müller-Enbergs, *Inoffizielle Mitarbeiter*, 2:88–89, 290–340.
120. BStU BV Suhl XI/196/76, 72, 184–187; BStU MfS HA-IX-2198, 173, 180.
121. BStU BV Suhl XI/196/76, 198–201, 218, 237–238.

122. Notable: "Vermutlicher Agent," *NP*, 4 Jun. 1953; "'Todesstreifen' war Treffpunkt," *NP*, 23 Jun. 1953; "Sowjetzonale Behörden," *NT*, 24 Jun. 1953; "Sowjet-Agentin in Coburg festgenommen," *NT*, 25 Jun. 1953.

123. Brückner, "Hin und her," in Kleindienst, ed., *Von hier*, 156.

124. BayHStA B-StK-10860, Riedl, 18 Jan. 1954.

125. SA-N 2050, Neustadt Police Chief, 4 Sep. 1953.

126. BayHStA BayObLG 072/1959.

127. BStU BV Suhl XI/212/76 II, 4–17, 86–87.

128. Some Neustadt communists did collaborate; one retired porcelain craftsman and a former KPD member had been under suspicion for eight years, and was finally caught in 1961 when an inquisitive journalist noticed him giving the local bus driver envelopes from different senders to post at the train station. File: BayHStA BayObLG 103/1961.

129. BStU BV Suhl XI/196/76, 191, 208–209, 301–304, GI "Lib," Oct.–Nov. 1959.

130. BayHStA PrBGP 120, BBP-Pressig, Interrogation—L. N., 29 Oct. 1954.

131. BStU BV Suhl XI/196/76, 198–199.

132. BayHStA BayObLG 120/1963, Deposition, 28 May 1963.

133. BayHStA BayObLG 120/1963.

134. Adler was not found out for two years, when another Stasi informant in Neustadt implicated him; the western court gave him a sentence of four months probation, BayHStA PrBGP 120, Wölfel, 15 Oct. 1958; (flight report) Riedl, 3 Jul. 1956; BayHStA BayObLG 108/1958.

135. Deposition, 28 May 1963, BayHStA BayObLG 120/1963.

136. BayHStA BayObLG 094/1955.

137. BStU BV Suhl XI/196/76, 239–240, 248–250. Overview of western operations in East Germany: Maddrell, "Western Espionage"; Schmidt-Eenbook, "Rise and Fall."

138. BArch-K B137-2416, "Überwachung von SBZ Flüchtlingen," 1951–56.

139. West German authorities did not even believe some who claimed Stasi involvement. When one man was arrested in 1961 for painting swastikas in Neustadt, he said that two East Germans had forced him, bragging once in a tavern that he had earned "a lot of money" from "over there." Western police believed he was making up these "fairy tales" for attention—but recent scholarship has revealed that the Stasi did incite anti-Semitic graffiti in the West, StA-C StAnw-430; Mertens, "'Westdeutscher' Antisemitismus?" in Epstein, "Stasi," 336.

140. BayHStA BayObLG 096/1960; "Die Wahrheit über den Spion Jakob Stegmann," *FW*, 11 May 1957; "Betrüger wurde gefasst," *DWg*, 3 Jul. 1957 (names changed).

141. Far less is known about the cross-border operations of West Germany's Bundesnachrichtendienst than about the activities of the Stasi in East Germany. Overview: Wagner and Uhl, *BND*, 61–120.

142. Reisenweber, *Reihe*, 1:30–32; Eisenkrätzer et al., *VPKA-Sonneberg*, 22–24; Kaufmann, *Schicksalsjahre*, 45.

Chapter 8: Home

1. StA-C BGS 145, "Flüchtlinge über die DDR-Grenzsperranlage," 1961–89. Similar: Schmidt, *BGS*, 116; Ritter and Lapp, *Grenze*, 173; BArch-B/SAPMO DY30 2507, 43–46, 353–354. Hertle and Sälter, "Todesopfer," 676. Prisoners' experiences: Knabe, ed., *Opfer*.

2. Overview: Sälter, *Grenzpolizisten*, 166–176; *Der Spiegel*, "Schießbefehl für DDR-Grenze entdeckt," 11 Aug. 2007.

3. Geographical planning: Nelson, *Ecology*, 27–28.

4. Pommerin, "General Trettner"; Eckert, "East."

5. Chin, *Guest Worker*; Herbert, *Ausländerpolitik*, 202–262.

6. Sarotte, *Dealing*; Patton, *Cold War*, 61–104.

7. Kopstein, *Politics*; Maier, *Dissolution*, 59–107.

8. Zatlin, *Currency*, 203–285.

9. Wierling, "Mission."

10. Betts, *Within Walls*; Fulbrook, *Anatomy*.

11. Effects on identity and private life: Borneman, *Belonging*.

12. Schake, "Broader Range"; Gray, *Cold War*, 95–102.

13. Flight per day: Hertle, Jarausch, and Kleßmann, *Mauerbau*, 313. By late July 1961, the Bundesnachrichtendienst warned West German leaders that East Germany would likely "blockade" Berlin's sector borders by force: Uhl and Wagner, "Möglichkeiten."

14. On Ulbricht's long-standing machinations to close the border in Berlin versus the Soviet preference for moderation: Harrison, *Driving,* esp. 74.

15. Harrison, *Driving,* 207–209.

16. Bobby Scott incident: "German Reds Seize G.I.," *NYT,* 30 Aug. 1961; "Vopos verhaften US-Soldaten an der Zonengrenze," *NP,* 30 Aug. 1961. Water: "Graben blieb ohne Wasser," *NP,* 2 Sep. 1961 (13 Sep., 25 Nov., 22 Dec. 1961); Fischer, *Ebersdorf,* 24–25; BayHStA PrBGP 506, BBP-Cbg, Correspondence, Sep. 1961; BArch-K B137-2507, Riedl, 22 Sep. 1961; Schätzlein, Rösch, and Albert, *Grenzerfahrungen,* 1:155; Schmidt, *Wir tragen,* 116.

17. Interview, Klaus Treichel.

18. "Zonengrenze war Ziel vieler Besucher," *NP,* 31 Aug. 1961; "Französische Gäste an der Zonengrenze," *NP,* 6 Sep. 1961; "Die Zonengrenze wird immer dichter," *NP,* 4 Nov. 1961.

19. "Vopos verhaften US-Soldaten an der Zonengrenze," *NP,* 30 Aug. 1961.

20. "Ob ihnen das wohl Spass macht?" "Tragödie an der Zonengrenze," *NP,* 8 Sep. 1961.

21. Interview, Ingrid Klinger, Neustadt/Ebersdorf, 13 Nov. 2009.

22. "Kein Abfall auf Todes-Streifen," *NP,* 2 Sep. 1961. E.g., "Todesstunde der Bergmühle am Muppberg," *NT,* 26 Aug. 1961; Fischer, *Ebersdorf,* 26–27; StA-M SED-KL-Sbg IV/4.07/207, Heiliger, 8 Sep. 1961; "Demontage an der Zonengrenze," *NP,* 24 Aug. 1961, updates 24, 25, 26, and 29 Aug. 1961.

23. Interview, Wilhelm Thaler, Coburg, 20 Jul. 2002, and Norbert Holzmann, Sonneberg/Oberlind, 25 Jun. 2002.

24. Interview, Frieda Gansel, Neustadt/Ketschenbach, 15 Nov. 2009.

25. "Todesstunde der Bergmühle am Muppberg," *NT,* 26 Aug. 1961.

26. E.g., SA-N: 2051, Ziebill, 17 Aug. 1961, and 5698, 62–63; "Hilfe für SBZ-Flüchtlinge," *NP,* 18 Oct. 1961.

27. Though more than a hundred westerners had travel permits to Sonneberg in late August, all but five had to cancel their trips. BArch-B/SAPMO DY30-3682, 154–156; "Interzonen-Reiseverkehr ging zurück," *NP,* 12 Sep. 1961.

28. "Neue Zonenrandprobleme durch Erweiterung der EWG," "Wenn Brandt nicht kommen kann, dann gehen wir zu ihm," "Bei Willy Brandt in Schöneberg," *NP,* 22, 26 Aug. 1961.

29. StA-M SED-KL-Sbg IV/4.07/101, Protocol, 6 Oct. 1961.

30. E.g., StA-M SED-KL-Sbg IV/4.07/207, Heiliger, 8 Sep. 1961; 164, SED-KL-Sbg, 30 Aug., 5, 11 Sep. 1961; BArch-B DO1 0.2.3. Nr. 20585, BDVP Suhl, 22 Aug. 1961.

31. Eisenkrätzer et al., *VPKA-Sonneberg,* 28–29; Mangold, "Einsatz," 59–60.

32. StA-M SED-KL-Sbg IV/4.07/100, Protocols, 18, 25 Aug. 1961.

33. Schoenau, *Sonneberg,* 278; Eckardt, "Augenzeuge," 11. Precautions: BArch-B/SAPMO DY30/J IV 2-2-784, Merkel, 13 Aug. 1961. Concerns lasted throughout the fall, e.g., StA-M RdBz-Su 464, Sollmann, 10, 14 Nov. 1961.

34. "Einwohner Lindenbergs geben Bonner Ultras kontra," *SB,* 24 Aug. 1961.

35. StA-M SED-KL-Sbg IV/A/4.07/172, "Informationsbericht," 15 Aug. 1961. Demonstrations: *SB,* Aug.–Sep. 1961.

36. StA-M SED-KL-Sbg IV/A/4.07/172, "Informationsbericht," 15 Aug. 1961; BArch-B/SAPMO DY30/IV 2/12-107, "Information," 18 Aug. 1961.

37. StA-M SED-KL-Sbg IV/A/4.07/172, "Informationsbericht," 15 Aug. 1961.

38. StA-M SED-KL-Sbg IV/4.07/164, "Informationsbericht," "Einschätzung," 16 Aug. 1961.

39. BArch-B/SAPMO DY30/IV 2/12-107, "Information," 18 Aug. 1961. People were likewise reluctant to publicize their endorsement of the October 3 evacuations; StA-M SED-BL-Suhl IV/2/12 1175, 7.

40. "Interzonen-Reiseverkehr ging zurück," *NP,* 12 Sep. 1961; BArch-K B106-15296, "Grenzschutzkommando Süd," 9 Oct. 1961, 9 Jan. 1962; StA-M SED-KL-Sbg IV/4.07/207, Heiliger, 8 Sep. 1961. Details: Sheffer, "Burned Bridge," 392–393.

41. E.g., StA-M SED-KL-Sbg IV/A/4.07/172, "Informationsbericht," 14, 28 Aug. 1961; 164, "Informationsbericht," 11 Sep. 1961; "Einwohner Lindenbergs geben Bonner Ultras kontra," *SB,* 24 Aug. 1961.

42. SED-KL-Sbg IV/4.07/164, "Abschlussbericht," 23 Sep. 1961; Wagner, 8:30 a.m., 22 Sep. 1961.

43. StA-M SED-KL-Sbg IV/4.07/101, Protocol, 6 Oct. 1961; 164, Wagner, 10 a.m., 22 Sep. 1961. There were seventy-nine local assemblies in Sonneberg County the night of September 22, drawing 12,384 people, with hundreds more turned away.

44. BArch-B/SAPMO DY30/IV 2/12/72, 177–180; SED-KL-Sbg IV/4.07/164, Wagner, 10 a.m. and 2:45 p.m., 22 Sep. 1961.

45. StA-M SED-KL-Sbg IV/4.07/101, Protocol, 6 Oct. 1961.
46. SED-KL-Sbg IV/4.07/164, Wagner, 2:45 p.m., 22 Sep. 1961; 171, "Informationsbericht für 16.00 Uhr," 22 Sep. 1961.
47. StA-M SED-KL-Sbg IV/4.07/171, "Informationsbericht für 16.00 Uhr," 22 Sep. 1961; 164, "Abschlussbericht," 23 Sep. 1961; 165, "Informationsbericht," 27 Jan. 1962.
48. The action went by other code names in different regions, known as *Aktion Blümchen*, or Action Floret, in the district of Suhl. Regional overview: Wagner, "Beseitigung."
49. Bennewitz and Potratz, *Zwangsaussiedlungen*, 127–128.
50. Schoenau, *Sonneberg*, 278.
51. StA-M SED-KL-Sbg IV/4.07/101, Wagner, 5 Oct. 1961.
52. StA-M SED-KL-Sbg IV/4.07/101, Wagner, 5 Oct. 1961, and SED-BL-Suhl IV/2/12: 1176, 1177; Moczarski, "Archivalische Quellen," 336.
53. Bennewitz and Potratz, *Zwangsaussiedlungen*, 132; interview, Waltraud Wagner.
54. Interview, Waltraud Wagner.
55. Freyer, "Mein Vater," 62; "Wir fragten nicht einmal, wo es hinging," *FW*, 4 Oct. 1996. Their fate: Sheffer, "Burned Bridge," 398.
56. Names changed, StA-M SED-KL-Sbg IV/4.07/101, Wagner, 5 Oct. 1961; SED-BL-Suhl IV/2/12 1175, 4. There were suicide and arson threats throughout the borderland, but no incidents reported; BStU MfS-BdL Nr. 000584, "Aktion 'Festigung,'" 1961.
57. StA-M SED-KL-Sbg IV/4.07/101, Protocol, 6 Oct. 1961.
58. Interview, Waltraud Wagner.
59. "Neue Sicherheitsmaßnahmen an der DDR-Staatsgrenze reibungslos abgewickelt," *FW*, 4 Oct. 1961; StA-M SED-KL-Sbg IV/4.07/207, Damaske, 10 Oct. 1961; Luthardt, *Geschichte*, 150–152.
60. StA-M: SED-KL-Sbg IV/4.07/101, Wagner, 5 Oct. 1961; Schoenau, *Sonneberg*, 280.
61. StA-M: SED-KL-Sbg IV/4.07/101, Wagner, 5 Oct. 1961; SED-BL-Suhl IV/2/12 1177, BV Suhl "Stimmung," 4 Oct. 1961.
62. StA-M SED-BL-Suhl IV/2/12 1175, 13, 135; SED-KL-Sbg IV/4.07/101, Wagner, 5 Oct. 1961; SED-BL-Suhl IV/2/12 1177, 19; BArch-B/SAPMO DY30/IV 2/12-80, 1.
63. BStU MfS-BdL Nr. 000584, "Aktion 'Festigung,'" 1961; StA-M SED-BL-Suhl IV/2/12: 1175, 7, 11; 1177, 30.
64. StA-M SED-KL-Sbg IV/4.07/101, Wagner, "Abschlußbericht," 5 Oct. 1961.
65. Interview, Frieda Gansel.
66. Only 174 East Germans were not evacuated, due to family or health complications, while seventy-six additional people were deported who were not on the original lists.
67. BArch-K B106-15296, Dippelhofer, 9 Oct. 1961. Rumors and reports: "Ulbricht räumt die Grenzdörfer," "Erste Aussiedlung hinter der Zonengrenze?" "Bockstadter Gestüt evakuiert," and "Neues von der Zonengrenze," *NP*, 6, 7, and 14 Oct. 1961.
68. Deportations included 920 targeted individuals plus 2,250 of their family members, 1,049 of whom were children. The 1961 deportations also placed greater emphasis on political reliability, purging more people with National Socialist histories and oppositional attitudes, in addition to returnees, immigrants, and those deemed "work-shy" and "asocial"; Bennewitz and Potratz, *Zwangsaussiedlungen*, 116, 133, 214, 285. Regime officials worried about resources, and successively reduced the lists to avoid civil unrest. The district of Suhl revised its targets from over 4,000 to just 562; Moczarski, "Archivalische Quellen," 331–341; Luthardt, *Geschichte*, 150–152.
69. Fifty-four were "targets" and 114 were relatives. Geographical breakdown: KrA-S In. 930-467, Report–1971.
70. StA-M SED-KL-Sbg IV/A/4.07/164, "Informationsbericht," 17 Oct., 3 Nov. 1961; Schoenau, *Sonneberg*, 281.
71. Schätzlein, Rösch, and Albert, *Grenzerfahrungen*, 1:168. Incorporated into the National People's Army in 1961, border guards were formally removed from the army in December 1973 and renamed "Border Troops of the GDR" so as not to be subject to international negotiations for force reductions. Offenders often received two-year sentences, with early release possible upon collaboration with the Stasi.
72. Lapp, *Gefechtsdienst*, 86.
73. East Germany's receipts are generally estimated up to 3.5 billion DM. Horster, 414–415; interview, Ingrid Dreyer.
74. West German BGS statistics are similar to those of East German border troops; however, both are significantly lower than the 40,101 escapees customarily estimated for the entire border, including transit routes, Berlin, and the Baltic Sea (see Appendix 3).

75. Each year, 100–600 border troops fled from 1961 to 1967, 30–90 from 1968 to 1973, and 5–25 from 1974 to 1989. Available statistics are largely in agreement: Lapp, *Gefechtsdienst*, 93; Schmidt, *BGS*, 116; StA-C BGS 145, "Flüchtlinge," 1961–1989; SA-N EAP 001-02, Arbeitsgemeinschaft 13 Aug.
76. BstU MfS 160, Nr. 141/69, 69–72, Mangold, "Einsatz," 15 Dec. 1969, plus an inventory of weak spots in Sonneberg's border.
77. "Signalzaun als neue Menschenfalle," *NT*, 15 Dec. 1965.
78. Thoss, *Gesichert*, 159.
79. BArch-MA GR15 11348, Schmidt, "Aufklärungssammelbericht, August 1982."
80. The total cost of the border remains an extremely complex calculation, roughly estimated at 1.5 million DM per kilometer by the 1980s; Schultke, *"Keiner,"* 92–96; Schätzlein and Albert, *Grenzerfahrungen*, 2:30, 66, 539.
81. Of the 4,956 people who attempted escape between January 1, 1974, and November 30, 1979, 4 percent were caught at the signal fence, and 15 percent were caught by border troops inside it: Ritter and Lapp, *Grenze*, 78; Lapp, *Gefechtsdienst*, 86. Border Helpers, and estimated troop arrests for the 1980s at around 24 percent: Schultke, *"Keiner,"* 38, 108.
82. BArch-MA GR15 11348, GR-15, 5 Oct. 1977.
83. BStU BV Suhl, KD SON 3687, MfS, "Kreis Sonneberg," 1967, 35–36; StA-M SED-KL-Sbg IV/A/4.07/162, Kreissl, 9 May 1963; KrA-S In. 445-132, Göhring, 25 Nov. 1965.
84. Mangold, "Einsatz," 59–60.
85. StA-M SED-KL-Sbg IV/4.07/207, "Bericht—Gemeindevertretersitzung," 18 Jan. 1962; 164, "Informationsbericht," 12 Dec. 1961; 165, Meußgeyer, 18 Jan. 1962.
86. SA-S C2-113, SbgSR-1, 27 Sep. 1961; BArch-B/SAPMO DY30/IV A 2/12-85, 5–11; KrA-S In. 930-457(II), "Ausgemeindung Hönbach," 13 Feb. 1972; StA-M SED-BL-Suhl IV/C-2/12 675, Linke, 27 May 1976.
87. E.g., *SR,* "Gegen die Grenzordnung verstoßen," 17 May 1966; BArch-MA GB13 8367, GR-15, 7 Nov. 1969.
88. Mangold, "Einsatz," 73; BArch-MA GB13 8367, GB-13, "Sitzung—KEL Sonneberg," 22 Sep. 1969.
89. StA-M SED-KL-Sbg IV/B/4.07/164, Sitter, 14 Nov. 1969; 162, "Sicherheitsbesprechung—4. Grenzkompanie Effelder," 21 Oct. 1966.
90. BArch-B/SAPMO DY30/IV B2/12/71, 29–36. The regime allowed internal traffic on certain borderland streets during curfew for "economical and social reasons," lengthened residence registration renewals from three to twelve months, simplified permit applications, and relaxed outside visitation allowances from extended family in exceptional circumstances, including sickness, deaths, births, weddings, and major anniversaries; BArch-B DO1 0.2.1. 420/2; "Auskunftsangaben," 1973.
91. E.g., StA-M SED-KL-Sbg IV/4.07/207, "Gemeindevertretersitzung in Mupperg," 18 Jan. 1962; 164, "Informationsbericht," 12 Dec. 1961; 165, Meußgeyer, 18 Jan. 1962; KrA-S Vors. 465-139, Walther, 26 Sep. 1973. Yet it got harder to appeal over time. Complaints about street and checkpoint closures in 1972 had little success, as did ongoing grievances about roads and transportation. Petitions: KrA-S In.: 930-457; 931–468; 593-210; Vors. 465-139; StA-M SED-BL-Suhl IV/C-2/12 675.
92. StA-M SED-BL-Suhl IV/C-2/2 26, "Protokoll—Grenzdirektive und Grenzordnung," 21 Jun. 1972.
93. BArch-B DO1 0.2.1. 420/2, "Auskunftsangaben," 1973; StA-M SED-BL-Suhl IV/C-2/6 480, Mueller, 1 Nov. 1972; KrA-S In. 930-457(I), "Entwicklung des gesellschaftlichen Lebens," 8 Mar. 1973.
94. StA-M SED-BL-Suhl IV/C-2/6 480, esp. Mueller, 1 Nov. 1972; C-2/12 675; KrA-S In. 930-457(II); BArch-B/SAPMO DY30/IV B2/12/71, 29–36.
95. BArch-B/SAPMO DY30/IV B2/12/69, 24–33; KrA-S Vors. 465-139, Reports, "Stimmungen und Meinungen," 1972–73. Escalations continued to raise hopes of relaxations; e.g., BStU BV Suhl, Abt. VII/899 Bd. 1, 116; BArch-MA GR15 11348, GR-15, 5 Oct. 1977.
96. Sonneberg's first 3.5-kilometer stretch of signal fence was built near Burned Bridge in 1965–1967, with most of the rest built in the 1970s.
97. Interviews, Frieda Gansel, Edgar Pfisterer, Neuhaus-Schierschnitz (Sonneberg), Jul. 2002. Planning: KrA-S In. 944-473(I); StA-M BT RdBz-Su, K2909, 2910; e.g., BArch-MA VA-03/38588, "Konzeption—Landwirtschaft und Nahrungsgüterwirtschaft," 23 Feb. 1971; StA-M SED-BL-Suhl IV/E-2/6 566, "Gestaltungskonzeption—Kreisstadt Sonneberg," 1 Jul. 1986.
98. And plans to remove businesses—StA-M SED-KL-Sbg IV/4.07/101, Stolze, 12 Oct. 1961; KrA-S In.: 533-157(IV), Greiner, 23 Oct. 1969; Vogel, 6 Jul. 1970; 930-467, Fischer, 25 Jun. 1970.
99. Schultke, *"Keiner,"* 66. Sonnebeg agricultural directives: KrA-S In. 593-210(1), "Information," 3 Oct. 1972.
100. Sonneberg's twenty-one towns in the (post-1972) Border Area had a total population of 14,084 in 1960, 13,891 in 1972, 13,044 in 1981, and 12,540 in 1987: KrA-S In. 930-457(II), population table, 1960, 1972; BStU BV Suhl, BdL/Dok 963, 4–8; StA-M BT RdBz-Su, K2720, Sauerteig, 20 Feb. 1989.

101. KrA-S In. 593-210(I), Rat der Gemeinde Roth, 11 Dec. 1972; StA-M SED-KL-Sbg IV/C/4.07/192, Hallier, 10 Jul. 1972.
102. Interview, Edgar Pfisterer; BArch-MA GB13 8367, NVA GR-11, Protocol, 27 Aug. 1969.
103. Interview, Harald Kunert, Almerswind (Sonneberg), 19 Jan. 2003.
104. StA-M: SED-KL-Sbg IV/A/4.07/162, Kreissl, 14 Sep. 1965; SED-BL-Suhl IV/C-2/2 26, "Proto-koll—Bezirksparteiaktivtagung," 21 Jun. 1972; KrA-S In. 967-481, "Feststellungen eines Kontrollein-satzes," 2 Aug. 1984. County campaigns: KrA-S In. 599-216, 1975–1982.
105. "Anerkennung für Heubisch," SZ, 19 Jun. 1989; BMiB, Wo Deutschland, 39.
106. StA-M SED-KL-Sbg IV/C/4.07/193, Lorenz, 31 Jan. 1975.
107. KrA-S In. 930-457(II), "Besichtigung Hönbach," Mar. 1972.
108. Sheffer, "Burned Bridge," 421–422; SA-S C2-111, Bunzel, 24 Oct. 1960; StA-M SED-KL-Sbg IV/4.07/163, Heiliger, 15 Jan. 1961, and 207, Heiliger, 9 Feb. 1961, and "Berichterstattung," 5 Jul. 1961; SA-S C2-113, SbgSR-495, 21 Jul. 1961.
109. BArch-B DC20 I/4, Ministry of Finance, 4 Nov. 1961. Resolutions: BArch-B/SAPMO DY30/J IV 2-2-797, 10–16.
110. KrA-S In. Ang. 144-51, "Einschätzung—Staatsgrenze," 18 May 1962.
111. E.g., KrA-S In. 931-468, "Beratung Staatsgrenze," 22 Jan. 1976; RdG Mupperg, 17 Nov. 1981.
112. Notable: KrA-S In.: 930-457(II), Heller, 14 Jun. 1972; 931-468, Hartung, 15 Jun. 1977; "Beratung—Sicherheit an der Staatsgrenze Koberorth," 9 May 1977; Mehlitz, 2 Mar. 1978.
113. KrA-S In. 967-481, "Feststellungen eines Kontrolleinsatzes," 2 Aug. 1984.
114. BStU BV Suhl, Abt. VII/895, Mangold, 15 Dec. 1969. KrA-S In.: 930-457(II), Oberthür, 5 Sep. 1974, plus reports and correspondence: 931-468(V); StA-M SED-KL-Sbg IV/C/4.07/193.
115. KrA-S In. 931-468(I). Also: Schätzlein and Albert, Grenzerfahrungen, 2:518–521 (Suhl's entire bor-der: 472–538); BStU BV Suhl, Abt. VII/899 Bd. 1, 63.
116. StA-M SED-KL-Sbg IV/4.07/164, "Informationsbericht," 27 Oct. 1961; BArch-B/SAPMO DY30/IV A 2/12-85, 56–59, 87–88; StA-M SED-BL-Suhl IV/C-2/12 675, Linke, 20 Jun. 1974.
117. StA-M SED-BL-Suhl IV/A-2/12 678, Heiliger, 10 Jun. 1963.
118. KrA-S In. 533-157(I), "Verbesserung von Gebäudeansichten," 27 May 1964; StA-M: SED-KL-Sbg IV/A/4.07/162, Kreissl, 11 Nov. 1963; SED-BL-Suhl IV/C-2/12 675, Linke, 20 Jun. 1974; BT RdBz-Su, K2909, Greiner, 23 Jul. 1973; Albert and Salier, Grenzerfahrungen Kompakt, 347–348.
119. Border authorities wanted to ensure that Liebau's destruction occurred in the "shortest possible time frame" because it was visible on three sides from West Germany; StA-M SED-KL-Sbg IV/C/4.07/193, "Oberflächenberäumung Mupperg, Ortsteil Liebau," 24 Jul. 1975; KrA-S In. 777-398, Greiner, 28 Oct. 1975, plus file: "Liebau—Abbruch," 1975.
120. Demolition budgets and plans: KrA-S In. 930-457, 930-467, 931-468, 967-481; StA-M SED-KL-Sbg IV/B/4.07/164.
121. The budget grew up to 685,000 marks in 1972; then, from 1972 to 1975 Sonneberg County logged 2.25 million marks in property purchases, demolitions, border signs, and barriers, during which time at least twenty-six households were evacuated. KrA-S In.: 533-157(II), Göhring, 7 Jan. 1966; 930-467, Schönheit, 16 Oct. 1970; 930-457(III), Wehner, 10 Sep. 1972; StA-M BT RdBz-Su, K3011, "Kosten Kr. Sonneberg," "Errichtung von Sperren & Beschilderung," 1972–1975.
122. KrA-S In. 930-457(III), Wehner, 10 Sep. 1972; StA-M SED-BL-Suhl IV/C-2/2 26, "Protokoll—Bezirksparteiaktivtagung," 21 Jun. 1972.
123. Interview, Ingrid Dreyer, Sonneberg/Hönbach, 11 Nov. 2009.
124. StA-M SED-KL-Sbg IV/4.07/165, Meußgeyer, 18 Jan. 1962.
125. E.g., StA-M SED-KL-Sbg IV/4.07/164, "Informationsbericht," 27 Nov., 12 Dec. 1961.
126. Border planning and protocols: KrA-S In. 445-132, 488-145, 593-210, 533-157(I).
127. KrA-S In. 445-132, "Bericht—entlang der Staatsgrenze," 7 Jul. 1970; BArch-MA GB13 8367, NVA GR-11, 27 Aug. 1969.
128. Interview, Ingrid Holzmann.
129. Interview, Gerd Jahn.
130. BArch-B/SAPMO DY30/J IV 2/2 1431, 69–70.
131. StA-M: SED-KL-Sbg IV/4.07/101, esp. Protocol, 6 Oct. 1961; 100; 162, Kreissl, 9 May 1963; BArch-B/SAPMO DY30/IV 2/12/72, 177–180. Interview, Fritz Nagel, Neuhaus am Rennweg (Sonneberg), 17 Jan. 2003, and memoir, in private possession; StA-M SED-BL-Suhl IV/C-2/12 676.
132. Participation: BStU BV Suhl, BdL/Dok 963, 13.
133. Berdahl, Where the World Ended, 48–49; interview, Elisabeth Dietzer.
134. StA-M SED-KL-Sbg IV/C/4.07/192, "Einschätzung—Emstadt," 1973.
135. Community assembly protocols: KrA-S In. 533-157(III).

136. E.g., *Der Lautsprecher,* "Zum Schutze Heimat bereit," "Unsere Taten," "Mit den Waffenbrüdern vereint," Oct., Nov. 1974, Jan. 1980.

137. Reisenweber, *Reihe,* 1:20, 52 (Horn, *Bewährung*); Schätzlein and Albert, *Grenzerfahrungen,* 2:572. Local successes, e.g., *Der Lautsprecher,* "Stern-Radio Jugend bereitet 25. Jahrestag der DDR würdig vor," Feb. 1974; KrA-S In. 612-228, Leibknecht, 26 Jun. 1986.

138. Albert and Salier, *Grenzerfahrungen Kompakt,* 158.

139. KrA-S In. 945-473, Rebhan, 26 Jun. 1985; Albrecht, 15 Dec. 1986. GSA figures: StA-M BT RdBz-Su, K2720, Sauerteig, 20 Feb. 1989; KrA-S In. 944-473, "Ankunftsbericht," 11 Aug. 1988; BStU BV Suhl, AKG/41 Bd. 2, 284–287.

140. KrA-S In. 612-228, Finger, 17 Jun. 1986.

141. KrA-S In. 612-228, Schröder, "Bericht—'Mariensee,'" Jan. 1987.

142. A total of 250 Border Helpers and 350 Police Helpers; StA-M SED-KL-Sbg IV/4.07/180, "Vorlage—Sicherheit und Ordnung," 1985; BStU BV Suhl, BdL/Dok 963, 18. Difficulties: *VPKA-Sonneberg,* 20–22; StA-M SED-KL-Sbg IV/4.07/172/3. Protocol: BPO SED-KL, 27 Dec. 1962; AA B38-II A1, 167, 291–309. Recruitment tallies: Reisenweber, *Reihe,* 2:52; BArch-B/SAPMO DY30: IV A 2/12-85, 8–11, 87–88; IV 2/12/73, 220–222; BArch-MA GB13 8367, GB-13, 22 Sep. 1969.

143. Interview, Beate Strassner, Sonneberg, 16 Jan. 2003.

144. E.g., Schultke, *"Keiner,"* 38; BArch-B/SAPMO DY30/IV 2-12/73, 221.

145. Evolution of restrictions in the 1950s: Sälter, *Grenzpolizisten,* 218–228.

146. "Beziehungen zu Soldaten und Bevölkerung herzlicher denn je," SR, 24 Feb. 1965, "Frauen betreuten Grenzsoldaten," 1 Jan. 1963, "Herzliche Freundschaft," 8 Mar. 1967. E.g., *25 Jahre,* 91–93; *Sonni-Express,* "Sicherung der Staatsgrenze jederzeit bereit, wachsam und standhaft," Dec. 1982.

147. Private possession, Schwartz: "1 Jahr Grenzdienst."

148. StA-M SED-KL-Sbg IV/4.07/101, "Informationsbericht," 8 Nov. 1961.

149. StA-M SED-KL-Sbg IV/B/4.07/164, Fischer, 13 May 1968.

150. BStU MfS JHS MF 98, 11–16.

151. BArch-MA GB13 8367, NVA GR-15, 13 Oct., 7 Nov. 1969; KrA-S In. 533-157(III), Protocol, "Gemeindevertretersitzung, Unterlind," 30 Oct. 1969; BArch-MA GB13 8367, NVA GR-15, 7 Nov. 1969; Grafe, *Grenze,* 188; Berdahl, *Where the World Ended,* 50.

152. KrA-S Vors. 465-139, Walther, 23 Aug. 1973; KrA-S In. 958-478, "Erfahrungsaustausch," 21 Jul. 1983; Schätzlein and Albert, *Grenzerfahrungen,* 2:572–573.

153. Interview, Götz Emrich, Siegfried Tenner.

154. "Wachsam an der Grenze," *FW,* 22 Sep. 1961.

155. "Was vorgestern 12.30 Uhr geschah," *FW,* 19 Aug. 1961.

156. StA-M SED-KL-Sbg IV/A/4.07/162, Kreissl, 11 Nov. 1963; e.g., "Betrüger wurde festgenommen," SR, 17 Jul. 1963. Sixty-three Sonnebergers fled in 1963, but the number was down to around forty-five in 1964 and thirty-nine in 1965; MfS JHS MF 149, Anl. 2–3, 6.

157. KrA-S In. 445-132, Göhring, 25 Nov. 1965.

158. *VPKA-Sonneberg,* 40.

159. Gross, *Revolution,* 117–122. E.g., BArch-MA GR15 11348, Gruber, 2 Jun. 1977; Schmidt, Aug. 1982; KrA-S In. 599-216, Höhn, 31 Jan. 1983.

160. KrA-S In. 593-210(1), SED-KL-Sbg, 22 Mar. 1973.

161. BArch-MA GR15 16177, GR-15, "Aufklärungssammelbericht," 22 Dec. 1986.

162. Schätzlein and Albert, *Grenzerfahrungen,* 2:572–573, 577.

163. Interview, Hendrik Richter, Sonneberg/Köppelsdorf, 26 Jun. 2002.

164. BStU Suhl AOP 196/76, 23–28. E.g., Koch, "Einsatz," 36.

165. Mangold, "Einsatz," 117–120.

166. Zeppei, "Einsatz," 9–10; Kalning, "Aufdeckung," 28.

167. Korn, "Aufgaben," 27–28.

168. Files: BStU Suhl AOP: 196/76; 385/76, Bd. 1, 2.

169. Pfadenhauer, "Staatsicherheit," 38.

170. Foucault, *Discipline and Punish,* 195–228.

171. Interview, Anna Emrich.

172. Mangold, "Einsatz," 40–41; Korn, 23.

173. Interview, Erich Klinger.

174. Eckardt, "Augenzeuge," 13.

175. Initial, wide-ranging deportation plans in Sonneberg: StA-M SED-BL-Suhl IV/2/12 1176, "Protokoll—Sitzung der BEL," 14 Oct. 1961. Rumors: e.g., StA-M RdBz-Su 464, 7, 10 Nov. 1961;

StA-M SED-KL-Sbg IV/4.07/166, 8; KrA-S In. Ang. 144-51, "Einschätzung," 18 May 1962; "Informationsbericht," 30 Aug. 1962.

176. StA-C BGS 76, BGS reports; AA B38-II A1, 49, 122–126; *Frankfurter Allgemeine Zeitung*, "Drei Häuser in Klein-Tettau vor drohendem Vopo-Zugriff geräumt," 26 Mar. 1962; Schmidt, *Adler*, 117–118; Grafe, *Grenze*, 115–116.

177. Overview: Bennewitz and Potratz, *Zwangsaussiedlungen*, 170–182.

178. Earlier: STA-M SED-KL-Sbg IV/A/4.07/172, "Täglicher Informationsbericht," 28 Aug. 1961; SA-S C2-113, SbgCC, 21 Sep. 1961.

179. E.g., BStU MfS Sekr. Neiber 115, 28–46; interview, Ingrid Holzmann, Sonneberg, 12 Nov. 2009.

180. E.g., BArch-MA GB13 8367, NVA 13; GrBr, 22 Sep. 1969; GR-15, 7 Nov. 1969; KrA-S In. 533-157(II), Heinze, 10 Nov. 1967.

181. KrA-S In. 533-157(I), "Sitzung der Kreiseinsatzleitung," 23 Feb. 1970.

182. BStU BV Suhl, KD SON 3687, 105.

183. BArch-B DC20 I/4 2855, "Protokollbeschluss—Nr. 02-44/II.3./73"; "Wohnsitzverlegung von Bürgern aus dem Grenzgebiet," 10 Jan. 1973; Koch, "Einsatz," 15.

184. KrA-S In. 930-467, "Zuzüge in den Kreis Sonneberg," 1971.

185. KrA-S In.: 473-229; 489-145; 931-468(V). For 1986–1988: 2683-1035, "Absprache mit Gen. Freiberg," 16 Jan. 1989.

186. Interview, Hendrik Richter. Similar: StA-M VPKA-Sbg 1031, VPKA Sonneberg, 12 Dec. 1963.

187. File: KrA-S In. 442-131; especially unusual is "Zurückschleusung der Familie D. nach Westdeutschland," 1964.

188. KrA-S In. 442-131, Eisenkrätzer, 16 Jan. 1964; Hey, 17 Oct. 1963; "Zurückschleusung der Familie [name changed] nach West Berlin," 1963.

189. Interview, Beate Strassner.

190. KrA-S In.: 488-145, "Protokoll—Ständigen Kommission der Kreistages," 19 Jan. 1967, and, e.g., 533-157(IV), Gottschild, "Zuzugsgenehmigung nach Liebau," Sep. 1970.

191. Interview, Jörg Trautmann.

192. Formal rejections ranged between 10 and 20 percent, though officials often informally denied or dissuaded people from applying, so the number of petitioners more than halved over the decades. KrA-S In.: 930-467, "Zuzüge," 1971, and 2683-1035, "Absprache mit Gen. Freiberg," 16 Jan. 1989; StA-M BT RdBz-Su, K2720, Sauerteig, 20 Feb. 1989.

193. Interview, Gerd Jahn.

194. StA-M SED-KL-Sbg IV/A/4.07/159, Western visits, 1967; BStU BV Suhl, KD SON 3687, 100.

195. BStU BV Suhl, KD SON 3687, 101.

196. StA-M BT RdBz-Su, K2720, Sauerteig, 2 Feb. 1987; KrA-S In. 599-216, VPKA Protocols, 1969–1975. GDR: BArch-B: DO1 0.2.1. 420/2, Anl. 1, 6; DY30/IV B2/12/71, 17–26; 37–38.

197. Interview, Jakob Ziegler.

198. E.g., KrA-S In. 930-457(II), Gottschild, 26 Nov. 1973; StA-M SED-BL-Suhl IV/2/12 1176, "Sperrzonenschwierigkeiten," 24 Oct. 1961.

199. Interview, Heike Wrobel, Sonneberg/Wolkenrasen, 10 Nov. 2009.

200. E.g., KrA-S Vors. 465-139, Walther, 24 May 1973.

201. Interview, Ingrid Holzmann.

202. Luthardt, *Geschichte*, 152.

203. KrA-S In. Ang. 144-51, "Bericht—Sicherheit und Ordnung," 10 Mar. 1962.

204. StA-M SED-BL-Suhl IV/C-2/2 26, 75, 82–83.

205. Discussion: Sheffer, "Burned Bridge," 463–467.

206. E.g., interviews, Heike Wrobel, Hendrik Richter, Beate Strassner.

207. Eckardt, "Augenzeuge," 11.

208. E.g., KrA-S In.: 533-157, "Arbeitswirksamkeit—Orten des Grenzgebietes," 1 Oct. 1970; files, 445-132, 593-210, 930-457, 944-473(II, III). The number of state-sponsored "cultural events" in Sonneberg County increased from 592 a year in 1958 to 1,709 in 1965; *Statistisches Taschenbuch*, 1960, 1966, 105; 147.

209. Kalning, "Aufdeckung," 13–14.

210. StA-M SED-KL-Sbg IV/C/4.07/193, Hitzner, 26 Apr. 1974.

211. The county closed seventeen taverns in the wake of August 1961; BArch-B/SAPMO DY30/IV 2/12-80, 47.

212. *VPKA-Sonneberg*, 43.

213. KrA-S In.: 489-145, "Bericht—Kriminalitätsbewegung," 30 Jan. 1970, Wolff, 16 Feb. 1971, 21 Feb. 1972; 488-145, 4; 490-145, "Beratung—Sicherheits- und Rechtspflegeorgnanen," 10 Mar. 1978; Kalning, "Aufdeckung," App. 1.

214. KrA-S In.: 533-157(I), "Bericht—entlang der Staatsgrenze West," 26 Apr. 1965; 930-457(I), "Bericht—entlang der Staatsgrenze," 10 Nov. 1973.

215. KrA-S In. 930-467, Heublein, 17 Jun. 1971; StA-M SED-BL-Suhl IV/C-2/2 26, "Protokoll—Bezirksparteiaktivtagung," 21 Jun. 1972.

216. KrA-S Vors. 2274-894, Günsche, 17 Nov. 1987; In. 944-473(II, III), In. 931-468(III).

217. E.g., KrA-S In. 930-467, Heublein, 17 Jun. 1971. Notwithstanding plans for material improvements in "Grenzplan 1990": KrA-S KrPK 2373-931, 1986–1989.

218. Foreseen in the 1961 expansion: BArch-B/SAPMO DY30/IV 2/12-80, 10–47.

219. Kalning, "Aufdeckung," 14; BArch-B/SAPMO DY30-2533, 60; KrA-S In. 465-139, "Referat—Bestätigung des Volkswirtschafts- und Haushaltsplanes," 22 Mar. 1970.

220. Heinersdorf's attempt to win back brighter lightbulbs because its dimness made a poor "political" comparison with the West: KrA-S In. 930-467, Fischer, 23 Nov. 1971.

221. KrA-S In. 533-157(III), VKPA Sonneberg, 3 May 1969.

222. StA-M SED-KL-Sbg IV/A/4.07/162, Kreissl, 11 Nov. 1963; KrA-S: In. 533-157(III), Greiner, 23 Oct. 1969. E.g., Neuhaus-Schierschnitz: In. 931-468(III), "Zuarbeit—Nr. 90/21/77," 28 May 1979; Vors. 2274-894, "Schriftverkehr—SED-KL," 1987–1989.

223. So common was the expression that Daphne Berdahl titled her seminal study *Where the World Ended*.

224. Fuchs, *Billmuthausen*, 54–55.

225. Grafe, *Grenze*, 251.

226. Versus 9 percent of Neustadt respondents; Sheffer, Survey, "Gebrannte Brücke."

227. Interview, Ingrid Dreyer.

228. Faber, "Auf Beerensuche im Sperrgebiet," in Schugg-Reheis, ed., *Grenzenlos*, 30.

229. Normalization: Fulbrook, ed., *Power*.

230. Interviews, Harald Kunert, Josef Jahn.

231. Interview, Antje Emrich.

232. Interview, Greta Geis.

233. Interview, Beate Strassner, Hendrik Richter.

234. Luthardt, *Geschichte*, 158; also Schultke, *Grenze*, 56.

235. The role of local identity in East Germany: Palmowski, *Inventing*.

236. Interview, Beate Strassner.

237. Interview, Edgar Pfisterer.

238. Interview, Wolfgang Mayerhofer.

239. Interview, Beate Strassner.

Chapter 9: Fault Line

1. "Im Minenfeld hilflos verblutet," *DW*, 27 Nov. 1968.

2. "Wounded Boy, Split Home, Split Land," *NYT*, 9 Dec. 1968.

3. Ibid. Diplomatic consequences: AA B38-II A1, 263, 699–707; Grafe, *Grenze*, 174–178. Also: StA-M VPKA-Sbg 1516, 3; StA-C BGS 76, "Bayerisches Angebot," 1968; BArch-K: B285-834, Oppermann correspondence, Nov.–Dec. 1968; B136-6642, "Hilfeleistung," 3 Dec. 1968. Initial press: *Bild*, "Ich bin doch erst 16," 27 Nov. 1968; "Mein Sohn in der DDR in besten Händen," *ND*, 30 Nov. 1968; "Vater von Günter Oppermann: Widerwärtige Propaganda," *ND*, 1 Dec. 1968; "Jede erdenkliche Hilfe geleistet," *Berliner Zeitung*, 20 Nov. 1968; "Was gilt in Bonn ein Menschenschicksal?" *Berliner Zeitung*, 1 Dec. 1968; "East Germans Say Mine Victim Lives," *NYT*, 29 Nov. 1968.

4. "Mit der Draht Schere in die Freiheit," *NP*, 2 Nov. 1961; "Erschütternde Tragik an der Zonengrenze," *NT*, 31 Dec. 1963.

5. BArch-MA: GT 8367, NVA GR-15, 8 Aug. 1969.

6. GT 4425, NVA GR-15, 19 Oct. 1966; BStU BV Suhl, KD SON 3687, 54–59; Kalning, "Aufdeckung," Anl. 6.

7. Korn, "Aufgaben," 28; Eckardt, "Augenzeuge," 12.

8. E.g., "Zwanzig Jahre Zonengrenze im Neustadter Raum," *NT*, 21 Sep. 1964; "Keine Hinweise auf Fluchtwege mehr," *SdZ*, 15 Oct. 1977.

9. BArch-K B137-6418, Einwag, 11 May 1966.

10. Hertle and Sälter, "Todesopfer," 672–674. The Coburg public prosecutor investigated at least seven border shootings in the 1960s: St-C StAnw 280 (NVA), 289, 291, 321, 434 (NVA), 435, 436.

11. BStU MfS ZKG 69/82, 7.

12. Interview, Heike Wrobel, Sonneberg/Wolkenrasen, 15 Aug. 2003.
13. Sonneberg installations: StA-C BGS 66, "Grenzsperranlagen," 31 Aug. 1989.
14. BArch-B/SAPMO DY30 2507, 43–46, 353–354; BArch-MA GB13 8367, NVA GR-15, 13 Oct., 2 Dec. 1969; KrA-S In. 593-210(1), SED-KL-Sbg, 22 Mar. 1973; Kalning, "Aufdeckung," Anl. 2, 3, 6; Lapp, *Gefechtsdienst*, 101. Schätzlein, Albert, and Salier, *Grenzerfahrungen*, 3:468–469.
15. Stasi records tend to report higher rates: BStU BV Suhl, BdL/Dok 963, 73; Koch, "Einsatz," 10, 35; Mangold, "Einsatz," 72; BStU BV Suhl, KD SON 3687, 54–59. Sonneberg sources portray fewer: KrA-S: In. 445-132, "Bericht," 7 Jul. 1970; In. 533-157(IV), VPKA Sonneberg, 25 Jun. 1970; In. 490-145, Coburger, 11 Nov. 1978; StA-M: VPKA-Sbg 1516, VPKA Sonneberg, 13 Jan. 1969; SED-KL-Sbg IV/4.07/180, "Bericht—Grenzsicherung," 1985; BArch-MA VA-03/38592, "Einschätzung," 19 Mar. 1974. West Germany's BGS reported the highest rates of all: StA-C BGS 128, "Flüchtlinge," 26 Sep. 1973.
16. Schätzlein and Albert, *Grenzerfahrungen*, 2:561.
17. Lucht, "Analyse," 120–121; Lischewsky, *Puppen*, 39.
18. E.g., NP-A 564-8(I), BBP-Nec, N., 9 Jan. 1973; B., 24 Sep. 1987.
19. NP-A 564-8(I), BBP-Nec, A., B., 28 Jun. 1978.
20. E.g., StA-C BGS 135, GSA Süd 2, 27 Oct. 1986; NP-A 564-8(I), BBP-Nec, D., 4 Oct. 1989; M., 20 Oct. 1989; StA-M SED-KL-Sbg IV/4.07/165, "Informationsbericht," 16 Feb. 1962; 039, "Protokoll—Kreisparteiaktivtagung," 20 Feb. 1962.
21. Interview, Dietmar Huber. E.g., NP-A 564-8(I), BBP-Nec, L., 22 Apr. 1988.
22. Western public narratives: Ahonen, "Benito Corghi," "Werner Weinhold."
23. Kalning, "Aufdeckung," 38, Anl. 2, 3 6; StA-M VPKA-Sbg 1516, "Analyse—Angriffe," 13 Jan. 1969; KrA-S In. 489-145, "Bericht—Kriminalitätsentwicklung," 1973.
24. Mangold, "Einsatz," 112; StA-M VPKA-Sbg 1516, 3. Conflicting accounts: Schätzlein, Rösch, and Albert, *Grenzerfahrungen*, 1:258, 331; Grafe, *Grenze*, 179.
25. BayHStA MInn 89954, Ziegler, 15 Sep. 1969; AA B38-II A1, 164-7, 399.
26. NP-A 564-8(I), BBP-Nec, W., 9 Sep. 1982.
27. BStU MfS Sekr. Neiber 115, 28–46. Fragmentary reports: StA-C BGS 135, GSA Süd 2, "Informatorische Angaben," 1983; Schätzlein and Albert, *Grenzerfahrungen*, 2:222–223, 232, 407, 3:463 (names changed); Grafe, *Grenze*, 275.
28. NP-A 564-8(I/II), BBP-Nec, S., 3, 23 Jan. 1969; Schätzlein, Rösch, and Albert, *Grenzerfahrungen*, 1:314 (name changed). Similar: NP-A 564-8(I), Raps, 7, 17 Jan. 1969.
29. E.g., NP-A 564-8: (I), BBP-Nec, I., 26 Jun. 1969; M., 26 Jun. 1968; (II), S., 13 Feb. 1968; BArch-B DO1 34.0.34653, Correspondence-R., Mar. 1963–Feb. 1964.
30. NP-A 564-8(II), BBP-Nec, Z., 16 Dec. 1970.
31. BStU BV Suhl, AKG/33 Bd. 2, 118–123; Schätzlein, Albert, and Salier, *Grenzerfahrungen*, 3:411.
32. E.g., NP-A 564-8(I), BBP-Nec, A., B., 28 Jun. 1978; G., 14 Apr. 1969.
33. NP-A 564-8(II), BBP-Nec, Z., S., 9 Nov. 1970; SA-N EAP 436-06, Correspondence-Z., 29 Oct.–9 Nov. 1970.
34. BArch-MA GB13 8367, GR-15, 26 Jun. 1969; StA-M: VPKA-Sbg 1031, "Übersicht—Rückkehrer und Zuziehenden," 26 Nov. 1964; SED-KL-Sbg IV/A.4.07/162, "Beratung—Grenzdurchbrüche," 16 Feb. 1965; BStU Suhl AOP 196/76, Jan. 1961–Jan. 1964.
35. Kalning, "Aufdeckung," 13, 23–24; StA-M SED-KL-Sbg IV/C/4.07/192, Müller, 20 Feb. 1972.
36. SA-N EAP 436-06, BMInn, 15 May 1964; correspondence, "Rückführung von Jugendlichen," 1964–1970. Pass falsification: e.g., NP-A 564-8(I), BBP-Nec, L., 1 Dec. 1966.
37. NP-A 564-8(II) BBP-Nec, W., 2 Jun. 1971 (R., 20 Mar. 1970); Schätzlein, Rösch, and Albert, *Grenzerfahrungen*, 1:190, 364 (name changed).
38. KrA-S In. 489-145, Liebermann, 6 Mar. 1972.
39. On "rowdies," Poiger, *Jazz*, e.g., 202–203; Fenemore, *Sex*.
40. Kalning, "Aufdeckung," 36; StA-M: SED-KL-Sbg IV/A/4.07/162, "Beratung—Grenzdurchbrüche," 16 Feb. 1965; VPKA-Sbg 1516, "Lageeinschätzung Staatsgrenze West," 28 Apr. 1969.
41. BArch-MA GR15 11348, GR-15, 9 Mar. 1978; StA-M SED-BL-Suhl IV/C-2/4 248, 93.
42. Interview, Siegfried Tenner.
43. Interview, Ingrid Dreyer.
44. Interview, Waltraud Wagner, and memoir, private possession.
45. E.g., StA-M: SED-KL-Sbg IV/A/4.07/162, "Maßnahmeplan—Republikverrat," 16 Mar. 1963; SED-BL-Suhl IV/2/12 1176-217, "Beschluss—Einsatzleitung," 19 Aug. 1961; VPKA-Sbg 1516; BStU BV Suhl, Abt. VII/899 Bd. 1, 114–119; KrA-S In. 489-145, "Ordnung und Sicherheit," 1963–1979.

46. When one of the boys snitched to a local Police Helper, though, Doerner was sentenced to seven additional months and permanent expulsion from Sonneberg County; after his year in jail, Roland went West—alone. NP-A 564-8(I), BBP-Nec-Meilschnitz, D., 7 Aug. 1967; similar: BBP-Nec, B., 24 Sep. 1969.

47. Interview, Edgar Pfisterer.

48. Interview, Beate Strassner.

49. E.g., NP-A 564-8(II), BBP-Nec, S., 4 Dec. 1966; G., 25 Oct. 1968; S., 13 Nov. 1968; StA-M VPKA-Sbg 1031, "Zahlenmäßige Übersicht," 26 Nov. 1964. Because Neustadt did not have a children's home, Sonneberg runaways typically wound up in Coburg or Nuremberg, though the city did pay 25,000–75,000 DM per year in aid to children whose fathers lived in East Germany, counting twenty-two children in state custody and thirty-one under state supervision in 1963; SA-N 5698, "Verwaltungs- und Tätigkeitsbericht," 31 Mar. 1963.

50. By the late 1960s, almost half of the returnees (227) had been deemed "political risks," 76 were under active "operative control" from the Stasi or Interior Ministry, and dozens more were tracked by the county police and administration; BStU BV Suhl, KL SON 3687, 91–98; KrA-S In. 296-81, 1961–1968; StA-M VPKA-Sbg 1031. Returnees in the 1950s had been allowed to resettle in the city of Sonneberg, which lay outside the Prohibited Zone. But the inclusion of the city in the 1960s then posed a major security challenge for local authorities.

51. KrA-S In. 489-145, "Bericht—Rückkehrer und Zuziehende," 20 Jun. 1964, and "Bericht—Eingliederung," 14 Feb. 1966. StA-M: VPKA-Sbg 1031, "Zahlenmäßige Übersicht," 26 Nov. 1964; SED-BL-Suhl IV/A-2/12 678, Vonderlind, 3 May 1965. Overview: Schmelz, *Migration*. District of Suhl: Neumeier, "Rückkehrer."

52. StA-M VPKA-Sbg 1031, "Zahlenmäßige Übersicht," 26 Nov. 1964; KrA-S In. 489-145, "Bericht—Kreiskommission," 20 Jun. 1964; SA-S C2-178, SbgCC, 24 Apr. 1964. Of Sonneberg's twelve returnees in 1965 (eleven under twenty-five-years-old), half became problems within the year; KrA-S In. 489-145, "Bericht—Eingliederung," 14 Feb. 1966.

53. Motives and overview: Schaad, *"Dann geh"*; Stöver, *Zuflucht*, 77–108.

    In the Sonneberg-Neustadt region, one to five people crossed illegally from West to East per month during the sixties, the number diminishing significantly by the end of the decade. However, it is difficult to disaggregate West German crossers because East German reports do not tend to distinguish between eastern returnees and western emigrants, nor between westerners' momentary territorial infractions and people intending to cross. According to West German estimates, the number of west-east crossings (including East German returnees) dropped from an average of 42,000 a year in 1950–1960 to around 5,000 a year by 1963–1965. And the number of westerners apprehended on the border was minuscule by the seventies and eighties, running around 1 to 2 percent of the number of easterners; the Sonneberg region typically saw zero to two a year. StA-M VPKA-S 1516, "Lageeinschätzung Staatsgrenze West," 1967–1969; Mangold, "Einsatz"; BArch-K B137-2078, "FRG-SBZ-Abwanderung," 3 May 1966; AA B38-II A1,92, 302; BStU BV Suhl, BdL/Dok 963, 73. Examples: Schätzlein, Albert, and Salier, *Grenzerfahrungen*, 3:205–223.

54. StA-M VPKA-Sbg 1516, "Sozialdemokrat" Nr. 2, 31 Aug. 1967; AA B38-II A1, 49, 182.

55. StA-M VPKA-Sbg 1516, VPKA Sonneberg, 30 Apr. 1967.

56. Sonneberg officials generously estimated political immigration at around 5 percent. West German authorities put it at less than 1 percent, stressing that it was based mainly on private considerations, with 85 percent of west-east crossers returning easterners, 60 percent purportedly leaving the West for family reasons, 12 percent for financial reasons, and 8 percent because of housing shortages; AA B38-II A1, 92, 302-204; BArch-K B137-2078, "Abwanderung," 3 May 1966.

57. Zeppei, "Einsatz," 25–26.

58. Scheuerich, *Geschichte*, 1:259–260.

59. Hartmann and Doering-Manteuffel, eds., *Grenzgeschichten*, 136–138. Similar: BArch-K B285-834, "R. E.," 4 Sep. 1969.

60. E.g., BStU BV Suhl, Abt. VII/899 Bd. 1, 61; "NVA klagte bei der Grenzpolizei," *NP*, 26 Aug. 1972; "Ost und West: Aug in Aug," *CT*, 4 Jan. 2003.

61. *Augsburger Allgemeine*, "An der grenze zur DDR gehen Zaungäste oft einen Schritt zu weit," 14 Aug. 1976; BStU Suhl AIM 130/93, Teil II, BD XII, 134–136.

62. E.g., AA B38-II A1, 263, 531; *DW*, "Verirrter Mann kehrte zurück," 18 Oct. 1969; Koch, "Einsatz," 10.

63. Schätzlein and Albert, *Grenzerfahrungen*, 2:290; 3:220.

64. StA-C BGS 76, "Über 3 Stunden irrte die kranke I. durchs Minenfeld," (publication removed), 31 Jul. 1965 (name changed); AA B38-II A1, 166-7, 641; Schätzlein, Rösch, and Albert, *Grenzerfahrungen*, 1:263.

65. BArch-B/SAPMO DY30/IV 2/12/73, 220-222.

66. Interview, Gerd Jahn.

67. StA-M SED-KL-Sbg IV/A/4.07/162, Heublein, "Untersuchungen—Liebau-Mogger," Aug. 1964; AA B38-IIA1, 52-4, 360; BArch-K B137-2507, Federal Finance Minister, 31 Aug. 1964.
68. AA B38-II A1 50, 223–243; interview, Hendrik Richter; "Zwanzig Jahre Zonengrenze im Neustadter Raum," *NT*, 21 Sep. 1964.
69. Restrictions: StA-M SED-KL-Sbg IV/A/4.07.162, "Kontrollplan," 25 May 1967; KrA-S In. 930–467, KEL Sonneberg, "Kontrollübersicht," Jul. 1971, and 533-157(I), Greiner, 23 Oct. 1969. Similar, Roth cemetery: BArch-MA VA-03/38587, Bergmann, 14 Aug. 1970.
70. Interview, Kurt Geis.
71. E.g., StA-M SED-KL-Sbg IV/A/4.07/162, Rückerswind report, 3 May 1966; Pfadenhauer, "Staatssicherheit," 28; BArch-MA GB13 8367, NVA GR-15, 1 Sep. 1969. File: BStU Suhl AOP 196/76.
72. Interviews, Ingrid and Erich Klinger; Herbert Schacht, Neustadt, 14 Nov. 2009.
73. AA B38-II A1: 50, 9–10, 114–115; 49, 154; interview, Erich Klinger.
74. Sälter, *Grenzpolizisten*, 196–203; training: 253–291.
75. StA-C StAnw-434, "Vernehmungsniederschrift—E.," 24 Mar. 1963.
76. StA-C StAnw-504, "Vernehmungsniederschrift—G., Z.," 14 May 1966; Schätzlein, Rösch, and Albert, *Grenzerfahrungen*, 1:269.
77. BStU MfS HA I 13037, 2–7; Lindner, "Einsatz"; e.g., BStU MfS HA I 14385. 1950s: Sälter, *Grenzpolizisten*, 293–322.
78. Especially the Sattelgrund incident: Schmidt, *Adler*, 117–118.
79. Interview, Uwe Heider, Berlin, 17 Jun. 2003.
80. Schätzlein and Albert, *Grenzerfahrungen*, 2:274–276, 285, 332; interview, Uwe Heider. Cartoons: private possession, Treichel.
81. Military defections dropped from 17,000 in the 1950s to 2,000 between 1961 and 1973 and to under 200 between 1974 and 1988.
82. E.g., BArch-MA GR15 4425, GR-15, 30 Mar., 7 May 1970; NP-A 564-8(I/II), BBP-Nec, P., 17 Jun. 1968; I., 26 Jun. 1969; N., 4 Aug. 1970. 1950s: Sälter, *Grenzpolizisten*, 323–360.
83. E.g., BStU BV Suhl, AKG/33 Bd. 3, 150-152; BStU MfS ZAIG 16187, 22–31.
84. Leaflet samples: Luthardt, *Geschichte*, 155–157.
85. Pfadenhauer, "Staatssicherheit," 26.
86. NP-A 564-8(II), BBP-Nec, V., 9 Nov. 1968. Threatening: NP-A 564-8(I), BBP-Nec, M., 23 May 1978; D., 14 Mar. 1982.
87. AA B38-II A1 49, 181. Similar: St-C StAnw: 280, 434.
88. StA-C BGS 76; e.g., "NVA-Unteroffizier von Kameraden angeschossen," *NP*, 4 Jan. 1972; "DDR-Soldat auf der Flucht angeschossen," *NP*, 5 Jan. 1972; "Tausend DM für Wolfgang Pommer," *NP*, 25 Jan. 1972; "Eine lobenswerte Tat," *NP*, 28 Jan. 1972.
89. Interview, Erich Klinger.
90. Ibid.
91. *Münchner Merkur*, "Todesmachine an DDR-Grenze," 4 Aug. 1978.
92. Scheuerich, *Geschichte*, 1:260; Fischer, *Ebersdorf*, 4; Hartmann and Doering-Manteuffel, eds., *Grenzgeschichten*, 176; BStU BV Suhl AIM 130/93, Teil II, Bd. II, 76–78.
93. E.g., AA B38-II A1, 50, 197 (223–243); StA-C BGS 76, Grenzschutzabteilung II/2, 10 Jul. 1968; "Three East German Soldiers Reported Victims of Mines," *NYT*, 22 May 1973.
94. Half were triggered by wildlife, 30 percent by weather, and the remainder by technical problems; Ritter and Lapp, *Grenze*, 72.
95. "Schneegewicht brachte 300 'DDR'-Minen zur Explosion," *DW*, 18 Feb. 1978. Around 1,500 mines exploded from snow along the entire Bavarian border in the winter of 1981–1982; Schätzlein and Albert, *Grenzerfahrungen*, 2:211.
96. "Signalzaun als neue Menschenfalle," *NT*, 15 Dec. 1965.
97. StA-M SED-BL-Suhl IV/B-2/12 570, Vonderlind, 27 Dec. 1967; Vonderlind, 11 Jan. 1968; Eichhorn, 16 Jan. 1968.
98. StA-M SED-BL-Suhl IV/B-2/12 570, Vonderlind, 4 Jan. 1968. Media: e.g., "Durch Eisensplitter verletzt," *CT*, 4 Jan. 1968. Thereafter westerners were kept further back (500 meters) from the border during mine clearances, but the tavern continued to see damage and broken windows throughout Sonneberg's 860 detonations that winter. AA B38-II A1, 263, 221–243; 442–444; StA-C BGS 76, Grenzschutzabteilung II/2, 10 Jul. 1968.
99. BStU BV Suhl AIM 130/93, Teil II, Bd. III, 195–198.
100. BayHStA MInn 89954, Stahler, 11 Jun. 1970; Scheuerich, *Geschichte*, 261. Correspondence: e.g., AA B38-II A1: 48, 136–145; 263, 487; BArch-B DA5–2304, Grenzkommission, 22 Apr. 1974.

101. StA-C BGS 129, Beyersdorfer, 13 Jun. 1985. Clearances inventory: StA-C BGS 66, "Minenüberprüfung," 1 Jun. 1992.

102. In the early nineties 1,104 GDR mines were cleared at a cost of around 250 million DM; Hunka, "DDR-Mine auf der Baggerschaufel," *NP*, 18 Jun. 2005; "Scharfe Mine im Wald gesprengt," *NP*, 4 Aug. 2010.

103. Interview, Helmut Traub.

104. StA-M: BT RdBz-Su, K612, "Anruf," 19 Sep. 1973; SED-BL-Suhl IV/C-2/4 248, 119; "Das Rödenproblem erst nach 20 Jahren vor einer Lösung," *SZ*, 24 Apr. 1986; FRG policies: SA-N EAP 030-39.

105. E.g., BayHStA PrBGP 506, BBP-Cbg, 7 Jul. 1967; BArch-K: B136-6641, BMI, 2 Sep. 1966; B137-6310, "Gemeinsame Regelung von Problemen," 18 Dec. 1969; BArch-B/SAPMO DY: 30 IV A 2/12-87, Borning, 10 Mar. 1966; 30-3388, 460–474; Hartmann and Doering-Manteuffel, eds., *Grenzgeschichten*, 134–135.

106. "Zwanzig Jahre Zonengrenze im Neustadter Raum," *NT*, 21 Sep. 1964; "Zonengrenzraum—Brückenkopf nach Thüringen," *NT*, 31 Dec. 1964.

107. StA-C BGS 117, Zweiwassermühle, Apr.–Aug. 1967; BArch-K B106-83941, Apr.–Sep. 1967.

108. Overview: BMiB, *Die innerdeutsche Grenze*, 51–57. Regional correspondence: SA-N EAP: 001-008(3); 3/060-02; StA-M SED-BL-Suhl IV/C-2/12 676; BArch-B DA5-2304, "Sitzungen der Grenzkommission."

109. E.g., BBP-Cbg, BayHStA PrBGP 506; StA-M BT RdBz-Su, K612; Köhler, *Zwischen*, 508. Particularly problematic path: AA B38-II A1, 166, 318–340; BArch-K B106-8394, 1966–1973; StA-M BT RdBz-Su, K612, Knauer, 20 Jul. 1973.

110. Controlling sewage and rat problems on the Sonneberg side had long been a priority. Neustadt polluted the Röden as well, particularly its large gas works; SA-N 024-10/1, Oct. 1958–Mar. 1959.

111. "Abwässer säubern die Röden," *NP*, 5 Oct. 1967; SA-N EAP 001-10, Bergmann, 23 Aug. 1968; BMiB, *Wo Deutschland*, 39; "Das Rödenproblem erst nach 20 Jahren vor einer Lösung," *SZ*, 24 Apr. 1986.

112. "Waldfrieden-See als Sandgrube?" *NP*, 7 Jul. 1982; StA-M BT RdBz-Su, K612, BBP-Cbg, 10 Sep. 1973; Schiesswohl, 10 Mar. 1976; Schätzlein and Albert, *Grenzerfahrungen*, 2: 373, 396; KrA-S In. 931–468(IV), Zöllner, 26 Jan. 1982.

113. "Unübersehbare Schäden an den Wiesen durch Hochwasser der Steinach ab Grenze der DDR," *NP*, 10 Mar. 1977; "Hochwasserschäden an der Steinach," *NP*, 15 Mar. 1977; SA-N EAP 001-11.

114. Scheuerich, *Geschichte*, 2:5–6; Bretschneider, *Geschichte*, 147–149, 168.

115. KrA-S In. 937-470, Sauerteig, 2 Aug. 1984.

116. SA-N EAP: 001-10; 001-11; 2051; StA-M RdBz-Su, KmAbz., 81.

117. E.g., "Soll Röthenbett weiterhin Marasstätte bleiben?" *SB*, 24 Aug. 1961; BArch-B DO1-0.2.0-Nr.7-1, Peter, 14 Jun. 1960. StA-M: SED-BL-Suhl IV/2/12 1176, 1; BT RdBz-Su, K: 2909, Müller, 28 May 1975; 2910, Greiner, 14 Jan. 1976.

118. After a West German offer of "generous funds" for Sonneberg's plant 1971 fell through, Neustadt received 3.4 million DM (counted as compensation for war damages) for its own. Scheuerich, *Geschichte*, 1:388–391; Bergmann, *Suchet*, 60–66, and 164–170.

119. Out of the purported 50–60 million DM cost for the project, 9 million DM came from federal funds and 9 million from Bavaria. "Röden-Abkommen," *NT*, 13 Oct. 1983; BStU MfS ZAIG 21483, 2–3, 24. Budgets and timetable: BArch-B DC20 I/4 5305, 112–119; "Die Kläranlage für Sonneberg geht in zwei Jahren in Betrieb," *SZ*, 17 Feb. 1986.

120. Schoenau, *Sonneberg*, 63–67; Tresselt, "Ein Tiroler Hut aus Sonneberg," *SZ*, 25 Jun. 1986.

121. Interviews, Lenz Pfisterer, Sonneberg/Köppelsdorf, 28 Jun. 2002, Volker Langer, Neustadt, 3 May 2003 (names changed); BStU BV Suhl, AKG/40 Bd. 2, 169–173.

Chapter 10: Disconnect

1. Interview, Elisabeth Dietzer; Friedrich, "Die Grenze war einfach da," in Schugg-Reheis, ed., *Grenzenlos*, 16.

2. For example, Sonneberg was entirely absent from East Germany's *DDR Reiseführer* while it was in the Prohibited Zone (1966 and 1971 editions) and received abbreviated and distorted mention in subsequent editions (1978, 1981). Grimm, ed., *Zwischen*; Eichhorn-Nelson, *Sonneberg*.

3. Decker, "Wall," 119–125. Border soldiers' short stories: Preissler, *Grüne Leuchtkugeln*, and *Stunden*.

4. Treichel and Hentschel, private possession.

5. KrA-S In. 533-157(I), Mangold, 19 Feb. 1970.

6. Western portrayals: Ullrich, *Geteilte Ansichten*, 85–132.

7. *Tages-Anzeiger, Regensburg,* "Blick von oben hinter die 'Todesgrenze,'" 6 May 1966; BayHStA MInn 89957.

8. E.g., SA-N: EAP 0-001-06/21; 2051, esp. Bergmann, 2 Dec. 1958; Martin, 21 Nov. 1957; Menzel-Bergmann, May 1962; e.g., "Eine sehr gut gelungene Werbung für die bayerische Puppenstadt," *NP,* 25 Nov. 1976.

9. E.g., cover, *Nord-Ost Bayerisches Grenzland Magazin,* Nov. 1961; "Am Stacheldraht ist für die Kinder die Welt zu Ende," *NP,* 8 Sep. 1961.

10. "Die Mauer zieht sich durch das ganze deutsche Land," *NT,* 13 Aug. 1965.

11. Friedrich, private possession: S. to Friedrich family, 7 Jan. 1964 (names changed); "German Boy, 2½, Walks Through Mines to West," *NYT,* 27 Aug. 1963; Scheuerich, *Geschichte,* 1:259.

12. *Time,* "A Cold War Fairy Tale," 6 Sep. 1963.

13. ". . . mit neuen Schuhen in die Zone zurück," *NT,* 27 Aug. 1963; interviews, Ingeborg Friedrich, Brigitte Laub.

14. Feig, "Das deutsche Puppenparadies am Stacheldraht," *Nord-Ost Bayerisches Grenzland Magazin,* Nov. 1961, 6–8.

15. Feldkeller, "Unner Heamet" (1961), *SZ,* 15 Dec. 1986; "Ein Blick über den Stacheldrahtzaun," *NP,* 2 Dec. 1961.

16. Leuenberger, "Constructions."

17. E.g., BayHStA PrBGP 121, Reithmeier, 14 Oct. 1958; Riedl, 22 Sep. 1959; "Grenzlandkundgebung," 19 Apr. 1960. StA-M SED-KL-Sbg IV/4.07/160, "Informationsbericht," 23 Sep. 1959.

18. E.g., StA-C BGS 117, BGS Coburg, 14 Jun., 10 Aug. 1971; Schätzlein, Rösch, and Albert, *Grenzerfahrungen,* 1:366. Notable: BayHStA PrBGP 120, Riedl, 23 Oct. 1953; StA-C LRA 14659, "Vorsprechung," 7 Nov. 1958.

19. BStU BV Suhl XI/196/76, 289–297; Eckardt, "Augenzeuge," 12.

20. SA-N EAP 001-02, Bergmann, 19 Mar. 1959; Schütz, 1 Jun. 1959.

21. SA-N: 2051, Weppler-Kaemmerer-Emmert, May–Jun. 1957; EAP 001-02, Bergmann, 9 Feb. 1960, and "Aktion Selbstbestimmung," 1 Jun. 1960; EAP 023-22, "Tag der deutschen Einheit," 1961–1970.

22. Schätzlein, Albert, and Salier, *Grenzerfahrungen,* 3:187 (197–205). E.g., BStU BV Suhl, AKG/33 Bd. 4, 64–66; Köhler, *Zwischen,* 518–520.

23. SA-N EAP 023-22, "Zweiter Grenzlandwandertag," Jun. 1969.

24. "Rekordbeteiligung bei der 5. Grenzlandwanderung," *NP,* 19 and 20 Jun. 1972. The Stasi estimated that Neustadt's June 17 walks drew 16,500 participants between 1976 and 1988, with Bad Harzburg second, drawing 10,500. Welitsch (opposite Sonneberg's Heinersdorf) itself ranked sixth in the FRG with 4,600 demonstrators; BStU MfS HA I 13625, 2–4. Reports: BArch-MA G15 11348 and BStU BV Suhl, Abt. VII/899 Bd. 1.

25. SA-N 024-10/1, NecSR, 2 Nov. 1961; Raiminger, "Kindheit und Jugend am 'Eisernen Vorhang,'" in *Grenzenlos,* Schugg-Reheis, 23–24; SA-N EAP 001-02, Schütz, 16 Dec. 1959; "Lichtergruss an die Zone," 1967; BayHStA B-StK 14184, Riedl, 19 Dec. 1956; Christmas packages: StA-C LRA 15433.

26. Scheuerich, *Geschichte,* 2:514; Bretschneider, *Geschichte,* 127–129.

27. Büschel, "Entgrenzte Heimat," 195–209.

28. "Isoliert—aber tapfer," *NP,* 13 Apr. 1957. E.g., *NT* series "Das Dorf am Stacheldraht," Jun.–Jul. 1960; *Grenzlandmagazin; Wie lange noch?*

29. Coverage: SA-N 2051.

30. SA-N 024-10/1, NecSR, 16 Apr. 1959.

31. "Zonengrenzraum," *NT,* 31 Dec. 1964.

32. "Aufklärung über die Spaltung unseres Landes," *NT,* 21 Jul. 1966.

33. SA-N EAP 001-06-2, "Arbeitsgespräch," 9 May 1966; Groebe, 3 Jun. 1966.

34. Correspondence and budget files: SA-N EAP 001-06-2, 3, 4, 5, esp. Giers, 8 Nov. 1966.

35. "Arbeiten für die Informationsstelle," *NP,* 11 Apr. 1968; "Informationsstelle Zonengrenze," *NP,* 11 May 1968; SA-N EAP: 001-06-21, Gwosdzik, 10 May 1972; Documentary: 0-001-06/29; press: 001-06-23.

36. SA-N EAP 001-06-7; "Improvisation an der Zonengrenze," *NT,* 19 Jun. 1968; "Goppel eröffnete Informationsstelle," *NP,* 16 Jun. 1968.

37. Operations: SA-N EAP: 001-06-21; 001-06-1; 320–27, "Grenz-Info," May 1985.+

38. SA-N EAP 001-06-01, "Studienfahrten Erwachsener an die Demarkationslinie," 1966.

39. Eckert, "Greetings"; EAP 0-001-06/25. GDR: BStU MfS ZAIG 16342, "Information," 25 Nov. 1977; Schätzlein, Albert, and Salier, *Grenzerfahrungen,* 3:178–186. Travel context: Koshar, *German Travel.*

40. Between 1962 and 1990, the BGS in Coburg ushered 235,977 people to the border through 6,422 tours (8,500 visitors a year), while Neustadt's Border Police escorted an average of 6,500 people a year.

StA-C: BGS 198, "Grenzführungen GSA Süd 2," Jan. 1991; BGS 130, BGS Tours, 1962–1980; SA-N EAP 001-06-17.

41. Frantzen, "Entwicklung"; Dlouhy, *Wirtschaft*, 323; SA-N: 5698, "Verwaltungs- und Tätigkeitsbericht," 31 Mar. 1963; 5699, 25; "Kreisfreie Stadt Neustadt," *Monatshefte des Bayerischen Statistischen Landesamts*, 1964–1965, 15, 24.

42. Borneff, "Bahnhof als Wochenendhäuschen," *NN*, 3 May 1967.

43. Itineraries: SA-N EAP 001-06-01; -17, -18.

44. Treichel, private possession. Additional: www.bergmuehle.de/start.htm.

45. This very image: Karl Borneff, "Aufsätze 1952–1988," and Rose, *Lost Border*, 21.

46. E.g., Borneff, *Zonengrenze*, 32–33.

47. "Küche, Service und Gast in Harmonie," *NP*, 16 Mar. 1988; "Zweites Wohnzimmer des Gastes wurde eingeweiht," *NP*, 18 Mar. 1988.

48. SA-N EAP 0-001-06/29. Stasi: BStU BV Suhl, KD SON 3688.

49. SA-N EAP: 0-001-06/1, NecSR, 28 Sep. 1981; 001-06-0, *NT*, 11 Feb. 1969; 001-06-17, Raps, 10 Aug. 1972.

50. E.g., Eckert, "Greetings." One American's tour: Rehyansky, "Letter from the Edge of Détente," *National Review*, 20 Feb. 1976, 141–142, 170.

51. "Verläuft der Metallgitterzaun wirklich durch ganz Deutschland?" *CT*, 28 Aug. 1980; Ritter and Lapp, 129–139, 132.

52. StA-C BGS 198, Entry, 16 Jul. 1979, BGS Visitors' Book, BGS Coburg.

53. BStU BV Suhl, Abt. VII/899 Bds. 1, 2, Wahl, monthly reports.

54. Koch, "Einsatz," 34; StA-C BGS 67, Judex, 6 May 1982; GR-15 reports: BArch-MA: 011348; GT 8367.

55. *Esslinger Zeitung*, "Hört hinter Neustadt die Welt auf?" 24 Mar. 1966; *Stuttgarter Nachrichten*, "Um 2.10 Uhr kam einer durch," 23 Mar. 1966.

56. Frantzen, "Entwicklung"; SA-N EAP: 000-09/0, 000-03, 001-008(3); Aumann, *Coburg*, 180–184.

57. Borneff, "Am Bahngleis Coburg-Eisenach," *Ost-West Kurrier*, 20 Apr. 1968.

58. Interview, Margarete Schacht.

59. Bailey, *Along*, 186–187, 197, 7.

60. Raiminger, "Kindheit," 23.

61. Dietzsch, *Grenzen überschreiben*?; Härtel and Kabus, ed., *Westpaket*.

62. E.g., *NP* columns "Nachrichten vom Rennsteig" and "Streifzug durch das Thüringer Land."

63. "Tagesausflüge immer beliebter," *NP*, 11 Oct. 1972; "Wiedersehensfreude und manch rührende Szenen," *NP*, 15 Sep. 1981.

64. Gallert, "Am Schlagbaum in Neustadt bei Coburg," *SZ*, 24 Apr. 1989; Mertin, "Affen im Käfig," in Schugg-Reheis, ed., *Grenzenlos*, 15. East German reactions to western tourism: Eckert, "Zaun-Gäste."

65. Statistics: "Kreisfreie Stadt Neustadt," 21–23; *Statistisches Taschenbuch*, 1966, 113–114; BArch-B/SAPMO DY30-2533, 60–61.

66. Significantly greater detail: Sheffer, "Burned Bridge," 543–560.

67. Interview, Brigitte Laub; Hofmann, "Industrie," 60–69, 75–81. SA-N: 5698, 90; 5699, 58–62; 4403.

68. Frantzen, "Entwicklung"; 83–86, 97–104; SA-N EAP 001-14. Toy industry workers remained around 1,500, between 20 and 30 percent of the workforce: Sperschneider, "Spielwarenindustrie," 128–138, 147, 161–165; Scheuerich, *Geschichte*, 1:285–286; SA-N EAP 000-08, 80; 2050, 2111. Region: Falkenberg and Dlouhy, *Wirtschaft*.

69. Andrä, "Fachgebietsleiter Staatliche Plankommission," *Fachbereich Standardisierung Spielwaren*, 1960; StA-M SED-KL-Sbg IV/4.07/086, 5–6; BArch-B DE1-6413, "Schwerpunkte—Spielwarenindustrie," 1960; Lischewsky, *Puppen*, 75–77; BStU BV Suhl AOP 385/76 I, 90–102. Overview: Zips, *Spielzeugmacher*.

70. Dora A., in Lischewsky, *Puppen*, 118. The number of Sonneberg workers employed outside nationalized entities in the early seventies was over twice the East German average (20 percent compared to 7.6 percent) and Sonneberg counted almost as many private toy companies as Neustadt (twenty-three compared to thirty), in addition to eleven fairly independent production cooperatives. By 1989, Sonni's revenue totaled 1.4 billion marks, the toy industry supporting roughly one in three families in the county. More than 50 percent of its production was exported, a quarter to "non-socialist" countries. SA-N EAP 320-27, Klöppel, Jan. 1989; BArch-B DC20 I/3 2023, 31–58.

71. Lischewsky, *Puppen*, 66–78, 118; Sperschneider, "Spielwarenindustrie," 143–144. Factory life in East Germany: Madarász, *Working*.

72. "Umsatz der oberfränkischen Spielwarenindustrie 70 Mill. DM," *NT*, 12 Dec. 1964; Scheuerich, *Geschichte*, 2:298–299.

73. BStU BV Suhl AOP 385/76 I, 306–310; BArch-B DC20 I/3 2023, 31–58; Damaske, "Heraus aus der Enge," *FW*, 23 Aug. 1958. Modern materiality in East Germany: Rubin, *Synthetic Socialism*.

74. E.g., SED-KL-Sbg, *25 Jahre*, cover.

75. Sperschneider, "Spielwarenindustrie," 148–150; KrA-S In. 465–139, "Referat," 22 Mar. 1970; BStU BV Suhl, KL SON 3687, 18; *Statistisches Taschenbuch,*156; "Kreisfreie Stadt Neustadt," 22.

76. Harsch, *Revenge*, 87–132.

77. By contrast, just seventeen foreign-born workers, from Vietnam, lived in Sonneberg in 1989. SA-N B-Akte Bl.18ff, "Einwohnerstand," 2003; SA-N EAP 0-001-03 Bd. 1, Grempel, 21 May 1971; KrA-S In. 2683-1035, Sauerteig, 12 May 1989.

78. "Die Abwanderung der Jugend aus dem Grenzlandgebiet bereitet große Sorgen," *NN*, 20 Feb. 1970.

79. Overviews: Offer, *Zonenrandgebiet*, 24–27; Jones and Wild, "Opening," 259–274.

80. SA-N: EAP 311-04, Bergmann, 2 May 1960; SA-N EAP 001-008 (1–2), 200; 5698, 26; 2052; BArch-K B137-3788.

81. Stephen Redding and Daniel Sturm, "The Costs of Remoteness: Evidence from German Division and Reunification," Social Science Research Network, Apr. 2005, CEPR No. 5015; Köhler, *Zwischen*, 532–533.

82. SA-N EAP 000-08, *Handelsblatt*, "Schwarzmalerei," 11 Jul. 1966.

83. SA-N 2051, "Denkschrift," 27 Apr. 1965.

84. SA-N 2050, Neustadter Tageblatt, 10 Dec. 1955; Schwämmlein, "Entwicklung," 170–171. Construction concerns: StA-M SED-BL-Suhl IV/2/12 1176, Protocol, 14 Oct. 1961; BArch-B/SAPMO DY30/IV 2/12-80, 24, 45; StA-M BT RdBz-Su, K1625, "Wolkenrasen," 12 Jul. 1973.

85. Bergmann, *Suchet*, 77–82; BayHStA StK 12831, Dünnbier, 6 Aug. 1964, and Wehgartner, 22 Oct. 1964.

86. "Kontraste einer Stadt," *NP*, 20 Aug. 1971.

87. StA-M SED-KL-Sbg IV/A/4.07/159, visit statistics, 1967. From 1962 to 1966, the number of westerners granted entry to Sonneberg County was higher, at 350–630 a month, roughly one-quarter of whom were allowed into the five-kilometer zone and 1 percent inside the five-hundred-meter zone; BStU BV Suhl, KL SON 3687, 100–103.

88. SA-N 5698, "Verwaltungs- und Tätigkeitsbericht," 31 Mar. 1963.

89. Hentschel, private possession: unstamped postcard, K., Oeslau-Rödental, 1 Aug. 1966.

90. Teßmer and Zien, *Sonneberger Geschichten*, 41.

91. Kalning, "Aufdeckung," 12, 22.

92. StA-M SED-KL-Sbg IV/A/4.07/109, "Informationsbericht," 15 Nov. 1963.

93. Negotiation: Sarotte, *Dealing*, 113–134. In addition to cases of sicknesses and death, East Germany allowed travel for relatives of any age for "urgent family matters," including births, weddings, major birthdays, and anniversaries.

94. Policy: McAdams, *Germany*, 102–103.

95. BArch-B/SAPMO DY30 2309, 46; Bretschneider, *Geschichte*, 133–134, (147–149).

96. Correspondence: SA-N: EAP 001-008(2, 3); 024-10/1. Four road checkpoints were opened between East and West Germany on June 21, 1973, for a total of eight along the inter-German border.

97. The majority were for multiple entry; SA-N EAP 000-03, "Information," 11 Apr. 1974; Bergmann, *Suchet*, 162. KrA-S Vors. 465-139, esp., SED-KL-Sbg, 14 Aug. 1973; Greiner, 31 Aug. 1973; StA-M SED-BL-Suhl IV/C-2/12 675, 6–7; Knespel, "Arbeit," 5, 20.

98. KrA-S Vors. 465-139, Walther, 24 Jul. 1973; BArch-B/SAPMO DY30 2310, 157; Lentz, "Daily Border Crossings by West Germans Decline," *NYT*, 30 Jun. 1974.

99. StA-C BGS 76, 1973–1985; SA-N EAP 000-03, "Grenzübergang," 11 Apr. 1974.

100. BArch-B/SAPMO DY30/IV B2/12/69, 24–33.

101. BArch-B/SAPMO DY30 2309, Albrecht, 28 Nov. 1973; KrA-S Vors. 465-139, Walther, 4 Dec. 1973.

102. "Scharfer Protest bei Bundesminister Heinrich Windelen," *CT*, 5 Jun. 1985.

103. KrA-S Vors. 465-139, Walther, 21 Jun. 1973; StA-M SED-BL-Suhl IV/C-2/12 675, 6–7; BArch-B/SAPMO DY30 2309, 59–60.

104. KrA-S Vors. 465-139, Walther, 4 Dec., (15) Jun. 1973.

105. KrA-S Vors. 465-139, esp. SED-KL-Abt Parteiorgane, 29 Aug. 1973.

106. KrA-S Vors. 465-139, Walther, (15) Jun. 1973.

107. KrA-S Vors. 465-139, Walther, 24 Oct. 1973.

108. KrA-S Vors. 465-139, SED-KL-Sbg, 14 Aug. 1973.

109. Riehl-Heyse, "Entdeckungsfahrt zu den fremden Verwandten," *SdZ*, 23–26 Dec. 1972.

110. Interview, Greta and Kurt Geis.

111. BStU MfS BdL/Dok. 001829MfS, "Befehl Nr. 21/73," 18 Jun. 1973; Knespel, "Arbeit," 21, 57; interviews, Lenz Pfisterer, Emrich family, Elisabeth Dietzer.
112. Riehl-Heyse, "Entdeckungsfahrt."
113. Ibid.
114. KrA-S Vors. 465-139, Walther, "Informationsbericht," Sep. 1973. Attendance at Sonneberg's Toy Museum skyrocketed after removal from the Prohibited Zone, from 12,000–24,000 a year in the 1960s to well over 200,000 after 1972, up to 40 percent of whom were westerners. BStU BV Suhl, KL SON 3687, 135; KrA-S In. 599-216, Gottschild, 20 Jul. 1977; Lischewsky, *Puppen*, 39.
115. "Sonneberg 1982," *NP*, 18 Sep. 1982; "Wo Deutchland geteilt ist . . . ," *NT*, 31 Aug. 1984.
116. "Die 'Sumbarger Säu,'" *SZ*, 19 Jun. 1989.
117. Interview, Margarete Schacht.
118. Interview, Elisabeth Dietzer.
119. E.g., Tresselt, "Ein Tiroler Hut aus Sonneberg," *SZ*, 25 Jun. 1986.
120. "Geistige Einheit dokumentiert," *NP*, 19 Sep. 1983.
121. Eichhorn, *Blick* [foreword]. E.g., Götz, *Humor*, 46–47; Truckenbrodt and Maaser, *Alt-Neustadter*.
122. Interview, Volker Langer.
123. StA-M SED-BL-Suhl: IV/C-2/12 675, Linke, 23 Jul. 1975; Sommer, 28 Nov. 1975; IV/D/4.07/175, "Beurteilung," 10 Apr. 1979; BArch-B/SAPMO DY30: 2310, 40; 2309, 108; IV/B2/12/69, 24–33; BStU BV Suhl, Abt. VII/899: Bd. 1, 75; Bd. 2, 54.
124. Interviews, Josef Jahn, Ingrid Holzmann, Inge Mulzer and Brigitte Laub. E.g., StA-M SED-BL-Suhl: IV/C-2/4 248, "Protokoll," 21 Sep. 1973; IV/C/4.07/192, "Einschätzung," 1973; KrA-S Vors. 465-139, Gottschild, 16 Aug. 1973.
125. E.g., Knespel, "Arbeit," 152–155; BArch-B/SAPMO DY30: 2309, 97; 2310, 157; IV/B2/12/69, 24–33; StA-M BT RdBz-Su, K612.
126. KrA-S Vors. 465-139, Walther, 3 Oct. 1973.
127. BArch-B/SAPMO DY: 30/IV B2/12/69, 24–33; 30 2309, 135; BArch-MA GR15 11348, Gruber, "Aufklärungssammelbericht," Aug. 1977.
128. Schätzlein, Albert, and Salier, *Grenzerfahrungen*, 3:532; BStU BV Suhl: AKG/33 Bd. 2, 76–79; AKG/40 Bd. 1, 35-38. 1989: BArch-B DO1 34.0 12/0, Höhn, Mar.-Jun. 1989; KrA-S In. 3059-1126.
129. Stasi activity in West Germany: Müller-Enbergs, *Inoffizielle Mitarbeiter*, 2; Knabe and Eisfeld, *West-Arbeit*. In the eastern borderland in Halberstadt, 1961–1989: Münkel, "Kontrolle."
130. Interview, Elisabeth Dietzer. Smuggling locations: BStU Suhl AOP 196/76, 52–53.
131. "Eiserner Vorhang mit Schlupflöchern," *NT*, 4–6 Jan. 2003. E.g., AA B38-II A1, 164–168, 619, 687; BayHStA BayObLG 120/1963, "Deposition—P.," 28 May 1963. Sonneberg installations: StA-C BGS: 88, "Schleusungsstellen," 30 Dec. 1983; 85, GSA Süd 2, 10 Jul. 1985; 129, Hagen, 11 Apr. 1988; "Wer benutzte den Tunnel zwischen Ost und West?" *NP*, 19 Jun. 1990; BStU BV Suhl, AFO 30/89, 269–277. Stasi fears of western infiltration: BStU MfS-HA IX Nr. 4020; Wachsmann, "Verantwortung," 18.
132. Interview, Herbert Schacht.
133. BayHStA BayObLG 115/1961, esp. BBP G-Cbg, 28 Sep. 1961.
134. E.g., BArch-K B285-834, E., 4 Sep. 1969; BStU Suhl AOP 196/76, 132; Zeppei, "Einsatz," 25–26.
135. BBP-Nec NP-A 564-8(II), Räder, 16 Feb. 1969; Raps, 20 Feb. 1969; File S., 4 Dec. 1966; File D., 16–20 Feb. 1969.
136. Coburg BGS intake: StA-C BGS 66, 128, 135, 136. West Germany reported apprehending twenty-three Stasi agents and collaborators in 1964, and questioning more than fifteen thousand; AfguBF Deutscher Bundestag, "Bericht über die Studienreise III in das Zonenrandgebiet," 10 May 1965, 30.
137. BStU MfS HA IX Nr. 2198, 5–12, 42–50.
138. Sonneberg-Neustadt soldier interrogations, 1961–1971: BStU MfS HA IX Nr. 2198.
139. Fuhrmann, "Suche"; Zeppei, "Einsatz," 18–19.
140. StA-C BGS 115, GSA IV/2, 16 Dec. 1969; interview, Johann Thull.
141. StA-C BGS 86, Oberlandesgericht Celle, 14 Apr. 1987. Others: Schätzlein, Albert, and Salier, *Grenzerfahrungen*, 3:279–281, 314–328.
142. Zeppei, "Einsatz," 24–26; StA-C BGS 115, Ammon, 8 Jul. 1963; GSA IV/2, 16 Dec. 1969. E.g., Schätzlein, Rösch, and Albert, *Grenzerfahrungen*, 1:232–236; StA-C BGS 127, Schmidt, 2 Sep. 1971; "Gespräch," 9 May 1974. BGS were instructed not to refuse Stasi overtures, but to play along, report the interactions, and drag out the communications.
143. Interview, Johann Thull, Herbert Schacht. E.g., BStU 25391/91, "Mal," 26 Jul. 1988.

144. Zeppei, "Einsatz," 3–4, 8, 17–18; BStU BV Suhl: AOP 196-76, 23–25; KD SON 3686, 109. By 1989, the district of Suhl was running 116 IMs in the "western border forefield," of whom twelve were permanent residents. This was in addition to the 322 IMs and 104 GMs involved in border security on the eastern side and the 3,388 IMs and 1,164 GMs active inside the district itself. Schätzlein, Rösch, and Albert, *Grenzerfahrungen*, 1:221; 3:134, 263.

145. StA-C BGS 115, GSA IV/2, 27 May 1970.

146. StA-C BGS 87, Kundörfer, 17 Sep. 1984; "US-Zeitung: Vermehrt Spione in Unterfranken," *NP*, 5 Jan. 1988.

147. Interviewees requested that incidents remain confidential.

148. "Das ist doch ein großer Feuerteich" *NP*, 22 Nov. 1995; Coburg region, *NP* series 20–23 Nov. 1995.

149. BStU BV Suhl, KD SON: 3684, 4–7, 30–32; 3686, e.g., 58–62, 104–109; 3688.

150. BStU BV Suhl, AFO 30/89, 104–107, 318–324.

151. BStU BV Suhl, AFO 30/89, 185–197, 269–277, 450–452. E.g., BStU BV Suhl, AFO 30/89, 159, 221–224; SA-N EAP 320-27. Overview of borderland Heimat clubs: BArch-MA VA-03/38594, Pommer, 9 Jul. 1976; Traut, "subversive Tätigkeit," 8; Schätzlein, Albert, and Salier, *Grenzerfahrungen*, 3:188–195.

152. IM "Giesela" was the best "source," traveling to Neustadt several times a year and collecting up to 800 DM a trip; BStU BV Suhl, AFO 30/89; "Feuerteich," *NP*. Reports: BStU BV Suhl: AFO 30/89; KD SON 3688, 40–42; Abt. VII/899 Bd. 2, 55; BArch-MA GR15 11348, Schmidt, 4 Oct. 1982.

153. Zeppei, "Einsatz," 20–25; interviews, Johann Thull, Jörg Trautmann.

154. Interview, Beate Strassner.

155. BStU BV Suhl AIM 130/93, Teil II, BD IX, 17–22.

156. BStU BV Suhl AIM 130/93, Teil II, BD XII, 132–133; II, 76–78; VII, 281–282; VIII, 176–178.

157. E.g., BStU BV Suhl AIM 130/93, Teil II, BD XII, 134–136; V, 6, 134–137.

158. Interview, Greta Geis.

159. Treichel, private possession: Letter, 4 Jul. 1987.

160. Interview, Inge Mulzer and Brigitte Laub.

161. BStU BV Suhl, AFO 30/89, 348–349.

162. BStU BV Suhl AIM 130/93, Teil II, BD IX, 17–22.

163. Interview, Jakob Ziegler.

164. Eckardt, "Augenzeuge," 12; interivew, Elisabeth Dietzer; Koch, "Einsatz," 17.

165. Hemmann, "Kleiner Grenzverkehr (1988)," in Schugg-Reheis, ed., *Grenzenlos*, 31.

166. Grams, *Als bei uns die Grenze*, 41–43.

167. Kaiser, "Ein kleines Wunder für die Deutschen," *DZ*, 1 Jan. 1988; Schätzlein and Albert, *Grenzerfahrungen*, 2:251.

168. Maier, *Dissolution*, 128.

169. BStU BV Suhl, AKG/41 Bd. 1, 67–68.

170. Grempel, "Grußwort," *SZ*, 25 Aug. 1988; Präcklein, "Zum Weihnachtseinkauf mal kurz in den Westen," "Großer Zustrom von jungen Leuten," and "Reger Reiseverkehr an DDR-Grenzübergängen," *NP*, 17 Dec. 1987, 5 Jan. 1988. By comparison, in the 1970s Sonnebergers made just 1,500 trips to all of West Germany.

171. Präcklein, "Zum Weihnachtseinkauf."

172. "DDR-Rentner kaufen für Weihnachten ein," *NP*, 27 Nov. 1987.

173. Präcklein, "Zum Weihnachtseinkauf."

174. Ibid.; "Großer Zustrom."

175. BStU BV Suhl, AKG/33 Bd. 2, 32–40.

176. "Städtepartnerschaft mit Sonneberg noch Utopie," *NP*, 21 May 1986; "SPD-Initiative für deutsch-deutsches Gasmodell," *NP*, 12 Jan. 1988; "DDR-Studientage durchgeführt," *SZ*, 24 Apr. 1986; interview, Volker Langer; BStU BV Suhl, Abt. XX/736 Bd. 1, esp. 17–28; Bd. 2, 69–78. City partnership: SA-N EAP: 023-35-0; 000-08, Cremers, 17 Apr. 1989. Directives: BArch-B DO1 34.0. Nr. 052115.

177. Kleiner, "Frieden," 113–115.

178. Interview, Hendrik Richter.

179. Mayer, *Flucht*, 438, 464.

180. The repercussions of 1984 relaxations: Major, *Berlin Wall*, 215–217.

181. Regional examples: Schätzlein, Albert, and Salier, *Grenzerfahrungen*, 3: 95, 470–481.

182. BStU BV Suhl, AKG/33 Bd. 1, 50–60.

183. Lapp, *Gefechtsdienst*, 90; BArch-B/SAPMO DY30/IV 2/2.039-309, 79–80. Details: Sheffer, "Burned Bridge," 593–594; StA-M BT RdBz-Su, K2889, esp. "Zuarbeit," 24 Nov. 1988; "Schlußfolgerungen,"

29 Oct. 1987; KrA-S In. 2914-1096, "Informationsmaterialien," 1988. Sonneberg administration: KrA-S In.: 3059-1126; 2683-1035, esp. Höhn, 9 Jun. 1989; Sommer, 22 Sep. 1989.

184. StA-M BT RdBz-Su, K2889, Sommer, 8 Sep. 1988; BStU BV Suhl, AKG/33 Bd. 1, 19–23, 50–60.

185. Growth of citizens' petitions in the 1980s: Zatlin, *Currency*, 286–320.

186. Sonneberg's border zone often claimed better election returns than the national average of 1.15 percent "no-votes," registering *one* dissenting vote in both the elections of 1981 and 1984. Even in May 1989, it claimed 99.98 percent voter participation, the county as a whole registering 99.48 percent. Schätzlein, Albert, and Salier, *Grenzerfahrungen*, 3:505–507, 510; KrA-S KrPK, 2373-931, Scheler, 3 Jul. 1989; BStU BV Suhl: Abt. VII/899 Bd. 2, 119–125; AKG/33 Bd. 3, 185–188.

187. E.g., BStU BV Suhl, AKG/33: Bd. 2, 147–151; Bd. 3, 140–149.

188. StA-M BT RdBz-Su, K2888, esp. Witter, 4 Jan. 1989; BStU BV Suhl, AKG/33 Bd. 1, 19–23.

189. BStU BV Suhl: AKG/33 Bd. 5, 146–152, and additional, 9–17, 88–89, 155–156; AKG/33 Bd. 3, 217–220; BArch-B/SAPMO DY30 2121, 39–45.

190. By this point, flight prompted change, as "private exit" now stimulated, rather than diminished, the expression of "public voice." Hirschman, "Exit," 197.

191. BArch-B DO1-40.0, Nr. 054024. Local opinion: BStU BV Suhl, AKG/33 Bd. 6, 140–157.

192. BStU BV Suhl, AKG/33 Bd. 5, 211–223, 216–217; interview, Elisabeth Dietzer.

193. BStU BV Suhl, AKG/33 Bd. 7, 31–41; "Bürgerforen am Wochenende," *FW*, 1 Nov. 1989; "Erst Friedensgebete in Sonneberg," *FW*, 30 Oct. 1999; KrA-S: In. 2910-1095, "Vereinigung 'Neues Forum,'" 9 Nov. 1989; Vors. 22276-895, Witter, 4 Nov. 1989.

194. Interviews, Hendrik Richter, Hermann Stöcker, Sonneberg, 3 Feb. 2003. 500 attended October 8: BStU BV Suhl, AKG/33 Bd. 6, 174–177. Sonneberg church surveillance: KrA-S In. 937-470; 938-471.

195. Reich, *Kirche*, 13 (minutes, 7–14).

196. BStU BV Suhl, AKG/33 Bd. 7, 50–61; "Demonstrationen im Bezirk Suhl," *FW*, 31 Oct. 1989.

197. BStU BV Suhl, AKG/33 Bd. 7, 177–179; Grams, *Die friedliche Revolution*, 12–13; "Kein Benzin für die 'roten' Suhler," *CT*, 25–26 Nov. 1989; KrA-S Vors. 22276-895, "Informationsbericht," 7 Nov. 1989.

198. Reich, *Kirche*, 17–18.

199. StA-C BGS 145, "Flüchtlinge über die DDR-Grenzsperranlage," 1961–1989. The number of crossing attempts in Sonneberg rose 70 percent in 1988 (seventy-seven people, one-third of them Sonnebergers), and the rate continued to climb during 1989. BStU BV Suhl, AKG/41 Bd. 2, 284–287; KrA-S In. 2683-1035, Stier, 25 Jan. 1989.

200. BStU BV Suhl, AKG/33 Bd. 5, 211–223. Individuals: "DDR-Familie gelang die Flucht bei Wildenheid," *NP*, 19 Oct. 1989. Chronology: Schätzlein, Albert, and Salier, *Grenzerfahrungen*, 3: 167–204.

Epilogue: New Divides

1. SA-N EAP 023-35/0, NecSR Meeting, 20 Nov. 1989.

2. Hertle, *Berlin Wall*, 146–151.

3. KrA-S Vors. 22276-895, Häfner, 11 Nov. 1989; GDR: BArch-B/SAPMO DY30-IV 1-2.039-320, 10–14.

4. Interview, Klaus Treichel, and scrapbook.

5. "Um 4.48 Uhr fiel der Schlagbaum an der 'Gebrannten Brücke,'" *CT*, 13 Nov. 1989; SA-N EAP 001-13/3d, Maaser, 17 Nov. 1989.

6. "Wir sind aus einem Holz," *CT*, 13 Nov. 1989.

7. Interview, Wolfgang Mayerhofer.

8. Video: Limmer, "Die Wunder-Wende: Neustadt und Sonneberg," 2009, and Mayerhofer, private possession.

9. Minutes: Reich, *Kirche*, 19–33. Between five thousand and seven thousand people on November 13: KrA-S Vors. 22276-895, Czmok, 14 Nov. 1989; BStU BV Suhl, AKG/33 Bd. 7, 231–234.

10. KrA-S In. 2683-1035, Scheler, 28 Nov. 1989; KrA-S StVors. 2927-1099; BStU MfS ZAIG 5746, 516/89, 1–8; StA-M BT RdBz-Su, K2723; SA-N EAP 001-13/2; StA-C BGS 112, 20 Nov. 1989.

11. Overview: Bretschneider, *Grenzen*, 90–132. E.g., private possession: Mayerhofer, Treichel, Müller, Kunert, Thaler. Subsequent celebrations: Bretschneider, *Freiheit*.

12. Roundtable: KrA-S Vors. 22276-895. Overview: "Im Dezember 1989 begannen in Sonneberg die Gespräche am Runden Tisch," *FW*, 15 Dec. 1999. City partnership: SA-N EAP 023-35/0. Political organization: Maier, *Dissolution*, 168–214.

13. "Ein ganz normales Wunder," *CT*, 18–19 Nov. 1989.
14. E.g., Fuchs, "Ist das nicht Wahnsinn?" *CT*, 18–19 Nov. 1989; Müller, ". . . so ich dir," *FW*, 20 Feb. 1990.
15. Interview, Erich Klinger. Opening: "Für 150 Minuten: das 'Wunder von Heubisch,'" *CT*, 27 Nov. 1989; StA-C BGS 112, 25 Nov. 1989.
16. SA-N EAP 023-35/0, NecSR Meeting, 20 Nov. 1989; "Grenzübergang in Richtung Heubisch verlegen?" *CT*, 22–23 Nov. 1989; SA-N EAP 001-13/3d, Fischer, 26 Nov. 1989, and file. Sonneberg complaints: "Verkehrswelle durch Hönbach," *FW*, 18 Nov. 1989.
17. E.g., "700,000 DDR-Bürger reisten bislang ein," *CT*, 7 Dec. 1989; Berger, "Tagsüber nur wenig Übersiedler," 11 Nov. 1989.
18. "Kein Benzin für die 'roten' Suhler," *CT*, 25–26 Nov. 1989.
19. "Die Tür nicht wieder schließen," *CT*, 14 Nov. 1989; KrA-S Vors. 22276-895: Weise, 15 Nov. 1989; Scheler, 17 Jan. 1990.
20. Reportedly, 12,658,320 DM was dispensed, SA-N EAP 001-13/5.2 Grempel, 15 Jan. 1990; e.g., "Vielerorts ging das Geld aus," *CT*, 13 Nov. 1989.
21. E.g., "Mit Disziplin ins Kaufgetümmel," *CT*, 14 Nov. 1989.
22. "Oberfranken nicht mehr im toten Winkel," *CT*, 14 Nov. 1989.
23. "Kauftrubel von früh bis abends," "Schlaf, Kindlein, schlaf," and "Vor allem die Kinder machen große Augen," *CT*, 13, 17 Nov. 1989
24. Interview, Wolfgang Mayerhofer.
25. Interview, Anna Emrich.
26. Interview, Edgar Pfisterer.
27. Interview, Götz Emrich.
28. "Hilfsbereitschaft ohne Grenzen," *CT*, 14 Nov. 1989; "Die größte Betreuungsaktion seit dem Zweiten Weltkrieg!" *CT*, 21 Nov. 1989.
29. "Die 'schnelle Mark' im goldenen Westen machen," *CT*, 25–26 Nov. 1989.
30. Koch, "Gäste mit langen Fingern?" *CT*, 25–26 Nov. 1989.
31. "Am Wochenende keine Begrüßungsgeld-Zahlung," *CT*, 30 Nov. 1989. Neustadt staffing and concerns: SA-N EAP 001-13/5.2, 13/5.3, and 10/0.
32. "Der 'graue Markt' entwickelt sich," *CT*, 15 Nov. 1989; "Einzelhandel warnt vor unfairen Preisaufschlägen," *CT*, 17 Nov. 1989; W., "Kommentar: Zollrestriktionen," 25–26 Nov. 1989.
33. Totals: SA-N EAP 001-13/0, "Grenzübergang Neustadt-Hönbach," 12 Jul. 1990.
34. "Schwimmen für Besucher aus der DDR nicht mehr umsonst," *NP*, 21 Dec. 1989; "Auszug aus einem Schreiben des OB Neustadt," *FW*, 11 Jan. 1990.
35. "Sonneberg sagte Dankeschön," *FW*, 3 Jan. 1990; "Sonneberg dankte Neustadtern mit Stelldichein," *CT*, 29 Dec. 1989.
36. Rieder, "Hallo," *CT*, 18–19 Nov. 1989.
37. "Betrüger sollen an den Pranger," *FW*, 5 Dec. 1989; Funke, "Kommentar geschenkt?" *FW*, 17 Feb. 1990; "Ungebrochener Volkswille in Sonneberg demonstriert," *CT*, 28 Nov. 1989; "Die Würde bei Westbesuchen bewahren," *CT*, 29 Nov. 1989; minutes: Reich, *Kirche*, 46–57.
38. Metz, "Wie ich dir—du mir?" *FW*, 27 Jan. 1990; interview, Inge Mulzer.
39. Kirbach, "Und wieviel kostest du?" *DZ*, 9 Mar. 1990.
40. Private possession, Müller: video, 1989–1990.
41. "Gülle-Lagune im Sperrgebiet," *CT*, 4 Jan. 1990; "Sperrgebiet aus dem Dornröschenschlaf erwacht," *CT*, 20 Nov. 1989.
42. Interview, Volker Langer, Jens Reichert.
43. Sexual culture in East Germany: Herzog, *Sex*, 184–219; McLellan, "Bodies."
44. Steichen, "Shopping Hordes Raid the East," *Times*, 27 Mar. 1990.
45. Metz, "Wie ich dir?" *FW*; Traut, "Ein besonderes 'Dankeschön,'" *FW*, 2 Feb. 1990; Feller, ". . . Gestürzte noch zu Boden treten," *FW*, 1 Mar. 1990.
46. International context: Sarotte, *1989*.
47. Interviews, Herbert Schacht, Josef Jahn.
48. New Sonneberg leadership: Interview, Hermann Stöcker; KrA-S: StVors. 2927-1099; Vors. 22276-895. Reform and rehabilitations: e.g., StA-M BT RdBz-Su, K2722; BArch-B DO1-0.1.2-55074, 93–96, 115–117. Inflation worries: BStU BV Suhl, AKG/33 Bd. 7, 247–252. Crime: SA-N EAP 120-02/8, "Ein ungeheuerer Anstieg," *CT*, 9 Apr. 1992. Streets: *NP*, 27 Mar. 1990.
49. Gerth, "In grosser Sorge um Zukunft," *FW*, 14 Dec. 1989.
50. Interview, Beate Strassner.
51. Photographs, private possession, Mayerhofer, Wrobel; StA-C BGS 116, 3-GSA Süd 2, 29 Nov. 1989.
52. E.g., StA-M BT RdBz-Su, K777. McAdams, *Judging*.

53. Public cases, e.g., Anonymous, "Getroffener Denunziant?" *NP*, 19 Dec. 1991; "Verleumdung," *CT*, 20 Dec. 1991. Additional: SA-N, *CT*, *NP* file, 1993–1995; "Immer noch neue Fälle," *FW*, 7 May 2002.
54. Private possession, Gansel: e.g., postcard, 1 Oct. 2001, plus newspaper classifieds, e.g., "Viele sahen ihre Heimat NIE wieder," *FW*, 24 Dec. 1993.
55. Interview, Ingrid Dreyer.
56. Interview, Helmut Traub.
57. Border trials: McAdams, *Judging*, 23–53; Grafe, *Gerechtigkeit*. Organizations supporting former troops: http://grenztruppen-der-ddr.org; www.grenztruppen-der-ddr.de.
58. Steinhäuser, "Der Mann in Schwarz," *Bild* (Thüringen), 5 Oct. 2001; "Gedenktafel erinnert an DDR-Unrecht," *FW*, 5 Oct. 2001.
59. E.g., "Keine Einladung zum Spielen," *ST*, 23 Jan. 1992.
60. Interview, Herbert Schacht; "In der Praxis wurde Partnerschaft durch Bürger schon vollzogen," *FW*, 23 Nov. 1989.
61. Interview, Herbert Schacht.
62. "Gesprächsforum," *FW*, 20 Nov. 2003; interviews, Volker Langer, Klaus Treichel, Lothar Hentschel, Neustadt, 17 Dec. 2002. Earlier: "Solidarität mit den DDR-Bürgern," *CT*, 4 Dec. 1989. Coordination: e.g., SA-N EAP 001-13/3d; StA-C BGS 66.
63. SA-N EAP 023-35/0, 35/2, esp. "Städtepartnerschaften," 17 Oct. 1990. E.g., "'Nikolaus' kam mit 10 000 Mark-Präsent," *NT*, 5 Dec. 1990; Koch, "Außer Spesen nicht viel gewesen," *NT*, 16–17 Feb. 1991; "Weitere Partnerschafts-Hilfe," *NT*, 19 Jul. 1991. The cities' formal partnership was signed February 10, 1990, and was contentious from the start; SA-N EAP 023-35/0, 35/1. Joint projects: SA-N EAP 023-35/7, 35/8.
64. Private possession, Schacht, petitions, and interview.
65. Interview, Wolfgang Mayerhofer.
66. Interview, Herbert Schacht.
67. Eghigian, "Homo Munitus."
68. Interview, Edgar Pfisterer.
69. Leuenberger, "Constructions," 27; Michael Linden et al., *Posttraumatic Embitterment Disorder* (Toronto: Hogrefe & Huber, 2007).
70. Interview, Ulrike Schwarz, Sonneberg, 13 Feb. 2003.
71. Interview, Ingrid Dreyer.
72. "Es war einmal . . . 'Der gute alte Osten' Kirmes in Bettelhecken," *Amadeus*, 21 Aug. 2002; "Bettelhecker Kirchweih," *Amadeus*, 19 Sep. 2002; "Sperrgebiet," *FW*, 31 Aug. 2002.
73. Controversy, 1991–1992: SA-N EAP 001-06/36, 06/38.
74. E.g., "Eine Beziehung mit unklarem Gefälle," *CT*, 22 Nov. 1991; "Frieden im Kleinen mit sich selbst schließen," *NP*, 22 Nov. 1991.
75. SA-N EAP 001-13/3, Fischer, 7 May 1990, plus file; "Großartiger Erfolg," *NP*, 3 Aug. 1990; SA-N EAP 140-40. Sonneberg: "Hönbacher fordern Umgehung," *NT*, 3–4 Nov. 1990.
76. "Plakataktion wird gestartet," *NP*, 29 Aug. 1991.
77. Regional overview: Jones and Wild, "Opening"; Kawka, "Development."
78. Scherzer, "Über zwei Städte, die dicht an dicht und doch weit voneinander entfernt liegen Herzens-Sachen," *FW*, 14 Jan. 2005.
79. E.g., "So gibt es keinen Aufschwung," *ST*, 24 Apr. 1991; "Hönbach-Kritik zurückgewiesen," *ST*, 29 Apr. 1991.
80. "Sonneberg-Neustadt," *NP*, 28 Mar. 2001.
81. E.g., "Grenzgänger aus Sonneberg in Neustadt um Erfahrung reicher," *FW*, 19 Nov. 1999; Brückmann, "Bayerische Schulen sind gar nicht so schlecht," *CT*, 1 Nov. 2009.
82. KrA-S In. 2683-1035, Sauerteig, 12 May 1989. "Culturized" racism in Europe: Eley, "Trouble."
83. Sources of remembrance: Sabrow, ed., *Erinnerungsorte*.
84. Sheffer, Survey, "Gebrannte Brücke," details in Bibliography.
85. Local prejudices appeared even stronger. Twenty-six percent of former westerners said they had a "positive" opinion of Sonnebergers, and 39 percent of former easterners had a "positive" opinion of Neustadters. Only 5 percent of former East Germans said that Neustadters saw Sonnebergers positively, and 9 percent of former West Germans said that Sonnebergers saw Neustadters positively.
86. Details: Sheffer, "Burned Bridge," 615.
87. Ibid., 613. For example, 44 percent of former easterners said they "agreed" with the East German government's values versus just 1 percent of former westerners; only 36 percent of easterners said they regarded the current Federal Republic as a "fair system," versus 72 percent of westerners. Both former westerners and easterners said they were disappointed at how reunification was "carried out" (63 and

49 percent, respectively) though they were nonetheless "happy that reunification happened" (76 and 85 percent). Seventy-four percent of former East Germans said that "more should have been incorporated from the GDR," versus just 20 percent of former West Germans.

88. The ratio of former westerners and easterners, respectively, stating that the following bore "no responsibility" for border escalation: the United States, 53 versus 28 percent; the Soviet Union, 5 versus 8 percent; West Germany, 73 versus 30 percent; East Germany, 7 versus 9 percent; Neustadters, 93 versus 90 percent; Sonnebergers, 81 versus 90 percent.

89. "Ein wenig mehr Eigenverantwortung," *NP*, 20 Jun. 2009; Friedrich, "Jeder kämpft für seine eigene Stadt," *NP*, 14 Nov. 2009.

90. Scherzer, "Acht gleiche Fragen an Jugendliche in Sonneberg und Neustadt," *FW*, 1 Feb. 2005; Scherzer, *Grenz-Gänger*, 132–142.

91. Scherzer, "Acht gleiche Fragen."

92. "Veranstaltungen zu '20 Jahre Grenzöffnung in der Region,'" *Amtsblatt des Landkreises Sonneberg*, 31 Oct. 2009.

93. Interview, Erich Klinger.

94. Interview, Ingrid Holzmann.

95. Germany as a continental border zone: Lindenberger, "Zonenrand."

96. The dissimilarity of these cases has yielded few comparisons: Stueck, "United States." Additional on Austria: Bischof, *Austria*; Rauchensteiner and Kriechbaumer, eds., *Gunst*. Korea: Cumings, *Korean War*; Stueck, *Rethinking*.

97. Judt, *Postwar*.

98. Sheehan, *Soldiers*.

99. Maier, "Transformations." From jurisdictional to territorial sovereignty: Sahlins, *Boundaries*, 2–7.

100. Hargreaves, "West African," 101.

101. Moon, *Divide and Quit*; Kumar, "Partition"; Schaeffer, *Severed States*, 41–55. Overview: O'Leary, "Partition."

102. Baud and Schendel, "Comparative History," 227–228.

103. Samaddar, "Last Hurrah."

104. Chandler, *Institutions*; Si-Woo, *Life*; Hahm, *Living*.

105. Martinez, *Border People*, 5–10.

106. Andreas, "Redrawing."

107. E.g., Andreas and Snyder, eds., *Wall*; Ganster and Lorey, *Borders*; Kahler and Walter, eds. *Territoriality*.

108. Brown, *Walled States*.

109. Torpey, *Invention*.

110. Brown, *Walled States*, 20.

111. Andreas and Snyder, eds., *Wall Around the West*.

112. Hundley, "The New Iron Curtain," *Chicago Tribune*, 30 Mar. 2008.

113. Davies, "Melilla: Europe's Dirty Secret," *Guardian*, 17 Apr. 2010.

114. Ganster and Lorey, *U.S.-Mexican Border*, 190.

115. Mackey, "Thousands Sign up for Virtual Border Patrol," *NYT*, 26 Mar. 2009; Texas Border Sheriff's Coalition, www.texasborderwatch.com.

116. By year: Stuart Anderson, "Death at the Border," *National Foundation for American Policy*, May 2010. www.nfap.com/pdf/0505brief-death-at-border.pdf; Hertle and Nooke, *Todesopfer*, 18.

117. Anzaldúa, *Borderlands/La Frontera*, 25.

118. E.g., Brown, *Walled States*, 8–20; Debusmann, "Around Globe, Walls Spring Up to Divide Neighbors," *Reuters*, 30 Apr. 2007.

119. In Sonneberg County, at Heinersdorf. Memorialization after 1989: Ullrich, *Geteilte Ansichten*, 163–292. Grünes Band in Sonneberg: http://www.lkson.de/gbw/index.html.

120. Mines still found: "Scharfe Mine im Wald gesprengt," *NP*, 4 Aug. 2010. Initial clearings: StA-C BGS 66, "Minenüberprüfung," 1 Jun. 1992.

121. Administration and dwindling attendance: SA-N EAP 001-06/20, 21, 23, 30.

BIBLIOGRAPHY

Archival Sources

AUSWÄRTIGES AMT, POLITISCHES ARCHIV (AA)
POLITICAL ARCHIVE OF THE GERMAN FOREIGN OFFICE

B10 Abt. 2 — Politische Abteilung
B38-IIA1 — Berlin und Deutschland als Ganzes

BUNDESARCHIV, BERLIN-LICHTERFELDE (BArch-B)
FEDERAL ARCHIVE, BERLIN-LICHTERFELDE

BY 1 — Kommunistische Partei Deutschlands—West
DA 5 — Staatsrat der DDR
DC 20 I/3 — Sitzungen des Ministerrates
DC 20 I/4 — Präsidium des Ministerrates
DE 1 — Staatsplankommission
DO 1 — Ministerium des Innern
DO 1 8.0 — Hauptabteilung Paß- und Meldewesen
DO 1 34.0 — Hauptabteilung Innere Angelegenheiten

STIFTUNG ARCHIV DER PARTEIEN UND MASSENORGANISATIONEN DER DDR IM BUNDESARCHIV (BArch-SAPMO)
ARCHIVES OF THE PARTIES AND MASS ORGANIZATIONS OF EAST GERMANY IN THE FEDERAL ARCHIVES

DY 30 — Zentralkomitee der SED
DY 30/IV 2/2 — Beschlüsse des Politbüros
DY 30/IV 2/12 — Abteilung für Sicherheitsfragen
DY 30/J IV 2/2 — Protokolle der Sitzungen des Politbüros
DY 30/J IV 2/2J — Büro Walter Ulbricht
DY 47 — Örtliche Wirtschaft
NY 4090 — Nachlaß Otto Grotewohl

BUNDESARCHIV, KOBLENZ (BArch-K)
FEDERAL ARCHIVE, KOBLENZ

B106 — Bundesministerium des Innern
B136 — Bundeskanzleramt
B137 — Bundesministerium für gesamtdeutsche Fragen
B285 — Gesamtdeutsches Institut—Bundesanstalt für gesamtdeutsche Aufgaben

BUNDESARCHIV, MILITÄRARCHIV FREIBURG (BArch-MA)
FEDERAL MILITARY ARCHIVE, FREIBURG

GR15	Grenzregiment 15, Sonneberg
GB13	Grenzbrigade 13, Rudolstadt
VA-03	Militärbezirk III

BUNDESBEAUFTRAGTE FÜR DIE UNTERLAGEN DES STAATSSICHERHEITSDIENSTES, AUßENSTELLE SUHL (BStU)
FEDERAL COMMISSIONER FOR THE RECORDS OF THE STATE SECURITY SERVICE OF THE FORMER GERMAN DEMOCRATIC REPUBLIC, SUHL

BV Suhl, Abt. VII	Abwehrarbeit in MdI und DVP
BV Suhl, Abt. XX	Staatsapparat, Kultur, Kirche, Untergrund
BV Suhl, AFO	Archivierte Feindobjektakte
BV Suhl, AIM	Archivierter IM-Vorgang
BV Suhl, AKG	Auswertungs- und Kontrollgruppe
BV Suhl, AOP	Archivierter Operativer Vorgang
BV Suhl, BdL/Dok	Büro der Leitung/Dokumentenstelle
BV Suhl, KD SON	Kreisdienststelle Sonneberg
BV Suhl XI	Bezirksverwaltung Suhl
MfS BdL/Dok	Büro der Leitung/Dokumentenstelle
MfS HA I	Abwehrarbeit in NVA und Grenztruppen
MfS HA VI	Passkontrolle, Tourismus, Interhotel
MfS HA IX	Untersuchungsorgan
MfS JHS	Juristische Hochschule Potsdam
MfS Sekr. Neiber	Sekretariat des Stellvertreters Gerhard Neiber
MfS ZAIG	Zentrale Auswertungs- und Informationsgruppe
MfS ZKG	Zentrale Koordinierungsgruppe

BAYERISCHES HAUPTSTAATSARCHIV, MÜNCHEN (BayHStA)
BAVARIAN CENTRAL STATE ARCHIVE, MUNICH

B-MInn	Ministerium des Innern
B-StK	Staatskanzlei
BayObLG	Bayerisches Oberstes Landesgericht
LflüV	Landesflüchtlingsverwaltung
MSo	Ministerium für Sonderaufgaben, Minister für Politische Befreiung
MWi	Ministerium für Wirtschaft, Infrastruktur, Verkehr und Technologie
OMGB-CO	Office of the Military Government of Bavaria, Coburg
PrBGP	Präsidium der Grenzpolizei
PrBLP	Präsidium der Landpolizei

KREISARCHIV SONNEBERG (KrA-S)
SONNEBERG COUNTY ARCHIVE

In.	Abteilung Inneres
KrPK	Kreisplankommission
St. Vors.	Stellvertretender Vorsitzender
Vors.	Vorsitzender des Kreises

POLIZEIINSPEKTION NEUSTADT BEI COBURG (NP-A)
NEUSTADT BEI COBURG POLICE OFFICE ARCHIVE

| 564-8 I and II | Flüchtlinge aus der DDR |

STAATSARCHIV COBURG (StA-C)
COBURG STATE ARCHIVE

AG-N	Amtsgericht Neustadt bei Coburg
BGS	Bundesgrenzschutz
LRA	Landratsamt Coburg
StAnw	Staatsanwaltschaft bei dem Landgericht Coburg

STADTARCHIV NEUSTADT BEI COBURG (SA-N)
NEUSTADT CITY ARCHIVE

SA-N	Altaktei
EAP	Einheitsaktenplan
MB	Manuskripte und Briefe
Obgm	Oberbürgermeister
StRPr	Stadtratsprotokolle

STADTARCHIV SONNEBERG (SA-S)
SONNEBERG CITY ARCHIVE

C2	Stadtrat und Bürgermeister
C3	Organisationsabteilung und Sekretär
C6	Wohnraumlenkung
C10	Sozialfürsorge
C16	Arbeit mit der Besatzungsmacht

UNITED STATES NATIONAL ARCHIVES AND RECORDS ADMINISTRATION, COLLEGE PARK, MD (NACP)

RG226	Office of Strategic Services
RG243	U.S. Strategic Bombing Survey
RG260	U.S. Occupation Headquarters, World War II
RG338	U.S. Army Operational, Tactical, and Support Organizations
RG407	Adjutant General's Office
RG466	U.S. High Commissioner for Germany

THÜRINGISCHES HAUPTSTAATSARCHIV WEIMAR (ThHStAW)
THURINGIAN CENTRAL STATE ARCHIVE, WEIMAR

BMPr	Büro des Ministerpräsidenten
GStAnw-E	Generalstaatswanwalt Erfurt
LBdVP	Landesbehörde der Volkspolizei Thüringen
Th-MInn	Ministerium des Innern

THÜRINGISCHES STAATSARCHIV MEININGEN (StA-M)
THURINGIAN STATE ARCHIVE, MEININGEN

Bib.	Bibliothek
BT RdBz-Su, K	Bezirkstag, Rat des Bezirkes Suhl
KR-S	Kreisrat des Landkreises Sonneberg
RdBz-Su	Rat des Bezirkes Suhl
RdBz-Su, In.	Innere Angelegenheiten
RdBz-Su, KmAbz.	Kommunale Auslandsbeziehungen
RdBz-Su, Sek.	Sekretär des Rates
RdBz-Su, Vors.	Vorsitzender
SED-BL-Suhl	SED Bezirksleitung Suhl
SED-KL-Sbg	SED Kreisleitung Sonneberg
VPKA-Sbg	Volkspolizei-Kreisamt Sonneberg

INTERVIEWS

Fifty-two interviews were conducted, with dates and locations cited in the notes. Tapes and transcripts are in the author's possession. Pseudonyms have been assigned to each.

PRIVATE COLLECTIONS

Twenty-four individuals shared private papers, photographs, and videos. Copies of personal collections are in the author's possession. Pseudonyms have been assigned to each.

Mailed Survey

"GEBRANNTE BRÜCKE: OST- UND WESTDEUTSCHLAND IM GRENZGEBIET SEIT 1945."

A nine-page survey was mailed in February 2003 to 500 people selected at random, half in Neustadt and half in Sonneberg. In total, 129 Neustadters and 130 Sonnebergers responded. All respondents except one stated they were of German nationality; a dozen recipients with non-German surnames did not answer. Because some respondents had moved from the former East Germany to Neustadt after reunification, results were most meaningful when analyzed by residence before 1989, rather than by current place of residence. Five respondents who had emigrated from East Germany to Neustadt before 1989 (in 1952, 1957, 1961, and 1975) were counted as "former West Germans."

The groups of 119 former West German and 140 former East German respondents were demographically similar. For both, the mean year of birth was 1950; 95 percent were over thirty years old at the time of the survey. Three-quarters of each group reported that one or both of their parents had been born in the region (around 10 percent born in the city opposite from where they now live), and half reported their ancestors lived in the region before 1900. The group of former westerners had slightly more men (57 to 53 percent), was more affluent (42 to 29 percent reporting a household net monthly income above 2,000 euros), and was more prone to claim religious affiliation (97 to 46 percent).

NEWSPAPERS AND PERIODICALS

Amadeus, Amtsblatt des Landkreises Sonneberg, Augsburger Allgemeine, Bayerische Staatszeitung, Bayerisches Volks-Echo, Berliner Illustrierte, Berliner Zeitung, Bild, Coburger Geschichtsblätter, Coburger Tageblatt, Echo der Woche, Esslinger Zeitung, Fachbereich Standardisierung Spielwaren, Frankenpost, Frankfurter Allgemeine Zeitung, Fränkischen Presse, Die Freie Wort, Freies Wort, Grenzlandmagazin, Kronacher Volksblatt, Der Lautsprecher (Stern-Radio, Sonneberg), Lebensmittelgroßhandel, Los Angeles Times, Monatshefte des Bayerischen Statistischen Landesamts, Münchner Merkur, Neue Presse, Neue Zeitung, Neues Deutschland, Neustadter Tageblatt, New York Times, Nord-Ost Bayerisches Grenzland Magazin, Nürnberger Nachrichten, Ost-West Kurrier, Rheinischer Merkur, Sonneberger Bauernzeitung, Sonneberger Kulturspiegel, Sonneberger Museums- und Geschichtsverein, Sonneberger Rundschau—Sonni-Express, Sonneberger Zeitung, Der Spiegel, Stuttgarter Nachrichten, Süddeutsche Zeitung, Südthüringer Heimatblätter, Südthüringer Tageblatt, Tageblatt Neustadt, Tages-Anzeiger Regensburg, Thüringer Tageszeitung, Thüringer Volk, Thüringer Volkszeitung, Time, Das Volk, Völkischer Beobachter, Washington Post, Die Welt, Der Wühlpflug, Die Zeit.

Books and Theses

25 Jahre Deutsche Demokratische Republik: Bilddokumente aus dem Kreis Sonneberg. Sonneberg: SED Kreisleitung, 1974.

Ackermann, Volker. *Der "echte" Flüchtling: Deutsche Vertriebene und Flüchtlinge aus der DDR, 1945–1961.* Osnabrück: Universitätsverlag Rasch, 1995.

Adam, Alfred. *Das Volk durfte wieder wählen: Das Wiederaufleben der parlamentarischen Demokratie von 1946 bis 1949 unter besonderer Berücksichtigung von Coburg, Kronach, Lichtenfels u. Ebern.* Coburg: Neue Presse, 1966.

Ahonen, Pertti. *After the Expulsion: West Germany and Eastern Europe, 1945–1990.* Oxford: Oxford University Press, 2003.

———. *Death at the Berlin Wall.* Oxford: Oxford University Press, 2011.

———. "Defending Socialism? Benito Corghi and the German-German Border." In "Migration: Crossing Borders," special issue, *History in Focus* 11 (2006).

———. "The Curious Case of Werner Weinhold: Escape, Death, and Contested Legitimacy at the German-German Border." *Central European History* (forthcoming).

Albert, Reinhold, and Hans-Jürgen Salier. *Grenzerfahrungen Kompakt: Das Grenzregime zwischen Südthüringen und Bayern/Hessen von 1945 bis 1990.* Leipzig: Salier, 2009.

Allinson, Mark. *Politics and Popular Opinion in East Germany, 1945–68.* Manchester: Manchester University Press, 2000.

Altrichter, Frank. "Im Schatten der Zonengrenze: Die Erschließung des bayerischen Grenzlandes 1945–1973—eine Nahaufnahme Oberfrankens." Ph.D. diss., Friedrich-Alexander-University of Erlangen, in preparation.

Amos, Heike. *Die Westpolitik der SED 1948/49–1961: "Arbeit nach Westdeutschland" durch die Nationale Front, das Ministerium für Auswärtige Angelegenheiten und das Ministerium für Staatssicherheit.* Berlin: Akademie, 1999.

Anderson, Malcolm. *Frontiers: Territory and State Formation in the Modern World.* Cambridge, UK: Polity, 1997.

Andreas, Peter. "Redrawing the Line: Borders and Security in the Twenty-First Century." *International Security* 28 (2003): 78–111.

Andreas, Peter, and Timothy Snyder. *The Wall Around the West: State Borders and Immigration Controls in North America and Europe.* Lanham, MD: Rowman & Littlefield, 2000.

Anzaldúa, Gloria. *Borderlands/La Frontera: The New Mestiza.* 2nd ed. San Francisco: Aunt Lute Books, 1999.

Applegate, Celia. *A Nation of Provincials: The German Idea of Heimat.* Berkeley: University of California Press, 1990.

Armbruster, Heide, and Ulrike H. Meinhof. "Working Identities: Key Narratives in a Former Border Region in Germany." In *Living (with) Borders: Identity Discourses on East-West Borders in Europe,* edited by Ulrike H. Meinhof, 15–32. Aldershot: Ashgate, 2002.

Aumann, Georg. *Coburg: Stadt und Land.* Coburg: Verkehrsverein Coburg, 1985.

Bachmann, Harald. "45 Jahre Teilung Deutschlands im fränkisch-thüringischen Grenzraum: Die innerdeutsche Grenze als Schicksal unseres Heimatraums in der Nachkriegsgeschichte." *Coburger Geschichtsblätter* 4 (99): 111–127.

———. "Coburgs Anschluß an Bayern vor 75 Jahren." *Coburger Geschichtsblätter* 3 (95): 104–118.

Bailey, Anthony. *Along the Edge of the Forest: An Iron Curtain Journey.* New York: Random House, 1983.

Ballinger, Pamela. *History in Exile: Memory and Identity at the Borders of the Balkans.* Princeton: Princeton University Press, 2003.

Baud, Michiel, and Willem Van Schendel. "Toward a Comparative History of Borderlands." *Journal of World History* 8 (1997): 211–242.

Baumgarten, Klaus-Dieter, and Peter Freitag. *Die Grenzen der DDR: Geschichte, Fakten, Hintergründe.* Berlin: Edition Ost, 2004.

Bennewitz, Inge. "'Das verurteilte Dorf': Ein Eigentor für die SED-Propaganda." *Deutschland Archiv* 5 (2003): 772–789.

Bennewitz, Inge, and Rainer Potratz. *Zwangsaussiedlungen an der innerdeutschen Grenze: Analysen und Dokumente.* Berlin: Ch. Links, 1994.

Berdahl, Daphne. *Where the World Ended: Re-Unification and Identity in the German Borderland.* Berkeley: University of California Press, 1999.

Berghahn, Volker. "Recasting Bourgeois Germany." In *The Miracle Years: A Cultural History of West Germany, 1949–1968,* edited by Hanna Schissler, 326–340. Princeton: Princeton University Press, 2001.

Bergmann, Ernst. *Suchet der Stadt Bestes! Gedanken und Sorge um Neustadt.* Neustadt bei Coburg: Patzschke, 1983.

Bessel, Richard. *Germany 1945: From War to Peace.* New York: HarperCollins, 2009.

———. "The Making of a Border: Policing East Germany's Western Border, 1945–1952." In *L'établissement des Frontières en Europe après les Deux Guerres Mondiales,* edited by Christian Baechler and Carole Fink, 199–214. Bern: Peter Lang, 1996.

———. "Policing in East Germany in the Wake of the Second World War." *Crime, Histoire et Sociétés* 7 (2003): 5–21.

Bessel, Richard, and Ralph Jessen. *Die Grenzen der Diktatur: Staat und Gesellschaft in der DDR.* Göttingen: Vandenhoeck & Ruprecht, 1996.

Beth, Hans-Joachim, and Hans Gotthard Ehlert. *Die Militär- und Sicherheitspolitik in der SBZ/DDR: Eine Bibliographie (1945–1995).* Munich: Oldenbourg, 1996.

Betts, Paul. *Within Walls: Private Life in the German Democratic Republic.* Oxford: Oxford University Press, 2010.

Beyersdorf, Peter. "Militärregierung und Selbstverwaltung: Eine Studie zur amerikanischen Besatzungspolitik auf der Stufe einer Gemeinde in den Jahren 1945–1948, dargestellt an Beispielen aus dem Stadt- u. Landkreis Coburg." Universität Erlangen-Nürnberg, 1967.

Bierer, Willy. "Die hausindustrielle Kinderarbeit im Kreise Sonneberg." Universität München, 1913.

Biess, Frank. "'Everybody Has a Chance': Civil Defense, Nuclear Angst, and the History of Emotions in Post-war Germany." *German History* 27 (2009): 215–243.

———. *Homecomings: Returning POWs and the Legacies of Defeat in Postwar Germany*. Princeton: Princeton University Press, 2006.

Biess, Frank, and Robert Moeller, eds. *Histories of the Aftermath: The Legacies of the Second World War in Europe*. New York: Berghahn, 2010.

Bischof, Günter. *Austria in the First Cold War, 1945–1955: The Leverage of the Weak*. New York: St. Martin's Press, 1999.

Black, Monica. *Death in Berlin: From Weimar to Divided Germany*. Cambridge, UK: Cambridge University Press, 2010.

Blackbourn, David, and Geoff Eley. *The Peculiarities of German History: Bourgeois Society and Politics in Nine-teenth-Century Germany*. Oxford: Oxford University Press, 1984.

Blackbourn, David, and James Retallack, eds. *Localism, Landscape, and the Ambiguities of Place: German-Speak-ing Central Europe, 1860–1930*. Toronto: Toronto University Press, 2007.

Blaive, Muriel, and Berthold Molden, *Grenzfälle: Österreichische und tschechische Erfahrungen am Eisernen Vorhang*. Weitra: Bibliothek der Provinz, 2009.

Blessing, Benita. *The Antifascist Classroom: Denazification in Soviet-occupied Germany, 1945–1949*. New York: Palgrave Macmillan, 2006.

Boehling, Rebecca. *A Question of Priorities: Democratic Reforms and Economic Recovery in Postwar Germany*. Providence: Berghahn, 1996.

Borneff, Karl. "Aufsätze 1952–1988." Coburg, 1989. Landesbibliothek Coburg.

———. *Zonengrenze 1945–1985: Grafik, Malerei, Fotos*. Coburg: Neue Presse, 1985.

Borneman, John. *Belonging in the Two Berlins: Kin, State, Nation*. Cambridge, UK: Cambridge University Press, 1992.

Bretschneider, Günter. "Es brennt, es brennt . . . !" In *Unsere Coburger Heimat: Erzählungen und Berichte*, edited by Walter Eichhorn, 54–55. Coburg: Verl. Blätter zur Geschichte d. Coburger Landes, 1987.

———. *Freiheit ohne Grenzen*. Neustadt bei Coburg: Patzschke, 1990.

———. *Die Geschichte des Neustadter Kinderfestes*. Neustadt bei Coburg: Patzschke, 1987.

———. *Grenzen öffnen sich: Neustadt und Sonneberg finden wieder zusammen*. Neustadt bei Coburg: Bret-schneider, 1990.

Brown, Kate. *A Biography of No Place: From Ethnic Borderland to Soviet Heartland*. Cambridge, MA: Harvard University Press, 2003.

Brown, Wendy. *Walled States, Waning Sovereignty*. New York: Zone Books, 2010.

Brubaker, Rogers. *Ethnicity Without Groups*. Cambridge, MA: Harvard University Press, 2004.

Bruce, Gary. *The Firm: The Inside Story of the Stasi*. New York: Oxford University Press, 2010.

———. "The Prelude to Nationwide Surveillance in East Germany: Stasi Operations and Threat Perceptions, 1945–1953." *Journal of Cold War Studies* 5 (2003): 3–31.

Buckow, Anjana. *Zwischen Propaganda und Realpolitik: Die USA und der sowjetisch besetzte Teil Deutschlands 1945–1955*. Stuttgart: Franz Steiner, 2003.

Bundesministerium für innerdeutsche Beziehungen. *Der Bau der Mauer durch Berlin: Die Flucht aus der Sow-jetzone und die Sperrmassnahmen des kommunistischen Regimes vom 13. August 1961 in Berlin*. Bonn: Gesamtdeutsches Institut, 1986.

———. *Die innerdeutsche Grenze*. Bonn: Gesamtdeutsches Institut, 1987.

———. *Die Sperrmassnahmen der DDR vom Mai 1952: Die Sperrmassnahmen der Sowjetzonenregierung an der Zonengrenze und um Westberlin*. Bonn: Gesamtdeutsches Institut, 1987.

———. *Wo Deutschland noch geteilt ist. Beiderseits der innerdeutschen Grenze*. Bonn: Gesamtdeutsches Institut, 1984.

Burg, Peter. *Die deutsche Trias in Idee und Wirklichkeit: Vom alten Reich zum Deutschen Zollverein*. Stuttgart: Steiner, 1989.

Büschel, Hubertus. "Entgrenzte Heimat: 'Emotives' im Herbst 1989." In *Differenzerfahrung und Selbst: Bewusst-sein und Wahrnehmung in Literatur und Geschichte des 20. Jahrhunderts*, edited by Bettina von Jagow and Florian Steger. Heidelberg: Winter, 2003.

Caldwell, Peter. *Dictatorship, State Planning, and Social Theory in the German Democratic Republic*. Cambridge, UK: Cambridge University Press, 2003.

Chandler, Andrea. *Institutions of Isolation: Border Controls in the Soviet Union and Its Successor States, 1917–1993*. Montreal: McGill-Queen's University Press, 1998.

Chin, Rita. *The Guest Worker Question in Postwar Germany*. Cambridge, UK: Cambridge University Press, 2007.

Coburg Mayor and Upper Franconian Chamber of Commerce, "Grenzland in Not." October 1952. Staatsbibliothek Coburg, 3.90 COB 67, 31.

Cohen, Stanley. *Folk Devils and Moral Panics: The Creation of the Mods and Rockers*. London: Routledge, 2002.

Confino, Alon. *The Nation as a Local Metaphor: Würtemberg, Imperial Germany, and National Memory, 1871–1918*. Chapel Hill: University of North Carolina Press, 1997.

Connelly, John. *Captive University: the Sovietization of East German, Czech, and Polish Higher Education, 1945–1956*. Chapel Hill: University of North Carolina Press, 2000.

———. "The Uses of Volksgemeinschaft: Letters to the NSDAP Kreisleitung Eisenach, 1939–1940." *Journal of Modern History* 68 (1996): 899–930.

Creuzberger, Stefan. *Kampf für die Einheit: Das gesamtdeutsche Ministerium und die politische Kultur des Kalten Krieges 1949–1969*. Düsseldorf: Droste, 2008.

Crew, David. *Consuming Germany in the Cold War*. Oxford: Berg, 2003.

Cumings, Bruce. *The Korean War: A History*. New York: Modern Library, 2010.

Daum, Andreas. *Kennedy in Berlin*. New York: Cambridge University Press, 2008.

Decker, Bernard H. "The Wall as Seen Through the Eyes of Border Guards: The Border as a Literary Topos Within the Framework of Socialist Defense Readiness Education." In *The Berlin Wall*, edited by Ernst Schürer, Manfred Keune, and Philip Jenkins, 119–125. New York: Peter Lang, 1996.

Dennis, Mike. *The Stasi: Myth and Reality*. London: Longman, 2003.

Derix, Simone. "Facing an 'Emotional Crunch': State Visits as Political Performances During the Cold War." *German Politics and Society Journal* 25 (2007): 117–139.

Diedrich, Torsten. *Waffen gegen das Volk: Der 17. Juni 1953 in der DDR*. Munich: Oldenbourg, 2003.

Dierske, Ludwig. *Der Bundesgrenzschutz: Geschichtliche Darstellung seiner Aufgabe und Entwicklung von der Aufstellung bis zum 31. März 1963*. Regensburg: Walhalla & Praetoria, 1967.

Dietzsch, Ina. *Grenzen überschreiben? Deutsch-deutsche Briefwechsel 1948–1989*. Cologne: Böhlau, 2004.

Dlouhy, Richard. *Die Wirtschaft im Coburger Grenzland*. Kulmbach: Baumann, 1982.

Döbrich, Wilhelm. "Wie wurde der Aufruf des Zentralkomitees vom 11. Juli 1945 in Sonneberg bekannt und wie wurde er den Burgern erläutert?" Bezirksparteischule Schleusingen, 1973. SED-BL-Suhl V/1/1/074.

Donnan, Hastings, and Thomas M. Wilson. *Borders: Frontiers of Identity, Nation and State*. Oxford: Berg, 1999.

Dorst, Tankred. "Die Villa." In *Deutsche Stücke*, 377–451. Frankfurt am Main: Suhrkamp, 1985.

Eckardt, Erich. "Ein Augenzeuge berichtet." In *Wider das Vergessen: 10 Jahre Grenzöffnung Heinersdorf-Welitsch*, edited by Sabine Bergmann-Pohl and Rudolf Pfadenhauer, 9–14. Kronach: Druck & Media, 1999.

Eckert, Astrid. "The East of the West." *Der Tagespiegel*, September 10, 2010.

———. "'Greetings from the Zonal Border': Tourism to the Iron Curtain in West Germany." *Zeithistorischen Studien* Studies in Contemporary History, Online Ausgabe, 8 (2011).

———. "'Zaun-Gäste.' Die innerdeutsche Grenze als Touristenattraktion." In *Grenz/ziehungen/erfahrungen/ überschreitungen. Niedersachsen und die innerdeutsche Grenze 1945–1990* [exhibition catalogue], edited by Detlef Schmiechen-Ackermann, Carl-Hans Hauptmeyer, and Thomas Schwark, 243–251. Darmstadt: WBG, 2011.

Effner, Bettina, and Helge Heidemeyer. *Flucht im geteilten Deutschland*. Berlin: Bebra, 2005.

Eghigian, Greg. "Homo Munitus: The East German Observed." In *Socialist Modern: East German Everyday Culture and Politics*, edited by Katherine Pence and Paul Betts, 37–70. Ann Arbor: University of Michigan Press, 2008.

Eichhorn, Walter. *Blick nach drüben: Coburg und seine thüringischen Nachbarn*. Coburg: Neue Presse, 1983.

Eichhorn-Nelson, Wally. *Von Sonneberg zur Rennsteighöhe*. Rudolstadt: Greifenverlag, 1968.

Eisenberg, Carolyn Woods. *Drawing the Line: The American Decision to Divide Germany, 1944–1949*. Cambridge, UK: Cambridge University Press, 1996.

Eisenkrätzer, Heinz, et al. *Aus der Geschichte des Volkspolizei-Kreisamtes Sonneberg: Von 1945 bis zum X. Parteitag der SED*. Sonneberg: Komm. zur Erforschung d. Volkspolizei-Kreisamtes, 1986.

Eley, Geoff. "The Trouble with Race: Migrancy, Cultural Difference, and the Remaking of Europe." In *After the Nazi Racial State: Difference and Democracy in Germany and Europe*, edited by Rita Chin, Heide Fehrenbach, Geoff Eley, and Atina Grossmann, 137–181. Ann Arbor: University of Michigan Press, 2009.

Elton, Catherine. "The Jivaro People Between Peru and Ecuador." In *Borders and Border Politics in a Globalizing World*, edited by Paul Ganster and David Lorey, 107–115. Lanham, MD: SR Books, 2005.

Engel, Jeffrey A., ed. *Local Consequences of the Global Cold War*. Washington, DC: Woodrow Wilson Center Press, 2007.

Epstein, Catherine. *The Last Revolutionaries: German Communists and Their Century*. Cambridge, MA: Harvard University Press, 2003.

———. "The Stasi: New Research on the East German Ministry of State Security." *Kritika* 5 (2004): 321–348.

Erdmann, Jürgen. "Anschluss war Akt der Zukunftssicherung: Coburg wahrte seine kulturhistorische Identität." In *Coburg: 75 Jahre bei Bayern*, 20–23. Coburg: Neue Presse, 1995.

Ermarth, Michael. *America and the Shaping of German Society, 1945–1955.* Providence: Berg, 1993.

Falkenberg, Jörg, and Richard Dlouhy. *Die Wirtschaft im Coburger Grenzland.* Kulmbach: E. C. Baumann, 1982.

Fehrenbach, Heide. *Race After Hitler: Black Occupation Children in Postwar Germany and America.* Princeton: Princeton University Press, 2005.

Fenemore, Mark. *Sex, Thugs and Rock 'n' Roll: Teenage Rebels in Cold-War East Germany.* New York: Berghahn, 2009.

Fischer, Julius. *650 Jahre Ebersdorf bei Neustadt im Landkreis Coburg.* Ebersdorf b. Neustadt: 1967.

Foucault, Michel. *Discipline and Punish: The Birth of the Prison.* Translated by Alan Sheridan. 2nd ed. New York: Vintage, 1995.

Frantzen, Günter. "Entwicklung Neustadt bei Coburg." Institut für Städtebau und Raumplanung: Technische Universität München, 1976–77.

Freyer, Elisabeth. "Mein Vater hat leidenschaftlich gern Kontra gegeben." In *Die Schuld der Mitläufer Anpassen oder Widerstehen in der DDR*, edited by Roman Grafe, 59–68. Munich: Pantheon, 2009.

Fromm, Hubert. *Die Coburger Juden: Geschichte und Schicksal.* Coburg: Evang. Bildungswerk Coburg, 1990.

———. *Eingliederung der Heimatvertriebenen im Coburger Raum.* Coburg: Landratsamt, 1986.

Fuchs, Norbert. *Billmuthausen: Das verurteilte Dorf.* Hildburghausen: Frankenschwelle, 1991.

Fugmann, Ernst. *Der Sonneberger Wirtschaftsraum: Eine Wirtschaftsgeographie des Südthüringer Waldes und seines Vorlandes.* Halle: Niemeyer, 1939.

Fuhrmann, Michael. "Suche, Auswahl, Aufklärung und Werbung von IM zur direkten Bearbeitung subversiver Kräfte aus dem Grenzvorfeld der BRD." Juristische Hochschule Potsdam, 1988. BStU MfS JHS 21115.

Fulbrook, Mary. *Anatomy of a Dictatorship: Inside the GDR 1949–1989.* Oxford: Oxford University Press, 1995.

———. *The People's State: East German Society from Hitler to Honecker.* New Haven: Yale University Press, 2005.

Fulbrook, Mary, ed. *Power and Society in the GDR, 1961–1979: The "Normalisation of Rule"?* Oxford: Berghahn, 2009.

Gaddis, John Lewis. *The Cold War: A New History.* New York: Penguin Press, 2005.

Ganster, Paul, and David Lorey. *The U.S.-Mexican Border into the Twenty-First Century.* Lanham, MD: Rowman & Littlefield, 2008.

Ganster, Paul, and David Lorey, eds. *Borders and Border Politics in a Globalizing World.* Lanham, MD: SR Books, 2005.

Gaus, Günter. *Wo Deutschland liegt: Eine Ortsbestimmung.* Hamburg: Hoffmann and Campe, 1983.

Gearson, John P., and Kori Schake, eds. *The Berlin Wall Crisis: Perspectives on Cold War Alliances.* New York: Palgrave Macmillan, 2002.

Gellately, Robert, "Denunciations in Twentieth-Century Germany: Aspects of Self-Policing in the Third Reich and the German Democratic Republic." In *Denunciation in Modern European History, 1789–1989*, edited by Sheila Fitzpatrick and Robert Gellately, 185–221. Chicago: University of Chicago Press, 1997.

———. *The Gestapo and German Society: Enforcing Racial Policy, 1933–1945.* New York: Oxford University Press, 1990.

Geyer, Michael. "Cold War Angst: The Case of West German Opposition to Rearmament and Nuclear Weapons." In *The Miracle Years: A Cultural History of West Germany, 1949–1968*, edited by Hanna Schissler, 376–408. Princeton: Princeton University Press, 2001.

Gieseke, Jens. *Das Mielke-Konzern: Die Geschichte der Stasi 1945–1990.* Stuttgart: Deutsche Verlags-Anstalt, 2001; 2nd expanded ed., Munich: Deutsche Verlags-Anstalt, 2006.

Glaser, Günther. *"Reorganisation der Polizei" oder getarnte Bewaffnung des SBZ im Kalten Krieg? Dokumente und Materialien zur sicherheits- und militärpolitischen Weichenstellung in Ostdeutschland 1948/1949.* Frankfurt: P. Lang, 1995.

Glassheim, Eagle. "Ethnic Cleansing, Communism, and Environmental Devastation in Czechoslovakia's Borderlands, 1945–1989." *Journal of Modern History* 78 (2006): 65–92.

Goedde, Petra. *GIs and Germans: Culture, Gender and Foreign Relations, 1945–1949.* New Haven: Yale University Press, 2003.

Götz, Walter. *Neustadter Humor.* Neustadt bei Coburg: Patzschke, 1988.

Grafe, Roman. *Deutsche Gerechtigkeit: Prozesse gegen DDR-Grenzschützen und ihre Befehlsgeber.* Munich: Siedler, 2004.

———. *Die Grenze durch Deutschland: Eine Chronik von 1945 bis 1990.* Berlin: Siedler, 2002.

Grams, Edgar. *Als bei uns die Grenze war: Geschichten und Erzählungen aus der Zeit der Teilung unseres Landes.* Kunter und Buntes. Sonneberg: Trautmann, 1996.

———. *Die friedliche Revolution: Erinnerungen.* Sonneberg: Trautmann, 1997.

Gray, William Glenn. *Germany's Cold War: The Global Campaign to Isolate East Germany, 1949–1969.* Chapel Hill: University of North Carolina Press, 2003.

Greiner, Albert. *Geschichte der Stadt Neustadt und ihrer Industrie seit 1650.* Coburg: Roßteutscher, 1911.

Gretzbach, Renate. *125 Jahre SPD Neustadt, 1876–2000.* Neustadt bei Coburg: SPD-Ortsverein Neustadt, 2001.

Grimm, Frankdieter, ed. *Zwischen Rennsteig und Sonneberg.* Berlin: Akademie Verlag, 1983.

Gross, Jan. *Revolution from Abroad: The Soviet Conquest of Poland's Western Ukraine and Western Belorussia.* Princeton: Princeton University Press, 1988.

Grossmann, Atina. *Jews, Germans, and Allies: Close Encounters in Occupied Germany.* Princeton: Princeton University Press: 2007.

Grund, Eberhard. "Fakten zur Arbeiterbewegung in Sonneberg." In *Stadt Sonneberg, 650 Jahre Stadt Sonneberg, 1349–1999*, 96–115. Sonneberg: Verlag Frankenschwelle KG, 1999.

Grünspan, Siegfried. "Die deutsche Spielwarenindustrie unter besonderer Berücksichtigung des Exportes und der ausländischen Konkurrenz." Universität Köln, 1931.

Hacke, Christian. "The United States and the German Question." In *The United States and Germany in the Era of the Cold War*, edited by Detlef Junker, 2:18–25. Cambridge, UK: Cambridge University Press, 2004.

Hahm, Kwang Bok. *The Living History of the DMZ: 30 Years of Journeys in the Borderlands.* Translated by Brian Kim. Seoul: Eastward, 2004.

Hambrecht, Rainer. *"Nicht durch Krieg, Kauf oder Erbschaft": Ausstellung des Staatsarchivs Coburg anläßlich der 75. Wiederkehr der Vereinigung Coburgs mit Bayern am 1. Juli 1920.* Munich: Generaldirektion der Staatlichen Archive Bayerns, 1995.

Hamlin, David. *Work and Play: The Production and Consumption of Toys in Germany, 1870–1914.* Ann Arbor: University of Michigan Press, 2007.

Hanisch, Wilfried. *Für den Schutz der Staatsgrenze der jungen Republik: Beiträge zur Geschichte der Grenztruppen der DDR.* Beiträge zur Geschichte der Grenztruppen der DDR, 2, 1988.

———. *Vom schweren Anfang: Beiträge zur Geschichte der Grenztruppen der DDR.* Beiträge zur Geschichte der Grenztruppen der DDR, 1, 1986.

Hargreaves, J. D. "West African Boundary Making." In *Borders and Border Politics in a Globalizing World*, edited by Paul Ganster and David Lorey, 97–104. Lanham, MD: SR Books, 2005.

Harrison, Hope. *Driving the Soviets Up the Wall: Soviet-East German Relations, 1953–1961.* Princeton: Princeton University Press, 2003.

Harsch, Donna. *Revenge of the Domestic: Women, the Family, and Communism in the German Democratic Republic.* Princeton: Princeton University Press, 2007.

Härtel, Christian, and Petra Kabus, eds. *Das Westpaket: Geschenksendung, keine Handelsware.* Berlin: Links, 2001.

Hartmann, Andreas, and Sabine Doering-Manteuffel, eds. *Grenzgeschichten: Berichte aus dem deutschen Niemandsland.* Frankfurt am Main: S. Fischer, 1990.

Havel, Václav. *The Power of the Powerless: Citizens Against the State in Central-Eastern Europe.* London: Hutchinson, 1985.

Hayward, N. F., and D. S. Morris. *The First Nazi Town.* Aldershot, UK: Avebury, 1988.

Hefele, Peter. *Die Verlagerung von Industrie- und Dienstleistungsunternehmen aus der SBZ/DDR nach Westdeutschland: Unter besonderer Berücksichtigung Bayerns (1945–1961).* Stuttgart: F. Steiner, 1998.

Heidemeyer, Helge. *Flucht und Zuwanderung aus der SBZ/DDR 1945/1949–1961: Die Flüchtlingspolitik der Bundesrepublik Deutschland bis zum Bau der Berliner Mauer.* Düsseldorf: Droste, 1994.

Heineman, Elizabeth. *What Difference Does a Husband Make? Women and Marital Status in Nazi and Postwar Germany.* Berkeley: University of California Press, 1999.

Herb, Guntram. "Double Vision: Territorial Strategies in the Construction of National Identities in Germany 1949–1979." *Annals of the Association of American Geographers* 94 (2004): 140–164.

Herbert, Ulrich. *Geschichte der Ausländerpolitik in Deutschland: Saisonarbeiter, Zwangsarbeiter, Gastarbeiter, Flüchtlinge.* Munich: C. H. Beck, 2001.

Herf, Jeffrey. *Divided Memory: The Nazi Past in the Two Germanys.* Cambridge, MA: Harvard University Press, 1997.

Hermann, Ingolf. *Die Deutsch-Deutsche Grenze: Von Posseck bis Lehesten, Ludwigstadt nach Prex.* Plauen: Vogtländischen Heimatverlag Neupert, 1996.

Herold, Emil. *Führer durch die "Bayerische Puppenstadt" Neustadt bei Coburg.* Neustadt bei Coburg: Verschönerungs- und Fremdenverkehrsverein, 1929.

Hertle, Hans-Hermann. *The Berlin Wall: Monument of the Cold War.* Berlin: Ch. Links Verlag, 2007.

Hertle, Hans-Hermann, Maria Nooke, et al. *Die Todesopfer an der Berliner Mauer 1961–1989.* Berlin: Ch. Links, 2009.

Hertle, Hans-Hermann, and Gerhard Sälter. "Die Todesopfer an Mauer und Grenze. Probleme einer Bilanz des DDR-Grenzregimes." *Deutschland Archiv* 39 (2006): 667–676.

Hertle, Hans Hermann, Konrad Jarausch, and Christoph Kleßmann, eds. *Mauerbau und Mauerfall: Ursachen—Verlauf—Auswirkungen.* Berlin: Ch. Links, 2002.

Herzog, Dagmar. *Sex After Fascism: Memory and Morality in Twentieth-Century Germany.* Princeton: Princeton University Press, 2005.

Heß, Julius. *Heimat und Volkstum: Mundartgedichte und Heimaterzählungen.* Sonneberg: Gräbe & Hetzer, 1936.

Hildebrandt, Alexandra. *The Wall: Figures, Facts.* Berlin: Haus am Checkpoint Charlie, 2008.

Hirschman, Albert. "Exit, Voice, and the Fate of the German Democratic Republic: An Essay in Conceptual History." *World Politics* 45 (1993): 173–202.

Hitchcock, William. *The Bitter Road to Freedom: A New History of the Liberation of Europe.* New York: Free Press, 2008.

Hochscherf, Tobias, Christoph Laucht, and Andrew Plowman, eds. *Divided, but Not Disconnected: German Experiences of the Cold War.* New York: Berghahn, 2010.

Hofmann, Alfred. "Industrie in peripheren Grenzräumen unter besonderer Berücksichtigung der industriellen Zweigbetreibe, dargestellt am Beispiel der Räume Coburg/Kronach und Cham." Institut für Geographie der Universität Würzburg, 1982.

Hofmann, Ernst. *Vom "Industrie- und Gewerbemuseum des Meininger Oberlandes" zum "Deutschen Spielzeugmuseum": Zur Geschichte einer kulturhistorischen Sammlung 1901–1945.* Sonneberg: Dt. Spielzeugmuseum, 2001.

Höhn, Maria. *GIs and Fräuleins: The German-American Encounter in 1950s West Germany.* Chapel Hill: University of North Carolina Press, 2002.

Horn, Karl. *Bewährung in den sechziger Jahren.* Berlin: Grenztruppen der DDR, 1985.

Horster, Maximilian. "The Trade in Political Prisoners Between the Two German States, 1962–89." *Journal of Contemporary History* 39 (2004): 403–424.

Hoßfeld, Adolf. *Die Geschichte der Strassen und Plätze der Stadt Sonneberg.* Mengersgereuth-Hämmern: Müller, 2002.

———, ed. *Sonneberg. Die Stadt im 20. Jahrhundert. Teil 1. Daten und Ereignisse im Überblick.* Sonneberg: Stadtarchiv Sonneberg, 2006.

———. "Sonneberg auf dem Weg in die nationalsozialistische Ära, 1929–1932." *Sonneberger Museums- und Geschichtsverein* 2 (2000).

———. "Sonneberg im Zweiten Weltkrieg, 1939–1944/45: Alltagsleben unterm Hakenkreuz." *Sonneberger Museums- und Geschichtsverein* 2 (1999).

———. "Sonneberg in den 'Goldenen Zwanziger Jahren' (1924 bis 1928)." *Sonneberger Museums- und Geschichtsverein* 2 (2001).

———. "Sonneberg und seine Spielzeugindustrie, 1932–1939: Von der roten zur braunen Hochburg." *Sonneberger Museums- und Geschichtsverein* 2 (1998).

———. "Sonnebergs Reaktionen auf den Anschluß Coburgs an Bayern." *Coburger Geschichtsblätter* 1–2 (2001): 29–33.

Hughes, Michael. *Shouldering the Burdens of Defeat: West Germany and the Reconstruction of Social Justice.* Chapel Hill: University of North Carolina Press, 1999.

Jarausch, Konrad. "Care and Coercion." In *Dictatorship as Experience: Towards a Socio-Cultural History of the GDR,* edited by Konrad Jarausch, 47–69. New York: Berghahn, 1999.

Jarausch, Konrad, and Michael Geyer. *Shattered Past: Reconstructing German Histories.* Princeton: Princeton University Press, 2003.

Johnson, Jason. "Dividing Mödlareuth: The Incorporation of Half a German Village into the GDR Regime, 1918–1989." Ph.D. diss., Northwestern University, in preparation.

Johnson, Molly Wilkinson. *Training Socialist Citizens: Sports and the State in East Germany.* Leiden: Brill, 2008.

Jones, Philip N., and Trevor Wild. "Opening the Frontier: Recent Spatial Impacts in the Former Inner-German Border Zone." *Regional Studies* 28 (1994): 259–74.

Judson, Pieter. *Guardians of the Nation: Activists on the Language Frontiers of Imperial Austria.* Cambridge, MA: Harvard University Press, 2006.

Judt, Tony. *Postwar: A History of Europe Since 1945.* New York: Penguin, 2005.

Junker, Detlef, ed. *The United States and Germany in the Era of the Cold War.* 2 vols. Cambridge, UK: Cambridge University Press, 2004.

Kahler, Miles, and Barbara Walter, eds. *Territoriality and Conflict in an Era of Globalization.* Cambridge, UK: Cambridge University Press, 2006.

Kalning, Karl. "Die Aufdeckung der Ursachen und begünstigenden Bedingungen für das Verlassen der DDR durch Jugendliche aus der 5-km-Sperrzone um Bereich der Kreisdienststelle Sonneberg sowie die sich daraus ergebenden Schlussfolgerungen für die Organisierung der vorbeugenden Arbeit des Ministeriums für Staatssicherheit." Hochschule des MfS, 1964. BStU MfS JHS MF 149.

Kalter, Isolde. "Neustadts Weg durch die Jahrhunderte." In *750 Jahre Neustadt*, edited by Wolfgang Braunschmidt, 4–12. Coburg: Neue Presse, 1998.

Kaufmann, Willi. *Schicksalsjahre: Spaltung—Wiedervereinigung 1922–1990*. Tettau: Willi Kaufmann, 1999.

Kawka, Rupert. "Regional Development Along the Former Inner-German Border After Unification." ERSA conference paper ersa03p245, European Regional Science Association, 2003.

Kleindienst, Jürgen, ed. *Mauer-Passagen: Grenzgänge, Fluchten und Reisen 1961–1989*. Berlin: Zeitgut, 2004.

———. *Von hier nach drüben: Grenzgänge, Fluchten und Reisen im kalten Krieg 1945–1961*. Berlin: Zeitgut, 2004.

Kleiner, Manuel. "Frieden im Kleinen." In *Coburger Friedensbuch*, edited by Karl Eberhard Sperl, 113–115. Meeder: Friedensausschuss der Gemeinde Meeder, 2001.

Kleinschmidt, Johannes. *"Do not Fraternize": Die schwierigen Anfänge deutsch-amerikanischer Freundschaft, 1944–1949*. Trier: WVT Wissenschaftler Verlag, 1997.

Kleßmann, Christoph, ed. *The Divided Past: Rewriting Post-War German History*. Oxford: Berg, 2001.

Knabe, Hubertus, ed. *Die Vergessenen Opfer der Mauer: Inhaftierte DDR-Flüchtlinge berichten*. Berlin: List, 2009.

Knabe, Hubertus, and Bernd Eisfeld, *West-Arbeit des MfS*. Berlin: Ch. Links, 1999.

Knespel, Herbert. "Die Arbeit mit IM/GMS zur Sicherung, Kontrolle und Überwachung des Einreiseverkehrs in grenznahe Gebiete der DDR als Bestandteil der Schwerpunktarbeit territorialer Diensteinheiten." Juristische Hochschule Potsdam, 1975. BStU MfS JHS 1 361/75.

Knop, Werner. *Prowling Russia's Forbidden Zone: A Secret Journey into Soviet Germany*. New York: Knopf, 1949.

Koch, Lothar. "Der Einsatz der IM/GMS zur Aufklärung und vorbeugenden Verhinderung von feindlichen Handlungen gegen die Staatsgrenze der DDR außerhalb der vorrangig zu sichernden Bereiche des Grenzkreises Sonneberg." Juristische Hochschule Potsdam, 1979. BStU BV Suhl, BdL/Dok 894.

Kocka, Jürgen. "Eine durchherrschte Gesellschaft." In *Sozialgeschichte der DDR*, edited by Hartmut Kaelble, Jürgen Kocka, and Hartmut Zwahr, 547–553. Stuttgart: Klett-Cotta, 1994.

Köhler, Heinz. *Zwischen Grundlagenvertrag und Wiedervereinigung: Die Entwicklung des Landkreises Kronach an der deutsch-deutschen Grenze*. Kronach: 1000 Jahre Kronach, 1998.

Kopstein, Jeffrey. *The Politics of Economic Decline in East Germany, 1945–1989*. Chapel Hill: University of North Carolina Press, 1997.

Korn, Manfred. "Die Aufgaben einer Grenzkreisdienststelle an der Staatsgrenze zur Bundesrepublik zur Feststellung und Kontrolle operative interessanter Personen im Grenzgebiet." Juristische Hochschule Potsdam, 1973. BStU MfS JHS 160 220/73.

Koshar, Rudy. *German Travel Cultures*. Oxford: Berg, 2000.

Kotkin, Stephen. *Magnetic Mountain: Stalinism as Civilization*. Berkeley: University of California Press, 1995.

Kufeke, "'Eine gewisse Unzufriedenheit in der Bevölkerung . . .': Erfolg und Misserfolg des SED-Regimes bei der Kontrolle der innerdeutschen Grenze am Beispiel des DDR-Kreises Hagenow." Paper presented at the annual meeting for the German Studies Association, Washington, DC, October 8–11, 2009.

Kumar, Radha. "The Troubled History of Partition." *Foreign Affairs* 76 (1997): 22–34.

Landsman, Mark. *Dictatorship and Demand: The Politics of Consumerism in East Germany*. Cambridge, MA: Harvard University Press, 2005.

Lansing, Charles. *From Nazism to Communism: German Schoolteachers Under Two Dictatorships*. Cambridge, MA: Harvard University Press, 2010.

Lapp, Peter Joachim. *Gefechtsdienst im Frieden—Das Grenzregime der DDR*. Bonn: Berard & Graefe, 1999.

Last, George. *After the "Socialist Spring": Collectivisation and Economic Transformation in the GDR*. New York: Berghahn, 2009.

Laufer, Jochen. "From Dismantling to Currency Reform: External Origins of the Dictatorship, 1943–1948." In *Dictatorship as Experience: Towards a Socio-Cultural History of the GDR*, edited by Konrad Jarausch, 73–90. New York: Berghahn, 1999.

———. *Pax Sovietica: Stalin, die Westmächte und die deutsche Frage 1941–1945*. Cologne: Böhlau, 2009.

Lebegern, Robert. *Mauer, Zaun und Stacheldraht: Sperranlagen an der innerdeutschen Grenze 1945–1990*. Weiden: Role-Verlag, 2002.

Leuenberger, Christine. "Constructions of the Berlin Wall: How Material Culture Is Used in Psychological Theory." *Social Problems* 53 (2006): 18–37.

Lindenberger, Thomas. "Die Diktatur der Grenzen: Zur Einleitung." In *Herrschaft und Eigen-Sinn in der Diktatur: Studien zur Gesellschaftsgeschichte der DDR*, edited by Thomas Lindenberger, 13–44. Cologne: Böhlau, 1999.

———. *Volkspolizei: Herrschaftspraxis und öffentliche Ordnung im SED-Staat 1952–1968*. Cologne: Böhlau, 2003.

——. "Home Sweet Home: Desperately Seeking Heimat in Early DEFA films." *Film History* 181 (2006): 46–58.

——. "'Zonenrand,' 'Sperrgebiet' und 'Westberlin'—Deutschland als Grenzregion des Kalten Krieges." In *Teilung und Integration: Die doppelte deutsche Nachkriegsgeschichte als wissenschaftliches und didaktisches Problem*, edited by Christoph Klessmann and Peter Lautzas, 97–112. Schwalbach: Wochenschau, 2006.

Lindner, Konrad. "Der Einsatz der IM/GMS während des Grenzdienstes in den grenzsichernen Einheiten eines Grenzbataillons zur Erarbeitung politisch-operativ bedeutsamer Information bei der politisch-operativen Absicherung des Personalbestandes sowie zur Aufdeckung, Vorbereitung und Verhinderung feindlicher Angriffe gegen die Staatsgrenze der DDR." Juristische Hochschule Potsdam, 1979. BStU MfS JHS 1 368/79.

Lischewsky, Ulrike. *Sonneberger Puppen- und Plüschspielzeugproduktion: Studien zum industriellen Arbeitsalltag in der DDR der 50er bis 70er Jahre.* Hildburghausen: Frankenschwelle, 1998.

Löffler, Stefan. "Auf in's Gelobte Land: Die Auswanderung aus dem Sonneberger Land nach Nordamerika." *Sonneberger Museums- und Geschichtsverein* 3 (2000).

Loth, Wilfried. *Die Sowjetunion und die deutsche Frage: Studien zur sowjetischen Deutschlandpolitik von Stalin bis Chruschtschow.* Göttingen: Vandenhoeck & Ruprecht, 2007.

Ludwig, Karl, and Rainer Zetzmann. "Organisation der Parteiarbeit der KPD und SPD unmittelbar in den Monaten Mai–Juli 1945 in Sonneberg." Bezirksparteischule Schleusingen, 1973. StA-M SED-BL-Suhl V/1/1/072.

Luedtke, Alf. "People Working: Everyday Life and German Fascism." *History Workshop Journal* 50 (2000): 75–92.

Luthardt, Jürgen. *Geschichte und Geschichten um 650 Jahre Sonneberg.* Sonneberg: Dyba-Werbung, 1998.

Macrakis, Kristie, Thomas Wegener Friis, and Helmut Müller-Enbergs, eds. *East German Foreign Intelligence: Myth, Reality and Controversy.* London: Routledge, 2010.

Madarász, Jeannette. *Working in East Germany: Normality in a Socialist Dictatorship, 1961–79.* Basingstoke: Palgrave Macmillan, 2006.

Maddrell, Paul. "Western Espionage and Stasi Counter-Espionage in East Germany, 1953–1961." In *East German Foreign Intelligence*, edited by Macrakis, Friis, and Müller-Enbergs, 19–33.

Maier, Charles. *Dissolution: The Crisis of Communism and the End of East Germany.* Princeton: Princeton University Press, 1997.

——. "Transformations of Territoriality, 1600–2000." In *Transnationale Geschichte: Themen, Tendenzen und Theorien*, edited by Gunilla Budde, Sebastian Conrad, and Oliver Janz, 32–55. Göttingen: Vadenhoeck und Ruprecht, 2006.

Major, Patrick. *Behind the Wall: East Germany and the Frontiers of Power.* Oxford: Oxford University Press, 2010.

——. *The Death of the KPD: Communism and Anti-Communism in West Germany, 1945–1956.* Oxford: Oxford University Press, 1997.

——. "Going West: The Open Border and the Problem of *Republikflucht*." In *The Workers' and Peasants' State*, ed. Patrick Major and Jonathan Osmond, 190–208. New York: Palgrave, 2002.

Major, Patrick, and Jonathan Osmond, eds. *The Workers' and Peasants' State.* New York: Palgrave, 2002.

Mangold, Bruno. "Der Einsatz des IM/GMS-Systems der KD Sonneberg zur wirksamen Sicherung der Staatsgrenze der DDR." Juristische Hochschule Potsdam, 1969. BStU MfS 160, Nr. 141/69.

Martínez, Oscar J. *Border People: Life and Society in the U.S.-Mexico Borderlands.* Tucson: University of Arizona Press, 1994.

——. *Troublesome Border.* Rev. ed. Tuscon: University of Arizona Press, 2006.

Marx, Karl. *The Eighteenth Brumaire of Louis Bonaparte.* Translated by Daniel de Leon. Chicago: C. H. Kerr, 1913.

Matthäi, Werner. *Die Anfänge des Wiederaufbaus und der antifaschistisch-demokratischen Neugestaltung im Kreis Sonneberg: Aus Akten, Protokollen, Mitteilungen und Schriften.* Sonneberg: SED Kreisleitung Sonneberg, 1966.

Mayer, Wolfgang. *Flucht und Ausreise: Botschaftsbesetzungen als wirksame Form des Widerstands und Mittel gegen die politische Verfolgung in der DDR.* Berlin: A. Tykve, 2002.

Mazower, Mark. *Dark Continent: Europe's Twentieth Century.* New York: Vintage Books, 2000.

McAdams, James. *Germany Divided: From the Wall to Reunification.* Princeton: Princeton University Press, 1993.

——. *Judging the Past in Unified Germany.* Cambridge, UK: Cambridge University Press, 2001.

McAllister, James. *No Exit: America and the German Problem.* Ithaca: Cornell University Press, 2002.

McLellan, Josie. "State Socialist Bodies: East German Nudism from Ban to Boom." *Journal of Modern History* 79 (2007): 48–79.

Merritt, Richard L. *Democracy Imposed: U.S. Occupation Policy and the German Public, 1945–1949.* New Haven: Yale University Press, 1995.

Meyfarth, Brunhild. *Die Sonneberger Spielzeugmacher: Zu den Arbeits- u. Lebensbedingungen der Sonneberger Spielzeugmacher Ende des 19. und Anfang des 20. Jahrhunderts.* Sonneberg: Spielzeugmuseum Sonneberg, 1981.

Miles, William. *Hausaland Divided: Colonialism and Independence in Nigeria and Niger.* Ithaca: Cornell University Press, 1994.

Miller, Barbara. *The Stasi Files Unveiled: Guilt and Compliance in a Unified Germany.* New Brunswick: Transaction, 2004.

Moczarski, Norbert. "Archivalische Quellen über die Vorbereitung und Durchführung der Zwangsaussiedlungen zu Beginn der 50er und 60er Jahr in Südthüringen." *Jahrbuch 1992 des Hennebergisch-Fränkischen Geschichtsvereins* (1992): 315–47.

———. *Der 17. Juni im Bezirk Suhl: Vorgeschichte, Verlauf und Nachwirkungen.* Erfurt: Landesbeauftragten des Freistaates Thüringen für die Unterlagen des Staatssicherheitsdienstes der ehemaligen DDR, 1996.

———, ed. *Die Protokolle des Sekretariats der SED-Bezirksleitung Suhl: Von der Gründung des Bezirkes Suhl im Sommer 1952 bis zum 17. Juni 1953.* Weimar: H. Böhlaus, 2002.

Moeller, Robert, ed. *West Germany Under Construction: Politics, Society, and Culture in the Adenauer Era.* Ann Arbor: University of Michigan Press, 1997.

———. *War Stories: The Search for a Usable Past in the Federal Republic of Germany.* Berkeley: University of California Press, 2001.

Moon, Penderel. *Divide and Quit.* Berkeley: University of California Press, 1962.

Müller, Adolf. *Mein Deutschland! Neue Lieder mit Tonweisen.* Sonneberg: Müller, 1938.

Müller-Enbergs, Helmut. *Inoffizielle Mitarbeiter des Ministeriums für Staatssicherheit: Anleitungen für die Arbeit mit Agenten, Kundschaften und Spionen in der Bundesrepublik Deutschland,* vol. 2. Berlin: Ch. Links, 1998.

Münkel, Daniela. "Überwachung und Kontrolle im Grenzraum—das Beispiel des Kreises Halberstadt." Paper presented at the conference "Grenze—Konstruktion Realität Narrative." Hanover, Germany, June 24–26, 2010.

Murdock, Caitlin. *Changing Places: Society, Culture, and Territory in the Saxon-Bohemian Borderlands, 1870–1946.* Ann Arbor: University of Michigan Press, 2010.

Muth, Walter. *Die Wirtschaft im Coburger Land.* Coburg: Coburger Tageblatt, 1952.

Naimark, Norman. *The Russians in Germany: A History of the Soviet Zone of Occupation, 1945–1949.* Cambridge, MA: Harvard University Press, 1995.

Nelson, Arvid. *Cold War Ecology: Forests, Farms, and People in the East German Landscape, 1945–1989.* New Haven: Yale University Press, 2005.

Neumann, Karl. *Spielzeugland Sonneberg.* Gotha: Engelhard-Reyher, 1939.

Neumeier, Gerhard. "'Rückkehrer' in die DDR: Das Beispiel des Bezirks Suhl 1961 bis 1972." *Vierteljahrshefte für Zeitgeschichte* 58 (2010): 69–91.

Niethammer, Lutz. *Die Mitläuferfabrik: Die Entnazifizierung am Beispiel Bayerns.* Berlin: Dietz, 1982.

Offer, Michael. *Das Zonenrandgebiet nach der deutschen Einigung: Wirtschaftliche Entwicklung und regionalpolitische Implikationen.* Mainz: Johannes Gutenberg-Universität, 1991.

O'Leary, Brendan. "Analysing Partition: Definition, Classification and Explanation." *Political Geography* 26 (2007): 886–908.

Ostermann, Christian F. *Uprising in East Germany 1953: The Cold War, The German Question, and The First Major Upheaval Behind the Iron Curtain.* Budapest: Central European University Press, 2001.

Palmowski, Jan. *Inventing a Socialist Nation: Heimat and the Politics of Everyday Life in the GDR, 1945–1990.* Cambridge, UK: Cambridge University Press, 2009.

Patton, David. *Cold War Politics in Postwar Germany.* New York: St. Martin's, 1999.

Pelkmans, Mathijs. *Defending the Border: Identity, Religion, and Modernity in the Republic of Georgia.* Ithaca: Cornell University Press, 2006.

Pence, Katherine. *Rations to Fashions: Gender and Consumer Politics in Cold War Germany.* New York: Cambridge University Press, forthcoming.

Pence, Katherine, and Paul Betts, eds. *Socialist Modern: East German Everyday Culture and Politics.* Ann Arbor: University of Michigan Press, 2008.

Petzold, "Entwicklung der Gas- und Stromversorgung in der Stadt Sonneberg von 1861–1998." In *Stadt Sonneberg, 650 Jahre Stadt Sonneberg, 1349–1999,* 299–314. Sonneberg: Verlag Frankenschwelle KG, 1999.

Pfadenhauer, Rudolf. "Die Staatssicherheit in Heinersdorf." In *Wider das Vergessen,* edited by Bergmann-Pohl and Pfadenhauer, 22–42.

Poiger, Uta. *Jazz, Rock, and Rebels: Cold War Politics and American Culture in a Divided Germany.* Berkeley: University of California Press, 2000.

Pommerin, Reiner, ed. *The American Impact on Postwar Germany.* Providence: Berghahn, 1995.
———. "General Trettner und die Atom-Minen: zur Geschichte nuklearer Waffen in Deutschland." *Vierteljahrshefte für Zeitgeschichte* 39 (1991): 637–654.
Port, Andrew. *Conflict and Stability in the German Democratic Republic.* New York: Cambridge University Press, 2007.
Potratz, Rainer. "Stigmatisierung der Opfer und Einschüchterung der Zurückgebliebenen: Die Zwangsaussiedlungen aus dem Grenzgebiet der DDR an der innerdeutschen Grenze als zentrales Element zur Durchsetzung einer Sicherheitszone." Paper presented at the annual meeting for the German Studies Association, Washington, DC, October 8–11, 2009.
Preissler, Helmut. *Grüne Leuchtkugeln: Erzählungen und Gedichte.* Berlin: Deutscher Militärverlag, 1969.
———. *Nur ein paar Stunden: Erzählungen.* Berlin: Deutscher Militärverlag, 1975.
Prieß, Benno. *Erschossen im Morgengrauen: Verhaftet, gefoltert, verurteilt, erschossen; "Werwolf"-Schicksale mitteldeutscher Jugendlicher.* B. Prieß, 2002.
Pritchard, Gareth. *The Making of the GDR 1945–53: From Antifascism to Stalinism.* Manchester: Manchester University Press, 2000.
Rau, Siegfried. "Die Entwicklung der Bündnispolitik der Arbeiterklasse unter Führung der Kreisparteiorganisation Sonneberg der SED mit den städtischen Mittelschichten und privaten Unternehmen, 1949–52." Bezirksparteischule Schleusingen, 1976. StA-M SED-BL-Suhl V/1/1/191.
Rauchensteiner, Manfried, and Robert Kriechbaumer, eds. *Die Gunst des Augenblicks: Neuere Forschungen zu Staatsvertrag und Neutralität.* Vienna: Böhlau, 2005.
Rausch, Ernst. *Die Sonneberger Spielwaren-Industrie und die verwandten Industrieen der Griffel- und Glasfabrikation unter besonderer Berücksichtigung der Verhältnisse in der Hausindustrie.* Berlin: Siemenroth & Troschel, 1901.
Reich, Jürgen. *Die Erinnerung verblaßt . . . aber es lebten auch in Sonneberg Juden.* Sonneberg: Arbeitsgemeinschaft Kirche und Judentum (Arbeitsgruppe Thüringen), 1988.
———, ed. *Kirche, Kerzen, Klassenkampf: Erinnerungen und protokollarische Notizen aus der Wendezeit im Raum Sonneberg (Thüringen) und Neustadt bei Coburg (Bayern).* Coburg: Coburger Tageblatt, 2000.
Reisenweber, Gerhard. *In vorderster Reihe für die Sache der Arbeiterklasse.* 2 vols. Sonneberg: Grenzregiment Herbert Warnke, 1985 and 1986.
Ritter, Jürgen, and Peter Joachim Lapp. *Die Grenze: Ein deutsches Bauwerk.* 6th ed. Berlin: Ch. Links, 2007.
Roggenbuch, Frank. *Das Berliner Grenzgängerproblem: Verflechtung und Systemkonkurrenz vor dem Mauerbau.* Berlin: de Gruyter, 2008.
Rose, Brian. *The Lost Border: The Landscape of the Iron Curtain.* New York: Princeton Architectural Press, 2005.
Ross, Corey. "Before the Wall: East Germans, Communist Authority, and the Mass Exodus to the West." *Historical Journal* 45 (2002): 459–480.
———. *Constructing Socialism at the Grass-Roots: The Transformation of East Germany, 1945–65.* New York: St. Martin's, 2000.
———. *The East German Dictatorship: Problems and Perspectives in the Interpretation of the GDR.* Oxford: Oxford University Press, 2002.
———. "East Germans and the Berlin Wall: Popular Opinion and Social Change Before and After the Border Closure of August 1961." *Journal of Contemporary History* 39 (2004): 25–44.
Rothe, Ilona. *Verraten, Vertrieben, Verkauft, Verhöhnt: Dokumente, Tatsachen, Hintergründe zur Aktion "Ungeziefer," "Kornblume."* Erfurt: Rothe, 1992.
Rothe, Ilona, and Lutz Jödicke, eds. *Zwangsaussiedlungen in Deutschland—Erlebnisberichte—Dokumente—Aktion "Ungeziefer" Juni 1952, Aktion "Kornblume" Oktober 1961.* Erfurt: Rothe, 1992.
Rubin, Eli. *Synthetic Socialism: Plastics and Dictatorship in the German Democratic Republic.* Chapel Hill: University of North Carolina Press, 2008.
———. "The Trabant: Consumption, Eigen-sinn and Movement." *History Workshop Journal* 68 (2009): 27–44.
Ruggenthaler, Peter. *Stalins grosser Bluff: Die Geschichte der Stalin-Note in Dokumenten der sowjetischen Führung.* Munich: Oldenbourg, 2007.
Sabrow, Martin, ed., *Erinnerungsorte der DDR.* Munich: C. H. Beck, 2009.
Sahlins, Peter. *Boundaries: The Making of France and Spain in the Pyrenees.* Berkeley: University of California Press, 1989.
Sälter, Gerhard. *Grenzpolizisten: Konformität, Verweigerung und Repression in der Grenzpolizei und den Grenztruppen der DDR 1952–1965.* Berlin: Ch. Links, 2009.
Samaddar, Ranabir. "The Last Hurrah that Continues." In *Divided Countries, Separated Cities: The Modern Legacy of Partition,* edited by Ghislaine Glasson Deschaumes and Rada Iveković, 21–35. New Delhi: Oxford University Press, 2003.

Sandner, Harald. *Coburg im 20. Jahrhundert: Die Chronik über die Stadt Coburg und das Haus Sachsen-Coburg und Gotha vom 1. Januar 1900 bis zum 31. Dezember 1999.* Coburg: Neue Presse, 2000.

Sarotte, Mary Elise. *1989: The Struggle to Create Post-Cold War Europe.* Princeton: Princeton University Press, 2009.

———. *Dealing with the Devil: East Germany, Détente, and Ostpolitik, 1969–1973.* Chapel Hill: University of North Carolina Press, 2001.

Schaad, Martin. *"Dann geh doch rüber": Über die Mauer in den Osten.* Berlin: Ch. Links, 2009.

Schaefer, Sagi. "Border-Land: Property Rights, Kinship and the Emergence of the inter-German Border in the Eichsfeld." In *Praktiken der Differenz: Diasporakulturen in der Zeitgeschichte,* edited by Miriam Rürup, 197–214. Göttingen: Wallstein, 2009.

———. "Hidden Behind the Wall: West German State-Building and the Division of Germany." *Central European History* 43 (2011).

———. "Ironing the Curtain: Border and Boundary Formation in Cold War Rural Germany." Ph.D. diss., Columbia University, 2010.

Schaeffer, Robert. *Severed States: Dilemmas of Democracy in a Divided World.* Lanham, MD: Rowman & Littlefield, 1999.

Schake, Kori. "A Broader Range of Choice? US Policy in the 1958 and 1961 Berlin Crises." In *The Berlin Wall Crisis: Perspectives on Cold War Alliances,* edited by John P. Gearson and Kori Schake, 22–42. New York: Palgrave Macmillan, 2002.

Schätzlein, Gerhard, Bärbel Rösch, and Reinhold Albert. *Grenzerfahrungen: Bayern-Thüringen 1945 bis 1971,* vol. 1. Hildburghausen: Frankenschwelle, 2001.

Schätzlein, Gerhard, and Reinhold Albert. *Grenzerfahrungen: Bezirk Suhl—Bayern/Hessen 1972 bis 1988,* vol. 2. Hildburghausen: Frankenschwelle, 2002.

Schätzlein, Gerhard, Reinhold Albert, and Hans-Jürgen Salier. *Grenzerfahrungen: Bezirk Suhl—Bayern/Hessen zur Zeit der Wende,* vol. 3. Hildburghausen: Frankenschwelle, 2005.

Scherzer, Landolf. *Der Grenz-Gänger.* Berlin: Aufbau-Verlag, 2005.

Scheuerich, Helmut. *Geschichte der Stadt Neustadt bei Coburg im zwanzigsten Jahrhundert.* 2 vols. Neustadt bei Coburg: Stadt Neustadt bei Coburg, 1989 and 1993.

Schindhelm, Waldemar. *Die Ortsnamen des Sonneberger Landes.* Rudolstadt: Hain, 1998.

Schissler, Hanna, ed. *The Miracle Years: A Cultural History of West Germany, 1949–1968.* Princeton: Princeton University Press, 2001.

Schleevoigt, Christa. "Von Heubisch nach Jena—Aktion 'Ungeziefer.'" Familientagebuch.de, 2000. Online. Available: http://familientagebuch.de/christa. January 2011.

Schmehle, Günther. "Coburg und die Deutsche Arbeiterbewegung." Universität Bamberg, 1980.

Schmelz, Andrea. *Migration und Politik im geteilten Deutschland während des Kalten Krieges: Die West-Ost-Migration in die DDR in den 1950er und 1960er Jahren.* Opladen: Leske and Budrich, 2002.

Schmidt, Hans-Jürgen. *50 Jahre BGS, 1951–2001: Daten—Menschen—Fakten.* Coburg: Fiedler, 2001.

———. *An der Grenze der Freiheit: Die US-Verbände am Eisernen Vorhang 1945–1990.* Coburg: Fiedler, 1999.

———. *Coburg und die amerikanischen Streitkräfte 1945–1990.* Coburg: Historische Gesellschaft Coburg, 1995.

———. *Wir tragen den Adler des Bundes am Rock: In Freiheit dienen.* Coburg: Fiedler-Verlag, 1993–94.

Schmidt-Eenboom, Erich. "The Rise and Fall of West German Intelligence Operations against East Germany." In *East German Foreign Intelligence,* edited by Macrakis, Friis, Müller-Enbergs, 34–47.

Schneider, Peter. *The Wall Jumper: A Berlin Story.* Chicago: University of Chicago Press, 1983.

Schoenau, Hanns. *Sonneberg: Geschichten, Gestalten, Geschichte.* Die Blaue Reihe, ed. Xing-hu Kuo. Böblingen: Tykve, 1994.

Schubert, Albin. *Das Ende des Zweiten Weltkrieges im Coburger Land.* Coburg: Riemann, 1985.

Schugg-Reheis, Claudia, ed. *Grenzenlos: Thüringer und Franken schreiben über 45 Jahre Grenzdasein.* Coburg: Neue Presse, 1992.

Schultke, Dietmar. *Die Grenze, die uns teilte: Zeitzeugenberichte zur innerdeutschen Grenze.* Berlin: Köster, 2005.

———. *"Keiner kommt durch": Die Geschichte der innerdeutschen Grenze 1945–1990.* Berlin: Aufbau, 1999.

Schwämmlein, Thomas. "Die Geschichte der Industrieschulen Sonneberg und Neustadt bei Coburg." *Coburger Geschichtsblätter* 4 (99): 28–41.

———. "Jüdische Bürger und jüdisches Leben im Sonneberg." In *Stadt Sonneberg, 650 Jahre Stadt Sonneberg, 1349–1999,* 351–352. Sonneberg: Verlag Frankenschwelle KG, 1999.

———. *Landkreis Sonneberg.* Langenweißbach, Beier & Beran, 2007.

———. "Landwirtschaft in und um Sonneberg." In *Stadt Sonneberg, 650 Jahre Stadt Sonneberg, 1349–1999,* 255–261. Sonneberg: Verlag Frankenschwelle KG, 1999.

———. "Sonneberg und Neustadt—Neustadt und Sonneberg: Historische Anmerkungen zur gemeinsamen Geschichte zweier Nachbarstädte." *Coburger Geschichtsblätter* 4 (1999): 128–138.

———. "Sonneberg zwischen 1918 und 1945." In Stadt Sonneberg, *650 Jahre Stadt Sonneberg, 1349–1999*, 79–87. Sonneberg: Verlag Frankenschwelle KG, 1999.

———. "Die Sonneberger Stadtgrenze: Die Vermerkung und Versteinung der Sonneberger Stadtflur 1730 und die Entwicklung der Gemarkungsgrenzen der Stadt Sonneberg." *Sonneberger Museums- und Geschichtsverein* 4 (99).

Schwarzkopf, Christoph. "Die Stadterweiterung Sonnebergs von 1830 bis zur Jahrhundertwende." In Stadt Sonneberg, *650 Jahre Stadt Sonneberg, 1349–1999*, 132–165. Sonneberg: Verlag Frankenschwelle KG, 1999.

Schwede, Franz. *Kampf um Coburg*. Munich: Zentralverlag der NSDAP, 1939.

Seipp, Adam. "Refugee Town: Germans, Americans, and the Uprooted in Rural West Germany, 1945–52." *Journal of Contemporary History* 44 (2009): 675–695.

Sheehan, James. *Where Have All the Soldiers Gone? The Transformation of Modern Europe*. Boston: Houghton Mifflin, 2008.

Sheffer, Edith. "On Edge: Building the Border in East and West Germany." *Central European History* 40 (2007): 307–339.

———. "Burned Bridge: How East and West Germans Made the Iron Curtain." Ph.D. diss., University of California, Berkeley, 2008.

Si-Woo, Lee. *Life on the Edge of the DMZ*. Translated by Myung-Hee Kim. Folkestone: Global Oriental, 2008.

Smith, Helmut Walser. *The Continuities of German History: Nation, Religion, and Race Across the Long Nineteenth Century*. New York: Cambridge University Press, 2008.

Smyser, W. R. *From Yalta to Berlin: The Cold War Struggle over Germany*. New York: St. Martin's Press, 1999.

Sonneberger Beobachter. *Sonneberger Kommunalpolitik in Versen: Lieder, Balladen und Glossen für Spießer, Bonzen, Genossen*. Sonneberg: Sonneberger Beobachter, 1931.

Sperber, Jonathan. "17 June 1953: Revisiting a German Revolution." *German History* 22 (2004): 619–643.

Sperschneider, Ingrid. "Beiträge zur geschichtlichen Entwicklung der Spielwarenindustrie in Neustadt bei Coburg." Pädagogische Hochschule Bayreuth, Universität Erlangen-Nürnberg, 1965.

Spevack, Edmund. "The Allied Council of Foreign Ministers Conferences and the German Question." In *The United States and Germany in the Era of the Cold War*, edited by Detlef Junker, 1:43–49. Cambridge, UK: Cambridge University Press, 2004.

Spilker, Dirk. *The East German Leadership and the Division of Germany: Patriotism and Propaganda 1945–1953*. Oxford: Oxford University Press, 2006.

Stacy, William. *U.S. Army Border Operations in Germany, 1945–1983*. HQ USAREUR and Seventh Army, 1984. Online. Available: www.army.mil/cmh-pg/documents/BorderOps/content.htm. January 2011.

Stadt Sonneberg. *650 Jahre Stadt Sonneberg, 1349–1999*. Sonneberg: Verlag Frankenschwelle KG, 1999.

Statistisches Taschenbuch—Kreis Sonneberg, Bezirk Suhl. Staatliche Zentralverwaltung für Statistik, Kreisstelle Sonneberg, 1960 and 1966.

Steege, Paul. *Black Market, Cold War: Everyday Life in Berlin, 1946–1949*. Cambridge, UK: Cambridge University Press, 2007.

———. "Ordinary Violence on an Extraordinary Stage: Incidents on the Sector Border in Postwar Berlin." In *Performances of Violence*, edited by Austin Sarat, Carleen Basler, and Thomas Dumm. Amherst: University of Massachusetts Press, 2011.

Stenbock-Fermor, Alexander. *Deutschland von Unten: Reise durch die proletarische Provinz*. Stuttgart: Engelhorn, 1931.

Stier, Gerhard. *Die letzten Tage und Wochen des II. Weltkrieges in der Stadt Sonneberg*. Sonneberg: G. Stier, 1997.

———. *Zwangsarbeit in Sonneberg: Das Beispiel Zahnradwerk*. Sonneberg: Museums- und Geschichtsverein, 2001.

Stiftung Haus der Geschichte der Bundesrepublik Deutschland. *Drüben: Deutsche Blickwechsel*. Leipzig: Zeifgeschictliches Forum, Leipzig, 2006.

Stoll, Ulrich. *Einmal Freiheit und zurück: Die Geschichte der DDR-Rückkehrer*. Berlin: Ch. Links, 2009.

Stöver, Bernd. *Zuflucht DDR: Spione und andere Übersiedler*. Munich: C. H. Beck, 2009.

Strang, William. *Home and Abroad*. London: Deutsch, 1956.

Stubenrausch, Andreas, and Hermann Förster. "Das Kabel- und Leitungswerk Neustadt." In *Unsere Coburger Heimat: Erzählungen und Berichte*, edited by Walter Eichhorn. Coburg: Verl. Blätter zur Geschichte d. Coburger Landes, 1987.

Stueck, William. *Rethinking the Korean War: A New Diplomatic and Strategic History*. Princeton: Princeton University Press, 2004.

———. "The United States, the Soviet Union, and the Division of Korea: A Comparative Approach." *Journal of American-East Asian Relations* 4 (1995): 1–27.

Teßmer, Angelika, and Gudrun Zien. *Sonneberger Geschichten*. Hildburghausen: Frankenschwelle Salier, 1995.

Thompson, E. P. *The Making of the English Working Class*. New York: Vintage Books, 1963.

Thoß, Hendrik, ed. *Europas Eiserner Vorhang: Die Deutsch-deutsche Grenze im Kalten Krieg*. Berlin: Duncker & Humblot, 2008.

———. *Gesichert in den Untergang: Die Geschichte der DDR-Westgrenze*. Berlin: K. Dietz, 2004.

Timm, Annette. *The Politics of Fertility in Twentieth-Century Berlin*. New York: Cambridge University Press, 2010.

Torpey, John. *The Invention of the Passport: Surveillance, Citizenship and the State*. Cambridge, UK: Cambridge University Press, 2000.

Trachtenberg, Marc. *A Constructed Peace: The Making of the European Settlement, 1945–1963*. Princeton: Princeton University Press, 1999.

Traut, Günther. "Die subversive Tätigkeit operativ bedeutsamer Institutionen, Organisationen, Einrichtungen, Personengruppen und Personen aus dem westlichen Grenzvorfeld gegen die Bevölkerung des Grenzgebietes und die Staatsgrenze und die daraus erwachsenden Aufgaben zur vorbeugenden Verhinderung, Aufdeckung und Bekämpfung feindlicher Aktivitäten." Juristische Hochschule Potsdam, 1980. BStU MfS JHS 1 289/80.

Truckenbrodt, Rolf, and Arno Maaser. *Alt-Neustadter G'schichtla*. Neustadt bei Coburg: Patzschke, 1982.

Uhl, Matthias. *Die Teilung Deutschlands: Niederlage, Ost-West-Spaltung und Wiederaufbau 1945–49*. Berlin: Bebra, 2009.

Uhl, Matthias, and Armin Wagner. *BND contra Sowjetarmee: Westdeutsche Militärspionage in der DDR*. Berlin: Ch. Links, 2008.

———. "'Die Möglichkeiten, aber auch die Grenzen nachrichtendienstlicher Aufklärung.' Bundesnachrichtendienst und Mauerbau, Juli–September 1961." *Vierteljahrshefte für Zeitgeschichte* 55 (2007): 681–725.

Ullrich, Maren. *Geteilte Ansichten: Erinnerungslandschaft deutsch-deutsche Grenze*. Berlin: Aufbau-Verlag, 2006.

van Melis, Damian, and Henrik Bispink. *"Republikflucht": Flucht und Abwanderung aus der SBZ/DDR, 1945 bis 1961*. Munich: Oldenbourg, 2006.

von Plato, Alexander, Sergej Vladimirovič Mironenko, and Lutz Niethammer. *Sowjetische Speziallager in Deutschland 1945 bis 1950*. Berlin: Akademie Verl., 1998.

Wachsmann, Manfred. "Die Verantwortung und Aufgabenstellung der HA I/Kommando der Grenztruppen/ Bereich Aufklärung für die Feststellung, Aufklärung und politisch-operative Bearbeitung der feindlichen Schleusungstätigkeit durch Menschenhändlerbanden u.a. feindliche Organisationen über die Staatsgrenze der DDR zur BRD und 'Westberlin.'" Juristische Hochschule Potsdam, 1981. BStU MfS JHS 1 294/81.

Wachter, Franz. "Umständliche Reise in die Nähe: Mit dem Bähnlein auf heimischer Entdeckungsfahrt." *Aus Coburg Stadt und Land*. Fränkischer Heimatkalender, 1961.

Wagner, Manfred. "'Beseitigung Des Ungeziefers…': Zwangsaussiedlungen in den Thüringischen Landkreisen Saalfeld, Schleiz und Lobenstein—1952 und 1961." Landesbeauftragte des Freistaates Thüringen für die Unterlagen des Staatssicherheitsdienstes der ehemaligen DDR. Erfurt, TLSTU-Verlag, 2001.

Weiner, Amir, ed. *Landscaping the Human Garden: Twentieth-Century Population Management in a Comparative Framework*. Stanford: Stanford University Press, 2003.

Weisbrod, Bernd, ed. *Grenzland: Beiträge zur Geschichte der deutsch-deutschen Grenze*. Hannover: Hahn, 1993.

Weitz, Eric. *Creating German Communism, 1890–1990: From Popular Protests to Socialist State*. Princeton: Princeton University Press, 1997.

Welsh, Helga. *Revolutionärer Wandel auf Befehl? Entnazifizierungs- und Personalpolitik in Thüringen und Sachsen (1945–1948)*. Munich: Oldenbourg, 1989.

Westad, Odd Arne. *The Global Cold War: Third World Interventions and the Making of our Times*. Cambridge, UK: Cambridge University Press, 2005.

Wierling, Dorothee. "Mission to Happiness: The Cohort of 1949 and the Making of East and West Germany." In *The Miracle Years: A Cultural History of West Germany, 1949–1968*, edited by Hanna Schissler, 110–125. Princeton: Princeton University Press, 2001.

Wiesen, Jonathan. *West German Industry and the Challenge of the Nazi Past*. Chapel Hill: University of North Carolina Press, 2001.

Willoughby, John. *Remaking the Conquering Heroes: The Social and Geopolitical Impact of the Post-War American Occupation of Germany*. New York: Palgrave, 2001.

Wilson, Thomas M., and Hastings Donnan. *Border Identities: Nation and State at International Frontiers*. Cambridge, UK: Cambridge University Press, 1998.

Wirth, Kurt. *Ein Kampf um Neustadt der "Dreschflegelkrieg" 1742 zwischen Coburg und Meiningen (Neustadt und Sonneberg)*. Sonneberg: Sonneberg Museums- und Geschichtsverein, 2005.

Witzel, Eron. *Disturbed Ground: Journeys Along the Remnants of the Iron Curtain*. opensource_media: 2006. Online. Available: www.archive.org. January 2011.

Wolter, Manfred. *Aktion Ungeziefer: Die Zwangsaussiedlung an der Elbe—Erlebnisberichte und Dokumente*. Rostock: Altstadt, 1998.

Zahra, Tara. "Imagined Non-Communities: National Indifference as a Category of Analysis." *Slavic Review* 69 (2010): 93–119.

———. *The Lost Children: Reconstructing Europe's Families After World War II*. Cambridge, MA: Harvard University Press, 2011.

Zatlin, Jonathan. *The Currency of Socialism: Money and Political Culture in East Germany*. Cambridge, UK: Cambridge University Press, 2007.

Zeppei. "Der Einsatz des Netzes der inoffiziellen Mitarbeiter der Operativgruppe Aufklärung im Bereich des 15. Grenzregiments zur Organisierung der offensiven Abwehrarbeit gegen Fahnenfluchten von Angehörigen der Grenztruppen." Juristische Hochschule Potsdam, 1964. BStU MfS JHS MF 98.

Zips, Inge. *Spielzeugmacher im revolutionären Aufbruch* and *Spielzeugmacher—aktive Gestalter der entwickelten sozialistischen Gesellschaft*. Sonneberg: VEB Sonni Sonneberg, 1983 and 1985.

Zogbaum, Max. *Weltspielwarenstadt Sonneberg am Thüringer Wald*. Berlin-Friedenau: Dt. Kommunal-Verl., 1931.

INDEX